Anti-Movements in America

This is a volume in the Arno Press series

Anti-Movements in America

See last pages of this volume for a complete list of titles.

THE RED NETWORK

A "Who's Who" and Handbook of Radicalism for Patriots

ELIZABETH DILLING

ARNO PRESS

A New York Times Company

New York / 1977

Editorial Supervision: JOSEPH CELLINI

Reprint Edition 1977 by Arno Press Inc.

Reprinted from a copy in
The Princeton University Library

ANTI-MOVEMENTS IN AMERICA
ISBN for complete set: 0-405-09937-1
See last pages of this volume for titles.

Manufactured in the United States of America

Library of Congress Cataloging in Publication Data

Dilling, Elizabeth Kirpatrick, 1894-
The Red network.

(Anti-movements in America)
Reprint of the ed. published by the author, Chicago.
1. Communism--United States--1917- 2. Socialism in the United States. 3. Socialists--United States. I. Title. II. Series.
HX83.D5 1977 335.4'0973 76-46073
ISBN 0-405-09946-0

THE RED NETWORK

A "Who's Who" and Handbook of Radicalism for Patriots

by

ELIZABETH DILLING
(Mrs. Albert W. Dilling)

Published by the Author

545 ESSEX ROAD . . KENILWORTH, ILLINOIS
53 WEST JACKSON BOULEVARD, CHICAGO

Printed in the United States of America

First Printing—April 1934
Second Printing—May 1934
Third Printing—July 1934
Fourth Printing—January 1935

DEDICATED TO THE "PROFESSIONAL PATRIOTS"

Without committing them to its statements, this book is admiringly dedicated to all those sincere fighters for American liberty and Christian principles who, because of their opposition to Red propaganda and the "new social order" of Marx and Lenin, are denounced as "professional patriots", super-patriots", "100 per centers", "patrioteers", and "Tories" by their Red opponents. Particular mention is gratefully made of those "patrioteers" who have aided and encouraged the author in her effort to bring to the sound but still sleeping portion of the American public the truth about the Communist-Socialist world conspiracy which, with its four horsemen, Atheism, Immorality, Class Hatred, and Pacifism-for-the-sake-of-Red-revolution, is boring within our churches, schools and government and is undermining America like a cancerous growth. Among these are:

The national headquarters of the staunch D. A. R. (of which the author, unfortunately, is not a member), which reprinted each article in her former pamphlet "Red Revolution" and sent copies to each chapter in the U. S. A. The D. A. R. members are the best informed body of women in America on this subject and are correspondingly detested by the Reds.

Senator Clayton R. Lusk, whose gift of the most valuable and complete 4,450-page four-volume Report of the Joint Legislative Committee of the State of New York Investigating Seditious Activities, a report based upon indisputable documentary evidence made by the committee which he headed, has made available the background and information concerning the Red movement up to the year 1920, when it was issued, which is incorporated within this book.

Lt. Nelson E. Hewitt, a super-expert-patriot who has devoted twelve years of his life to active statistical work and study on Red subversive activities, who edits the Advisory Associates weekly Bulletins which every "super-patriot" needs (P. O. Box. 403, Chicago) and who has given the greatest personal aid of all, having devoted a number of full days of his time to checking and supplying information used in this book.

Francis Ralston Welsh, Philadelphia attorney and research expert on subversive activities—a real "super-patriot"—who has sent many excellent reports.

Miss Margaret Kerr, executive secretary of the "professional patriots' " Better America Federation, which placed and has kept the Criminal Syndicalism Law on the statute books of California despite the frantic efforts of the Reds to repeal it—who has sent valuable data.

Mr. Walter Steele, manager of the "100 per centers' " National Republic magazine (511 11th St. N. W., Wash., D. C.) and author of its articles on subversive activities which are unsurpassed, who has sent excellent special information. All "patrioteers" need the "National Republic" (price $2.00 yearly).

Mr. Harry Jung, a "professional patriot", of the American Vigilant Intelligence Federation, sufficiently annoying in his anti-Red "free speech" to be honored by intimidating libel suits filed by the notorious "free-speech-for-Reds-only" A. C. L. U. (whose Chicago office is the office of its member, Carl Haessler of the Communist school of Red revolution and the Reds' Federated Press). Mr. Jung kindly loaned the author some documents.

Mr. John B. Chapple, editor of the Ashland (Wis.) Press, author of "La Follette-Socialism," etc., whose courageous exposure in the face of death threats of the Socialist-Communist network in Wisconsin defeated the La Follette dynasty in the 1932 election for the first time in forty years, who sent his helpful book and pamphlets to the author.

Those who have assembled large and distinctive audiences to hear the author's lectures, among them: Paul G. Armstrong, Vice Commander Dept. of Ill., American Legion, and many other valiant Legion Commanders; U. S. Army and Navy Officers Club; the men of the Chicago Military Intelligence; leaders of: the Illinois Federation of Women's Clubs; Moody Church and Bible Institute; Women's Patriotic League; Catholic organizations; Fundamentalist and other anti-Bolshevik, anti-Atheist Churches; Clubs; Community mass meetings; etc., etc.

Col. Sidney Story, lecturer and fiery patriot; W. H. Chesbrough, Wisconsin Commander of the G. A. R.; Maude Howe of the Canadian Christian Crusade (against atheism); Nesta Webster, world famous English historian and author of "Surrender of an Empire", "World Revolution", "French Revolution", etc.; my friends Mr. and Mrs. George Cretors, residents of Soviet Russia while Mr. Cretors was employed there as an engineer; Mr. John E. Waters, also a former engineer for the Soviet Government, whose true story entitled "Red Justice" is available at 50c (P. O. Box 242, Madison, Wis.); Mr. Carveth Wells, famous lecturer and author of "Kapoot", a graphic account of his Russian experiences; Mrs. C. D. Shipley, tireless patriotic worker in Waukegan, Ill., a Red stronghold.

After reading the author's pamphlet "Red Revolution", David Kinley, the brilliant and loyal-American president-emeritus of the University of Illinois, wrote in part: "I congratulate you on your clear and earnest exposition of the situation, and I quite agree with you that it is time something were done to prevent the evil influence of the advocates of Communism and their allies. The allies include a good many people who would refuse to be called Communists, but whose influence, through various associations, tends to strengthen the work and claims of that group. I agree with you that it is time that parents should look more closely into the influence of the teachers of the schools and colleges which their children attend."

Mr. and Mrs. James H. Watt of Chicago declare: "From a viewpoint gained through our recent residence of fifteen months in an American engineering colony in Soviet Russia, the statements of Mrs. Albert W. Dilling concerning conditions prevalent in that country are found to be absolutely authentic and of invaluable import."

May "professional patriots" increase and multiply; may they cease to be lone voices crying in the wilderness; may their number and activities grow strong enough to avert now threatening Socialism or Fascism, and to preserve for America, Christianity, the American Constitution, and American liberty. (See "Professional Patriots" under Organizations herein.)

TABLE OF CONTENTS

PART III

"Who's Who"

ADDENDUM

(Fourth Printing)

INDEX

Facsimile Illustrations

PART I

MISCELLANEOUS ARTICLES

RUSSIAN REVOLUTION

Do We Want It Here?

To one who has seen Russia, unblinded by the propaganda of a few "model" institutions shown to tourists and built by foreign brains and capital, this talk of "revolution" here to better economic conditions strikes terror to the heart. One recalls those great civilizations in history which were laid to waste and were then for centuries unable to rise again.

In the Moscow "Museum of the Revolution", I saw racks and racks of photographs taken during the Russian Revolution and its attendant famine. These pictures of people who starved to death lying in the streets where they fell, cannibalistic views of dead mothers and babies with half-eaten bodies, and revolutionary scenes of stark horror and misery, were revolting past description.

The Soviet government woman-guide showing us these said she had lost two members of her own family in this famine and had seen worse scenes herself around Odessa. Later I shuddered as I heard her announce: "There is no use to waste time here in the Foreign Department (of the Museum). You people all read newspapers. You know what we are doing in China, Spain, and in your own country—our strikes and all. *Our world revolution will start with China and end with the United States."* In this Department is a map of the United States re-districted and with our cities renamed as they are expected to be "when the red flag waves over the White House." On this map Cleveland is renamed "Ruthenberg", Detroit is "Lewistown", etc. Since I heard these ominous words of our guide, the December 24, 1931, issue of "Inprecorr" announced that "the Soviet power has already been set up over a sixth part of China"; the Communist "Daily Worker" of April 5, 1932, in an article entitled "The Growth of the Soviet Power in China", gave details of great new Red Army victories in China. No wonder Communists demonstrate in front of Japanese embassies against "imperialist" war on China.

In January 1933, authorities reported seven provinces and at least 80,000,000 Chinese Sovietized, and an inner Chinese Soviet state which had an army of many thousand troops trained by German and Russian officers. Officers, arms and supplies were being sent from the U. S. S. R. by an ancient caravan route through Outer Mongolia, a large territory practically annexed to the U. S. S. R. after a revolution was engineered there in 1921, a point the League of Nations remained strangely silent about. Sovietization is increasing steadily in China.

The dirty, drab dilapidation of Russia, with its uncurtained, broken windows and unrepaired roofs, but with idle crowds roving the streets, bespeaks the loss of private ownership which always fosters personal interest and initiative. Communism has indeed abolished wealth in Russia. The wealth of those "liquidated" millions of the intelligentsia, aristocratic, middle, and small-land-holding classes, who have been killed or leveled down, has made way for universal poverty. Thirty per cent of the poorer portion of the 160,000,000 Russian population still remain to be dispossessed or "liquidated", and so, unceasingly, great train loads of those resisting "collectivization" travel the rails to Siberia. Ellery Walter counted, recently, in four weeks' time, seventeen train loads, some forty cars long, of such people. Men, women and children peered out at him through the bars. They were enroute to hard labor, prison camps, or death in Siberia.

Siberia is now populated as never before with exiled peasants who have spoken bitterly about, or resisted, the giving up of their pigs, cows, or little homes, or nearly all of their grain, or have offended by upholding religion, and consequently are being punished as "counter revolutionaries" or "damagers".

Tourists in Moscow may see, near their hotels, during late night and early morning hours, the "wild" or deserted children sleeping in doorways. These are not the same wild hordes of children seen during the revolution sixteen or more years ago, for those would now be grown. These are a new crop, produced not only by low living conditions but also by conditions of low living, fostered by the Communist government destruction of faith in God, religion, and morality. Lenin's wife said in "Pravda" (the official organ of the Communist Party of Russia): "We have seven million deserted children officially registered and eighty thousand who have been gathered into our asylums. How many more are wandering about Russia?" Couples may simply live together or register quickly as married or divorced by payment of a ruble. These can hardly support the children of several successive unions on incomes barely sufficient for their own existence.

Of course, a hospital we visited bragged of forty abortions performed that morning, and an "educational" movie viewed by a friend showed pictorially, to a mixed audience, old and new abortion methods and the benefits of the latter.

While visiting a "model" institution for children at the Tsar's old summer palace at Tsarskoye Selo, we photographed the little tots, naked from the waist up, running around in our party. Some not over six years old had learned enough English to beg "Gimme a cigarette, gimme a cigarette!" In this, and in other respects, our American institutions for six-year-olds are unlike the "model" products of the Russian Revolution. Concerning the Russian conditions, the U. S. Fish report on Communism says: "Documents and books presented to the committee indicate that the most terrible kinds of vice are encouraged among the young school children in order to break down their family influence which is the foundation of all religion." Siemashko, Soviet Commissar of Health, confessed at one time that venereal disease "had reached the proportions of a terrible plague".

My friends Mr. and Mrs. George Cretors have returned from Russia, where he, an American engineer, was in charge of 475,000 acres as agricultural expert for the Soviet government. They tell of the openly free sex relations among the 700 children between the ages of 11 and 17 in the "model" cooperative children's institution on this project, and of indecent practices taught in the school there by a Soviet official from Moscow, and of the long line of these children who waited in line to be treated for social disease when a doctor and nurse came there for that purpose.

All of the churches our guides took us to visit had been converted into anti-religious museums. Life-size manikins are dressed up in church robes and the most revolting interpretations of religious subjects are portrayed by them and by colored cartoons tacked up on large bulletin boards so that the crowds of young workers who are taken through may see and have explained to them by Soviet guides how ridiculous religious faith is. The most exquisite church of all, the Church of the Redeemer in Moscow, was then about to be dynamited to make way for a "Palace of the Soviets". I have movies of nude bathing in the river taken in the heart of Moscow, men and women together, with the Church of the Redeemer in the background. Beautiful St. Isaac's Cathedral in Leningrad, then an anti-religious museum, is now used as an atheist theatre as part of the new five-year plan to close all houses of worship by 1937 and to eradicate even the thought of God from the minds of the people by a militant anti-God campaign.

Our guides took us to the Torgsin stores for foreign tourists, where gold trinkets, paintings, art objects, church robes and ikons, looted from their former owners, are sold by the Soviet government for foreign gold only. But no visitor or proletarian Russian gets inside the Soviet officials' special stores, where the best is sold to the higher-ups at lowest prices. The windows of these stores are whitewashed and a guard with a gun stands out in front. Nor did our guides take us to visit the poor, miserable workers' stores, where long lines wait whenever merchandise is offered at prices the worker can afford to pay. My friends living there did take me, however. Goods on the half-empty shelves were labeled in several stores "For Display Purposes Only". Only counter supplies were for sale. An oil barrel in one had a sign "There is no more", which had been there for eight months, I was told. In one store, buzzing flies fought over three cheeses, priced at eight, ten, and twelve rubles (four, five, and six dollars) per pound. Three fish displayed were priced at $3.75 per pound. A thin, fly-specked box of candy was priced at $5.00, small individual pieces priced about twenty cents each, although a Woolworth buyer in New York was offered all the Soviet candy he could use at a penny a pound delivered. Incidentally, he patriotically bought American candy at five cents a pound instead.

The products of Russian workers are dumped abroad to break the markets of capitalistic countries, to pay for some machinery which is rusted and unfit for use in a short time, and to pay for propagandizing Communist revolution throughout the world.

There was no meat in the stores when I was there, as it was August and there is no ice. Everything is strictly rationed. Soap was $1.30 a bar and limited to two bars a month. Black bread, dried herring, and cucumbers seemed to be the actual purchases of the average buyer, except at one store which offered carrots and at another which offered tomatoes, both of which had previously been impossible to procure. Long lines waited to buy these specialties. Milk is sold at a special store and only to those with certificates showing that they have infants.

I saw scaffoldings on numerous buildings, but while there saw no one working on them. An American engineer who had been there three years said nobody in that time had worked on a scaffolding across the street from our hotel. I saw buildings which had been slopped over outside with whitewash a long time before, to judge by their soiled appearance, and yet the windows, splotched and streaked with the whitewash, still remained unwashed. I saw no window curtains anywhere, but I am told there are a few in Russia.

Two of the three busses we rode in in Leningrad broke down. The streets and roads were very much torn up and rutted, and the government cars rented to our party were trembling and unsure. On one trip, a wheel came off of one, and an axle broke on another. However, one day we had the use of some very good Packards and Buicks. These were the private cars of minor Soviet officials, loaned to us. I was told there were over seventy Rolls-Royces then in use in Moscow as the private cars of Soviet officials. Of course, the poor bundle-laden proletarian who walks or hangs out of an over-crowded street car is told that these cars are not the officials' "private" cars but are only for their "private use". The Socialist slogan is "Production for use, not for profit." (Whose use, whose profit?) Outside the towns, people poured out of old, dilapidated houses to see us go by. Auto traffic is a novelty.

The incessant propaganda about Communism and about what Russia is *going to do* is the only lively feature about Russia. So many of the widely-publicized and supposedly photographed projects are merely on paper. Dinginess, bad smells, and a sense of fear pervades everything. The last manager of the Grand Hotel in Moscow with his wife and children had been awakened at three o'clock in the morning by the G. P. U. (secret police) and had not since been heard of. They have a saying "Only the G. P. U. works fast in Russia." My friends showed me their letters, which plainly had been opened and glued together again before reaching them. All dispatches by foreign newspaper correspondents are censored before entering or leaving Russia. Our ship was not allowed to use its radio while within Russian waters.

Russian workers pay out about 30% of their earnings in taxes, such as the "culture tax" (for the privilege of reading newspapers and hearing propaganda at Workers' Clubs), a "housing tax" (to build houses for others), a "cooperative store tax" (for the privilege of buying at government stores), and an income tax. Besides, all workers must occasionally "voluntarily" give their whole month's wages to the government as a loan. Russians are forbidden to possess foreign money. Guards, barbed wire, spies, and heavy penalties inflicted on relatives left behind deter Russians from leaving Russia.

The bedbugs in the Grand Hotel were wild about me, the listless waiters not interested at all. Some beautiful marble statues, large Sevres vases, fly-specked crystal chandeliers, and massive old furniture remained, contrasting sharply with bare floors and cheap new iron beds. The hotel elevator ran once in a while, when not out of order. The dingy-windowed empty stores which line the streets (for only here and there a government store is operating) give a dismal appearance to the large cities. The few outcast private peddlers who remained when I was there were ragged and wretched looking individuals and were soon to be strictly dealt with and banned.

The hotel food was the best Russia provides for its tourists who pay precious foreign money and was infinitely better than the Russians get, but it had a kinship with the smelliness of everything connected with it and affected the digestion peculiarly—due it was said to benzoate of soda preservatives used.

Ragged proletarians loaded with bundles fill the railroad stations. The mattress and pillow tickings of the special first-class sleepers we rode on were revoltingly dirty. On the train, unwrapped black-bread sandwiches were handed to us out of a basket by a girl with soiled hands about 9 A. M. Regular breakfast was served at the hotels between 10 and 11 A. M., luncheon between 3 and 4, and supper between 10 and 11 P. M. Fresh fruit was non-existent; it is exported.

We were constantly told how much better off the Russians are now than they were before the Revolution. To be sure, we visited suburban homes formerly owned by well-to-do families now in use as "Workers' Clubs," or "Homes of Rest and Culture," as they are called. In one of these, workers in undershirts were sitting around, one hammering on the grand piano. Their old hats were hung on an elaborate old lamp and the marble statuary. Beautiful paintings of the former owners still hung at each end of the paneled dining room. The floors were bare and none too clean and there were iron cots in living room and dining room. The dining table was covered with soiled oil cloth and set with black bread and soup for the noonday meal of the inmates. A plaster bust of Lenin with a red necktie tied slightly askew graced the window seat in the living room. Out of the window, we saw and photographed girls very scantily clad lying in the tall grass of what had once been the garden, near an ornamental pool then filled with trash.

I was never in Russia before the Revolution. But as I passed miles of homes along the roads now neglected and nearly falling down and noted how many of them had ginger-bread carvings on them, it occurred to me that someone must have cared for them more than their present occupants do, or else they would never have bothered to carve them. As I watched the workers in the stores and noted what they were buying, I concluded that if they had formerly had less to eat than they were now getting they would not have survived. I met Russian bourgeois exiles in Switzerland who had escaped only with their lives and whose relatives had been killed after the Revolution. I believe that those exiles and the millions who were killed are more fortunate than the poor Russian proletarian left behind living as a mere cog in a Godless, slavedriving state machine.

Stepping from Russia into Esthonia is like stepping from the slums into a comfortable neighborhood. Until only fifteen years ago, Esthonia was a part of Russia; but it has since had democratic government and private trade. The clean window curtains and potted flowers, and the busy bustle of trade and traffic, and the general air of well being contrast sharply with gloomy Russia.

When over one thousand Communists rioted in front of the Chicago School Board offices (March 27, 1932), they bore a placard: "We Want Soviet Conditions Here." Some misguided Americans, openly or covertly, are echoing this sentiment. The universities seem to have joined the gutter Communists in "going Red." They unite in using the argument that inasmuch as the American "economic system" has "collapsed" we must have Russian revolution to right matters.

Owing to the spirit of Christian (not atheist) mercy, deeply ingrained in the American people, no one is starving, or will starve, here, who asks for aid. I compare the miserable food and living conditions of Russians who work, with the rations of our county and charity unemployed poor, to the latter's advantage. Moreover, no free-born American can conceive of the Soviet despotic regulation of the smallest personal matters of conduct and conversation, nor understand the haunting fear of the terrorist secret police which even the American tourist in Russia senses. Much less would Americans want to live under such "Soviet conditions" here.

While I was in Moscow, factory workers who had long protested bad working conditions decided to strike. At once soldiers and machine guns surrounded the factory. The workers were given fifteen minutes to decide whether to work or be blown to bits. They worked.

The present economic depression or "collapse" is not as unprecedented as was the era of prosperity which just preceded it. No other country at any time has ever had a standard of living, a condition of general welfare, to compare with ours. Since our struggling little thirteen colonies pioneered through to the foundation of this nation, we have survived wars and many depressions (or "collapses") without halting our upward march and without ceasing to be the mecca of the whole world. Immigration barriers have been necessary to hold back the multitudes drawn here by the opportunities and liberty offered under our form of government. Africa, South America, and other lands have soil and resources as rich, but they have lacked our government and those American principles which have inspired progress in the people of all nationalities who have come here to make America their home.

Macauley, the historian, said: "Your Republic will be pillaged and ravaged in the twentieth century, just as the Roman Empire was by the barbarians of the fifth century, with this difference, that the devastators of the Roman Empire came from abroad, while your barbarians will be the people of your country, and the *products of your own institutions.*"

Within each person lies the spirit and the power to help guide events in this nation either toward Russian revolution, with all its horrors, or upward toward firmer American principles and new American progress. Will our people rise in this crisis, as they have before, or will they at last fall? That depends upon you and me.

HAVE WE RECOGNIZED RUSSIA?

Have we recognized the poor Russian peasants deprived of food cards and deliberately "liquidated"—starved to death—by the Soviet Government within the last year as "class enemies," a number estimated at three million by Ralph Barnes of the N. Y. Herald Tribune, four million by Henry Chamberlain of the Manchester Guardian of England, and five million by pro-Soviet Walter Duranty of the N. Y. Times?

"At the recent London Economic Conference Maxim Litvinov . . . calmly admitted to an European diplomat that the sacrifice of fifteen to twenty million more people will be readily agreed to by the Soviet Government in order to transform Russia into a real Communist State" (from "America" of Nov. 25, 1933).

Anna Smirnova, Moscow factory worker, answering questions about Russia in the communist Daily Worker of Nov. 10, 1933 says: "It is true that we are unmercifully driving from our ranks and from our enterprises all those 'wreckers' and counter revolutionary forces in our midst—those forces that are using all their intelligence and physical strength to hold us back and to establish a capitalist society among us. . . . To take the place of the Church we have given the workers the theatre . . . club houses, etc. To take the place of the Bible and the priests, books concerning the class struggle by Lenin and Stalin. There are quite a few churches left in the U. S. S. R. It is true that with each year the number grows less . . . little by little through their contacts with this culture of ours they" (the believers) "are being won over to the cause of the workers' struggle to establish a Socialist Society and they find little place or time in their lives to think of religion." (Won over by the example of the "liquidated.")

Have we recognized the hapless Christians or the helpless majority of the Russian people now living under the iron dictatorship of their Communist Party which comprises but 1% of the population?

We have not. We have recognized the Communist Party Government of Russia and its Communist International, which are one and which are striving for similar power in America. We are financing agitations for our own destruction and supplying millions of dollars worth of cotton to be used for explosives for a war, perhaps, against anti-communist Japan, Asia's only bulwark against Communism now. We have made a pact with Hell to help provide the Cross upon which to crucify Christian civilization.

"Tut tut—be broadminded!" says the man educated beyond his own intelligence. One is reminded of two prisoners discussing a fellow prisoner in a motion picture. One asked "What is he in for? Didn't he kill his mudder?" "Sure," replied the other, "he cut his old lady's t'roat—but he's sor-ry. He's a *good* guy!"

The most broadminded can not say that the Soviet Government is sorry. It is proud and hopeful of similar opportunities for revolution in America and fifty-eight other countries. As the world's outstanding nation that withheld recognition of the murder regime for 16 years, we now capitulate and provide it with new hope, new pride, new funds for the fulfillment of its aims.

As a reward the communist Daily Worker editorially promises us the following (Nov. 20, 1933):

"The success of recognition, which the workers throughout the world will celebrate and greet as a harbinger of greater advances for the workers of the Soviet Union, and the revolutionary proletariat throughout the world, was made possible by the stalwart and brilliant leadership of the Communist Party of the Soviet Union, the Party of Lenin and Stalin, a section of the Communist International.

"Revolutionary Way Out of Crisis"

"The Communist Party of the U. S. A., section of the Communist International, points out that the only guarantee of peace is the abolition of capitalism. Its main task is the abolition of capitalism in the United States.

"The deepening of the crisis of American capitalism, the growing sympathy for the Soviet Union, gives the Communist Party of the U. S. A. the widest possibilities of convincing and winning the American toiling masses for the revolutionary way out of the crisis.

"In this country, the Communist Party, section of the Communist International, basing itself on the principles of Lenin and Stalin, will more determinedly than ever strive to win the American workers for the revolutionary way out of the crisis, for the emulation of the Soviet Union and its revolutionary victories."

M. J. Olgin, member of the central committee of the Communist Party, and editor of the Jewish Communist organ, "Freiheit," has written a pamphlet *since* recognition of Russia by the United States, entitled "Why Communism," which is even clearer in its open advocacy of violent destruction of the United States government. It should be read by everyone, particularly by those who have any belief in the piffle printed in the daily press about cessation of Soviet communistic activities in the United States. To quote but a small part of it:

"The Communist Party of the Soviet Union is affiliated with the Communist International. It is the most influential but not the only influential party in the International. It is one part but not the whole of the International. Its advice is highly precious because it has long accomplished what the Communist Parties of the world are only striving at—the proletarian revolution. The advice and experiences of the other parties, however, is also of great value in determining the policies of the Comintern. The seat of the Comintern is Moscow because this is the capital of the only workers' and peasants' government in the world, and the Comintern can meet there freely. As the workers become rulers of other countries, the Comintern will not have to confine its meetings to Moscow alone.

"The Communist Party of the U. S. A. is thus a part of a world-wide organization which gives it guidance and enhances its fighting power. Under the leadership of the Communist Party, the workers of the U. S. A. will proceed from struggle to struggle, from victory to victory, until, rising in a revolution, they will crush the capitalist State, establish a Soviet State, abolish the cruel and bloody system of capitalism and proceed to the upbuilding of Socialism."

"O, LET THEM BLOW OFF STEAM—AS THEY DO IN ENGLAND"

Before obligingly parroting this subtle Red propaganda:

1. Read the Communist press and the Workers Schools leaflets and see there the headlined quotation: "'*Without revolutionary theory there can be no revolutionary practise.*' Lenin." Thousands of dollars are continually raised for the Red press in order to "blow steam" *into* the Red movement, with this statement of Lenin's heading the printed pleas for funds.

2. Read: "The Surrender of an Empire" by Nesta Webster, "Potted Biographies" (of British statesmen), and the weekly "Patriot" of London, to gain some actual picture of England's blind grapple with Socialism-Communism within. (Boswell Pub. Co., 10 Essex St., London, W. C. 2.)

3. Read in this book, in the daily press, and A. C. L. U. reports, of the determined fight the A. C. L. U. (directed by Communists, Socialists and

sympathizers) wages to secure the "free speech" for Reds to "blow steam" *into* the Red movement, whereas Michael Gold's statement in the Daily Worker, Oct. 28, 1933, is typical of the Communist-Socialist view of "free speech" for others. To quote: "This whole controversy over free speech is an academic one with these ivory-tower liberals. To the worker it is something as real as murder. It is part of the class war, not something in the clouds. Free speech is not an inalienable right, but something to be fought for—a class weapon. It is not to be given up to scabs in a strike, or to Nazis and Ku Kluxers. We are not interested in hearing what they have to say—we only wish to labor that they *may not exist*." Read herein what Robt. Briffault says of "liquidating" dissenters in the article "Recovery Through Revolution" under "Organizations."

4. Take note that the Garland Fund appropriation "to investigate spy activities of the U. S. Department of Justice" and the National Popular Government League's false charges resulted in successfully shutting off the appropriation of U. S. funds to the Dept. of Justice for the purpose of investigating Red activities in the U. S. A. This was in 1925. We have since had no actual protection from the Government against Reds except some barring and deportation of Reds by the late Mr. Doak through the Dept. of Labor. "Miss" Perkins has now changed that. Then note that the Communist Party (see Communist Organization in the U. S. A.), which was illegal and was raided at Bridgman, Michigan in 1922, after 1925 came out more boldly, until in 1928 all camouflage was thrown aside and it labeled itself "Communist Party of the U. S. A. (Section of the Communist International)." Since 1928, it has increased its organizing Party workers to 27,000 members and enlisted a membership in its subsidiary organizations of 1,200,000 members, approximately the number of Communists now holding down Russia's 160,000,000 people who, however, were put in bondage by not over 79,000 Communists (by working the "united front"). Many of these members of Communist subsidiaries are our college presidents, professors, ministers, and public idols.

5. Study various revolutions and learn what a small number of determined agitators can actually govern a country. Observe what is being done in Washington now.

6. Ask yourself if in recent years sex, pacifistic, atheistic, and socialistic propaganda has increased in America—and why.

7. First familiarize yourself with the names of leaders and the principles of Socialism-Communism, then visit your son's or daughter's college. Read the college paper and look at the college bulletin board. Observe the insidious High School journals. Then start looking elsewhere with "seeing" eyes.

8. Finally try "blowing off" some anti-Red, anti-pacificst, anti-sex-trash, patriotic "steam" and watch who opposes you. You will be surprised!

COMMUNIST ORGANIZATION IN THE U. S. A.

The World Communist movement is organized by three super-organizations. The *supreme head* is the *Communist Party of the U. S. S. R.* The two equal and subordinate organizations are the *Soviet government* and the *Third International.*

The ruling inner circle of the C. P. U. S. S. R. is a group of nine men forming the *Polit-Buro* (Political Bureau). This inner circle rules the Soviet government and the Third International. *All* of the nine members of the Polit-Buro are high officials of the Soviet Government and *all* are high officials of the Third International. The supreme head is Joseph Stalin, secretary of the C. P. U. S. S. R.

"The Communist Party of U. S. A. (section of the Communist International)," which is the title of Moscow's American branch, is one of about 59 national branches of the Third International.

To quote from the leaflet "Revolutionary Greetings," which is presented to each new Party member in the U. S. A.: "The Communist Party was organized Sept. 1, 1919, by the revolutionary workers who were expelled from or left the Socialist Party when it became a reformist organization.

"The Party was declared illegal by the Federal government in January, 1920, when thousands of its members were arrested.

"The Party functioned illegally up to Dec. 26, 1921, when it changed its name into Workers Party.

"The name was subsequently changed to Workers (Communist) Party and finally again to Communist Party, in April, 1928.

"The Party has been a section of the Communist International from the day of its organization."

The Central Committee of the C. P. of U. S. A. receives its orders directly from the Third International and in turn sends out its orders through district committees in the U. S. and the Communist press to Communist members.

The United States is now (1934) divided into 20 districts each with its own committee. Each district is divided into sections and sub-sections with Section Committees, mapped out in accordance with the residential location of Communist members.

The district in which I live is district No. 8 and comprises all of Illinois and part of Indiana and small section of Mo. (St. Louis). The district headquarters are in Chicago (101 South Wells St., Room 705) and the district Party school for training organizers, agitators, functionaries, etc. is called the "Workers School" (2822 S. Michigan Ave.).

New York City is in district No. 2 and houses also the headquarters for the entire U. S. and part of Latin America. New Haven, Conn., is in district No. 15, Boston in district No. 1, etc.

Each section is divided into Units. The Units establish Nuclei (two or three members), in various neighborhoods and shops. There are two kinds of Nuclei: Shop Nuclei, made up of those working in one establishment, and Street Nuclei, made up of scattered membership in one neighborhood.

Each Unit has its own "Functionaries," such as Organizer, Agit-Prop (agitational propaganda) Director, Literary Agents, etc. The Units after they number more than 25 members, are frequently divided. Meetings of these Units are held in the homes of members and admittance is solely by membership identification (now a numbering system, 1934). General meetings of functionaries of Units are held at a Party headquarters with admittance only by membership identification. Since the Communist Party is a *secret society* it is impossible to know, with the exception of certain open leaders and organizers, whether or not any individual is or is not a Party member. He may or may not be. Only a small percentage of Communist Party members are known as such.

All Party members must engage in active Communist work. Otherwise they are expelled. The Communist Party regularly cleans house of slothful or dissenting members. One word against Party commands and out they go. Often, if an expelled member shows contrition, he is taken back or put on probation more humble and tractable than he was before. This strict discipline is exercised even against the highest Party leaders. Wm. Z. Foster himself is not exempt. The offshoot Communist Parties are largely composed of expelled Communist Party members who refused to "knuckle" to Moscow. This military organization gives the Party a cohesive, united driving force which increases its power a thousand fold and makes it "only the distilled essence of revolution," as Wm. Z. Foster once said.

"The Communist" for Aug. 1933 (p. 716) complains that thousands are ready for Party membership "but we do not bring them in. . . . During 1932 our membership was doubled." For a number of years it had hovered around 8,000 members. The present active number is given as 27,000 members (Clarence Hathaway, Jan. 21, 1934). "When we consider the composition of the mass organizations under our influence, with the 100,000 members and the more thousands in the left-wing oppositions, the 150,000 readers of the language press, then we immediately realize that we have already thousands upon thousands of potential forces inside of hundreds of factories in the country, among the millions of unemployed," etc.

Earl Browder, general secretary of the Communist Party, at the Trade Union Cleveland conference August 29-30, 1933, stated that the membership in Communist Party *subsidiary* organizations was 1,200,000 members. This figure is considered fair by neutral experts. Russia is now being held down by about this number of Communists. The revolution in Russia was put over by not over 79,000 Bolshevik fighters.

The figure of 1,200,000 members in Communist subsidiaries probably does not include the membership of the allied Socialist Party which polled about 800,000 votes at the last election (in addition to the heavy Socialist and Communist vote given to Roosevelt as the radicals' most practical hope), nor the I. W. W. and Communist opposition parties' complete memberships. Jan. 1934 the Communist Friends of the Soviet Union claimed over the radio to have 2,000,000 members.

Under Soviet Supervision

Communist Revolutions do not just happen. They are officered and planned. From Soviet sources the Better America Federation compiled the following information: The *Polit-Buro* of the U. S. S. R. (the executive committee of the central committee of the Communist Party of Russia; nine men) controls the *Torgpred* or controlling organization for the Soviet government's activities in the U. S. Torgpred is organized in three depts.: one is the *Razvedoupr,* the military or naval espionage, having as heads two "Voenspetz" military or naval specialists of high rank. Razvedoupr is composed of three sections; Sec. 1 has charge of gathering information relative to the army and navy; Sec. 2 has charge of organizing Communist "centuries" or "100's," which are to be the framework of the Revolutionary army. Sec. 3 has charge of abolishing military power, also the organized espionage; it is further composed of nine branches:

1. Operations branch; 2. Information branch; 3. Disarmament branch; 4. Naval branch; 5. Aeronautical branch; 6. Transportation branch; 7. Bacterio-Chemical branch; 8. Anti-militaristic branch; 9. Liason with Moscow.

Another of three sections of Torgpred is the *Tcheka* (O. G. P. U.) or State political police, secret in practically all of its activities and personnel and with the following functions: A. Dept. of investigations; B. Education of anti-revolutionary masses; C. Organization of assaults on individuals condemned by the Tcheka; D. Protection of prominent Communist offiicials who are at any time in the U. S. whether on open missions or, as is usually the case, incognito.

Qualifications required of Tchekists in the U. S. are as follows:

1. Must speak and write English correctly; 2. Must know American history and political economy; 3. Must study minutely and in minute detail the political activity of the parties in the U. S.; 4. Must send a daily report to Torgpred; 5. Must dress correctly and in style; 6. Must hide their identity as well as their functions; 7. Must never have on their persons, in case of arrest, anything which will compromise the Party or anyone connected with the Party; 8. When doing a job must be certain they are not being watched, but if watched, escape at all costs; 9. Never speak of their assignments, even to comrades; 10. Never call a comrade in public; 11. In case arrested never confess not even when told their fellows have confessed; 12. Before appearing in court prepare defense carefully beforehand, then speak as little as possible; 13. When arms or explosives are found on an arrested Tchekist, he will swear that he found them on the street, or they were handed him by an unknown person; 14. In prison do not speak to anyone, not even those arrested with you, they may be spies; 15. Get a Communist lawyer if possible; speak only in his presence; 16. How to maneuver policemen and judges is the first duty of an arrested Communist. Violations of any of the above rules cause the Tchekist so violating to be considered and treated as anti-revolutionist.

The third branch under Torgpred is *Amtorg* (so-called Commercial agency of the Soviet Govt. in the U. S.), under which is *Ikki* (the executive committee) under the control of the Komintern (Communist International). In the U. S., Ikki's mission is to direct the action of the American Communist Party. It studies the possibilities of action. The functions of Ikki are as follows: 1. Organizes centuries (A) in "clashing" or strife groups and (B) in combat groups (armed Communists) (20,000 arms had already been imported, in 1930, for this purpose); 2. Obtains arms in foreign countries; 3. Organizes specialist corps to manufacture grenades, bombs and explosives; 4. Formulates plans for disarming the police and loyal troops; 5. Operates to break up all groups of loyal fighting workmen when the revolution starts, and to destroy, when unable to capture, all tanks, cannon, machine guns and other weapons which the loyal proletariat might use; 6. Details and instructs reliable men who at the zero hour will arrest you and put to death magistrates, police heads and police officers; 7. To seize quickly all barracks, city halls, public buildings and newspapers; 8. To seize and strongly occupy all public means of transportation, stations and piers; 9. To use sabotage on all state equipment, bridges, telegraphs and telephones, railroads, army trucks, powder mills, aviation camps, barracks, police stations, banks and newspapers—which if left undestroyed will aid the State to quell the revolution.

The Ikki Section must be entirely composed of *American citizens* who must conform themselves strictly to instructions from Moscow.

Clarence Hathaway of the central committee of the Party spoke one hour Jan. 21, 1934 at the Chicago Coliseum on Leninist policies for seizure of power and said they already had men in the Army and Navy ready to turn their guns on their officers and the "capitalist class" (as they did in the Russian revolution) and turn any war into Red revolution. He emphasized the point that "We must be ready and prepared to DESTROY everyone who puts up any struggle against us." An audience of 10,000 Reds cheered him and booed the American flag as it was paraded up and down the aisles, by men dressed as U. S. soldiers, led by a man dressed to represent a capitalist holding a big yellow bag with a dollar mark on it. A huge Red flag was then dropped from the top of the stage and the audience applauded enthusiastically.

RED ARMY IN THE U. S. A.

Now recruiting fighters to train for bloody revolutionary action. "Red Front," the monthly publication for the Red Army in the U. S. A., is published by the "Central Executive Committee, Red Front Fighters League of U. S. A., 95 Ave. B, N. Y. City." The November 1933 issue was distributed at the Communist mass meeting Nov. 7, 1933 at the Chicago Coliseum and is headlined *"Mobilization!"* After telling of the need for fighting Fascism in the U. S. A., it says, to quote from p. 1: "We revolutionary workers who at all strikes, demonstrations, and picket lines have a share in the tear gas and the clubs of capitalistic lackeys are also not more anxious for terrorism and beatings without *returning them their due.* We live in a new time, when any day may be the beginning of the struggle. . . . WE RED FRONT COMRADES HAVE A GREAT RESPONSIBILITY" (emphasis in original) "in winning over the unemployed for the fight against Hunger and Frost and to *open food storage places.* New methods for the defense of strikers must be discovered. At the same time the question of anchoring the Red Front in different factories and shops, railroads, etc. are of the greatest importance. *The dashing to pieces of the whole apparatus of government, is, in the period of revolutionary uprising, thus easier to accomplish.*" (Emphasis supplied). On p. 8: "What is the Red Front?—The Red Front is composed of workers and farmers as poor, downtrodden and exploited as proletarians of all other working parties and organizations. . . . With Red Front against hunger regime! With Red Front for a Socialist Soviet Republic of America! Comrades: Decide on which Front you are willing to fight." The Fist (Red Front emblem) is "a symbol of irreconcilable battle."

And on p. 7: "Join Our Ranks! . . . The Chicago Red Front is the section of the Red Front Fighters League, an International Workers Defense Organization. Send in your applications to Red Front, care Young Communist League, Room 707, 101 S. Wells St., Chicago."

"Join the Red Front for Anti-Fascist Action: Los Angeles, Calif., 224 S. Spring St., Rm. 304; New York District: East Manhattan, 95 Ave. B. Every Wed., 8 P. M.; West Manhattan, 108 W. 24 St.; Yorkville and Harlem, 350 E. 81 St.; Bronx, 2800 Bronx Pk., East, Every 1st, 2nd and 4th Wed's.; Brownsville, Bklyn., 1440 E. N. Y. Ave. Every Fri., 8 P. M.; South Brooklyn, 291 Wyckoff St.; Brighton Beach. Inquire at 95 Ave. B, N. Y. C.; Jamaica (same); Red Front Pioneers, 95 Avenue B. Every Friday."

The May 1934 issue of "Red Front" announced opening of its summer training camp at Phillipsport, N. Y., and showed pictures of its Red troops drilling in uniform and of the Jiu Jitsu tricks taught to enable Reds to "disarm the enemy and with one grip put him out of commission."

Is there no sedition law in the U. S. A.? Must citizens now simply train themselves in target practise to combat these revolutionaries bent on seizing plants (as at Austin, Minn.), farmers' produce, and private property?

In November 1933, Litvinov, the arch conspirator and bank-robbery aid who represents these, our would-be Red assassins, was feted and dined by Pres. Roosevelt as an honored guest in our American White House.

COMMUNIST PARTY AND RELIGION

The Union of Soviet Socialist Republics, "Mother of harlots and abominations of the earth" (Rev. 17:5), is the world's first government to raise the flag of absolute hatred and enmity to God Almighty. It not only makes no secret of its satanic Marxian atheism but finances and boastfully backs immoral sex and militant atheist movements the world over. In addition to surpassing the worst days of pagan Rome in its wholesale murder, persecution, and exile of Russian Christians, it endeavors to kill the souls of the young generation by prohibiting all teaching of God to children; by urging children to publicly disown non-atheist parents; by urging parents to turn over children to atheist state control; by blaspheming God and Jesus Christ always and everywhere in the Communist press, in plays, in anti-religious parades and pageants and in nauseous cartoons placed in former churches. Its birth control societies, there and in America, are for the purpose of facilitating immorality and encouraging promiscuity and the abolition of Christian marriage. Communism blasphemes not only against the "Son of Man" and all churches but against the Divine Spirit under any name or form whatever.

I heard Neil H. Ness of the sinister Russian O. G. P. U. speak at the radical Seven Arts Club, Chicago, Oct. 14, 1933. His outstanding boasts were that Soviet Russia in 15 years under Communism had risen to first place as the greatest military power in the world, and that "*Godless* Russia" had done more in fifteen years than *Christianity* had in nineteen hundred. He said he had been often asked about promiscuity in Russia and that in reply he would say it had been his observation that the "ladies of shame" had all turned good Bolsheviks after the revolution and were now "handing out their commodity in a Comradely manner." Truly this accomplishment of changing vice from a segregated, commercialized pursuit to a free and general habit is something Christianity has *not* achieved in nineteen centuries, nor have the savages in thousands of years. They are less degenerate.

"The Church and the Workers" is pamphlet No. 15 in the series of International Pamphlets published for Communist Party use. It proudly says: "The Soviet Union, under a workers and peasants government, is the only country in the world where religion and the churches are being combatted with the active cooperation of the government. . . . As militant materialists, the Soviet leaders are uncompromising in their scientific and atheist position. . . . It is necessary to link the fight against the church and religion with the fight against capitalism and imperialism. As long as capitalism exists, religion and the churches will be used. . . . In the United States, as in all capitalist countries, the churches by developing law-abiding citizens through the appeal to fear of an avenging god, become part of the repressive apparatus, equally with the police, the army, the prisons, for the purpose of attempting to prevent rebellion. . . . As the anti-religious campaign in the Soviet Union succeeds, the religious forces of the world are organizing and supporting interventionist movements to destroy the worker's state. . . . A militant worker's anti-religious movement must be organized . . . "; etc.

In the official Communist Chicago newspaper "Workers Voice" of Mar. 1, 1933, was an article by Joseph Stalin, dictator of Russia, entitled "Communists and Religion", in which he says: "The Party cannot be neutral towards religion and does conduct anti-religious propaganda against all and every religious prejudice. . . . The Party cannot be neutral toward the bearers of religious prejudices, toward the reactionary clergy who poison the minds of the toiling masses. Have we suppressed the reactionary clergy? Yes, we have. The unfortunate thing is that it has not been completely liquidated. Anti-religious propaganda is a means by which the complete liquidation of the reactionary clergy must be brought about. Cases occur when certain members of the Party hamper the complete development of anti-religious propaganda. If such members are expelled it is a good thing because there is no room for such 'Communists' in the ranks of our Party." Great placards with the words of Marx, "Religion is the opium of the people," are widely displayed in Russia.

The "A. B. C. of Communism" by N. Bucharin and E. Preobraschensky is a standard work for use in Communist Party schools. It says: "Religion and communism are incompatible. 'Religion is the opium of the people,' said Karl Marx. It is the task of the Communist Party to make this truth comprehensible to the widest circles of the labouring masses. It is the task of the party to impress firmly upon the minds of the workers, even upon the most backward, that religion has been in the past and still is today one of the most powerful means at the disposal of the oppressors for the maintenance of inequality, exploitation and slavish obedience on the part of the toilers. Many weak-kneed communists reason as follows: 'Religion does not prevent my being a communist. I believe both in God and communism. My faith in God does not hinder me from fighting for the cause of the proletarian revolution!' This train of thought is radically false. Religion and communism are incompatible, both theoretically and *practically*." (To this I agree!)

SOCIALIST PARTY AND RELIGION

The 1908 Convention of the Socialist Party adopted a plank in its platform which stated: "The socialist movement is primarily an economic and political movement. It is not concerned with the institutions of marriage and religion." Agnostic Victor Berger backed this plank, as did Unterman, delegate from Idaho, who started off his speech in its favor by declaring himself to be a thorough atheist but argued: "Would you expect to go out among the people of this country, people of different churches, of many different religious factions and tell them they must become atheists before they can become Socialists? That would be nonsense. We must first get these men convinced of the rationality of our economic and political program."

Arthur M. Lewis, delegate from Illinois, who opposed this plank stated: "I know that the Socialist position . . . in the question of religion does not make a good campaign subject . . . therefore I am willing that we should be quiet about it. But if we must speak, I propose that we shall go before this country with the *truth* and not with a *lie* . . . I do not propose to state in this platform the *truth* about religion from the point of view of the Socialist philosophy as it is stated in almost *every book of standard Socialist literature*; but if we do not do that, let us at least have the good grace to be silent about it, and not make hypocrites of ourselves."

The official proceedings of this convention quote Morris Hillquit as saying that 99% of the Socialists were agnostics (Lusk Report. p. 1127). The International Socialist Review at that time said "Religion spells death to Socialism, just as Socialism to religion . . . the thinking Socialists are all free thinkers." The New Yorker Volkzeitung later said: "Socialism is logical only when it denies the existence of God."

In 1912, the Socialist Party Convention dropped this plank and adopted a resolution on "Our Attitude Towards the Church" in which this language appears: "The ethics of Socialism and religion are directly opposed to each other." (See official proceedings National Convention held at Indianapolis, Ind., May 12 to 18, 1912, pages 247-8).

The May 9, 1920 Socialist Party Convention adopted a "Declaration of Principles" which urged complete separation of church and state and allowed freedom of conscience to worship or not as one pleased. At this same time David Berenberg of Socialist Rand School reported to the Socialist Party international executive committee on the book to be published that August by the Socialist Schools Publishing Assn. connected with the Rand School. It was entitled "Socialist Sunday School Curriculum." The Lusk Report sums up its review by saying the purpose of this book was "to inculcate in the minds of children from a very early age a distrust in the government of this country as now constituted, a belief that religion is one of the instruments invented by capitalists for the oppression of workers and to lead them to accept the revolutionary principles of the Socialist movement." (p. 1791).

The Socialist Educational Society of New York more recently published a pamphlet entitled "Socialism and Religion." It was sold at the Rand School Book Store, 7 E. 15th St., the same address at which the official Socialist weekly "New Leader" is published (mouthpiece of the clever "Rev." Norman Thomas and his fellows). In the preface the Socialist Educational Society says: "Our position is clear. There can be no compromise between Socialism and religion." Chapter headings include "The Exodus of Religion," "The Materialist Explanation of Society," and "Quackery and Confusion."

The booklet sums up its point of view on the last page with the statement: "The decay of religion is, indeed, a measure of the advance of humanity."

Herr Bebel, German Socialist leader and classic Socialist writer, announced in the German Reichstag that his party aimed "in the domain of economics at socialism and in the domain of what is called religion at atheism" (Mar. 31, 1881), and again he said, "Christianity and socialism stand toward each other as fire and water. . . . Christianity is the enemy of liberty and civilization . . . it has kept mankind in slavery and oppression."

Today the works of atheists Lenin, Trotsky, Scott Nearing, Robt. W. Dunn, etc. are recommended and standard Socialist literature (see L. I. D.), as are the "Little Blue Books of Socialism" of Socialist Haldeman-Julius which are also recommended by the Socialist "Christian Social Action Movement" of the Chicago Methodist Church hdqts. To quote the National Republic of Sept. 1933:

"In January the radical and filthy minded Haldeman-Julius launched a new publication. His pockets already overflowing with gold collected through sales of his various socialist, communist, sex, trial marriage, atheist and birth control propaganda periodicals and pamphlets, the new publication known as the 'Militant Atheist,' was begun in January with a circulation of 1,540. The September number had reached 4,051, a gain of 2,511 subscribers within only eight months. This sacrilegious sheet, the size of a daily newspaper, is edited by E. Haldeman-Julius and 'Rev.' Jos. McCabe. It contains ballyhoo articles on atheism, on Russia, on Prof. Einstein, on Karl Marx, on Revolution, and derides Catholicism, Protestantism, the Church, and God Himself."

Among books sold and recommended by the Socialist Party hdqts. in 1932-5 are: "Socialism the Utopia of Science" by Engels, in which he says: "Nowadays in our revolutionary conception of the universe there is absolutely no room for either a Creator or ruler" (English edition, 1901, p. 17); "Socialism in Thought and Action" by Harry W. Laidler, L. I. D. student lecturer, in which he says: "the philosophy of Socialism is itself diametrically opposed to the principles of revealed religion" (p. 155); the atheist Communist Manifesto, alone price 10c; with Norman Thomas' commendatory introduction and an essay added (Socialist L. I. D. edition) price 25c; "Songs for Socialists," leaflets "Printed by the Socialist Party of America," contain the "Red Flag," "When the Revolution Comes," the international Red anthem, "The International," with its anti-religious verse, "We want no condescending saviors to rule us from a judgment hall, we workers ask not for their favors," etc.

Two friends of mine attended a public Socialist meeting at Highland Park, held in behalf of the candidacy of Norman Thomas and Rev. Roy Burt, a Methodist minister in good standing and connected with world-wide Methodist religious education. As they entered, they were given a copy of "America for ALL," the official Socialist campaign paper (issue of August 13, 1932), and noted with surprise that, under the heading "Yes, but WHICH shall I read? Our Recommendations are:", the first recommendation was "The Communist Manifesto by Marx and Engels." The price was given as ten cents and the footnote said: "Send order with remittance to Socialist Party of America, 549 Randolph, Chicago." During the question period, they asked Rev. Burt, who presided and spoke, whether Socialism and Communism were the same. He replied lengthily that their aims were the same but that their methods of attainment differ. They then asked him why the Socialists recommended the Communist Manifesto for reading. Burt replied that *the Communist Manifesto is the basis of Socialism.* After reading this Manifesto, a copy of which is before me, I was unable to understand how anyone could presume to be a disciple of both Christ and Marx. Since it is the "bible" of Socialism-Communism, it is sold at all Communist and Socialist book stores. It is printed in pamphlet form, about forty-eight pages. It was drawn up first in 1848 by Marx and Engels, later re-edited by Engels in 1888. Class hatred is, of course, the dominating note. Society is divided into two classes, proletarian and bourgeoisie (or middle class, such as small merchants and land owners). The bourgeoisie are represented throughout as the villains who exploit the proletarians. The proletarians, or lowest class, are represented as the noble heroes who must fight to the finish for dictatorship in order to make everything equal. According to Marxian argument, people are necessarily worthy of ruling all society because they are poor.

To quote (page 20): "The proletariat, the lowest strata of our present society, cannot raise itself up without the whole super-incumbent strata of official society being sprung into the air. . . . the struggle of the proletariat with the bourgeoisie is at first a national struggle. The proletariat of each country must, of course, first of all settle matters with its own bourgeoisie . . . up to the point where that war breaks out into open revolution, and where the violent overthrow of the bourgeoisie lays the foundation for the sway of the proletariat."

(Page 23): "The theory of the Communists may be summed up in the single sentence: Abolition of private property."

(Page 24): "And the abolition of this state of things is called by the bourgeois, abolition of individuality and freedom! And rightly so. The abolition of bourgeois individuality, independence and freedom is undoubtedly aimed at. By freedom is meant, under the present bourgeois conditions of production, free trade, free selling and buying."

(Page 25): "In a word you reproach us with intending to do away with your property. Precisely so; that is just what we intend."

(Page 26): "Abolition of the family! . . . On what foundation is the present family, the bourgeois family, based? On capital, on private gain. In its completely developed form this family exists only among the bourgeoisie. But this state of things finds its complement in the practical absence of the family among the proletarians, and in public prostitution. The bourgeois family will vanish as a matter of course . . . with the vanishing of capital."

(Page 27): "But you Communists would introduce community of women, screams the whole bourgeoisie in chorus! . . . Bourgeois marriage is in reality a system of wives in common and thus, at the most, what the Communists might possibly be reproached with is that *they desire to introduce, in substitution for a hypocritically concealed, an openly legalized community of women.*"

Communizing women for free use was tried repeatedly in Russia until the outcries against it temporarily halted this program, which for the time being is now largely limited to encouragement of free relations, legalized abortions, and state care for children. The private "ownership" of one man for one woman is called "capitalism" and is frowned upon. The teaching is: "Break down the family unit to build national Communism, break down nationalism (or patriotism) to build international Communism."

To resume quoting from the Manifesto (Page 29): "But Communism abolishes eternal truths, it abolishes all religion, and all morality, instead of constituting them on a new basis; it therefore acts in contradiction to all past historical experience. What does this accusation reduce itself to? . . . The Communist revolution is the most radical rupture with traditional property relations; no wonder that its development involves the most radical rupture with traditional ideas." (Thus does Marx defend the destruction of all morality and all religion.)

The proceedings of the Socialist Ministers Conference held in Evanston, Ill., 6/25-28/34 (price 10c from Rev. W. B. Waltmire, 1717 N. Fairfield Ave., Chicago) quotes communist Carl Haessler as saying: "Marxists believe in atheism . . . they are materialists of the Hegelian dialectical variety. According to this philosophy, the world is full of opposing forces or trends which give way to new trends but never come to rest. . . . Religion has no place in this perpetual clashing and remaking of forces. They are material forces only. Of course there is room for the play of consciousness but there is no room for God or for conscience outside the forces which are in conflict. Neither is there room for truth or moral verities. The purer the religion the deadlier it is because it is so effective in blurring the class divisions. Q. Why cannot dialectical materialism fit in with theistic idea of the universe? A. Because theism involves a force outside the powers of the conflicting forces. The result would be determined not by the power of the forces but by the power of the supernatural force."

WOMEN AND SOCIALISM

The Socialist authority August Bebel in "Women and Socialism," pp. 466-467, says: "In the new society women will be entirely independent both socially and economically. . . . In the choice of love she is as free and unhampered as man. She woos or is wooed and enters into a union prompted by no other consideration than her own feelings. The union is a private agreement without interference of functionary. . . . No one is accountable to anyone else and no third person has a right to interfere. What I eat and drink, how I sleep and dress is my own private affair, and my private affair also is my intercourse with the person of the opposite sex."

Friedrich Engels' "Origin of the Family" (p. 91-92) says: "With the transformation of the means of production into collective property the monogamous family ceases to be the unit of society. The private household changes to a social industry. The care and education of children becomes a public matter. Society cares equally well for all children, legal or illegal. This assumes the care about the consequence which now forms the essential social factor hindering the girl to surrender unconditionally to the beloved man."

Helen R. Marx, daughter of Karl Marx (quoted Chgo. Tribune, Nov. 14, 1886), said: "Love is the only recognized marriage in Socialism. Consequently no bonds of any kind would be recognized. Divorce would be impossible as there would be nothing to divorce; for when love ceases, separation would naturally ensue." Eleanor Marx, another daughter, never married her "husband" Dr. Aveling. A consistent Socialist woman would neither marry nor bear her "husband's" name. (Note the leading Red women who do not bear the husband's name.)

"CHRISTIAN" SOCIALISM

The American Association for the Advancement of Atheism (4A), which cooperates in its own World Union of Atheists with Moscow's International of the Godless and other Communist groups, in its official reports proudly relates how the socialist Debs Memorial Radio Station (WEVD) staunchly aided it in regularly broadcasting the 4A Atheist propaganda. It states that it has but two real foes, Fundamentalist Christianity and Roman Catholicism, and adds that it welcomes the aid of Modernists in paving the way for Atheism (and, one might add, Communism). Jeeringly, it asserts that the reason Fundamentalists do not dare openly to expose heresy within the Protestant Churches is because they are afraid of a split and that the Churches are thus held together "by real estate." To this one might reply that Christ's faith was started without any real estate in the first place and it can flourish and acquire real estate any time that it burns with living power.

Modernist Protestant Churches, united under the influence of the radical Federal Council of Churches, penetrated with communistic propaganda, unsure of allegiance to Christian doctrines, are weak and divided foes, when not actual allies, of the advancing menace of Bolshevism and Atheism now assailing America from the schools and universities, the press, the pulpit, the lecture platform, and radical politicians.

Three facts stand out:

1. *Marxism is Atheism.* Both Socialism and Communism are Marxism, the only difference being that Socialism covers over its Atheism with a garment of "Christianity" when camouflage is expedient, while Communism does not.

2. *Coöperation with Marxism is cooperation with Atheism.* Christ has warned us against trying to serve two masters, saying "he who is not with Me is against Me." Also, "Be ye not unequally yoked together with unbelievers: for what fellowship hath righteousness with unrighteousness? and what communion hath light with darkness. . . . Wherefore come out from among them, and be ye separate, saith the Lord, and touch not the unclean thing; and I will receive you." (II Corinthians 7:14-17.) The Communist and Socialist Parties of Spain, Germany, Saar, France, and numerous American cities are officially acting jointly 1934-5.

The "A. B. C. of Communism" has truly stated that it is impossible for a man both to believe in God and to serve the Marxian cause. Even though a Christian may believe that he is no less a Christian—or that he in fact is even a more "practical" Christian—through accepting Marxism with a mental reservation concerning its immorality and atheism, still the fact remains that he is aiding those who have no such mental reservation but whose fixed, immediate, and ultimate purpose is the destruction of Christianity and its moral principles everywhere. The intermediary stage of true Socialism, which is called "Christian" Socialism, is a smeary mess of conflicting

Marxism and religious sentimentality which is referred to facetiously by real Communists and Socialists as "the kindergarten of Red radicalism." Socialists agree that a consistent Socialist must lose his Christian faith. The pity is that so many who have lost it continue to usurp pulpits.

3. *"Christian Socialists" do cooperate actively with atheist Communists.* This whole book is an illustration of that fact. One may search in vain for the prominent "Christian" Socialist who is not working with and for Atheist Communists. As one becomes familiar with the names in the various Red organizations, the truth becomes apparent that "Christian" Socialism and Communism are branches of the same movement. Their members mingle on the same committees; they are arrested in the same strikes and riots; they share funds from the same sources; they unite in defending Satan's Base—Godless Soviet Russia.

My most vigorous opponents are "Christian" Socialists, even those who are only sympathizers with the Red movement. My first experience was with the Rector of the Episcopal Church which I formerly attended and in spite of this I believe him to be a sincere, tho misguided, believer in Christ. I was lecturing about Russia and I told him about the Soviet government's dreadful blasphemous anti-Christian displays I had seen there, of their open boast that they would accomplish from within the same thing in America, and offered to come and show my Russian pictures to the Women's Guild, gratis. Of course, I expected his sympathetic indignation and cooperation. Instead, to my surprise and bewilderment, he started talking about "Christian" Socialism and about its being "quite different" from Communism; he stated that he had once belonged to a small Socialist group at Oxford "just for the benefit of the social order." Later, he asked if an anti-communist lecturer who was to speak in the vicinity was "one of those terrible American Legion men" and asked if I did not agree with him that Norman Thomas' Socialist campaign platform was "pretty good." His instantaneous, almost automatic, efforts to shield godless Communism and his refusal to allow me to warn of its atheistic Christ-crucifying plans came as a shock to me at the time, but I soon found it to be but a mild manifestation of "Christian" Socialism.

Try, I say, attacking Soviet Russia's godlessness, and see where your "Christian" Socialist will stand. He will screen Sovietism and attack *you*!

As we observe how "Christian" Socialist Reinhold Niebuhr advocates Marxian revolution and how he occupies the platform with atheist Communist Party officials controlled by godless Moscow; as I have observed the constant procession of Communist notices tacked on "Christian" Socialist Tittle's Evanston M. E. Church bulletin board and read his printed sermons praising Communist revolutionaries as the ones God "spoke through"; as one observes with what zeal Harry Ward, Bishop McConnell, and other "Christian" Socialists serve the A. C. L. U. legal defense of atheists and Communist criminals, and how pleasantly McConnell serves the Socialist campaign while Winifred Chappell serves the Communist campaign and signs a Manifesto subscribing to Communist principles, and all of these unite in the Methodist Federation for Social Service, headed by McConnell, in getting out the Bulletin edited by Ward and Winifred Chappell—after a thousand more observations like these—the airy soap-bubble castle built upon arguments that "Christian" Socialism has nothing to do with and is "quite different from Communism" vanishes into thin air!

The Catholic Church, strangely, seems unaware that it has a few Red-aiders in its midst, but in spite of these no such headway has been made by radicals with Catholics as has been made with Protestants.

Gerard B. Donnelly, S. J., wrote, in "America," a Catholic publication (1932), a statement which should be framed and put on every church door in this land. He held that a vote for Norman Thomas for President would be in direct violation of Catholic doctrine and said: "No Catholic can accept the Marxian philosophy or the denial of the right of property. Socialism cannot Christianize itself merely by soft-pedaling or even by dropping entirely its dogmas on class warfare and property rights. Rome's ban against Socialism is not withdrawn. . . . The Socialist Party proposes recognition of the Soviet Union. Now the Soviets are publicly and explicitly hostile to God. To vote for their recognition, or, what is tantamount, to vote for a party which advocates their recognition, is once more formal cooperation with evil and obviously something no Catholic can do."

Tactics

The Socialist method of attaining power has been the inspiration for the adjective which Communists popularly bestow upon their Socialist brothers. They call the Socialists "yellow" and the Second International the "yellow" International. This Socialist method, says Hearnshaw, is "the method of sapping rather than assault; of craft rather than force; of subtelty rather than violence. 'Permeation' has been their watchword. . . . Above all they have tried to bemuse the public mind into the belief that 'socialism' and 'collectivism' are synonymous terms; and that all they are aiming at is a harmless and beneficent extension of state and municipal enterprise."

Even Friedrich Engels, collaborator of Karl Marx, writing to his friend Sorge in America (who collected Florence Kelley's letters from Engels and placed them in the New York Public Library) in commenting on the camouflage, subterfuge and indirection of Fabian Socialists said: "Their tactics are to fight the liberals not as decided opponents, but to drive them on to socialistic consequences; therefore to trick them, to permeate liberalism with socialism, and not to oppose socialistic candidates to liberal ones, but to palm them off, to thrust them on, under some pretext. . . . All is rotten." (Socialist Review, vol. 1, p. 31).

Even more rotten is the attempt of mis-named "Christian" Socialists to deceive Christians into believing that Marxism is like Christianity. The Daily Northwestern of Dec. 13, 1932, under the heading "Niebuhr Claims Marxian Theory Like Christian," reviews Niebuhr's book, "Moral Man and Immoral Society," which has been praised by both the Communist and Socialist Red press for its correct Marxian position in setting forth the necessity for bloody class hate and revolution. It quotes him as saying: "The religio-political dreams of the Marxians have an immediate significance which the religio-ethical dreams of the Christians lack." Yes, indeed! The religio-political dreams of the Marxians include the destruction of Christianity and of the very moral principles Christ held dear. Whenever and wherever Marxians attain power, as in Mexico, Russia, or Spain, Christian churches are "significantly" and immediately closed or destroyed and Christians persecuted.

Reinhold Niebuhr is one of America's outstanding "Christian" Socialists. In company with Harry Ward and others of the same kind who adorn platforms at Communist meetings, he teaches at Union Theological Seminary, where the L. I. D. conference on "Guiding the Revolution" was held and from whence Arnold Johnston went forth to Kentucky last year as representative of the A. C. L. U., to be arrested for criminal syndicalism. Niebuhr was honored with a place on the platform as speaker for the Communist-controlled U. S. Congress Against War, held in N. Y. City, Sept. 29, 1933, in company with Earl Browder, General Secretary of the Communist Party, and Henri Barbusse, French Communist, guest of honor (Daily Worker).

The Phila. Record of October 14, 1933 reported: "Reinhold Niebuhr, Union Theological Seminary Professor, last night advocated the *use of force* to bring about a *new social order*. . . . His open leaning toward revolution was expressed at the opening of a three-day joint regional conference of the Women's International League for Peace and Freedom and the Fellowship of Reconciliation at Swarthmore College" (A "Pacifist" conference).

Karl Marx, the idol of Reinhold Niebuhr, denies the existence of God or Supreme Spirit in any form. He teaches: the desirability and inescapable necessity of class hatred, class revolution, envy and covetousness; the abolition of the family unit and of marriage; the communizing of women; state ownership of children; that matter and force constitute all of creation; that only materialistic circumstance guides destiny, character, and history; that man's spirit is as material as a chemical effervescence or an electric spark which flickers out or rots with the body; that "Religion is the opium of the people"; that with the vanishing of property rights, religion and morality will vanish, along with other "bourgeois sentimentalities"; that a governmental proletarian dictatorship must be set up by violence; and that any theory that the two classes can get together is only a dodge on the part of the bourgeoisie who wish to avoid having their throats cut in a bloody proletarian revolution.

Jesus Christ teaches: that God is the Father of all life; that the family unit and marriage are indissoluble; that parents should love their children and children honor their parents; that Christians should exercise love and charity toward their neighbors; that no political kingdom of worldly power should be sought by Christians, as such, but rather personal kindness and a mastery over self.

Any government will be good if it is composed of good persons and no government can be good that is built by persons of Godless and immoral principles. Goodness is a day to day personal achievement, a contest with evil which constantly breaks down, and must be taken up again.

Anyone who says that the theories of Marx and Christ are alike is either a hopeless idiot or a wilful deceiver. But the siren call of Marxism to the altruist, who clings to the title of "Christian" for the sake of lingering sentiment, or financial or political expediency, is that it promises to obtain by foul means a pure, just, classless, equalitarian society; by means of rage and hate to usher in the reign of brotherly love; by means of plunder and gory class war to achieve peace; and by means of anti-moral propaganda to elevate mankind. By discouraging the lazy, incompetent and debauched man from the belief that his condition is in any way the result of his own faults, but rather that all sufferings and inequalities are due to capitalism, it promises to eradicate these sufferings through revolution.

The kindly man cannot see that, as Hearnshaw says: "Socialism debilitates and demoralizes those whom it seeks to succor." It "is the cry of adult babyhood for public nurses and pap bottles" and "by means of doles, poor relief, free meals, free education, free medical services, free everything—all paid for by the industrious and careful—it breeds and fosters a vast demoralized mass of paupers and vagrants . . . battening contentedly and permanently upon the industry of their more efficient and self-respecting neighbors."

"The ultimate source of our social evils is not economic," says T. W. Headley (in "Darwinism and Modern Socialism"), "and as soon as we realize that whatever social malady we have to deal with, it originates with human weakness and folly more than with outward circumstances, we have a principle that will guide us."

"Socialism" That Is Christian Is Not Socialism

There is an epigram to the effect that "Socialism is Christian only in so far as it is not Socialism and Socialism only in so far as it is not Christian."

Modern predatory Socialism despises and ridicules as "only sham Socialism," the religious, purely voluntary "Associations for Cooperative Production" which were formed in England subsequent to 1848 by Christian groups calling themselves "Socialists." Dr. Robert Flint says of these Christian "Socialists": *"They did not teach a single principle or doctrine peculiar to socialism* but rather by their ethical and religious fervor struck at the very roots of socialism." They had no quarrel with the existing social system as such; they gave no countenance to projected raids on land and capital; they utterly rejected the doctrine that character and destiny are determined by materialistic circumstance; above all, they repudiated with abhorrence the idea of the class war and the ferocious savagery of the Communist Manifesto of Marx and Engels.

Dr. C. E. Raven's "Christian Socialism" tells the pathetic but ridiculous story of forty-one of these community enterprises all of which failed disastrously and failed in a short time. He illustrates and specifies as causes of their uniform collapse: the vicious principle of equality of reward irrespective of output or ability; lack of business capacity; quarrels; indiscipline; greed; dishonesty; slackness; inefficiency—it was said, for example, "you could always tell a Christian socialist by the cut of the cooperative trousers." When the incentive of competition and private profit is removed only compulsion remains as a driving force. Without dictatorship and force, any form of Socialism collapses. As Socialist-Communist G. B. Shaw has said: "Compulsory labor with death as the final punishment is the keystone of socialism" (Fabian Tract No. 51, 1906).

F. J. C. Hearnshaw in "Survey of Socialism" (1929) says: "It is a profound truth seen equally clearly by keen sighted Christians and by keen sighted socialists that the principles of the religion of love are wholly incompatible with the only operative form of socialism viz.—that which incites the proletariat to attack all other classes; which seeks to drag down the prosperous to the level of the base; which lusts for confiscation of capital; which projects the extermination of landowners; which envisages the eradication of competition by the reintroduction of slavery under a criminal dictatorship. 'In their strictest sense Christianity and socialism are irreconcilable,' said the Rev. T. W. Bussell in a recent Bampton lecture. 'It is a profound truth that socialism is the natural enemy of religion,' echoed the *British Socialist Party* in its *official manifesto.*"

"Marxism . . . sublimated robbery into 'restitution.' It enabled the impecunious to regard themselves as 'the disinherited'; the ne'er-do-wells as 'the defrauded'; the unsuccessful as 'the oppressed'; the unskilled as 'wage slaves'; the incompetent as 'the exploited'; the unemployed as 'the sole creators of wealth and value'; the proletariat as 'the people'; and the violent revolutionaries as 'vindicators of the rights of man.' "

"Marxian socialism is potent just because of its appeal to the primitive individualism of the subnormal man. It excites his passion for plunder; it stimulates his love of fighting; it bemuses his rudimentary conscience, making him believe that he is out for justice and not for loot; it muddles his immature mind with ineffable nonsense concerning complicated economic theories of value and surplus value. Of the potency and efficacy of its appeal there can be no doubt. It is the only really effective type of socialism in existence. It entirely supersedes its utopian predecessors; for they postulate self-sacrifice and hard work, and depict an ideal community which provides its own modest sustenance by cooperative toil—a most unattractive paradise to a cave-man. Only Marxian socialism offers brigandage—systematized, rationalized, moralized, glorified. Hence, as Thorstein Veblen says: 'The socialism that inspires hopes and fears today is of the school of Marx. No one is seriously apprehensive of any other so-called socialistic movement. . . . In proportion as the movement in any given community grows in mass, maturity, and conscious purpose, it unavoidably takes on a more consistently Marxian complexion. . . . Socialists of all countries gravitate toward the theoretical position of avowed Marxism.' So, too, Clayton: 'Modern socialism is Marx and Marx modern socialism: there is no other foundation.' . . . Prof. Ely concludes: 'In socialism Karl Marx occupies a position . . . all going before him in a manner preparing the way for him and all coming after him taking him for a starting point.' " (Hearnshaw).

The Lusk Report says: "In fact the only scientific, concrete and perfectly systematic scheme" (of Socialism) "is the scheme of Karl Marx. This is the basis for materialism inherent in present day socialism, for its antagonism to religion, to ethics, to all idealism based on principles . . . that do not relate to purely material life and wealth interests."

"METHODISTS TURN SOCIALISTIC"

If the great voice of John Wesley with its call to Christianize individual souls should finally be stilled by the voice of Karl Marx with its call to class war—disguised as a call to preach the "social gospel of economic justice"—not only Methodism but the whole world will suffer.

Ominously, the Socialist "Christian Social Action Movement" of Chicago

Methodist Church headquarters says of its opportunities for teaching Socialism-Communism: "Our most fruitful field of accomplishment we believe to be within and through the agency of the Church of which we are a part. It is difficult to overemphasize the significance to the *social and economic* movement in America if the Methodist Church should be won to whole hearted advocacy and support of the social gospel. To this endeavor . . . we pledge ourselves." (p. 41 of its Handbook).

"Methodists Turn Socialistic" is the title of an article written by Socialist Chas. C. Webber (jailed in a radical strike in 1930 and defended by the A. C. L. U.), which appears in the Socialist, Garland-Fund-aided "World Tomorrow" of July 1933. In it he felicitates the Annual Conference of the M. E. Church held at Central Church, Brooklyn, N. Y. for its report on "The Necessity of Social Change—from capitalism to a socialistic economic system," and says that the motion to change the words "social ownership" (complete Socialism) in the final report to "social control" just barely passed. He says: "This debate clearly showed that the majority of the members of the N. Y. East Conference of the M. E. Church are convinced that 'capitalism' must be brought under some form of social control."

The Northeast Ohio Conference of the M. E. Church exhibited similar tendencies when "Socialized ownership and control of the country's financial and industrial system as a substitute for capitalism were recommended" (Associated Press report, Sept. 20, 1932). Other conferences have likewise adopted communistic-socialistic resolutions.

The Methodist Federation for Social Service is headed by Bishop Francis J. McConnell, Socialist, A. C. L. U., etc., and its Bulletin is edited by Harry Ward, of radical fame, and Winifred Chappell, frankly of the Communist Party campaign committee. As an ex-Communist said to me, "Most of those Bulletins sound like the Daily Worker, only more so." The April 15, 1932 Bulletin, which I have, not only frankly admitted Federation cooperation with *Communist* organizations but under the heading "Is it a Coincidence?" said: "The nature of the membership of the Federation and the *penetration of the church by this movement* is indicated in part by the fact that entirely without design one third of the Delaware Conference membership belonged to the Federation. This overlapping included every member of the commission on 'Modern Business and Industry,' 10 of the 14 commission chairmen, and two secretaries of the Board of Foreign Missions who were largely responsible for the conference, and the presiding officer, the president of the Federation."

Of the "Call to Action," which had just then resulted in the formation in Chicago of the Socialist Methodist "Christian Social Action Movement," it also proudly observed that "most of the sponsors—were members of the Federation." Concerning the Federation's financial support it said the Rock River Conference had originated and systematically used the plan of donating "one half of one per cent of the preacher's salary including house rent" to the Federation (for its Socialist and Communist-cooperating activities) and that "Philadelphia uses it in modified form."

The editorial of Dr. E. P. Clarke, editor of the Riverside Daily Press and himself a prominent Methodist layman, is reprinted in the National Republic of October 1933. To quote from it:

"The Methodist conference at Long Beach adopted resolutions urging the pardon of Mooney. It seems rather pertinent to ask what these ministers know about the Mooney case. The evidence has been reviewed by four governors—Stephens, Richardson, Young and Rolph—and they all refused to pardon Mooney. The courts have also acted unfavorably on his case in several hearings. The average citizen may well give some heed to the findings of these various investigations; and it looks as if the Methodist conference went far afield in seeking some subject on which to adopt resolutions.

"For centuries of human progress and recession it has been a controversial question as to the supremacy of church or state, but the Methodists apparently have no fear of stepping over the line. The action on the Mooney question might seem to line up the Methodists with the unsavory and violent element of Russia and America.

"Other resolutions were of similar dubious propriety. To issue its demands upon the mayor of Los Angeles to abolish the 'Red squad' of police, foe of communistic rioters, and to investigate the Better American Federation, and other organizations outside of church affiliation is hard to reconcile with the teachings of the gentle Carpenter from Nazareth, which the church is supposed to further.

"The Methodist Church is probably the most powerful of all religious denominations. It has done a marvelous good, but when their conference presumes to rule on things religious, moral and political without regard to courtesy or courts of justice we fear the church's popularity is endangered, especially with the youth of the land."

The communist Daily Worker of May 13, 1933 under the heading "Negro Bishops Back I. L. D. Fight" says: "The General Board of the Colored Methodist Episcopal Church in session in Jackson, Tenn. with 8 Bishops and 9 general officers, with more than 250 pastors and lay representatives throughout the U. S. went on record. . . . The resolution reads in part: 'The Bench of Bishops and the General Board of the Colored Methodist Church in Annual Session desire to issue the following statement to the nation with reference to the Scottsboro and Peterson cases in Alabama, and the Angelo Herndon case in Georgia. . . we feel it our duty . . . to call upon our entire congregations throughout the Nation to contribute funds and moral support to aid in such able defense as shown by the *International Labor Defense* organization; and that such donations be given concertedly, and funds sent to a designated committee and in turn to the headquarters of the *International Labor Defense.*' " (Godless Moscow's Communist organization using this means to hook Christian Negroes into the revolutionary movement). "The Bishops of the bench are: Elias Cottrell, Holly Springs, Miss.; C. H. Phillips, Cleveland, O.; R. C. Carter, Chicago; R. T. Brown, Birmingham, Ala.; J. C. Martin, Memphis; J. A. Hamlett, Kansas City, Kans.; and J. W. McKinney, Sherman, Texas."

The colored people are a sincerely religious race. As long as they stayed in Africa un-Christianized, they remained, as did pagan white men, savages. Their pagan brothers in Africa today are savages, while in a comparatively few years, under the opportunities of the American government and the inspiration of Christianity, the American Negroes have acquired professions, property, banks, homes, and produced a rising class of refined, home loving people. This is far more remarkable than that many Negroes are still backward. The Reds play upon the Negroes' love of their own people and represent them as persecuted in order to inflame them against the very white people who have in reality given the colored race far greater opportunities than their fellow negroes would give them in Africa today. Only recently the U. S. government was protesting slave holding by colored officials in Liberia. The Reds look upon the Negroes as their greatest hope. They want them to do their dirty work in stirring up bloody revolution and to bear its brunt. Then whether the Reds win or lose the Negroes will be the losers, for Sovietization is slavery. (See Lg. Strugg. Negro Rts. p. 188.)

The U. S. Fish report states: "The task of the Communists among the negro workers is to bring about class consciousness, and to crystallize this in independent class political action against the capitalist class; to take every possible advantage of occurrences and conditions which will tend to develop race feeling with the view of utilizing racial antagonism. At every opportunity the attempt is made to stir up trouble between the white and negro races.

"The negroes are made to believe that the Communists practice complete racial and social equality and that only when a Communist Government is set up in the United States will the negroes obtain equality and freedom from exploitation by the 'white bosses,' and in order to attract and impress the negro, the Communists make a point of encouraging mixed social functions where white women Communists dance with negro men and white men Communists dance with negro women. It is openly advocated that there must be complete social and racial equality between the whites and negroes even to the extent of intermarriage."

Put yourself in the Negro's place. Would you not be flattered by Dr. Tittle's act in putting over a Negro social equality plank in the 1932 General M. E. Conference in Atlantic City, following similar action by the Federal Council of Churches, even though you knew in your heart that social equality is guided entirely by human desires and feelings and that no law or plank can alter this. Neither a white nor a colored person will invite another person to supper in his home unless he wishes to. Sociability is won, not forced. Force on this point only engenders real antagonism, even bloodshed.

To quote the Chicago Tribune report of May 8, 1932 concerning this Conference, headed "Racial Question Jars Methodist Church Session": "Doctor Tittle's resolution stated that future general conferences will be held 'only in cities where there is no segregation of racial groups, no discrimination in hotels, hotel lobbies, hotel dining rooms, restaurants, or elevators.' . . . In his argument for the passage of the resolution Dr. Tittle . . . stated that the wording of his resolution 'followed closely a resolution recently adopted by the Federal Council of Churches.' . . . Such possible inability to find a city that would entertain the conference, Dr. Tittle said, would focus the attention of church and nation on the 'cause of racial equality.' . . . The M. E. Church South seceded from the northern church on the slavery issue nearly a century ago. It was pointed out in debate that 'The passage of this resolution would forever end all possibility of reunion of the two American branches of Methodism.' "

Dr. Tittle went out of his way to solicit support for Jourdain, a colored candidate for Alderman, but not of Tittle's ward. He signed a letter sent out for this purpose during the 1932 spring campaign and Jourdain was elected.

The time was, when Methodism in its zeal for personal purity frowned upon dancing. Some Methodists nowadays who are little opposed to dancing even in a church were a bit surprised, however, when several colored men were introduced into circle dances at a dance given in the parish house of Tittle's church and were thus forced upon the young white girls as partners. An M. E. Guild member whose daughter attended this dance reported that when she phoned the assistant pastor about this he said that these colored men had been invited by Dr. Tittle himself (one of them being the son of a classmate of his at college), who felt that it was now time that the young people learned to mingle with other races. (God created separate races, but Communism insists upon racial inter-mixture and inter-marriage.)

The great American colored man, Booker T. Washington, voiced the sentiment of the best elements in both races when he said the races should be as separate and distinct as the fingers of a hand and as united for the service of all humanity. Why should either race wish to lose its distinctive characteristics? Neither the races nor the sexes can ever be equal. They will always be different and have distinctive functions to perform in life.

Most shocking is the constant procession of Red and outright Communist posters and notices which disgrace the bulletin board of this gorgeous M. E. church, coupled with the fact that the minister himself is a "book editor" of the National Religion and Labor Foundation and responsible for distribution of such Communist literature as "Toward Soviet America" by Wm. Z. Foster, "Little Lenin Library," etc.

One such poster advertised "We, the People," a play by Elmer Rice, for the benefit of the militant Socialist L. I. D., in which Tittle is a leader. This play is praised by the Communist press as "an argument for revolution." Others advertised: lectures by George Soule of the "New Republic," on such subjects as "The Chances for Revolution," at the Chicago City Club, Mar. 6, 7 and 8, 1933, under the auspices of the Chicago Forum Council, of which Tittle is a member; Scott Nearing's (Communist) lectures under the same auspices; Reconciliation Trips to radical headquarters; and the Oct. 23, 1933 mass meeting for the visiting French Communist, Henri Barbusse, whose "pacifistic" cure for war is bloody Red revolution. Perhaps most incongruous of all was the large poster advertising the *"Proletarian Arts Ball"* of April 15, 1933, given for the benefit of the communist *International Labor Defense,* Moscow's propaganda and legal defense agency to aid Communist criminals—a *dance* given for the defense of Communism, which means destruction of Christianity, and advertised in a Methodist Church!

One can only regret that men like this minister possess the gifts of glorious oratory, of charm and culture to bestow upon the Socialist cause and that their humanitarian sincerity gives them additional power. For no hate-filled grimy Communist, however sincere, cursing God and capitalism from a soap box, could ever lure the Church-going "bourgeoisie" into Marxism as can a truly sincere and altruistic "Christian" Socialist. Yet both are leaders to the same ugly end—Marxism. Those repelled by the crude who would shudder at raw Marxian doctrine, sit enraptured in a church to hear Marxism falsely embellished with adornments stolen from Christianity. Under the spell of soft organ music and dim religious light, they feel that whatever the preacher's direction it *must* be toward heaven and they remain oblivious of the fact, or uncaring, that the Communist notices sent out by Satan's publicity bureau hanging in their very Church are calls to Christ's flock to hear Communists like Henri Barbusse, advocates of Christ crucifixion and throat-slitting Red revolution, preach *Communism* as the "Way and the Truth." As one sees the blind leading the blind into the ditch, one realizes that Hell must indeed live up to its reputation of being "paved with good intentions."

That some Methodists are awakening to the issue now being forced within the church by radicals, and that they wish to cleave to the "faith once delivered" and to the Rock of Ages, rather than to the new social order of Marx and Lenin, is shown by statements such as that of Methodist Bishop Leete which I have quoted under "Christian Century." The survey of Bishop Lake revealing that the Methodist Church had lost 2,000,000 members between 1920 and 1932 should also provide food for thought. The fault certainly does not lie with the drawing power of Jesus Christ, "the same yesterday, today, and forever."

"NEWS"

There is a saying: "When a dog bites a man, that is not news, but when a man bites a dog, that is news." Red meetings are constant occurrences in Evanston, Illinois. People either do not sense their significance or are used to them. It is not considered "news" that James M. Yard should at the same time be Dean of *Religious Education* of the Methodist Northwestern University, an active Communist-defending A. C. L. U. committeeman, an advertised John Reed Club speaker, and an official sponsor of the communist revolutionary Chicago Workers Theatre. (Once Methodists frowned upon the ordinary worldly theatre.) Nor, when the post of Dean of Religious Education was abolished and Yard lost his position, was the public announcement by Pres. Walter Dill Scott that Yard was *not* let go because of his radicalism, in itself, considered news. That Max Otto, a leader of the atheist movement, should be engaged in successive years by this Methodist University to lecture to its students on such subjects as "Can Science Recognize God" (Oct. 1933) and be praised and honored by the college paper for these addresses, is not news; nor is Harry Ward's address in praise of Godless Russia at Garrett *Biblical* Institute, or the sale of I. W. W. and other Red literature at this Methodist college Y. M. C. A., news. But when, following only two of the many Red meetings held in Evanston churches, a group of patriotic Americans gathered outside and sang "America" in protest against the sedition they had heard preached within, this was indeed as though a man had bitten a dog. It was *news* and the newspapers featured it!

The first of these was an A. C. L. U. meeting held in Tittle's Evanston M. E. Church and addressed by Carl Haessler, a teacher and official of the Communist Party's school of revolution at 2822 S. Michigan Ave., Chicago, and a fellow A. C. L. U. committee member with Dr. Tittle. Haessler ended his talk with a little story illustrating the A. C. L. U. viewpoint, frankly saying "And so what we want is not more *liberty* but more *license*!" On the Church bulletin board hung an announcement of Communist Scott Nearing's lectures. Tittle attended this meeting. Inside the door of the church at the close of the meeting a Communist handed out leaflets reading: "A Lecture of Vital Importance!—by Romania Ferguson who recently returned from the Lenin Institute of Moscow. On Tuesday, January 17th, 8 P. M., at The Unitarian Church of Evanston—Fight for the freedom of the Scottsboro boys! Join with the International Labor Defense! Auspices: International Labor Defense, Scottsboro Branch of Evanston."

The patriotic crowd who had attended this A. C. L. U. meeting out of curiosity, indulged afterwards in some arguments on the church lawn with Red sympathizers, among them Catherine Waugh McCulloch of the A. C. L. U., who had presided at the meeting. But this would not have merited publicity, only that a young Red who intruded himself into the conversation I was holding with friends attempted to slap my face when I contradicted him, and he was chased by my husband and some Legionnaires. The attempted but unsuccessful *slap* was news!

At the announced communist I. L. D. meeting which followed, the Reds were prepared to defend themselves against any patriotic utterances. Police were stationed inside the Unitarian Church. And one menacing looking Negro in front of us pulled out his gun and looked it over before returning it to his pocket. Others had bulging pockets. A colored woman as officer of this I. L. D. branch announced that regular meetings were held in this Unitarian Church every first and third Tuesday of the month; also that all of the 18 north side branches of the I. L. D. were expected to participate in a Communist demonstration to be held before the Japanese consulate in Chicago the following week as a protest against Japan's war against the Chinese Soviets and Chinese revolution. When this demonstration actually took place, an army of steel-helmeted policemen was required to disperse the surging crowds of Red rioters which formed and reformed to advance on the building. Several policemen were injured and one without a steel helmet had his skull fractured by Communists.

Romania Ferguson, the colored girl advertised as speaker for this I. L. D. meeting, who had been trained at Moscow's Institute for Red agitators from all countries, was then teaching with Haessler (speaker in Tittle's church) at the Communist Chicago school of revolution. She spoke of the Scottsboro case and then contrasted the wonderful life and race relations of Soviet Russia, and said that the only way for the 12,000,000 colored people in the United States to obtain a similar "paradise" was to unite with the white Communist "workers" in the "revolutionary way out" and set up a Soviet government in the United States as the Russians had done. (Pure sedition and in direct violation of the Illinois sedition law).

She was followed by Albert Goldman, fellow teacher with herself and

Haessler at the Chicago school of revolution. He said that it was a good thing the capitalistic class in America were building fine homes and other buildings as these would then be ready for the "workers" to take over and occupy by revolution in from six months to a year. He said that only old people cared for churches in Russia now; that no one under 35 went to church and, as the old people would soon die off, churches would soon be extinct there. He pointed out that children could be taught anything and that the same thing could be accomplished in America by training the young generation against religion. (A fine meeting to advertise in a Methodist Church!) Red cards were passed out at this meeting advertising a Scott Nearing lecture for the benefit of the Communist school of revolution. Nearing's lectures had been advertised on *white* paper on the bulletin board at the Methodist Church, a slight difference—in paper.

The police who had so staunchly stood by while Romania talked sedition, at once attempted to disperse the patriotic crowd that stopped to discuss the meeting outside. They were told to go back inside the church, but the group objected saying they were not wanted inside the church, that the police allowed sedition inside why not patriotism outside? When one policeman kept insisting they must either go back inside the church or go home, some in the crowd said "All right we *will* go back in. Come on!"; but as they started to do so, a woman of the church aided by a policeman barred the door of the church and flourished her arm at me and said: "You shan't come in." I said: "Keep your hands off me" as she waved dangerously near my nose and this flourishing falsely reported as "hitting" furnished the "news" for the next burst of publicity, which, however, did some really enlightening educational work. People who had been actually unaware of the Red movement in Evanston started wondering and inquiring what it was all about.

Soon after this, a patriotic group in Evanston published a pamphlet of authentic and indisputable information revealing the purposes of the organizations these ministers support. They distributed a copy to practically every home in Evanston at their own expense with the result that—? O, no, they received no praise whatever! On the contrary the patriotic editor who gave the situation in Evanston some truthful publicity and participated in preparing the pamphlet lost his position owing, so he said, to the pressure brought by M. E. Church supporters upon the wealthy "patriotic" men of national reputation who owned the newspaper!

And what did the dear smart successful American capitalist Church trustees, who collect $85,000 or more each year to support Tittle's activities, do? They issued a public statement rebuking those who would interfere with the "free" speech of the M. E. Church pulpit and expressing their staunch admiration for and support of Dr. Tittle.

One feels like snickering at the thought of the triumph of Socialism, which Tugwell, in the National Religion and Labor Foundation (see) Bulletin, (of which Tittle is an editor) says will literally *do away with* private business. One can picture with amusement these capitalists who support Socialism having had their businesses "done away with." But the sad part is that we "bourgeoisie" and the hopes and futures of the present rising "proletariat" and of their and our children would all suffer as well with the sweeping away of the American system. That is why a public political propaganda pulpit becomes a public affair and deserves public and political opposition.

The communists' Federated Press news service, Mar. 29, 1933, stated:

"The trustees of the Unitarian Church of Evanston, where the Intl. Labor Defense has been renting a hall for its fortnightly meetings, declare that they 'consider it against the spirit of the church to deny the use of its church house to any group of people who might wish to rent it for political, economic, social or educational purposes, except those whose meetings would be objectionable on moral grounds or those whose meetings might be definitely forbidden by the law of the land.'

"The Rev. R. Lester Mondale of the church had been criticized by professional patriots for allowing the I. L. D. to rent the church hall. Trustees of the First Methodist Church of Evanston similarly supported the Rev. E. F. Tittle when he was rapped by the patrioteers for permitting a civil liberties meeting in his church hall."

The Advisor of March 15, 1933, stated:

"Following the activities of the American Legion and Paul Revere Clubs in exposing the affiliations and red-supporting activities of the Reverend Ernest Fremont Tittle, pastor of the First Methodist Church, Evanston, Illinois, the government board of the church has issued a statement expressing 'absolute confidence in Dr. Tittle's Christian character and his deep unselfish devotion to his country and humanity.' We note that these profound expressions of support come from Fred Sargent, president of the Northwestern Railroad, William A. Dyche, donor of Dyche Stadium to Northwestern University, R. C. Wieboldt, and others.

"This is quite typical of the warning we have voiced continually in our bulletins. Knowing little or nothing of the ramifications of Communism and Socialism, these 'Captains' of industry listening to the siren voice of this misleader, come to his support with a vote of confidence. The average man would sing pretty hard to get the support of the millions represented by the three men named above. The moral and financial support which is given the Communist and Socialist movements by the very class that would suffer most if these agencies should win control, is one of the principal factors in the perpetuation of these movements in this country. Without this support Communism and Socialism would collapse of their own weight.

"Men like Tittle are more valuable to the Communist movement than if they were actual members of the Party. Lenin's injunction 'Get things done and paid for by others' has been fulfilled to a remarkable degree. The unfortunate part of things is that should either Communism or Socialism succeed in their objectives the loyal would have to suffer for the mistakes of the misguided. The more we study Lenin, the more we appreciate his diabolical shrewdness and psychology."

JAIL OR ASYLUM FOR ME—SUGGESTS "LIBERAL" MONDALE

The September, 1933 issue of the communist magazine "Anti Fascist Action," published by the Chicago Committee to Aid Victims of German

Fascism of the communist W. I. R., contains, in addition to material by Communist authors, a section headed "Correspondence," which invites "the true expression of workers everywhere" and says: "Here is the space! Voice your indignation, your protest, etc." To quote:

The following letter comes from R. Lester Mondale, Evanston, who takes this opportunity to answer a worker who had written to him, asking "How is it possible for Mrs. ——— (a notorious red-baiter) to insult every worker in this country, calling them 'gutter adherents,' without being thrown into a prison or insane asylum?":

> "Dear Frank:
>
> "You ask, 'How is it possible that this woman can insult every honest wage earner in this country without being thrown in a prison or insane asylum?
>
> "Permit me to tell you how it is possible for these respectable women to insult you and to get away with it. My answer will sound stranger than fiction. But Frank, the reason it sounds strange is that you have been fed up on the lies you read every day in the newspapers and the lies you were taught in the public schools—lies about every American being born free, and equal to the richest.
>
> "The lady you speak of is a well-known North Shore 'patriot.' She speaks before fashionable churches; the Legionnaires admire her; the D. A. R. ladies introduce her at speaking engagements. Now, Frank, there is a man in Chicago (another patriot, who has an organization for spying on communists and liberals) who also speaks before churches, Legionnaires and D. A. R. conventions. This man is a great friend of the lady who insulted the working men. In fact, Frank, this lady and this man more often than not are seen together in public gatherings, and the style of her anti-red pamphlets strikingly resembles the style of the reports sent out by his spy organization.
>
> "One sentence will explain why they insult you, Frank. This man I speak of was for years a professional strike-breaker in the Clay Products Industries. Do you see the connection now? By pretending to be super-patriots these people can break up the workingman's unions, keep him in poverty, and call all liberals like myself un-American Communists because we would like to see these ladies get a little less of the country's income and honest workers like yourself get your just share.
>
> "To these respectable ladies, you are a 'gutter adherent.' To them, the wife you love, 'stinks of the gutter'; to them, the babies you bring into the world are 'rats of the gutter' and they can use the gutters (whenever the super-patriots haven't parked their Packards) for their playgrounds. You 'gutter' people should be glad to kiss the hands of the wealthy for their willingness to be compelled to pay enough in taxes to keep you starving to death on the installment plan on the dole. You 'gutter' people should be glad to get a fifteen dollar week minimum wage and to starve and freeze through life while the government dumps wheat in China, plows under the cotton crops, closes coal mines, and slaughters hogs. You 'gutter' people who complain if the Citizens Committee (whose

own children go to private schools) destroy the public schools with their economies, when thousands of contractors would be willing to put up new buildings and thousands of unemployed teachers would gladly teach your 'gutter' children—you who complain are trouble makers, un-American!

"You and I know, Frank, that the 'gutter' people of New York and New England made the rulers of Cincinnati and Cleveland; that the 'gutter' people of Europe and Ohio made the rulers of present day Chicago; that the 'gutter' people of Indiana and Illinois made the pioneers of the great West. But Frank, now there is no West where you can show the world the fight there is in you; now you must not complain, you must not demonstrate, you must not strike—to do so would be to disturb the peace and be un-American. You stay where you are—*in the gutter.*

"But Frank, I have been a 'gutter' person myself. I know that you have the intelligence not to be fooled for long by the lies of the insulting 'patriots' and their schools and their newspapers.

"Your fellow workers in Germany were not fooled. They saw the German patriots grinding the life out of the working men at a time when their country was over-flowing with milk and honey, and they organized. In Germany the respectable people, such as insult you in this country, became afraid that the working man would get justice, that the working man would seize the factories in which he worked and use them for all the people, rather than for the respectable patriotic few, the owners. Today, the German relatives of those American women who insult you, are making their last desperate stand under the leadership of that madman and enemy of the worker, Hitler. They are making one last desperate stand to keep the working man in the gutter. The German workers need your help. If you can help the German working man today, help to overthrow Hitler Fascism, then, when the time comes for you to get justice in this country, they will stand ready to help you.

"The day is coming, Frank, when those who insult honest working men will be cast into prison or into the hospitals for the insane. And you, Frank, are the one to set the date.

"Very Sincerely yours,
"R. LESTER MONDALE."

Since I too may be besieged by Red Workers asking my help and advice, I now take this opportunity to answer a Red who may write to me:

Dear Red Worker:

You ask me why Rev. ——— puts on such a show of sympathy for the Communist cause and of hatred for its enemies while at the same time he himself does not come out and stand by your side as an avowed comrade? You want to know why he calls himself a "Liberal" instead of a Communist? I will explain this to you, Red. You see Rev. ——— has a much better education than you have and he likes North Shore bourgeois comforts, the title of "Rev.," an income from capitalistic sources, and he does not want to lose these nor to risk his head in Red demonstrations, nor to spend his time in smelly jails with you. Don't you see how much safer it is for him to peek out from behind the skirts of respectability, to sic you on to do the dirty work? In that way he gets the thrill without paying the bill.

After the Revolution is over, of course, I shan't blame you, Red, if you do with his kind just what your brothers in Russia did after their Revolution. They made truces with some of their outright Czarist enemies but they cleaned out as so much bourgeois trash the yellow little professors and ministers who had tried to play both sides and were true to neither, especially when it came to making sacrifices. This was right. One cannot depend on a man who is not loyal to his colors—be they Red or White.

Mike Gold has the right idea. In his communist Daily Worker column, Oct. 24, 1933, he says of these arm-chair warriors:

"One of the basic dangers has been that these intellectuals come into the movement bringing a great deal of worthless bourgeois baggage in their minds and trying to sell this junk to the movement. They sometimes demand positions of leadership, and try to revise and pervert the proletarian character of the Communist movement. . . . One of the most amazing sights to me has been to watch some of the recent recruits to Marxism around New York. Their progress is sometimes as rapid and humorous as that of an old Keystone comedy. On May 1 they suddenly discover the proletarian revolution. It had been present in the world for over 60 years but the boys shout and whoop as though they were original Columbuses. . . . By the next May Day these heroes have been completely disillusioned. Now they have a whole new program for Communism and they share the 'betrayed' feeling of a Trotsky. Really it is no wonder intellectuals get a bad name. The worker earns his Communism and the right to make mistakes by hard and dangerous experience. Do these intellectuals really EARN their right to criticize? They know nothing, actually nothing, of the revolutionary practise. It is all in their heads."

The next day he took another crack at them, saying: "the truth for which one is ready to die or (more dreadful) the truth for which one is ready to go ragged and poor . . . this really is the Integrity that the vacillating Stuart Chases cannot permit themselves to see or announce. This is the true luxury of integrity—the guts to speak out and say *'Capitalism is dead, Long live Communism!'* "

One cannot dispute Rev. ———'s statement that he belongs in the gutter; but if I felt about Communism as he *says* he feels, I would quit peddling the "opium" of religion, as Marx calls it, from a bourgeois North Shore pulpit and call myself a Communist not a "Liberal."

But wasn't it kinda cute and deteckatif-like for him to find out all by himself that a big strong man is seen with me "more often than not?" Of course he only infers—you know. Wouldn't he be surprised if he could see the door close on that man and me night after night when he brings me home? He has stayed with me for fifteen years, and, while law and engineering are supposed to be his professions, still he *does* break spinach-eating and neck-washing "strikes" on the part of our children.

Like the rotten bourgeois that I am, I bear his name. But what's in a name when one is facing at best the penitentiary or asylum as I am?

On the door of the A. C. L. U. Chicago hdqts., Room 611, 160 N. La Salle St., of which Rev. ———— and Carl Haessler are both members is printed "Institute for Mortuary Research, The Director, Carl Haessler, Federated Press," etc. Do you not see the connection, Red? While Haessler capably runs the communists' Federated Press and teaches leaders for Red revolution at the communist Workers School, his and Rev. ————'s A. C. L. U. committee in his office defend his pupils when they participate in little riot practise skirmishes. But with the Institute for *Mortuary* Research under the same capable Haessler direction, how can people like me have hope of the asylum or penitentiary after the Revolution?

Yours until I clasp a White's lily,
MRS. A. W. DILLING.

WHO ARE THEY?

Those who read newspapers these days without some knowledge of Red propaganda and its propagandists miss much of the significance of what they read. Lectures, forums and debates, advertised in such a way as to make it appear they are impartial educational entertainments of general public interest, are the mediums constantly used for subversive propaganda among the intelligentsia.

Stuart Chase, when he lectured before the society Town Hall audiences was advertised as an "economist" and author, not as a Socialist propagandist and former associate of the Berkman anarchist gang. Scott Nearing, the Communist mouthpiece of Moscow, is also referred to in the press as a lecturer and "economist." In the press notices announcing Horace Bridges as the speaker for a North Shore audience, his connection with the Ethical Society was emphasized, but no mention made of his connection with the Communist-aiding American Civil Liberties Union. He is on the Chicago Committee which has been pushing suits against the City of Melrose Park because its police, when attacked and defied by Communist rioters, were forced to uphold law and order and use guns. If these suits are successful, no one will be safe, for naturally the police will not dare to interfere with Communist agitators.

Gandhi

Vithalbhai J. Patel, speaker at the Wilmette Sunday Evening Club and Union League Club of Chicago last year was the Gandhi aid released from jail and "welcomed out" of India. He was the house guest while in Chicago, of Herbert J. Friedmann, who is on the executive board of the Chicago Civil Liberties Committee. Patel was listed in the Communist Moscow News of August 30, 1932, as the delegate for India to the Communist "World Congress Against War" which convened in Amsterdam in August, 1932.

"The Surrender of an Empire" (by Nesta Webster, published by Boswell, London), in writing about Gandhi's Moscow-financed agitations in India, has bits like this: "In 1928, the Bardoli No-Tax Campaign was carried out by Vithalbhai Patel. This agitation, though ostensibly industrial, was directly inspired by Communist agents. . . . Meanwhile money had been sent continually from Moscow to the strike leaders. In May it was publicly announced that £1575 had been sent. . . . In August a sum of £5500 . . . on September 5, £1000 from Moscow. 'The Statesman' confessed itself puzzled as to the policy of the British government in allowing Soviet Russia to remit these sums through British banks in order to foment agitation. . . . In March, Pravda (Moscow official paper) had declared that the battles in India 'are now part of the World Revolution, led, organized and watched over by the Communist International . . . in July it devoted eight columns to an analysis of the position in India, showing that Moscow was not only heavily subsidizing the revolutionary movement there, but maintaining its own spies and agents, and again admitting that it was out to destroy British power in India." (The British government sent an appeal to the Indian people saying the government and Viceroy were in entire accord with Indian desire for self-government. Gandhi, Nationalist leader, replied demanding a conference.) "The violent elements in the Nationalist camp replied more forcibly by placing a bomb on the rails outside Delhi, with the object of blowing up the Viceroy's train, which was carrying him, on December 23rd, to a meeting with Gandhi and other Nationalist leaders. The plot, however, failed in its effect . . . (1930) Savage rioting broke out in Calcutta; a raid, accompanied by the murder of British officials and every form of violence, was made on the armories of Chittagong; loyal Indian police were massacred and burned by brutal mobs at Sholapur; the Afridis descended from the hills and Peshawar burst into flame. As Gandhi peacefully observed to the 'Times' correspondent 'Non-violent and violent movements always go hand in hand.'

"Then and then only, when India was in a blaze from end to end, the Viceroy took alarm and resolved on firmer action. . . . On May 5 Gandhi was arrested. His successors to the leadership, the aged Abbas Tyabji and Mrs. Naidu, then the Pandit Motilal Nehru and Vithalbhai Patel followed him into imprisonment later."

Glenn Frank

When a radical forum wrote a local paper asking that in its columns "particular attention" be given to Glenn Frank, their lecturer to be, the paper asked me to write this publicity and published the following (Oct. 28, 1932), which complied with the letter if not the spirit of the request.

Those who have paid "particular attention" to the Red movement know that Glenn Frank, president of the U. of Wis., is on the Mooney-Billings Committee organized by the American Civil Liberties Union, which fights for Communists and upon whose national board sit such Moscow-controlled Communists as William Z. Foster, Scott Nearing, and Robert W. Dunn. They know also of the exposures made by John B. Chapple, fiery Wisconsin editor, whose revelations showing the connections between radicalism and atheism at Wisconsin University and Communism-Socialism-La Folletteism resulted in such an uprising at the last election that for the first time in forty years the La Follette dynasty was overthrown. The Wisconsin voters registered their unwillingness to surrender to the threefold Red onslaught against (1) the right to own property, (2) the American home and Christian moral standards, (3) the American form of government.

Harry Elmer Barnes, who said "There is no such thing as sin, scientifically speaking, and hence it disappears into the limbo of outworn superstitions. The Bible deserves no reverential awe," etc., founded the Wisconsin American Civil Liberties Union chapter with headquarters at the University. Governor La Follette, and Prof. Meiklejohn, head of the Wisconsin University Experimental College, are committee members. Meiklejohn's pupils on the Communist Labor Day, May 1, 1931, were flying the Red flag and singing the Internationale without known protest from him. One of his pupils, Fred Bassett Blair, now running for governor on the Communist ticket, was sentenced to serve a year for rioting in Milwaukee. Meiklejohn worked diligently to have him released. Governor La Follette pardoned and released him before his term expired.

Bill Haywood House, named in honor of the Anarchist-Communist and occupied by radical students, a large proportion being self-professed Communists, has been situated on University property. A large photo of Lenin, sent from Russia, decorated the walls. (U. P. Dispatch.)

The Wisconsin University Zona Gale Scholarship was awarded to a young Communist, David Goronefsky, alias Gordon. He led a Communist parade at Madison which resulted in the injury of two persons. He wrote an obscene poem against the United States, printed in the communist Daily Worker, which was so vile that he was sentenced to serve three years in the New York State Reformatory. Zona Gale, one of the Wisconsin University Regents wrote the New York Parole Board begging for Gordon's early release saying in part (U. of Wis. Cardinal, May 8, 1928): "I am interested in the future of David Gordon. Mr. Gordon was the winner of a scholarship in competition with many other applicants, a scholarship which he held at the time of his conviction for an offense committed *before he entered the University of Wisconsin.* As the donor of this scholarship I want you to know that with the approval of the president the scholarship will continue to belong to Mr. Gordon upon his release from the reformatory."

In a notorious case involving student immorality at Wisconsin University, Prof. William Ellery Leonard defended the actions of the immoral students in a long letter to President Frank, saying their actions were "founded on the decent instincts of human nature." Dean Nardin in upholding marriage and morality stated: "Prof. Leonard is an advocate of free love and a contributing force to unsanctified marriage." President Frank was evasive. It was noted, however, that after notoriety died down somewhat, Dean Nardin was discharged while Prof. Leonard continued to hold his position. (See Chapple's "La Follette-Socialism.")

Victor Berger, the Milwaukee Socialist, in a speech before a radical group, said: "The ballot box is simply a humbug. Now I don't doubt that in the last analysis we must shoot, and when it comes to shooting Wisconsin will be there." He advised radicals to have good rifles and the necessary ammunition. He died before his dreams materialized. This announcement appeared in the Chicago Daily News (March 20, 1931): "The Victor Berger Foundation is preparing to launch a drive next month for a $100,000 fund as a nucleus for a national chain of daily newspapers 'for the promulgation of liberal thought and public welfare.' Prof. John Dewey of Columbia University is one of the leaders of the foundation. Associated with him are Clarence Darrow, Jane Addams, *President Glenn Frank of the University of Wisconsin,* Upton Sinclair, and Elizabeth Gilman of Baltimore."

The Communist Daily Worker looked with such approval upon Maurice Hindus' book about Russia, "Broken Earth," that they ran it serially. John Dewey wrote the introduction to Hindus' next book. Hindus dedicated his last book about Russia to Glenn Frank.

Harry Ward, A. C. L. U. leader, with Harry Elmer Barnes and Sherwood Eddy, sent a demand to the United States War Department that the ban on the Communist party in the Philippines be lifted. This was after 300 Communists had been arrested charged with sedition. One month after this, at the commencement exercises, President Frank bestowed an honorary degree upon Harry Ward saying: "As chairman of the American Civil Liberties Union you have valiantly defended those basic rights of free speech, free press, and free association, without which neither scientific advance nor social progress is possible."

A short time after this the New York Times (August 22, 1931) reported: "The American Civil Liberties Union announced yesterday it had cabled $500 to the Philippines to aid the legal defense of Communists indicted there for sedition." The next spring (May 19, 1932) a New York Times report on rioting, revolt and arson in the Philippines said: "Fourteen Communists, free on appeal and assisted by the American Civil Liberties Union, are declared to be leading general agitation."

Prof. Max Otto, well known for his atheistic ideas, is prominent at Wisconsin University. His picture appeared in a periodical with the heading: "Is there a God?" and below this: "Max Otto says—NO."

One who has paid "particular attention" to Glenn Frank is not surprised that he thought it necessary to announce publicly that he is not a Communist, and that he believes in the existence of a God. The Chicago Tribune commented editorially upon this announcement.

Einstein

One of the best press-agented men in the world is Albert Einstein, who dares to tell the smart professors that his Relativity theory is so far beyond their intelligence that they cannot understand it—and gets away it! They know, sure enough, that they cannot understand it but evidently figure that the best thing to do is to keep quiet and leave him undisturbed on his self-erected scientific throne, lest perchance his theory might be found to have some basis some day, in which event they would be classed as ignoramuses for having doubted it in the first place.

Fellow workers in the Red movement are glad, of course, to magnify Einstein's importance in order to point out with pride that the greatest most un-understandable scientist in the world is one of their number.

But no publicity for some reason is given to those sober courageous scientific authorities who with proof deride Einstein's theory. Dr. Nikola Tesla takes sharp issue with Einstein, saying: "The Einstein theory in many respects is erroneous." Charles Lane Poor, Ph. D., Professor of Celestial Mechanics at Columbia University, states: "The supposed astronomical proofs of the theory as cited and claimed by Einstein do not exist." Prof. Thomas Jefferson See, a distinguished scientific authority, says: "Einstein is neither astronomer, mathematician nor physicist. He is a confusionist. The Einstein theory is a fallacy. The theory that ether does not exist, and that gravity is not a force but a property of space can only be described as a crazy vagary, a disgrace to our age." Prof. Dayton C. Miller lectured before the Western Society of Engineers on his experiments in complete refutation of the Einstein theory.

Perhaps the most exhaustive treatise on the Einstein theories is the volume entitled "The Case Against Einstein," written by Dr. Arthur Lynch, a very eminent English scientist. While much of this treatise is a technical analysis of the mathematical and philosophical fallacies of Einsteinism from a scientific standpoint, part of it is of interest to the layman. Dr. Lynch cites such critics of Einstein as the noted mathematicians, M. Picard, Henry Poincaré, "perhaps the most celebrated of his race since Cauchy," G. Darboux, "who received the Nobel prize for mathematics," M. Paul Painleve, LeRoux, the German Klein, the Italians Ricci and Levi Civita, "who have done most to develop the mathematical instrument used by the Relativists" and who reject Relativity, and the American "framers of the case which is the corner stone of the theory, the Michelson-Morley experiment. Michelson rejected the Relativist theory."

Dr. Lynch analyzes Einstein's popular vogue and says: "Yet as I cast my eye over the whole course of science I behold instances of false science, even more pretentious and popular than that of Einstein gradually fading into ineptitude under the searchlight; and I have no doubt that there will arise a new generation who will look with a wonder and amazement, deeper than now accompany Einstein, at our galaxy of thinkers, men of science, popular critics, authoritative professors and witty dramatists, who have been satisfied to waive their common sense in view of Einstein's absurdities."

Personally I shall not forget the merry evening my husband and I spent at a University round table lecture devoted to the Einstein theory. As our instructor diagrammed space-time as a circle and visioned us meeting ourselves as infants again coming around the circle of time, and demonstrated the speed of a locomotive and its beams of light in accordance with relativity and in contradiction to all accepted mathematical rules, we all, including the instructor who admitted he could not understand it himself, howled with glee. We felt as though we had spent an evening in a mental madhouse.

While I am unable to understand the scientific value of the Relativity theory, I can understand the "relativity" of Einstein to his daughter who married a Russian and lived in Russia following her marriage. I can also see the "relativity" of the atheist book he endorses and of the "Down with War, Up with Revolution" pacifism of the War Resisters International, of which he is a leader, to the communist Congress at Moscow, which he attended (he appears in a photograph published by the Better America Federation), and the relativity of the communist Workers International Relief, which he sponsors, the communist Congresses against War and in favor of Red revolution (see his "Who's Who"), which he has helped to assemble, and the communist International Committee for Struggle Against War, upon which he serves (1933) with Maxim Gorki, Romain Rolland, Henri Barbusse, etc., Moscow's world leaders for bloody Communist revolution. Atheism, pacifism for capitalist countries, and militarism for Russia are Communist principles.

The League of Nations Chronicle, published in Chicago, March 1931, reporting Einstein's address to 400 "peace" advocates in Chicago said: "No one mentioned relativity. . . . Militant opposition to militarism was his keynote. . . . 'It is my conviction that the *only way* is actual refusal of military service,' he said. . . . 'What I propose is *illegal*, but whenever a government demands criminal actions from its citizens, they have a very real right to *oppose* it and we must uphold them.' "

In his speech to the War Resisters conference at Lyon, France, he not only urged defiance of the government authority which requires citizens to bear arms in defense of their government, but also said: "I have authorized the establishment of the Einstein War Resisters Fund. Contributions should be sent to the treasurer of the W. R. I., 11 Abbey Road, Enfield, Middlesex, England." This fund is for the defense of "militant war resisters."

"The Patriot" of London, Nov. 30, 1933, said: "It is reported from Berlin that the entire seized property of Prof. Einstein and his wife has been confiscated under the law regulating the seizure of property of Communists."

When Hitler started his campaign against Communists and Einstein's Jewish relatives, Einstein demonstrated his "relativity" theory in a perfectly understandable way by reversing his "pacifist" position and urging Belgian war resisters to go to war against Germany.

When the Woman Patriot Society tried in 1932 to bar Einstein from entering the United States, the whole company of Red intellectuals rose up in wrath. Jane Addams' W. I. L. P. F. sent a message criticizing the American consul for even questioning the idol, Einstein.

Yet, legally, Einstein's membership in only one of these communist organizations was sufficient to exclude him from admission to the United States.

The United States Immigration Act of February 5, 1917, requires: "That the following classes of aliens shall be excluded from admission into the United States: Anarchists or persons who believe in or advocate the overthrow by force or violence of the government of the United States, or who disbelieve in or are opposed to organized government . . . or who are members of or affiliated with any organization entertaining and teaching disbelief in or opposition to organized government. . . . The giving, loaning or promising of money or anything of value to be used for the advising, advocacy or teaching of any doctrine above shall constitute the advising, advocacy or teaching of such doctrine." Etc. (Section 3.)

Nor is it necessary to prove he "had knowledge of the contents of the programs . . . or any one of them. It is sufficient if the evidence showed that he was a member of, or affiliated with, such an organization as contemplated by the statute." (Case of "Kjar vs. Doak," page six.)

The Supreme Court of Pennsylvania in the Robert F. Clark case (301

Pa. 321) held: "Anarchy will stalk in unmolested if individuals, because of superior education, age or mental reservation, are to be permitted to resist or to modify the laws of Congress according to their own individual beliefs." That was a naturalization case where the fundamental principle of the United States Constitution, namely, the power of government to defend its existence and enforce its laws by force of arms, was at issue.

The program of Einstein's War Resisters International, which is actually affiliated with at least three Anarchist-Communist societies, is in entire conformity with the teachings of Karl Marx as quoted by Lenin: "Not merely to hand on from one set of hands to another the bureaucratic and military machine . . . but to shatter it, and it is this that is the preliminary condition of any real people's revolution."

Jane Addams

Greatly beloved because of her kindly intentions toward the poor, Jane Addams has been able to do more probably than any other living woman (as she tells in her own books) to popularize pacifism and to introduce radicalism into colleges, settlements, and respectable circles. The influence of her radical protegées, who consider Hull House their home center, reaches out all over the world. One knowing of her consistent aid of the Red movement can only marvel at the smooth and charming way she at the same time disguises this aid and reigns as "queen" on both sides of the fence.

I was impressed with her charm and ability (and subterfuge) at my only meeting with her, which was at a Legislative Hearing held at the Chicago City Hall, May 29, 1933. She was there to testify against the passage of the Baker Bills, which aimed only at penalizing the seditious communistic teaching of overthrow of this government in Illinois colleges. One would not have believed any person wishing to appear decently law abiding could have objected to these Bills which easily had passed the Senate; but the vehement fight the college presidents (Hutchins, Scott, McClelland, and McGuire of St. Viator's) put up against them at the first Hearing in Springfield was in itself a revelation.

At the second Hearing in Chicago, in reply to a gentleman's testimony concerning Prof. Lovett's revolutionary speeches, Miss Addams, after pleading for freedom to teach Socialism and Communism in schools because these are world movements, said she was sure Prof. Lovett (who lives at Hull House) had never advocated the overthrow of this government by force and violence; in fact, said she, "I don't believe I ever heard of any member of the Communist Party doing so! Of course you all know I am a pacifist and would not advocate the overthrow of *anything* by force and violence." (Lovett writes the introduction of "Recovery Through Revolution" [see].)

I arose to remark that Communists *do* advocate such overthrow as she should know since she had been associated with enough of them, reminding her that she had spoken only in December on the same program with Communist Scott Nearing at the Student Congress Against War (see) at the University of Chicago. She started to deny this, but I held up the program of the Congress with her name on it. Then she said: "But Prof. Nearing is not a member of the Party any more." I replied: "He is lecturing under the auspices of the Friends of the Soviet Union and for the benefit of the communist Chicago Workers School of revolution at 2822 S. Michigan Ave." "O, I didn't know," she murmured. (I had the announcement card with me.)

During this Hearing, Carl Haessler of this same school of revolution sat taking notes, probably for his communist Federated Press, and when it adjourned he came along with Jane Addams as she magnanimously sought me out, her "enemy," to introduce herself. Graciously she said, "I don't believe we have ever met, Mrs. Dilling, I am Miss Addams." We shook hands and I said "I believe you have a *very* kind heart for the poor, Miss Addams, but why is it you have been helping the Communist movement all these years? Communism only pulls people down!" She said "I am not a member of the Communist Party." "No, of course not," said I, "You can do so much more good from the outside. But you have belonged to every outstanding Red-aid society from the American Civil Liberties Union with its terrible record in aid of sedition down to this last National Religion and Labor Foundation which uses atheist Soviet cartoons and talks plain revolution." She said, "I make no apology for my connection with the Civil Liberties Union. It was quite necessary during the war. But what is this National Religion and Labor Foundation you mention?" I dug down into my brief case and drew out its letterhead and pointed to her name on its national committee. Mildly she professed to know nothing about it, and her woman companion at her request copied off the address, presumably to chide the organization for "using her name."

Only a few weeks later (July 21) the Chicago Daily News carried the story of a radical strike in which three patrol wagons full of strike pickets were arrested for "hurling missiles at returning workers and the police," and stated that Lea Taylor of Chicago Commons (who had also testified against the Baker Bills at this same Hearing), Karl Borders of Chicago Commons, and Annetta Dieckman of the Chicago Y. W. C. A., along with Francis Henson, Victor Brown, Norman Sibley, and Ralph Barker, *four delegates to the national conference of the National Religion and Labor Foundation then being held at Hull House,* had joined the picket lines. So, after "discovering" her membership and making inquiries, Miss Addams must evidently have approved of the National Religion and Labor Foundation sufficiently to sanction its convention at Hull House.

Newspaper photographers approached asking to take our pictures, as Miss Addams stood talking with me after the Hearing, with Carl Haessler grinning like a little Cheshire cat at her side. He had written me up in the communist Federated Press as a "rabid D. A. R.," following our previous encounter (see article "Red Ravinia").

To the photographers Miss Addams said: "If Mrs. Dilling is broadminded enough to have her picture taken with me, you may take it providing you will call the picture 'Two D. A. R.'s' " and to me, "You know I *also* am a D. A. R." But before a Haessler-Addams-Dilling photo could be snapped then and there I truthfully spoke up and said "I am not a D. A. R., I am sorry to say," which upset her plan.

Roland Libonati, chairman of the Legislative committee holding the Hearings, was impressed no doubt by the array of talent ("important" personages such as college presidents and Jane Addams) which opposed the Baker Bills and favored freedom for communistic teaching in our schools. Living as he does within a block of Hull House, he must also realize the influence Jane Addams wields in his political district. At any rate, the Bills were killed, as he then intimated to reporters that they would be.

Miss Addams wields great influence also at the Chicago Woman's Club, where the communist Chicago Workers Theatre (see) play "Precedent" was given in May, 1933. Its Feb. 1934 play was presented at Hull House.

The communist Daily Worker, Saturday, Oct. 21, 1933, said: "Today the John Reed Club will hold a banquet for Henri Barbusse at the Chicago Woman's Club, 72 E. 11th St. . . . Jane Addams internationally known social worker, winner of the Nobel Peace Prize and head of the Women's International League for Peace and Freedom, writes that although illness will prevent her from attending the mass meeting, she expects to be present at the banquet and is anxious to meet M. Barbusse. . . . B. K. Gebert, district organizer of the Communist Party, and Herbert Newton, editor of the Workers Voice, are also scheduled to speak at the banquet. . . . Barbusse will be accompanied by Joseph Freeman, editor of the New Masses and Prof. H. W. L. Dana, noted author."

(See "Who's Who" for affiliations of Jane Addams.)

G. Bromley Oxnam

Louis Adamic, radical, in an article entitled "Liberals in Los Angeles" in "Plain Talk" magazine for December, 1929, said: "A few years ago there was in town a Methodist minister, Methodist only in name—Bromley Oxnam, a man of tremendous personal force, who ran a dingy institution called the Church of All Nations, preaching in a vacant storeroom in an out-of-the-way street, interesting himself in all sorts of liberal and radical movements, fighting for the atheistic wobblies who got into jail, pacifists, anarchists and other victims of police persecution, running for office on independent tickets, speaking from all sorts of platforms five or six times a week. He wanted to stay in Los Angeles, but it was no place for a man of his sincerity and capacity and so when he received an offer of the presidency of De Pauw University in Indiana he wisely accepted it."

The Daily Worker, Communist newspaper, Oct. 26, 1926, stated: "Rev. Oxnam, one of the American delegation of 24" (Sherwood Eddy's delegation) "just returned from Soviet Russia spoke at the open forum of the Civil Liberties Union at Music Arts Hall to a large audience. After reciting what he had seen in that immense country he urged that the American government recognize the Union of Socialist Soviet Republics. . . . Such statements as 'priests are considered parasites and are therefore disenfranchised' and 'tho there is absolute religious freedom in Soviet Russia yet there are no young people in the churches' were greeted with enthusiastic applause."

The American Vigilant Intelligence Federation of Chicago reprints the charges which Leroy Smith, a member of the M. E. Church of Los Angeles, laid before the M. E. Southern California Bishop, A. W. Leonard, on Sept. 22, 1923. To quote from these charges, specifications and mass of data concerning Oxnam's radical activities: "I hereby charge that G. Bromley Oxnam,

. . . has proven by many and varied public activities, by many personal affiliations and by numerous spoken and printed utterances that he is utterly unfit to represent the Methodist Episcopal Church as one of her ministers."

"Specification 1" cites details of a meeting held April 13, 1921, in behalf of prisoners convicted for sedition at which Oxnam "had as a fellow speaker Harriet Dunlop Prenter, the well known Communist."

Specification 2 tells how Oxnam spoke at "a protest mass meeting against the Criminal Syndicalism Act of the State of Calif."; and at this same meeting it was publicly advertised that "members of the I. W. W. now on trial would address the meeting and did address said meeting, six of these men being introduced as martyrs."

Specification 3 charges that May 19, 1923 under A. C. L. U. auspices in the interest of Upton Sinclair and in defense of so-called "Freedom of Speech," in company with specified notorious radicals, "Mr. Oxnam opened the meeting with prayer and as he started to pray, several in the gallery called out 'Cut out the prayer'; one of these men said, 'Who the hell is that Bird?' One of the others answered, 'That's Oxnam, the Wobbly Preacher.' The first one asked, 'Is he with us?' The second one replied, 'Is he? You ought to hear the blankety blank blank preach sometimes.' Then the third man broke in—'That's the dope—that's great, once we get a few of these Holy Joes coming our way, we'll be able to put the skids on the whole damned works, president, constitution, government and all'—others agreed with fine fervor"; etc. (Note: "Wobblies" is the slang term for "I. W. W.'s.")

Specifications under the second charge concerning Oxnam's unfitness for the ministry include: "One of Mr. Oxnam's trusted Lieutenants, an enthusiastic teacher in his Sunday School, has been Mrs. Kashub. Mrs. Kashub entertained Harriet Dunlop Prenter and other numerous Communists and I. W. W.'s on visits to this city. Mrs. Kashub has been teaching the children from 9 to 11 years of age in the Church of All Nations; she has been using Walter Thomas Mills' book called 'The Struggle for Existence' as a text book. This book is wonderfully adapted to make it easy to understand Socialism. On a certain Sunday morning not long since, in the Sunday School Class of Mrs. Kashub, the following program was carried out: First—The studies in Socialism lasted one hour. Second—There was one hour of dancing. Third —There was twenty minutes of singing—the meeting closed by singing 'The Workers' Flag is the Red Flag.' "

Specifications No. 2 states: "The Boy Scout movement of the Church of All Nations (Methodist Episcopal) is in charge of a young Russian Socialist by the name of Klussman."

Specification 3: "The Church has a library of most up-to-date Socialist and Communist books," etc.

Specification 4: "His religious services have not been religious services." (See "Who's Who" for affiliations.)

"Red Ravinia"—Carl Haessler

Several years ago, because of the activities of a certain "Red" clique, Ravinia acquired the nickname "Red Ravinia" in neighboring communities.

Carl Haessler spoke at the Ravinia Woman's Club April 13th, 1932, in favor of Communism and violent Red revolution in America. His audience was composed of well-dressed women who enjoy the comfortable homes, great new inventions, and educational benefits of church and school which the American "capitalistic" system has fostered as never before in the world's history. To be sure, Haessler is a past master at the art of revolutionary propaganda. His own account of how he and a few others incited the strike of 3,200 fellow prisoners in Leavenworth Penitentiary demonstrates practical ability which no doubt helped him to secure his present position as Chicago head of the Communistic propaganda news-gathering agency, The Federated Press.

In appearance, Haessler is harmless, even effeminate, and before the Woman's Club he employed to perfection the manner of a sweet startled deer beseeching its captors for mercy, which is so appealing to the mother instinct. He told the ladies he wanted to avoid offending anyone, and apologetically asked that his propaganda be regarded as an academic question (not a question of life and death to all of us). By all the subtle arts of indirection and innuendo he proposed a revolution of terror and confiscation as smoothly as though he were offering his listeners a charming prospect or a chocolate cream, and most of them seemed to accept it as such.

Haessler's introductory remarks were that, while he was not a member of the Club (laughter), he felt that he had *taken part in its life through his wife,* who had acted as Program Chairman, Secretary of the Board, etc., for over ten years. After hearing this, I could well understand the difficulty patriotic citizens and club members have had in trying to combat "Red" influence in Ravinia, where the Haesslers live.

Briefly, his arguments were for the confiscation of all private wealth and property, and for putting these under state control (control by state political machines being purer, supposedly, than private control). He said that while the Socialist and Communist systems were interchangeable, Socialists think they can win by peaceable means, while "history tells Communists" that violence is necessary, and that his sympathies were with Communism. He said Communism is inevitable and we had only to choose between "dragging along" for several generations or "having it over with" by quick, violent revolution. He deceptively compared this proposed revolution with our own Revolutionary War for independence (as Communists always do). He nonchalantly observed that while revolutions undoubtedly "pull down houses," many of these need pulling down anyway, and while they undoubtedly kill people, all of these would have to die later anyway, so that, after a few generations this violence becomes immaterial. He omitted to say that property destruction and death would be very material to *this generation.* However, as Haessler's appearance is harmless and appealing, the ladies applauded him enthusiastically; they had "listened," evidently, to his appearance.

It is interesting to note in Communist literature that criminal violence is always promoted and excused under a cloak of supposed martyrdom. Negroes are urged to fight their white "oppressors," who actually have freed them and given them better jobs and opportunities than exist in Africa. Mooney is the Anarchist convicted of bombing the 1917 Preparedness Day Parade at

San Francisco, when many were killed and injured. To the Communists, Mooney is "framed" by his "capitalistic oppressors," and freeing him is a popular Communist cause. Freeing the Scottsboro Negroes convicted of raping two white girls is another Communist enthusiasm (in order to stir up race hatred). Patriotic citizens of Ravinia speak with despair and indignation of their futile efforts to combat "Red" influences in Ravinia and of the persistence required to keep the United States flag displayed there. As soon as a "Ravinia Red" is reproached for disloyalty to America, he or she at once assumes the martyr role, giving the role of "oppressor" to the patriotic person, who is then referred to slightingly as a "hundred-per-center," "a narrow-minded D. A. R.," or a "super patriot." To praise the American Legion in "Red Ravinia" society circles, would be the social faux pas inexcusable.

No one in Ravinia has ever accused Brent Dow Allinson of being a "super patriot." He is the infamous slacker who refused to serve his country in the World War and, like Haessler, is a penitentiary alumnus. His mother is an active member of the Ravinia Woman's Club.

Haessler served twenty-six months in Leavenworth and Alcatraz Prisons (between June 1918 and August 1920), for refusal to serve the United States during the World War. His reasons for refusing to serve, and his activities while confined in prison, are clearly set forth in his article describing the strike incited by the "political prisoners" of whom he was one. This article appeared in the Communist "Labor Defender" (issue of January, 1927), and is entitled "The Fort Leavenworth General Strike of Prisoners—An Experiment in the Radical Guidance of Mass Discontent." It says in part: "Not every convict took part in the general strike that brought the War Department of the strongest nation on earth to its knees. But those who scabbed will remember the surging of overwhelming cooperative action that all but engulfed them." (He tells how the 500 out of 3,700 prisoners who did not join were afraid to return to their cells for fear of the strikers.) "How was this feeling brought about? It is an interesting experiment in the solidarity of mobilizing and directing mass discontent. A small but highly organized and highly conscious body of prisoners led the great majority *almost without the knowledge of anybody but the leaders and their opponents,* the military command of the prison. This small body of leaders were the political objectors to the Wilson war. . . . *Their purpose was general revolutionary propaganda, and,* if the occasion proved favorable, *revolutionary action* . . . The politicals as a rule *had no conscience* so far as means of furthering their *main purpose* was concerned. They deemed Socialism, or *Communism,* as many of them began to call it after the Russian revolution, as more important than any specially ordained way of achieving it . . . Where the commandant used spies and propaganda the politicals did likewise with better effect. In a few months they had the roughneck ordinary military convict *tatooing red flags instead of the national emblem* on their arms and chests. In some weeks more they had them rejecting every chance to shorten their terms by reinstatement with the colors." (He describes the riots in which arms were broken, teeth knocked out, and prisoners "bruised to a jelly.") "That night the commandant surrendered. The men then returned to work. Their strike had been successful beyond their dreams. . . . The political prisoners had not produced the mob but they had supplied the direction for it. The two factors cooperated in a *neat little revolutionary experiment* behind the walls and under the guns of Fort Leavenworth. *When the tide of events produces similar conditions on a national scale, it may be that men of national calibre will be ready to carry out a similar experiment on national and international lines."* (All italicising mine). He was the spokesman for the strikers, as is proudly stated in the radicals' Am. Labor Who's Who.

In 1922, Haessler became Managing Editor of the Federated Press, which is described in the U. S. Government Fish Committee report on Communism (2290). The Communist Party of America considers the Federated Press its own press service organization, and upwards of 200 papers in the U. S. are affiliated with it. It represents and is closely associated with the Soviet Union Telegraph Agency. Louis P. Lochner is European director and has an office in Berlin where he is in close touch with the International Propaganda Bureau of the Communist International of Moscow. Haessler is also an official of the communist Workers School (of revolution).

Haessler, while lecturing August 12, 1926, is said to have referred to his sister Gertrude as being then in Moscow studying "Journalism." Gertrude Haessler writes not only for Communist papers but also for the Communist "Party Organizer." She is an authority on publications of "shop nuclei," or revolutionary units in shops. The April, 1932, issue of that startling Communist paper, the "Labor Defender," bears an article by her entitled "In Blue Blood Kentucky." In it, she ridicules the "capitalistic" Lindberghs and their lost baby, as Communist papers have been doing ever since the kidnapping. She upholds Mooney and the convicted Scottsboro Negro rapists and says: "Lindbergh shaking hands with the czars of the underworld in the frantic effort to get back his 'chubby, golden-haired son' doesn't give a damn for the nine terrified little dark skinned Scottsboro lads . . . Lindbergh, the ideal of American boyhood, never made a move to see that Mother Mooney got her son back during the entire fifteen years of his legal kidnapping."

After Haessler's talk at the Ravinia Woman's Club, one of the "Red Ravinians" said to a friend of mine who has the honor, which I have not, of being a D. A. R. member; "I don't understand you D. A. R.'s at all. You are all for that old 1776 Revolution but against this *new* revolution." Communists delight in making it appear that our Revolutionary War for Independence and the second Russian, or Bolshevik, revolution, as well as the proposed international "Red" revolution, are all similar. They are not similar. Our Revolutionary War of 1776 was to establish only the right of this nation to govern itself. The first Russian revolution which overthrew the Czar in February, 1917, formed the Kerensky government, patterned somewhat after our own, and was a revolution concerning only Russia. The U. S. was the first nation to officially recognize the Kerensky government. But eight months later, in October, 1917, about 36,000 Russian Communist Bolsheviks overthrew the Kerensky government and proceeded to repudiate all national debts and set up a dictatorship *over*, not *of*, the "proletariat," more autocratic than any Czar's. They confiscated all private property, murdered at least 3,000,000 persons of the upper classes and of those resisting dispossession. They abolished all religion, for Communists everywhere must not only be atheists themselves but also militantly anti-religious. They set up and financed, as part of the Soviet government, the Third International, whose purpose is (quoting U. S. Government Report 2290) "the stirring up of Communist activities in foreign countries in order to cause strikes, riots, sabotage, bloodshed and civil war . . . The ultimate and final objective is by means of world revolution to establish the dictatorship of the so-called proletariat into one world union of Soviet, Socialist Republics with the capital at Moscow."

As this U. S. report says (page 65): "There is a sharp distinction between the right to advocate in an academic way any doctrine we like and the right, which is not right, under any reasonable interpretation of our Constitution, to preach and plan the overthrow of our republican form of government by force and violence." This report says in regard to the Soviet "five-year plan": " 'Pravda,' the Communist organ, of August 29, 1929, fully defines its purpose: 'It is a plan tending to undermine capitalist stabilization. It is a great plan of world revolution.' " In spite of the efforts of radical Senators with Soviet sympathies, like Brookhart, Borah, La Follette, etc., the U. S. Government long refused to officially recognize the Soviet government.

Atheism and Communism go hand in hand. The February 14, 1928, issue of the Communist "Daily Worker" announced an illustrated lecture by Carl Haessler on "The Twilight of Religion in Soviet Russia" under the auspices of the Russian branch of the American Association for the Advancement of Atheism at Workers' Home, 1902 West Division Street, Chicago. On January 7, 1932, Haessler gave a lecture "The Twilight of the Gods in Russia" at the Communist atheist forum at 109 West Chicago Avenue, Chicago.

Haessler is a committeeman of the American Civil Liberties Union, of which the U. S. Report (2290) says: "The A. C. L. U. is closely affiliated with the Communist movement in the U. S. and fully ninety per cent of its efforts are in behalf of Communists who have come into conflict with the law. It claims to stand for free speech, free press, and free assembly; but it is quite apparent that the main effort of the A. C. L. U. is to attempt to protect the Communists in their advocacy of force and violence to overthrow the Government, replacing the American flag by a red flag and erecting a Soviet government in place of the republican form of government . . . Roger Baldwin, its guiding spirit, makes no attempt to hide his friendship for the Communists and their principles." It was this same Roger Baldwin who recently threatened to sue Henry Ford for "countenancing the injury" of the Communist rioters at the Ford plant.

Roger Baldwin was the speaker for the Ravinia Woman's Club January 14, 1931. Mrs. Haessler was then the Club's Program Chairman. Ravinia residents tell of the community dinner which preceded the evening meeting of the Ravinia Woman's Club March 3, 1926, at which the honored speaker was Scott Nearing, the well known Communist lecturer and a director of the communistic Garland Fund. They tell how a patriotic school teacher challenged Nearing's statements about Russia and how this challenge was brushed aside. Scott Nearing and Arthur Fisher of Winnetka (A. C. L. U. Chicago Chairman) staged a debate on a favorite Communistic subject, "Imperialism" with Carl Haessler acting as chairman, at Plumbers' Hall, 1340 Washington Boulevard, Chicago, on March 10, 1928.

During the question period which followed Haessler's talk at the Ravinia Woman's Club, I asked a question which showed my antipathy for Haessler's proposed revolution. The audience at once broke into a surging tumult of angry comment against me. Then, defying this hostility, I said: "Oh, you have been listening to the insidious propaganda of the voice of Moscow, whose government is attempting to overthrow our Government, etc. Just as in Russia, you would be the class first to be murdered in case of a revolution here. This meeting is an insult to a loyal American citizen!" Then, indeed, there was a near riot. The Club President (Mrs. Robt. L. Grinnell, wife of the President of the local school board) quieted the meeting momentarily by apologizing to Haessler. Most of the audience applauded this act vehemently. She then came to me, and to prominent members of patriotic organizations who were with me, to criticize and to demand by what right we were there. I was the invited guest of two members but I refused to divulge their names, feeling that they had been persecuted enough in Ravinia for their patriotic leanings. At Ravinia, once again, as in the Leavenworth Prison revolt, Haessler "led the majority almost without the knowledge of anybody but the leaders and their opponents."

This is a time when the entire world is feeling the unrest caused by the strikes, sabotage, and revolutionary activities of Communists in India, Germany, England, South America, New Zealand, America, and so on. Wealthy Americans are now losing their fortunes, aging with worry, and turning to despair and to suicide. Every American is feeling the economic pinch caused by deflation and by the Communist "plan of economic unstabilization" or "plan of world revolution." The person who joins Communists in accusing our capitalists of closing their factories and ruining themselves for the purpose of ruining the poor is either blind or willfully seditious. We do need the Jeffers and Bachmann Federal Bills for our protection, but when loyal fighting Americans unite in insisting that our elected officials enforce the Illinois statutes covering sedition, then organizations like the Ravinia Woman's Club, Y. M. C. A., and University of Chicago (a hotbed of similar speakers) will lose their taste for hiring men of Haessler's calibre to preach revolution to audiences who are also held responsible under these laws for attending such meetings.

The Illinois Criminal Code (Chapter 38, Sections 558-564) provides a penalty of one to ten years in the penitentiary for advocating the overthrow of our Government by unlawful means, and a fine of $500 to $1,000 and imprisonment for six months to one year for knowingly attending a meeting at which such overthrow is advocated.

"I AM NOT INTERESTED"

Police line the streets when the Red flag is paraded down the streets of Chicago, in defiance of the Illinois sedition law. Any week one may attend immense revolutionary Red meetings, which are given ample police protection.

In fact, the Daily News last year reported that the only unseemly incident in one Communist parade was when a Red flag was snatched from the hands of a marcher by a bystander, but that it was quickly restored to the Red by the police.

The Chicago police department granted a permit for a parade Sunday, December 17th, 1933, of loyal Ukrainian-Americans who, after a service in their church, wished to march to a hall to hold a meeting and raise funds to try to save their relatives in the Russian Ukraine, now being "liquidated" —deliberately starved to death—by the Soviet government. Even pro-Soviet news reporters estimate the deaths by such starvation during the last year as numbering in the millions, while the American Communist press maintains that such "liquidation" of bourgeois elements who object to Soviet tyranny and destruction of religion, must go on until Russia is a "pure" Communist state.

Dr. Emil Tarnawski, loyal American citizen, and president of the affiliated Ukrainian-American societies of Chicago, with some 10,000 members, also Lt. Nelson E. Hewitt, warned the Chicago police department, asked for special police protection for this parade, and told them that a secret meeting of the Reds had been held to plan an attack on the parade and that Dr. Tarnawski and many of his people had been personally threatened with death if they marched.

But only *two policemen* were with the 3,000 Ukrainian-American marchers at the time the Reds attacked them by first throwing Communist leaflets from above, then, as they looked up, throwing down bricks in their faces from an elevated station platform. Hundreds of Communists along the sidewalks simultaneously rushed in from both sides, and assaulted them with iron pipes, tools, brass knuckles, etc. They tore the American flag to pieces, and about 100 were injured. I personally saw many bandaged heads at the Ukrainian meeting which I addressed. Dr. Tarnawski received a severe leg injury and for some time was unable to walk. The communist Daily Worker reported the attack jubilantly as a Communist triumph.

Judge Gutnecht (see Robt. Morss Lovett in "Who's Who"), who heard the cases the next day, was reported in the press as criticizing the police for having only arrested Communists, and not the Ukrainians whom they had attacked as well! When their cases were tried only two received ten and two received thirty days in jail for this bloody attack!

When sixteen of us, including Mrs. Tarnawski, as a delegation representing various patriotic societies, called upon Chief of Police Allman the following Tuesday and laid the facts before him, I attempted to show him a copy of the "Red Front of U. S. A.," a Communist revolutionary military publication which boldly lists recruiting stations in New York, Los Angeles, Chicago, etc. where Reds are urged to sign up for military training for just such attacks, and in order to give the police "their due" in strikes and riots, to "open food storage places," and says, "Any day may be the beginning of the revolutionary struggle" and that "the dashing to pieces of the whole apparatus of government is in the period of revolutionary uprising, thus easier to accomplish. The Chicago office, 101 S. Wells St., Room 707 . . . meets at 2322 W. Chicago Avenue" (near where the attack occurred). Chief Allman said, "We have recognized those people now." (We have not recognized the overthrow of this government.) He refused to look at this Red publication, saying very coldly, *"I am not interested."*

While Chief Allman has been often praised by radicals and by the 1932 report of the Red-aiding Chicago Civil Liberties Committee for his "enlightened attitude" toward "civil liberties" for Communists, some of us are still interested in civil liberties for Americans, in the protection of the *American* flag, and the enforcement of the Illinois State sedition law. The attorney for the Ukrainian-Americans called upon the Federal authorities the same day and was told that they are no longer interested in Communist activities. Is anyone interested? Are you? What are *you* going to do about it?

I. SO-CALLED "PACIFISM"—IS IT CHRISTIAN OR RED?

(II Cor. 7:14) "Be ye not unequally yoked together with unbelievers: for what fellowship hath righteousness with unrighteousness? and what communion hath light with darkness?"

(Matt. 12:29) "How can one enter into a strong man's house and spoil his goods unless he first bind the strong man? and then he will spoil his house. He that is not with me is against me; and he that gathereth not with me scattereth abroad."

The sincere Christian pacifist, determined in spite of Biblical prophecy to immediately invoke Christ's final reign as Prince of Peace on earth by disarmament, buries his head in the sand like an ostrich, blindly ignoring the fact that those most dominant in influencing, financing, boring from within, if not actually controlling the great majority of pacifist societies are Socialists and Communists who appear in the clothing of sheep crying "Peace! Peace! when there is no peace" while they themselves, like ravening wolves, are agitating "class struggle," "class war," civil wars and bloody revolution.

"Beware of false prophets," said Jesus Christ (Matt. 7:15), "which come to you in sheep's clothing but inwardly they are ravening wolves. Ye shall know them by their fruits. Do men gather grapes of thorns or figs of thistles?" —or peace of civil war or godliness of atheistic Socialism-Communism? one might add.

Jesus Christ, who so militantly fought sin and so tenderly sought to save sinners from the inescapable penalties of their sins, taught that "wars and rumors" of wars would continue, "for these things must first come to pass. And nation shall rise against nation and kingdom against kingdom" (St. Luke 21:10), until a final era of great tribulation and warfare against Christianity (such as Communism is preparing) would culminate in a mighty conflict ushering in HIs second coming and real reign as Prince of Peace. Throughout the Scriptures, it is foretold that one of the signs preceding that era would be the return of the Jews, scattered over the earth, to Palestine, their homeland.

The great conflict, as visioned by St. John (Revelation, Chap. 17, 18), will take place on the plains of Armageddon in Palestine, between lovers of God and ten blasphemous kingdoms, in power but a short time, under the control of "that great city which reigneth over the kings of the earth" called

"The Mother of Harlots and Abominations of the Earth" (a description perhaps of Moscow and its blasphemous anti-God, anti-moral hordes now plotting to control all governments). "These shall make war with the Lamb and the Lamb shall overcome them: for He is Lord of Lords and King of Kings: and they that are with Him are called and chosen and faithful." "For her sins" (the city's) "have reached unto Heaven and God hath remembered her iniquities." In regard to this final conflict, Jesus said (St. Luke 21:20): "And when ye shall see Jerusalem compassed with armies, then know that the desolation thereof is nigh." (Verse 22): "For these be the days of vengeance, that all things that are written be fulfilled." (St. Luke 21:12): "But before all these, they shall lay hands on you and persecute you delivering you up to the synagogues and into prisons, being brought before kings and rulers for My name's sake." (Christians are now persecuted by the Russian government and similar persecutions are under way in Mexico and Spain. Churches closed, ministers banished, Marxian education enforced '35.)

St. Paul (Timothy 3:1-7) says: (1) "This know also, that in the last days perilous times shall come." (2) "For men shall be lovers of their own selves, covetous, boasters, proud, blasphemous, disobedient to parents, unthankful, unholy." (3) "Without natural affection, truce-breakers, false accusers, incontinent, fierce, despisers of those that are good." (4) "Traitors, heady, high-minded, lovers of pleasures more than lovers of God." (5) *"Having a form of godliness, but denying the power thereof:* from such turn away." (6) "For of this sort are they which creep into houses, and lead captive silly women laden with sins, led away with divers lusts." (7) *"Ever learning, and never able to come to the knowledge of the truth."*

One is forced to think, in this connection: of those present-day, Moscow-loving, intellectual ministers who rewrite the Bible and teach it in modernist style so as to leave faith in little besides its covers—"having a form of godliness but denying the power thereof"; of those, "Ever learning and never able to come to the knowledge of the truth," who follow, like a will-of-the-wisp, every conflicting theory, so uncertain, so wobbly in their own faith that they willingly yoke their Christian faith equally together with the agnostic, the depraved Hindu and similar cults, in a "Fellowship of Faiths," which applauded Wm. M. Brown (unfrocked Bishop) when he said: "We must banish capitalism from the earth and gods from the skies!"; of Russia falsely *boasting* of its "new social order," Communism-Socialism, which teaches, in Russia and abroad (subsidized by the Soviet Govt.): Atheism and *blasphemy; disobedience to parents* (Children of parents disenfranchised because of being Christians are urged to publicly disown their parents in Russia); *want of natural affection* on the part of parents (who are urged to put their children into state orphanges for "mass education" (because of the lack of such orphanages, thousands are deserted); *trucebreaking* (Moscow makes "Non-Aggression Pacts" with nations within which she is maintaining Moscow-directed schools training agitators to stir up bloody revolution and civil war); *incontinence* or "free love" (taught by Marxian Socialists-Communists as "freedom from bourgeois sentimentality" and from the "capitalistic private ownership of one man and one woman for each other," and propagandized everywhere by such sympathizers with the Red movement as: Communist Dreiser, Bertrand Russell, Bernard Shaw, Havelock Ellis, Judge Ben Lindsey (aided by the Garland Fund), Freud, etc., etc.; by "sex" publishers such as the Eugenics Publishing Co.; by some radical and numerous commercially-greedy motion picture producers whose pictures glorifying prostitution and vice inspire people "to be led away with divers lusts"—and so on.

"Pacifist" Clarence V. Howell, director of Reconciliation Trips, announced that he was voting for and supporting the Communist Party in its 1932 campaign. "Pacifist" J. B. Matthews, exec. sec. of the "Pacifist" Fellowship of Reconciliation, and a militantly revolutionary speaker at many Communist meetings, was booked as co-chairman, with Communist Donald Henderson, of the communist U. S. Congress Against War, Sept. 29, 1933, and fellow speaker with Communists Earl Browder and Henri Barbusse at its sessions (Daily Worker, Sept. 8, 1933).

That the "Pacifist" Fellowship of Reconciliation deliberately uses the name of Christ to propagandize communistic theories among Christians is shown in its release to members advising: "Position A. Keep Central and Typical the Reference to Jesus—Brief A. (1) To omit all reference to Jesus from our public statement of purpose or to make our reference to Him incidental, so that it might be inferred that the Fellowship began with central emphasis on the way of Jesus but has now substituted a wider basis, are positions both subject to the following objections: . . . The Fellowship would have less chance to *influence churches and the Christian Student Movement and to secure their cooperation in spreading radical Christian views on war, economics, and race issues*. . . . Many members might feel compelled to start a new organization to regain the advantages of the original unequivocal basis of the Fellowship *for demonstrating 'left-wing' Christianity*. (3) Much practical work of the Fellowship would be jeopardized. *Hitherto our leadership and support have come mainly from Christian sources*. These sources especially have made possible the extension of our work in Europe, Central America and Southern United States. If the leadership and support of them is seriously diminished *what evidence is there that other pacifist groups can take over this work and carry it on?*" . . . But stating our objective in terms of His type of love, has in addition to the advantages implied above such reasons as the following: (1) *The unique fitness of Jesus of Galilee to be a world wide symbol of pacifism . . . the utter conflict between His way and the way of military preparedness and war*," etc., etc.

But Jesus Christ was not a "left-wing" proponent of "radical views on war, economics and race issues." While teaching love and pity in the heart for enemy or sinner, He said (St. Luke 11:21-23): "When a man armed keepeth his palace his goods are in peace. But when a stronger than he shall come upon him, and overcome him, he taketh from him all his armour wherein he trusted, and divideth the spoils. He that is not with me scattereth against me." In St. Luke 22:35, He said: "When I sent you without purse, and scrip and shoes, lacked ye anything? And they said, nothing. (Verse 36): Then said he unto them But now, he that hath a purse, let him take it, and likewise his scrip: and he that hath no sword, let him sell his garment, and buy one. (Verse 38): and they said, Lord behold here are two swords. And he said unto them, It is enough." He also said (Matt. 10:34-37): (34) "Think not that I am come to send peace on earth, I came not to send peace, but a sword. (35) For I am come to set a man at variance against his father, and the daughter against her mother, and the daughter-in-law against her mother-in-law. (36) And a man's foes shall be they of his own household. (37) He that loveth father or mother more than me is not worthy of me."

Nor was He pacifistic in His denunciations of sin and hypocrisy, for when they came to Jerusalem "Jesus went into the temple, and began to cast out them that sold and bought in the temple, and overthrew the tables of the money changers, and the seats of them that sold doves; And would not suffer that any man should carry any vessel through the temple. And he taught, saying unto them, Is it not written, My house shall be called of all nations the house of prayer? but ye have made it a den of thieves." (St. Mark 11:15-17.)

I think of that when I see Communist posters on the bulletin boards of Christian Churches.

Jesus taught that the Kingdom of God is within the individual heart. He rebuked the idea of making His Kingdom a political system over this world until after the final culmination of evil in the great Armageddon conflict and the defeat of that "mystery of iniquity" which works to keep this world in strife. (Eph. 6:12): "For we wrestle not against flesh and blood, but against principalities, against powers, against the rulers of the darkness of this world, against spiritual wickedness in high places."

During His fast (Matt. 4), He was "led up of the spirit into the wilderness to be tempted of the devil . . . the devil taketh Him up into an exceeding high mountain and sheweth Him all the kingdoms of the world and the glory of them: And saith unto Him, All these things will I give Thee, if Thou will fall down and worship me. Then saith Jesus unto him, Get thee hence, Satan: for it is written, Thou shalt worship the Lord thy God, and Him only shalt thou serve." Today some "Christians" are *not* turning a deaf ear to this bid for temporal power made by the satanic Marx.

They came asking Him whether they should revolt against Caesar's government by refusing tribute and said: (Matt. 22:17-21): "Is it lawful to give tribute unto Caesar, or not? But Jesus perceived their wickedness, and said, Why tempt ye me, ye hypocrites? Show me the tribute money. And they brought unto him a penny and He saith unto them, Whose is this image and superscription? They say unto Him, Caesar's. Then saith He unto them, Render therefore unto Caesar the things which be Caesar's; and unto God the things that are God's."

None of Christ's disciples taught a political revolution either in the name of Christ or of "social justice." But the traitorous or misguided Christians of today are doing so in teaching the "social gospel" of Socialist-Communist revolution for the sake of the political "new social order" of atheist Karl Marx. In warning against the false prophets that shall "deceive the very elect," Christ said: "For wheresoever the carcass is there will the eagles be gathered." So Christian pacifists today, dead to the realization that they are cooperating with Jesus Christ's crucifiers when they cooperate with Marxians for the "pacifism" of civil war, merely serve as the carcasses for these revolutionary eagles to feed upon.

How earnestly Christ asked his disciples three times in the Garden of Gethsemane to watch with Him and to pray lest they fall into temptation! But three times He came to find them sleeping. The last time, sadly, He said (Matt. 26:45): "Sleep on now and take your rest: behold the hour is at hand, and the Son of man is betrayed into the hands of sinners." Then Judas approached with those who were to crucify Him and betrayed Christ to them with a kiss. So again today with the kiss of supposed friendship for Christ the Judas "Christian" worker for atheist Socialism-Communism betrays our Lord within His own sanctuary to the Socialists-Communists who wait only for the power to destroy the Christian faith. It is as unsuitable to yoke Christianity to Socialism as it is to yoke Christianity to atheism or to yoke Christ's teaching of the indissolubility of marriage and the family unit to the Marxian teaching of "free love." The "class struggle" and "class war" of Karl Marx have nothing in common with "Love your neighbor as yourself" and frequent admonitions against coveting "anything that is his." Karl Marx very correctly stated, in respect to the success of his *own* teachings, that the Christian "Religion is the opium of the people." It deadens people to the call of the "Mother of Harlots and Abominations of the Earth" to follow the Marxian way of hate and lust and class war. Instead, the teaching of the "Light of the World" offers them "The Way, the Truth and the Life" everlasting. Christians should read the Parable of the Talents on the unworthiness of doing nothing, and be sure that they are aligned on God's side in this conflict to "fight the good fight" against satan's "whited sepulchres," the Red pacifists.

II. PACIFISM AND ITS RED AIDS

Anyone willing to peruse the dry documentary evidence by reading, for example, the lists of Communist organizations and leaders named side by side with "Peace" organizations and leaders, as cooperating and official supporters of such Communist-organized and controlled affairs as the various Congresses against War (World, U. S., Youth, Student), cannot doubt that the Pacifist and Revolutionary movements are linked together by hoops of steel.

One might wonder why revolutionaries support Pacifism. That they *do* back Pacifism with good hard cash is shown by reading the Garland Fund Reports. One sees, for example, that the Fund's directors: Communists Wm. Z. Foster, Robt. W. Dunn, Scott Nearing, Eliz. Gurley Flynn, and Benj. Gitlow (the first American Communist sentenced during the war), and their close associates and fellow directors Socialist Norman Thomas, Harry Ward, Roger Baldwin, etc., voted large sums of money in successive years to Jane Addams' Women's International League for Peace and Freedom (see), which agitates against all R. O. T. C. and C. M. T. C. Camps, all military training and armament for the United States but advocated recognition of militaristic Russia and sweetly suggests abolition of property rights (Communism).

One is surprised that a "peace" leader like Miss Addams could serve with these same men for 10 years on the national committee of the American Civil Liberties Union, 90% of whose efforts are in defense of Communist revolutionaries, and not realize that their first plan is for bloody world revolution and not "peace." One may choose to believe either that Miss Addams was too dull to comprehend this, or that she believed a Communist revolution would aid peace eventually, or draw one's own personal conclusions.

These same Garland Fund Communists and their associates voted "To a group of students at Northwestern University and Garrett Biblical Institute, Evanston, Ill.—April, 1924—for anti-militarist movement, $497.41," recording in the same official report sums given: to the Anarchist school at Stelton, N. J.; to the Communist press; to the American Civil Liberties Union for its Communist defense activities; to the communist Labor Defense Council to aid their own director Wm. Z. Foster and his fellow Communists arrested at Bridgman, Mich.; etc.

In the 1925-28 Report, we see they voted: to the "Optional Military Drill League, Columbus, Ohio—for one half expense of campaign against compulsory military training, $250"; to the "Wyoming State Conference Methodist Church, Laramie, Wyo.—for publication of literature against compulsory military training, $300"; and to the "Committee on Militarism in Education, New York City (1) For preparation and distribution of pamphlet on 'Military Training in Schools and Colleges in the U. S.' $5,400 (2) Toward general budget, $5,000," and later another $2,000; at the same time voting to the Young Communist League at Superior, Wis., $2,000; another $2,400 to Jane Addams' W. I. L. P. F. and $6,122.10 to the communist Workers School of New York City, which trains leaders for violent Communist revolution on the United States. Are these gifts for contradictory purposes?

Pacifists frequently refer to Soviet Russia's disarmament proposal as a proof of its peaceful intentions. Maxim Litvinov, as Soviet "Peace Envoy," proposed to the League of Nations, in 1928, that all nations, including Russia, immediately and completely disarm. This Maxim Litvinov, who is Meyer Genoch Moisevitch Wallach (also alias Finklestein, Graf, Maximovitch, Buchmann, Harrison), "In 1908 was arrested in Paris in connection with the robbery of 250,000 rubles of Government money in Tiflis. . . . He was deported from France." The bomb thrown by Stalin in this robbery killed or injured fifty people. Litvinov's secretary Fineberg "saw to the distribution of his propaganda leaflets and articles. At the Leeds Conference, 2 June, 1917 (to hail the Russian Revolution to organize British Democracy to follow Russia, and establish Soviets to replace our Government), Litvinov was represented by Fineberg" (London Patriot, July 20, 1933). Litvinov was barred from England for his seditious activities; admitted back under Ramsay MacDonald's Red Socialist government. Interception of Litvinov's messages from Moscow caused the raid on Arcos, Ltd., and the severing of diplomatic relations between England and Russia (resumed again under Ramsay MacDonald).

Lord Cushendum, aware of the persistent and flagrant violation of Russia's Trade Agreement to cease revolutionary propaganda in England questioned Litvinov before the League of Nations, asking him whether his "peace" proposal of disarmament would include the cessation of Soviet government fomentation of civil war in all countries. To this Litvinov replied (N. Y. Herald Tribune, Mar. 23, 1928): "It had never occurred to us and we had no grounds for believing that the League intended to include under the questions of disarmament and security the prevention of *civil war* and the *class struggle.* I may say without the slightest hesitation that the Soviet government would never have agreed to participate with the British or any other government here represented in working out questions regarding the class war or the struggle against *revolution.* It would be naive to expect such work from a government which owes its existence to one of the greatest revolutions in history."

The communist Daily Worker, in a thesis entitled "The Struggle Against Imperialist War and the Task of the Communists" (Jan. 3, 1929), emphasized the point that this Soviet disarmament proposal was in harmony with, not opposed to, the world revolutionary movement, saying: The aim of the Soviet proposal is not to spread pacifist illusions, but to destroy them, not to support capitalism by ignoring or toning down its shady sides but to propagate the fundamental Marxian postulate that disarmament and the abolition of war are possible only with the fall of capitalism. The difference between the methods of combating pacifism employed by the proletariat in the Soviet Union and those adopted by the working class in capitalist countries does not mean there is a contradiction between the two; nor does it follow that Communists in capitalist countries must not make use of the Soviet Government's declaration on disarmament in carrying on agitation among the masses. On the contrary the disarmament policy of the Soviet Government must be utilized for purpose of agitation much more energetically and to a wider extent than has been done hitherto . . . as a means (1) For recruiting sympathizers for the Soviet Union—the champion of peace and socialism; (2) For utilizing the results of the Soviet disarmament policy and its exposure of the imperialists in the effort to eradicate all pacifist illusions and to carry on propaganda among the masses in support of the only way toward disarmament and abolition of war, viz., *arming of the proletariat, overthrowing the bourgeoisie and establishing the proletarian dictatorship.*" (Emphasis supplied.)

Under the title "What Is True Is True," Izvestia (official Soviet govt. organ), Mar. 1, 1928, quoted the accusation " 'As for Russia, in reality it is striving to destroy civilization in all countries of the world and at the same time proposes disarmament'—From a speech by John Hicks," presenting below it a poem of reply by Damian Byedny,

Bela Kun, member of the Communist International, says in the Daily Worker (Sept. 14, 1934): "The Soviet Union does not pursue a League of Nations policy any more than revolutionary workers, when they conclude a collective agreement are pursuing a policy of class collaboration. The Soviet Union when it enters this League of Nations will pursue a Soviet policy just as revolutionary workers in an enterprise where they are working on the basis of a collective agreement pursue a policy of class struggle."

The Daily Worker Sept. 19, 1934, states editorially:

"The task of mobilizing for the defense of the Soviet Union is not weakened in any way, either by United States recognition or entry into the League of Nations. The Soviet Union, as Izvestia in its leading article points out, is strengthening its own mighty arm of defense of Socialism through the Red Army. . . . The greatest strength of the Soviet Union lies in the vigilance of the militant toiling masses throughout the world who are ready to spring to the defense of the victorious proletarian revolution. . . . We must demand a stop be put to shipment of arms to Fascist Germany, to Japanese Imperialism. . . . We must rally the masses for defense of the Soviet Union. . . . One of the chief questions before the U. S. Congress Against War and Fascism to open in Chicago on Sept. 28, '34, will be this very point." (See communist Am. L. Ag. War & Fascism (p. 124) formed by Communist Party and very active all over the U. S., 1934.)

When military training was added to the program of the Young Communist League the communist Daily Worker, (Aug. 6, 1928) explained:

"Our Leninist position on militarism and war is very clear and certain. We are NOT against war and against militarism as such. We are against IMPERIALIST war; we are against BOURGEOIS militarism (i. e. the militarization of the proletarian and farmer youth to fight in the interests of the bourgeoisie). But we are in favor of REVOLUTIONARY wars (wars of oppressed colonial peoples against the imperialist powers, civil wars of proletarian revolution); we are in favor of the military training of the proletarian youth to learn to use arms in the interests of their class and against the bourgeoisie. 'An oppressed class that does not strive to learn to use arms . . . deserves to remain in slavery.'—(Lenin.) We are therefore opposed to pacifism (which opposes, as a matter of principle *All* war and *All* military training). . . . Our main task of course is to prevent the young workers who are being militarized from becoming traitors to their class; it consists in winning them for the proletarian class struggle and getting them to use their training *for the benefit* of the workers and not against their own class . . . and this attitude is in no contradiction to—on the contrary it clearly falls in with our bitter and most determined struggle against new imperialist wars and bourgeois militarism. . . . We realize very well that under present conditions and for the next period of time, the chief way for us to obtain military instruction is in the military organizations of the bourgeoisie (regular forces, National Guard, military schools, R. O. T. C., C. M. T. C., etc.); of course, as Comrade Gorki points out (Jugend Internationale, May, 1928) the sending of our comrades into these bourgeois military institutions 'implies no rejection whatever of the attempt to set up a class organization of the proletariat to provide military training for young workers.' "

The communist Daily Worker editorial of Sept. 30, 1933 was addressed to the Communist-called U. S. Congress Against War, then in session in N. Y. City, Earl Browder, nat. sec. of the Communist Party, and Henri Barbusse, French Communist who came to America especially for this Congress, being the headlined speakers to share the platform (according to Daily Worker, Sept. 28, 1933) with Mrs. Annie Gray, speaking as director of the *Women's Peace Society*, Emil Rieve, A. J. Muste, Devere Allen of the World Tomorrow (*War Resisters' organ*), and others; five delegates had been elected from the Pa. Branch of Jane Addams' W. I. L. P. F. to attend. (Sept. 29, 1933 Daily Worker.)

This editorial said: "The Communist Party urges upon the Congress a real united front on the basis of a fighting program against war—a *revolutionary* working class program. . . . Serious systematic work must be undertaken in every factory, on every dock, on every ship, arousing these workers against war, exposing every detail of the war preparations for them, setting up Anti-war committees, hampering and working to prevent the manufacture and shipment of war material and munitions. . . . Phrase mongering, empty peace talk—this is not the road. *Mass action behind a revolutionary program* is the road the congress should follow, starting now against the N. R. A. All the honest elements, all persons and organizations *ready to fight* can unite behind such a program."

"The A. B. C. of Communism" (by N. Bukarin and E. Preobrazhensky, English translation by Eden and Adar Paul, issued by Communist Party of

Great Britian) is a standard Communist text book used everywhere in Party schools. It states on p. 83: "The proletariat is fighting solely on behalf of the new social order. Whatever helps the struggle is good; whatever hinders, is bad." . . . "We must promote disintegration in an army which is ranged against the workers and is at the orders of the bourgeoisie, even though the latter consists of our fellow countrymen. Failing this the revolution will succumb . . . a revolutionist who destroys the State apparatus of the bourgeoisie may consider that he is doing excellent service." On p. 129: "To think that the revolution can take place without civil war is equivalent to thinking there can be a 'peaceful' revolution."

The formation of Soviet nuclei throughout our armed forces is covered under "Soviet Organization in the U. S."

The seditious pronouncements of the Socialist Party and the jailing of numerous Party leaders during the war, the attempts of the Socialist Independent Labour Party of England (see "English Red's") to cause revolution, and present Socialist Party activities, are covered more fully under the title "Socialist Party (and the New Deal)."

SOCIALIST PARTY (AND THE NEW DEAL)

Because the Socialist Party generally favors the taking over of the government first by legislative means, relying on a throat-cutting revolution principally as a finishing touch when it becomes necessary, it is called "yellow" by the Communist Party and "practical" by its followers. Chameleon-like, the Socialist agitator colors himself to fit the group he is addressing, appearing as a delicate-pink, "Christian" social reformer in Churches, and as a throat-cutting capitalist-hating revolutionary and a genuine Marxian atheist in militant labor circles. Since 1912 the Socialist Party has achieved practically its entire 1912 platform, passing hundreds of socialistic laws and "stealing" regular party elections by electing Socialists as regular party candidates, until now in 1933 the entire Socialist Party rejoices at the socialistic New Deal and radical "Roosevelt Appointees" (see).

Under the heading "Longuet Urges All Socialists to Support N. R. A.," the Chicago Daily News, Sept. 15, 1933 reported: "Jean Longuet, French Socialist leader and grandson of the founder of socialism, Karl Marx, declares today in the French socialist organ Populaire that socialists everywhere should approve President Roosevelt's program because it is rapidly trade-unionizing the United States." Without more extensive unionization than America has ever had the Reds believe a general strike would be unsuccessful. Communists, anarchists and I. W. W.'s have always advocated the general strike as the prelude to revolution. Most revolutions are preceded by the general strike. The English general strike, altho planned to result in Red revolution, failed. The Daily News, Sept. 21, 1933 quotes Clarence Senior just home from the Second Internationale conference in Paris as saying: "For the first time in its history the Socialist and Labor internationale indorsed the general strike as a means of thwarting an outbreak of war." (Or turning war into revolution.)

Norman Thomas writing in the socialist New Leader, Aug. 19, 1933 issue, says: "The Roosevelt program has achieved certain things . . . these things do not constitute Socialism but State capitalism, although a kind of State capitalism unquestionably influenced by Socialist influence and agitation. . . . The great hope of the New Deal is that it may make it a little easier . . . to advance toward a truly Socialist society." Says the Socialist "World Tomorrow" (Aug. 31, 1933 issue): "When the aims of the Ickes-Perkins-Richberg forces at the Capital are compared to those of the previous Administration, the change is indeed breath-taking. Most of the pet nostrums progressives have advocated throughout the last two decades are now being tried on a huge scale at Washington. To consider the formation of a new party at such a time, a party that seeks to fit in between Rooseveltian liberalism and that of the Socialist Party of America seems to us the sheer madness. . . . Whatever the weaknesses of the Socialist Party in the past or in the present, it has been making gigantic strides in the right direction."

Upton Sinclair, active in both Socialist and Communist organizations, the press reports, is to run for governor on the 1934 Democratic ticket in California. Socialist La Guardia was elected as the "fusion" candidate for Mayor of N. Y.

The Socialist and Communist Parties fight like brothers. Just as the Communist Party fights Socialist leadership everywhere, but at the same time cooperates with and works for the same ends as Socialists, so the Communist Party is now bitterly fighting the socialistic New Deal, in which it considers Socialists are sitting too prettily, and is insisting that the "revolutionary way out of the crisis" is the only way. Each Party accuses the other of disrupting the Socialist-Communist movement.

Norman Thomas is one of the "militant" members of the National Executive Committee (N. E. C.) of the Socialist Party who voted in 1933 for an immediate "united front" with the Communist Party, according to the May, 1933 issue of "The Communist" (p. 428), which states that of the N. E. C. members Norman Thomas, Albert Sprague Coolidge, Powers Hapgood, Darlington Hoopes, and Leo M. Krzycki voted for immediate formal cooperation with the Communist Party, while Morris Hillquit, James D. Graham, Daniel W. Hoan, Jasper McLevy, John L. Packard and Lilith M. Wilson, the "old guard," voted to wait for action by the two Internationals. The vote evidently went by a very close margin, 6 to 5, against immediate formal cooperation. So, April 17, 1933, Clarence Senior, exec. sec. of the Socialist Party, sent the following reply to the Communist Party which was printed in "The Communist" (same issue): " 'The national executive committee has voted to comply with the request of the Labor and Socialist International not to enter into united front negotiations with national sections of the Communist International until the L. S. I. and the Comintern have reached an agreement for an international united front.' (quoted in full—C. A. H.)" (Clarence A. Hathaway.)

The Socialist Party's New Leader, Apr. 8, 1933, stated: "In answer to a request by a committee of the Communist Party for a so-called 'united front' against fascism, the Conference stated that it lacked authority from any of its national and international parent bodies to unite with a party which, while making gestures in the direction of a united front, has since its inception followed a policy of disuniting and disrupting the laboring elements of the world. As soon as the Communist Party 'discontinues its policy of destruction of our united strength, a united front will be possible not only against fascism but against all the forces of capitalism which are grinding down the strength of labor.' "

"But Norman Thomas puts the case for the 'militants' most clearly," says "The Communist" (May 1933), and reprints Thomas' letter, which was sent out by the Socialist Party N. E. C., in which Thomas says (the voting was by mail): "I am voting *Yes* on Comrade Krzycki's motion for the appointment of a sub-committee to discuss with the sub-committee of the Communist Party the question of united front. *I cannot too strongly urge the adoption of this proposal.* I have recently been traveling rather extensively in New England and elsewhere and know that in our own Party and outside of it we shall suffer very considerable harm if we can be made to appear to be blocking any kind of united front action. Frankly, I am skeptical whether the Communists will undertake united action on honorable terms. But for the sake of our own members, especially our younger people, it must be made obvious that it is they who sabotage the united front, not we who disdainfully reject it," etc. "The Communist" adds that the united front proposal "requires more than here and there a joint meeting or now and then a joint conference." Socialists and Communists have had these all along.

Though jealous of each other, Socialists and Communists since their division in 1919 have worked together, intermingled, and quarreled like a family. When they split in 1919, Morris Hillquit, the "conservative" N. E. C. member, always a Socialist Party executive, said (New York Call, Sept. 22, 1919, also Lusk Report): "Our newly baptised 'Communists' have not ceased to be Socialists even though in a moment of destructive enthusiasm they have chosen to discard the name which stands for so much in the history of the modern world . . . they have not deserted to the enemy. The bulk of the following is still good Socialist material and when the hour of the real Socialist fight strikes in this country we may find them again in our ranks."

In a letter appearing in the New York Call, May 21, 1919 (also Lusk Report, pp. 524-30), headed the "Socialist Task and Outlook," Hillquit referred to the Socialist-Communist impending split and said: "Let them separate honestly, freely and without rancor. Let each side organize and work its own way, and make such contribution to the Socialist movement in America as it can. Better a hundred times to have two numerically small Socialist organizations, each homogeneous and harmonious within itself, than to have one big party torn by dissensions and squabbles, an impotent colossus on feet of clay. The time for action is near. Clear the decks."

When five Socialist members of the N. Y. State Legislature were expelled on the ground that the Socialist Party was not an American political party but a revolutionary organization, the 1920 Socialist Party national convention issued a report which "modified the relations with the Third Internationale of Moscow so as to permit association with that institution while giving to the Socialist Party in America the opportunity to carry out its campaign in this country by parliamentary methods" (Lusk Report p. 1780).

Benj. Glassberg, a leading socialist Rand School instructor, in a letter published in the N. Y. Call, July 26, 1920, commented on this Socialist Party report and "modification" saying in part: "It has 'Albany' written all over it. It was framed, ostensibly, to meet the objections which were raised by Sweet against the Socialist Party so that the next delegation of Assemblymen will not be unseated. It is intended to paint the Socialist Party as a nice, respectable, goody-goody affair, rather than a revolutionary organization whose one aim is to overthrow a dying social order and replace it with a Cooperative Commonwealth."

Morris Hillquit, speaking as a Socialist Party leader Sept. 25, 1920 (Lusk Report p. 1789), said of this supposed "change": "We have never at any time changed our creed. Never certainly to make ourselves acceptable to any capitalist crowd. . . . As international Socialists we are revolutionary, and let it be clearly understood that we are out to overthrow the entire capitalist system."

Eugene V. Debs, while in prison for seditious activities, was nominated as the Socialist Party candidate for President of the U. S. A. The Socialist Party bulletin for June 1, 1920 contained the official report of Debs' speech of acceptance upon notification of his nomination in which he said: "Before serving time here, I made a series of addresses, supporting the Russian Revolution which I consider the greatest single achievement in all history. I still am a Bolshevik. I am fighting for the same thing here that they are fighting for there. I regret that the Convention did not see its way clear to affiliate with the Third International without qualification."

While the 1920 National Convention report (before referred to) "soft pedaled" its revolutionary program for expediency's sake saying it was opposed to the "Dictatorship of the Proletariat in the form of Soviet," it at the same time passed a resolution reading as follows: "Resolved, That this convention favor the election of representatives to all legislative bodies by industries as well as by geographical units," which is an endorsement of the Soviet form of government, which is "based upon territorial units and representation through industries" (Lusk Report).

Press reports of the Socialist International congress held at Paris, France, Aug., 1933, stated that Maynard C. Krueger advocated the arming of the proletariat for violent revolution and that the American delegation was the most militant of those present. Aug. 21, 1933, the Chicago Tribune reported: "Comrade Levinson of the executive body will tell the congress how the new deal is going to lead to Socialism in America."

Russia is honored as the first Socialist country. Its name is now the Union of Soviet *Socialist* Republics (U. S. S. R.) It is held up as the example of Socialism in action. Leaders of both Communist and Socialist Parties state that their principles and aims are identical but that they differ as to choice of leadership and tactics.

The Socialist Party of America is not an American political party in the sense that the Democratic and Republican Parties are. Its control lies not solely with Americans but also with alien members in America as well as abroad. The opening statement in the Constitution of the Socialist Party (also Lusk Report, p. 563) says: "The Socialist Party of the U. S. is the political expression of the interests of the workers in this country and is part of an *international working class movement.* . . . The workers must wrest the control of the government from the hands of the masters and use its powers in the upbuilding of the new social order—the cooperative commonwealth. . . . To accomplish this aim it is necessary that the working class be powerfully and solidly organized also in the economic field to struggle for the same Revolutionary goal."

The Preamble to the Socialist Party Constitution adopted in 1919 says: "The Socialist party seeks to organize the working class for independent action on the political field not merely for the betterment of their condition, but also and above all with the revolutionary aim of putting an end to the exploitation or class rule."

When the U. S. declared war, the Socialist Party convention at St. Louis, April 7-14, 1917, adopted a lengthy disloyal resolution favoring seditious activities, saying: "The Socialist Party of the U. S. in the present grave crisis solemnly declares its allegiance to the principles of internationalism and working class solidarity the world over, and proclaims its unalterable opposition to the war just declared by the government of the United States. . . . As against the false doctrine of national patriotism, we uphold the idea of international working class solidarity. We brand the declaration of war by our government as a crime." (The U. S. Govt. was finally forced to jail many Socialists whose seditious activities were camouflaged as "peace" work.) "The acute situation created by the war calls for an even more vigorous prosecution of the class struggle and we recommend to the workers and pledge ourselves to the following course of action: Continuous and active public opposition to the war through demonstrations, mass petitions and all other means in our power. Unyielding opposition to all proposed legislation for military or industrial conscription. . . . Vigorous resistance to all reactional measures such as censorship of the press and mails, restriction of the right of free speech, assemblage and organization, or compulsory arbitration and limitation of the right to strike. Consistent propaganda against military training and militaristic teaching in the public schools. . . . We recommend the National Executive Committee extend and improve propaganda among women." One delegate is reported to have said "If I knew we could sway the boys when they got guns to use them against the capitalist class I would be for universal training."

The 1932 Socialist Party election platform similarly called for total disarmament of the United States, no deportation or barring of alien Reds, free speech, free press, and "civil liberties" (for revolutionaries), recognition of militant bloody Soviet Russia, etc.

The New York Call, June 28, 1921, printed the following Resolution, passed by the Socialist Party, which was offered by Morris Hillquit: "Resolved that the incoming national executive committee be instructed to make a careful survey of all radical and labor organizations in the country with the view of ascertaining their strengths, disposition and *readiness to cooperate with the Socialist Movement* upon a platform not inconsistent with that of the party, and on a plan which will preserve the integrity and autonomy of the Socialist Party." This was headed *"Text of Hillquit Resolution that Ends Isolation of Socialist Party."* With this, the "boring from within" other parties began in earnest. (See under Internationals; also August Claessens, Victor Berger, Debs, etc.)

Socialist Party National Hdqts., 549 Randolph St., Chicago.

THE NEW DEAL AND ROOSEVELT APPOINTEES

(See page 256 for facsimile of letter.)

The average brainy American business man, whose capable concentrated efforts have raised the American standard of living to a preeminent place in the world's history, feels that he is too busy running his own business to bother with politics. He wants "George" to do it and a Red "George" has been working to do "it" and do *him* out of his business for a long time.

Only, perhaps, when Red George and his political cronies step in to completely run his business for him will he awaken to find time to attend to politics.

Mr. Successful American bountifully endows Colleges teaching Socialism and supports ministers teaching Socialism, but objects to voting for a "crack-brained radical" on the Socialist ticket, as the radicals know. So they arrange matters so that he votes for the "crack-brained" Socialist on a conservative ticket. The Conference for Progressive Political Action (see) since 1922 has been successfully boring from within to "steal" elections for radical candidates. They are organizing more energetic and deceptive programs for future elections right now.

Americans who are alarmed at the present Socialist administration, labeled as "Democratic," may easily turn out "Democrats" and vote in Republicans at the next election, but how many of the elected "Republican" officials will be radicals of the same stripe?

Many of the radicals now making this Democratic administration a Socialist one only left the Republican Party during the last campaign at the invitation of Mr. Roosevelt, their kindred soul. While the radicals have a keenly organized, well planned program, American conservatives have practically none. If they wait until election day, they may find themselves in the predicament of having a choice between Tweedle-Dum and Tweedle-Dee, between Socialists, Communists, Democratic-Socialists, or Republican-Socialists, because the radicals are also active within both conservative parties and "practical", short-sighted politicians seem to believe that by compromising with them and pampering them they are increasing the Party's hopes of success. *"Marx versus Washington" will be the real issue in the next election, and this issue transcends former partisanship.* If the fight were clear-cut, Americanism would win with the people hands down, but a fight with radicals is a fight with snipers. They do not fly their true colors willingly.

The only propaganda now dinned into an American's ears is that, because of "emergency," or "collapse of capitalism," he must either accept Socialistic measures or have Communist dictatorship thrust upon him. (This is Socialist propaganda.) Why does almost no one propagandize a return to Washingtonian principles which built this country's greatness? Bureaucracy and the load of governmental taxation have been steadily increasing of late years under Socialist manipulation, until under depressed trade conditions business came nearly to a standstill. Now, inside of a few months, more billions in taxation have been heaped upon American taxpayers than our share of the cost of the World War. How many years will it take to pay off the present load of indebtedness which this administration has only started to incur? During this process the American taxpayer is apt to lose his property as the Socialists intend that he shall. Between forfeited loans and heavy taxation, it is hoped to confiscate farms, homes, banks and utilities by legal means.

As Communist V. F. Calverton says in "Recovery Through Revolution" (see): . . . "what with the state practically supporting and subsidizing the industrial and financial set-up of the nation by means of monies afforded by the Reconstruction Finance Corporation, in time, if such subsidies continue, and the railroads and industries which have accepted them cannot meet the obligations that they necessitate, there will be no other recourse than for the State to take them over." (Our "peaceful revolution.")

Wm. E. Sweet, whom the Conference for Progressive Political Action claimed credit for electing Governor of Colorado (See "Who's Who"), is one of Pres. Roosevelt's radical appointees in the Public Relations Division of the N. R. A. He was very prompt in having published in the Daily News, Oct. 30, 1933, his protest against a "white" Daily News editorial of Oct. 26. His was a lengthy letter sent from Washington, D. C., in which he said: "The editorial 'Back to the Constitution' printed on the front page of the Daily News, Oct. 26, would be highly important if it voiced the sentiments of any considerable inarticulate body of citizens as the Daily News seems to think it does. . . . Has the time come in America when a man may not do as he pleases with his oil? It has. But this is clearly unconstitutional. . . . The Constitution was based on security and privilege for the *owners of property,* but this is no reason for confusing it with holy writ. . . . If these revolutionary changes in our economic system work out satisfactorily, they will be found to be constitutional. . . . When former Pres. Hoover made his concluding speech in Madison Square Garden he said: 'This campaign is more than a contest between two parties, it is more than a contest between two men, it is a contest between two fundamentally different theories of government.' Mr. Hoover rightly appraised the issues of the campaign. The people have placed their seal of approval for the present on the theory of government advanced by Franklin D. Roosevelt and they are following his leadership with loud acclaim. As yet there is no sign of any diminution in his popularity." (?)

"The radicals you complain of have been chosen by the President. He may not agree with all their theories but he would rather have their counsel, noise and all, than that of the *traditionalists,* 'money changers,' and reactionaries who surrounded and dominated his predecessor. Wm. E. Sweet, Washington, D. C."

Senator Warren R. Austin of Vermont said, (Sept. 18, 1933, Chgo. American): "Only one step further need be taken to destroy the Constitution and overthrow the government, namely, to remold the judiciary." And Senator Henry D. Hatfield of W. Va. declared, (Chgo. Tribune, Oct. 20, 1933): "President Roosevelt's executive order threatening N. R. A. violators with $500 fines and six months' imprisonment means that economic serfdom has become a grim reality in the United States."

The attitude of radicals with regard to the recent U. S. Supreme Court decision in the Minnesota mortgage moratorium case is clearly indicated in the following excerpts from the January 18, 1934 "World Tomorrow":

"TOWARD PACIFIC REVOLUTION

"The five-to-four decision of the Supreme Court of the United States in the Minnesota mortgage moratorium case enormously increases the possibility of revolution in this country without another civil war. If the principles enunciated therein are incorporated in forthcoming decisions, the NRA, the AAA and other aspects of the New Deal are likely to be upheld. In this event the creditor and property-owning class will lose billions and billions of dollars. The validation of recent state and national legislation by the Supreme Court will result in the redistribution of wealth on an almost unimaginably colossal scale.

"The law under review authorized owners, when about to lose their property through foreclosure, to apply in court for a two-year extension of time in which to redeem their holdings. The invalidating decree of the district court was reversed by the Minnesota Supreme Court, and the latter's decision was upheld at Washington." (Chief Justice Hughes and Justices Brandeis, Cardozo, Roberts, and Stone [radicals, three of whom were appointed by Pres. Hoover], against Justices Butler, McReynolds, Sutherland, and Van Devanter [Constitutionalists]).

"Pacifists who are struggling for radical changes in the present social order have reason to be encouraged by the Court's decision in the Minnesota case. Once more it has been demonstrated that the Supreme Court tends to follow public opinion. Progress has often been slowed down, but the highest tribunal of the land is not likely to become a permanent barrier to revolutionary change. As a last resort its powers may be shorn or its decision changed by increasing the size of the Court and the appointment of new Justices who are in sympathy with radical legislation."

This last brazenly gives voice to a radical threat that has been propagandized under cover ever since Pres. Roosevelt took office and has reference to the emergency power which the President has of increasing the number of Supreme Court Justices. For example, it is alleged that in case of any adverse decision, say 5 to 4, against any phase of the "New Deal," the President will appoint two more radicals (possibly Felix Frankfurter and Donald Richberg, or at least men of their persuasion) to the Supreme Bench, insuring a reversal or favorable decision of 6 to 5, in favor of the proposition when it again comes up for action.

In passing, it should be noted that Pres. Roosevelt's "first assistant," Secy. Ickes, served on the National Campaign Executive Committee when Chief Justice Hughes ran for President in 1916.

Norman Thomas in "Student Outlook" for Nov., 1933 (p. 5) proceeds to tell how N. R. A. must be turned into permanent Socialism. He says: "Only social ownership of natural resources and the great means of production and distribution, their management according to plan for the use of the great company of people and not *for the profit* of any" (true enough) "can fulfill the promise of N. R. A. . . . The codes must not only be improved but correlated under a general economic plan.

"We can scarcely have experts plan for us unless we own the things which are vital to this plan. We must acquire rapidly our banking system, our coal, oil, electric power and railroads. Speedily we must add other natural resources and basic industries and utilities. We should socialize marketing machinery of what farmers buy and sell. The milk situation, for instance, cannot be solved without socially owned milk distributing companies in place of the present trusts. Taxation of incomes and inheritances in a transitional period should meet most costs of government, though the land values tax can and should be used to *end private landlordism.* A capital levy must be employed to help reduce debt, care for the unemployed, and facilitate the transfer of the industries to be socialized. In general, *under present conditions,* compensation for socialized industries—usually in notes or bonds of these industries—*plus such taxation* as I have outlined is likely to prove more equitable and practicable than *piecemeal confiscation.* For the immediate present we need a far bolder plan of unemployment relief and public works, including housing. Such a program plus social insurance will aid not only in terms of social justice but in economic recovery by its help in *redistributing* national income a little more equitably.

"No program can be carried out merely by wishing. It requires effective organization. . . . The party which represents the workers is *still to be built.* It is that party which the Socialist Party wishes to help to create or become. There is an unfortunate tendency among radicals to spend in their own discussions more time on an attempt to prophesy the *degree of violence* which will bring about a desirable social revolution than on working on a dynamic organization without which ballots or bullets are equally futile."

This, then, is the Red program for confiscating private property and American liberty *"under present conditions"* and under the flag of patriotism. Later on—well that is still another story.

It is significant that Socialist Basil Manly (See "Who's Who"), long a noisy voice for public ownership of Muscle Shoals and kindred projects, who in 1927, announced (See People's Legislative Service) that proper strategy in the 1928 elections would secure radicals a real voice in the choice of President in 1932, is now Pres. Roosevelt's appointee as chairman of the Federal Power Commission, in charge of these very projects, now threatening extermination of the privately-owned competing power industries and saddling taxpayers with the extravagant expense of political ownership.

Roosevelt, in his Detroit campaign speech, frankly told the American people he was as "radical as the Federal Council of Churches" (see), which meant a great deal more than the average person realized.

John Boettiger, Washington correspondent of the Chicago Tribune, Oct. 1, 1933, wrote: "One recovery policy seems to reduce while another promotes larger production. Millions are spent to take farm lands out of production. Millions are spent to put farm lands into production. Food and cotton are destroyed, while many people hunger and go ill-clothed. Prices are sky-rocketed and people are told to buy more. Water power is planned to take the place of steam while thousands of coal miners are jobless. Waterways are projected while the railroads go bankrupt and thousands of rail workers go jobless. . . . For all this the tax payers bear the brunt at both ends, paying processing taxes to pay the farmers for destroying produce; paying for the dole to feed the hungry; paying for power plants whether their communities benefit or not; paying more and more taxes to support the ever growing bureaucracy, which invokes all the schemes at Washington.

"These paradoxes and many others are held inevitable in a government which almost overnight has essayed to control farming, industry, finance and transportation, which is starting to spend three billions of public moneys for a thousand and one widely diversified projects, most of which are leading the government into endeavors to paternalism, government-in-business and socialism.

"In a single year the consuming Americans must pay additional taxes aggregating approximately $364,500,000 for farm products. That money is to be paid to farmers in return for their agreement to curtail wheat acreages, plow-up cotton, send pigs and sows to slaughter, cut production of tobacco, butter, and cheese, to raise prices paid to farmers who are accused of increasing productively to get the federal funds.

"Reclamation to make more arable land, and power projects for more electrical power than required, thus far approved by Secretary Ickes call for the expenditure of $166,000,000 . . . will compete with steam produced power for the cities of the northwest, and will drive more nails into the coffin of feeble old King Coal.

"The Tennessee valley authority dream of Pres. Roosevelt and Sen. George Norris of Nebraska with $50,000,000 to spend this year, is a combination of these described paradoxes, bringing new lands into cultivation, creating new water power where there is insufficient demand for what is available." This, of course, will tend to force privately-owned utilities into ruin by governmental competition and thus into political ownership.

The Chicago Tribune of Sept. 16, 1933 says: "In the rate structure announced by David E. Lilienthal, director of the Tennessee experiment in charge of power, there is no provision for repaying to the federal treasury a net loss of $43,590,619 which the hydro-electric power plant at Muscle Shoals already has cost the tax payer. Besides waiving past expenditures as money already 'gone over the dam,' Director Lilienthal has computed his rates which undersell existing commercial companies by 75 percent on a quasi-socialistic basis . . . by disregarding the original investment, making no provision for profits, avoiding taxes and computing interest at the low rate available to the government, the Muscle Shoals officials have given themselves a 75 percent advantage in rates over commercial companies. . . . These rate schedules . . . are being held up as models to commercial companies which have to meet all these costs."

While the average non-radical American knows so little about Socialism and its symptoms that he fails to recognize them when he sees them, the Federated Press which supplies communist and socialist papers with news is no such novice. To quote its release of Aug. 10, 1934: *"Few people realize that the Roosevelt administration has socialized more industry in 18 months than the Socialist Labor Party ever did in Great*

Britain or the Social Democrats of Germany or even the more revolutionary Socialists in Spain—or all of them combined."

The communist Daily Worker, Oct. 6, 1933, under the heading "A Socialist Invitation," said: "Yesterday Franklin D. Roosevelt, President of the United States, was invited to join the Socialist Party. . . . Over ten thousand New York workers heard Abraham Cahan, one of the oldest leaders of the Socialist Party, and editor of the Socialist paper, the 'Forward,' invite him in. Here are his actual words set down for every worker to see: 'The NRA has been handled in a democratic way, and the President has earned the gratitude of every thinking man in the country . . . on the basis of his work so far he really should be a Socialist.' On one side of Cahan sat Norman Thomas. On the other sat the Tammany Police Chief. . . . This was the setting for the invitation to Roosevelt to join the party of Eugene Victor Debs. Thomas seconded the invitation—with the typical Thomas reservations. Thus the Thomas 'left-wing' and the Hillquit-Cahan 'right-wing' of the Socialist Party joined hands. . . . Cahan's invitation is only the logical culmination of the congratulatory visit that Thomas and Hillquit paid Roosevelt at the White House in April. The Socialist leaders have looked Roosevelt over. And they find him good. . . Cahan sees in Roosevelt a fellow-socialist. He is right. They are both socialists—of the same calibre. Of the calibre of Hindenburg, the fascist butcher." (Pres. Roosevelt sent his condolences to Mrs. Morris Hillquit when Hillquit died recently.)

This last is typical of the insults Communists and Socialists hurl at each other. No insult could be more far fetched than the epithet of "fascist" or anti-Red applied to Socialists, whose leaders serve on the selfsame anti-fascist committees with Communists; but it conveys the intended meaning that the Socialism of Socialists is a farce, that only the Socialism of the Communist Party is the "pure goods".

Why this continual horse play between Red parties with identical principles and objectives? Were it entirely due to bitter Party rivalry and jealousy the Party leaders would not be on the close friendly terms that they are. The Garland Fund illustrates their chummy interlocking cooperation. The "hymn of hate" publicity policy is undoubtedly mutually understood. It helps to keep the rank and file members in separate camps, gives the disgruntled Red another place to go to help the movement, spurs members on to rivalry, confuses and ensnares some of the bourgeoisie into believing Socialism different from Communism, and enables the Parties, like two flanks of an army, to carry on separate, even apparently hostile, coordinated Red movements—one penetrating, the other agitating.

While the Socialist Party in a practical, gentlemanly manner has bored from within and secured governmental power and now guides NRA as far toward complete Socialism as the leash of legalism will stretch, sanctions destroying food and confiscating property, has forced upon the A. F. of L. its former enemy, the pro-Soviet Amalgamated Clothing Workers unions, and is aiding the A. F. of L. to unionize America in the expectation of using the enlarged organization as an instrument for the general strike as suggested by the Second International Conference at Paris 1933, the Communist Party has adopted the definite program of utilizing the deepening discontent NRA is creating, and is agitating rabid hatred against the NRA "slave regime," and, with hundreds of violent strikes to its credit already within the past few months, hopes with increasing strikes to finally bring on a psychological moment of chaos and despair, in which that taut leash of legalism may be broken by a united front General Strike culminating in Red seizure of power. Then would Socialists and Communists hold this power together, and with violence. For, as Socialist Norman Thomas says in "Why I am a Socialist" (p. 11): "Socialists are not non-resistants. We want to minimize violence and place the onus of it *when it comes* where it belongs: On an *owning class* that will not give up while it can hypnotize anyone to fight in its behalf."

Concerning the "General Strike" (the I. W. W. specialty), the Communist International, May 25, 1928, stated: "The task of the party (Communist) is to lead the working class into the revolutionary struggle for power. When the revolutionary tide is flowing, when the dominant classes are disorganized . . . and the masses are prepared for action and for sacrifice, the task of the party is to lead the masses into the direct attack upon the bourgeois state. This is to be achieved by propaganda in favor of all transition slogans . . . to which all other branches of party work must be subordinated. This includes strikes, strikes combined with demonstration, the combination of armed demonstrations and strikes, and finally *the General Strike* conjointly with the armed uprising against the political party of the bourgeoisie. This struggle must be subjected to the rules of *military art;* it must be conducted according to a *plan of war* and in the form of a military offensive. . . . Communists do not think it necessary to conceal their views and aims. They openly declare that their goal can be achieved only by the violent overthrow of the whole of the present social system." Both the Russian and the Cuban Red revolutions were preceded by a "General Strike".

In the communist Daily Worker, Oct. 21, 1933, appears the headline "Roosevelt Invites Soviet Envoy, U. S. S. R. Decides to Send Litvinov," and an editorial saying: "The chief conflict in the present-day world is between the system of advancing Socialism and of decaying world capitalism. . . . The United States is now forced to step aside from its traditional policy of non-recognition and undertake diplomatic negotiations with the workers' fatherland. . . . The Roosevelt regime now grasps for this market." Other captions are typical of Communist opposition to NRA and include: "New Revolt Looms As Miners Sense Deception of NRA"; "NRA Cuts Wages at Sheffield Steel Mills"; "Farms Rise in Strike Against NRA"—this last over the gloating announcement that "Government officials are unable to conceal their alarm at the unusual depth and prevalence of the farmers' bitterness against the Roosevelt regime"; and announcement that the next convention of the National Farmers Committee of Action would take place under Communist auspices Nov. 15-18 in Chicago (to stir up further strikes).

Page 4 (same issue) is entirely devoted to the speech of the Communist Party general secretary, Earl Browder, before the Central Committee of the C. P. U. S. A., in which he said: "We point out the increased and more effective participation in strikes" (against NRA); and, after covering the communist Anti-War Congresses and other Party activities, he terminated with this advice: "An essential part of the whole propaganda of the revolutionary solution of the crisis, the proletarian dictatorship, is the example of the successful revolution and building of socialism in the Soviet Union. . . . A large number of our leading comrades in many districts who think they can get a larger number of workers to join the Party by talking to them only about the immediate demands, and who soft-pedal the ultimate program of our Party in order to be popular, are making a big mistake. Precisely this line is what keeps workers out of the Party, because it doesn't give them the essential reason why the Party is necessary and why they must join . . . it is essential to bring forward the revolutionary program, the revolutionary character of our Party, to propagandize the revolutionary way out of the crisis, the problem of *seizure of power,* the problem of building socialism in America as a problem of the next future of the United States."

An article in the Daily Worker of Sept. 30, 1933 by Joseph Stalin, head of the Soviet government, of the Communist Party of U. S. S. R., and of the Third International, is entitled "The Peace Policy of the U. S. S. R." He states: "Our policy is a policy of peace and strengthening of trade relations with all countries" and refers to the U. S. S. R. as the "citadel of the revolution". Then in the adjoining column is this quotation from Lenin:

"*'We do not only live in one State but in a system of States, and the existence* of the *Soviet Republic side by side with the imperialist States is inconceivable for any considerable length of time. Eventually, one or the other must win.'* " (Emphasis in original), with the following comment: "The Communist Party of the Soviet Union and the *Communist International, under the leadership of Comrade Stalin,* have worked untiringly for the realization of this bequest. To win over the workers and peasants of the imperialist powers, . . . to obtain the sympathy of the petty-bourgeoisie and the intellectual middle class, to *utilize the imperialist antagonisms* in the interest of Socialist construction and the extension of peace, *of the breathing space*—this has been, and still is, the meaning of the policy of the Soviet Union . . . because the peace policy of the Soviet Union was linked up with the realization of the First Five Year Plan, and the beginning of the realization and carrying out of the Second Five Year Plan."

The "breathing space" is the Communist term for Russia's present period of preparation. Propaganda abroad and industrialization in the U. S. S. R. must both be supported in order that the Red Army's millions, now training, may be supported when they step forth to fulfill their promise to the "Workers of the World" to aid them in overthrowing such capitalist governments as have not by that time already been overthrown by means of revolutions inspired by Red propaganda. Communists everywhere confidently hope that if sufficient credits can be secured from capitalist governments—particularly from rich Uncle Sam—to aid in this preparation, that the end of the Second Five Year Plan will find Russia able to support its Red Army in the field.

"Long live the American proletariat! Long live the Communist International, the general staff of the World Proletarian Revolution," says the Daily Worker in the column adjoining Stalin's article, while Rooseveltian supporters are now flooding the press with the statement that Stalin now ignores the Third International which he heads, and the embargo against slave-made Soviet products (1934) has been lifted!

Communist leaders long ago said that capitalists would commit suicide for the sake of temporary profits (on paper). American patriotic societies, I know, have flooded Pres. Roosevelt with information concerning the oneness of the Soviet Government and Third International which spreads sedition in the U. S. A. for the purpose of overthrowing this government and setting up a Socialist Soviet one. The U. S. S. R. has "cried" for recognition, as a baby cries for a bottle. It needs credits for industrialization and the subsidization of world revolutionary propaganda. It wants above all else this freedom in America, world prestige, and money to strengthen itself for our assassination, all of which recognition will give.

Then why does Pres. Roosevelt, against all precedent, in effect say "Nice kitty!" to this man-eating tiger which would devour America's government and invite him over to feed and roam in America? Is he stupid, blind, badly-informed and played-upon by radicals, or well-informed and deliberately playing the Red game as socialist Ramsay MacDonald and every other clever socialist statesman plays it?

The Literary Digest, Nov. 4, 1933, quotes the editor of "L'Echo de Paris" as stating: "'Doubtless Roosevelt was influenced by members of the "brain trust" and by intellectual snobs who believe that Communism would be a diverting experiment.'" It must be assuring to our capitalistic Reds to read that Litvinov, the proletarians' spokesman, sailed for America occupying the Royal Suite on the Berengaria.

Concerning Soviet Recognition, the Chicago Daily News, Oct. 24, 1933 (Paul Mallon), says: "The real inside negotiations were handled by Wm. C. Bullitt, special assistant to Hull. He is the man who made a secret trip to Europe last spring. . . . Bullitt's real mission was to sound out European governments as to how they were getting along with the Reds. His report was favorable." It would be, as Pres. Roosevelt must have known.

Bullitt, Roosevelt appointee as special adviser of the State Department, and now as Ambassador to the U. S. S. R., was, until recently, married to Louise Bryant Reed, widow of John Reed, a founder of the American Communist Party. Louise Bryant and Lincoln Steffens of the Anarchist-Communist group sent a joint telegram, quoted in the Lusk Report, asking Lenin and Trotsky to appoint a man in America with whom they could cooperate in aiding the Russian revolution. After this, Bullitt and Lincoln Steffens went over on a confidential mission to Russia. To quote magazine "Time" of May 1, 1933: "Wm. C. Bullitt went to Sweden on Henry Ford's Peace Ship in 1915. . . . In Feb., 1919, Diplomat Bullitt, with Journalist Lincoln Steffens, was entrusted with a confidential mission to Russia to make peace terms with the Soviet. . . . Mr. Bullitt spent a week in Moscow and came to terms with Dictator Lenin. On his return to Paris his peace proposal, involving recognition of the Bolshevist regime was suddenly tossed into the waste basket by Messrs. Wilson and Lloyd George. . . . He impulsively resigned from the Peace Commission after Pres. Wilson refused to give him an audience. An admirer of Lenin, he predicted that the Reds would oversweep all Europe.

. . . Mr. Lloyd George referred to 'a journey some boys were reported to have made to Russia' and flayed the Bullitt report as a tissue of lies. After a Paris divorce in 1923 Bullitt married Anne Moen Louise Bryant Reed, widow of Red John Reed of Greenwich village who went to Russia and today lies buried in the Kremlin wall."

Paul Mallon states in the Daily News of Sept. 13, 1933: "The Communists used to have no shoulder on which to weep in Washington. They have one now. It's Louis Howe's." (Roosevelt's secretary.) "A Washington detective tried to cross-question several well-known Reds a few days ago. 'We don't want to talk to you' they said. 'We are going to see Howe.'—They got in. Howe is also credited with the appointment of two former leaders of the bonus army to the department of justice. What they do is not generally known in the department, but they are on the payroll." The bonus army was Communist-led. Einstein, barred as a Communist from Germany, in Jan., 1934 was an over night guest of the President at the White House.

Under the heading "An Alarming Appointment," Francis Ralston Welsh reports: "In 'Science' for Sept. 6, 1933 is the following notice: 'Prof. Vladimir Karapetoff, of the department of electrical engineering of Cornell University, has been appointed Lieutenant Commander in the Naval Reserve and has been assigned to the Volunteer Naval Reserve for engineering duties.' " Karapetoff is and has been vice president of the League for Industrial Democracy, the left-wing Socialist organization spreading Socialist and Communist propaganda in schools and colleges. To quote Mr. Welsh: "Appointee Karapetoff should be kept under closest scrutiny."

Under the heading "A Shameless Appointment," Mr. Welsh reports the appointment of Frederic Clemson Howe as chairman of the Consumers' Board of AAA. When Mr. Welsh brought about an investigation of Howe's activities when Howe was Commissioner of Immigration at the Port of New York, Howe resigned, but the Congressional investigation brought out letters showing Howe's close connection with Emma Goldman, Eliz. Gurley Flynn and other Anarchists and Communists and his aid to their cause. "Byron H. Uhl testified that he had issued orders to the Ellis Island officials to stop the circulation of radical literature among inmates of Ellis Island, but that this order was held up under Howe's regime and the circulating of I. W. W. and Anarchist literature permitted. Howe was shown also to have held up deportation proceedings against the Reds brought to Ellis Island and that various Reds were released without giving bail and permitted to travel about the country continuing their Anarchist and Communist work. The proceedings of the committee were reported at the time in the 'New York Times'. Just before Howe resigned as Commissioner, information came to me that he had been tipped off that there would be a Congressional investigation. This information came from inside the Berkman anarchist gang. From whence they got it is not disclosed." (Welsh) (See also "Who's Who").

"Miss" Perkins, who is the mother of Mr. Paul Wilson's daughter, follows the custom popular with Red married ladies who refuse to acknowledge the "private ownership" of marriage and show that they "wear no man's collar" by refusing to use a husband's name. The cry of the Socialists and Communists had long been "Down with Deportation Doak". Secy. Doak utilized the machinery of the Department of Labor to deport and bar certain notorious Red alien agitators. "Miss" Perkins, his successor as Roosevelt's Secretary of Labor, ended this activity at once. Tom Mann, notorious English Red agitator, jailed in England, barred from Ireland, and previously absolutely barred from the United States, recently (1933) preached sedition and Red revolution in the United States, with his temporary visa extended, due to the new policy. Henri Barbusse, Communist agitator, has lectured in many American cities advocating Red revolution, and Frank Borich, vicious Communist agitator slated for deportation, has been turned loose to create violence and disorder.

Yet, because the smokescreen must ever be kept before the public, the Daily Worker of Oct. 5, 1933 actually "razzes" Secy. Perkins; to quote: "The lady, Miss Perkins, whom the wily Roosevelt chose as the liberal window-dressing for his cabinet" . . . "claims to have 'liberalized' the immigration regulations regarding the admittance of foreign visitors to the United States. The hypocrisy of her claims can find no better proof than the *delay* in granting Tom Mann's visa. . . . Mann's visa was not granted by the American Consul in London until too late for him to attend the U. S. Congress Against War"; and again, slightingly, the Daily Worker of Oct. 18, 1933 refers to "Miss" Perkins as a former member of the Socialist Party. She was an executive and fellow worker with Mrs. Roosevelt in the New York National Consumers League.

Of the Blue Eagle, which Senator Schall (Minn.) calls "the Soviet Duck," P. H. Hatch, writing in the Literary Digest of Nov. 4, 1933 asks: "I would very much like to know why the Soviet eagle is selected, that bears electricity in its talons, and is placed here, there and everywhere, instead of our American eagle, carrying an olive branch, and which is shown on the obverse side of the great seal of the United States?"

The Daily Worker, Sept. 8, 1933, found it necessary to take Communist Theodore Dreiser to task for not following the Party line of attack on NRA, saying: "Theodore Dreiser has come out with a statement of his conversion to NRA on the grounds that the New Deal comes to us direct from Moscow."

Rexford Guy Tugwell (see "Who's Who"), whose radical speech on doing away with private business entirely is quoted under "National Religion and Labor Foundation," said in Chicago, Oct. 29, 1933: "We are passing through a fairly sensible mass revolution," to which the Chgo. Daily News replied with a great editorial, Nov. 1, 1933, headed *"Did You Vote for Revolution?"* He is Pres. Roosevelt's Assistant "Commissar" of Agriculture and one of the principle spokesmen for the administration.

To quote Cong. Hamilton Fish's speech before the House of Representatives, May 2, 1933: "Mordecai Ezekiel, Economic Adviser to the Secretary of Agriculture, is a real shadow of Prof. Tugwell so far as the Russian farm plan is concerned. He appears to be the Professor Einstein of the administration and carefully elaborates the working of the 'new deal' to Congress by the use of logarithms, letting a hog equal X, the squeal equal Y, and the price equal Z. If it works out 'everything will be all right'. Prof. Ezekiel has visited Russia, where he made a considerable study of the Gosplan. . . . Here is a clipping from the greatest propagandist of Soviet Russia in the world, a writer for the N. Y. Times, Mr. Walter Duranty, who says that after 15 years the agricultural plan in Russia has failed. . . . The heading of this article in the N. Y. Times is 'All Russia suffers shortage of food, supplies dwindle, two-thirds of people are not expected to get sufficient allowances for winter; crops below 1930; live stock reduced more than 50 percent from 5 years ago, with fodder lacking; new plans dropped'. These are the agricultural plans that were commended by Mr. Tugwell and probably are the plans now being suggested or copied from Soviet Russia in the pending farm bill. If its purpose is to reduce production of farm products, as has happened in Soviet Russia, then this farm bill ought to succeed at least in that respect, although that was not the intention of the framers of the Soviet Gosplan in Russia.

"Where did the 'new deal' come from? . . . is it possible that the 'new deal' was borrowed from the Socialist book 'A New Deal,' from which apparently a large part of the proposed legislative program has been taken? . . . in which Stuart Chase says that 'in a way it is a pity that the road to revolution is temporarily closed'." I note that the last line of this same book is "Why should Russians have all the fun of remaking a world?"

When Smith Wildman Brookhart, defeated radical Iowa Senator, Roosevelt's Foreign Trade Adviser of Agricultural Adjustment Administration, debated with Hamilton Fish in Chicago, 1932, under L. I. D. and A. S. C. R. R. auspices, with Prof. Paul H. Douglas, executive of both, presiding, he took the side of Soviet Russia and of Soviet recognition. He spoke in friendly familiar terms of his friend Boris Skvirsky, unofficial Soviet representative in Washington, and to judge by the plaudits of the audience he might well have been born in Russia instead of the United States. The hall was packed with Reds who cheered Brookhart and hissed Fish.

Among other radical Roosevelt appointees is Robert M. Hutchins, self assured young president of the University of Chicago, under whose administration the U. of C. has become a hotbed for Communist propaganda. The Student Congress Against War with Scott Nearing and Earl Browder of the Communist Party as speakers, mass meetings with Wm. Z. Foster, Carl Haessler, and others, advocating overthrow of our government in defiance of the Illinois sedition law, are not only held in University auditoriums, but the communist National Student League is an officially recognized U. of C. student activity. Hutchins, accompanied by Victor Olander of the Illinois Federation of Labor, Pres. Walter Dill Scott of N. U., etc., opposed me in testifying before the Illinois Legislative hearing at Springfield on the Baker Bills, aimed at curbing sedition in colleges. Jane Addams opposed me at the second Chicago hearing. I was in the unique position at Springfield, at Senator Baker's invitation, of being the only person to testify in favor of curbing sedition. The presidents of St. Viator's College, and Northwestern and Chicago Universities were pitted against me, with Mrs. Ickes, wife of Secy. Harold L. Ickes, leading Roosevelt appointee, applauding on the sidelines the remarks of the opponents of the sedition bills.

When I showed documentary proof of my charges that Communism is allowed to flourish at the U. of C., young Hutchins came back with the very good answer that he did not know why Communism should *not* be a student activity at the U. of C., since Wm. Z. Foster and the Communist Party were allowed on the ballot of the State of Illinois (and a scandal that it is true!), and that he taught Marxism and Leninism himself. Hutchins heads the Chicago Mediation Board of NRA. Jane Addams was invited to serve also but declined, but Victor Olander, his ally at the Springfield Hearing, serves under him, as does James Mullenbach (see "Who's Who") and John Fitzpatrick (appointed through Leo Wolman), president of the Chicago Federation of Labor and a member of the Chicago Committee for Struggle Against War, which put over the huge Communist mass meeting I attended Oct. 23, 1933 in honor of Communist Henri Barbusse. Only the Red flag was displayed and the Internationale sung, and Revolution was cheered. Fitzpatrick's committee were seated on the stage and a Communist pamphlet sold at the meeting stated that Fitzpatrick had been asked to address the meeting but had not dared do so as a representative of the A. F. of L.

This Chicago Labor Board (according to the Chicago Tribune, Oct. 20, 1933) was chosen from nominations submitted to Senator Robt. E. Wagner, chairman of the National Board. Wagner himself is a warm advocate of Russian recognition and a contributor to the radical Survey, Graphic and Nation.

According to the Daily Worker of March 19, 1934, Sen. Brookhart praised Soviet agriculture at the New School for Social Research (Mrs. F. D. Roosevelt was on its Advisory Board, 1931) and said similar collectivisation could be achieved here by means of his Bill. To quote: " 'My Bill is the revolution. A couple of Bills like that and there would be no more Wall Street!' Brookhart suggested that the audience read Stalin's speech on agriculture mimeographed copies of which he distributed free."

We are not surprised at Mrs. Roosevelt's lavish praise of Jane Addams, her friend, with whom she shared the program led by Newton D. Baker, in a drive for relief funds, Oct. 30, 1933 in Chicago, nor to read: "Mrs. Franklin D. Roosevelt and Mrs. Henry Morgenthau, Jr., motored from the summer White House at Hyde Park, N. Y., to pay a visit tonight to Miss Lillian Wald, welfare worker and sociologist. The President's wife and her companion joined Miss Jane Addams . . . and Dr. Alice Hamilton . . . as dinner guests of the founder of Henry St. Settlement, New York." (Chicago Tribune, Aug. 8, 1933.)

The A. S. C. R. R., a Communist subsidiary, was formed at Henry St. Settlement. Lillian Wald and Mrs. Roosevelt served together on the Non-Intervention Citizens Committee, 26 of the 75 members of which were outright Socialists or Communists, and the others all more or less connected with the pacifist movement. Rose Schneidermann (see "Who's Who"), who has objected to the nickname, the "Red Rose of Anarchy," was also one of this committee and is a Roosevelt appointee on the Labor Advisory Board.

Rose Schneidermann, Lillian Wald and Mrs. Roosevelt are associated together also in the National Women's Trade Union League (radical enough to merit Garland Fund support and the Garland Fund plainly states it gives only for radical purposes).

"Miss" Frances Perkins was formerly executive secretary of the socialist National Consumers League, of which, in 1931, Mrs. Roosevelt, Jane Addams, Newton D. Baker and Alice Hamilton were vice presidents.

Nor is it strange that Leo Wolman and Sidney Hillman, two outstanding radicals (see "Who's Who"), should be Roosevelt appointees to the Labor

Advisory Board. They were both directors of the Garland Fund, which aided two of the organizations of which Mrs. Roosevelt is a member (National Consumers League and National Women's Trade Union League).

Paul Douglas left his work at the U. of Chicago to go to Washington as Roosevelt's Adviser to NRA. His radical record (see "Who's Who") is lengthy. Sam Hammersmark, the head of the Chicago Communist Book Store at 2019 W. Division St. and a Communist Party district executive, knows him well enough to call him "Paul". A columnist quoted Douglas, commenting on the present change in administration, as saying: "And to think but a short time ago we were called radicals!" He left his wife and children in recent years and married the daughter of Lorado Taft, the sculptor. Taft now serves on the Red "Chicago Committee for Struggle Against War".

Wm. E. Dodd (see "Who's Who"), a member of the executive committee of the Chicago A. C. L. U., is Pres. Roosevelt's appointee as Ambassador to Germany. How Hitler must love that!

Harold L. Ickes, radical "Republican," is Roosevelt's Secretary of the Interior. He owns a gorgeous Winnetka, Ill. estate and has been active in "reform" politics for many years. He is held up as the model "honest" politician. He is in Paul Douglas' utilities-baiting, socialist Utility Consumers and Investors League and is either a member of or contributor to the A. C. L. U. His wife, a member of the Illinois Legislature, is said to be an ardent pacifist.

Donald Richberg, another member of Paul Douglas' Utility Consumers and Investors League, is Pres. Roosevelt's General Legal Advisor of NRA. Said the Chgo. Daily News, Sept. 5, 1933: His position in NRA "can be measured by the fact he gets $12,500 while the others (including Johnson) get $6,000." He was chairman of the resolutions committee of the radical Conference for Progressive Political Action in Cleveland, 1924, which "steals" elections for radical candidates (Am. Labor Who's Who). (See also this "Who's Who").

Henry Wallace, the radical Roosevelt Secretary of Agriculture, was a member of the Nat. Citizens Committee on Relations with Latin America and Nat. Save Our Schools Com.

Sophonisba P. Breckenridge and Anne Guthrie (see "Who's Who") were U. S. delegates to the Pan-American Conference, Nov., 1933, with the official party.

Wm. H. Leiserson, Secretary of the National Labor Board, is a fellow author with Norman Thomas and Harry Laidler of the book "Socialism of Our Times". His section is entitled "Socialist Theory and the Class Struggle".

Prof. Raymond Moley, Roosevelt's appointee as Assistant Secretary of State, is a close friend of Wm. C. Bullitt. According to "Time" of May 8, 1933: "At Western Reserve he is still well remembered as the professor who required his classes to read the New Republic when that journal of parlor liberalism was considered Red." (It is still considered Red).

John F. Sinclair, of the Garland Fund Committee on Imperialism and of the A. C. L. U. national committee, was reported by the press to be engaged in confidential work for Pres. Roosevelt (Chgo. Tribune, May 9, 1933). He was appointed member of the NRA review board, March 1934, with Clarence Darrow, chairman (See "Who's Who" for both).

Heywood Broun and Joseph Wood Krutch, well known radicals (see "Who's Who"), were appointed as NRA industrial advisors for codes of fair competition in the theatre industry (Chgo. American, Aug. 8, 1933).

If McKee, 1933 candidate for Mayor of New York, was, as he claimed, a Roosevelt man, and the accounts in the Daily Worker of Sept. 13, 15, 17, 1933 concerning Pres. Roosevelt's aid to La Guardia are correct, then the non-Tammany voter indeed had a Tweedle-Dum and Tweedle-Dee choice between Rooseveltian candidates. To quote the Daily Worker; "Wm. J. Schiefflin, known as the founder of the Fusion movement, is a wily demagogue who has considerable distinction among capitalist politicians. On May 17, 1931 Schiefflin paid verbal tribute to Norman Thomas. He said that Thomas was 'a man excellently capable and fitted for the office of Mayor. . . . But in the Fusion fight Schiefflin feared that Thomas might handicap his capitalist political wing through his Socialist tag." And then: "By Aug. 2" (1933) "the whole Fusion movement seemed to be at the point of collapse. It was then that Roosevelt's personal advisor was rushed upon the scene to save the day. Adolph A. Berle, Jr., a member of Roosevelt's so-called 'brain trust,' went into hurried conference. Another such gathering was called the following night and it was at this session that La Guardia was chosen as standard bearer. Since that time Roosevelt's personal advisor has helped La Guardia to draft the City Fusion Party platform. . . . Fusion's standard bearer is a former Republican, a former Socialist, a former Progressive, a former well paid advisor of the Tammany administration" (legal services in 1923). "In the following autumn" (1924) "he entered the race for Congress on the Socialist ticket. . . . As a Socialist La Guardia had often expressed his opposition to war . . . ," etc.

The National Labor Tribune for June 22, 1933 states that Adolph A. Berle, Jr. and the radical Congressman Fiorello H. La Guardia wrote the Railroad Corporation Reorganization Bill. A. A. Berle, Jr. and Paul Blanshard, for 15 years a leading Socialist, and an executive of the Socialist L. I. D., are now members of the La Guardia cabinet.

The Daily Worker failed to give La Guardia credit for his Socialist consistency in boring from within these various parties and at the same time that he was the Fusion candidate for conservatives joining in issuing the call for the Conference for Progressive Political Action held in Chicago, Aug. 29, 1933, to plan radical nation-wide action along the same political lines.

A. A. Berle, Jr., Special Advisor of Reconstruction Finance Corporation, is the the son of A. A. Berle, who served on the executive committee of the Civil Liberties Bureau (Lusk Report, p. 1083). He was formerly in the law office of Louis D. Brandeis, radical Supreme Court Justice (see), whose decision in the Oklahoma Ice Case is cited by radicals as a victory for Socialism.

Louis E. Kirstein of the National Advisory Board is the socialistic associate of Edward A. Filene of Boston. "Incidentally it was learned today that the Century Fund endowed by Edward A. Filene, Boston merchant, paid all the expenses of the industry control administration, including salaries of many publicity men, etc. . . . during the organization before the industrial control bill had been passed by Congress." (Chgo. Tribune, July 30, 1933).

Judson King, Research Investigator for Tennessee Valley Authority; James P. Warbasse of the Consumers Board of NRA; Wm. F. Ogburn, resigned member of Consumers Advisory Board; David E. Lilienthal, connected with Tennessee Valley Authority; Henry T. Hunt, General Counsel, Federal Emergency Administration of Public Works (of Communist and Socialist committees); and Arthur E. Morgan, Director, Tennessee Valley Authority; all have radical affiliations listed in this "Who's Who," as has Felix Frankfurter, at whose request Jerome Frank was made Gen. Counsel of AAA, Wm. L. Nunn, Nathan Margold, Chas. Edw. Russell, etc.

"The safety of the country rests on the provision it makes for adult education George F. Zook, United States Commissioner of Education, declared today before the Adult Educational Council of Chicago" (Chgo. Daily News, Oct. 20, 1933). (The Adult Educational Council provides Socialist and Communist lecturers for adult education which should make America safe for Socialism.) "Mr. Zook added that the orders of the Federal Employment Relief Service to the effect that public funds be made available for employment of unemployed persons in adult education projects grew out of a conference sponsored by the education office and prompted in part by successful adult education projects in New York under Harry Hopkins, now Federal Director of Relief."

The speech of Hopkins, who shared the program with Mrs. Roosevelt and Newton D. Baker at the Stevens Hotel, Chgo., Oct. 30, 1933 (as reported in the Chgo. Daily News, Oct. 31), may be summed up in his statement: "A *new social order* is to come out of the new deal." No socialistic speaker ever forgets that phrase "new social order," which of course differentiates Marx' social order from the American social order.

The Roosevelt administration mouth piece "Today" (of Raymond Moley) said editorially, Jan. 27, 1934, concerning President Roosevelt:

"To the Philippine Islands he sent Frank Murphy, the colorful and progressive Mayor of Detroit. Frank Murphy, sharing some of Father Coughlin's ardent progressivism, is, in his thinking, *rather to the left*."

Father Coughlin, who said over the radio, Jan. 14, 1934, that he would rather live in Russia under the heel of Stalin than in America under the lash of Morgan, has been hailed with glee by the socialist Public Ownership League (see). His radio propaganda is deeply appreciated by radicals. Father John A. Ryan of the Public Ownership League and the national committee of the infamous Communist-aiding American Civil Liberties Union declares that Father Coughlin "is on the side of the angels," while other Catholic dignitaries have dubbed him a "rabble rouser".

When Pres. Roosevelt was Governor of New York, he appointed Frank P. Walsh, one of the most valuable friends the Red movement has had, to the N. Y. Commn. on Revision of Public Utility Laws, June, 1929, and chmn. of Power Authority of the State of N. Y., May, 1931. The radical activities of Frank P. Walsh and Felix Frankfurter, one of the insiders of Pres. Roosevelt's "brain trust," have been extensive. See Fred Biedenkapp (notorious Communist agitator) in "Who's Who" for aid given him by F. D. Roosevelt while Governor.

The Chicago Daily News, Dec. 26, 1933, under the caption, "Hails 1500 Yule Pardons As Victory for Free Speech," quotes the words of praise of Harry N. Weinberg, the attorney who defended Anarchist Emma Goldman, for the action of Pres. Roosevelt in extending pardon and amnesty to 1500 Reds, who had been convicted of seditious activities against the U. S. government —a gesture of friendship following close upon recognition of Russia, not unappreciated by revolutionaries. It is noteworthy, however, that at the same time the nation's newspapers, after months of haggling, were still unsuccessful in securing a clause guaranteeing *them* "freedom of speech" in their NRA code. As a consequence, Emma Goldman, deported Anarchist-Communist and free love exponent, has now returned and is spreading her ulcerous doctrines again.

Pres. Roosevelt recently pardoned Robert Osman, Brooklyn corporal, convicted in 1931 of communicating military secrets to Communists (see Louis Waldman in "Who's Who").

An Associated Press dispatch of Dec. 15, 1933, stated that "Raymond Moley, former assistant Secretary of State, criticized his former chief, Secretary of State Cordell Hull, for terming the administration's relief and recovery measures 'temporary and extraordinary' measures . . . saying that 'we are building permanently and not for a mere purpose of recovery,' urged the reconstruction of the Democratic Party to carry on the principles of the administration's recovery and relief measures."

Pres. Hutchins, who shared the Sinai Temple program of Oct. 30, 1933, with Mordecai Ezekiel and Norman Thomas, pleaded for federal funds and a federal secretary of education in order that education might be more and more state subsidized and controlled. Norman Thomas, of course, supplemented this socialistic idea with other Socialist plans and Ezekiel said that the long term aim of the U. S. agricultural program is to "place the best farmers on the best land," placing the surplus farmers in city factories.

I think when Ezekiel comes to shifting farmers around, as Russia does, and telling a farmer who loves his home that he is a "surplus" farmer he may find that the "loud acclaim" which Wm. E. Sweet's letter asserts Roosevelt is receiving will change to something like the statements of Gov. 'Alfalfa Bill' Murray, as recently reported in the press. Having heard that the panhandle section of his State's lands were to be declared unfit for farming and the settlers moved elsewhere, he declared he would call out the National Guard and "not one d— settler would be moved". The residents themselves declared they had lived on and loved their land for many years and knew more about its possibilities than the government appointees and did not care to be moved. Of course the more probable and smoother method of making the farmers move peaceably would be to pay for the land and load the bill onto the taxpayers. Any measure which raises taxes is a means of socialization or doing away with private ownership.

Abraham Lincoln said that any issue should be judged not by whether it is all good or all bad, but by whether it is preponderantly good or bad, as no issue or individual is wholly good or bad.

American government along Washingtonian lines has demonstrated its worth. It is as perfect a form of government for any age as human nature will allow it to be. It spurs initiative and offers incentive with a maximum of freedom and a minimum of coercion. Until recent years, when radical tamperers started saddling it with bureaucracy, it maintained its people at the highest level ever known.

No former depression was able long to halt the upward surge of American progress. Given back their real liberty, their freedom to work for something except the tax collector, Americans would again down this depression. Socialism in Austria, England and Australia has kept those countries depressed for years by the vicious cycle of taxation, more unemployment, more unemployment, more taxation. For every rich employer "swatted," many wage earners were thrown on the dole, then more people on the dole required more taxation.

The many thousands of middle class, or "bourgeois," American citizens who have a financial interest in the packing industry, or the public utilities, through the ownership of stock, bonds, life insurance policies, etc., may well look with apprehension upon the recently announced plan of the Roosevelt administration to take over the packing industry as a "basic industry." And yet, if quick, drastic and concerted action in opposition is not taken, that is what may possibly be done, as one of the various steps toward complete socialization of the Country under the guidance of "Commissars" Morgenthau, Richberg, Perkins, Ickes, Wallace and Tugwell.

A comparison between the **Communist Manifesto's ten measures** for socializing a state, the **1932 Socialist Party platform,** and the **Rooseveltian Bills passed by Congress** 1933-4, is shocking. It is significant that Postmaster General Farley, Administration spokesman and still head of the Democratic National Committee, insists (summer 1934) that **every feature of the "New Deal" was conceived in the mind of Franklin Roosevelt before he was even nominated for the Presidency,** and deplores the popular vogue of giving the credit **(or blame)** to the "Brain Trust."

Not partisanship, but "Socialism versus Americanism" is the issue before America now. No Socialist-Democrat, no compromising willy-nilly Republican torn between innate American conservatism and internationalist radical-pacifism deserves support. We need a rockbound old American or an anti-Marxian Democrat (with a Congress to match) to lead America. Who is he? Even though he is found, he will not relieve individuals of responsibility in picking local election slates before "George" does it for them.

Every American who values his home, his liberty and the future of his children should give himself heart and soul in the next election to the Party which gives *proof* that its candidates will uphold the American principles which have made America great and will offer American voters the opportunity to vote "Karl Marx" out of office.

CAPITALISM—HEWER AND "CHISELER" OF AMERICAN GREATNESS

The slogan of socialism is "Production for use and not for profit," but the spirit of capitalism is production for use *and* for profit. Socialists everywhere are as familiar with the Soviet cartoons and myths concerning the ugly, fat, heavy-jowled old man in the frock coat and high hat, greedily clutching bags of gold, whom they label "Capitalism" as we all are with cartoons and myths about fat, jolly, old Santa Claus with his pack of toys. The myths built up around each of these imaginary old gentlemen are childish, but no less satisfying to certain mentalities.

What could be simpler in time of economic stress and bewilderment than to imagine a few greedy old fat capitalists clutching all of the nation's wealth in their money bags, while exulting maliciously over the hardships of the unemployed, the unemployed advancing upon them, cracking them over their heads and "re-distributing the wealth" in their bags to the needy? An ending as simple and happy as the arrival of Santa Claus with toys, with the added satisfaction of taking revenge on the villain.

In reality millions of Americans, a greater proportion of the population than in any other country, own farms, homes, property, stock, savings, or a business of some sort and are capitalists on a larger or smaller scale. When a Socialist tells the "old one" about a half dozen or so capitalists controlling all of the wealth in the United States, he should be sent to read the volumes of names of owners of property listed on the tax books of various districts and to poll the store keepers and business men of any "Main Street" to ask them how many of their concerns are owned by the half dozen big, bad, capitalists, and how many are privately owned.

Anyone who owns any investment, property, or business nowadays knows that profits are doubtful, dividends and interest are not being paid, taxes are almost confiscatory, that capitalists who have large holdings are distressed, tax eaten and gloomy, and that some of them commit suicide. The Socialists' mythical capitalist exulting over the present depression is not to be found in real life, nor is it conceivable that any capitalist would deliberately deprive himself of profits in order to deprive his employees of the prosperity wages paid when business is run at prosperity speed.

Who, then, should be cracked over the head? How can wealth that is not produced be re-distributed? Property, tools, business, factories, cannot be eaten, hoarded in bags, or hidden under the bed. These produce wealth only when they can function at a profit for everyone. When they do not, their owners are "property poor."

Russians are told they must suffer deprivation in order that the goods they produce may be exported abroad to pay for machinery (soon rusted through carelessness), to industrialize Russia.

Ellery Walter, fascinating author and lecturer who, after living under the "planned society order" of Russia, became depinked, told how he stood looking at a long line of tractors which were out of commission and asked his Russian girl guide what was the matter with them. She said they had broken down from lack of greasing. Noting a peasant's cart rumbling along with a bucket of grease swinging from the axle, he pointed it out and said to her: "Those peasants know enough to grease their wagons. What is the matter with them that they don't know enough to grease the tractors?" She happened to know the peasant and merely replied, "O! that wagon belongs to *him*."

America, the world's greatest industrial nation, industrialized itself under private capitalism, for use *and* for profit, not only without deprivation, but while enjoying increasing prosperity and highest wages. American sufferings started only when capitalism took sick. Like a sick horse, the decrepit economic system back of which we are now crawling along is not Capitalism himself, but a Capitalism loaded down with Socialism. Quietly, step by step since 1912, one socialistic measure after another has been passed, one state or federal bureau after another has been put into operation at the expense of the tax payer. It is estimated that a generation ago a man worked one day in every fifty to pay taxes, whereas just before the New Deal he worked one day in every five to pay taxes. A mere list of governmental activities run at the expense of the taxpayer would fill a good sized booklet.

America's horse "Capitalism," or private industry, carried his steadily mounting load very well until recent years, when his back caved in alarmingly and his gait became labored. Promising to cure this overloaded back and slow gait by "balancing the budget," the New Deal has instead piled onto him a further load of billions of dollars in socialistic taxation. Socialists gleefully predict that our horse will die. They exult that "Capitalism has failed." He probably will die unless he is rescued. If he does, it will not be his fault, but the fault of those deliberately aiming to kill him with Socialist burdens. Unload Capitalism and give him a sniff of oats for his profit, and he will trot along as he did before. He has proven what he can do in the past.

What have socialistic experiments ever achieved, except deficits or failure? While Russia was primitive under the Czars, it danced on holidays and worshipped God with a full stomach. The Ukraine, now starving, was, in fact, called the bread basket of Europe. Famine, spy and shot gun ridden Russia now turns out more propaganda than produce.

Dr. H. Parker Willis, Columbia U. professor, one of the authors of the federal reserve act, and a monetary authority, said before the American Economic Association, Dec. 28, 1933, that he had had difficulty in analyzing the recovery program because of "a lack of consistency and frankness on the part of those identified with its origin and administration. One fully accredited spokesman of the recovery administration stated that the New Deal was devised after a careful study of European Socialism, Russian Communism, and Italian Fascism. But almost at the same time, another equally high and equally authoritative spokesman denied that there was anything revolutionary in the undertakings.

"But taking the most recent and official exposition of the recovery, I find it based upon a fundamentally false premise. It rests upon the assumption that the depression was due to a breakdown of laissez faire. When did industry lose its freedom? Certainly not on March 3, 1933, but many years earlier.

"As a matter of fact, the panic of 1929 grew out of the existence of too much interference with some industries and nursing, spoon-feeding, and coddling others. It is not true that uncontrolled excessive individualism has destroyed itself. What we are suffering from today is an undue governmental interference with business." (Chicago Tribune, Dec. 29, 1933).

I listened to Henry A. Wallace, Secretary of Agriculture, telling the world over the radio on Christmas morning that governmental "planning" under the New Deal must go on in ever broadening measure, to secure for the people of America a more "equitable redistribution of wealth," to abolish the "profit motive," the "greed" and "rugged individualism" (all good Socialist phrases), which had ruined this country. He said that nothing that governmental "planning" could do in the future could fail as America had failed in the past, and that nothing it could do could ruin America as we Americans had already ruined it.

I wondered if Mr. Wallace were unaware of the fact that America and its capitalism is the greatest success in history, that the "rugged individualism" of our American pioneering ancestors "chiseled" from the forests of a vast wilderness, no richer than similar vast wildernesses in South America, Africa and Asia, which remain, however, wildernesses today, a nation which is the envy of every nation on earth, and this in the space of only about 150 years. The freely released energies of those who fled the autocracies of European countries created the miracle of modern times—America.

I wondered how Mr. Wallace could call America a failure unless perchance he had never seen the rest of the world to draw his comparisons. Anyone who has traveled over the world knows that the greatest part of its surface is still untouched by "Capitalism" or "rugged individualism," that its minerals lie unmined, that the feet of countless millions go bare, that mud or straw huts and a few rags remain in style century after century, for the *majority* of human beings, that insect-bitten, comfortless poverty on a bare subsistence level reigns unchallenged over the vast stretches of Africa, Asia, South America, and China, where famines also regularly kill off millions, that these millions never experience depressions because they never have any prosperity. They cannot drop because they remain down.

Enroute to the Orient last year when I facetiously jibed a kerosene lamp salesman about his business being out of date, he came back with very exact figures on the millions of inhabitants in India, Asia, Africa, Pacific Islands, etc., who have never had gas or electricity, could not afford it if it were available, who live countless miles from the few foreign settlements where it is available, and are now using far more primitive lighting devices than kerosene lamps. He assured me that his business was in its infancy!

City Americans naturally look upon those who have had their gas and electricity shut off during the depression as sufferers. Yet our own parents had none. My mother, during Christmas holidays, was reminescing with an old friend about their youthful days in Ohio. She recalled the horse and buggy days. He, a prominent Chicago physician, said: "I go you one better. Remember you lived in northern Ohio, which with its lake port, Cleveland, developed ahead of Southern Ohio where I lived. I travelled by ox cart at a time when you, in northern Ohio, had advanced to horses and carriages."

To "rugged individualism" and capitalism we owe machines, road and transportation developments, and countless other comforts unknown in any previous age.

If capitalism and capitalists are a blight to humanity, then a land like Egypt—where its sore-eyed fellaheens, who live in mud huts, till the fields with the same style crooked stick plows, raise water from the Nile with the same old water wheels, and sail the Nile in the same old model dahabeahs as are pictured on the walls of King Tut's tomb which was sealed centuries ago—should be a happy spot. But the happiest event which has befallen

Egypt in many centuries came with the British "imperialism" and "capitalism" which built the Assuan Dam to control Nile floods, increase tillable land, and prevent famines. While the dam may have been built for the profit of British capitalism, it has, no less, profited the Egyptians by filling their stomachs with food.

If capitalism is "greed" and a blight to humanity, then why are the savage and miserable lands which have no capitalism, not blessed? Why is the standard of living of the *whole* people in any land raised in proportion to the success and development of its capitalistic enterprises?

How inconsistently the very people who welcome the advent of a factory to their home town and mourn its closing as a catastrophe, who glory in the memory of the $10 per day wages it once paid and the silk shirts, radios and Fords they were able to buy when capitalism was pulsing with life, who themselves hope for nothing so much as the legitimate chance to again make profits, and the sooner the better, will applaud the thrilling experienced "rabble-rouser," with his ever popular appeals to envy, when he denounces as the source of all evil the "profit-motive" of the capitalist who built or ran that factory for their *mutual* benefit. When he made profits they profited also.

There is, of course, an alternative to the "profit-motive" for spurring human beings on to perform hard, worrisome, or distasteful labor. It is the shot gun. As Bernard Shaw put it: "Compulsory labor with death, the final punishment, is the keystone of socialism." Business men are not apt to voluntarily get too "tired" working for the State, nor are laborers on public works noted for their over exertion. Try calling on a politician early in the day. "He is not down yet" is what you will probably be told. We may reward or punish people to make them work, "crack down" on them, employ a G. P. U. spy system to enforce Socialism, or return to the American Capitalistic principle of production for use *and* for profit.

A capitalist business must efficiently produce goods for *use* or it can make no profit. State works on the other hand, need not be either useful, necessary, or efficiently run, since the tax payers pay the bills out of the proceeds from private efficiency. Even the U. S. Post Office piles up a large yearly deficit (112 million dollars in 1933). Capitalism is a system of spending which pumps profits into every part of society. Buying goods is spending for the products of industry, while buying investments is spending to maintain and develop industry. Even savings are loaned out to be spent for home building and business enterprise, or else the banker realizes no profit. New investment means new industry, new employment, new spending, new investing, and so on around the circle again.

Have you ever had your wants completely satisfied? Other Americans have not had theirs satisfied either. There is no limit to new wants, new developments, new possibilities, within America itself, while other lands have been scarcely touched with modern equipment. Wash bowls and pitchers formed the entire window display in a prominent London store when I visited there only a few years ago. There is no over-production and there never has been. Yet Rex. Tugwell, our "brain trust" leader, says new industry should not be allowed to arise unless it has first been planned for and considered probably desirable by the government. (See under Nat. Religion and Labor Found.)

In Russia, where Marxism rules, employees do not receive the full value of their products in wages, according to the accepted Marxian theory of value. Someone there, as everywhere, must take part of the sale price of products and spend it to develop processes, build and maintain the factory and tools, with which the product is made. The government is that someone in Russia or under Socialism anywhere. Individual owners are the "someones" under capitalism. Which is the more efficient? No capitalist can actually use for himself a great amount of the world's goods. As the old British jingle about being able to sleep in only one bed or wear one hat at a time goes:

"You can only wear one eye-glass in your eye,
Use one coffin when you die—don't you know!"

The rest of a capitalist's profits are not hoarded in bags, but invested, and that is spent, for further development of industry and further profits for others as well as himself.

Many business men, now harassed by the evident animosity of socialistic "New Dealers" toward private business for profit, warned to keep prices down, wages up, hours of business long (for themselves), hours of employees short, to compute sales taxes and to expect to lose their blue eagle if they err, would gladly, but for the hope of future change, rid themselves of the worrisome burden of running a profitless business for others, and become employees themselves. Many people who saved to buy investments for their own "old age security," which are now almost worthless, wish they had squandered the money instead. Even the movies portray all mortgage owners as villains. Many of these villains are widows, orphans, and aged people dependent for support on this income. Insurance policies depend largely upon mortgages.

Many Chicago home owners, straining to pay preposterous state, county, sanitary district, and other taxes on their homes and furniture, would now gladly change places with renters of furnished apartments and give up the struggle of meeting taxes.

When it no longer "pays" to own property or run a business, it means that capitalism or "private ownership" is being squeezed to death. Socialism is killing it. Only when Socialism is throttling legitimate profits does the big and little capitalist stop investing, that is, spending, and try to hide a little of his fast disappearing money from the tax collector, but "New Dealers" have devaluated even money now. The State seems about ready to gobble up all private ownership rights.

In the face of all evidences of the success of capitalism and of the failures of Socialism, one can but marvel at the ever gushing zeal of Socialist propagandists. Their appeals to abolish the profit motive are as sweet as the rustle of angels' wings. Who could remain unmoved by the following from "Toward A New Economic Society" by Kirby Page and Sherwood Eddy? (p. 83): "What can religion as the champion of personality do to give our economic activities an ethical content and place them in their proper sphere? . . . The profit motive must be supplanted by the motive of service or production for use, which in turn means that ownership as soon as practicable, should rest in the hands of the community. . . . The Columbia Conserve Company in Indianapolis, owned and controlled by its employees, is a rare but enlightening example of this form of organization." (Soulful, is it not?)

The Columbia Conserve Company, from a thousand pulpits, lecture platforms, and class rooms, has long been heralded as the most advanced form of industrial democracy, an example to youth, a reproof to the American business man. Yet, the socialist World Tomorrow (Dec. 21, 1933) itself publishes this story of its debacle: About 15 years ago Mr. Wm. P. Hapgood with the cooperation of his brothers, Norman and Hutchins, established a canning factory with the avowed purpose of demonstrating the possibilities of democracy in industry. A system was also devised whereby the ownership of the company would pass by stages into the hands of the employees. About a year ago, the quarrel between Mr. Hapgood and some of the ablest veteran workers became so acute that in February, with the consent of all parties concerned, Sherwood Eddy, Jerome Davis, Paul H. Douglas, and James Myers (all radicals) were requested to serve as a committee for the purpose of investigating the whole situation. An agreement was reached which was to remain in force until April, 1934. Nevertheless, within two months Mr. Hapgood requested of the committee that the company be released from the agreement. Opposition was offered to this by a group of employees, etc. (Wm. M. Leiserson, Roosevelt appointee as secy. Nat. Labor Bd., was chosen as arbitrator.)

To quote from the reply of this Committee of Four who charged breach of faith and of contract: "During our own experience with the Columbia Conserve Company during recent weeks, we have observed with deep regret that Mr. Wm. P. Hapgood, although in his philosophy, democratic, seems to have proved autocratic in dealing with the workers. . . . It seemed to the Committee that the leaders of those who dared openly to differ with the management were forced out or impelled to resign until effective industrial democracy had disappeared" (as in Russia).

The socialist World Tomorrow draws from this "disappointing outcome of a notable experiment" the conclusion that "genuine democracy in industry cannot be achieved by isolated efforts. . . . Nothing short of the socialization of natural resources and basic industry will suffice. . . . Therefore it seems to us that deeper wisdom has been displayed by Powers Hapgood who left his father's plant to become a national organizer for the Socialist Party. The collapse of the experiment in industrial democracy at the Columbia Conserve Company is partly the result of the failure of the human spirit, but much more it is the consequence of an inadequate social philosophy and an incorrect social strategy."

Jail or the shot gun is the "correct social strategy" in the Soviet Socialist paradise. These take the place of competition, under capitalism, in settling wage and other controversies. Had the United States been completely socialized at the time this quarrel broke out, governmental forces would have been used to "crack down" on these disgruntled workers.

Socialist appeals for complete Socialism, sharing, and abolition of the "profit motive" would be so much more winning if Socialists first voluntarily proved the success and practicability of their theories, instead of insisting upon the necessity for brute force to achieve and hold Socialism in power.

One notes that even such a zealous "Christian" Socialist as Rev. E. F. Tittle of Evanston, while denouncing Capitalism and social inequality between whites and negroes, yet continues to enjoy his capitalistic salary, home and car, instead of sharing them with poor evicted negroes, and sends his own daughter through Roycemore, the most exclusive private school on the North Shore, although Evanston has good public schools.

Morris Hillquit, national executive of the Socialist Party for many years, died recently, leaving a fortune of some $200,000, which according to his Socialist principles, should be "redistributed." He should have shared it long ago.

Bernard Shaw, one of the world's most outstanding propagandists for Communism-Socialism, lives in England where he can enjoy the huge profits from his writings and other capitalistic ventures. Portly Maxim Litvinoff, who visited the United States while hunger was rampant in Russia, bore no marks of suffering, nor, as the Chicago Tribune remarked at the time, was there any direct evidence that he had been "especially fattened for the occasion." He demonstrated the well-known fact that political commissars, everywhere, eat, regardless of whether others starve or not. The cure for the temptations inherent in politics which give rise to its widespread corruption, is not *more* political offices, *more* temptation, *more* politicians, *more* political power, *more* graft, *more* taxes—in other words *more* Socialism—but *less*, and a return to the individualistic sense of responsibility, the private initiative and capitalism which has actually hewn and chiseled American greatness out of a primitive wilderness and given its people the highest standard of living of any people in history.

The National Republic (Dec. 1933 issue) under the heading "The Failure of Socialism" states:

"Persons socialistically inclined often point to the present world-wide depression as 'a failure of the capitalist system,' that is, of the system of private ownership of property and liberty and from this argue in favor of fundamental changes in the economic order as a means of improving the lot of the people.

"But the present world-wide breakdown could more properly be charged to a collapse of the socialist system. Every important power in the western world today, except the United States, is under either socialist parliamentary control, or that dictatorship to which socialism leads as in Italy, Poland, Germany and Russia.

"Beyond this effect of direct socialist control, the menace of political ownership of property and destruction of individual liberty and enterprise, and the meddling with the established monied systems, are the chief factors in the slowing down of business enterprise. It is not to be expected that productive enterprise will go ahead full steam when enemies of all private enterprise are busily engaged in trying to tear up the tracks and burn the bridges just ahead.

"In western Europe, under the threat of socialism and bolshevism, money was withdrawn from productive enterprise in thousands of cases and went into hiding. In this country political demagogues and doctrinaires who are at heart socialists whatever their outward party profession, have been busily engaged in threatening all business enterprise, and hampering and hamstringing it wherever possible. What they cannot immediately destroy by socialist legislation, they try to tax and restrict and handicap to the point of extinction. In this they are joined by those international adventurers of capitalism who seek by this method to kill off all independent enterprise in the belief that they may gain profits not only through national but world-wide mergers. . . .

"The failures of socialism in the Old World are resulting in dictatorships. Socialism centralizes all power in the politicians. It hands over to them complete control of the life, property and liberties of the people. Thus it builds up a giant machine ready for the hand of dictators. Will we venture into such chaos?"

FASCISM

Fascism, the bitterest enemy of Socialism-Communism, resembles Socialism in the respect that it gives great power to the State and dictatorship over all industry, employment, education, freedom of the press, etc. The points of difference which make it violently hated by the Reds are: its opposition to the "class struggle" and the subjugation of the bourgeoisie by the dictatorship of the proletariat. Rather, it seeks a harmony between all classes and concedes to industrialists, white collar, professional, as well as laboring workers, a place in the social order as necessary parts, not "class enemies," of the whole, but under State control. It defends some property rights and religion. It opposes Marxist philosophy and the Communist and Socialist Marxian parties. Fascism in Italy is not anti-Semitic. The problem of the large number of revolutionary Russian Jews in Germany doubtless contributed toward making Fascist Germany anti-Semitic.

Fascism arose in Italy and Germany as the result of the weakness of Democracy in combatting the Marxian poison which had been allowed to disintegrate the entire social fabric of these nations with agitations for strife and disunity. It took over power at a time in both countries when the choice lay between Fascist or Red dictatorship. It is the only enemy feared by the Reds, because it is the only system which opposes militancy with militancy and puts down one dictatorship by means of another.

The price of Democratic freedom is eternal vigilance. When a people are too indifferent to the loss of their liberty, too blind to see that unchecked Marxism will result in complete chaos, disunity and national helplessness, too lazy to bother to protect their form of government, or to govern themselves, then some form of dictatorship will arise to take over the task for them.

Unless large numbers of Americans shake off their present indifference to fast disappearing liberty and to danger from within, and combat Socialism-Communism vigorously, some form of Fascism will arise in America to do battle with Socialism for the dictatorship over the indifferent. As the strength of Socialism-Communism increases, the chance to preserve Democracy decreases, until eventually Fascism becomes the only alternative to Socialism-Communism. It is late, but not too late to save American Democracy if Americans will awaken—*now!* Where are America's leaders?

UNEMPLOYMENT PREVENTION NUMBER

Economic Justice

BULLETIN OF THE NATIONAL RELIGION AND LABOR FOUNDATION

Application for Entry as Second Class Matter Pending

VOL. 1—NO. 3 304 CROWN STREET, NEW HAVEN, CONN. JANUARY, 1933

THE BASIC CAUSE OF UNEMPLOYMENT*

(Professor Tugwell has made a masterful and clear analysis of the nature of the choice before mankind. Humanity, religious insights, and the economic forces are working together in the movement toward a world order in which our collective life will be organized, according to a plan, to meet the predetermined needs of all people. Everyone must take a stand on this basic issue. Assumed neutrality is actually tacit support of the status quo. *The Editors.*)

The greatest economic event of the nineteenth century occurred when Frederick W. Taylor first held a stop watch on the movements of a group of shovelers in the plant of the Midvale Steel Company. And we must have understood, when *Shop Management* was published in 1903 that, perhaps a generation later, the world would be overwhelmed with goods. Taylor had already done his greatest work by then, and notice of it had been sufficiently public if there had been economic ears to hear. Instead of that, writing and teaching went on undisturbed the subject matter becoming more and more traditional. Perhaps most ironical of all, in view of the coming surplus, was all the emphasis on laws

A Soviet Poster

THE TRIUMPH OF ORGANIZED RELIGION?

Facsimile of portion of Jan. 1933 issue of "Economic Justice," showing a typical Soviet atheist cartoon, a pictorial plea to workers bowed under the Cross and pulling Capitalism (the fat man driving them), led by Christ, to throw off the Cross and Capitalism.

(See page 201)

PART II

ORGANIZATIONS, ETC.

Descriptive data concerning more than 460 Communist, Anarchist, Socialist, I. W. W., or Radical-Pacifist controlled or infiltrated organizations and other agencies referred in the "Who's Who" (Part III):

A

ABRAHAM LINCOLN CENTER—"UNITY"

Anyone reading the bulletins posted in the entrance hall of the six-story building entirely occupied by Abraham Lincoln Center (a social settlement) would believe that he had entered a Communist institution. For example, in Sept. 1933, one placard read: "Enroll Now! Chicago Workers School, 2822 S. Michigan Av." (Communist school of revolution); another announced new issues of "New Masses" (Communist magazine) and said "You can get it from M. Topchevsky here at desk!" (M. Topchevsky teaches art at the communist Workers School); another headed "John Reed Club" (Communist club at 1475 S. Michigan Av.) listed lectures to be given there, among others "Eugene Bechtold Sat., Sept. 23, at 8:30" (another teacher at communist Workers School); another notice addressed to "All Organizations—Save Our Schools Committee," etc., signed by Sam Lessitz, secretary of the communist National Student League, urged all those interested to come to a meeting to be held Sept. 22, 1933, at 3223 W. Roosevelt Road, Room 302, for the purpose of planning further agitations against Chicago school economies and pointed out that the National Student League "a non-partisan organization" (!) was already responsible for recent strikes in two schools. Lincoln Center is the meeting place for such Communist groups as the I.L.D., national convention of John Reed Clubs 1932, etc. Players from Lincoln Center helped to form the communist Chicago Workers Theatre (see) of which Curtis Reese, head of Lincoln Center, is an official sponsor. The communist Workers' Laboratory Theatre School (see) is conducted at Lincoln Center for the purpose of training actors for revolutionary plays.

Unity Publishing Co., of Lincoln Center, also headed by Curtis Reese, publishes a weekly magazine, of which the editor is John Haynes Holmes, which has long had a reputation for radicalism. The Lusk Report in 1920 (p. 1129) said: "Such Unitarian ministers as J. M. Evans and A. L. Weatherly" (on Unity staff 1933) "can abjure God without leaving their ministry. John Haynes Holmes changed the name of his so-called church from 'Church of the Messiah' to 'Community Church' as an outward mark of his change of heart from Christianity to Communism. An insidious anti-religious campaign is being carried on by these men and their colleagues in such reviews as 'The World Tomorrow' (New York) and 'Unity' (Chicago)."

"A Song of Revolt," a poem by Communist Robert Whitaker with his footnote explaining "how I can accept the Communist position with my opposition to War," appears in Sept. 4, 1933, issue of "Unity." To quote from page 12: "This significant fast of Gandhi—to me is second in significance only to the crucifixion of Christ" (Gandhi is a pet of the Reds). Words of praise for Harry Ward's book on Russia are written by J. B. Matthews; another review says "Once again we are favored with a book from the pen of that fearless Methodist preacher, Ernest Fremont Tittle" (see this "Who's Who"). The "New Humanist" magazine featuring Harry Elmer Barnes (vice pres. atheist Freethinkers Society) exchanges advertisements with "Unity" and a cut-rate is offered for subscriptions to both.

Sidney Strong, radical, father of Anna Louise Strong (the Communist editor of the Moscow Daily News in Moscow) and of Tracy Strong (whose communistic activities in the Y.M.C.A. were widely commented upon by the press), is one of the board of directors of Unity. In his article in the Sept. 18, 1933, issue he says: "More than a year ago Litvinoff of the Soviet Republic made proposals that involved a drastic reduction of arms all around—in fact at one instance he proposed that steps be taken towards total and general disarmament" (see page 66). "Unfortunately his proposals were not heeded. . . . Everyone should be encouraged to take a personal stand—to be a war resister. . . . Anti war congresses should be held. There cannot be too many public protests."

The editorial in this issue voices the usual Red "anti-imperialist," anti-American-government attitude in reviewing red Carleton Beals' book on Cuba, saying in part: "We are made to see our own country, the United States, as the chief offender against the Cuban people. In 1898 we did not free Cuba, but only transferred her from the bondage of Spain to the exploitation of America. It is to the everlasting credit of President Roosevelt and Secretary Hull that they not only did not interfere with the revolutionists, but actually gave them friendly counsel and assistance."

In 1933, "Unity" lists the following:

Unity Publishing Co., Abraham Lincoln Center, 700 Oakwood Blvd., Chicago, Ill. John Haynes Holmes, Editor; Curtis W. Reese, Managing Editor; Board of Directors: Mrs. Salmon O. Levinson, President; Mrs. E. L. Lobdell, Vice President; Mrs. Irwin S. Rosenfels, Treasurer; Mrs. Francis Neilson (Helen Swift Neilson, daughter of the capitalistic packer, Gustavus F. Swift, and sister of Harold Swift, pres. of the bd. of trustees of the Univ. of Chicago, where Communism is a recognized student activity); Mrs. Ella R. Nagely; Mrs. O. T. Knight; Mrs. Irwin Rosenfels; Mr. Curtis W. Reese; Miss Mathilda C. Schaff; Mrs. E. E. Smith; Mr. Francis Neilson; Secretary, May Johnson; Editorial Contributors: W. Waldemar W. Argow; Dorothy Walton Binder (Wife of Carroll, editorial assistant to publisher of the Chicago Daily News, which urged recognition of Soviet Russia); Raymond B. Bragg; Edmund B. Chaffee; Percy M. Dawson (advisor in Alex Meiklejohn's ultra radical Experimental College at U. of Wis., 1927-29); Albert C. Dieffenbach (chmn. for Boston of the Fellowship of Faiths "Threefold Movement"); James A. Fairley; Zona Gale; A. Eustace Haydon; Jesse H. Holmes; Louis L. Mann; Jos. Ernest McAfee (of Union Theological Seminary, dir. for John Haynes Holmes Church of "community service" since 1924); Henry R. Mussey; Max C. Otto; Alson H. Robinson; Robt. C. Scholler; Clarence R. Skinner; Sidney Strong; Jabez T. Sunderland (of Union Theol. Sem.; Pres. of various Indian Freedom Organizations); Arthur L. Weatherly; James H. West. Poetry Editors: Lucia Trent, Ralph Cheyney. Foreign Representatives: Australia —Chas. Strong; Austria—Stefan Zweig; Bulgaria—P. M. Mattheff; England—Harrison Broun, Fred Hawkinson, Reginald Reynolds; France—G. Demartial, Romain Rolland (Communist); Germany —Theodor Hahn; India—Rabindranath Tagore; Japan—Nobuichire Imaoka; Palestine—Hans Kohn; Russia—Alina Huebsch.

ADULT EDUCATION COUNCIL
(of Illinois)

See Chicago Forum Council.

AGRICULTURAL WORKERS INDUSTRIAL UNION

A communist T.U.U.L. Union; rec'd $3,000 from the Garland Fund; A. E. Sanchez, 1643 Lawrence St., Denver, Colo., organizer of beet workers; Donald Henderson, sec.

ALL AMERICA ANTI IMPERIALIST LEAGUE

(ALSO INTERNATIONAL LEAGUE AGAINST IMPERIALISM)

A.A.A.I.Lg.

Name now is Anti Imperialist League, American section of Moscow's International League Against Imperialism; an "All America" Communist subsidiary which in 1928 had 12 sections established in the U. S. and 11 Latin American countries spreading "vicious and false propaganda in Mexico, Central and South American countries against the United States, depicting this country as a big bully trying to exploit Latin America. This campaign has been successful in arousing hatred among Latin Americans against the United States" (U. S. Fish Report); it agitates against the Monroe doctrine and forms "Hands Off Committees" (see) to propagandize against U. S. interference whenever the Communists are endangering American lives and property by stirring up trouble and revolution in Cuba, China, Mexico, Nicaragua, etc. This propaganda is echoed by such A.C.L.U. affairs as the Committee on Cultural Relations with Latin America, Non Intervention Citizens Committee, National Citizens Committee on Relations with Latin America (see), etc. Works in close association, though not affiliated, with the Chinese Students Alliance (mid-west section), Conference for Filipino Independence, Monsang (Chinese Waiters Union of Chicago), Sun Yat Sen Society, etc. The official report of the Communist Party's convention held in Chicago Aug. 21-30, 1925 (then called Workers' Party), where it was formed, stated: "Under the present Central Executive Committee the Worker's Party of America has for the first time made anti-imperialist work one of its basic activities—the most important step in this direction being the successful organization of the All America Anti-Imperialist

League. . . . The A.A.A.I.Lg. was endorsed by the Comintern and Profintern." (page 19). The Garland Fund, in 1927 and later, not only donated $1,500 to the A.A.A.I.Lg. itself but spent thousands and thousands of dollars for "research work on imperialism" and appointed and paid "the Garland Fund Committee on American Imperialism" (see) for its efforts along this line; Roger Baldwin, a director of both Garland Fund and A.C.L.U., went with Wm. Pickens of the N.A.A.C.P., Richard Moore (director of Communist Negro work) and Communist Manuel Gomez, Nat. Sec. of the A.A.A.I.Lg., to Brussels, Belgium, in 1927 as a delegate to the communist World Congress Against Imperialism, which organized Moscow's International League Against Imperialism, the coordinating body of all communist Anti Imperialist League branches throughout the world. (Daily Worker, Mar. 9-22, 1927). This Congress, according to Baldwin, "was conceived by the same Communists and near-Communists who were active in the International Workers' Aid, working in close cooperation with the European representatives of the Kuomintang party and the Mexican workers."

The A.A.A.I.Lg.'s first official report stated that "direct contact with Mexico was maintained through the visits of Comrades Johnstone, Gomez, and Lovestone to Mexico." Lovestone was then head of the Communist Party of the U. S. A., called then the "Workers Party."

Paul Crouch, the Communist convicted of sedition in Hawaii, has been an active leader. He issued a manifesto in behalf of the A.A.A.I.Lg. printed in the Daily Worker Nov. 2, 1928. Communist Manuel Gomez, who first headed the A.A.A.I.Lg. as nat. sec. and acted as active organizer in 1927, was replaced in 1929 by Wm. Simons, who is still nat. sec. (1933), and Communist Scott Nearing became nat. chmn. The Chicago hdqts. were at 156 W. Washington St. with the Federated Press and units were established in large cities like New York, Chicago, San Francisco, etc.

Soon after the recent Communist-fomented Cuban revolution broke out, the "Daily Worker" headlined "Hands Off Cuba" and Wm. Simons and a delegation visited Pres. Roosevelt to protest against the sending of warships to Cuba (Sept., 1933). The Mar. 1933 issue of National Republic reported that about 150 members of the A.A.A.I.Lg. took part in a demonstration of 1,000 Reds in New York City and paraded before the Chinese consulate to protest against the imprisonment in China of a Communist leader Huang Ping.

Members of committees supporting Washington, D. C. conference of A.A.A.I.Lg. (Daily Worker, Dec. 14, 1926) were:

Clarence Darrow, Waldo Frank, Scott Nearing, Frank Weber (pres. Wis. Fed. Labor), Henry Teigan (sec. Minn. Farmer-Lab. Party), R. C. Wiggin (Asst. City Atty. Mpls.), Albert F. Coyle (ed. Locomotive Engrs. Journal), Rev. J. H. Holmes, Robt. W. Dunn, E. G. Flynn (nat. chmn. I. L. D.), Manuel Gomez, Jac Frederick (Machinists' Un.), Guy Anderson (Electricians Un.), Ernest Untermann (edtl. writer Milw. Leader), Wm. F. Dunne (ed. Daily Worker), Paul Jones (Fell. Recon. assoc. dir.), Prof. Ellen Hayes (Wellesley Coll.), H. W. L. Dana, Robt. M. Lovett, Carl Haessler, Wm. Pickens (N. A. A. C. P.), Dorothy Gary (chmn. Minn. State Fed. Lab. ed. dept.), John Stockwell, Arthur Fisher (sec. Emer. For. Pol. Conf.), Ex-Cong. Clyde M. Tavenner (ed. "Philippine Republic"), Mike Gold (New Masses), V. F. Calverton (ed. "Modern Quarterly"), Ralph Chaplin (I. W. W.), Rev. David Rhys Williams, Eliz. Glendower Evans, Lucia Ames Mead (W. I. L. P. F.), Wm. H. Holly, Prof. H. S. Bucklin (Brown U.), Justine Wise (Yale U. Law Sch.), John F. Markey (U. of Minn.), "Bishop" Wm. M. Brown, Cirilo Mavat (Filipino Assn. of Chgo.), Marx Lewis (sec. to Cong. Victor L. Berger), Lawrence Todd (Wash. corr. Fed. Press), Rev. Sidney Strong (Seattle).

The Daily Worker, April 18, 1928, stated concerning an A.A.A.I.Lg. conference:

"The Conference voted unanimously for the immediate formation of a permanent All-America Anti-Imperialist League branch to be composed of the organizations present. The provisional executive committee with many additional names was made the permanent executive of the Chicago League with William H. Holly as chairman, Ray Koerner as vice-chairman and Harry Gannes as secretary.

"The complete committee of the Chicago All-America Anti-Imperialist League is as follows: Anacleto Almanana, Filipino Association of Chicago; Zonia Baber, chairman, Pan-American Relations Committee, Women's International League for Peace and Freedom; John Bielowski, United Brotherhood of Carpenters and Joiners, Local No. 1367; Clarence Darrow, lawyer and publicist; Henry Duel, League for Industrial Democracy; Arthur Fisher, Secretary, Emergency Foreign Policy Conference; Harry Gannes; A. Gans, Jewish Marxian Youth Alliance; Alice Hanson, secretary, Chicago Liberal Club; Sam Herman, Young Workers (Communist) League; Lillian Herstein, Teacher's Union; William H. Holly; T. Y. Hu, Sun Yat Sen Lodge 492; Peter Jenson, pres. Machinists lodge 492; Arnulfo E. Jimenez, Sociedad Mutulista; Benito Juarez; Ray Koerner, secretary Boilermakers Lodge 626; Dr. John A. Lapp; Prof. Robert Morss Lovett, associate editor, New Republic; C. J. Martell, Chicago Watch and Clock-makers Union; Walter Rienbold, president, Boilermakers 626; F. Scriben, Filipino Workers Club; Mordecai Schulman, Workmen's Circle 516; Arne Swabeck, Painters Union; Otto Wangerin, editor, Railroad Amalgamation Advocate; Dr. David Rhys Williams."

The official organ (1933) is "Upsurge"; pub. by Wm. Simons; editor is Martin Kaye. Hdqts. 90 East 10th St., N. Y. City.

The letter-head, 1928, lists:

"Secretary, Manuel Gomez; National Committee: Clarence Darrow, James H. Maurer, Alexander Howat, Roger Baldwin, Socrates Sandino, Charlotte Anita Whitney, H. H. Broach, Lewis S. Gannett, Harriet Stanton Blatch, Scott Nearing, John Brophy, William Blewitt, William Mahoney, S. A. Stockwell, William Z. Foster, Paxton Hibben, W. E. B. Du Bois, William Pickens, L. J. De Bekker, Louis F. Budenz, Robert W. Dunn, Albert Weisbord, Robert Morss Lovett, Arthur Garfield Hays, Pablo Manlapit, Ben Gold, Anacleto Almanana, Freda Kirchwey, Lillian Herstein, Hugo Oehler, Max Schachtman, Harry Gannes, Arthur C. Calhoun, Fred T. Douglas, Ernest Untermann, William F. Dunne, Harriet Silverman, Eduardo Machado, P. T. Lau. National office, United States Section—39 Union Square, New York City."

The International League Against Imperialism, the parent organization, has branches in all parts of the world and is Moscow's agency for spreading revolutionary doctrines among colonial peoples. It urges those still primitive peoples who are now united with and defended by strong civilizing powers such as the U.S., England, Holland and France, to throw off "foreign imperialism" in order that they may more easily be captured piecemeal for *Moscow* imperialism—an imperialism which by comparison with the modern, liberal, so-called "imperialism" of the nations it attacks is like a penitentiary reform school compared with a Montessori Kindergarten (where freedom of "self expression" for each little personality is the rule). It not only urges the Philippines to break away from United States "imperialism," and Latin America to throw off the Monroe Doctrine, but it tries to persuade the citizens of all ruling countries that civilizing and keeping order in savage countries is brutal bullying "imperialism" on the part of their governments and that they should urge their governments to keep "Hands Off" regardless of danger to the lives or property of other nationals. Communist sympathizers naturally help this propaganda along.

Willi Muenzenberg, German Communist, has been its head or international secretary. Bertrand Russell has been head of the English section and Henri Barbusse, French Communist, head of the French section. Albert Einstein, Mme. Sun Yat Sen (China), Upton Sinclair, Willi Muenzenberg, Maxim Gorki (U.S.S.R.), Sen. Katayama, artist Diego Rivera (then mem. cent. com. Communist Party of Mexico), Prof. Wm. Pickens, James Maxton of England, with various Negro and Asiatic Communist leaders from all parts of the world were photographed and featured as members of the League presidium and leaders of the Leagues' Anti-Imperialist World Congress held at Frankfort-on-Main, July 20, 1929, by the Communist organ "Illustrierte Arbeiter Zeitung" (of Berlin) (reproduced also in Hadley's "T.N.T.").

The World Congress against War (Amsterdam 1932), U.S. Congress against War, Student Congress against War (see) and their various off-shoots—Anti-War Committees, etc., etc., are controlled by the League Against Imperialism and its various leaders. See its Intl., American and Chicago Committees for Struggle Against War, Hands Off Committees, Mexican Propaganda.

ALL WORLD GANDHI FELLOWSHIP

Headed, since 1929, as president, by John Haynes Holmes; a radical pacifist organization upholding "pacifist" Gandhi, whose agitations resulting in strikes, murder and violence, are so useful to Moscow; closely related to the Threefold Movement—Union of East and West, League of Neighbors and Fellowship of Faiths (see); sponsors "Fellowship Center," opened 1933 as a "House of Retreat" for pacifists under the management of Wm. H. Bridge, at Crow Hill Road, near Mt. Kisco, New York.

AMALGAMATED BANKS

Of New York and Chicago, operated by the Amalgamated Cloth. Workers Unions; agents for Soviet American Securities Corp., which sells bonds of the Soviet government.

AMALGAMATED CLOTHING WORKERS OF AMERICA

Amalg. Cloth. Wkrs. of Am.

A pro-Soviet labor union of about 100,000 members organized, according to Jane Addams' book, at Hull House; "Like all other subversive organizations its tactics are those of the class struggle. Its ultimate object is to take possession of the industry. It has gained control of the clothing industry in the State of N.Y. and in many other of the industrial centers" (Lusk Report); formed by Socialist delegates, excluded because of extreme radicalism from the A.F. of L. United Garment Workers Union convention Oct. 1914, who then constituted themselves a separate organization under Sidney Hillman, using the same name until legal action by the United Garment Workers forced them to choose a new name, Dec. 1914; formed Russian-American Industrial Corp. to aid and finance clothing industry in Russia;

celebrate the Communist Labor Day—May 1 (A.F. of L.'s is in Sept.); predominantly Jewish; anti-American during the war; closely affiliated with Amalg. Textile Wkrs. and Intl. Ladies Garm. Wkrs.; official organ "Advance." Hdqts. address: Jos. Schlossberg, 11 Union Square, N.Y. (See Intl. Ladies Garment Wkrs.); joined with A.F. of L. 1933.

AMALGAMATED CLOTHING WORKERS INDUSTRIAL UNION

A Communist labor union; part of T.U.U.L.

AMALGAMATED TEXTILE WORKERS OF AMERICA

Amalg. Textile Wkrs.

"An industrial union under the domination of the Socialist Party and having a revolutionary objective is the Amalg. Textile Wkrs. of Am. This organization is an outgrowth of the Lawrence, Mass. strike in 1919, which was promoted and assisted by the Amalg. Cloth. Wkrs. of Am. The relationship therefore . . . is very close . . . the principal agent sent there for that purpose was Paul Blanshard" (pp. 947, 951, Lusk Report). "Wm. Z. Foster attended the first Congress of the Red Trade Union Intl., at Moscow, in June 1921, as a representative of the Amalg. Textile Wkrs. of Am." (Whitney's "Reds in Am.")

AM.-DERUTRA TRANSPORT CORPORATION

Official Soviet shipping agency; transport agents of Amtorg.

AMERICAN ANTI-BIBLE SOCIETY, INC.

Organized by 4A; Mr. Recht, who attended to the papers of incorporation, was the legal representative of the Soviet Govt. in this country (see N.Y. Herald-Tribune, Aug. 3, 1927); officers: pres., James I. Elliott; vice pres., O. H. Bailey; nat. sec., Wm. S. Bryan. It announces: "The object of the Am. Anti-Bible Soc. is to discredit the Bible. The budget for the first year calls for $83,000. Headquarters for Anti-Biblical Literature: If it's against the Bible we have it. Catalogue free on request"; 119 East 14th St., N.Y.C.

AMERICAN ASSOCIATION FOR ADVANCEMENT OF ATHEISM (4A)

"The Fool hath said in his heart, There is no God." But the 4A, whose slogan is "Kill the Beast" (religion), says: "To Hell with compromise—The 4A is here to ensure a complete job in the wrecking of religion. . . . Killing the Beast is rough work and those who are afraid of its claws might at least keep quiet. We shall ignore their wailings. We offer no apology for our tactics. We sneer and jeer at religion and shall continue doing so until it is laughed out of existence. . . . The supernatural does not exist. There is no God. Religion deserves no more respect than a pile of garbage. It must be destroyed."

Beneath this article on "Tactics" in the 1929 Official Report of the 4A, appears the picture of the misguided youth, then national secretary of the Junior Atheist League of the 4A, who has now returned to Christianity—Albert Dehner Bell. He tells me how he was drawn into Atheism and Communism by propagandists planted in the very Seminary in which he was studying for the ministry.

A severe automobile accident which brought him to death's door and long semi-consciousness seemed also to bring to him the guilty consciousness of what he was doing.

From Mar. 1929 to July 1931, he served as nat. sec. of the Junior Atheist League of the 4A, at the same time acting as N.Y. sec. of the Young Communist League under his Communist Party name (his own spelled backwards) of L. R. Trebla. During that time, he met many "Christian" ministers and others on the friendly terms of fellow opponents of Christ. (!) His note book, kept to jot down the affiliations of office callers and correspondents, contains names which if published with proof should blow the lid off of certain Church organizations. He was shocked even before his conversion, he says, when a high official of the Federal Council of Churches (now serving openly on a communistic committee) came in to his office and gave him, as secretary, a $50 donation for atheist Communist camps.

He tells me that the 4A while maintaining its public offices and Atheist Book Store at 307 E. 14th St., N.Y.C., also maintains six floors of offices with unlettered doors at 347 Madison Ave.; that it has about 3,000 actual members, about 500,000 contributors, and had an income of $2,200,000 in 1931, its official report of around $15,000 being the accounting only of its New York funds, as required of New York corporations. The 4A was incorporated in New York in 1925.

Missionary Work

In conjunction with the World Union of Atheists, which it helped to form at Moscow 1931, it maintains atheist missionaries in various countries. The official 4A Reports say: "New Years day 1927 was signalized by the sailing of our first foreign representative. On that day Mr. Edwin Bergstrom, who had organized a branch in British Columbia, left New York to spread the 4A message in Sweden. A delegation was at the pier to see him off." The work of Chen Tsai Ting, 365 Hennessy Road, Hong Kong, and of Felix Borbon, director of the Spanish division, is also commented upon. The 1928 Report says: "We have established the Confederacion Americana del Ateismo with hdqts. in Mexico City. Nanni Leone Costelli, a man of extraordinary ability, already has done much in advancing Atheism. He is now organizing branches in all Central and South American countries. His address is Apartado Postal 1065, Mexico D. F., Mexico." . . . "We are pleased to have as a member Prof. Alphonse A. Herrera of Mexico City, director of Biological Studies of the Republic of Mexico and *in charge of the National Museum.* He has under his supervision a chimpanzee nearly old enough to be utilized in a hybridization experiment." (With a human being). Elsewhere in the same Report: "To demonstrate the truth of Evolution and particularly to prove the kinship of man and ape a fund has been started to hybridize the two by artificial fecundation. Mr. Geo. T. Smith has opened the fund with a $100 contribution."

Societies Formed

These official Reports point with pride to the formation of many "Damned Souls Societies," "Liberal clubs," "Truth Seekers Societies," in high schools and colleges all over the U.S. The 1928 Report says its first "Damned Souls Society" was organized at Rochester University (N.Y.). The Junior Atheist League for high school students was established with many branches in 1927-8. The 4A divides the United States into areas. Each area has a director who is supposed to organize nuclei in schools of his area. The photo of Robert Conine, of Tulsa, appears in the 1930 report, for example, as director of the Fifth Area.

Elated reports are made of the formation also of such sex and blasphemy societies as: the Thespian Society, an actors' guild, "to offset the Actors' Guild, a Catholic society"; Church Taxation League: "We must either tax ecclesiastical possessions or confiscate them"; Conception Control Society, to "Conduct an aggressive propaganda for the repeal of Section 211 of the U.S. Penal Code and similar laws in 24 States. . . . The next great battle will be for the elimination of venereal disease and *greater sex freedom* of which the Church has been and is the greatest enemy. . . . *Free prophylactic* stations should be maintained in every city. Scientific sex instruction should be given in every high school. There is ample room for another organization opposed to ecclesiastical bigotry concerning sex."

The Feb. 1928 Report stated: "The greatest achievement of the year was the founding in August by the officers of the Assn., together with other leading anti-religionists, of the American Anti-Bible Society. This new organization . . . has made a good beginning, and under the leadership of Tennessee's Grand Old Man, Wm. S. Bryan, historian and humorist, should soon make a laughing stock of the Christian fetish book, causing people to smile whenever it is named."; "Atheist Training School: The national office has established in New York a training school with meetings for the present once a week. Young men and women and boys and girls are given practise in public speaking . . . "; "Foreign Language Groups have been organized among the non-English speaking groups, such as the Russian, Lithuanian, Bohemian, which hold regular meetings."

Virtually all branches conduct Forums, say the Reports; one at Communist Party hdqts. (see Red Army), 224 S. Spring St., Los A., Cal., having held meetings since 1925. One of the best known of the Ingersoll Forums is in New York, "meeting in Pythian Temple (70th St., East of Broadway) Sunday evenings the year round"; "The Atheist Society of Chicago under the direction of Mr. James E. Even ran two weekly forums during the past season." (One at Communist Party local hdqts., 357 W. Chicago Ave.) "Regular meetings (Open Air) were held almost every weekday evening along Broadway (N.Y.) with a battery of speakers including Messrs. Smith, Teller, Bedborough, Murphy, Blanchet, Wright, Mieler, Portal, Goldberg, Kewish, Goldsmith, Sklaroff, Peiser and others." (May 1932 Report).

Phonograph records of parodies on

hymns, atheist words to the tune of the International, etc. are made for the 4A and distributed by them. A gold "A" within a *red* five-pointed *star* on a background of blue was adopted as the official 4A insignia in 1931.

Atheist Aids

The A.C.L.U. is frequently mentioned as suing in behalf of, or cooperating with, the 4A in suits. In the Anthony Bimba case (Communist Party functionary tried for blasphemy), the Garland Fund, A.C.L.U., and 4A all cooperated in his defense.

The Socialist Debs Memorial Radio Station (W.E.V.D.) fittingly proved itself a true friend of Atheism, according to the Apr. 1929 Report: "We have outwitted the bigots and now broadcast regularly over Station W.E.V.D., New York (231.6-1300 K.C.), Saturdays, 6 P.M. The recent increase in this station enables us to reach a much larger audience. Because of our sending Atheism over the air through its transmitting plant, Franklin Ford of Station W.H.A.P. terminated his contract with Station W.E.V.D., which now has its own plant." The June 1930 Report says: "Mr. Kenneth Blanchet is the official broadcaster for the Association over Radio Station W.E.V.D., New York."

Atheist Literature

"Tons of tracts" are sent out. The June 1930 Report says: "At the last printing of leaflets and folders, a total of 300,000 copies was run off. Previous to that and during the year 1929 we had printed 50,000 copies of 'Uncle Sams Mistress'" (the Church), "100,000 copies of 'Read Without Fear,' 20,000 copies of 'What is Religion?'" 110,000 copies of "The Bible in Balance" were sold. "Most of this literature is sold to members and friends at cost or less than cost and by them given away. . . . Now that we have a ground floor store on one of the city's busiest streets a considerable number of leaflets and folders is given away each day to passersby who are invited by a large sign to help themselves."

Atheist literature specializes in obscenity. The title of an article in the Apr. 1929 Report is "The Cohabitation of Church and State." "Uncle Sam's Mistress," the leaflet mentioned above, says in part: "The Church calls herself the bride of Christ. But as he does not support her, she is forced into dishonorable relations. This kept woman of the State is supposed to repay those from whom the State collects money by looking after their morals. But what is the conduct of the Church worth as a moral example? We might as well hire one of those females called gold-diggers to train our daughters in virtue."

The same Report reprints from its 4A organ "Truthseeker" two items which had aroused opposition from a minister. One, an obscene birth control suggestion for government supervised prostitutes, another a "Holy Ghost joke" which is typical of the atheist anti-religious literature of Jos. Lewis and his ilk: "A very pious young lady had died and had gained admittance into heaven. Saint Peter took her around and presented her to God, Christ and various other notables. Being left alone, she strolled around and admired the scenery, but noticed she was being followed by a very small, mean looking fellow, who kept bowing to her and was evidently trying to 'pick her up.' Much alarmed, she ran back to St. Peter, told him what had happened, and asked him who this little fellow could be. Looking up and seeing who it was, Peter replied: 'Oh, that's the Holy Ghost, but we don't introduce him to ladies since he had that little affair with the Virgin Mary.'" This draws a picture which reminds one of the blasphemous Soviet cartoons of Christ and the Holy Ghost which fill Russian Churches (see Proletarian Party).

Befriending Blasphemy and Communism

Under the heading "Hypocrites Howl About Russia," the June 1930 Report tells how President Smith of the 4A, in defense of Soviet Russia's persecution of Christians, addressed an audience of 15,000 at the N.Y. Coliseum, Mar. 16, 1930.

"The First Annual Trial of God—A Blamegiving Service held in New York Nov. 26, 1931, under the auspices of the 4A, Inc., on the assumption for the day only that God exists. Blamegiving Day has been officially established by the Association as a day of protest against Thanksgiving services. . . . It is hoped and expected many such services will be held in each State of the Union next Blamegiving Day and in coming years until Thanksgiving is abandoned." A parody of the Lord's Prayer to be said in unison follows and a Modern Doxology of numerous verses beginning: "Blame God from whom all cyclones blow, Blame Him when rivers overflow, Blame Him who swirls down house and steeple, who sinks the ship and drowns the people," and ending: "For clergy who with hood and bell, Demand your cash or threaten hell, Blame God for earthquake shocks, and then, Let all men cry aloud, 'Amen.'"

The report of the mock trial for 1931 follows, in which God is called "Public Enemy No. 1." Woolsey Teller opened it saying: "I am sorry to announce that God cannot be with us this afternoon . . . as there is a law in N.Y. state against his personal appearance on the platform. His son, Jesus, is absent also—peacefully being digested in the stomachs of those pious persons who ate him this morning at early mass. We can picture Jesus today as being mixed up with turkey and cranberry sauce"; etc., etc. A verdict of guilty was rendered against God for his malevolence and another such trial was held 1932. "When recently the Ingersoll Forum, our N.Y. branch, announced that in a lecture by Mr. Woolsey Teller on 'Crazy Jesus' the Atheist would impersonate the New Testament character, the more clearly to demonstrate the absurdities of his actions and teaching, we were warned by our lawyer that representation of the deity of a religious sect is prohibited in this State." (1930 Report).

CHRISTIAN SERMONS FROM ATHEISTS

There is much food for thought on the part of Christians in the following dissertations taken from 4A Reports on the "Church Drift to Atheism." Ironically enough, they are powerful sermons—from Atheists.

"The religious forces have cause for alarm. Divided by internal strife, they possess neither the power nor the courage to expel heretics. Christians cannot agree upon anything except their name. Protestantism is breaking up, and whenever its adherents attempt to cooperate with Catholics they get a slap in the face."

Atheism in America today may be likened unto a huge iceberg, of which the visible peak is but a small part of the submerged mountain.

"Churches are becoming secular, preaching anything except the oldtime orthodox religion. They are becoming social centers with just enough of nominal religion to escape taxation. Sermons on books are more popular than those on the barbaric doctrine of the Atonement. The Clergymen are bewildered. They do not know what to preach. Evolution explodes their doctrines. They are declining in number and quality. Church leaders now even oppose missionizing the Jews, thereby confessing, in effect, that Christianity is only *a* religion, not *the* religion."

"The clergy are so honeycombed with heretics that they are powerless to expel known heretics. The only real cleavage is between the Modernists and Fundamentalists. They cannot force the issue in their conventions and they dare not withdraw from the denominations. Most college graduates are godless. The number of churches is increasing in which the monologue called prayer is omitted." (Apr. 1929.)

"The spread of Atheism was never faster. It is not measured by the growth of Atheist groups but by the decline of religious belief as a controlling factor in the lives of men. The drift of the age is away from religion." (Is this the "falling away" and "spiritual wickedness in high places" prophesied for the era before Armageddon?)

"This loss of faith causes consternation among the Orthodox, who are powerless to arrest the movement. The reconcilers, the Liberals and the Modernists—are heroically saving the ship of Christianity by throwing her cargo overboard. With what zeal the Fosdicks, the Matthews and the whole crew of rescuers toss out, first the Garden of Eden and the Flood, followed by the Virgin Birth, Atonement, and the Resurrection. Then they gain a victory by getting rid of Hell and Heaven and of the Devil and God, tho with much ado they keep the name of the last. They may save the vessel of ecclesiasticism, but how long will man sail the seas in an empty ship? They will go ashore and enjoy life with the Atheists. We welcome the aid of the Modernists and pledge them our fullest cooperation in ridding the world of Fundamentalism—of any serious acceptance of Christian theology."

"The supreme literary honor was conferred last year upon an avowed Atheist, when the Nobel Prize was given to Sinclair Lewis, author of 'Main Street' and 'Elmer Gantry' . . . a terrific indictment of evangelical religion." (Apr. 1931 Report).

"There is much Atheism in the Church. Heresy is rampant among the clergy, a few of whom openly express their rejection of religious dogma, without fear of expulsion. Even the Methodist Church now tolerates clergymen, such as the Rev. James Hardy Bennett of N.Y., who preach that Jesus was physically the son of Joseph and Mary, who told the Virgin story to shield themselves." (Feb. 1928) ". . . Why do these men stay in the pulpit? Some of them must stay or starve. They know no trade. Among them are Atheists and even members of the 4A." A letter is then quoted from an atheist minister wishing to leave the ministry with this comment: "If any member or friend will contribute $200 for the special purpose of freeing this prisoner of the pulpit, the 4A will liberate him and announce his name."

"Most denominational schools are hotbeds of heresy, as it is impossible for any educational institution to maintain any degree of dignity without teaching Evolution which inevitably undermines religion. These schools, even when controlled by Fundamentalists, are often compelled to employ Infidels, who are hypocrites from necessity. *Members of the 4A are teaching in Catholic and Fundamentalist Colleges.*"

"The growth of what is called Humanism, together with the establishment of a few churches and societies for its propagation, caused considerable discussion during the year. However much Humanists, for reasons of expediency shun the title 'Atheist,' they are Godless. Consequently, we welcome their aid in overthrowing Christianity, and all other religions based on the supernatural." (June 1930 Report).

"There is a marked increase in the use of the word Atheist to designate the opponent of religion. The change is for the better. Atheist is the logical title for whoever has no god. Formerly for weighty reasons the titles of Liberal, Rationalist and Freethinker were adopted because of their uncertainty of meaning. . . . Under cover timid Atheists are helping to undermine religion by demanding a new concept of God. These critics profess to be searching for the true God. They might as well search for the true witch or a true hobgoblin."

"Modernism is unworthy of serious notice. It is intellectual mush, a disgusting mass of figurative language. . . . The downfall of Christianity is presaged by the passing of Hell which inevitably drags Heaven with it, since the two have the same foundation. If the one is figurative, so is the other."

"Much as we dislike Modernists because of their illogical compromising, we must recognize that for many Modernism is but a stopover on the road to Atheism. Perhaps we should have a little more patience with these our weaker brothers who are unable to go straight from Orthodoxy to Atheism without resting at the camps of Liberalism along the way. Modernism being no abiding place for a reasoning mind, some of them will yet arrive. For the present we should train our guns principally on such religious standpatters as the Roman Catholic Church and the Protestant hotbeds of Fundamentalism. The American Tract Society deserves special attention."

"The Modernists seem to attack Atheism only to screen their own unbelief. No better proof of our contention that the Church is losing ground can be given than that the Modernists are now in control of all the larger Protestant denominations and, working from the inside, discredit the basic teachings of Christianity in the name Christianity. . . . we now hear of that absurdity, 'a creedless faith'—of persons who believe, without believing anything. Thus Christianity slowly dissolves. But the good work of Modernists not only does not lessen the need of Atheist propaganda . . . the Advance Guard is always the most important unit in the army. We must continue to lead the way." (June 1933 Report).

"The Ten Demands of the 4A:

(1) Taxation of church property. (2) Elimination of chaplains and sectarian institutions from public pay rolls. (3) Abrogation of laws enforcing Christian morals and restricting the rights of Atheists. (4) Abolition of the oath in courts and at inaugurations. (5) Non-issuance of religious proclamations by chief executives. (6) Removal of 'In God We Trust' from coins and the cross from above the flag. (7) Exclusion of the Bible as a sacred book from the public schools. (8) Suppression of the bootlegging of religion through dismissing pupils from religious instructions during school hours. (9) Secularization of marriage, with divorce upon request. (10) Repeal of anti-evolution and anti-birth-control laws."

"The Five Fundamentals of Atheism:

(1) Materialism: The doctrine that Matter, with its indwelling property, Force, constitutes the reality of the universe. (2) Sensationalism: The doctrine that all ideas arise out of sensation, and that, therefore, man can have no conception of an infinite God, or of ultimate causation, or that absolute moral imperative which certain philosophers have made the foundation of Theism. (3) Evolution: The doctrine that organisms are not designed, but have evolved, mechanically, through Natural Selection. (4) The existence of Evil: The patent fact that renders irrational the belief in a beneficent, omnipotent being who cares for man. (5) Hedonism: The doctrine that happiness here and now should be the motive of conduct."

The Report of May 1932 (officers same in 1933) lists:

Officers: Pres., Chas. Smith, Vice Pres., Woolsey Teller; Gen. Sec., Freeman Hopwood; Treas., Freda Rettig; Board of Directors: O. H. Bailey, Ohio; Geo. Bedborough, N.Y.; Wm. S. Bryan, Mo.; Louis J. Bergson, Pa.; Felix Borbon, Mich.; John A. Bremner, Wash.; Ira D. Cardiff, Wash.; Stanley J. Clark, Okla.; J. Howard Cummins, Tex.; N. Louis Dorion, N.Y.; Mary E. Elliott, N.Y.; Howell S. England, Mich.; James E. Even,

NATIONAL COMMITTEE

Charles F. Amidon
Harry Elmer Barnes
Herbert S. Bigelow
Edwin M. Borchard
Richard C. Cabot
John S. Codman
Clarence Darrow
John Dewey
James H. Dillard
Robert W. Dunn
Sherwood Eddy
Elizabeth Glendower Evans
John F. F[illegible]
Elizabeth Gurley Flynn
Walter Frank
Felix Frankfurter
Ernst Freund
Kate Crane Gartz
Norman Hapgood
Powers Hapgood
[illegible] C. Herring
Morris Hillquit
John Haynes Holmes
Frederic C. Howe
James Weldon Johnson
George W. Kirchwey
John A. Lapp
Julia C. Lathrop
Agnes Brown Leach
Arthur LeSueur
Henry R. Linville
Robert Morss Lovett
Mary E. McDowell
Anna Martin
Alexander Meiklejohn
Henry R. Mussey
A. J. Muste
Walter Nelles
William L. Nunn
Julia S. O'Connor Parker
William Pickens
Amos Pinchot
Jeannette Rankin
Edward A. Ross
Elbert Russell
John A. Ryan
John Nevin Sayre
William Scarlett
Joseph Schlossberg
Vida D. Scudder
Abba Hillel Silver
John F. Sinclair
Clarence R. Skinner
Norman M. Thomas
Edward D. Tittmann
Millie R. Trumbull
William S. U'Ren
Oswald Garrison Villard
B. Charney Vladeck
David Wallerstein
George P. West
Peter Witt
L. Hollingsworth Wood

Free Speech *Free Press* *Free Assemblage*

American Civil Liberties Union

100 Fifth Avenue, New York City

TOmpkins Square 6-4230

OFFICERS

Chairman
Harry F. Ward
Vice-Chairmen
Helen Phelps Stokes
James H. Maurer
Fremont Older
Treasurer
B. W. Huebsch
Directors
Roger N. Baldwin
Forrest Bailey
Counsel
Arthur Garfield Hays
Morris L. Ernst
Research Secretary
Lucille B. Milner
Washington Counsel
Edmund D. Campbell

Attorneys and correspondents in leading cities

February 27, 1932.

To the members of the Senate and
House Immigration Committees.

Gentlemen:

We send you herewith a pamphlet in regard to a bill pending before you intended to carry into effect the opinion of Chief Justice Hughes in a case recently decided, 5 to 4, by the U.S. Supreme Court. Justice Hughes' opinion is set out almost in full.

We trust that the proposed change in the law in accordance with Justice Hughes' opinion may have your support.

Very truly yours,

John Haynes Holmes

Chairman

JHH/IE
Enc.

Facsimile of a letter typical of constant efforts of A.C.L.U. to influence legislation favored by radicals. Signed by John Haynes Holmes, acting Chairman while Harry F. Ward was in Russia. Note names of National Committee and Officers.

Ill.; Linn Gale, D.C.; E. Haldeman-Julius, Kans.; Robt. F. Hester, S.C.; John T. Kewish, N.Y.; Geo. T. Marclay, N.Y.; Philip G. Peabody, Mass.; M. A. Stolar, Ill.; Walter Van Nostrand, N.Y.; Clark H. Yater, N.Y. Organ: "Truthseeker," 49 Vesey St., N.Y.; 4A Hdqts. 307 E. 14th St., N.Y. City.

AMERICAN ASSOCIATION FOR LABOR LEGISLATION

Am. Assn. Lab. Legis.

"There are doubtless many people who have contributed to the support of the Am. Assn. Lab. Legis. who are far above the charge of consciously desiring the success of a subversive movement. If we subtract these . . . there remains a large number who are prominently connected with the radical movement and in some instances indirectly with the Communist Party of America. . . . It beseeches legislators for the adoption of social insurance by the state. To it we owe the present workmen's compensation laws which are on the statute books of the various states. Compulsory health insurance is a part of its legislative program. . . . 'En passant' it should be said that these measures were born of revolutionary Socialism in the decade following 1860. The effect of its adoption means a lightening of responsibility on the part of labor in the maintenance of a healthy, well balanced society, and quick adaptation of the working classes to the idea of dependency on the state. Samuel Gompers, at one time a member of the Am. Assn. Lab. Legis., resigned, repudiating all its words and works. Social insurance legislation is class legislation and socialistic. . . . Among its conspicuous officials are or have been in the past such well known radicals as Mrs. Raymond Robins, organizer and pres. Wom. Tr. Un. Lg. . . . her associates Miss Agnes Nestor and Miss Mary Anderson; the Rev. John Haynes Holmes, the radical pacifist, and his friend and co-worker Stephen S. Wise; Owen Lovejoy . . . Miss Lillian Wald . . . Miss Jane Addams . . . and a host of others of like thought. In general there is a mutual sympathy for the objects which this class of organizations desire to attain, an interlocking personnel in the directorates, and programs which dovetail into each other that suggest common inspiration and mutual financial resources. They present the appearance of a united front, and might be deemed the shock troops of an insinuating army of borers, whose province it is to wedge ignorant inertia aside and make room for advancing Communism. To call such organizations 'socialistic' as opposed to communistic is in reality a distinction without a difference. These systems differ in degree and not in principle." (Whitney's "Reds in America," p. 182); similar to A.A. for O.A.S.; hdqts.: John B. Andrews, 131 East 23rd St., N.Y.

AMERICAN ASSOCIATION FOR OLD AGE SECURITY

A.A. for O.A.S.

Organized to promote old age pensions at the expense of state and nation, among the immediate objectives of the Socialist program which aims ultimately to put every possible human activity, as well as all property, under state (political) control. (See Am. Assn. Lab. Legis.) Officers 1931: pres., Bishop Francis J. McConnell; exec. sec., Abraham Epstein; treas., Nicholas Kelley; exec. com.: Eliz. Gilman, Agnes Brown Leach, Mary K. Sinkovitch, Stephen S. Wise; vice presidents: Jane Addams, Herbert S. Bigelow, Edw. T. Devine, Glenn Frank, John A. Lapp, James H. Maurer, Wm. A. Neilson, I. M. Rubinow, John A. Ryan; hdqts.: Abraham Epstein, 22 East 17th St., N.Y.

AMERICAN BIRTH CONTROL LEAGUE

Interaligns with the atheist movement; cooperates with other radical groups; aided by Garland Fund; pres., Margaret Sanger; affiliated with communist Intl. Conf. Ag. War & Fascism, Paris '34 (Inprecorr. 8/3/34).

AMERICAN CIVIL LIBERTIES UNION

A.C.L.U. See also page 336.

"FREE SPEECH"

"Your actions speak so loud I can't hear what you say!" said Ralph Waldo Emerson, and this quotation exactly fits the A.C.L.U., which *says* it is a non-communist organization interested only in maintaining the rights of "free speech, free press and free assembly as guaranteed by the Constitution of the U.S." while drowning out its words by its actions. Any one who has taken the trouble to investigate what the A.C.L.U. is and does, knows that it is directed by Communist and Socialist revolutionary leaders and their sympathizers, and that it works untiringly to further and legally protect the interests of the Red movement in all of its branches—Red strikes, Atheism, sex freedom, disarmament, seditious "academic freedom," deportation and exclusion of Reds, rioting, etc., constantly supporting and cooperating with Moscow's open legal defense agency, the I.L.D., for this purpose. It plays the "white collar" role in the movement.

One is amused at the A.C.L.U. highbrow appeals, its constant cries for unlimited "freedom of speech" for Reds "as guaranteed by the Constitution," which the Reds aim to destroy, while at the same time it is suing for libel, patriotic anti-Red defenders of this Constitution who make comparatively petty criticisms of its own members.

The sort of "freedom of speech" defended by the A.C.L.U. seems to cover the Red's right to conduct a libelous, obscene, and seditious press against our American government and its loyal supporters, the right to not only advocate sedition, violence and murder but to commit these deeds as well, for after a Red commits these crimes the A.C.L.U. redoubles its efforts to secure his release. The statement of Tom McKenna, a busy little spectator at Communist riots and secretary of the Chicago A.C.L.U., that the Chicago Committee had devoted one day a week and reviewed some 1300 cases, practically all Communist, in Cook County during 1932, taking part of these cases up with Police Commissioner Allman and filing suit in behalf of some, would indicate a more than mere theoretical interest in "free speech" on the part of the A.C.L.U. It is impossible to believe that A.C.L.U. bureaus and lawyers all over the United States are maintained at great expense for the purpose of fighting countless legal battles in behalf of Reds merely because of a love for defending "free speech" for everyone including "those with whose opinions we disagree," particularly in view of the A.C.L.U. petty libel suits against Anti-Reds who actually dare to disagree with the A.C.L.U.

The U.S. Fish Report says: "During the Gastonia strike there was a bloody conflict between the communist-led workers and the police, in which the chief of police was shot and killed and two of his assistants wounded. Seven communists were sentenced to long terms in prison. . . . During the trial of the communists at Gastonia, not for freedom of speech, of the press, or assembly, but for conspiracy to kill the chief of police, the A.C.L.U. provided bail for five of the defendants, amounting to $28,500, which it secured from the Garland Fund. All of the defendants convicted jumped their bail and are reported to be in Russia. The $28,500 bail was forfeited, including $9,000 more advanced by the International Labor Defense" (Communist).

Chief Aderholt was murdered by the Communists and the murder was planned three days before the event, yet the 1929-30 A.C.L.U. Report jauntily and brazenly says: "The *only* violence by strikers occurred in a shooting affray on the strikers' lot in Gastonia in which *Chief of Police Aderholt of Gastonia was killed and one policeman and one striker were wounded;* and at Marion where a few strikers were caught *dynamiting private property* without however injuring any person" (A mere trifle, of course, compared to bloody Red revolution). And this same Report adds with pride: "The Civil Liberties Union *was active from the beginning* of the trouble in the cases both at Marion and Gastonia."

The N.Y. State Lusk Report says: "The American Civil Liberties Union, in the last analysis, is a supporter of all subversive movements; its propaganda is detrimental to the State. It attempts not only to protect crime but to encourage attacks upon our institutions in every form." To this indictment, based upon barrels of incontestable documentary proof, the A.C.L.U. leaders blithely answer: "O! the Lusk Report is discredited" (by the A.C.L.U.). Asked for proof, they have and offer none. Financed by the Red Garland Fund, the Reds campaigned while patriots slept and secured the repeal of the N.Y. State Criminal Syndicalism Law which had been sponsored by the Lusk Committee and since that repeal N.Y. has become one of the great centers of World revolutionary activity. South American Communist work is controlled from N.Y. Meetings of 22,000 Reds are held in N.Y. City nowadays.

The U.S. Committee appointed by the 71st Congress to investigate Communist Propaganda, headed by Hon. Hamilton Fish, officially reported Jan. 1931: "The A.C.L.U. is closely affiliated with the communist movement in the United States, and fully 90% of its efforts are on behalf of communists who have come into conflict with the law. It claims to stand for free speech, free press, and free assembly; but it is quite apparent that the main function of the A.C.L.U. is to attempt to protect the communists in their advocacy of force and violence to overthrow the government, replacing the American flag by a red flag and erecting a Soviet Government in place of the republican form of government guaranteed to each State by the Federal Constitution."

"Roger N. Baldwin, its guiding spirit, makes no attempt to hide his friendship for the communists and their principles. He was formerly a member of the I.W.W. and served a term in prison as a draft dodger during the war. This is the same Roger N. Baldwin that has recently issued a statement 'that in the next session of Congress our job is to organize the opposition to the recommendations of the Congressional Committee investigating communism.' In his testimony before the Committee he admitted having said at a dinner in Chicago that 'the Fish Committee recommendations will be buried in the Senate.'" (And they have been, and are!)

"Testifying on force and violence, murder, etc. the following is quoted: The chairman: Does your organization uphold the right of a citizen or alien—it does not make any difference which—to advocate murder? Mr. Baldwin: Yes. The Chairman: Or Assassination? Mr. Baldwin: Yes. The Chairman: Does your organization uphold the right of an American citizen to advocate force and violence for the overthrow of the Government? Mr. Baldwin: Certainly; in so far as mere advocacy is concerned. The Chairman: Does it uphold the right of an alien in this country to urge the overthrow and advocate the overthrow of the Government by force and violence? Mr. Baldwin: Precisely on the same basis as any citizen. The Chairman: You do uphold the right of an alien to advocate the overthrow of the Government by force and violence: Mr. Baldwin: Sure; certainly. It is the healthiest kind of thing, of course, for a country to have free speech—unlimited."

Both Communist and Socialist Party platforms stand for this same unlimited "free speech" (for Reds) and so it seems very picayunish, to say the least, that Maynard C. Krueger, member of the Socialist Party executive committee, should be suing, as is now reported, the Chicago Tribune for calling him a "jackass" and that the A.C.L.U. should be suing Mr. Jung of the American Vigilant Intelligence Federation for calling one A.C.L.U. member, Karl Borders (see Who's Who), a "propagandist of the Bolshevik murder regime" and John Haynes Holmes, another A.C.L.U. member, an "exponent of free love." If I believed the Constitution guaranteed unlimited free speech to everyone to advocate force, violence and assassination I would certainly not be so fussy as to sue anyone for using his Constitutional right to call me a mere "propagandist" or an "exponent" of an idea. Instead I would be flattered that he had not advocated boiling me in oil, cutting my throat, or assassinating me. Of course, every organization hews to its own line. Perhaps if those whom the A.C.L.U. sues would fall into line and advocate assassinating the A.C.L.U. and its members in cold blood, the A.C.L.U. would feel more sympathetic and be impelled itself to defend them (?). This would be an intriguing and novel experiment for patriotic Americans who, ordinarily, consider murder and its advocacy a little out of their line.

What possible interest could such Moscow-directed Communists as Wm. Z. Foster, Robt. W. Dunn, Scott Nearing, Anna Rochester, etc., etc. (who help direct the A.C.L.U.), have in merely promoting free speech for everyone, since their chosen career is to work for a Soviet United States *barring* free speech? The A.C.L.U. nicely explains this fight for "free speech" in its 1929-30 Annual Report, p. 5: "Our services are essential for whatever degree of tolerance we can achieve, and will be until a political and economic opposition *arises* strong enough to defend its own rights. . . . These early months of 1930 have produced a larger crop of court cases" (for the A.C.L.U. to defend) "involving civil liberty than any *entire year* since the war. This is due to the wave of *suppression* by officials of the *militant activities of the Communist Party and left-wing strikes.*" In other words, under the guise of free speech, etc., by means of legal battles, revolutionary Communism-Socialism must be defended until it gains power, and the large crop of A.C.L.U. cases was due to *defense of Communist militant activities.* "Minorites" is also a favorite A.C.L.U. term for revolutionaries.

What the A.C.L.U. Says of Itself

One need not accept the conclusions of the U.S. Fish Report, N.Y. State Lusk Report, Better America Federation, or other expert reports concerning the A.C.L.U. One who carefully reads the daily newspapers or who reads the Communist press may gain constant evidence of A.C.L.U. activities in support of the Red movement.

Doubting Thomases should read for themselves the official yearly Reports of the A.C.L.U. Since a 40-60 page pamphlet is required each year to report merely the outstanding cases handled by the A.C.L.U. and its branches in the United States, it is obvious that only a smattering of these can be given in this article. Each Report might easily have a volume written about its cases. Each case aids some phase of the Red program, while 90% are out-and-out Communist-defense cases. Patriotism is always sneered at by the A.C.L.U.; hence the 1931-32 Report is sarcastically entitled "Sweet Land of Liberty." To quote from it:

"Among the professional patriots, the American Legion and the D.A.R. stood out as the most active inciters against pacifists and radicals." . . . "Local patriots continue to function, often to our annoyance. In Chicago the Vigilant Intelligence Federation continually prods the authorities to bring proceedings against Communists and sympathizers, but with much less open and reckless charges since libel suits were lodged against its secretary by John Haynes Holmes and Karl Borders" (filed by A.C.L.U. against H. A. Jung).

"The professional patriots were particularly active in attacking in Congress the bill to admit alien pacifists to citizenship and in pushing the bill for deportation of Communists as such. . . . John W. Davis of N.Y., former Ambassador to Great Britain, who served as Prof. Macintosh's personal counsel and who appeared before the Senate Committee to argue for a change in the law, was attacked by these organizations as unpatriotic, along with the other spokesmen at the hearing—Bishop Francis J. McConnell of the Federal Council of Churches, Rabbi Edward L. Israel of Baltimore, and the Rev. Richard A. McGowan of the National Catholic Welfare Conference."

"Conflict between Communists, sympathizers, and the Philippine government continued, with prosecutions for sedition—etc. The Civil Liberties Union has endeavored to aid at long distance and has lodged protests with the War Dept. at Washington and with the Philippine Govt. *A representative of the Union in the Philippines, Willard S. Palmer, aids in cooperation with Vincente Sotto of Manila, Attorney for the Communists and their sympathizers.*" Under "New Loans made 1931," is listed: to "Philippine representatives of Civil Liberties Union—for defense of sedition cases $500," and under "Expenditures": "For defense of sedition cases in Philippines $571.50." (Good practical support of "civil liberties," that!)

Concerning these "civil liberties," a 1932 New York Times dispatch (reprinted in Chgo. Tribune), headed "Rioting Spreads in Philippines; Revolt Feared—Manila, P.I., May 19," said: "Unrest, rioting and the threat of a Communistic uprising in the northern Luzon provinces took a more serious turn today when Secretary of the Interior Honoris Ventura ordered provincial constabulary commanders at Bulacan, Pampanaga and Nueva Ecija to report instantly at Manila to check the threatened danger—in which arson and a general revolt is threatened. Fourteen Communists, convicted of Manila sedition, *free on appeal and assisted by the American Civil Liberties Union,* are declared to be leading general agitation in Nueva Ecija which has already resulted in destruction of property of those refusing to join the movement. . . . " etc.

Perhaps the newly appointed Gov. of the Philippines, Ex-Mayor Murphy of Detroit, the Roosevelt appointee, will establish another record for non-interference with communists' "civil liberties" and relieve the A.C.L.U. of its tasks. The A.C.L.U. Report (p. 41) eulogizes Murphy saying: "A break in the *year's record of Detroit under Mayor Frank Murphy's administration in no police violence against street meetings* occurred in November *while the Mayor was out of the city.* Police attacked a Communist meeting at a point where they had been accustomed to assemble, but for which permits had been refused. Protests of the committee resulted in an *order by the Mayor changing the system from permits to mere notification to the police,* except at a few designated points."

The A.C.L.U. cooperates with the 4A and Freethinker Atheist societies in their attacks on religion. The destruction of religion is an objective of Socialism-Communism. Supposed ministers of Christ who serve on the A.C.L.U. boards must be undecided as to which master they are serving. No minister could convince me that he can both be yoked together with atheist Communists and aid in filing suits for atheists and atheist Communists and be serving Jesus Christ. The letter of Joseph Lewis, the self-styled "Enemy of God," threatening suit to stop Bible reading in N.Y. public schools appears in this book under "Freethinkers of America." The A.C.L.U. Report, p. 34, says: "An attempt to stop Bible reading in the public schools through a suit in court was lost in N.Y. City when the Freethinkers of America raised the constitutionality of a charter provision of New York City." (which permits Bible reading in schools). "The Civil Liberties Union supported the suit. The Court of appeals upheld the provision. A directly contrary provision in the constitution of the State of Washington prohibiting the reading of the Bible in the schools was sustained by the State Supreme Court and review was refused by the U.S. Supreme Court" (a triumph for the Atheists).

The Atheist 4A Report of 1932 states that seven atheists in the New Jersey Levine case who refused to take an oath, since they deny the existence of God, were barred from testifying, and that the 4A and A.C.L.U. were sharing costs of an appeal. The A.C.L.U. Report under "Expenditures" lists: "Appeal in test case New Jersey on rights of atheists as witnesses $206.35."

The Atheist 4A Report for 1927-8 (p. 11) said: "Last spring Meyer Koninkow and Meyer Applebaum members of the Society of the Godless, the Greater N.Y. branch of the Junior Atheist League, wrote Miss Christine Walker, Nat. Sec. of the League, asking for her assistance in freeing them from compulsory attendance at Bible reading in the high school assembly... Harold S. Campbell, Supt. of High Schools, refused to excuse Applebaum and on his remaining away expelled him. But a threat of Court action with the aid of the *American Civil Liberties Union* recalled the school officials to their senses... they reinstated young Applebaum. The victory reestablished a valuable precedent."

The A.C.L.U. promised to send Arthur Garfield Hays to Little Rock, Ark., to fight against Arkansas anti-Atheist laws, says the 4A April 1929 Report. Also when the contract for use of the Huntington, West Va., auditorium for an Atheist lecture by Chas. Smith, Pres. of 4A, was cancelled, the A.C.L.U. wired protests, according to the 4A 1927-8 Report. "A Court Victory for Atheists" is the heading of the account in the 4A 1931-2 Report of the case won Mar. 23, 1932, "argued by Mr. Albert E. Kane of 381 Madison Ave., a rising young New York lawyer . . . who represented the American Civil Liberties Union" (Chas. Smith, Pres. of the 4A, had been arrested for conducting Atheist street meetings without a permit). To quote: "As a result of our reopening the streets for Atheist propaganda numerous free lance speakers began holding anti-religious meetings of their own all over the city. This spread of Atheism caused the city authorities to attempt to suppress it by one of the most absurd prosecutions ever instituted." The A.C.L.U. Report also jubilates and lists under the heading of its "Gains": "6. Decision of Court of Appeals in New York that atheists' street meetings are not religious gatherings within the meaning of the law and require no permit."

In suits like this, as a 4A Report said of a similar contest, "Not Mr. Smith, but Atheism is on trial." The A.C.L.U. rejoices and "Gains" when Atheism wins, evidently.

Concerning violent Red revolutionary agitation in the Kentucky Coal fields, the A.C.L.U. Report says (p. 26): "The Civil Liberties Union early in the struggle in 1931, raised money and aided the defense committees *both of the I.W.W. and the International Labor Defense*" (Communist). "The Civil Liberties Union sent into this district in July, 1931, Arnold Johnson, a Union Theological student, who after a few weeks of activity was arrested and held under bail on a charge of criminal syndicalism." "The Union also took charge of a proposed damage suit by Tom Connors, I.W.W. organizer, against the sheriff of Harlan County. . . . Finally when repeated efforts to establish civil rights in the area had failed the Civil Liberties Union undertook a mission of its own. A party headed by our general counsel, Arthur Garfield Hays, announced its intention to go into Bell and Harlan Counties. The prosecuting attorney of Bell County at once countered with threats of violence to the party. The Union thereupon sought an injunction in the federal court in Ky. to restrain violence to the party. . . . He denied the injunction, warned the party to stay out and held that Bell and Harlan Counties had a right to be 'protected from free speech.' The Union has taken an appeal. The party made an effort to go into Bell County, but was blocked by force at the boundary. Mr. Hays, returning to the seat of the Federal court, sued the county officials for damages" (Atty. Smith of Bell County challenged the A.C.L.U., calling it an egotistical atheistic communistic menace, to dare spread their propaganda in Bell County. He said Bell Co. had as much right to be protected from Communism as it had from a mad dog. The A.C.L.U. so far has not dared pass him!).

(p. 19) "The Civil Liberties Union works on the Mooney-Billings case from our office, and particularly this year through attorney Aaron Shapiro . . . spending some $1500 more than the A.C.L.U. raised toward his expenses" (for freeing the Anarchist-Communist dynamiter Mooney).

Jubilantly the A.C.L.U. lists as "Gains": "The parole of two of the remaining six men in Centralia, Wash., I.W.W. case" (convicted of murdering six Legionnaires in an Armistice Day parade). Says the A.C.L.U.: "The State Board of Parole is evidently slowly releasing the men one by one in order not to arouse political opposition from the American Legion" (Harry Ward and Bishop McConnell, of both Federal Council of Churches and A.C.L.U., have long kept up a campaign for the release of these Reds).

(p. 16) "The chief campaign in Congress revolved around bills aimed at aliens backed by the professional patriots. The fight centered on registering aliens, on deporting Communists as such, and on the admission of alien pacifists to citizenship. The Civil Liberties Union mobilized its forces against the proposal to register aliens and to deport *Communists* as such, enlisting the support of well-known men and women throughout the country in opposition to both proposals. Neither has passed." (True enough. And where the alien registration law did pass, in Michigan, the newly-elected Atty. Gen. O'Brien, an A.C.L.U. atty., immediately aided in nullifying it.)

The case of "Twenty-seven Communists arrested at Bridgman, Mich. on criminal syndicalism charges, and still awaiting trial" is listed under "Defense Cases Awaiting Trial in the Courts" (Atty. Gen. O'Brien after his election called these cases and aided in having them dismissed. About $100,000 in bond money which had been held by the State was thus released for the use of the Communist Party.) (See Bridgman Raid.)

The A.C.L.U. lists in its Report as "Issues Pending June 1932": its "Appeal from order upholding indictments against six Communist organizers in Atlanta, Georgia on charges of 'incitement to insurrection' and 'distributing insurrectionary literature.'" (See "Nat. Com. for Defense of So. Political Prisoners," formed to defend them); its "Argument in the U.S. Supreme Court against the conviction of seven Negro boys at Scottsboro, Alabama" (Case being handled largely by the communist I.L.D. and used as Communist propaganda to incite Negroes against American "justice" and government); its "Appeal to the U.S. Supreme Court to review the deportation order against Edith Berkman, National Textile Workers Union organizer" (a most virulent Communist organizer of a Communist union); its "Appeal from the conviction for sedition at Media, Pa. of two young Communists for a speech in the 1931 election campaign"; its "Appeal from decision of Common Pleas Judge Wanamaker holding Ohio criminal syndicalism law constitutional in case of Paul Kassey." (This Hungarian Communist was caught, and admitted sabotaging the U.S. airship Akron. He was declared liable under the criminal syndicalism law, which the Ohio Supreme Court later upheld, but in the meantime by some unknown means and unknown influence Kassey was not prosecuted and secured a passport and skipped the country in the Spring of 1933.)

Among A.C.L.U. "Defense Cases Awaiting Trial in the Courts" listed are: "Twenty Philadelphia May Day demonstrators charged with inciting to riot, assault and battery, parading without permit, etc." (May Day, the Reds' labor day in celebration of the anarchists' Haymarket Riot, is a day of Communist violence.)

"Kentucky coal miners and sympathizers for 'conspiracy to murder,' 'criminal syndicalism' and other charges." (Communists—I.W.W.'s.)

"Fifty-eight charged with riot and inciting to riot at Melrose Park, May 6th, 1932." (Communist riot called and advertised by the I.L.D. and carried out in defiance of the police. When the Reds attacked, the police shot several in the legs. The Chicago A.C.L.U. is also suing Melrose Park for injuring these Communists. The police undoubtedly *did* make a mistake in shooting the Reds—in the legs.)

"Two members of the Young Communist League, arrested in July, 1931 on sedition charges for distributing literature at *Fort Logan* military camp" (trying to make Red traitors of our soldiers).

"Seven Communists indicted in Franklin County, Ill. for criminal syndicalism in connection with coal strike activities."

"Three Communists held for 'inciting to riot' at a demonstration at New York City Hall in April."

"Two I.W.W.'s arrested in Ohio, June, 1931, for criminal syndicalism for distributing literature."

Under "Damage Suits Handled Through the A.C.L.U." listed are: "Against the village of Melrose Park, Ill. in behalf of nine persons shot by police on May 6th at a meeting."; "In behalf of Paul Brown, representative of the Unemployed Council" (Communist) "and his friend John Kaspar, against Chief of Police Cornelius J. O'Neill . . . "; "In behalf of Russian Workers Cooperative Association in Chicago. . . . " (16 suits listed.)

Activities in behalf of "Political Prisoners" listed include: "Campaign for pardon of Tom Mooney and Warren K. Billings" (Anarchist-Communist dynamiters); "Parole of the four remaining Centralia I.W.W. prisoners" (murderers of 6

Legionnaires); "Pardon application for Israel Lazar, *also known as Bill Lawrence,* sentenced to two to four years under the Pennsylvania sedition act"; "Pardon applications for two Pennsylvania prisoners serving two-year sentences for 'inciting to riot' at Wildwood in the 1931 coal strike"; "Parole instead of deportation for Carl Sklar, Russian-born, and voluntary departure to Russia for Tsuji Horiuchi, Imperial Valley, Calif. prisoners whose terms expire July 1932." (Sklar was a convicted Communist revolutionary agitator. A Japanese Communist deported to Japan would be jailed; hence the A.C.L.U. request for his "voluntary departure to Russia").

Exultantly, the A.C.L.U. lists under its *"Gains"* for the year:

"Decision . . . permitting Tao Hsuan Li, Chinese Communist, and Guido Serio, anti-Fascist Communist, to go to Soviet Russia instead of to certain death or imprisonment in their home lands. Eduardo Machado, slated for deportation to Spain, also was granted voluntary departure to Russia."

"Ruling of U.S. Judge Woolsey that Dr. Marie C. Stopes book 'Contraception,' is moral and can legally be imported . . . the first book on specific birth control information admitted since 1890. The Courts overruled the Customs Bureau in admitting it. It cannot however be sent by mail."

"The acquittal of Communists held in East St. Louis, arrested for meeting in private house, and the establishment of the right to hold Communist meetings without interference."

"Final discharge of ten Communists held in Portland a year under the Oregon criminal syndicalism law."

"Frank Spector freed from prison, his conviction in Imperial Valley, Calif., strike criminal syndicalism case having been reversed." (Communist organizer.)

"Defeat of bills sponsored by the D.A.R. in Mass. and Minn. for special oaths of loyalty by school teachers." (Reds do not wish to take an oath of loyalty to this government.)

"Alabama Syndicalism bill designed to outlaw Communists rejected in Committee." (A "Gain" indeed for the Reds.)

"Decision of New Jersey Vice Chancellor upholding rights of Communists to utter views." (No Red movement without Red propaganda is possible.)

"Release of Theodore Luesse, Communist, confined on an Indiana prison farm in default of $500 fine, for Unemployed Council activities."

"Refusal of U.S. Supreme Court to review a case from Washington in which Bible reading in public schools was sought to be established." (No Bible reading, say the Reds.)

The A.C.L.U. lists among its *"Setbacks"*: "The violent police attacks on street demonstrations, Communist-led, before offices of the Japanese government in Chicago and Washington," but does not mention the fact that the only real violence in the Chicago Japanese consulate riot was the shooting by a Communist of three policemen merely performing their duty in dispersing a Red army of rioters. The Reds were bent on violence against Japanese officials in protest against Japan's war on Communist China. Banners were carried saying "Defend the Chinese Revolution," "Down with Japanese Imperialism," etc. Three policemen were seriously wounded by Communist "Chuck," who was given only two years in prison for this. I met one of the policemen recently who is still under treatment as the result of three vicious wounds inflicted by this Communist. The A.C.L.U. boasts that it has Chicago Police Chief Allman behaving nicely and considerately toward the Reds nowadays, so much so that some policemen are wondering which pays the best: to be the Red who smashes in Relief Stations and yells for Red revolution and is treated as an innocent martyr by "leading Chicagoans" of the A.C.L.U. Committee, or to be the Police defender of law and order and be cut with razor blades, have red pepper thrown in one's eyes, have one's word discounted at Court, be sued for "roughness" to Communists by the A.C.L.U., and be shot by Reds, without receiving thanks and without appropriate punishment being given the Reds. No protest committee ever waits on Chief Allman when the Reds fracture a policeman's skull, as they do frequently.

The legislative program of the A.C.L.U. is stated as:

"1. To enact in each state a model anti-injunction bill along the lines of the new federal bill." (Sponsored by the A.C.L.U. It gives Red strikers freedom to make employers helpless.)

"2. In New York State to repeal the moving picture censorship, the theatre padlock law" (allowing padlocking of a theatre for showing obscene plays), "to take away special police powers from the Vice Society" (why repress vice?), "and in Massachusetts to set aside free speech areas in public parks; to take away from

Boston officials the power of censorship over meetings in private halls and over theatres." (Then Red, atheist and obscene affairs in parks and theatres could not be interfered with.)

"3. In Pennsylvania, to repeal sedition act" (against Reds), "to take police out of strikes, to abolish the coal and iron police and to force the incorporation of company towns." (This would put Red strikers in power.)

"Among other issues tackled by the Chicago Committee were the barring of minor" (Communist, etc.) "political parties from the ballot in Illinois, compulsory military training at the State University . . . " etc. (Weakening national defense is a Red objective.)

Significant indeed is the Report of the A.C.L.U. "Bail Fund" and "Expenditures." To quote: "Bonds amounting to $29,050 were cancelled in 22 cases, 18 of which involved Communist defendants, and 4 I.W.W.'s . . . Bail bonds amounting to $16,750 are still outstanding. $13,000 of these are placed on six defendants in the Atlanta, Ga. insurrection case. Of the 12 persons now bonded, 8 are Communists, 2 are members of the I.W.W. and 2 are independent of any affiliation."

"Expenditures for the ordinary operations of the Union were $25,300, against $24,808 the year previous."

"Special Fund expenditures totaled $23,300. . . . $15,589 went to carrying the expenditures in excess of receipts of the three auxiliary organizations created by the Union, the *National Mooney-Billings Committee,* the *National Committee on Labor Injunctions,* and the *National Council on Freedom from Censorship.* The remainder of the special funds outside of the specific grants from the American Fund for Public Service" (Garland Fund) "went into court cases."

Under "Loans" are listed: to *"General Defense Committee* $500" (I.W.W.); to *"International Labor Defense,* national office $1518.30, Philadelphia office $450, Boston office $50." (Communist.)

"Expenditures" for: "Cases of Ky. Miners and sympathizers, defense in court $1269.55." (Communists and I.W.W.'s); "Toward expenses of appeal to U.S. Supreme Court conviction of Yetta Stromberg in the California anti-red flag law $263.25." (The leader of a Communist camp for children teaching sedition, atheism, etc., was convicted of displaying the Red flag); "Defense of National Miners Union members, West Va. $250." (Communist union); "Court costs, deportation case against Guido Serio $526.95." (Communist); "Suit against Glendale, Cal. police and American Legion $100" (for breaking up a Red Socialist's meeting); "For appeal from convictions of two Communist girl leaders at a Children's summer camp, Van Etten, N.Y. $71.35"; etc., etc., etc.

Concerning its branches the A.C.L.U. Report states that:

"In Pennsylvania, the work is organized on a state-wide basis with headquarters at Harrisburg, in charge of Allan G. Harper, state secretary, and local committees at Philadelphia, Pittsburg, and other centers. The committee tackles repression on many fronts—by legislative act, public and private police and by local officials . . . The Committee *won pardons for two men serving five-year sentences under the sedition act.* Other *sedition convictions* in which men are serving sentences will be taken before the board," etc.

"In Seattle a local Civil Liberties Committee was formed in 1931 with Edward E. Henry as secretary, and has since been active in efforts to get downtown meeting places and permits to parade for Communist-led organizations . . . The Committee has participated in defense of *deportation cases;* . . . and has taken part in the movement to *abolish compulsory military training* at the state university."

"In Cincinnati the local committee with Mrs. Mary D. Brite as secretary took part in the protest against the expulsion of Prof. Herbert A. Miller from the state university" (for radicalism) "and later had him as speaker at a meeting; has backed *repeal of the criminal syndicalism* law, and aided in *obtaining dismissal of cases* brought in Cincinnati under that law. A protest meeting against treatment of" (Communist) "Kentucky coal miners was held. The attitude of the present City Manager of Cincinnati toward public meetings by radicals is such that no issue has arisen during the present year." (Nice man!)

"A small committee was formed in Wash., D.C. to aid in work with Congress and the departments as occasion demands."

"The Union continues to prepare a page for the monthly issues of the Arbitrator, published by Wm. Floyd, thus reaching a large number outside the Union's membership." (Wm. Floyd is one of the gentle "pacifists" who decry violence so earnestly that they oppose all national defense—for the U.S.)

What the Better America Federation Says of the A.C.L.U.

Among the numerous Red pamphlets and publications put out by the A.C.L.U. is "Professional Patriots," edited by Norman Hapgood. Its distribution was reported as A.C.L.U. "Work in Hand" for 1927, and the Communist Daily Worker published it serially as good Communist propaganda. It took the customary shots at all who dare criticize its activities giving particular mention to the Better America Federation, which is responsible for the enactment and retention of the California Criminal Syndicalism Law, in spite of the frantic and united efforts of the A.C.L.U., I.W.W. and Communist and Socialist Parties to repeal it. The Better America Federation came right back with a published reply which is a classic. Reading it gives one the desire to yell "Hurrah for you!" and throw a hat into the air. To quote:

"The B.A.F. is pleased to say this:

"The American Civil Liberties Union is the 'respectable front' in the United States of America for the organized forces of revolution, lawlessness, sabotage, and murder. It is so recognized and acknowledged by these forces. It numbers among its board of control not only the Moscow-appointed chief of the American Branch of the Communist International, but also an assortment of Socialists, Defeatists, and Slackers.

"It was spawned to give aid and comfort to the enemies of this Republic.

"Its first organized movement was that of encouraging the youth of the United States to defy their country's laws.

"Its consistent policy is one of breeding hatred and suspicion and hostility toward this country in the minds of all it can influence.

"It consistently preaches the doctrine proven false in the Supreme Court of the United States and many state Courts, namely, that inciting to crime is not a crime.

"Its literature and its representatives are characterized by flagrant dishonesty, mendacity, and categorical lies.

"It spends each year more money for its program of moral and civic sabotage than the entire stipends of those it evilly dubs 'professionals patriots.'

"It has been in bad odor with many governmental and educational agencies in this Republic from its birth.

"It is the god-mother of slackerism, the chum of Socialism, the tried and true friend of the I.W.W., the helpful hand-maiden of Communism, and the attorney-in-fact for obscenity, criminal syndicalism, and anarchy.

"It has a 100% record of aiding persons and movements about whose character, lawful practices, and statutory patriotism there have been grave official doubts.

"It has never caused a single human being's heart to turn toward the love or even the decent respect for this Republic; on the contrary, it has been from the beginning, is today, and blatantly promises to continue to be a breeder of disaffection and a protector of revolutionary movements aimed at the life of this Republic.

"And it is an enemy many fold more detestable than any we have fought in any war; for those foes were proud to wear a uniform and to die in open battle for their flags; while the American Civil Liberties Union is a rascally, skulking foe, operating under a camouflage, and marshalling the lewdest fellows of the basest sort to secret sapping of the foundations of this Republic.

"The Better America Federation will be proud to be a 'Professional Patriot,' and will continue, in company with its many allies, to fight the American Civil Liberties Union organization, program, and personnel—Clergymen, Communists, Bishops, Slackers, Revolutionaries, I.W.W.'s, and all."

FORMATION OF A.C.L.U.

American League to Limit Armaments

Says the Lusk Report (p. 1077): "To compel American neutrality and to still the growing demand for military preparation by the United States, it became necessary for German propagandists to stimulate pacifist sentiment in this country. . . . Among the active organizers of the *American League to Limit Armaments* will be found the names of many who were at the same time active in the movement directed by Louis Lochner in Chicago, under the name of the *Emergency Peace Federation.* Among them are: Jane Addams, Rev. John Haynes Holmes, David Starr Jordan, Dr Jacques Loeb, Dr. George W. Nasmyth, George Foster Peabody, Oswald Garrison Villard, Morris Hillquit, Hamilton Holt, Elsie Clews Parsons, Lillian D. Wald, Stephen S. Wise, and L. Hollingsworth Wood, secretary." . . .

American Union Against Militarism

"In the early part of 1915 the members of the executive committee of this league felt that its scope was not wide enough and, therefore, the *anti-preparedness* committee was formed, which later became the *American Union Against Militarism* with hdqts. at 70 Fifth Ave., New York" (which in May 1917 carried on a vigorous Anti-Conscription Campaign in conjunction with the Socialist Party, Woman's Peace Party, Emergency Peace Federation); etc.

Civil Liberties Bureau

"The passage of the draft act, after our entry into the war caused the American Union Against Militarism to increase its activities. It immediately undertook to assist all persons desiring to avoid the draft, and to protect all persons from so-called 'infringement of Civil liberties,' opening branch offices under the name of the *Civil Liberties Bureau,* both in Washington and New York, for this purpose."...

"Since both the conscription and espionage bills were soon passed by Congress it was not very long before the American Union Against Militarism virtually withdrew leaving the field in the hands of its branch offices" (the Civil Liberties Bureau).

"Though the ostensible object of the Civil Liberties Bureau was to protect free speech and civil liberties during war times, an exhaustive examination of its files shows . . . some of the real objects were: 1. Encouraging naturally timid boys and discontents to register as conscientious objectors. 2. To assist any radical movement calculated to obstruct the prosecution of the war, as evidenced by the bureau's activities in collecting funds for the I.W.W. and 'Masses' defense. 3. Issuing propaganda literature . . . to influence public sympathy toward the I.W.W., conscientious objectors and radical organizations. 4. To discourage in every possible way any conscientious objector from doing his military duty in the war; and pointing out to mothers and friends the means employed by others to escape military service. 5. To furnish attorneys for conscientious objectors and persons prosecuted for violation of the Espionage act. . . . 6. 'Boring from within' in churches, religious organizations, women's clubs, American Federation of Labor, etc., in order to spread radical ideas. . . . 7. Working towards an after-the-war program, usually referred to as 'a democratic program of constructive peace.'"

"A full list of the officers and executive committees of the *Civil Liberties Bureau* was as follows:

Lillian D. Wald, chmn.; Amos Pinchot, vice-chmn.; L. Hollingsworth Wood, treas.; Crystal Eastman, exec. sec.; Chas. T. Hallinan, edtl. dir. Executive Committee: Roger Baldwin, director of Civil Liberties Bureau; Jane Addams, A. A. Berle, Frank Bohn, Wm. F. Cochran, John Lovejoy Elliott, John Haynes Holmes, Paul U. Kellogg, Alice Lewisohn, Frederick Lynch, James H. Maurer, Scott Nearing, Oswald Garrison Villard, Emily Greene Balch, Herbert S. Bigelow (of Cincinnati), Sophonisba P. Breckenridge, Max Eastman, Zona Gale, David Starr Jordan, Agnes Brown Leach, Owen R. Lovejoy, John A. McSparran, Henry R. Mussey, Norman M. Thomas, James P. Warbasse, and Stephen S. Wise."

National Civil Liberties Bureau

"In October 1917 the Civil Liberties Bureau enlarged both its offices and scope under the name of *National Civil Liberties Bureau.* The Am. Union against Militarism in announcing this separate establishment enclosed significantly a reprint of the Russian Council of Workmen's and Soldiers' Delegates' peace terms" (the Soviets of today).

Roger Baldwin, director of the enlarged organization was soon convicted under the Selective Service Act and sent to prison. While he had said in his letter to Socialist Lochner concerning the infamous People's Council: "We want to look like patriots in everything we do. We want to get a good lot of flags, talk a good deal about the Constitution and what our forefathers wanted to make of this country, and to show that we are really the folks that really stand for the spirit of our institutions," he was in reality a "philisophical anarchist," according to the sworn testimony of his friend Norman Thomas during his trial, and a radical to the bone. He said (quoted from leaflet issued by his friends, Nov. 1918): "The Non-Partisan League, radical labor and the Socialist Party hold the germs of a new social order. Their protest is my protest" (against the war).

American Civil Liberties Union

After Baldwin's conviction, the *National Civil Liberties Bureau* continued its activities, and in March 1920 changed its name to its present one—*American Civil Liberties Union,* with the following list of officers:

Harry F. Ward, chmn.; Duncan McDonald, Ill., and Jeannette Rankin of Montana, vice chairmen; Helen Phelps Stokes, treas.; Albert de Silver and Roger N. Baldwin, directors; Walter Nelles, counsel; Lucille B. Lowenstein, field secretary; Louis F. Budenz, publicity director; National Committee, Jane Addams; Herbert S. Bigelow;

Sophonisba P. Breckenridge, Robt. M. Buck, Chgo.; John S. Codman, Boston; Lincoln Colcord, Wash., D.C.; James H. Dillard; Crystal Eastman; John Lovejoy Elliott; Edmund C. Evans and Edward W. Evans, Phila. Pa.; Wm. M. Fincke, Katonah, N.Y.; John A. Fitch, N.Y. City; Eliz. Gurley Flynn; Felix Frankfurter, Harvard U.; *Wm. Z. Foster;* Paul J. Furnas, N.Y. City; Zona Gale; A. B. Gilbert, St. Paul, Minn.; Arthur Garfield Hays; Morris Hillquit; John Haynes Holmes; Frederic C. Howe; James Weldon Johnson; Helen Keller, Forest Hills, L.I.; Harold J. Laski, Cambridge, Mass. (now England); Agnes Brown Leach; Arthur LeSueur; Henry R. Linville; Robt. Morss Lovett; Allen McCurdy; Grenville S. MacFarland, Boston; Oscar Maddaus, Manhasset, L.I.; Judah L. Magnes; James H. Maurer; A. J. Muste; Geo. W. Nasmyth; Scott Nearing; Julia O'Connor; Wm. H. Pickens; Wm. Marion Reedy, St. Louis; John Nevin Sayre; Rose Schneidermann; Vida D. Scudder; Norman M. Thomas; Oswald G. Villard; L. Hollingsworth Wood; Geo. P. West, Oakland, Cal.

A.C.L.U. Directors and Branches 1932

To quote the 1932 Report: "The National Committee which controls the Union's general policies now numbers 69. Former Federal Judge Geo. W. Anderson of Boston was added to the committee during the year. The committee suffered the loss by death of Dr. David Starr Jordan for many years a vice chairman of the Union; Julia C. Lathrop of Rockford, Ill. and A. M. Todd of Kalamazoo, Mich. Former U.S. Senator Thos. W. Hardwick of Georgia resigned because of a difference with the policies outlined in our pamphlet 'Black Justice.' Anna Rochester" (Communist) "resigned from the National Committee, but *remains on the board of directors;* Jos. Schlossberg, Dr. Henry R. Linville and Hubert C. Herring resigned from the board of directors but remain on the National Committee."

"The Board of Directors, meeting weekly, in active charge of the union's affairs, is now composed of:

Dr. Harry Elmer Barnes, Robt. W. Dunn" (Communist), "Morris L. Ernst, Walter Frank, Arthur Garfield Hays, Rev. John Haynes Holmes, Ben W. Huebsch, Dorothy Kenyon, Corliss Lamont, William L. Nunn, Frank L. Palmer, Amos R. Pinchot, Eliot Pratt, Roger William Riis, Anna Rochester" (Communist), "Rev. Wm. B. Spofford, Dr. Harry F. Ward, and the executive staff: Forrest Bailey, Roger Baldwin and Lucille B. Milner. The officers are unchanged. Dr. Ward has been absent abroad on his sabbatical year" (spent in Soviet Russia) "and his place taken by John Haynes Holmes as Acting Chairman."

(Wm. Z. Foster's and Scott Nearing's names disappeared from the letterhead in 1931. They became possibly too conspicuous. Jane Addams, after 10 years of service on the nat. com., removed hers also at this time. She had been repeatedly attacked for this connection.)

A.C.L.U. National Officers 1932:

Chmn., Harry F. Ward; Vice Chmn.: Helen Phelps Stokes, James H. Maurer, Fremont Older; Treas., B. W. Huebsch; Directors: Roger N. Baldwin, Forrest Bailey; Counsel: Arthur Garfield Hays, Morris L. Ernst; Research Sec., Lucille B. Milner; Washington Counsel, Edmund D. Campbell.

National Committee 1932:

Chas. F. Amidon, Geo. W. Anderson, Harry Elmer Barnes, Herbert S. Bigelow, Edwin M. Borchard, Richard C. Cabot, John S. Codman, Clarence Darrow, John Dewey, James H. Dillard, Robt. W. Dunn, Sherwood Eddy, Eliz. Glendower Evans, John F. Finerty, Eliz. Gurley Flynn, Walter Frank, Felix Frankfurter, Ernst Freund, Kate Crane Gartz, Norman Hapgood, Powers Hapgood, Hubert C. Herring, Morris Hillquit, John Haynes Holmes, Frederic C. Howe, James Weldon Johnson, Geo. W. Kirchwey, John A. Lapp, Agnes Brown Leach, Arthur LeSueur, Henry R. Linville, Robt. Morss Lovett, Mary E. McDowell, Anne Martin, Alexander Meiklejohn, Henry R. Mussey, A. J. Muste, Walter Nelles, Wm. L. Nunn, Julia S. O'Connor Parker, Wm. Pickens, Amos Pinchot, Jeannette Rankin, Edw. A. Ross, Elbert Russell, Father John A. Ryan, John Nevin Sayre, Wm. Scarlett, Jos. Schlossberg, Vida D. Scudder, Abba Hillel Silver, John F. Sinclair, Clarence R. Skinner, Norman M. Thomas, Edw. D. Tittmann, Millie R. Trumbull, Wm. S. U'Ren, Oswald Garrison Villard, B. Charney Vladeck, David Wallerstein, Geo. P. West, Peter Witt, L. Hollingsworth Wood.

Local Committee Officers 1932:

Cincinnati Branch, 845 Dayton St., Cincinnati; Dr. W. O. Brown, chmn.; Mary D. Brite, sec.

Detroit Branch, 1976 Atkinson St., Detroit; Walter M. Nelson, chmn.; Fannie Ziff, sec.

Maryland Civil Liberties Committee, Inc., 513 Park Ave., Baltimore; Dr. A. O. Lovejoy, chmn.; Eliz. Gilman, sec.

Massachusetts Civil Liberties Committee, 1241 Little Bldg., Boston; John S. Codman, chmn.; David K. Niles, sec.

New York City Committee, 100 Fifth Ave., N.Y. City; Dorothy Kenyon, chmn.; Eliz. G. Coit, sec.

Pennsylvania Civil Liberties Committee, 219 Walnut St., Harrisburg; Rev. Philip David Bookstaber, chmn.; Allan G. Harper, sec.

Philadelphia Civil Liberties Committee, 318 S. Juniper St., Phila.; J. Prentice Murphy, chmn.; Ada H. Funke, sec.

Pittsburg Civil Liberties Committee, 1835 Center Ave., Pitts.; Ralph S. Boots, chmn.; Sidney A. Teller, sec.

Seattle Branch, 515 Lyons Bldg., Seattle; H. E. Foster, chmn.; Edward E. Henry, sec.

Southern California Branch, 1022 California Bldg., Los A.; John Beardsley, chmn.; Clinton J. Taft, sec.

St. Louis Branch, 3117 Osage St., St. Louis; Dr. Albert E. Taussig, chmn.; Richard C. Bland, sec.

Wisconsin Civil Liberties Committee, Univ. of Wis., Madison; Wm. G. Rice, chmn.; W. Ellison Chalmers, sec.

Chicago Civil Liberties Committee, Room 611, 160 N. La Salle St., Chicago (Office of Carl Haessler, Federated Press and Chgo. Com. for Struggle Against War); pres., Arthur Fisher; vice pres., Wm. H. Holly; treas., Duane Swift; exec. sec., Thomas M. McKenna.

AMERICAN CIVIL LIBERTIES UNION
100 FIFTH AVENUE, NEW YORK CITY

March 23, 1932.

To our Washington friends:

May we ask you to make an effort to attend a hearing to be held this Saturday morning at 10:30 in Room 450, Senate Office Bldg. on Senator Cutting's bill to admit alien pacifists to citizenship without promising to bear arms? The hearing is before a sub-committee of the Judiciary Committee composed of Senators David A. Reed of Pennsylvania, chairman; Marcus A. Coolidge of Massachusetts and Roscoe C. Patterson of Missouri, -- a not too hopeful group.

This hearing is solely for the opponents of the measure. We had our field-day yesterday, and according to reports, it was a highly effective presentation of the case for the bill. John W. Davis, counsel for Prof. Macintosh, led off, followed by Bishop McConnell, president of the Federal Council of Churches, Father McGowan of the National Catholic Welfare Conference, Rabbi Israel of the Central Conference of American Rabbis and Francis Taylor of the Society of Friends. The committee room was crowded with members of "patriotic" societies who had gotten wind of the hearing, although we had done our best to keep it quiet so there would not be the high-tension emotional atmosphere which marked the Griffin bill hearings. Apparently there is no escape from that conflict at hearings. We are therefore asking all our friends to be out in force on Saturday morning to hear what the "patriots" have to say!

A good turnout will help offset them. We trust you will make an effort to be present.

Sincerely yours,

Roger Baldwin

RNB/GH

Facsimile of A.C.L.U. letter urging support of a Bill to admit alien pacifists to citizenship without promise to bear arms (sponsored by Senator Cutting of the Senate radical bloc). Any measure which will weaken the power of a capitalist government to defend itself receives radical support. Note the bit about offsetting the patriots. Signed by Roger Baldwin (see this "Who's Who").

Executive Board:

The officers and Helen Ascher, Margaret B. Bennett, Jessie F. Binford, Karl Borders, Raymond B. Bragg, Herbert J. Friedman, Charles W. Gilkey, Lloyd H. Lehman, Robt. Morss Lovett, Curtis W. Reese, Wm. E. Rodriguez.

Committee:

Frederick Babcock, Melbourne P. Boynton, Percy H. Boynton, Sophonisba P. Breckenridge, Horace J. Bridges, A. J. Carlson, Eliz. Christman, Clarence Darrow, Samuel Dauchy, Wm. E. Dodd, Paul H. Douglas, Margaret Furness, Carl Haessler, Alice Hamilton, Florence Curtis Hanson, A. Eustace Haydon, Lillian Herstein, Paul Hutchinson, A. L. Jackson, Esther L. Kohn, John A. Lapp, Harold D. Lasswell, Frederic W. Leighton, Clyde McGee, Louis L. Mann, Mrs. G. M. Mathes, Wiley W. Mills, Catherine Waugh McCulloch, Fred Atkins Moore, R. Lester Mondale, Chas. Clayton Morrison, Robt. Park, Ferdinand Schevill, Chas. P. Schwartz, Amelia Sears, Mary Rozet Smith, T. V. Smith, Clarence Starr, Ernest Fremont Tittle, Arthur J. Todd, Edward M. Winston, James M. Yard, Victor S. Yarros.

Claims about 2000 members.

Committees and Auxiliary Organizations of A.C.L.U.:

Committee on Academic Freedom; Prof. Wm. H. Kilpatrick, chmn.; Forrest Bailey, sec.

Committee on Indian Civil Rights; Nathan Margold, chmn.; Robt. Gessner, sec.

National Committee on Labor Injunctions; Former U.S. Judge Chas. F. Amidon, chmn.; Dr. Alexander Fleisher, sec.

National Council on Freedom from Censorship (see); Prof. Hatcher Hughes, chmn.; Gordon W. Moss, sec.

National Mooney-Billings Committee (see); Henry T. Hunt, chmn.; Roger N. Baldwin, sec.

AMERICAN COMMITTEE FOR CHINESE RELIEF

AMERICAN COMMITTEE FOR FAIR PLAY TO CHINA

AMERICAN COMMITTEE FOR JUSTICE TO CHINA

These committees were organized, when the Communists were in control of the National Party of China, in order to prevent U.S. intervention in behalf of American citizens and property in jeopardy there. See "Hands Off Committees."

AMERICAN COMMITTEE FOR STRUGGLE AGAINST WAR

See under "Intl., American, and Chicago Committees for Struggle Against War," also "World Congress Against War."

AMERICAN COMMITTEE ON INFORMATION ABOUT RUSSIA

Am. Com. on Inf. About Russia.

A group spreading pro-Soviet propaganda; formed 1928 with hdqts. Room 709, 166 W. Washington St., Chicago.

Chmn., John A. Lapp; sec.-treas., Lillian Herstein; Jane Addams, A. Barton (of Machinists Union 492), Prof. Paul H. Douglas, Carl Haessler, Felix Hauzl (Bus. Agt. Woodcarvers Assn.), Mary McDowell, Peter Jensen (Chmn. System Federation 130), Hyman Schneid (pres. Amalg. Cloth. Wkrs. Ill.), Wm. H. Holly, Prof. Robt. Morss Lovett, Thos. A. Allinson (father of Brent Dow), Ray Korner (sec. Boilermakers Union 626), Ed. Nelson (sec.-treas. Painters Union 194), J. Schnessler (Photo Engravers Union 5), John Werlik (sec. Metal Polishers Union 6).

AMERICAN FEDERATION OF LABOR

A.F. of L.

Up to this time the A.F. of L. has been a bitter disappointment to Moscow, which long ago expected to take it over. Continuously, however, the warfare of "boring from within" to bring the A.F. of L. under Communist control goes on. Wm. Z. Foster and Robt. W. Dunn were long ago expelled; other Communists are from time to time expelled and licenses of Locals "going Red" are revoked. Many A.F. of L. leaders deserve unstinted praise for their pro-American efforts against Red domination. Certain A.F. of L. unions are under Red control, however, others are well penetrated and influenced, and in practically every "united front" Communist activity, A.F. of L. Locals and representatives participate. It is to be hoped the Red element will not eventually gain control. Lillian Herstein of the radical Am. Fed. of Tchrs., an A.F. of L. affiliate, who is a Socialist and a member of two Communist subsidiary organizations, serves on the executive board of the Chicago F. of L. of which John Fitzpatrick of the red Chgo. Com. for Struggle Against War is president. Victor Olander, Illinois F. of L. executive, made a most bitter speech against the Baker Bills (to curb teaching of sedition and overthrow of the Govt. in Illinois schools and colleges), quoting Hapgood's "Professional Patriots," etc., at a public hearing in Springfield, May 1933, yet saying he was opposed to Communists. Press reports concerning the proposed union of the radical "outlaw" Amalgamated Clothing Workers with the A.F. of L. stated that this movement indicated an increasing "liberalization" of A.F. of L. policy. The Communist Daily Worker Sept. 6, 1933 contained a message from Earl Browder (sec. Communist Party) in which he said: "Now, more than ever, it is necessary to seriously build up our forces inside the A.F. of L. There is still the remnants in all districts of the old mistaken idea that we cannot both build the militant unions of the T.U.U.L. and at the same time the left wing opposition inside the A.F. of L. *More attention than ever must be given to this problem.*" (Emphasis in original.) See David Dubinsky vice. pres. '34, p. 338.

A.F. OF L. COMMITTEE FOR UNEMPLOYMENT INSURANCE

Full name is the "A.F. of L. Trade Union Committee for Unemployment Insurance and Relief"; hdqts., 799 Broadway, Room 336, N.Y.C. (Communist hdqts.). A Communist movement in the A.F. of L. for the purpose of disruption; "organized in N.Y. City on Jan. 27, 1932 at a Conference representing 19 A.F. of L. Unions"; headed by Communist Harry Weinstock expelled by the A.F. of L. Painters Union, N.Y.C., Feb. 1933, for Communist membership, assisted by Walter Frank, a Minneapolis Communist; endorsed heartily in letter from Tom Mooney published by this committee; barred by order of Wm. Green from participation in A.F. of L. Convention at Wash., D.C., Oct. 4, 1933.

AMERICAN FEDERATION OF TEACHERS

Am. Fed. Tchrs.

Radical; stands for abolition of R.O. T.C.; recognition of Russia; full "academic freedom" to teach anything, including Socialism, Communism or Atheism; closely allied to A.C.L.U.; received financial aid from the Garland Fund, which gives only to radical agencies; monthly organ "The American Teacher"; pres., Henry R. Linville, N.Y.; sec.-treas., Florence Curtis Hanson, Chgo.

AMERICAN FRIENDS SERVICE COMMITTEE

Am. Friends Serv. Com.

A Quaker relief organization; part of the War Resisters International Council of international anti-militarist organizations having their first meetings in Holland, linked together "working for the supersession of capitalism and imperialism by the establishment of a new social and international order" (see W.R. Intl. Coun.); cooperates with L.I.D., Fell. Recon., Y.M. C.A. and Y.W.C.A. in recruiting students to "investigate industry" and in holding conferences featuring radical pacifist, socialistic speakers; conducted an Institute at N.U., Evanston, June 1932, with hdqts. also at Tittle's M.E. Church; Herbert A. Miller, Tucker P. Smith, Kirby Page, Harry D. Gideonse, Louis L. Mann and E. F. Tittle were Institute faculty members; see connections of Robt. W. Dunn, Karl Borders, Paul Douglas, W. K. Thomas, and Institute faculty members in "Who's Who"; National Office: 20 S. 12th St., Phila., Pa.; Midwest hdqts.: Room 902, 203 S. Dearborn St., Chgo., Ill.

AMERICAN FUND FOR PUBLIC SERVICE

See under Garland Fund.

AMERICAN LABOR YEAR BOOK

Published yearly by the Rand School Press, 7 E. 15th St., N.Y.C., formerly financed by the Garland Fund; reports activities of radical organizations.

AMERICAN LEAGUE AGAINST WAR AND FASCISM

Am. Lg. Ag. War & Fascism

Communist; the Communist International's magazine (Jan. 15, '34, p. 78) states: "Our most successful application of the united front has been in the anti-war and anti-fascist movement. We led a highly successful U. S. Congress Against War" (see) "which brought together 2,616 delegates from all over the country. . . . The Congress from the beginning was led by our Party quite openly. . . . The Congress set up a permanent organization on a federative basis called the American League Against War and Fascism." Its second congress (Sept. 28, 29, 30, 1934), which I attended, was decked with Communist banners. Messages from "many nuclei of the Communist Party in the National Guard" and two masked army officers in full uniform pledged seditious cooperation to turn any U. S. A. war into Red revolution (described by communist "New Theatre" magazine, Nov., '34). Hayes Beall of the nat. com. of the Am. Lg. and chmn. Nat. Coun. Methodist Youth pledged the cooperation of 1,400,000 Methodist youths to this Congress program (Daily Wkr., 9/28/34). Leading Communist agitators, "jailbirds" and "religious" leaders mingle on the National Committee listed in Daily Worker of Aug. 4, 1934, as follows: Dr. Harry F. Ward, Chairman; Robert Morse Lovett, Vice-Chairman; Lincoln Steffens, Vice-Chairman; Earl Browder, Vice-Chairman; Anna N. Davis, Treasurer; Israel Amter, Roger Baldwin, Max Bedacht, Ella Reeve Bloor, Winifred L. Chappell, George A. Coe, Barnett Cooper, Prof. George S. Counts, Malcolm Cowley, H. W. L. Dana, Dorothy Detzer, Margaret Forsyth, Maurice Gates, Rabbi Benjamin Goldstein, Dr. Israel Goldstein, Annie E. Gray, Gilbert Green, A. A. Heller, Donald Henderson, Francis A. Henson, Harold Hickerson, Roy Hudson, Langston Hughes, Rabbi Edward L. Israel, James Lerner, E. C. Lindeman, Rev. R. Lester Mondale, William L. Patterson, Rev. A. Clayton Powell, Jr., Henry Shepard, William Spofford, Maxwell S. Stewart, Alfred Wagenknecht, Prof. Colston E. Warne, Louis Weinstock, Ella Winter, Charles Zimmerman. The National Committee members of the Youth Section as listed in Daily Worker of Oct. 8, 1934, are: James Lerner, present National Chairman; Edith Turner, Indiana, Y. W. C. A.; James Wexler, Editor Columbia University "Spectator"; Ed Strong of the International Negro Movement; Wm. Miller of the Young Circle League; Paul Streich of the Eden Seminary; Waldo McNutt of the Rocky Mountain Y. M. C. A.; Richard Whitten, National Chairman of the Student League for Industrial Democracy; Alex Hamilton of the Epworth League; Ellen Condra, Christian Hapke of the Nebraska Holiday Assn.; Franz Ultz of the Gillespie Y. P. S. L.; Rev. Kelly of the Pilgrim Baptist Church; Virgil Morris of the Marine Workers Industrial Union; X of the Youngstown, Ohio, National Guard; Buela Lee of the Indianapolis Y. W .C. A.; Martha Lawandowska, a Chicago Stock Yards worker; Helen Housch, of the St. Louis Neighborhood House; Beall Hayes, Chairman of the Methodist Youth Council; Futterman Mille of the N. S. L.; Bleil David of the Ann Arbor, Mich., City Council of Boy Scouts; Gershtenson, Director of the Y. M. H. A. in Washington Hghts.; Frank Meyers of England, Representative of the World Youth Committee; James Ashford of the L. S. N. R. and Gil Green, National Secretary of the Young Communist League.

AMERICAN LEAGUE TO LIMIT ARMAMENTS

See under A.C.L.U., section on "formation."

AMERICAN LITHUANIAN WORKERS LABOR SOCIETY

A Communist subsidiary (U.S. Report 2290).

AMERICAN NEGRO LABOR CONGRESS

Official Communist Negro subsidiary organized in Chicago, Oct. 1925; name changed at the American Negro Labor Congress at St. Louis, Nov. 16, 1930, to its present title "League of Struggle for Negro Rights."

AMERICAN NEUTRAL CONFERENCE COMMITTEE

See "Emergency Peace Federation."

AMERICAN NEWSPAPER GUILD

For newspaper writers; organized by Heywood Broun (see "Who's Who"), Sept. 1933, aided by Morris Ernst and other radicals; demands 5-day week NRA code, etc.

AMERICAN RATIONALISTS ASSOCIATION

Atheistic: Dr. Percy Ward, pres. 1926—; Independent Rationalists Assn. of Chgo. founded by M. Mangasarian, changed name to Chgo. Humanist Society, Jan. 12, 1934 (Burdette Backus, leader).

AMERICAN-RUSSIAN CHAMBER OF COMMERCE

For aiding American-Russian trade; agitated recognition of U.S.S.R.; sponsor of American-Russian Institute; cooperates with the Soviet Union Information Bureau; now preparing a Handbook of the Soviet Union, in Russia, to be published by the John Day Co. of the U.S.A.; pres. Hugh L. Cooper.

AMERICAN RUSSIAN INSTITUTE

Of New York; affiliate of the American Russian Chamber of Commerce and A.S. C.R.R.; sponsors exhibits of Russian goods, etc.

AMERICAN SOCIETY FOR CULTURAL RELATIONS WITH RUSSIA

A.S.C.R.R.

A Communist subsidiary (U.S. Report 2290); the American affiliate of the Russian V.O.K.S. (Bureau of Cultural Relations between U.S.S.R. and Foreign Countries), operating in several countries and very active in England; formed to break down antipathy toward the Soviet government; the "Nation" announced Jan. 14, 1925: "The establishment of closer cultural relations between the United States and the Soviet Union is the mission of Mr. Roman Weller of Moscow who has just arrived in this country as representative of the Bureau of Cultural Relations established in Moscow about a year ago"; the N.Y. Herald Tribune, April 24, 1927, reported: "With the announced intention of bringing together Americans who are interested in Russian life and contemporary culture the A.S.C.R.R. was formed yesterday. The first meeting will be at the administration building of the Henry Street Settlement" (of Lillian Wald) "on Wednesday evening. The speakers will be Leopold Stokowski, Robt. J. Flaherty, Lee Simonson, Graham Taylor and Elizabeth Farrell. Mrs. Norman Hapgood will preside. The Society is planning many activities including lectures by Russian scientists. A Russian exhibit is also being arranged . . . the Society will have a permanent program of work which will include the collection and diffusion in the U.S. of developments in science, education (etc.) . . . and an exchange of students and professors as well as scientists, artists and scholars as 'a practical way of promoting cultural relations between the two countries' is contemplated." In 1929 were listed:

President, William Allan Neilson (of Smith College); Vice-Presidents: John Dewey, Leopold Stokowski, Stephen P. Duggan, Floyd Dell, Lillian D. Wald; Treasurer, Allen Wardwell; Secretary, Lucy Branham; Chairman Executive Committee, Graham R. Taylor; Directors: Thos. L. Cotton, Jerome Davis, Ernestine Evans, Mrs. Norman Hapgood, Arthur Garfield Hays, Horace Liveright, Underhill Moore, Ernest M. Patterson, James N. Rosenberg, Lee Simonson, Edgar Varese, and the officers; Advisory Council: Jane Addams, Carl Alsberg, Franz Boas, Phillips Bradley, Stuart Chase, Haven Emerson, Zona Gale, Frank Golder, Mrs. J. Borden Harriman, David Starr Jordan, Alexander Kaun, Susan Kingsbury, Julia Lathrop, Eva Le Gallienne, Howard Scott Liddell, E. C. Lindeman, Jacob G. Lipman, Robert Littell, H. Adolphus Miller, Walter W. Pettit, Boardman Robinson, Clarence S. Stein, Lucy Textor, Wilbur K. Thomas, Harry Ward, William Allen White, and Lucy Wilson. Others listed in the various committees are: Joseph Achron, Sergei Radamsky, Kurt Schindler, Joseph Freeman, Oliver Sayler, Kurt Richter, Benj. M. Anderson, Jr., Gamaliel Bradford, Dorothy Brewster, Louise Fargo Brown, V. F. Calverton, Kate Holladay Claghorn, George A. Dorsey, W. E. Burghardt Du Bois, Edward Meade Earle, Haven Emerson, John Erskine, John Farrar, Harry Hansen, Sidney Howard, Horace M. Kallen, Joseph Wood Krutch, Joshua Kunitz, Fola LaFollette, Sinclair Lewis, Alain Locke, Robt. H. Lowie, Eugene Lyons, Chas. E. Merriam, Wesley C. Mitchell, Raymond Pearl, Walter W. Pettit, James Harvey Robinson, Mrs. K. N. Rosen, Edwin R. A. Seligman, Clarence Stein, Walter Stewart,

Louis Untermyer, Carl Van Doren, Mark Van Doren, Hendrik Willem Van Loon, Robert Woolfe, Stark Young, and Rosalind A. Zoglin. *The Chicago branch*: Chairman, Paul H. Douglas; Directors: Jane Addams, Clarence Darrow, Henry J. Freyn, Chas. E. Merriam; Executive Committee: Karl Borders, Chairman, Wm. Burton, Arthur Fisher, Lillian Herstein, Agnes Jacques, Stewart Leonard, A. D. Noe, Fred L. Schuman, Arvid B. Tanner; Treasurer, S. Jesmer. Chicago Hdqts. (1933), 38 S. Dearborn St., Room 765.

AMERICAN TEACHER

Monthly organ of the American Federation of Teachers; Florence Curtis Hanson, Executive Editor; Advisory Editorial Board: Henry R. Linville; Chas. B. Stillman, Chgo.; A. D. Sheffield, Wellesley College; Ruth Gillette Hardy, N.Y.; Selma M. Borchardt, Washington; Mary C. Barker, Atlanta; Lucie W. Allen, Chgo.; Editorial office, 506 S. Wabash Ave., Chgo.; features radical articles and upholds the principles of its organization (See "Am. Fed. of Tchrs.").

AMERICAN WORKERS PARTY

New name for A. J. Muste's Conf. for Prog. Lab. Action (see) 1933; a militant revolutionary party adhering neither to Second or Third International.

AMKINO

American representative of Sovkino, the Soviet government motion picture distributing agency.

AMKNIGA

Official book distributing agency of Soviet State Publishing House; N.Y. City.

AMNESTY COMMITTEE OF PEOPLES FREEDOM UNION

See "People's Freedom Union."

AMTORG TRADING CO.

The official Soviet government trading organization in the U.S.; sister organization of Arcos, Ltd., of England, which was raided in 1927 by British authorities and proven to be the headquarters and branch of the Communist International in England.

ANARCHISM AND ANARCHIST-COMMUNISM

Many anarchist groups (such as the Nihilists of Russia) might be described and their differences shown, but the first important anarchist movement in the U.S., which established several newspapers ("The Anarchist" at Boston, "The Arbeiter-Zeitung" at Chicago, and the "Voice of the People" at St. Louis), in 1883 at Pittsburg, issued, through twenty representatives, the following program: "(1) Destruction of the existing class rule by all means, i.e., energetic, relentless, revolutionary and international action. (2) Establishment of a free society, based upon cooperative organization of production. (3) Free exchange of equivalent products by and between productive organizations, without commerce and profit-mongering. (4) Organization of education on a secular, scientific and equal basis for both sexes. (5) Equal rights for all, without distinction of sex or race. (6) Regulation of all public affairs by free contacts between the autonomous (independent) communes and associations, resting on a federalistic basis." This, together with an appeal to workmen to organize, was published in Chicago (1883) by the local committee, among whom was August Spies, later convicted and executed for murder in connection with the anarchist Haymarket Riot of 1886. His widow spoke and was honored with a standing ovation at the Communist Mooney meeting May 1, 1933, at the Chicago Stadium. Anarchism has many points in common with the Socialist and Syndicalist programs, as is shown in the above Anarchist Manifesto. Subsequent American groups led by Emma Goldman and Alexander Berkman called their movement Anarchist-Communism (Lusk Report). Their official organs were "Mother Earth," "The Blast" (of Tom Mooney), and "Freedom." In the March 15, 1919 issue of "Freedom," Emma Goldman defined as follows: "Anarchist-Communism — Voluntary economic cooperation of all towards the needs of each. A social arrangement based on the principle: To each according to his needs; from each according to his ability."

The Garland Fund donated to the anarchist Ferrer School at Stelton, N.J., founded by Leonard D. Abbott, a N.Y. City branch of which was organized by Emma Goldman and Berkman. The Ferrer Assn. and Colony of about 300 houses was located at Stelton, but had branches in many parts of the country. The Ferrer Assn. was created as a memorial to the Spanish anarchist Francesco Ferrer, who was executed by his government. Harry Kelley was one of the trustees of the association and colony at Stelton, and editor (as he still is) of the Freedom magazine, published formerly at 133 E. 15th St., N.Y., the same place which housed the Union of Russian Workers, another anarchist association. The June 1, 1920 issue of Freedom praised the Liberator, Rebel Worker, Revolutionary Age, the Dial, World Tomorrow, Nation, New Republic, Survey, etc., saying: "These publications are doing excellent work in their several ways, and with much of that work we find ourselves in hearty agreement. They are, however, either liberal in the best sense of the word, Bolshevik or Socialist, and we are none of these, even if we look with a kindly eye on all of them. We are Anarchists, because we see in the State the enemy of liberty and human progress; and we are Communists, because we conceive Communism as the most rational and just economic theory yet proposed . . . As Anarchists we seek the abolition of the State or organized government, and would substitute for it a society founded upon the principles of voluntary association and free Communism. The Left Wing Socialists now advocate the same thing. So our differences are merely in the tactics pursued."

Emma Goldman in her essay "Anarchism," on page 59, said: "Religion, the dominion of the human mind; Property, the dominion of human needs; and Government, the dominion of human conduct, represent the stronghold of man's enslavement and all the horrors it entails"; and on page 134: "Indeed conceit, arrogance and egotism are the essentials of patriotism."

In her essay "Marriage and Love," she says, on page 242: "Love, the freest, the most powerful molder of human destiny; how can such an all-compelling force be synonomous with that poor little state and church-begotten weed, marriage?"; on page 72: "Direct action, having proven effective along economic lines is equally potent in the environment of the individual . . . Direct action against the authority in the shop, direct action against the authority of the law, direct action against the invasive meddlesome authority of our moral code" (she herself writes of the many men with whom she had intimate relations in her book "Living My Life") "is the logical, consistent method of Anarchism. Will it lead to a revolution? Indeed it will. No real social change has ever come without a revolution. People are either not familiar with their history, or they have not yet learned that revolution is but thought carried into action."

Acts of violence, such as her amour Berkman's stabbing and shooting of Frick, the steel magnate, as a protest against capitalism, are called "attentats" by Emma Goldman and her followers and are revered as heroic deeds in behalf of the "class struggle."

The Lusk Report cites an intercepted telegram of March 2, 1918 addressed to Leon Trotsky, Smolny Institute, Petrograd, from Leonard Abbott for the Ferrer Association, as follows: "Ferrer Association is with you to the death. Are forming Red Guards to help you defend the Revolution"; and another cablegram sent the same date by M. Eleanor Fitzgerald to Wm. Shatoff, Smolny Institute, Petrograd: "Mother Earth groups with our lives and our last cent are with you in your fight"; Lincoln Steffens was another of this group who sent a cablegram to Russia (March 4, 1918) with Louise Bryant, formerly wife of Communist John Reed and until recently wife of Wm. C. Bullitt, a radical who in 1919 was accompanied on an official mission to Russia by Lincoln Steffens. Bullitt has been chief advisor of the U.S. State Dept. by appointment of Pres. Roosevelt and is now Ambassador to Bolshevik Russia (1934). The Bryant-Steffens cablegram, addressed to Lenin and Trotsky, Smolny Institute, Petrograd, said: "Important you designate unofficial representative here who can survey situation, weigh facts and cable conclusions you might accept and act upon. Will undertake secure means of communication between such man and yourself." (Evidently Bullitt was the man.)

The Lusk Report (p. 860) says of Anarchist-Communism: "the interesting feature of this movement is the similarity of its methods and tactics with those of the Socialist Party, Communist groups and I.W.W. (1) It stands for the international solidarity of the working class. (2) It advocates industrial unionism as the best instrument for affecting the social revolution. (3) It advocates direct action, meaning thereby the general strike and sabotage. (4) It sympathizes with and supports Soviet Russia. (5) It advocates amnesty for so-called political prisoners. (6) It advocates the raising of the Russian blockade."

When Emma Goldman and Berkman were arrested for their seditious anti-war activities, the League for Amnesty of Political Prisoners was organized by their supporters. (See "Lg. for Amn. of Pol. Pris.")

Anarchists now and always cooperate with the Communists, Socialists and I.W. W.'s, in "united front" class war revolutionary activities. See "Free Society" and "Intl. Workingmens Assn.," American anarchist societies.

ANTI-FASCISTI LEAGUE OF NORTH AMERICA

A communist subsidiary (U.S. Fish Report). The German Anti-Fascisti League, Italian Anti-Fascisti League, etc., are sections.

ANTI-HORTHY LEAGUE

A Communist subsidiary (U.S. Fish Report).

ANTI-IMPERIALIST LEAGUE

The present title of the All-America Anti-Imperialist League (see).

ANTI-IMPERIALIST LEAGUE DELEGATION TO CUBA

The communist Daily Worker, Nov. 9, 1933, says, "a delegation representing the Anti-Imperialist League of the United States is sailing today for Cuba," and states that "the delegation plans to arrange numerous mass demonstrations in Havana and other cities" and is "bringing banners, letters and other expressions of warm revolutionary greetings and solidarity. . . . " The delegation consists of J. B. Matthews, Henry Shepard of the T.U.U.L., Geo. Powers, sec. shipyards division of Steel and Metal Wkrs. Indust. Union (Communist), Joe Thomas (T.U.U.L.), Harry Gannes of the Daily Worker, chmn., and Walter Rellis, student member already in Havana.

ARCOS, LIMITED

The Soviet government trading company of England; a sister organization to Amtorg in the U.S.; was raided in 1927 and documents seized revealed it to be the headquarters of the Communist International in England and gave proofs of the Red conspiracies against our own as well as England's government; because of this raid trade relations were severed between England and the U.S.S.R. until a Socialist Labor government again renewed them.

ASIATIC ASSOCIATION FOR THE ADVANCEMENT OF ATHEISM

Oriental atheist "missionary" society of the American Assn. for the Advancement of Atheism.

ASSOCIATION OF NEW CUBAN REVOLUTIONARY EMIGRANTS

Founded by Julio Antonio Mella, Cuban Communist leader; active in New York in association with the Spanish Workers Center. Mella was killed in Mexico some time ago and rioting occurred in Cuba, 1933, when Communists attempted to bring his remains back for a big Red burial demonstration.

ATHEIST PIONEERS

To promote atheism among primary school children; a 4A society.

AUTO WORKERS INDUSTRIAL UNION

Communist T.U.U.L. union; hdqts.: 4819 Hastings St. and 4210 Woodward Ave., Detroit, Mich., etc.

B

BAHAI INTERNATIONAL

An internationalist, pacifist, "religious" organization professing to accept and include persons of any or all religious beliefs—in other words the religion of the individual is his own affair; takes part in War Resisters International (see) conferences; the World Tomorrow, July 1933 issue, stated: "Members of the Bahai religion have recently been arrested in Turkey and will be brought to trial charged with 'aiding communism and internationalism' "; one branch is at Wilmette, Ill.

BERGER (VICTOR L.) NATIONAL FOUNDATION

Berger Nat. Found.

A Socialist organization "organized to honor the memory of the late Victor L. Berger. Its founders believe that this can be done best by rendering effective aid to those *minority causes* to which he devoted himself for four decades . . . by the building of a newspaper press which will mobilize public opinion in behalf of the ideals for which liberals, progressives and peace advocates contend." (From announcement of Victor L. Berger Foundation Dinner held at Morrison Hotel, Nov. 12, 1931.) The announcement does not dwell on Victor Berger's conviction for sedition and speeches favoring direct action and revolution, although "minority causes" is a polite phrase for "revolutionary causes." The "Statement of Clarence Darrow on accepting the presidency of the Victor L. Berger National Foundation" is printed as: "It is of paramount importance we establish our own press as quickly as possible. There is every evidence of the emergence of working class forces in this country. . . . I think the splendid work started by the late Victor L. Berger, of whose fearless independence I was an admirer, should be pushed with all possible energy"; it was founded Mar. 1, 1931 at the National Press

Club, Wash., D.C.; incorporated under the laws of the District of Columbia and its Dinner Announcement which scheduled as speakers at the Morrison Hotel, Nov. 12, 1931, Gov. Philip F. LaFollette, Mayor Daniel W. Hoan, Mrs. Meta Berger (Regent of Wis. U. and widow of Victor), Donald R. Richberg, Clarence Darrow, presiding, also listed as Officers:

Clarence Darrow, pres.; Jane Addams, John Dewey, Glenn Frank, Eliz. Gilman, James H. Maurer, Upton Sinclair, vice presidents; Marx Lewis, exec. dir.; Stuart Chase, treas.; B. C. Vladeck, Meta Berger, E. J. Costello, Thos. M. Duncan, Wm. T. Evjue, Sidney Hillman, Morris Hillquit, Daniel W. Hoan, Norman Thomas, Howard Y. Williams, as Board of Trustees, and a National Council as follows:

William J. Adames, Bernard M. Allen, Devere Allen, Rev. Peter Ainslie, Oscar Ameringer, Wood F. Axton, Forrest Bailey, Emily G. Balch, Joseph Baskin, Morris Berman, Rev. Herbert S. Bigelow, S. John Block, Cong. Gerald J. Boileau, Gladys Boone, William Bouck, A. P. Bowers, Paul F. Brissenden, Heywood Broun, Lewis Browne, Howard Brubaker, John P. Burke, Abraham Cahan, Stuart Chase, Henry S. Churchill, George A. Coe, Mabel Dunlap Curry, Jerome Davis, Paul H. Douglas, Daniel R. Donovan, W. E. B. Du Bois, Sherwood Eddy, George Clifton Edwards, Morris L. Ernst, Frederick V. Field, William Floyd, Zona Gale, Adolph Germer, Helen B. Gilman, Carl Henry Gleeser, Mrs. Henry Francis Grady, Florence Curtis Hanson, Rev. Otto R. Hauser, Dr. A. Eustace Haydon, Max S. Hayes, Arthur Garfield Hays, Adolph Held, Rabbi James G. Heller, Arthur E. Holder, Rev. John Haynes Holmes, Frederick C. Howe, Arthur Huggins, Fannie Hurst, Rabbi Edward L. Israel, Bishop Paul Jones, Vladimir Karapetoff, Paul U. Kellogg, Frederick M. Kerby, Casimir Kowalski, Elmer Krahn, Leo Krzycki, Harry W. Laidler, Prof. John A. Lapp, William Leiserson, Henry R. Linville, Owen R. Lovejoy, Robert Morss Lovett, Benjamin C. Marsh, John T. McRoy, Lucia Ames Mead, Alexander Meikeljohn, Darwin J. Meserole, Jacob C. Meyer, Henry Neumann, Reinhold Niebuhr, Edward N. Nockels, Henry J. Ohl, Jr., Joseph A. Padway, Kirby Page, Jacob Panken, Clarence E. Pickett, Amos R. E. Pinchot, Rabbi D. De Sola Pool, Jeannette Rankin, W. N. Reivo, Milo Reno, E. A. Ross, Charles Edward Russell, Mary R. Sanford, Benjamin Schlesinger, Rose Schneiderman, Vida D. Scudder, Emil Seidel, Rabbi Abba Hillel Silver, George Soule, Seymour Stedman, Morris Stern, Spencer Stoker, Helen Phelps Stokes, Augustus O. Thomas, Oswald Garrison Villard, H. J. Voorhis, Grace D. Watson, S. F. Weston, Rev. Eliot White, Charles H. Williams, James H. Wolfe, Abel Wolman, Leo Wolfsohn, S. N. Ziebelman, Phil E. Ziegler.

The following are listed in the dinner announcement as "Sponsors":

Mary M. Abbe, Jane Addams, Robert C. Beers, Carl Borders, M. O. Bousfield, Fritz Bremer, Charles H. Burr, Ralph Chaplin, Agnes B. Clohesy, Lenetta Cooper, Mrs. E. C. Costello, William A. Cunnea, Clarence Darrow, Paul E. Darrow, George E. Dawson, Arthur Fisher, John Fitzpatrick, John Fralick, Herbert J. Friedman, Judge E. Allen Frost, Denton L. Geyer, Rev. Charles W. Gilkey, M. Gitlitz, Morris Gold, Rabbi S. Goldman, Dr. R. B. Green, Margaret A. Haley, M. V. Halushka, Leon Hanock, N. M. Hanock, Florence Curtis Hanson, Dr. A. Eustace Haydon, Josef L. Hektoen, Lillian Herstein, Samuel H. Holland, William H. Holly, Paul Hutchinson, Newton Jenkins, M. B. Karman, Jesse T. Kennedy, S. J. Konenkamp, Casimir Kowalski, Carl Laich, Lloyd Lehman, Samuel Levin, Victor I. Levinson, Fay Lewis, Abraham Lidsky, Robert Morss Lovett, Theodore H. Lunde, Franklin Lundquist, Maurice Lynch, Mary E. McDowell, A. D. Marimpetri, Prof. Chas. E. Merriam, Agnes Nestor, Rev. J. Pierce Newell, Edward N. Nockels, Edwin P. Reese, Wallace Rice, Donald R. Richberg, William E. Rodriguez, Hayden J. Sanders, Stephen Skala, Dr. Ferdinand Schevill, Clarence Senior, Jacob Siegel, Morris Siskind, Peter Sissman, Donald Slesinger, Prof. T. V. Smith, Morris Spitzer, J. Edward Stake, Seymour Stedman, L. P. Straube, Duane Swift, Carl D. Thompson, Rev. Ernest Fremont Tittle, Irwin St. John Tucker, S. Turovlin, Daniel A. Uretz, Ethel Watson, Dorothy Weil.

National hdqts.; 907 15th St., N.W., Wash., D.C.; Western Office: 308 W. North Ave., Milwaukee, Wis.

BEZBOSHNIK

Russian Godless society; American branch of the official militant Communist anti-religious society; section of Proletarian Anti-Religious Lg.

BLUE BLOUSES

Communist agitational propaganda dramatic groups affiliated with League of Workers Theatres.

BONUS EXPEDITIONARY FORCES RANK AND FILE OF AMERICA

Formed by communist Workers Ex-Service Men's League; supporting org. of U.S. Congress Against War.

BRIDGMAN RAID

"The most colossal conspiracy against the U.S. in its history was unearthed at Bridgman, Mich., Aug. 22, 1922, when the secret convention of the Communist Party of America was raided by the Michigan constabulary, aided by county and Federal officials. Two barrels full of documentary proof of the conspiracy were seized and are in possession of the authorities. Names, records, checks from prominent people in this country, instructions from Moscow, speeches, theses, questionnaires—indeed the whole machinery of the underground organization, the avowed aim of which is the overthrow of the U.S. government, was found in such shape as to condemn every participant in the convention. . . . It is known that agents of Communists are working secretly through 'legal' bodies in labor circles, in society, in professional groups, in the Army and Navy, in Congress, in the schools and colleges of the country, in banks and business concerns, among the farmers, in the motion picture industry—in fact in nearly every walk of life. These agents are not 'low brows' but keen, clever, intelligent educated men and women. . . . They range from bricklayers to bishops and include many prominent official and society people. There were present besides Wm. Z. Foster, C. E. Ruthenberg, three times candidate for mayor of Cleveland; Ben Gitlow, N.Y. labor leader; Ella Reeve Bloor, who says she has been arrested more than a hundred times for radical agitation among workers; Robert Minor; J. Lovestone; Ward Brooks, direct representative of the Communist Intl., of Moscow; Boris Reinstein, representing the Red Trade Union Intl. of Moscow; Rose Pastor Stokes; Wm. F. Dunne; and many others. The seventeen arrested at or near Bridgman were Thos. Flaherty of N.Y.; Chas. Erickson, Chas. Krumbein, Eugene Bechtold" (Chgo. Wkrs. School now), "and Caleb Harrison of Chicago; Cyril Lambkin, W. Reynolds, Detroit; Wm. F. Dunne of Butte, Mont. and N.Y.; J. Mihelic, Kansas City; Alex. Ball, Phila.; Francis Ashworth, Camden, N.J.; E. McMillin, T. R. Sullivan and Norman H. Tallentire, St. Louis; Max Lerner, Seattle; and Zeth Nordling, Portland, Oregon," (from Whitney's "Reds in America"). This revolutionary Party frankly aiming to overthrow the U.S. Govt., compelled to meet in secret in 1922, is now on the ballot in 39 states, is mailing tons of treasonable literature through the U.S. mails, and is conducting schools of revolution without interference; after ten years, these Communists then arrested have had their cases brought up by Patrick H. O'Brien, A.C.L.U. attorney elected Attorney General of Michigan in 1932, and dismissed, thus releasing the bond money for the benefit of the Communists and other radicals; see Labor Defense Council and Garland Fund, for aid to Bridgman conspirators.

BROOKWOOD LABOR COLLEGE

A left wing Socialist school for training radical Negro and white agitators; located at Katonah, N.Y.; the American Labor Year Book states:

"During the summer of 1931, four members of the Brookwood staff assisted at the West Va. Mine Workers strike. Other faculty members taught at Barnard and Bryn Mawr summer schools and lectured at various summer institutes. Faculty for 1931-32 consisted of A. J. Muste, Chairman, Josephine Colby, David J. Saposs, Helen G. Norton, Mark Starr, and J. C. Kennedy, instructors; Cara Cook, Katherine Pollak and Lucile Kohn, assistants; Tom Tippett, extension director. Lecturers on special topics include Louis Budenz, Herbert S. Bigelow, Frank Palmer and Carl Haessler," and states that the American Federation of Teachers, the Conference for Progressive Labor Action, and Eastern States Cooperative League held conferences at Brookwood, 1931-32; see Garland Fund for bountiful aid it received.

After a row over policies in 1933, A. J. Muste resigned and Tom Tippett left to become educational director of the Progressive Miners Union at Gillespie, Ill., and Tucker P. Smith (of the C.M.E.) became director of Brookwood, and James H. Maurer, Pres.; Fannia M. Cohn, Vice Pres.; Bd. of Directors: Abraham Lefkowitz, John Brophy, Phil E. Zeigler, A. J. Kennedy, plus officers; Faculty: Tucker P. Smith, Director; Josephine Colby; David J. Saposs, Sec.; Helen G. Norton; Mark Starr, Extension Dir.; J. C. Kennedy, Dir. of Studies.

BROTHERHOOD OF SLEEPING CAR PORTERS

See under "Messenger."

BUILDING MAINTENANCE WORKERS UNION

Communist union of the T.U.U.L.

C

CAMPS NITGEDAIGET

Communist camps near N.Y., Chicago, Lumberville, Pa., Wash., D.C., Detroit, Birmingham, etc.; run by the communist Jewish "United Workers Cooperative Assn." The camp near Chicago for example is located on Paddock Lake 14 miles west of Kenosha, Wis. and occupies about 205 acres; accommodates 500 to 600 people from July 4, to Nov. 1; a Young Pioneer Camp has been held here for the past two years (under direction, 1933, of Comrade Levine of the Young Communist League); vicious dogs guard the place and no autos except those belonging to the camp are allowed in the grounds; there is an auditorium seating 500 people with stage, piano, etc.; has new bath house, a swimming tank, 5 boats; Comrade Hels of Chgo. in charge of it is reported to have claimed "the damned dirty Legion burned it"; it has been burned three times and each time rebuilt bigger and better; Miss Litzinger of Kenosha is reported to be office secretary.

CAMP UNITY

At Wingdale, N.Y.; Communist T.U.U.L. Camp.

CATHOLIC ASSOCIATION FOR INTERNATIONAL PEACE

Pacifist - internationalist organization; composed, no doubt, for the most part of perfectly sincere, non-radical, Christian pacifists. However, Rev. John A. Ryan, chmn. of its Ethics Committee, is at the same time one of three book editors (with E. F. Tittle and Edw. Israel) of the very radical National Religion and Labor Foundation and responsible for distributing such Communist literature as Wm. Z. Foster's "Toward Soviet America"; John A. Lapp, of its Intl. Law and Organization Committee, is on the exec. com. of the same National Religion and Labor Foundation; Both Lapp and Ryan were, in 1923, on the Labor Defense Council (see) (now Communist I.L.D.), formed to defend Wm. Z. Foster and other Communists; James E. Hagerty, of its Economics Relations Committee, is at the same time Hon. Pres. of the National Religion and Labor Foundation, which also disseminates red revolutionary propaganda, Communist cartoons of Jesus, etc. (see); and Patrick H. Callahan, of its Com. on Dependencies, is also on the exec. com. of the same National Religion and Labor Foundation; Prof. Carlton J. H. Hayes (see "Who's Who"), whose activity in behalf of the I.W.W. is cited in the Lusk Report, serves as chmn. of one and member of several other of its committees; Rev. R. A. McGowan, a committee chmn., was the fellow spokesman with the A.C.L.U. group (Edw. I. Israel, Bishop Francis J. McConnell, etc.) at the Hearing on admission of Prof. Macintosh, radical pacifist, to U.S. citizenship without promise to defend this Govt. by arms (June 1932 A.C.L.U. Report, p. 36; also see facsimile of A.C.L.U. letter); Parker T. Moon, pres., is author of "Imperialism and World Politics," which was part of the socialist L.I.D. program of reading for 1927-8; Edw. Keating (see "Who's Who"), active member of radical organizations, serves on its Com. on Economic Relations; Rev. Francis Haas, a vice pres., is classified as "radical" by Advisory Associates, serving in radical company as Roosevelt appointee to the NRA Labor Board (with Leo Wolman, Rose Schneidermann, etc.).

I heard Rev. J. W. Maguire of its Com. on Economic Relations, who is pres. of St. Viator's College, in action when he oratorically and vehemently pleaded at the Springfield Legislative Hearing, May 1933, in company with Pres. Hutchins of the U. of Chicago (where Communism is a recognized student activity), against the passage of the Baker Bills (to penalize the teaching of seditious Communism in Illinois colleges). He said that if passed these Bills might even make him trouble as some people considered him a dangerous radical. He also advanced the anarchistic argument that no one should be forced to obey a law against his own conscience. At this, Senator Barr asked him which of our laws he would refuse to obey. After this Hearing, at which I testified in favor of the Bills to curb Communism, I expressed to Rev. Maguire my respect for his Church, having attended a convent school myself, and my surprise and disappointment to find him on the side of those fighting for freedom to teach Communism and destroy Christian faith in our colleges.

There is however no finer, truer Christian and American than Rev. Edmund A. Walsh, author and opponent of Soviet recognition, who is a member of this Catholic Assn. Whether or not its Esperanto connections are with the international Red Esperanto groups I have not ascertained.

CENTRAL COOPERATIVE WHOLESALE (FORMERLY CENTRAL COOPERATIVE EXCHANGE)

Of Superior, Wis.; affiliated with the Workers and Farmers Cooperative Alliance, which is a branch of the communist T.U.U.L.; a communistic group that has had three Communist Party members on its board of directors; sells food products to 97 member societies with the Soviet emblems, hammer and sickle and red star, branded on them; maintains organizers and conducts conferences and summer schools with the affiliated Northern States Cooperative League; is dedicated to the "class struggle"; it, and its affiliates, the Cooperative League of U.S.A. and Northern States Cooperative League, received money from the Garland Fund; its affiliated Cooperative Trading Co. of Waukegan, Ill., organized Cooperative Unemployed Leagues, affiliated with Borders' Communist - I.W.W. - controlled Federated Unemployed Leagues (see), in every community in Lake County, 1932-3; the 1932 American Labor Year Book reports internal friction over control of the administration between Socialists and Communists; the report of the Communist International of 1928 said on p. 346; "the Central Cooperative Exchange is a left wing organization." . . . (See Cooperative Lg. of U.S.A.); its organ "Cooperative Builder" is sold at Communist bookstores.

CHICAGO ATHEIST FORUMS

It is estimated that some fifteen or sixteen atheist forums are being conducted at various of the 70 local Chicago Communist headquarters, Sunday afternoons. One, which is plainly advertised each Saturday in the Chicago Daily News, is conducted by the American Assn. for the Advancement of Atheism, at 357 Chicago Ave., Communist Party local hdqts. Speakers for 1933: Haldeman-Julius, Rev. Norman Barr, Prof. Frank Midney, Dr. Percy Ward, Neal Ness, Rev. Aronson, etc. Only atheist literature and the Communist Daily Worker are sold at these meetings. On Nov. 12, 1933, the atheist speaker used vile obscene language in ridiculing the Christian religion, and the existence of God. His opponent, Rev. L. Hoover, made a weak plea for the existence of a power called God as evidenced in viewing sunsets, etc. This the atheist was given the opportunity to ridicule vigorously. The hall is decorated with communist Russian posters, I.L.D. and T.U.U.L. local branch signs, Workers Theatre announcements; a big red paper bow drapes the top of the stage; and a black board lists meetings and speakers of the communist Unemployed Councils, which meet there. On Nov. 12, the name of "James M. Yard, D.D." was chalked up as speaker for Nov. 15. (See under "Who's Who.")

CHICAGO CITY CLUB CONSTITUTIONAL RIGHTS COMMITTEE

Purposes similar to and cooperates with A.C.L.U.; formed 1932; hdqts.: City Club, 315 Plymouth Court, Chgo. At the City Club, the "Workers Training School" of the C.W.C. on Unemp., A.C.L.U. and L.I.D. meetings are also held.

CHICAGO COMMITTEE FOR STRUGGLE AGAINST WAR

See under "Intl., American and Chicago Committees for Struggle Against War."

CHICAGO COMMITTEE TO AID VICTIMS OF GERMAN FASCISM

Chicago section of the Nat. Com. to Aid Victims of German Fascism (see) of communist W.I.R.; hdqts. Room 310—208 N. Wells St., Chicago; organ "Anti-Fascist Action."

CHICAGO EMERGENCY COMMITTEE FOR STRIKERS RELIEF

See under Emergency Committee for Strikers Relief.

CHICAGO FORUM COUNCIL

An intellectual agency propagandizing socialistic communistic doctrines; organized about 1925; merged with the Adult Education Council, about 1929; directed then and now by Fred Atkins Moore (of the Chicago A.C.L.U. Committee and communist Nat. Council for Protection of Foreign Born Workers); operates the Chicago Forum, which features the reddest of Communist and Socialist speakers; publishes "Educational Events," a bulletin widely distributed, announcing radical meetings and forums; sponsors radio broadcasts of radical speakers and conducts a speakers bureau. In 1928 among council members were:

Arthur Fisher, Louis L. Mann, John A. Lapp, Herbert J. Friedman (president), Wm. H. Holly, Jessie Binford, Horace Bridges, Wm. E. Dodd, Paul Douglas, Rev. Chas. W. Gilkey, A. L. Jackson, Robt. Morss Lovett, Mary E. McDowell, Chas. Clayton Morrison, Curtis Reese, Amelia Sears, Jane Addams, Rev. E. F. Tittle, Harold L. Ickes, (all A.C.L.U.), Henry P. Chandler, "liberalizer of the Union League Club," Rev. Norman Barr, John Fitzpatrick, Ann Guthrie, Solomon B. Freehof, Mrs. B. F. Langworthy, Salmon O. Levinson, Frank Orman Beck (Reconciliation Trips director), James Mullenbach, Agnes Nestor, Mordecai Shulman, Graham Taylor, David Rhys Williams, Dr. Rachelle S. Yarros, Samuel Levin, Charles E. Merriam (see "Who's Who" for these), S. J. Duncan-Clark, etc.

The 1933 program featured as speakers:

Communists Anna Louise Strong and John Strachey; Socialists Sherwood Eddy, Norman Thomas, etc.; our Assistant "Commissar" of Agriculture, Rex. G. Tugwell; Dr. Alfons Goldschmidt, Red professor "welcomed" out of Germany; James Weldon Johnson of the Garland Fund, etc. and names as the managing committee: Wm. H. Holly, chmn. and Lillian Herstein, vice chmn. (both members of Communist and Socialist organizations); Mrs. Beatrice Hayes Podell, sec.; R. G. Sathoff, treas.; Chas. W. Balch, Benj. Baltzer, Howard S. Bechtolt, Edith Benjamin, R. E. Blount, Fred Chayes, Mrs. Eli Daiches, Rev. Theodore C. Hume,* Chas. E. Lewis, Mrs. Fred Lowenthal,* Abraham Nechin, Mrs. M. D. Neufield, Mr. and Mrs. Edw. W. Ohrenstein, Geo. C. Olcott, Mrs. Glenn E. Plumb, Chas. A. Snyder, C. Francis Stradford, Chas. E. Suiter, Grace W. Weller, W. H. Wickersham, Dr. Walter Verity; Hdqts.: 224 S. Michigan Ave.; Director, Fred Atkins Moore.* (*Listed in this "Who's Who.")

CHICAGO LABOR RESEARCH

Chicago branch of the Labor Research, Inc.; collects material for Communist speakers, trade unions, organizers, etc.; hdqts. Chicago Workers School, 2822 S. Michigan Ave.

CHICAGO LAWYERS CONSTITUTIONAL RIGHTS COMMITTEE

Purposes similar to and cooperates with A.C.L.U.; formed 1932; Hdqts.: Leon M. Despres, 77 W. Washington St., Chgo.

CHICAGO WORKERS COMMITTEE ON UNEMPLOYMENT

C.W.C. on Unemp.

Claims sixty Locals with 20,000 members in Chicago; headed by Karl Borders and organized by him originally as a subsidiary of the socialist League for Industrial Democracy (L.I.D.) Chicago branch to capitalize upon unemployment by organizing the unemployed, ostensibly to aid them but at the same time to endoctrinate and finally align them with the Socialist movement. It is represented on the board of the Federation of Unemployed Organizations of Cook County headed by Communist Karl Lochner and both organizations are affiliated with the national Federation of Unemployed Workers Leagues (See) of which Karl Borders was national chairman until May 1933, when the convention held at Lincoln Center, Chicago, May 13, 14, 15, elected a controlling board of Communist, Proletarian (communist-supporting) and I.W.W. officers. This indicates the present marked drawing together of revolutionary forces for united action (See this also under Socialism, U.S. Congress Against War, etc.). The C.W.C. on Unemp. conducted a "Workers Training School" beginning March 30, 1933 at the Chicago City Club with Prof. Maynard C. Krueger teaching "New Economics for Old," Lillian Herstein "The Class Struggle in American History," W. B. Waltmire "How to Organize," etc., at which representatives of the Educational Committees of the Locals were expected to be present. Fortnightly Executive Committee meetings are held at Graham Taylor's Chicago Commons, 955 W. Grand Ave., of which Karl Borders is assistant head resident. W. B. Waltmire is chairman of this "Workers Training School" and when the C.W.C. on Unemp. cooperated with the Communist Party in staging the Chicago Oct. 31, 1932 "Hunger March" in which hundreds of revolutionary placards and Soviet emblems and flags were carried, Waltmire was spokesman before the Mayor for the demonstrators. The official organ is the "New Frontier," a fortnightly paper which publishes such propaganda as the Communist revolutionary songs "Red Flag" and "Internationale" and the I.W.W. song "Solidarity" by Ralph Chaplin (who served 5 years in the Penitentiary for seditious activities), and urges members to paste these songs in their hats, sing them in the bathtub, and learn them so they can "raise the roof" with them at the meetings (See Mar. 4, 1933 issue). Published at 20 W. Jackson Blvd., Chicago, L.I.D. headquarters; editor Robt. E. Asher; mg. ed. John Paul Jones; circ. mgr. C. W. Fisher; ed. bd.; Karl Borders, W. B. Waltmire, Glenford Lawrence, Chas. Williams, Harry Roberts.

The 60 Chicago C.W.C. on Unemp. Locals meet according to the "New Frontier" at the following places:

Lincoln Center; New England Congl. Church, 19 E. Delaware Place; Jefferson Pk. Congl. Church, 5320 Giddings St.; Baptist Church, 670 E. 39th St.; Graham Taylor's Chicago Commons; Olivet Institute; Ogden Park Meth. Church; Chase House (Episc.); Workers Progressive Club, 608 N. Leavitt St.; Pilgrim Congl. Church; Hyde Pk. Neighborhood Club, 1364 E. 56th St.; Hull House; Christopher House; Marcy Center; Hermosa Park Field House; Howell Neighborhood House; Garibaldi Institute; Trumbull Pk. Field House; Association House; Eli Bates House; U. of Chgo. Settlement; Emerson House; etc., etc.

The *Executive* is Karl Borders, 20 W. Jackson Blvd., Chicago; *Committee Chairmen:* L. C. Brooks, G. B. Patterson, W. D. Hogan, W. H. Seed, Glenford Lawrence, D. S. Howard; *Executive Committee:* Rev. W. B. Waltmire, Lester Dewey, vice chmn., Winifred Frost, sec., Frank W. McCulloch (son of Catherine Waugh), treas., Norman Buending, E. J. Cook, Annetta Dieckmann, Ray Jacobson, John Paul Jones, G. B. Patterson, Moderato Renzi, Hyman Schneid, T. M. Torgerson, Vincent Wojdinski; *Advisory Committee:* Rev. Norman Barr, Jessie Binford, Prof. Sophonisba P. Breckenridge, C. F. Case, Geo. E. Chant, Prof. Paul Douglas, Hilda R. Diamond, Prof. Aaron Director, Adolph Dreifuss, Arthur Fisher, A. L. Frost, Anton Garden, Frank Z. Glick, Edw. Hammond, Prof. Arthur E. Holt, Mrs. H. R. Henshaw, Paul Hutchinson, Florence Jennison, Harold Kelso, Marjorie Kemp, Rev. Harold O. Kingsley, A. M. Krahl, Dr. John A. Lapp, Glenford Lawrence, Samuel Levin, Judith Lowenthal, Prof. Robt. Morss Lovett, David McVey, Rev. Victor Marriott, Dr. James Mullenbach, Rev. D. M. Nichol, Rev. Raymond P. Sanford, Sarah B. Schaar, William Seed, Clarence Senior (nat. sec., Socialist Party), Lea D. Taylor (daughter of Graham), Harriet Vittum, John Werlik, Edward Winston, Dr. James Yard.

CHICAGO WORKERS THEATRE

Local branch of the Communist "League of Workers Theatres of the U.S.A.," which is the American section of the "International Union of the Revolutionary Theatre" headed at Moscow; Chicago headquarters John Reed Club (Communist), 1475 South Michigan Ave.; the official Chicago Communist newspaper, "Workers Voice," announced Jan. 21, 1933: "The Workers Theatre of Chicago, a revolutionary group and the first of its kind in the city was launched by John Reed Club which took the lead in its formation and which regarded the step as a potent weapon of the toiling masses in their struggle against capitalism. . . . Leading players from the universities, Lincoln Center and the Jewish Peoples Institute crowded John Reed Club headquarters, 1475 S. Michigan Ave., on a bitterly cold night to discuss plans for the theatre. A production committee . . . was elected to carry out . . . casting for the first play 'Precedent,' a drama by I. J. Golden dealing with the Tom Mooney frameup." This play was presented at the Goodman Theatre, Grant Park, as the first of the series. Patriotic efforts, it was reported, caused the Goodman Theatre to cancel the lease after two performances, but at the Communist May Day Mooney Rally at the Chicago Stadium, May 1, 1933, tickets were being sold for this play to be given at the Chicago Woman's Club that same week; sponsors of the communist Chicago Workers Theatre as listed by their announcements are as follows:

Sherwood Anderson, Waldo Frank, Prof. Eustace Haydon, Prof. Scott Nearing, Prof. Louis Wirth, Malcolm Cowley, Michael Gold, Mary McDowell, Dr. Curtis Reese, Prof. James M. Yard, Jacob L. Crane, Albert Goldman, Prof. Harold Lasswell, Prof. Fred L. Schuman, Prof. Robt. Morss Lovett.

CHINA FORUM

Communist Shanghai publication (in English) published by an American, Harold R. Isaacs, 23 Yuen Ming Yuen Road, Shanghai, China.

CHINESE ANTI-IMPERIALIST ALLIANCE

Branch of A.A.A.I. Lg. of U.S.

CHRISTIAN CENTURY

Classified by Smith-Johns (in "Pastors, Politicians and Pacifists") as a "pro-Russian, revolutionary, religious weekly"; features Socialist and Communist articles such as "The Communist Way Out" by Communist Scott Nearing (Oct. 12, 1932 issue), etc.

Editor, Chas. Clayton Morrison; mng. ed., Paul Hutchinson; lit. ed., Winifred Ernest Garrison; contrib. eds.: Lynn Harold Hough, Alva W. Taylor, Herbert L. Willett, Fred Eastman, Reinhold Niebuhr, Joseph Fort Newton, Thos. Curtis Clark, Robt. A. Ashworth; hdqts.: 440 S. Dearborn Street, Chicago.

Chas. Clayton Morrison presided at the huge Communist meeting, Oct. 23, 1933, at the Chicago Coliseum, held to honor and hear Henri Barbusse, French visiting Communist, founder of the Ex-Service Men's International, which teaches soldiers of all armies to "turn an imperialist war into a civil war" or red revolution by shooting their officers in the backs, as they did in Russia, and blowing up their country's ammunition, etc. at the right moment. Only the red flag of revolution was displayed and the International sung at this meeting, attended by about 9,000 Reds (and myself). Morrison was cheered when he said we would never have peace until the capitalist system was abolished! In introducing the various Communist speakers, he referred to Joseph Freeman of the communist "New Masses" as his "fellow editor."

"The Christian Century," March 29, 1933, p. 433, under the heading "Methodist Bishop Attacks The Christian Century," stated: "In a mid-year letter to Methodist ministers in the Omaha area Bishop Frederick D. Leete warns them against reading The Christian Century and certain books, unspecified, published by the Methodist book concern: 'Fellow-preachers,' says the bishop, 'we will do better work if our reading is spiritual rather than materialistic, critical and weak in faith in the great essentials. I find evidence and hear reports which I feel I ought to pass on to the effect that The Christian Century is doing Methodism and the church in general little good. Some of our pastors tell me they have decided not to support it further. Some books even from our own firm, seem to me injurious. I am determined to supply my mind with the most strengthening food.' "

CHRISTIAN SOCIAL ACTION MOVEMENT

Chr. Soc. Act. M.

A movement to introduce Socialism-Communism into churches, according to its "Leaders Handbook," sold at Methodist Board of Education hdqts., 740 Rush St., Chicago (price 15c); organized April 1932 by a conference of 84 ministers, their wives, and laymen, fourteen of these giving "740 Rush Street" as address; the handbook anounces that "A Socialist Minister's Protective Association, with 21 charter members was formed. . . . The purpose of the Assn. is to provide emergency maintenance for any member who loses his job because of social interest and activity. For detailed information inquiry may be made of the Rev. W. B. Waltmire, Humboldt Pk. Community Church, Chicago."

This precaution is not surprising in view of the program outlined in the handbook, which gives detailed instructions for conducting unemployed "hearings," conferences, mid-week discussion meetings, dramatics, games, calling attention in sermons to a rack of Communist and Socialist literature to be placed in the Church for reading, and numerous other schemes for definitely propagandizing the belief that our American "capitalistic" social system has permanently collapsed and that Socialism must be substituted for it. The books recommended for reading by Church people are by such authors as Atheist-Socialist Haldeman-Julius, atheistic Communists Robt. W. Dunn, Scott Nearing, Grace Hutchins, Anna Rochester, Charlotte Todes, and M. Ilin of Russia (Geo. S. Counts' translation), and radicals Norman Thomas, Harry Ward, Kirby Page, Sherwood Eddy, James Weldon Johnson, Winthrop Lane, Oscar Ameringer, Paul Douglas, the Webbs (English radicals), G. B. Shaw, H. W. Laidler, Maurice Hindus, Stuart Chase, Arthur Garfield Hays, Raushenbush, Meiklejohn, etc.; and also A.C.L.U. pamphlets.

Under "Resource Agencies," are listed the leading radical organizations such as the League for Industrial Democracy, Fellowship of Reconciliation, Committee on Militarism in Education, Methodist Federation for Social Service, etc. Observance of the "first of May Labor Day" (the Communist Labor Day) is advised.

The following are characteristic excerpts from this "Leaders Handbook": "Progressive Steps Toward Socialism (1) Uplift and coercion. Our task is to get underneath the victims of our present order and lift up and get above and *press down.*" (Most capitalists are well pressed down now it would seem and because of that the job holders suffer.) "Industrial Justice cannot be secured without coercion." (Coercion is a polite word for a Socialist program); "(4) Political Organization: Workers must be organized into a political party." (The un-American idea of joining church and state in politics); (p. 58). "Foment Discontent. There is great danger religion may be 'the opium of the people'" (quoting atheist Karl Marx), "it is the duty of the Church to stimulate the spirit of protest and revolt within the breasts of impoverished men and women; (12) That all ministers who are willing to participate actively in the industrial conflict register with the Methodist Federation for Social Service . . . to act as arbitrators or as actual participants in the distribution of literature, parading, speaking, picketing," etc.; (p. 58) "Minority groups: The local church should cooperate with all those organizations in the community which are seeking basic changes in the economic order." (Socialists, Communists, Anarchists, I.W.W.'s are such "minority groups," and advocate "basic changes" involving sedition and revolution.) "The church building should be made available as a meeting place for such groups whenever there is a denial of free speech. Wherever there is no agency to call a meeting of protest in the event of violation of human rights and civil liberties, ministers and churches should take the initiative in so doing." ("Free speech" is the battle cry of all Reds favoring sedition and revolution.) The conference, in this handbook, thanks those who "so generously contributed time, effort and expert information" to make it a success, naming as "good angels": Kirby Page, Arthur E. Holt, J. Stitt Wilson, Paul Hutchinson, Clarence Tucker Craig, Karl Borders, David Shillinglaw, Wm. C. Bonner, F. S. Deibler and Clarence Senior.

The chairman of the Christian Social Action Movement is Gilbert S. Cox; Secretary, Owen M. Geer, 740 Rush St., Chgo.; Executive Committee: Ross Conner, Whitewater, Wis.; J. Pierce Newell, Rockford, Ill.; Paul Hutchinson, Chgo.; John C. Irwin, 740 Rush St., Chgo.; Douglas Anderson, Illiopolis, Ill.; W. B. Waltmire, Chgo.; B. E. Kirkpatrick, 740 Rush St., Chgo.; Wade Crawford Barclay, 740 Rush St., Chgo.; O. W. Auman, 740 Rush St., Chgo.; Editorial Committee: Alice B. Mallory, Elmhurst, Ill., and several of the executive committee members. Other committee members listed are: Gross W. Alexander, Fresno, Cal.; Lester Auman, Jamaica, N.Y.; E. W. Blakeman, Wesley Foundation, Ann Arbor, Mich.; Karl Borders, Chicago; E. A. Brown, Cleveland, Ohio; Harold C. Case, Glencoe, Ill.; Richard Decker, Auburn, Wash.; R. O. Hills, Casper, Wyo.; Theo. Miner, Saltsburg, Pa.; R. B. Porter, Eugene, Ore.; Harry O. Ritter, St. Louis, Mo.; Chas. Schofield, Ft. Collins, Colo.; Benj. Schwartz, Muscatine, Ia.; Carl C. Seitter, Los Angeles, Cal.; Paul J. Snyder, Minneapolis, Minn.; J. Stitt Wilson, Berkeley, Cal.

Other conference members listed are:

James Asher, St. Paul, Minn.; Carl Asmus, Stevens Pt., Wis.; G. E. Bailey, Minneapolis, Minn.; Chas. F. Boss, Jr., 740 Rush St., Chicago; Mr. and Mrs. Chester L. Bower, Chgo.; Ina C. Brown, Nashville, Tenn.; Dan B. Brummitt, 740 Rush St., Chgo.; Geo. A. Burcham, Evanston, Ill.; Roy E. Burt, 740 Rush St., Chgo.; Mrs. Roy E. Burt, Chicago; Fay Butler, Los Angeles, Cal.; Mark Chamberlain, S. Milwaukee, Wis.; Clarence Tucker Craig, Oberlin, O.; Lewis H. Davis, Long Island, N.Y.; Nellie M. Day, Chicago; Merle N. English, 740 Rush St., Chicago; Mrs. M. N. English, Chicago; Carl Gamer, Mazon, Ill.; Ruth C. Geer, Elmhurst, Ill.; Mrs. U. S. Grant, Evanston, Ill.; W. E. J. Gratz, 740 Rush St., Chicago; Earl C. Heck, Westchester, N.Y.; Chas. Hempstead, Cleveland, Ohio; E. C. Hickman, St. Paul, Minn.; Carl Hutchinson, Chicago; Geo. B. Jones, Brook, Ind.; C. C. Jordan, Gary, Ind.; Andrew Juvinall, Evanston, Ill.; Clyde Keegan, Boulder, Colo.; H. R. Kelley, Centralia, Ill.; Roy Kelley, 740 Rush St., Chgo.; A. E. Kirk, 740 Rush St., Chgo.; Mrs. B. E. Kirkpatrick, Chgo.; Clyde

Little, DeSoto, Mo.; Wm. Matson, Huntington Beach, Cal.; Frank M. McKibben, Evanston, Ill.; Wendell Miller, Harbor City, Cal.; Lester R. Minion, Polo, Ill.; Floyd Morris, Jacksonville, N.Y.; Ruth Morton, Chicago; T. Otto Nall, 740 Rush St., Chicago; Kirby Page, N.Y. C.; Mary Randolph, 740 Rush St., Chicago; Victor H. Reiser, Waveland, Ind.; Paul A. Schlipp, College of the Pacific, Stockton, Cal.; Joseph Sefl, Chicago; Russel Stroup, Balboa, Cal.; A. E. Tink, West Bend, Wis.; Mrs. Geo. H. Tomlinson, Evanston, Ill.; Frank Toothaker, Hynes, Cal.; Vernon C. Tyree, Delta, Colo.; W. D. Waller, Santa Fe, N.M.; E. C. Wareing, Cincinnati, Ohio; Morgan Williams, Chicago, Ill.; Roland Wolseley, Evanston, Ill.; James M. Yard, Evanston, Ill.

The handbook states on page 48 that invitations to this conference were sent "only to those who were socially awakened; had already done a good deal of thinking on social and economic questions; who were ready to start with the assumption that the present system is basically wrong, . . . " etc.

CHURCH EMERGENCY COMMITTEE FOR RELIEF OF TEXTILE STRIKERS

Ch. Emer. Com. Rel. Textile Strik.

Formed to aid the jointly-conducted Communist and Socialist strike at Danville Va., of the United Textile Workers Union and communist National Textile Workers Union; hdqts.: 287 4th Ave., N.Y.C.; includes: Dr. Alva W. Taylor, chmn., Rev. Wm. B. Spofford, treas., Rev. James Myers, Rev. W. Russel Bowie, Winifred Chappell, Jerome Davis, Mary Dreier, Rev. Hubert Herring, Rev. Ronald Tamblyn, Rev. Worth M. Tippy, Rev. Chas. Webber.

CHURCH LEAGUE FOR INDUSTRIAL DEMOCRACY

Ch. L.I.D.

An Episcopal Socialist organization using L.I.D. literature; it absorbed the Church Socialist League (see); was formed in 1920 by members of the A.C.L.U. and L.I.D.; the pres. was Rev. Edw. L. Parsons; chmn. Vida Scudder; treas. Geo. Foster Peabody; asst. treas. Rev. Horace Fort; sec. Rev. Wm. B. Spofford; now headed by Rev. Wm. B. Spofford; claims about 1,000 members.

The following excerpts are from the "Statement of Principles" of the Church L.I.D.: "We face a world in revolution. . . . We believe that the Church is ready and anxious to discover how it can best be useful in forwarding the New Order; and we therefore pledge ourselves to help the great mass of Church people who are as yet uncertain how to find the way. . . . In case of teachers and preachers in our communion whose positions are endangered by reason of their social radicalism we promise . . . to give moral and practical support to those who shall clearly be seen to have incurred persecution through advising of social change. . . . We further intend to assist in recruiting such candidates for the ministry as shall enter it with desire for socialized leadership."

To quote from an "Open Letter to Members of the Protestant Episcopal Church," issued by The Movement Against Socialism in the Church, 18 Tremont Street, Room 732, Boston, Mass. (Page 8): "The first convention of the Church League for Industrial Democracy, at New York, was addressed by the conspicuous radical agitators, the Rev. Harry F. Ward, Chairman of the American Civil Liberties Union (hereinafter called A.C.L.U.); Lincoln Steffens, magazine writer; James H. Maurer, of the communist Trades Union Educational League, who seems to have signed the call for the convention, and others. Professor Vida D. Scudder, of Wellesley College, an officer of both the League for Industrial Democracy (hereinafter called L.I.D.) and A.C.L.U., and the Rev. Horace Fort, also of the L.I.D., are, or were, officers of the Church League for Industrial Democracy (hereinafter called C.L.I.D.). Its Executive Secretary, the Rev. William B. Spofford, wrote of it under date of June 1, 1926, in answer to an inquiry, as follows: 'The Church *Socialist* League, to which you addressed your letter, was disbanded last year; the members at that time joining the C.L.I.D. We felt that there was hardly room in the Episcopal Church for two organizations with ***practically the same aim***. . . . We are people who are classed all the way from liberals to *communists*.' (Italics ours.) Another letter from Mr. Spofford, printed in the Twentieth Aniversary booklet of the L.I.D. says: 'At a meeting of the Executive Committee of the C.L.I.D. recently, it was decided that there was little use for publications of our own, so long as the L.I.D. continued to get out such splendid pamphlets, which could be purchased for distribution at low cost.' "

CHURCH SOCIALIST LEAGUE (EPISCOPAL)

Organized 1911 by Episcopal clergy and laymen; its national secretary, Rev. Byron-Curtiss, in a report in the radicals' American Labor Year Book (volume II, pp.

358-60) said: "In spite of the conservatism of the Episcopal Church and its members yet that church has officially adopted radical and even revolutionary resolutions and the influence of the Church Socialist League is discernible as giving color to them. A considerable share of the clergy are tinctured with Socialism. With but 6,000 clergy, several hundred are avowed Socialists and nearly one hundred are members of the Socialist Party"; the official organ was the quarterly "The Social Preparation," which asserted: "We are not reformers trying to patch up an out worn garment but revolutionists"; a meeting of the League held at the Rand School, June 29, 1919, issued a radical manifesto calling for a "complete revolution of our present economic and social disorder," etc., and sent a message to Pres. Wilson expressing absolute sympathy with the Soviet government of Russia and asking him to cease intervention in Russia (Lusk Report). Those who signed this manifesto and in whose behalf Reverends Smiley and Spofford sent the message to Pres. Wilson were: Reverends John Paul Jones, J. P. Morris, Chas. H. Collett, James L. Smiley, Wm. B. Spofford, J. G. Mythen, Alfred Pridis, Irwin St. John Tucker (convicted that year of sedition), A. L. Byron-Curtiss, Horace Fort, Robt. Johnson, Richard M. Doubs, Alfred Farr, Geo. J. Miller, and John M. Horton; the League was absorbed by the Church League for Industrial Democracy about 1920 (see above).

CHURCH TAXATION LEAGUE

Sponsored by 4A and other radicals.

CHU SING YOUTH ASSOCIATION

Chinese Communist subsidiary; headquarters H. T. Chang, P. O. Box 2454, San Francisco, California.

CLARTÉ

French Communist club, 30 W. 58th St., N.Y. City; part of the Clarté Movement formed by Henri Barbusse. Associated with him were the writers: Anatole France, Jules Romains, Thos. Hardy, and H. G. Wells (Daily Worker, Sept. 29, 1933).

CLEANERS, DYERS AND PRESSERS UNION

Communist T.U.U.L. union; 223 Second Ave., N.Y. City.

CLEVELAND TRADE UNION CONFERENCE

Aug. 29-30, 1933; called by about thirty Communist Party leaders, joined by some A.F. of L. local officers; 10 Progressive Miners Union representatives; Full Fashioned Hosiery Wkrs. officers; Francis Henson of the Nat. R. & L. Found.; etc.

CLOTHING WORKERS INDUSTRIAL UNION

A Communist T.U.U.L. union.

COMINTERN

Abbreviation for Communist International (see Internationals; also Communist Organization in the U.S.A.).

COMMITTEE ON ACADEMIC FREEDOM

Of the A.C.L.U.; defends the right of teachers to teach Red revolutionary doctrines in the class room; Prof. Wm. H. Kilpatrick, chmn.; Forrest Bailey, sec.

COMMITTEE ON COAL AND GIANT POWER

Com. on Coal & Giant P.

A Socialist-controlled organization subsidized by the Garland Fund (see "Garland Fund"), working for public ownership of utilities and the coal industry, which is part of the Socialist program. Italicized names in the following list of its advisory council members (1926) were also League for Industrial Democracy (L.I.D.) officers or directors: Oscar Ameringer, *Robt. W. Bruere, Stuart Chase, McAlister Coleman, H. C. Cross,* Morris Ernst, Clinton J. Golden, Robt. L. Hale, Arthur Garfield Hays, *A. S. Holcombe,* A. B. Jones, Milton Jones, *H. W. Laidler,* J. H. McGill (vice pres. Pub. O. Lg. of Am.), *Evelyn Preston,* Donald Richberg, Champlain Riley, J. H. Ryckman, *George Soule, Norman Thomas,* Edw. Wieck, U.S. Sen. Geo. W. Norris, Delso Wilcox (vice pres. Pub. O. Lg. of Am.), *H. W. Raushenbush* (secretary).

COMMITTEE ON CULTURAL RELATIONS WITH LATIN AMERICA

Com. Cult. Rel. Lat. Am.

An A.C.L.U. - dominated committee organized about 1928-29 with Hubert C. Herring (A.C.L.U., nat. com.) as executive director; is antagonistic toward the Monroe Doctrine and deplores U.S. "imperialism"; in this respect its program is identical with that of the communist All America Anti-Imperialist League, which, among other activities, directs its propaganda shafts at U.S. "imperialism" and the Monroe Doctrine; a letter sent out Oct. 26,

1931 by the Chicago Branch soliciting attendance at a dinner at the Chicago Woman's Club, Nov. 9th, to be addressed by Herring, stated in part: "Among other features will be a description by Mr. Herring of some proposed short conducted trips in December and January and a Seminar in the Carribean in February. These should appeal to many people who have been charmed with what they have read and seen of Mexico and the Carribean, especially those who have been reading recent volumes such as that of *Stuart Chase.*" On the letterhead, executives of the Chicago branch were listed as: "Mrs. Frank H. McCulloch, chairman, 231 S. La Salle St." (Catherine Waugh McCulloch, A.C.L.U. Chgo. Com.); "Clyde C. McGee, vice chairman, 1755 W. 103rd St." (A.C.L.U. Chgo. Com.); "Mrs. Henry W. Austin, treasurer, 1022 Lake Street, Oak Park; Rudolph A. Clemen, secretary, 650 Garland Ave., Winnetka."

Officers: John Dewey, Hon. Chmn.; Stuart Chase, Chmn.; Walter Frank, Treas.; Edward A. Ross, Florence E. Allen, Henry Goddard Leach, Father Frederic Siedenburg, Vice-chmn.; Hubert C. Herring, Exec. Dir.

COMMITTEE ON MILITARISM IN EDUCATION (ILLINOIS ALSO)

C.M.E. and C.M.E.Ill.

Supporting organization of Communist-organized and controlled U.S. Congress Against War and represented on similar World Congress of Youth Against War and Fascism by Edwin C. Johnson.

Received $12,400 from the "Red" Garland Fund to propagandize against military training in the schools, $5,400 of which, according to the Garland Fund 1925-28 official report, was "for preparation and distribution of pamphlet on Military Training in Schools and Colleges in the U.S." by Socialist Winthrop D. Lane. This pamphlet was widely distributed by the closely associated Fellowship of Reconciliation, the League for Industrial Democracy, Women's International League for Peace and Freedom, American Civil Liberties Union, *all financed in part by the Garland Fund,* and to some extent by the Federal Council of Churches. Quarters adjoined the Fellowship of Reconciliation (Room 383) at 387 Bible House, Astor Place, New York City (until the Fell. Recon. moved, 1933).

Alvin C. Goddard, Treasurer; Tucker P. Smith and Edwin C. Johnson, Secretaries; Executive Board: George A. Coe, Chairman, Harry A. Overstreet and John Nevin Sayre, Vice Chairmen, and Roswell P. Barnes, Leslie Blanchard, Mrs. J. Henry Callister, Inez Cavert, Mrs. Bennett Epstein, Mrs. J. Malcolm Forbes, William B. Harvey, E. C. Lindeman, Patrick Malin, Norman Thomas, Wellington H. Tinker, Walter Van Kirk, Kenneth Walser; National Council: Will W. Alexander, Rev. W. Russell Bowie, Howell Hamilton Broach, John Brophy, Bayard H. Christy, J. Elwood Cox, Albert F. Coyle, Mrs. J. Sergeant Cram, Prof. Jerome Davis, James H. Dillard, Sherwood Eddy, Rev. Noble S. Elderkin, Prof. Charles Ellwood, Zona Gale, Lindley V. Gordon, Rev. Joel Hayden, Prof. Carlton J. H. Hayes, Pres. John M. Henry (Coll. Pres.), Rev. John Herring, Prof. Manley O. Hudson, Hannah Clothier Hull, Prof. Rufus Jones, James Weldon Johnson, Frederick Libby, Prof. Robert Morss Lovett, Halford Luccock, Frederick Lynch, James H. Maurer, Prof. Alexander Meiklejohn, Bishop Francis J. McConnell, Mrs. John F. Moors, Orie O. Miller, Pres. Arthur E. Morgan (Coll. Pres.), Pres. S. K. Mosiman (Coll. Pres.), A. J. Muste, Rev. Reinhold Niebuhr, Frank Olmstead, Pres. Bromley Oxnam, (Coll. Pres.), Kirby Page, Pres. Marion Park (Coll. Pres.), Bishop Edward L. Parsons, Carl Patterson, Prof. Ira M. Price, Justice James Hoge Ricks, Prof. W. Carson Ryan, Dean William J. Scarlett, Henry Seabury, Mary Seabury, J. Henry Scattergood, Charles M. Sheldon, Rabbi Abba Hillel Silver, Katherine V. Silverthorn, Thomas Guthrie Speers, Rev. Ernest F. Tittle, Henry P. Van Dusen, Oswald G. Villard, Rabbi Stephen S. Wise, Prof. Luther A. Weigle, Pres. Mary E. Woolley (Coll. Pres.), William Allen White; *Illinois Committee on Militarism in Education:* Jane Addams, Jos. C. Artman, Rev. Orrin W. Auman, Zonia Baber, Rev. James C. Baker (Champaign), Rev. Norman Barr, Rev. (Prof.) Frank O. Beck, Alice Boynton, Rev. Dan B. Brummitt, Rev. A. J. Burns (Champaign), Dr. Geo. A. Coe, Rev. Gilbert Cox, Prof. Paul H. Douglas, A. J. Elliott (Evanston), Prof. Fred Eastman (Chgo. Theological Seminary, contrib. "Christian Century"), Arthur Fisher, Marion Fisher, Prof. R. Worth Frank (McCormick Theol. Sem., radical pacifist), Rev. Chas. Gilkey, Wilbur D. Grose (Wesley Found. U. of Ill.; organizer of Com.), Ann Guthrie (exec. sec. Chgo. Y.W.C.A.; Fellowship for a Christian Social Order), Maude Gwinn, Frederick Hall (contrib. "Christian Century").

COMMITTEES FOR HUMAN RIGHTS AGAINST NAZIISM

National movement for boycotting Germany, supposedly because of its anti-Jewish activities, organized by Samuel Untermyer of N.Y. City. No one who treasures American freedom wants fascism or Hitlerism for America, but it is only fair to note that Germany had 6,000,000 Communists bent on Red terrorist revolution and that Russian Jews had made themselves prominent in the Red movement, and that Naziism has directed its attacks more against conspiring, revolutionary Communist Jews, than against nationalist German Jews who aided Germany during the war; if it has discriminated against the innocent also, it has been with no such ferocity and loss of life as the planned and imminent Communist revolution would have wreaked upon the German population, had it been successful as in Russia. Those making altruistic appeals for human rights for Jews in Germany, should at the same time raise their voices urging boycott of atheist Russia in behalf of its persecuted Christians and millions of "liquidated" starved Ukrainians, in order to escape the suspicion that they are protesting for Communist rather than "human" rights.

Chicago officers: Chmn. Salmon O. Levinson (pres. of red Abraham Lincoln Center); pres. Paul Hutchinson (active in various pro-Soviet activities); exec. sec. Prof. James M. Yard (backer of various Communist activities).

Committee: Dr. Preston Bradley, Gen. John V. Clinnin, Dr. Copeland Smith, Dr. Arthur O. Black, Gen. Frank A. Schwengel, Chas. Sincere, Mrs. Ella Alschuler, Mrs. Paul Steinbrecher, Mrs. Geo. V. McIntyre, Dr. Willard Hotchkiss, Samuel H. Holland, Dr. Horace J. Bridges (A.C.L.U.), Mrs. Clark Eichelberger; see "Who's Who" for John A. Lapp, Chas. Clayton Morrison, Curtis W. Reese (of A. Lincoln Center), Col. Raymond Robins, Mrs. B. F. Langworthy, John Fitzpatrick.

Hdqts.: Room 437, 30 N. La Salle St., Chgo.

COMMITTEES FOR THOMAS

Com. for Thomas

Committees organized to aid the perennial campaigns of Norman Thomas as Socialist candidate for Governor of New York, President of the United States and other offices bear names such as "Non-Partisan Committee for Norman Thomas," "Educators'" (also Professional Men's, Writers', Artists' and Publicists', Trade Union, Intercollegiate) "Committee for Thomas and Maurer," etc.

COMMON SENSE

A very radical new magazine; mouthpiece of the League for Independent Political Action (L.I.P.A.) and its Conf. for Prog. Pol. Action and cooperating with the National Religion and Labor Foundation, Christian Social Action Movement, and Emergency Committee for Strikers Relief; organized and edited by Alfred M. Bingham of the national committee of the communist F.S.U., son of Hiram Bingham, former U.S. Senator from Connecticut; Editors: Alfred M. Bingham, Selden Rodman; Contributors include: Communists John Dos Passos, V. F. Calverton, Robt. Cantwell, Max Eastman, Albert Weisbord, Chas. Yale Harrison, James Rorty; Communist-Socialist Upton Sinclair; former Communists Ludwig Lore, J.B.S. Hardman, etc.; Carleton Beals; also Socialists Stuart Chase, George Soule, A. J. Muste, Robt. S. Allen (L.I.P.A. dir.), Henry Hazlitt (ed. "Nation") and other radicals. (The communist "Anvil," Sept.-Oct. issue, 1933.)

COMMONWEALTH COLLEGE

At Mena, Arkansas; a communistic, coeducational, cooperative labor college to train radical labor agitators and organizers; has about forty-three students and ten faculty members, whose delegation to Kentucky in 1932 were arrested as Communists; received $24,580 between 1924-8 from the Garland Fund, and when this support stopped, Communists, Socialists, I.W.W.'s and intellectual sympathizers were called upon to help maintain it; the Federated Press, N.Y., Sept. 1, 1926, stated: "Legal services of the American Civil Liberties Union are offered to Commonwealth College to resist the attempt of the Arkansas American Legion executive committee to investigate the teaching and maintenance of the institution"; the Feb. 1931 issue of the National Republic said: "In a recent issue of Fortnightly" (the bulletin of Commonwealth College) "Prof. Zeuch declared that he wished the Fish Committee would visit Commonwealth College so that they could be told of 'the many good things about red, red Russia and the many evil things about the U.S.,' and printed a letter from a longshoreman engaged in trying to teach negroes atheism and to organize 'the right kind of labor unions under Communist auspices'"; the same National Republic issue also contained the following: ". . . the 13th anniversary of the 'first workers' democracy—Soviet Russia—was celebrated at the Commons, Commonwealth College, Mena, Arkansas, on Nov. 9. The meeting concluded with singing of the Internationale. Under the caption 'Fellow Builders,' the 'Fortnightly' says that 'since the last issue the Brandeises'" (Justice and Mrs. Brandeis) "'and Floyd Dell have repledged for the 1931-32-33 period'"; among the officers of Commonwealth College (1931) besides W. E. Zeuch were: Kate Richards O'Hare; Covington Hall, an I.W.W. writer and poet; Albert E. Coyle; William Bouck, radical agricultural leader; Alice Stone Blackwell; U.S. Sen. Lynn J. Frazier; John Haynes Holmes; Ernest R. Meitzen, member of the Communist I.L.D. and Communist United Farmers Educational League; and Upton Sinclair, "a violent literary Socialist" (Lusk Report) and Communist writer.

Among 1933 financial contributors were Harry Ward, Max Eastman, Aaron L.

Shapiro, Roger Baldwin, Prof. Ernest W. Burgess (U. of Chgo.). The Oct. 1932 Nat. Republic quotes from the Commonwealth Bulletin the ironical news that the capitalistic Carnegie Corporation had donated funds for modernizing the Commonwealth plant. How capitalists do love to help the Reds! Lucien Koch was director 1933 and the following telegram was sent dated Nov. 7, 1933 to "M. Litvinoff. In care of Boris Skvirsky, Washington, D.C.":

> "Commonwealth has long recognized Soviet Russia and its tremendous significance to the future of economic planning. It extends greetings and felicitations to Soviet Russia's able representative and invites him to visit and inspect Commonwealth, a worker's college at Mena, Arkansas, which supports itself by running a Kolhoz or collective farm. Wire answer collect. Commonwealth College, Mena, Arkansas."

While the wire states that Commonwealth *supports itself* another column of the college paper announces that Lucien Koch is in the East begging funds to carry on.

COMMUNIST, THE (Magazine)

The official monthly magazine of the Communist Party of U.S.A. theory; address: P.O. Box 148, Station D., N.Y. City; 20c per copy.

COMMUNIST CAMPS

A former Communist Party executive estimates that during 1933 there were about 300 Communist camps in the United States including Camps Unity (of the T.U.U.L.), Camps Nitgedaiget, Young Pioneer, W.I.R., Young Communist League Camps, etc.

COMMUNIST HEADQUARTERS

The St. Denis Bldg., N.Y. City, is located on the S.W. corner of 11th and Broadway, with addresses of 80 East 11th St. on one side and 799 Broadway on the other. Suite 436 is the national hdqts. of the communist Unemployed Councils now agitating in 36 states. In the same building are located the offices of the communist F.S.U., I.L.D., I.C.O.R., Nat. Com. for Defense Political Prisoners, Labor Research Assn., Workers Health Service, Proletarian Anti-Religious League, United Council of Working Class Housewives, United Council of Working Class Women, and League of Struggle for Negro Rights. The main hdqts. is an eight story building owned and completely occupied by the Communist Party. It has two addresses: 35 E. 12th St., and 50 E. 13th St. 26-28 Union Square is owned by the Party and houses the Freiheit and Daily Worker printing plants.

Chicago district hdqts. were moved, July 1933, from 1413 W. 18th St. to 101 South Wells St., Room 705.

COMMUNIST INTERNATIONAL, THE

See under Internationals (1st, 2nd and 3rd); also it is the semi-monthly official organ of the Executive Committee of the Communist International (10c copy; order from Workers Library Publishers).

COMMUNIST LEAGUE OF AMERICA

American adherents of the expelled Trotsky faction in the Communist International; organized 1928; while not affiliated with the Communist Party of U.S.A. it supports the Communist T.U.U.L. strikes and participates in other "united front" activities; is more violently revolutionary in theory than even the parent Communist Party. In 1930 the national committee included Martin Abern, James P. Cannon, Vincent Dunne, Albert Glotzer, Hugo Oehler, Max Schactman, Carl Skoglund, Maurice Spector, Arne Swabeck; issues Youth and Jewish papers besides the English weekly "Militant"; 1933 hdqts. 126 E. 16th St., N.Y.C. (Conf. for Prog. Lab. Action offices adjoin); Chicago hdqts.: 2559 W. North Ave.

(COMMUNIST) LEAGUE OF PROFESSIONAL GROUPS FOR FOSTER AND FORD

Communist Lg. P. G. for F. & F.

A group pledged to vote Communist and aid the Communist Party program and campaign; its pamphlet (published by the Communist Party Workers Library Publishers, P.O. Box 148, Sta. D., N.Y. City, Oct. 1932) stated: "In Sept. 1932, a group of over fifty American writers, painters, teachers, and other professional workers declared their support of Foster and Ford and the Communist ticket in the 1932 national election. . . . In October this group was organized as the League of Professional Groups for Foster and Ford. An editorial committee was appointed and instructed to expand the original statement into a 10,000 word 'Open Letter,' and publish it as an election pamphlet. This pamphlet is now issued under the title of 'Culture and the Crisis.' . . . As responsible intellectual workers, we have aligned ourselves with the frankly revolutionary Communist Party. . . . The Communist Party of America proposes as the real solution of the present crisis the overthrow of the system which is responsible for all crises. This can only be accomplished by the conquest of political power and the establishment of a workers' and farmers' government which will usher in the socialist commonwealth. The Communist Party does not stop short merely with a proclamation of its revolutionary goal. . . . Its actions and achievements are impressive evidence of its revolutionary sincerity. . . . We call upon all men and women—especially workers in the professions and arts to join in the revolutionary struggle against capitalism under the leadership of the Communist Party . . . and join us in this move to form 'Foster and Ford' Committees throughout the country." Etc. Signed by:

Leonie Adams, Sherwood Anderson, Newton Arvin, Emjo Basshe, Maurice Becker, Slater Brown, Fielding Burke, Erskine Caldwell, Robert Cantwell, Winifred L. Chappell, Lester Cohen, Louis Colman, Lewis Corey, Henry Cowell, Malcolm Cowley, Bruce Crawford, Kyle S. Crichton, Countee Cullen, H. W. L. Dana, Adolf Dehn, John Dos Passos, Howard N. Doughty, Jr., Theodore Dreiser, Miriam Allen De Ford, Waldo Frank, Alfred Frueh, Murray Godwin, Eugene Gordon, Horace Gregory, Louis Grudin, John Hermann, Granville Hicks, Sidney Hook, Sidney Howard, Langston Hughes, Orrick Johns, William N. Jones, Matthew Josephson, Alfred Kreymborg, Louis Lozowick, Grace Lumpkin, Felix Morrow, Samuel Ornitz, James Rorty, Isidor Schneider, Frederick L. Schuman, Edwin Seaver, Herman Simpson, Lincoln Steffens, Charles Walker, Robert Whitaker, Edmund Wilson, Ella Winter.

Hdqts.: 35 East 12th St., N.Y. City (the Communist "Workers School").

COMMUNIST LEAGUE OF STRUGGLE

A Communist party which broke away from the Communist Party of U.S.A. led by Albert Weisbord; organized Mar. 15, 1931; participates in "united front" Communist strikes, etc.; its official organ is "Class Struggle"; it puts out a shop paper in the Brooklyn Navy Yard ("Red Dreadnought"); favors many of Trotsky's ultra revolutionary theories; hdqts. Albert Weisbord, 212 9th St., N.Y. City.

COMMUNIST NEWSPAPERS

The "Workers Voice" is the official "midwest organ of the Communist Party of the U.S.A. Published at 2019 W. Division St., Chicago, Ill." Herbert Newton, colored Communist, is its editor. The "Southern Worker," "Western Worker," and "Michigan Worker," with the "Daily Worker," all Communist newspapers, together, rather thoroughly cover United States Communist activities (in English). The Foreign Language Groups publish 8 daily and 18 weekly newspapers.

COMMUNIST PARTY (OPPOSITION)

Another separate Communist party formed by members of the official Communist Party of U.S.A.; organized about 1931, led by Communists Jay Lovestone and Benj. Gitlow (of Garland Fund). The Am. Labor Year Book 1932 says: that it "fully endorses the general course of the Communist Party of the Soviet Union in economic construction although it criticizes the inner party methods used by the Stalin leadership"; that its official organ "Revolutionary Age," although supported by the American Civil Liberties Union, finally was barred by the Post Office authorities from second class mailing privileges, the "Workers Age" replacing it as the official weekly; that "the anniversaries of the Russian Revolution and death of Chas. E. Ruthenberg were the occasions of large meetings"; that "energies of the group were concentrated on individual unions in the needle trades and among the anthracite and marine workers, Locals 1 and 22 of the Intl. Ladies Garm. Wkrs., as well as in the Amalgamated Clothing Workers and Furriers left-wing elements"; that "The rebuilding of the left-wing in the Workmen's Circle also occupied the attention" of the Party; and that in the Nov. 1931 elections instructions were given members to vote the official Communist Party tickets." Jay Lovestone, editor, Will Herberg, mg. ed., and Bertram D. Wolfe, assoc. ed., are given as Staff members of its "Workers Age." Hdqts. 51 W. 14th St., N.Y. City.

COMMUNIST PARTY OF THE U.S.A. (SECTION OF THE COMMUNIST INTERNATIONAL)

The main powerful Moscow-directed world party of Communists. See under Communist Organization in the U.S.A.

COMMUNIST-RECOMMENDED AUTHORS

These authors and their writings are officially endorsed and recommended for reading by the "Soviet Union Review," organ of the official Soviet government agency in Washington, D.C., the "Soviet Union Information Bureau," headed by Boris Skvirsky, known as the "unofficial ambassador" of the Soviet Union in Washington. Considering the strictness of Soviet censorship, an author's propaganda necessarily must be pro-Soviet in order to receive official Soviet endorsement.

Ralph Albertson, R. Page Arnot, W. J. Austin, Newton D. Baker, Roger N. Baldwin, John Becker, May L. Becker, Karl Borders, Margaret Bourke-

White, H. N. Brailsford, Eugene Braudo, Adams Brown, David A. Brown, Joseph Budish, Wm. C. Bullitt, Emile Burns, George A. Burrell, Thomas D. Campbell, John M. Carmody, Huntley Carter, Wm. H. Chamberlain, Stuart Chase, Mrs. Cecil Chesterton, W. P. Coates, Alzada Comstock, Hugh Lincoln Cooper, H. M. Dadourian, Ruth Dadourian, Jerome Davis, Vera Micheles Dean, John Dewey, Maurice Dobb, Theodore Dreiser, Louis I. Dublin, Robert W. Dunn, Walter Duranty, Hans von Eckardt, Clough Williams Ellis, Ernestine Evans, Michael Farbman, Arthur Feiler, Alice Withrow Field, Louis Fischer, Joseph Freeman, Elisha Friedman, Edgar S. Furniss, General Wm. S. Graves, Mordecai Gorelik, Frederick Griffin, G. T. Grinko, Anna J. Haines, Jeyhoun Bey Hajibeyli, Talbot Faulkner Hamlin, Jack Hardy, Samuel N. Harper, Julius F. Hecker, Maurice Hindus, A. Ford Hinricks, John Haynes Holmes, Calvin B. Hoover, Bruce Hopper, William Kistler Huff, M. Ilin, Albert A. Johnson, John A. Kingsbury, H. R. Knickerbocker, Joshua Kunitz, Ivy Lee, Dr. Richard Lewinsohn, E. C. Lindeman, Ray Long, Louis Lozowick, Anatole Lunacharsky, Eugene Lyons, Robert McManus, Valeriu Marcu, V. M. Molotov, Albert Muldavin, Scott Nearing, Reinhold Niebuhr, Albert Parry, Ashley Pettis, Boris Pilniak, Albert P. Pinkevitch, Walter N. Polakov, George M. Price, George Earle Raiguel, Arthur Ransome, John Reed, Geroid T. Robinson, Edward A. Ross, Walter Arnold Rukeyser, Leonid Sabaneyef, A. A. Santalov, Prof. Fred L. Schuman, Louis Segal, Wm. Philip Simms, Jessica Smith, Gregory Sokolnikov, George Soule, Maxwell S. Stewart, Anna Louise Strong, Valentine V. Tchikoff, Rex. Guy Tugwell, Sidney Webb, Walter Wells, William C. White, Robert Whitten, Albert Rhys Williams, Frankwood E. Williams, Ella Winter, Thomas Woody, Victor Yakhontoff, Y. A. Yakovlev, Avram Yarmolinsky, A. Y. Yeghenian, Judah Zelitch, and Lucien Zacharoff.

See International Pamphlets, International Publishers, and Workers Library Publishers for further lists.

CONCEPTION CONTROL SOCIETY

A branch of the Am. Assn. for Advancement of Atheism (4A).

CONCOOPS

N.Y. City Communist organization operating cooperative apartments, camps, etc. Autos leave their Cooperative Restaurant, 2700 Bronx Park, East, regularly for Nitgedaiget Hotel, Beacon, N.Y., Camp Unity, etc.

CONFERENCE FOR PROGRESSIVE LABOR ACTION

Conf. Prog. Lab. Act.

A very militant left-wing Socialist trade union organization somewhat similar to the communist T.U.U.L.; cooperates with the Trotskyite Communists in labor strikes and struggles; is under the leadership of A. J. Muste, until recently head of Brookwood Labor College, and Louis Budenz, professional labor organizer and agitator. Its Unemployed Citizens Leagues have been active in "united front" activities with the Communists throughout the country. A report Sept. 28, 1933 from Seattle, where this League virtually controlled the last Seattle municipal election, stated that the Unemployed Citizens League of Seattle was "affiliated with the National Committee of the Unemployed Councils" of the Communist Party; supporting organization of Nat. Com. to Aid Victims of German Fascism (of communist W.I.R.) of which Muste is nat. chmn., and of U.S. Congress Against War; forming, 1934, the American Workers' party.

CONFERENCE FOR PROGRESSIVE POLITICAL ACTION

A radical political organization formed in Chicago, Feb. 20, 1922 by the LaFollette organization of Farmers, Amalgamated Clothing Workers, People's Legislative Service (of LaFollette), Women's Trade Union League, Farmer-Labor Party, Non-Partisan League, Communists, Socialists, I.W.W.'s, and radicals of all hues, for the purpose of running and electing radical candidates on regular party tickets. The organizing conference praised Soviet Russia, damned capitalism, and endorsed (in 1922 and 1923) Senators LaFollette, Brookhart, Norris, Ashhurst (Arizona), Dill, Frazier, Kendrick, Ralston, Swanson, and Howell on the Republican and Democratic tickets, and Shipstead and Johnson (Minn.) on the Farmer-Labor Party ticket, *all of whom were elected* (See Whitney's "Reds in America").

Wm. H. Johnston (Sec.-Treas. of the People's Legislative Service and Nat. Popular Govt. League) called the second Conference for Progressive Political Action at Cleveland, Dec. 11, 1922, with Edw. Keating (1933 Roosevelt appointee) as chmn. of the Committee on Program and Resolutions, Judson King (1933 Roosevelt appointee) as delegate from the Pop. Govt. Lg., Morris Hillquit, Victor Berger, Seymour Stedman, Geo. E. Roewer, B. Charney Vladeck, Otto Branstetter and James O'Neal, as delegates from the Socialist Party, Norman Thomas, Robt. Morss Lovett and D. J. Meserole, as delegates from the Socialist L.I.D., etc.

Conferences held in St. Louis, Feb. 11, 12, 1924 and July 4, 1924, prepared the Socialist platform and nominated LaFollette and Wheeler to run as the choice of the combined radical forces on a ticket dubbed as the "Progressive." Carl D. Thompson, Norman Thomas, and Morris Hillquit of the Socialist Party, and innumerable other well known radicals, were delegates to these Conferences called by Wm. H. Johnston.

Early in August 1933, a call for a United Conference for Progressive Political Action to be held at Judson Court, University of Chicago, Sept. 2-3, 1933 was issued by the socialist League for Independent Political Action to about a hundred Socialist, farmer-labor, racial, radical organizations. The call was signed by Prof. John Dewey, Congressman LaGuardia (one time Socialist candidate then running for Mayor of N.Y. City on Fusion ticket), Howard Y. Williams (exec. sec. of socialist Lg. for Independent Political Action), Congressman F. H. Shoemaker, Milo Reno (leader of farm marches and riots), Upton Sinclair (Socialist and Communist leader then running on Democratic ticket in California), Prof. Paul Douglas (chmn. Socialist Party campaign 1932, now on President Roosevelt's "Democratic" Planning Board), Prof. Robt. Morss Lovett (leader of Socialist and Communist organizations), Vida Scudder, and similar radicals.

Paul Douglas presided as temporary chmn. and the former LaFollette Congressman, Thos. R. Amlie, of Wis., was made permanent chmn. Addresses were delivered by W. R. Truax, Estelle Sternberger, Jos. Schlossberg, Mayor Wm. Mahoney of St. Paul (Socialist), John W. Wirds (pres. United Farmers of Am.), Alfred Bingham, editor of the radical "Common Sense" Magazine, and other radicals.

The conference adopted a platform calling for "public ownership of the means of wealth production" as the "ultimate objective" of the movement and as a step in this direction the nationalization of money and credits, of public utilities and of various "basic industries." The collapse of our present system was predicted and the scrapping of our Constitution proposed, to abolish what they call "absentee ownership of property." The establishment of national unemployment, maternity, sick, accident, and old age insurance, heavier taxation on wealth, on incomes and inheritances, etc., and a foreign trade monopoly similar to the Russian plan was advocated. The masses were urged to "rise and take control."

"Cautious and conservative" measures were adopted to "insure the realization of their purposes" says a release from the N.Y. City office of the movement. A promotional "Committee on Action was set up to be known as the *Farmer-Labor Political Federation* with representatives in every section of the country, authorized to call national and state conventions on or before July 1, 1934, and charged with organizing farmer-labor units similar to those now existing in Minnesota and other states. Committees almost at once were set up in 16 states.

Howard Y. Williams, exec. sec. of the L.I.P.A., will remain as executive secretary of the newly formed group.

John Dewey is hon. chmn. of the "Committee on Action"; Oswald Garrison Villard, treas.; and ex-Congressman Thos. K. Amlie, Henry Ohl (Pres. Wis. Fed. Labor), Congressman Ernest Lundeen (of Minnesota), John H. Bosch (pres. Minnesota Farmers Holiday Assn.), Hjalmore Peterson of Minn., Alfred Dale (state treasurer of N.D.), E. E. Green of the Farmers' Union of N.D., John T. Wirds (pres. United Farmers of Iowa), E. E. Kennedy (sec. Nat. Farmers Union of Ill.), Prof. Paul Douglas, Wm. J. Joyce (of Chgo. Workers Com. on Unemp.), Howard Y. Williams (exec. sec. L.I.P.A.), Alfred Bingham (editor of "Common Sense"), Stephen Raushenbush (director of Security Lg.), and C. G. Lubrand of Mich., are among the Committee members.

(Nov. 1933), United Action Campaign Committee:

Thos. R. Amlie, chmn.; Howard Y. Williams, nat. organizer; Alfred M. Bingham, exec. sec.; Wm. A. Anderson, Hon. Henry Arens, Alfred M. Bingham, Kath. Devereux Blake, LeRoy E. Bowman, Paul Brissenden, Heywood Broun, Lucy P. Carner, Stuart Chase, Geo. A. Coe, Eleanor G. Coit, Jerome Davis, Edw. T. Devine, Dorothy Detzer, Paul H. Douglas, Sherwood Eddy, Morris Ernst, Helen Everett, Henry Pratt Fairchild, Walter Frank, Zona Gale, Wm. P. Hapgood, John Herring, Sidney Hillman, Julius Hochman, Jesse H. Holmes, Ben Howe, Hannah Clothier Hull, Fannie Hurst, Edw. L. Israel, Hon. Magnus Johnson, C. F. Keeney, Emily R. Kneubuhl, Fiorello H. LaGuardia, Corliss Lamont, Caroline Lamonte, Benson Y. Landes, John A. Lapp, Abraham Lefkowitz, Jos. Lilly, Edward C. Lindeman, Robt. Morss Lovett, Hon. Ernest Lundeen, Hon. Wm. Mahoney, John McLaren, Lois Hayden Meek, Alexander Meiklejohn, Henry Neumann, Reinhold Niebuhr, Bishop Edw. L. Parsons, Augustus Pigman, Mercedes M. Randall, Ira De A. Reid, John Nevin Sayre, Hon. F. H. Shoemaker, Estelle M. Sternberger, Alva W. Taylor, Oswald Garrison Villard, Howard Y. Williams, Max Zaritsky.

CONGREGATIONAL EDUCATION SOCIETY

Closely affiliated with the League for Independent Political Action and other radical organizations; similar to and cooperates with Methodist Federation for Social Service; Hubert C. Herring of the A.C.L.U. nat. com. has been sec. of its Dept. of Social Relations since 1924; its hdqts. in 1932 occupied the same office with the League for Independent Political Action, 112 E. 19th St., N.Y. City.

CONGRESSIONAL EXPOSURE OF RADICALS

The Congressional Record of the 69th Congress, First Session, Volume 67, number 12, Dec. 19, 1925, states:

"Exposed in the Senate investigation as war obstructors, red, etc., was long list, and afterwards another list was given out in January, 1921 by the Department of Justice, of radicals who controlled radical organizations in the United States. On both lists we find the names of many of the A.C.L.U. officers and committee, including:

"Rev. Norman M. Thomas, Roger N. Baldwin, Morris Hillquit, Scott Nearing, James H. Maurer, Helen Phelps Stokes, Rabbi Judah L. Magnes, Edmund C. Evans, Rev. John Haynes Holmes, Frederick C. Howe, Oswald Garrison Villard, Agnes Brown Leach.

"Other A.C.L.U. names on the first list are those of:

"Jane Addams and Sophonisba P. Breckenridge (Women's International League for Peace and Freedom), John Lovejoy Elliott, Elizabeth Gurley Flynn, Rev. John N. Sayre, Rev. Harry F. Ward, L. Hollingsworth Wood.

"While on the second list are:

"Max Eastman, Crystal Eastman, Vida D. Scudder, Joseph D. Cannon, George P. West, Robert Morss Lovett, Benjamin L. Huebsch, Lincoln Colcord, Allan McCurdy.

"We also find on both lists the names of:

"Prof. Emily Green Balch, H. W. L. Dana of the Workers' Education Bureau, Lillian D. Wald of the Foreign Policy Association, Amos R. E. Pinchot, Louis P. Lochner.

"Other noteworthy names on one or the other lists are:

"Harold Evans, Prof. Wm. I. Hull of Swarthmore and the Rand School, Rev. Frederick Lynch, Kate Richards O'Hare, Jacob Panken, Alexander Trachtenberg, James P. Warbasse, Eugene V. Debs, Mrs. Florence Kelley of the Consumers' League, Charles Recht, Rebecca Shelley (friend of Jane Addams, Lochner, etc.), Isaac A. Hourwich, Lincoln Steffens, J. A. H. Hopkins, Harry A. Overstreet, Dudley Field Malone, Elsie Clews Parsons, Owen R. Lovejoy."

"Connected with the communist American Civil Liberties Union by a system of interlocking committee memberships are a number of other organizations that play into the hands of the communists. Among them are the old Intercollegiate Socialist Society with its name changed to League for Industrial Democracy. This tries to poison the minds of college youths, sponsors college forums, the youth movement, etc. Others are the American Committee for Chinese Relief; the Fellowship of Reconciliation which practically owns the Fellowship of Youth for Peace; the Rand School of Social Science; the Trades Union Educational League (now the Trade Union Unity League); the National Popular Government League; the Foreign Policy Association; the Worker's Education Bureau; the Public Ownership League; the Old Labor Defense League; the Conference to Perfect Plans for the Committee of Forty-Eight; the People's Council; Berkman's League for Amnesty of Political Prisoners; Friends of Soviet Russia; People's Reconstruction League; the Labor Publication Society; the People's of American Society; Conference for Progressive Political Action and International Labor Defense."

Since the above list was published in the Congressional Record, there have been changes in name of some of the agencies, and many additional groups have been organized.

CONTINENTAL CONGRESS OF WORKERS AND FARMERS FOR ECONOMIC RECONSTRUCTION

Organized by Socialist Party in state units; advocates abolition of Capitalism and state ownership of all means of production, etc. Hdqts. Moxley Bldg., Clinton Street, Chicago.

(NATIONAL) CONSTRUCTION WORKERS UNION

A Communist T.U.U.L. labor union.

COOPERATIVE LEAGUE OF U.S.A.

The cooperative movement is intended to eliminate the private store, private industry and individual initiative. The Cooperative League of U.S.A. is part of the National Federation of Consumers Cooperatives and member of the International Cooperative Alliance of which Centro Soyus, the Russian Cooperative, is a member; was approved and financially aided by the Garland Fund; has 145 affiliated societies with approximately 135,000 members; its president, J. P. Warbasse, says in his book "Cooperative Democracy," pp. 258-9: "The ultimate aim of the Consumer's Movement should be to purchase the land from the farmers and employ the latter as an agricultural worker" (abolishing private ownership of property is of course a fundamental principle of Socialism-Communism); hdqts.: 167 W. 12th Street, N.Y. City. (See Central Cooperative Wholesale, a member society.)

The "Communist International," published July, 1928 by the Communist Party of Great Britain, p. 346, stated: "The

Cooperative League of North America contains considerable Left Wing elements —The Central Cooperative Exchange (Superior, Wisconsin) serving 100 retail stores is a Left Wing organization. The Left Wingers in the Cooperatives have succeeded in securing some relief for the striking coal miners and recently called a conference to extend this work. In New York City is the United Workers' Cooperative Association which is controlled by the Left Wing. This cooperative has spread recently to other cities, Boston, Philadelphia, Chicago and Los Angeles. It is building a series of houses, controls a number of camps for workers, conducts cultural work on a Communist basis," etc.

COOPERATIVE UNEMPLOYED LEAGUES

Of Highland Park, Waukegan, and Lake County, Ill.; section of Federated Unemployed Workers Leagues (see).

CRISIS

Monthly organ of the N.A.A.C.P. Geo. W. Streator, Mg. ed. 1934, Mem. Revol. Policy Com. Socialist P. (See page 337.)

D

DAILY WORKER

"Central Organ of the Communist Party U.S.A. (Section of the Communist International)" is its heading; pub. daily except Sunday in English at 50 E. 13th St., N.Y.C.; Washington Bureau, Room 954, National Press Bldg., 14th and G St., Wash., D.C. (Seymour Waldman and Marguerite Young in charge); Clarence Hathaway, editor, Harry Gannes, etc., assts. Sold at all Communist stores and meetings.

The front page, Nov. 4, 1933, under the heading: "Towards a Soviet America!", says: "You can help hasten the day when we shall celebrate a Victorious Workers' and Farmers' Soviet Republic in the United States by building strong the Daily Worker, which agitates, organizes and mobilizes the forces for the destruction of capitalism in America."

That is plain enough sedition, is it not?

DEBS MEMORIAL RADIO STATION

Radio station WEVD named after Eugene V. Debs, "started and continued by Socialists and radicals," was, according to 1932 Am. Labor Year Book, "finally allowed to keep its license after a hard fight, and was heavily endowed by the Jewish Daily Forward" (Socialist newspaper). The third annual report of the American Association for the Advancement of Atheism (issued April 1929) announced (p. 3): "We have outwitted the bigots and now broadcast regularly over Station WEVD, New York (231.6-1300 K.C.), Saturdays, 6 P.M. The recent increase in the power of this station enables us to reach a much larger audience."

DEPARTMENT STORE WORKERS UNION

A Communist T.U.U.L. union.

DISARM

A League for Industrial Democracy (L.I.D.) publication which, like all Socialist-Communist publications, advocates complete disarmament of the United States for the purpose (as it has stated) of achieving international Socialism, urged recognition of militaristic Russia, urges internationalism in place of patriotism, and features articles advocating the establishment of the Socialist state and the abolition of capitalism (or private ownership of property).

DOLL MAKERS INDUSTRIAL UNION

Communist T.U.U.L. union.

DREISER COMMITTEE ON COAL

A Communist - controlled committee formed in 1931, headed by Theodore Dreiser, to investigate mining conditions in the Pittsburg coal district, then a center of strike activities under the influence of the National Miners Union (Communist); the committee included: Malcolm Cowley, Robt. W. Dunn, John Dos Passos, Mary Heaton Vorse, Anna Rochester, Horace B. Davis, Frank L. Palmer.

DRUG CLERKS UNION, NEW

Communist T.U.U.L. union.

E

ECONOMIC JUSTICE

Bulletin of the National Religion and Labor Foundation; discussed under that title.

ECONOMIC REVIEW OF THE SOVIET UNION

Communist semi-monthly magazine published by Amtorg Trading Corporation (of the Soviet Government), 261 Fifth Ave., N.Y. City.

EDUCATIONAL WORKERS INTERNATIONAL

A Communist international union of educators; American section is the Educational Workers Leagues affiliated with the T.U.U.L., with branches in N.Y., Pa., Cal., Chicago, etc. The N.Y. League publishes "Education Worker," an agitational publication for teachers; address Box 79, Station D, New York City.

EMERGENCY COMMITTEE FOR SOUTHERN POLITICAL PRISONERS

Emer. Com. So. Pol. Pris.

A Communist committee (U.S. Report 2290), formed by the John Reed Club and International Labor Defense (I.L.D.) to assist the I.L.D. in raising funds for the defense of six Communists arrested in Atlanta, Georgia, in 1930, for seditious activities (Herbert Newton, colored, Henry Storey, Joe Carr, Anne Burlak, Mary Dalton, and M. H. Powers); out of this committe grew the National Committee for Defense of Political Prisoners; hdqts. 80 E. 11th St., N.Y. City;

Theo. Dreiser, chmn.; John Dos Passos, treas.; members: Sherwood Anderson, Wm. Rose Benet, Witter Bynner, Malcolm Cowley, John Dos Passos, Waldo Frank, Josephine Herbst, Sheila Hibben, Alfred Kreymborg, Suzanna LaFollette, Scott Nearing, Burton Rascoe, Lola Ridge, Boardman Robinson, Upton Sinclair, Louis Untermyer, Carl Van Doren, Edmund Wilson.

EMERGENCY COMMITTEE FOR STRIKERS RELIEF (ALSO CHICAGO)

Emer. Com. Strik. Rel.

Organized in 1926 by Norman Thomas and other American Civil Liberties Union (A.C.L.U.) and League for Industrial Democracy (L.I.D.) members, with financial aid from the Garland Fund, to assist the Passaic textile strikers in the so-called Communist "first lesson in revolution," led by Communist Albert Weisbord; it next aided the Communist Gastonia strike; is now aiding the left wing Socialist-Communist penetrated Progressive Miners Union strike in Illinois and is soliciting funds through the National Religion and Labor Foundation and other cooperating agencies for this purpose;

1933 chairman, Norman Thomas; treasurer, Reinhold Niebuhr; committee members: McAllister Coleman, Anna N. Davis, Morris L. Ernst, Elizabeth Gilman, Bishop F. J. McConnell, Evelyn Preston, H. S. Raushenbush, Lillian D. Wald, Bertha Poole Weyl, John Herling, exec. sec.

Special Committee: Helen L. Alfred, Algernon Black, Paul Blanshard, Harriot Stanton Blatch, Susan Brandeis, Heywood Broun, Mrs. George Burnham, Jr., Rev. Edmund B. Chaffee, John Chamberlain, Stuart Chase, Dr. Bernard C. Clausen, Dr. Morris R. Cohen, Marc Connelly, Max Danish, Margaret De Silver, Mary Dreier, Sherwood Eddy, John Lovejoy Elliott, Charles Ervin, Elizabeth Glendower Evans, Frederick V. Field, Louise Adams Floyd, Walter Frank, Dr. A. L. Goldwater, Powers Hapgood, Arthur Garfield Hays, Adolph S. Held, John Haynes Holmes, J. A. H. Hopkins, Rev. Clarence V. Howell, Rev. Paul Jones, Nicholas Kelley, Paul U. Kellogg, Freda Kirchwey, Corliss Lamont, Rev. Leon Rosser Land, E. C. Lindeman, Dr. Henry R. Linville, Robert Morss Lovett, Mrs. James Marshall, Rev. J. Howard Melish, Darwin J. Meserole, Mary Raoul Millis, Dr. Wesley C. Mitchell, Mrs. Herbert Mitler, Dr. Henry Neumann, Irving S. Ottenberg, Amos Pinchot, Margaret Pollitzer, Caroline Pratt, George D. Pratt, Jr., Mrs. William I. Rosenfeld, Jr., Helen G. Sahler, John Nevin Sayre, Rose Schneidermann, Mrs. Arthur J. Slade, Rex T. Stout, Genevieve Taggard, Alva W. Taylor, Samuel Untermyer, Oswald Garrison Villard, James P. Warbasse, Rev. Charles Webber, Rev. Eliot White, Mrs. Stephen S. Wise.

The 1928 committee membership was largely the same. Communists John Dos Passos, Eliz. Gurley Flynn, Paxton Hibben, and Clarina Michelson were then members, and Forrest Bailey was treas. In 1930 Roger Baldwin, Florence and Dr. Gertrude B. Kelley were members, also Herbert Croly.

The Chicago branch of the Emer. Com. Strik. Rel. hdqts. are at 20 W. Jackson (L.I.D. hdqts.).

Robt. M. Lovett, chmn.; Karl Borders, sec.-treas.; members: Mrs. Inez Asher, Alice Boynton, Roy Burt, Hilda Diamond, A. Dreifuss, Prof. Thos. D. Eliot, Rev. Chas. W. Gilkey, Mrs. Alfred Hamburger, Mrs. Esther Henshaw, Lillian Herstein, William H. Holly, Paul Hutchinson, Mrs. Alfred Kohn, Glenford Lawrence, Hilda Howard Lawrence, Sam Levin, Lola Maverick Lloyd, Mrs. Judith Lowenthal, Rabbi Louis Mann, Wiley W. Mills, James Mullenbach, Mrs. Andrew McLeish, Rev. U. M. McGuire, Mrs. Murry Nelson, Frances Paine, Mrs. James F. Porter, Curtis W. Reese, Donald R. Richberg, Ethelyn Potter Rolfe, Mrs. M. E. Simpson, Graham Taylor, Mrs. Walter Vose, Chas. Weller, Edw. Winston, Victor Yarros.

EMERGENCY COMMITTEE FOR STRIKERS RELIEF NOW WORKING FOR SOUTHERN TEXTILE STRIKERS

Emer. Com. Strik. Rel. N.W.F.S.T.S.

The name given the Emergency Committee for Strikers Relief (see above) during one of its activities.

EMERGENCY PEACE FEDERATION

Oct. 1914 to Mar. 1915, and revived Feb. to May, 1917 as a rejuvenation of American Neutral Conf. Com.; organized first by Rosika Schwimmer, Louis Lochner, Jane Addams, and representatives of six Socialist and fifteen Socialist-sympathizing organizations, to propagandize a peace favorable to Germany (Lusk Report); the 1917 revival was aided as well by Mrs. Henry Villard (mother of Oswald Garrison Villard), Emily Greene Balch, Mrs. J. S. Cram, Norman Thomas, Mrs. Warbasse,

Lola M. Lloyd, etc.; a "peace demonstration" of 250 was staged Feb. 12, 1917 at the White House; $76,000 was raised in three months and a nation-wide propaganda organization perfected; a letter condemning it, which was received by Congressman Chandler and is reproduced in the Lusk Report, ends: "I cannot believe you will give a moment's consideration to the pro-German propaganda of the so-called Emergency Peace Federation, but I feel that you should hear from those who condemn it as traitorous and dangerous not alone to the United States, but to world civilization." (See also under A.C.L.U. Formation.)

EMMA GOLDMAN CIRCLES

Anarchist-Communist groups.

ENGLISH REDS

"The dividing line between Socialism and Communism is an imaginary one, like the equator. The Socialist ('Labour') Party sometimes publicly repudiates Communism; and then elects Communists to its own Executive; and Communists run the Labour Research Department. Socialists find excuses for all crimes of the Bolsheviks, who direct and finance Communism all the World over," says the authentic "Potted Biographies" (of Boswell Publishing, Ltd., 10 Essex St., London, W.C., price 6 d), which gives startling facts and extremely interesting political record of 49 Socialists (some belonging to the Communist Party). These "Socialists" are:

C. G. Ammon, Norman Angell, R. Page Arnot, Miss Margaret Bondfield, H. N. Brailsford, A. Fenner Brockway, John Bromley, W. J. Brown, C. Roden Buxton, W. M. Citrine, J. R. Clynes, G. D. H. Cole, A. J. Cook, Herbert Dunnico, J. H. Hayes, Arthur Henderson, George Hicks, Frank Hodges, J. F. Horrabin, F. W. Jowett, Jos. Montague Kenworthy, George Lansbury, Harold J. Laski, J. Ramsay MacDonald, C. J. L'Estrange Malone, Tom Mann, James Maxton, Sir Oswald Mosley, H. Pollitt, A. A. W. H. Ponsonby (Lord Ponsonby), Bertrand A. W. Russell, Dora Russell, S. Saklatvala, Tom Shaw, Emanuel Shinwell, Robert Smillie, Herbert Smith, Philip Snowden, H. H. Thomas, E. Thurtle, Ben Tillett, C. P. Trevelyan (Sir), R. C. Wallhead, Sidney Webb (Lord Passfield), J. C. Wedgwood, Miss Ellen C. Wilkinson, Robert Williams, and Edward F. Wise.

Leeds Conference

"The Patriot" (of London) for June 1, 1933 says: "that Litvinoff—who left this country for this country's good fifteen years ago—is to be permitted re-entry to attend the Economic Conference is unfortunate. . . . His presence will be a national insult. . . . He is a Jew whose real name is Finklestein, and he lived in the East End before the war. He attracted the notice of Scotland Yard in June, 1917, as one of six members of the Moscow Soviet who arrived in London—apparently by invitation—in order to witness the overthrow of constitutional government by Ramsay MacDonald's Leeds conference, which was a treasonable attempt to destroy our Constitution—in the midst of the war in our national defense—by setting up Soviets here under the name of Soldiers' and Workers' Councils. Litvinoff took an office at 82 Victoria Street, which he called the Russian Embassy. There were a number of complaints of Litvinoff's offences against the Defense of the Realm Act in 1917 and 1918, but he was merely sent to Brixton Gaol and had his fingerprints taken and was then deported as an undesirable alien."

"This attempt to organize a revolution to end the war was supported by the U.D.C." (wartime organization of the Socialist Ind. Labour Party), "Independent Labor Party, British Socialist Party, Women's International League" (Jane Addams', under Mrs. Pethwick Lawrence), "Herald League (an offshoot of the Daily Herald), the Clyde Workers Committee, etc. Sinn Feiners also attended the convention. Among the supporters of the scheme were Tom Mann, Arthur MacManus, W. Gallacher (Clyde), Noah Ablett, and other Syndicalists from South Wales." (Morning Post, Nov. 1918.)

The "Socialist Network" by N. Webster says: "Amongst the most active supporters of the movement were Ramsay MacDonald, the Snowdens and C. G. Ammon, all Ind. Labour Party; Chas. Roden Buxton, Pethwick Lawrence and Bertrand Russell, U.D.C.; E. C. Faerchild and Mrs. Dora Montefiore, British Socialist Party; and Sylvia Pankhurst of the Workers Socialist Federation" (which became Communist in 1920).

"It was in May of the same year, 1917, that Ramsay MacDonald applied for a passport to go to Russia in order to consult with the Workmen's and Soldiers' Soviets, but in view of his Pacifist activities during the war the National Seamen and Firemen's Union under Havelock Wilson refused to carry him."

"Potted Biographies" says: "In June 1917, MacDonald, assisted by Snowden, Smillie, Ammon, Anderson, Roden Buxton, Mrs. Despard, Mrs. Snowden, and many East End Jews, held a conference at Leeds, and agreed to the formation of Workmen's and Soldiers' Councils, on Russian lines, to end the war by outbreak of a revolution which would paralyze our military operations. MacDonald said: 'Now is the turn of the people; we must lay down our terms; make our own proclamations; establish our own diplomacy.' *He was appointed to the committee for acting and creating thirteen soviets.* In April 1918, a huge mass meeting at Woolwich passed this resolution, reported in the Times: 'That this meeting says: "To Hell with Ramsay MacDonald and Philip Snowden. . . . that the engineers of Woolrich Arsenal are Englishmen and they demand to be led by men who love their country."' . . . Mr. MacDonald was Prime Minister in the nine months Socialist Government of 1924, inflicted on us by Mr. Asquith. In the Govt. were twenty-seven members of the Ind. Labour Party, and it was responsible for recognition of the atrocious Soviet Govt. with the consequent enormous extension of the preparations for World Revolution and with active promotion of strikes and labour unrest here. . . . In March, 1924, he was recipient of 30,000 shares in McVitie and Price Biscuit Co. and a Daimler car."

General Strike

"In 1925 delegates from Moscow were in England arranging with members of the Trades Union Congress for strikes which might develop into revolution; and on May 1, 1926, the great General Strike was declared at a meeting of trade union leaders, when MacDonald said: 'We (the Socialist Party) are there in the battle with you, taking our share uncomplainingly until the end has come and right and justice have been done.' He and J. H. Thomas then joined in singing 'The Red Flag'; and he became a co-opted member of the Strike Committee, which was later charged in a Cabinet paper with 'having held a pistol at the head of Constitutional Government.' . . . Mr. Baldwin said: 'The General Strike will remain forever a stain on the annals of our country.' . . . Miss Ellen Wilkinson" (a Communist made an Ind. Labour Party executive) "took a very active part in the General Strike. . . . She toured the country addressing strike meetings. . . . MacDonald in Oct. 1928 said the strike 'as the manifestation of human solidarity was one of the most glorious things that this 20th Century had produced' . . . during the Miners' strike he wrote Miss Ellen Wilkinson in the U.S. . . . ;" etc.

See Independent Labour Party also.

EUGENICS PUBLISHING CO.

Affiliate of Freethought Press (anti-religious), having identical addresses and companion catalogues. Dr. Wm. J. Robinson, author of "the scathing denunciation of religion" so lauded by Albert Einstein in the atheist catalogue, is also author of several of the sex books. "Sane Sex and Sane Living" by H. W. Long, purporting to be written to benefit "married couples," uses some medical language, wallows apparently in enthusiastic licentiousness with descriptive erotic suggestions, and recommends and condones masturbation. The advertising leaflet for this book states that it is "Recommended by Union Theological Seminary." (!) Vile advertisements are sent out offering lewd books about sex perversions and atrocities fully illustrated. Why the Post Office Dept. allows such material to go through the mails is a mystery. Hdqts. 317 E. 34th St., N.Y. City.

EX-SERVICE MEN'S INTERNATIONAL

Communist veterans' organization with which the Workers Ex-Service Men's League (of the U.S.) is affiliated, formed by Communist Henri Barbusse, of France, its president; its purpose is "to make war on war" by bloody Red revolution; teaches soldiers to "turn an imperialist war into civil war."

F

FABIAN SOCIETY

An English "drawing room Socialists'" society; founded 1884 by Prof. Thomas Davidson, "an ethical Anarchist-Communist," who was quickly superseded by G. B. Shaw, then a clerk, and Sidney Webb, son of a London hairdresser, Annie Besant and H. G. Wells later becoming leading members; "by its method of middle class permeation, notably in the Civil Service, has done more to accelerate the revolutionary movement than the crude agitation of the Socialist Democratic Federation" (from "Socialist Network" by Nesta Webster); its program states: "The Fabian Society consists of Socialists. It therefore aims at the reorganization of Society by the emancipation of Land and Industrial Capital from individual ownership," etc.; aided in forming the very red Independent Labour Party of Great Britain in 1893 (see Ind. Lab. Party).

FARMER LABOR PARTY

Is virtually synonymous and interchangeable with the Socialist Party, each supporting candidates of the other party for certain offices; strong in Minnesota.

FARMER LABOR POLITICAL FEDERATION

Formed by the Conference for Progressive Political Action (see); pres. Thos. R. Amlie; Alfred M. Bingham, exec. sec.

FARMERS NATIONAL COMMITTEE OF ACTION

See under United Farmers League.

FEDERAL COUNCIL OF CHURCHES OF CHRIST IN AMERICA

Fed. Coun. Chs.

The Federal Council's claim that it represents the will of 22,000,000 Protestant Church members is ridiculous. Members of Protestant congregations do no voting on the policies of this Council. While about 400 delegates meet once every four years, appointed on the basis of four from each of twenty-eight denominations, plus one for each 50,000 communicants, these are entertained by a well planned steam-rollered program. The executive committee meets only once a year. In the interim, an Administrative Committee of twenty-eight members largely appointed by the Council's President issues the radical pronouncements in favor of Birth Control, disarmament, Negro social equality, League of Nations, World Court, prohibition, and against "sanctioning war" and the Naval Bill, against deportation or exclusion of alien Reds (in cooperation with the A.C.L.U.)—all matters upon which the 22,000,000 Protestant Church members never vote at all. S. Parkes Cadman, now on the nat. com. of the very red Nat. Religion and Labor Foundation, president of the Federal Council 1924-8 and radio minister of the same since, has shocked many denominational leaders into agitating for withdrawal from the Federal Council by his radio talks in contravention of essential New Testament Christian doctrines. Bishop Francis J. McConnell, president from 1929-33, has a long record for radicalism (see this "Who's Who"). Many denominational and Congressional protests have been registered concerning radical Council activities, but "The evidence shows that the Federal Council will continue to function regardless of any activity by the membership denominations respecting financial support since 75 per cent of its income is donated from outside the churches, a condition which tends to support the charge that it is serving these interests instead of the denominations." (From "Tainted Contacts" by E. N. Sanctuary, 156 5th Ave., N.Y. City, price 50c and $1.00, an exposé of the Federal Council.)

The Marion Star stated: "'They have been hand in hand with the Civil Liberties Union which has been doing its utmost to oppose, hinder and hamstring the Government in every activity in which it has engaged to protect American lives and property from the foes of all governments . . . from the I.W.W., the agents of Soviet Russia, from Communists and Direct-actionists of every label and variety. It was responsible for the sending out to 125,000 Clergymen the Kirby Page anti-war service pledge 'I never again will sanction or participate in war' and 'will not give financial or moral support to any war.' It is to the everlasting credit of the clergy that the 125,000 largely refused to sign the seditious pledge. It is indeed heartening to know that one of our Federal lawmakers has the backbone . . . to ask that this organization, which has been so consistently fighting the government and all its policies for the protection of American ideals, be investigated. The country should know the people at the head of it and the forces behind them, and the manner in which they are making dupes of the memberships of many denominations of the Christian Church of the land."

In 1914 Carnegie endowed the Church Peace Union, a self perpetuating board of 29 trustees practically all of whom are in some way identified with the Federal Council, "which gave the controlling group in the Federal Council an annual income which has enabled it to run the budget for the Federal Council and its cooperating organizations up into the millions. Among these organizations are the Church Peace Union, World's Alliance for International Friendship Through the Churches, The Commission on International Friendship and Good Will, the National Council for Prevention of War, American Civil Liberties Union." ("Pastors, Politicians and Pacifists" by Smith-Johns.)

The Federal Council admittedly violates the American ideal of separation of Church and State. In relating the work of its Washington Committee (on page 217 of the Federal Council "Handbook of the Churches"), it states that it "Serves as a center for the cooperating work of the churches in their relation to agencies of the government. It is a clearing house of information concerning governmental activities which affect moral and social conditions and also a medium for interpreting to the government from time to time the point of view of the churches."

FEDERAL COUNCIL SEX PAMPHLET

"Young Peoples Relationships" is a disgusting sex manual for "leaders of young people between the ages of 16 and 19" written by "a Conference convened by the Federal Council of Churches. Issued under the auspices of the Conference on Preparation for Home Making, Instituted by the Federal Council of Churches" . . . (quoted from its title page). General Amos Fries, in his booklet "Sugar Coating Communism" (price 25c; address: 3305 Woodley Road, Washington, D.C.), hails this sex manual as "A crowning achievement of the Federal Council controlling group along the line of preparing the way for atheistic communism." Perhaps because of Gen. Fries' exposure, the reference, in the second printing of the manual, to the Federal Council sponsorship has been carefully deleted. Otherwise it is the same and is sold by the Pilgrim Press (14 Beacon St., Boston and 418 S. Market Street, Chicago, price 75c).

Full detailed instructions and tests for studying various phases of sex and sexual intercourse by the "discussion method" in an "atmosphere" that is "informal," "frank," and "open minded" are given with the advice that "some leaders report good results in mixed groups." Model "opinion" and "word" tests are given to analyse the reactions of the young people individually to suggestive words and sentences such as: "Light Petting, Heavy Petting, Sex Consciousness in Girls, in Boys, Birth Control, Unmarried Mother, Flaming Youth, Modesty, Free Love, Necking; What sensations come from spooning?; On the basis of the stimulation experienced by men at the touch of some girls what is the stimulation in the girl and is that stimulation more intense at some times than at others?; What can a girl do when she is out with a boy in a car and he stops along the road, turns off the light and says 'Now we can have a good time?' "; etc., etc., etc. The Birth Control report of the Federal Council "Committee on Marriage and the Home" is quoted in this pamphlet with this addition: "This report contemplates only the use of contraceptives by married people, the facts stated however are of universal interest and apply with still more significance to sexual intercourse outside of marriage." The infamous Mary Ware Dennett pamphlet "The Sex Side of Life" is endorsed as "indispensable." Gen. Fries states: "Anyone reading the whole pamphlet cannot fail to get the idea that when all is said and done sexual intercourse is a personal matter and if two want to indulge therein it is nobody else's business. . . . Had this pamphlet come out of Russia direct as one of their means of breaking down all morality, the family, and the home, as the final step toward communism, we would have felt it well qualified to carry out the intent of its authors." What a manual for use, as it recommends itself, for "Denominational Summer Conferences, Young People's Societies and Study Groups in Churches, in Hi-Y Clubs and Girl Reserves!" It was "prepared by Benj. S. Winchester," who is secretary of the Federal Council and contributing editor of the official Federal Council Bulletin, while Federal Council officials Rev. Samuel McCrea Cavert (executive secretary of the Council and Editor of the Bulletin) and Rev. Worth M. Tippy (secretary of the Council and contributing editor of its Bulletin) were fellow members of the Conference which assisted and sponsored its preparation and publication. The average parent would sicken with disgust to take part in such licentious discussions as are presented in this manual for decent young church people who normally would never hear or become interested in a tenth part of the sexual trash presented for them to "study" in this manual.

FEDERATED PRESS

Fed. Press.

Claimed by Communists as their own press service; headed by Carl Haessler of the communist Chgo. Workers School; supplies news to Communist, Socialist, radical, revolutionary papers in the United States; was handsomely aided by the Garland Fund (see "Garland Fund"); the Lusk Report (1920) quotes Roger Baldwin as saying "There was organized sometime in 1908 largely through the activity of Scott Nearing, a small press association known as the International Labor News Service with headquarters at 7 East 15th Street. The active management of the news service was in the hands of Louis P. Lochner.... In December 1919 (it) became the Federated Press. The Federated Press is now serving something over one hundred papers . . . has international connections with and cable news service from England, Scandinavia, France and Australia. Its news service deals primarily with the labor movement and with *revolutionary progress*"; U.S. Report 2290 points out that Tass, the Soviet Union Telegraph Agency, has one and the same office and representative at Washington, D.C., with the Federated Press; E. J. Costello, its first manager, after visiting Russia and European countries, to establish connections with revolutionary organizations, was deported from England (1920) as a Red. Louis P. Lochner took charge of the Berlin office used as a publicity outlet by the Third International of Moscow; Carl Haessler supplanted Costello as manager from 1922 on; in 1927 members of the Federated Press executive board were Earl Browder and Arne Swabeck of the executive committee of the Communist Party, W. Maloney, Joseph Schlossberg, Phil Ziegler, John McGivney, Math Tenhunen (prominent Communist), Albert F. Coyle and Frank Palmer; in order to collect funds to aid the Federated Press, a Federated Press League was organized in Chicago, Feb. 4, 1922, with Robert Morss Lovett as president. Wm. Z. Foster was then a member of the executive board of the Federated Press.

The Chicago office of Carl Haessler and the Federated Press is (1933) also the office of the A.C.L.U. Chgo. Committee, the Chgo. Com. for Struggle Against War, the Acme News Syndicate and the "Institute for *Mortuary* Research" (whatever that is), of which Haessler is director.

FEDERATION OF UNEMPLOYED ORGANIZATIONS OF COOK COUNTY

Fed. Unemp. Org. Cook Co.

A Communist-officered committee with hdqts. at 1910 South Kedzie Ave., Chicago, and, according to its letterhead, "Affiliated to the National Federation of Unemployed Workers Leagues of America" (Borders'); a letter dated July 12, 1933, signed by the Communist chairman, Karl Lochner, was addressed "To All Workers Organizations in Cook County," and said in part: "The newly organized Federation of Unemployed Organizations of Cook County is organizing a Hunger March to force an answer from the bosses for next July 26th. . . . We want your organization to endorse this march, to participate in it under your own signs and banners, and to help popularize it. . . . Further, this action will require the issuing of a great deal of publicity matter at considerable expense. We want to ask your organization to help us in this by making a generous donation. We can send you speakers for meetings. You can get publicity material from our headquarters after July 19. Fraternally yours, Karl Lochner."

This letterhead lists as officers:

Chmn., Karl Lochner, Unemployed Council (of Communist Party); vice chmn., Bernard Klein, Chicago Workers Committee (Expelled Local No. 2); secretary, L. Armstrong, Unemployed Council; treas., J. Kasper, Chicago Workers Committee on Unemployment; exec. com.; Harry D. Weiser, Melting Pot League of America; G. Reeves, Unemployed Council; May Delin, Women's Committee, Unemployed Council; Albert Simon, Chicago Workers Committee (Expelled Local No. 2); Norman Satir, Workers League of America (of communist Proletarian Party); Paul Tucker, Unemployed Council; O. Heckner, Single Men's Committee, Unemployed Council.

FEDERATION OF UNEMPLOYED WORKERS LEAGUES OF AMERICA (NATIONAL)

Fed. Unemp. Wkrs. Lgs. Am.

A communist-I.W.W.-controlled "united front" federation of unemployed organizations first organized all over the U.S. in 1932-33 by Karl Borders, who also headed it as nat. chmn. until its national convention, held at Lincoln Center, Chicago, May 13-15, 1933, at which time Tom Dixon (of the Proletarian Party's (Communist) "Workers Leagues") became nat. chmn.; A. Guss (of the Communist Party's "Unemployed Councils") became vice chmn.; Eddy Stattman (organizer of I.W.W. "Unemployed Unions") became treas.; George Leach (of Border's "Chicago Workers Committee on Unemployment" (chmn. Local 34)) became sec. The I.W.W., Proletarian and various Communist parties are, of course, all openly revolutionary bodies. An executive committee was also elected consisting of Hugo Oehler (of the nat. exec. com. of the Communist League, known as "Trotskyites," and representative of the Unemployed Unions of Gillespie Ill., center of recent Communist agitation and hdqts. of the Progressive Miners Union); Warren Lamson (chmn. of the Communist Cook County, Ill. "Unemployed Councils," teacher at the Chicago Workers School of revolution); Zimmerman of the Proletarian Party's (Communist) "Workers Leagues"; V. Didwell (of People's Council of Bellingham); D. Harrington (of United Producers of Wash.); Wm. R. Truax of the "Unemployed Citizens Leagues" of the Conference for Progressive Labor Action (militant left-wing-Socialist, Communist-cooperating "Musteites"); Lore (of the S. E. Missouri "Unemployed Leagues" of the same Conference for Progressive Labor Action); Welsh (of the N.Y. "Association of Unemployed" of the Communist Party (opposition) "Lovestoneites"); Mattock (of the Proletarian Party's (Communist) "Workers Leagues"); Conners (of the Allen County, Indiana "Unemployed Assn." of the Communist Party (opposition) "Lovestoneites").

The "New Frontier" (April 19, 1933), organ of the Chicago Workers Committee on Unemployment, which was also organized by Karl Borders, stated: "Jobless leagues throughout the country have been asked by the Federation of Unemployed Workers Leagues of America to send delegates to a convention in Chicago, May 13-15. The Workers Committee on Unemployment and the Workers League, Chicago branches of the Federation, have agreed to act as hosts. They will feed and lodge the delegates. Sessions will be held at Lincoln Center, 700 Oakwood Blvd."

The May 3, 1933 issue said: *"Federation Still Growing*—Affiliations are still coming in daily. The list now includes:

"Chicago Workers Committee; Workers League of America (branches in Chicago, Buffalo, and Los Angeles); Racine County Workers' Committee on Unemployment; Downers Grove Unemployed Council; Unemployed Citizens' League of Michigan (branches at Detroit, Lansing, Owosso, Battle Creek, Bay City, Grand Rapids); Unemployed Citizens' League of St. Louis; Arbeiter Kultur Sport Verein; Waukegan Cooperative Unemployment League; Dayton Cooperative Production Units; Eastern Ohio Unemployed Leagues (18 branches); Unemployment League of Des Moines County; Houston Unemployment League; Community Cooperative Farms (Visalia, Cal.); Memphis Unemployed Citizens' League; South Bend Unemployed Council; Buffalo League of the Unemployed; Indianapolis Unemployment League; People's Unemployment League of Maryland; Unemployed Union of Boston; Tenants and Unemployed League of Washington, D.C.; Socialist Unemployed Union of Richmond, Virginia; Workers' Unemployed Leagues of New York; United Men and Women Workers of Terre Haute; Dauphin County (Pa.) Workers' Committee on Unemployment; Unemployed League of New Bedford, Mass.; Summit County (Ohio) Workers' League; Fall River Unemployed Union; New York Workers' Committee on Unemployment; Unemployed Union of New Jersey."

FEDERATED UNEMPLOYED WORKERS LEAGUES OF NEW YORK

Fed. Unemp. Wkrs. Lgs. N.Y.

Federated Feb. 1933 as part of the Federated Unemployed Workers Leagues of America (see); associated in New York with the Y.M.C.A., Y.M.H.A., Urban League, N.A.A.C.P.; Committee (as announced in the Communist press): Paul Blanshard, Fannia Cohn, Heywood Broun, Rose Schneidermann, Morris Hillquit, Walter Frank, Arthur Garfield Hays, Freda Kirchwey, Morris Ernst, J. Howard Melish, Bishop Francis J. McConnell, Rabbi Stephen Wise, John Haynes Holmes.

FELLOWSHIP FOR A CHRISTIAN SOCIAL ORDER

Fell. Christ. Soc. Order

Merged about 1929 with the Fellowship of Reconciliation; Kirby Page was chairman of the executive committee.

FELLOWSHIP OF FAITHS

"Be ye not unequally yoked together with unbelievers; for what fellowship hath righteousness with unrighteousness? and what communion hath light with darkness?" (II Corinth., 6:14.)

Like the Reconciliation Trips (see) of the Fell. Recon., it seeks to propagandize the anti-national internationalism and "reconciliation" of all races and creeds into one, or none, that is part of the program of Communism and Socialism. "How Expand Patriotism into World Consciousness" is a typical program subject. Speakers for the debasing and degrading Hindu, Mohammedan, Pagan and Agnostic Cults are placed in "fellowship" and on an equal footing with speakers for Jesus Christ. The audiences chant a mixture of prayers and ritual from all of these. The savage Mohammedan call of the muezzin as heard in darkest Asia is mingled with the propaganda of the Hindu, Jew and agnostic. Negro choirs and performers give an interracial touch to the meetings. This jumbling of contradictory beliefs leads only to confusion and unbelief, and robs Jesus Christ of His rightful place as *the* Light of this World. Its bulletins were handed out by the Communist booksellers at the A.S. C.R.R.-L.I.D. Brookhart-Fish debate Mar. 21, 1932. Ignorance of the purposes of its radical sponsors enables it to draw in numerous non-radical dupes who see only the supposed beauty of "fellowship" and "brotherly love" (with paganism).

Radicals of all hues addressed its World Fellowship of Faiths Parliament, held in Chicago, Aug. 27 to Sept. 17, 1933, including Raja Jai Bahadur Singh of India, "founder of the Humanistic Club," an atheistic movement, W. P. Hapgood, Rabbi Hillel Silver, Dean Roscoe Pound, Karl Borders, James M. Yard, Philip LaFollette, Carl D. Thompson, Rosika Schwimmer, Jesse H. Holmes, Charlotte Perkins Gilman, Jabez T. Sunderland of A. Lincoln Center "Unity," Rabbi Chas. E. Shulman, Eliz. Gilman, Curtis Reese, Mary E. McDowell, Mrs. M. H. Ford (Bahaist speaker), Margaret Sanger ("Crusading Freethinker"), Ex-Sen. Brookhart, Benj. C. Marsh, Norman B. Barr, etc., etc.

The speaker for the Parliament at two sessions was the unfrocked "Bishop" Wm. Montgomery Brown, author of atheist books for children and head of the communist W.I.R., which runs the anti-religious Red revolutionary Young Pioneer camps. He sacrilegiously wore a Bishop's tunic with a cross. To quote from the Bulletin of Advisory Associates: "Brown soon launched into a glorification of Soviet Russia stating there was one place in the world where they had dared to end the exploitation of man. . . . He said that in Russia science had replaced supernaturalness and religion was gradually being stamped out and that the new generation being reared there was free from the old shackles of religious beliefs in God in the skies . . . that the youth were not permitted to have their minds filled with reverence for abstract deities up in the skies and that science was replacing religion for the new generation. . . . He said that the U.S.S.R. was just the forerunner of an international Communist state which would gradually absorb all capitalist states which were gradually decaying away. Brown said that the only way to attain this international Communist state was through revolution and that he used the term advisedly knowing full well the cost attached to revolution but that the results were worth all. He said that the present corrupt and decayed capitalist systems must be torn down in order to build wholly anew, and that if any *government, church* or institution opposed or stood in the way of the attainment of this Communist state, they must be ruthlessly *overthrown and destroyed.*

"These utterly seditious remarks were received with enthusiastic applause by the audience and as he stressed his various points many of the audience could be seen vigorously nodding their heads in approval. In concluding his remarks 'Bishop' Brown said that if world unity were to be attained it must be through International Communism and could be arrived at by *banishing the Gods from the Skies and capitalists from the Earth* (his slogan) and then, and only then, would there exist a complete *World Fellowship of Faiths.*

"His conclusion was greeted with a wild round of applause. Charles Frederick Weller then arose and Brown was asked to repeat his concluding remarks, which he did. Then Weller thanked the 'Bishop' for his 'stirring' message and said that the audience, irrespective of individual viewpoints, could not help but admire the courage and stirring quality of 'Bishop' Brown's message and he was sure that others felt the same as he did, that they had been of the same belief as Brown for some time but did not have the courage to come out and admit it and he wanted to say at this time that he was in thorough agreement with the sentiments as expressed by 'Bishop' Brown."

This Chas. F. Weller and Kedarnath Das Gupta are the *"General Executives"* of the Fellowship of Faiths, with hdqts. at Room 320, 139 N. Clark St., Chicago. Das Gupta is "one of the three General Executives of the Threefold Movement—Fellowship of Faiths, Union of East and West, League of Neighbors."

"National Committee of 300": Hon. Pres.: Jane Addams; Vice Presidents: Newton D. Baker, Prof. John Dewey, Glenn Frank, Dr. John A. Lapp, Dr. R. A. Millikan, Frank Murphy (Gov. of the Philippines), Chester Rowell, Mary Woolley; Chmn., Bishop Francis J. McConnell; Vice Chairmen: Rabbi Stephen S. Wise, Prof. E. R. A. Seligman, Patrick Henry Callahan.

"Chicago Committee of 200": Chmn., Dr. Ernest F. Tittle; Vice Chairmen: Dr. Preston Bradley, Dr. Albert Buckner Coe. Other Chicago Committee members are: Dr. Chas. Gilkey, chmn. South Side; Rev. Irwin St. John Tucker, chmn. Northwest Side; Rev. E. F. Tittle, chmn. North Shore; Chas. Clayton Morrison, Chmn. Chicago general committee; Rabbi Chas. E. Shulman, James Mullenbach, Rabbi S. Felix Mendelsohn, Chandra Seena Gooneratne (see China Committees), Thos. W. Allinson (father of Brent Dow), W. Frank McClure, Frank Orman Beck (Recon. Trips), Mrs. B. F. Langworthy, Rev. Norman Barr, and the following who are also A.C.L.U. committeemen: Rabbi Louis L. Mann, Mary McDowell, Robt. Morss Lovett, Fred Atkins Moore, Horace J. Bridges, A. Eustace Haydon, Amelia Sears, Curtis Reese, Wm. H. Holly, Clarence Darrow, Jane Addams (an A.C.L.U. founder), etc., etc.

Communist Brown's talks before the Fell. Faiths 1933 Parliament in Chgo. are now printed and being advertised by him in his atheist children's book. They are entitled "Communism—the New Faith for the New World" (price 10c, Bradford Brown Edu. Co., Galion, Ohio). He calls them "Two outspoken appeals on behalf of communism."

FELLOWSHIP OF RECONCILIATION

Fell. Recon.

A radical-"pacifist" organization of about 10,000 members employing Christian terms to spread communistic propaganda; conducts Reconciliation Trips (see); widely circulated, in 1932, petitions for Recognition of Russia (see); affiliated with socialist Pioneer Youth of America; a section of the ultra-radical War Resisters International; sponsored the Lane Pamphlet against military training for the publication and distribution of which the red Garland Fund spent $5,400; a supporting organization, in conjunction with revolutionary Communist, I.W.W. and Socialist bodies, of the communist-called and controlled Congresses Against War (U.S., Student, World Congress of Youth); its executive secretary, J. B. Matthews, took an active part in these Congresses either as chairman, speaker, or organizer. I heard him cheered at the huge communist Mooney meeting, May 1, 1933, when he expressed his friendship and solidarity with the Reds and said he wished Mooney's chances of getting out of jail were as good as his were of leaving the Socialist for the Communist Party. His selection as co-chairman, with Communist Donald Henderson, of the U.S. Congress Against War, to preside over the two platforms from which the Communist Party's outstanding revolutionary agitators were to speak was an "honor" indicating reciprocal esteem for him on their part. The Feb. 1933 issue of "Student Outlook" (militant Socialist L.I.D. organ), of which he is editor, stated that he is "not opposed to a war that would end capitalism" (for his further remarks see under Student Congress). Henri Barbusse, Tom Mann, Earl Browder, Michael Gold, "Mother" Bloor, Jack Stachel, all Communist leaders, and J. B. Matthews were the speakers at the dinner given in honor of Tom Mann's arrival from England, Oct. 6, 1933, at Hotel Paramount, N.Y. City.

A Fell. Recon. leaflet stating the position and purpose of the Fell. Recon. admonishes: "Position A. Keep Central and Typical the Reference to Jesus" in order "to influence churches and the Christian Student Movement and to secure their cooperation in spreading *radical Christian views on war economics and race issues*" and "for *demonstrating left-wing Christianity*" as "hitherto our leadership and support have come mainly from Christian sources. These sources especially have made possible the extension of our work in Europe, Central America, and Southern United States" (quoted in first article on Pacifism).

It sponsored and called the conference for the communist All-America Anti-Imperialist League at Wash., D.C., Oct. 29-30, 1926 (Federated Press, Oct. 21, 1926). It is one of the branches of the International Fellowship of Reconciliation which originated in Holland about 1914. The American branch was organized 1917 by Norman Thomas aided by his fellow radicals Jane Addams, Harry Ward, Emily Greene Balch, Jessie W. Hughan, W. Raushenbush, Oswald G. Villard, etc., later joined by Scott Nearing, Anna Rochester, Paul Jones, John Nevin Sayre, etc. It participates in International War Resisters (see) conferences.

The International Fellowship of Reconciliation conference, held at Lyons, France, Aug. 29, 1929, issued a pamphlet, widely distributed by the American branch. It is entitled "Christ and the Class War" and states: "We are agreed in our conviction that the class war is a fact; that, whether we will or not, each one of us is involved; that, as a Fellowship, we must work toward a radical reorganization of society"; recommendations for activity include: "Joining political movements which aim at the replacement of private capitalism by a system of collective ownership" (Communism-Socialism); "aiding movements for the freeing of exploited colonial peoples from alien control by imperialist powers, for opposing race discrimination," (same as revolutionary Socialist-Communist propaganda), "supporting movements for disarmament, the abolition of compulsory military service and the settlement of conflicts by judicial method or conciliation realizing that *so long as military force is maintained for possible international war there is grave danger that it will be used in the class war*" (the very meat of Socialist-Communist so-called "pacifism"); "We urge on Fellowship members the study of the experiment of Soviet Russia in relation to the class struggle and in those countries which do not yet recognize the Soviet Union we urge them to support efforts to establish normal diplomatic relations" (with the Soviet Union which aims for world bloody revolution); etc. 1933 Chairman: Reinhold Niebuhr (the Marxian, also U.S. Congress Speaker).

Executive Secretaries: J. B. Matthews and John Nevin Sayre; Secretary: For South, Howard A. Kester; for Latin America, Chas. A. Thomson; for Industry, Chas. C. Webber; Vice Chairmen: Adelaide T. Case, Edmund B. Chaffee, Kirby Page; Treas. Wm. C. Biddle; Asst. Treasurers: James M. Boyd and Tucker P. Smith; Chmn. Exec. Com. Wm. C. Bowen.

National Council members whose terms expired 1929: Jane Addams, Don M. Chase, Elmer Cope, Juliette Derricotte, Carol Hyde, A. J. Muste, James Myers, Roy Newton, Wm. B. Spofford, Grace Watson, Theresa Wilson; terms expired 1928: Devere Allen, Kath. Ashworth Baldwin, Roger Baldwin, Gilbert Beaver, Helena Dudley, Benj. Gerig, Harold Hatch, Caroline LaMonte, Scott Nearing, Edw. Richards, Galen Russell,

Tucker P. Smith, Chas. Webber. Recent executives: A. J. Muste (militant labor agitator and Socialist), Paul Jones, George Collins, Amy Blanche Greene, etc.

European headquarters: 2126 Doublergasse, Vienna; 17 Red Lion Square, W.C.I., London. New York City hdqts., until recently, 383 Bible House Astor Place, now 29 Broadway.

FELLOWSHIP OF RECONCILIATION PETITION FOR RUSSIAN RECOGNITION

Fell. Recon. Pet. Russ. Recog.

A petition headed "For the Recognition of Soviet Russia" circulated in 1932 by the Fellowship of Reconciliation, in behalf of the Soviet government, which proudly announces that it intends to overthrow ours by bloody Red terror and Communist revolution, stated: "In the interests of World Peace and as a measure of mutual economic advantage I urge the immediate recognition of the Soviet government of Russia by the United States." The letter inclosed with this petition stated that "shortly after the November election" the petition would be presented to the President-elect" and was signed by J. B. Matthews, as exec. sec., who is so prominently featured as speaker at Communist affairs in company with Communist Party leaders. Attached was the following list headed: "The following college and university presidents have signed this request":

W. A. Neilson, Smith Coll.; Marion E. Park, Bryn Mawr Coll.; Ellen F. Pendleton, Wellesley Coll.; G. Bromley Oxnam, DePauw U.; Horace D. Taft, The Taft Sch.; John Hope, Atlanta U.; Daniel W. Morehouse, Drake U.; H. C. Bedford, Penn. Coll.; J. A. C. Chandler, William and Mary Coll.; Earl E. Harper, Evansville Coll.; Howell A. King, U. of Baltimore; M. H. Knudsen, Snow Coll.; Clyde L. Lyon, Eureka Coll.; Henry T. Moore, Skidmore Coll.; Earl A. Roadman, Dak. Wesleyan U.; Chas. J. Smith, Roanoke Coll.; Paul F. Voelker, Battle Creek Coll.; John H. Wood, Culver-Stockton Coll.; Paul H. Buchholz, U. of Dubuque; Arlo Ayres Brown, Drew U.; W. J. Hutchins, Berea Coll.; W. Douglas Mackenzie, Hartford Sem.; F. E. Eiselen, Garrett Bibl. Inst.; Arthur E. Morgan, Antioch Coll.; Wallace W. Attwood, Clark U.; I. N. McGash, Phillips U.; W. H. Hall, Wilmington Coll.; William T. Holmes, Tougaloo Coll.; H. L. Kent, N. M. Coll. of Agr. and Mech. Arts; Lucien Koch, Commonwealth Coll.; Robt. Williams, Ohio Northern U.; C. P. McClelland, MacMurray Coll.; W. O. Mendenhall, Friends U.; Margaret S. Morriss, Pembroke Coll.; Wm. H. Powers, S.D. State Coll.; John O. Spencer, Morgan Coll.; Wm. J. Wilkinson, Colby Coll.; Harry A. Garfield, Williams Coll.; Daniel L. Marsh, Boston U.; Henry Sloane Coffin, Union Theol. Sem.; Thomas E. Jones, Fisk Univ.; Henry J. Doenmann, U. of Toledo; Wm. Pearson Tolley, Allegheny Coll.; B. I. Bell, St. Stephens Coll.; Harvey N. Davis, Stevens Inst.; Ralph K. Hickok, Western Coll.; O. E. Kriege, New Orleans U.; H. L. McCrorey, Johnson C. Smith U.; John S. Nollen, Grinnell Coll.; Albert B. Storms, Baldwin-Wallace Coll.; Robert E. Blackwell, Randolph-Macon Coll.; Albert W. Palmer, Chicago Theol. Sem.; Ernest H. Wilkins, Oberlin Coll.; W. P. Behan, Ottawa U.; Norman F. Coleman, Reed Coll.; Franklin S. Harris, Brigham Young U.; V. F. Schwalin, McPherson Coll.; C. W. Tenney, Gooding Coll.; Arthur Braden, Transylvania U.

Some of the 350 Professors who signed are: Earle Eubank, Cincinnati U.; Jerome Davis, Yale U.; Gordon W. Allport, Harvard U.; Ernest F. Tittle, Garrett Bibl. Inst.; T. V. Smith, U. of Chgo.; Daniel A. Prescott, Gen. Edu. Bd.; H. A. Overstreet, City Coll. of N.Y.; Paul Monroe, Teachers Coll.; Frederick Efershuer, Butler U.; Charles P. Howland, Yale U.; Charles W. Gilkey, U. of Chgo.; D. F. Fleming, Vanderbilt U.; John Dewey, Columbia U.; Zechariah Chafee, Harvard U.; Benj. H. Williams, U. of Pitts.; Ida Sitler, Hollins Coll.; Ernest Minor Patterson, U. of Pa.; Reinhold Niebuhr, Union Theol. Sem.; James C. Miller, U. of Pa.; Robert Morss Lovett, U. of Chgo.; S. Ralph Harlow, Smith Coll.; Arthur N. Holcombe, Harvard U.; Herbert F. Fraser, Swarthmore Coll.; Stephen P. Duggan, Inst. of Intl. Edu.; John R. Commons, Wis. U.; Thomas Woody, U. of Pa.; Edwin R. A. Seligman, Columbia U.; O. Myeing Niehus, No. Tchrs. Coll.; Edward C. Lindeman, N.Y. Sch. of Soc. Wk.; Hugh Hartshorne, Yale U.; Wm. Trufant Foster, Pollak Found.; Horace A. Eaton, Syracuse U.; Phillip W. L. Cox, N.Y. U.; Henry Nelson Wieman, U. of Chgo.; Alva W. Taylor, Vanderbilt U.; Wm. F. Russell, Columbia U.; Paul Jones, Antioch Coll.; Wm. H. Kilpatrick, Columbia U. Tchrs. Coll.; Harry Emerson Fosdick, Union Theol. Sem.; Harold U. Faulkner, Smith Coll.

FELLOWSHIP OF SOCIALIST CHRISTIANS

A Union Theological Seminary (see) movement. (See page 336.)

FELLOWSHIP OF YOUTH FOR PEACE

Became the Youth Section of the Fellowship of Reconciliation, about 1928.

FELLOWSHIP PRESS

Formerly published the Socialist "World Tomorrow" and rec'd. money from the Garland Fund for this purpose.

FINNISH CULTURAL FEDERATION

Section of the Revolutionary Writers Federation (Communist).

FINNISH PROGRESSIVE SOCIETY

A Communist Party affiliated group.

FINNISH WORKERS AND FARMERS LEAGUE

Affiliated with the Workers and Farmers Cooperative Alliance of the communist T.U.U.L.

FINNISH WORKERS FEDERATION, INC.

Of the Communist Party Foreign Language Groups (see); includes Finnish

Workers Clubs, Finnish Women's Club (Chicago), and groups in various cities; conducted Young Pioneer Camp at Lake Zurich, Ill. 1933; its publishing plant in N.C. City printed the "Pioneer Song Book" for Young Pioneers 1933.

FIRST AMERICAN TRADE UNION DELEGATION TO RUSSIA

1st Am. Tr. Un. Delg. to Russia

In Aug.-Sept. 1927; was exulted over by the Communist Party; repudiated and denied the sanction of the A.F. of L. because of its communistic character; its trip was reported for the Federated Press and Daily Worker; its first report "Russia After Ten Years" was published by the communist International Publishers; its later report entitled "Soviet Russia in the Second Decade" sold by Communist book stores and recommended by the Soviet Union Information Bureau (see Mar. 1931 issue of its official publication "Soviet Union Review"); this book report was edited by Stuart Chase, Rex. Tugwell and Communist Robert W. Dunn, fellow members of the delegation, and is a mass of misleading communistic propaganda; Frank P. Walsh, counsel for the expedition in a letter soliciting funds, dated July 12, 1927 (reproduced in the Better America Federation Bulletin of July 27, 1927) said in part:

"Dear Comrade: We are running into strong opposition from the reactionary president, Wm. Green, of the A.F. of L., who has learned about our planned mission to Russia and has refused to this date to sanction and authorize our commission to be a representative body of the A.F. of L." (gives names of members, etc.). "We have picked these men personally and there is no danger of sabotaging the mission by any one of the delegation's rostrum, for the majority is in our hands. However, I do expect opposition from Johnson, Ziegler" (these evidently did not go) "and Fitzpatrick but since I am the Counsel for the mission you may trust the rest to me. The American Trade Union Delegation . . . feels justified in calling upon all persons outside the ranks of the organized labor movement to defray the cost of our traveling expenses and of covering the publication of our report. . . . Knowing your relations with the Liberal movement of California especially with Mrs. K. C. Gartz" (see this "Who's Who") "I am forced to ask you for financial contribution to the amount of at least $5,000, which I figure should be California's contribution to this greatest of all undertakings for the cause of Russia. . . . Remember we need $20,000 and by the end of July. For cooperation, Sincerely Yours, Frank P. Walsh, Counsel, The American Trades Union Mission to Russia."

Efforts of the Delegation to pose as officially representative of the A.F. of L. were quickly spiked by Wm. Green, President of the A.F. of L., who on May 27 issued a statement asserting in part:

"For the purpose of relieving any wrong public impression which may prevail, this delegation is not clothed with authority to speak for American labor, or for the American Federation of Labor." (Chicago Tribune, May 28, 1927).

At the Workers Party (the name of the Communist Party at that time) Convention held Sept. 1927 in N.Y. City, Jay Lovestone, then national secretary of the Communist Party, called special attention to the fact that the Communists had been able over the protest of the A.F. of L. to send a "labor" delegation to Soviet Russia (Marvin Data Sheets); during the tour Frank Palmer (see this "Who's Who") wrote reports for the Federated Press, the first from aboard ship appearing in the "Federated Press Labor Letter," August 18, 1927, and headed "Labor Mission on Way to Europe and Russia"; the Daily Worker published an article Oct. 12, 1927, after their return, headed "Palmer Praises Labor in U.S.S.R."; in 1930 Palmer was made field secretary of the Chicago A.C.L.U. committee headed by Arthur Fisher, a fellow delegation member and president of the A.C.L.U. Chicago branch. Fisher is a Winnetka neighbor of Carleton Washburne of the delegation, who is Supt. of Winnetka Public Schools.

The book report "Soviet Russia in the Second Decade—a Joint Survey by the Technical Staff of the First American Trade Union Delegation, edited by Stuart Chase, Robt. Dunn and Rexford Guy Tugwell," lists as labor members of the American Trade Union Delegation to the Soviet Union: James H. Maurer, John Brophy, Frank L. Palmer, Albert F. Coyle, James W. Fitzpatrick; and as "technical staff" members: Stuart Chase, Robt. W. Dunn, Jerome Davis, George S. Counts, Rexford Guy Tugwell, Paul H. Douglas, Arthur Fisher, Carleton Washburne (all listed in this "Who's Who") and a few other pro-Soviets; the preface states that "The members of the party did not travel or work singly and at all stages of the tour there was discussion and exchange of experience. . . . Some of us were in Russia for over two months, one or two remained only a fortnight. We visited Moscow, Leningrad and then split into five small parties. . . . Collectively we interviewed the most important figures in the country, including Stalin, Menjhinsky, Kalinin, Chicherin, Lunacharsky, Schmidt, Trotsky," etc.

Washburne in his section of the book on "Soviet Education" says, p. 305: "This study was made unfortunately in August (1927) when most schools were not in session. . . . This fact, the shortness of the time available and the necessity of talking through *interpreters* constitute the principal and most serious limitations of the study"; yet, he sympathetically says on the same page: "We almost never felt any attempt to suppress unfavorable facts or to exaggerate favorable ones" (!) and feels able to enthuse on p. 306 that "Today Soviet Russia as a whole probably has the most modern and progressive school program and methods of any country in the world," a conclusion labeled as just pure "bunkum" by those unbiased by communistic sympathies.

Washburne's "alibi" for his membership in this delegation (see North Shore Topics, Winnetka, Apr. 7, 1933) was: "I was crossing the Atlantic to speak to an Educational Conference in Locarno, Switz., in the summer of 1927. On the same ship were some university professors who had been asked by a group of trade unionists to make an *unbiased* study of the situation in Russia." (Note Walsh's letter) *"They had no one to study Russian schools* and asked if I would go with them and do this job." As a matter of fact, George S. Counts, Washburne's associate in the Progressive Edu. Assn., and a member of this staff, writes the companion section of the book on education, of which Washburne in his part says: "This section of the report confines itself to what is called in Russia 'Social Education'—the regular education of children from 3 to 16 or 17 years of age. Prof. Counts' report takes up the other phases of education—higher education, factory schools, the abolition of illiteracy, etc."

FOOD WORKERS INDUSTRIAL UNION

Communist T.U.U.L. union; 4 W. 18th St., N.Y. City.

FORD PEACE PARTY

"To get the boys out of the trenches by Christmas," according to its slogan; organized by Rosika Schwimmer with Louis P. Lochner acting as general secretary; financed by Henry Ford, who not only paid all expenses of the exposition but handsome honorariums to the delegates besides; sailed on Oscar II, the Peace Ship —Dec. 4, 1915; the Lusk Report says: "Among the passengers . . . we find the names of some thirty-odd men and women afterward active in furthering 'peace' pro-German or inter-nationalist movements, many of whom are active revolutionaries today"; Jane Addams whose place because of illness was taken by Emily Balch, Wm. C. Bullitt "well-known radical" (adviser of U.S. State Dept. and now Ambassador to Soviet Russia), Lola Maverick Lloyd and her brother Lewis Maverick, Carl D. Thompson, etc., are listed among members "afterwards active in radical movements." Altho Ford and Lochner finally broke, "Lochner considered a great deal had been gained for the cause through the Ford Party. . . . The 'Conference of Neutral Internationalists and Pacifists' entirely financed by Mr. Ford was held in Stockholm from about March to July, 1917" (two years later); "Miss Balch was appointed to organize an American Neutral Conference Committee in New York on her return; the Central Organization for a Durable Peace was enriched by at least $2,000," etc., "though the Ford Peace trip was generally ridiculed as the irresponsible venture of nebulous dreamers, Lochner and Mme. Schwimmer had in the undertaking a perfectly practical object. This was to effect a powerful international 'Conference of Neutrals' to which the Ford Pilgrims were to be delegates and the foreign delegates of the Central Organization for a Durable Peace a sort of steering Committee. . . . Miss McMillan is still an officer of the International Suffrage Alliance; and Mme. Schwimmer has had the distinction of being the first Bolshevik Ambassador from Hungary to Switzerland in 1919, her career being cut short by the fall of Bela Kun . . . perhaps then the Ford Peace Party may have served a useful purpose not generally understood."

FOREIGN LANGUAGE GROUPS

The Communist Party central committee operates about 16 Bureaus which control foreign language federations of Lettish, Italian, Hungarian, Finnish, Chinese, Ukrainian, Czechoslovak, Albanian, Polish, Jewish, Esthonian, Lithuanian, Russian, Spanish, Armenian, Japanese groups. Each federation is composed of various "Workers" clubs, cultural and insurance societies, etc., called "mass organizations," officered and controlled by "Party fractions" (or "nuclei" of Party members). These "fractions" hold separate meetings and are expected to control, in accordance with instructions, the "mass" group. The Federation pays a per capita membership fee to the Communist Party as a federation. Many of the federation members are not individual members of the Party. The policy in fact of the Communist Party is that all party members must be active Party workers and organizers and control from ten to fifty or more non-party members each by officering and boring from within mass groups in order to influence, bring and hold these groups under Communist control. Each federation has a secretary and an official Communist publication in its own language. A secretary of all the federations directs activities from N.Y. City. There are 8 daily foreign language Communist newspapers published in the United States and, besides the publications of the foreign language federations named above, there are Greek, Armenian, Bohemian, German, Bulgarian, Rumanian, Portuguese, Slovak, Jugo Slav, Yiddish, communist publications.

The "Party Organizer" (for Communist Party members), June-July, 1930 issue, page 10, in an article entitled "Shortcomings of Party Fractions in Language Work," stated: "Reports given by 16 Language Bureaus of the Central Committee uncover many weaknesses in our language fractions. . . . The fractions directed by 16 bureaus and numbering about 5000 Party members control organizations having about 50,000 members. About 800 Party members work among 140,000 workers in organizations in which we have influence. . . . Work in small, Party controlled organizations in which in some cases the Party members are the majority of those present at the meetings develop a tendency of giving these organizations almost a role of the Party, at least similar political functions. . . . A redistribution of these forces so that most of the Party members shall be organized in real mass organizations for struggle against reaction, for Party policies and leadership, is necessary."

FOREIGN POLICY ASSOCIATION

For. Pol. Assn.

Named in "Congressional Exposure of Radicals" (see) as one of the organizations interlocked by membership with the American Civil Liberties Union "that play into the hands of the Communists"; it organized the National Council for Prevention of War 1921; changed its own name from League of Free Nations 1921; claims 11,000 members and stated in 1932: "Last year 41,000 men and women met at 108 meetings in 19 cities"; in order to "educate public opinion" conducts long series of radio addresses, Institutes, study groups, discussion meetings, luncheons, lectures; issues pamphlets, maintains a "research staff." In its 1932 pamphlet series such authors are listed as Morris Hillquit, Paul Douglas, John A. Ryan, Harry D. Gideonse, Geo. H. Blakeslee (Am. Friends Peace Institute faculty member at Evanston), Max Eastman, Maurice Hindus, George Soule, John Dewey, Wm. E. Borah.

In an able and lengthy paper Matthew Woll, vice pres. of the A.F. of L., in April 1929, referred to the Foreign Policy statements favoring recognition of Russia and its pamphlets prepared by Vera A. Micheles (Dean) of the Foreign Policy research staff, saying in part: "These pamphlets are not merely partisan in adopting the Soviet view on this question but by wholly repressing important sections of the U.S. documents quoted and by giving other sections out of their context, have misrepresented our State Dept. policy to the point of presenting it as being the very reverse of what it actually is."

James G. McDonald, who has been the Foreign Policy Assn. chairman since 1919 and who gives radio addresses for the Assn. about foreign affairs, in a speech before the Phila. branch stated that Soviet Russia wished to maintain peace, "But intentions are hampered frequently by the activities of the Russian Communist Party and the Third International *neither* of which the government has power to control." To this false statement, long used by the Communists when trying to side step retaliation for their own activities, patriotic Ralph Easely retorted by showing that the executive committees of the Third International, the Soviet Government and the Communist Party of Russia are practically identical, Stalin, Buhkarin, Tchitcherin, Rykoff, for example, being on all three, also by quoting Pravda's official statements concerning their plans for world revolution. He commented on McDonald's statement that he had never felt he knew enough about alleged Bolshevik activities in America to warrant the expression of a positive opinion, by saying: "If you can display such ignorance in the matter of Red propaganda in a country where you have lived for years, how reliable would you be likely to be in telling what is happening in Europe and Asia where you spent only a few months on a tour last summer?"

Francis Ralston Welsh says: "Of course there are some respectable fronts in the Foreign Policy Assn., of course they do not realize what it is, and equally of course it is the object of the Foreign Policy Assn. to have respectable fronts as part of their camouflage. There is no room for doubt that it belongs in the class with the American Civil Liberties Union, the League for

Industrial Democracy, the Fellowship of Reconciliation, the International League for Peace and Freedom, the Peoples Lobby, the National Popular Government League and others of the sort as some of the well camouflaged organizations of the American Civil Liberties Union crowd which help the Communist cause."

Among those on the national council are: James G. McDonald, chmn., Jane Addams, Stephen P. Duggan, Bishop Francis J. McConnell, Wm. A. Neilson, Roscoe Pound, Rev. John A. Ryan, Wm. Allen White, Wm. Scarlett, Capitalist Thos. Lamont (a member of the firm of J. P. Morgan, international bankers, and father of Corliss, who is a radical). Among the directors are Mrs. Thos. Lamont, Lillian D. Wald, Mrs. Henry Goddard Leach, Paul U. Kellogg (chmn. finance committee), Bruce Bliven of the New Republic, Francis Biddle (signer of appeals for Sacco and Vanzetti, whose verse was published in the Liberator, of which his wife was a stockholder when Max Eastman was editor), etc.

Branches are in Albany, N.Y., Baltimore, Boston, Buffalo, Columbus, Elmira, N.Y., Hartford, Conn., Phila., Pittsburgh, Providence, R.I., Richmond, Va., Rochester, N.Y., St. Paul, Minn., Springfield, Mass., Toledo, O., Utica, N.Y., Worcester, Mass. National headquarters: 18 E. 41st St., N.Y. City.

FORWARD (JEWISH DAILY)

A Socialist publication; Abraham Cahan, editor, N.Y. City.

FRAZIER AMENDMENT

Senator Lynn Frazier's proposal to amend the Constitution of the U.S. so as to disarm and render the U.S. virtually defenseless; introduced for the third time at U.S. Senate Judiciary Committee hearing April 13, 1930; backed by the Women's Peace Union, Women's International League for Peace and Freedom, Fellowship of Reconciliation, War Resisters International, American Friends Service Committee, Pa. Committee for Total Disarmament; the Amendment reads: "War for any purpose shall be illegal, and neither the U.S. nor any state, territory, association or person subject to its jurisdiction shall prepare for, declare, engage in or carry on war or other armed conflict, expedition, invasion or undertaking within or without the U.S. nor shall any funds be raised, appropriated or expended for such purpose."

FREE SOCIETY

Anarchist-Communists—that is, believers in a cooperative society without state government. To quote from the Nov. 11, 1933 manifesto of the Chicago group:

"Nov. the 11th marks an epoch in the history of the working class in America . . . four anarchists were hanged in Chicago. . . . Forty-six years ago Nov. 1887 Parsons, Linng, Fischer, Spies, believed in a society without the state . . . the abolition of private property, the abolition of the state and the establishment of a masterless, stateless society. They were anarchists. . . . We the Free Society Group of Chicago, followers of the ideal for which Parsons and his comrades stood . . . pledge ourselves to continue their noble and libertarian work."

At the meeting at which this manifesto was distributed, Ben Reitman spoke and in answer to questions declared that he is still an Anarchist. He read a letter from his old amour, Emma Goldman, who expressed hope of returning to the U.S.A. under the Roosevelt administration. She was planning to organize meetings in Canada and meet the comrades from the U.S.A. on Canadian soil meantime. Her "slip of paper" marriage for the purpose of giving her English citizenship would admit her to Canada. Ben criticized her for being temporarily downhearted at her exile from the U.S.A. and for her antagonism toward Russia (which he favors). Her wonderful work for Anarchism should be enough to keep her happy, he declared. He said that he was most optimistic, after having spoken in a Theological Seminary, at Chicago University, and to a Methodist group during the preceding week, at the way the students and particularly the theological students were coming along in radicalism. The seizure of the whole Hormel Plant at Austin, Minn., by red strikers was another encouraging sign of the times, he said.

M. Olay (Spanish anarchist) presided. He represents the Chicago anarchists in united front activities, such as the Ky. Miners Def. and Relief Com. of the I.W.W., Nat. Mooney Coun. of Action of the Communists, etc., and as a contributor to the book "Recovery Through Revolution" (see).

The Chicago groups are conducting weekly forums for the 4th year every Sunday night at the socialist Workmen's Circle school, 1241 N. California Ave. Other anarchist forums (in English) are at:

Free Workers Center, 219 Second Ave., N.Y. City, Harry Kelley in charge; Jack London Guild, 1057 Steiner St., near Golden Gate Ave., Friday night forums, Clubrooms International Group, 2787 Folsom St., San Francisco, Cal.; Freedom Forum every Thursday, at 224 S. Spring St., Hall 218, Los Angeles, Cal.; Roseland Educational Forum every Sunday, 2:30 P.M., Dutch Hall, 233 111th St., Chicago; Cleveland, O. Libertarian Forum, every Sunday night, Garment Workers Hall.

American 1933 Anarchist publications: "Freedom," a monthly, 219 Second Ave., N.Y. City. Harry Kelley, M. Jagendorf, editors; "The Vanguard," N.Y. City; "Free Arbeiter Stimme," N.Y. City; "L'Adunata," Newark, N.J.; "Alba," Pitts., Pa.; "Man," San Francisco, Cal., 1000 Jefferson St., Marcus Graham, editor; "Cultura Proletaria," N.Y. City; "Eresia," N.Y. City; "Dielo Truda," Chicago.

FREETHINKERS OF AMERICA

National Atheist organization in New York City linked with the International Freethought Union of Europe; headquarters are with the Freethought Press Association (for anti-religious books), and the Eugenics Publishing Co. (for sex literature of the most revolting type), which have the same cable and street address (317 E. 34th St., New York City, formerly 250 W. 54th St.). The president is Joseph Lewis, whose biography, written by an admiring atheist, A. H. Howland, with introduction by Prof. H. E. Barnes, is entitled "Joseph Lewis, Enemy of God." Joseph Lewis threatened Mr. Wm. J. O'Shea, Supt. Dept. Education, City of New York, 59th and Park Ave., N.Y. City, on Dec. 21, 1928, as follows:

"Sir:

"It is generally known that the practice prevails, in the Public Schools of this City, of opening the sessions by reading selections from a book commonly known as 'The Bible,' together with the singing of religious hymns,****

"As a resident of the City of New York, a property owner and a taxpayer, I hereby notify you that I demand that this illegal practice be discontinued, and that the reading of 'The Bible,' and all other religious exercises, in the schools, be stopped.

"Unless this is promptly done, and I am advised by you within the next 10 days, or two weeks, that 'Bible' reading and psalm singing in the Public Schools will be prohibited and ended, I shall file a Taxpayer's Suit to enjoin this illegal practice.

"Yours sincerely,
(Signed) "Joseph Lewis,
"President."

The suit was filed and was being carried on to the Supreme Court by the American Civil Liberties Union (see) (May 3, 1932 issue "American Teacher"). One wonders how minister members of the A.C.L.U. can hold up their heads for shame who presume to serve Jesus Christ and the Bible while paying for and backing such a suit!

Officers: Pres. Joseph Lewis; 1st Vice-Pres., Dr. Charles A. Andrews; 2nd Vice-Pres., Garabed Locke; Sec., J. G. Tallon; Treas., Julius Janowitz; Attorney, Maj. Joseph Wheless; Honorary Vice-Presidents: J. F. D. Hoge, Herbert Asbury, Rupert Hughes, Clarence Darrow, Clarence H. Low, Prof. Ellen Hayes, Mme. Olga Petrova, Phillip G. Peabody, Theodore Schroeder, Prof. Harry Elmer Barnes, Mrs. Maude Ingersoll Probasco. (See page 337.)

FREETHINKERS INGERSOLL COMMITTEE

To quote: "In recognition of Col. Robt. G. Ingersoll's most noteworthy contributions to the emancipation of mankind from religious superstition," an "International Committee" was formed by the Freethinkers to collect funds for an Ingersoll monument to be erected in Washington, D.C., and to stage a memorial celebration during 1933, the hundredth anniversary of Ingersoll's birth. Maude Ingersoll Probasco, chmn.; W. McLean Probasco, treas.; Jos. Lewis, sec. Officers of The Am. Assn. for the Advancement of Atheism assisted at the celebration and served on the committee.

FREETHOUGHT PRESS

See Freethinkers of America; catalogue lists 180 anti-religious books. Among these are: "Twilight of Christianity," by Prof. H. E. Barnes; "Infidels and Heretics," by Clarence Darrow and Walter Rice; "To the Pure," by Morris Ernst and Wm. Seagle ("A study of obscenity and the censor—A valuable contribution to the literature of Man's struggle with his sex complex, and the efforts of organized religion in politics to stifle his attempts to acquire information"); "The Mistakes of Jesus," by Wm. Floyd; "Let Freedom Ring," by Arthur Garfield Hays; "Joseph Lewis, Enemy of God," by Arthur H. Howland (catalogue quotes preface by Prof. H. E. Barnes, who calls Lewis "the most aggressive and effective leader of irreligion in America today" and adds: "Interesting in every line this book by Mr. Howland (once a Methodist minister) makes clear the aims and aspirations of Atheism as expounded by Jos. Lewis"); "The Bible Unmasked," by Jos. Lewis ("Its analysis of so many of the perversions, liaisons and licentious escapades of biblical characters is a brilliant and daring feat of honest scholarship . . . despite the censorship which has been placed on it in some countries—notably Canada, where its sale is still prohibited—over 50,000 copies have been printed"). (Author's note: I have this disgusting obscene book which not only portrays Christ as a bastard and Mary as immoral but imputes immoral conduct to the angels in visiting Mary); "The Tyranny of God," by Jos. Lewis (". . . a devastating attack on the theistic conception of the universe. . . . Says Clarence Darrow, 'The book is bold and true beyond dispute. I wish I were the author.'"); "Atheism—What It Is, What It Means," by Jos. Lewis ("Rev. John Haynes Holmes, famous minister of the Community Church New York City calls it 'brilliant in the extreme, altogether the best statement on Atheism I have ever heard.' "); "If I were God," by Dr. Wm. J. Robinson, who is a sex writer for Eugenics Pub. Co. also ("Albert Einstein, the great discoverer of the Theory of Relativity admires this book so much that, as he wrote the author, a copy is on his desk at all times. It is a sweeping criticism of religion with its bigotry and intolerance."); "Marriage and Morals," by Bertrand Russell (containing "sufficient dynamite to blast a carload of ordinary sex popularizers from the face of the earth. Mr. Russell deals most competently and completely with practically every rámification of sex and sex life."); "Forgery in Christianity," by Maj. Jos. Wheless (" . . . proves more than 1000 notorious frauds and forgeries in the Bible"); "Thinker or Believer," by W. H. Williamson; "The History of Prostitution," by Dr. Wm. W. Sanger ("shows that this social evil had its origin in obscure religious rites . . . tends to prove that prostitutes of our own times come generally from those classes of society where religion is taught most thoroughly and that prostitutes themselves are generally ultra devout"); "My Fight for Birth Control," by Margaret Sanger ("In this wonderful book Margaret Sanger tells how she as a Crusading Freethinker has struggled," etc.); "Up from Methodism," by Herbert Asbury (" . . . He is descended from a long line of clergymen; one of his ancestors being Bishop Francis Asbury, who founded the American branch of the Methodist Church. How Mr. Asbury rose above the faith of his fathers is a story every American must read"); and "Bible Comically Illustrated—A book as good as a farce yet as instructive as a schoolmaster. Both text and illustrations help to expose the absurdities of the Bible from Genesis to Revelation"; hdqts. 317 E. 34th St., New York City.

FREIHEITS

Communist Jewish "Foreign Language Groups" (see) conducting Freiheit Singing Societies, Freiheit Workers Clubs, etc., etc., in N.Y., Chicago and other cities. The official Jewish Communist newspaper (published in Yiddish) is the Jewish Daily Freiheit; Moissaye J. Olgin is editor. The building of this newspaper, which in 1930 had a daily N.Y. sworn circulation of 64,067 copies, adjoins the building of the official communist Daily Worker (published in English). They use the same presses. Communist banners, recently, decorated the front of both buildings, 26-30 Union Square, N.Y. City. Those on the Freiheit building read: "Organize Anti-War Committees in Shops and Factories," "Not a Cent for Armaments—All Funds for the Unemployed," and "Demonstrate on Union Square, Aug. 1, Friday at 5 P.M." Similar banners decorated the Daily Worker building.

FRIENDS OF SOVIET RUSSIA

F.S. Russia.

Formed by the Central Committee of the Communist Party 1921; changed name to Friends of the Soviet Union 1929.

FRIENDS OF THE SOVIET UNION
(Carveth Wells Boycott)

F.S.U.

A Communist subsidiary (U.S. Report 2290); formed as noted above; propagandizes Soviet Russia as the workers' paradise; sponsors lectures; in 1933 driving for a million signatures for recognition of Russia by the U.S.; staged the Reception for Soviet Flyers 1929 (see); publishes magazine Soviet Russia Today; claims, Jan. 1934, 2,000,000 members.

J. C. Coleman of the California section of the F.S.U. (June 13, 1933), as well as Ella Winter (Mrs. Lincoln Steffens), lecturer for F.S.U., wrote letters protesting and threatening Mr. Sol Lesser of Principal Pictures, 630 9th Ave., N.Y.C., causing this firm to halt the release of a truthful moving picture of Russia taken by Carveth Wells. Our theatres are flooded with Soviet propaganda films. For example, three N.Y. Theatres at one time, Sept. 2, 3 and 4, 1933, were showing a Communist propaganda film "The Strange Case of Tom Mooney" advertised in the "Daily Worker." But organized Red opposition quickly silences the truth about Soviet Russia.

Ella Winter's letter, written on stationery headed "Lincoln Steffens, Carmel, California, The Gateway, Box 855," is significant. She says:

"Dear Mr. Lesser: I am shocked and astounded to read the news that you are releasing a picture on Russia called "The Truth About Russia" by Carveth Wells. . . . Such a showing as you contemplate can only discredit your studio as every American correspondent in Russia and such well-known figures in American literary, professional and business-life as Sherwood Anderson, Col. Hugh Cooper, Governor Philip LaFollette, Louis Fischer, Maurice Hindus, Curtis Bok, Margaret Bourke White, Cecil de Mille, Mrs. Cecil de Mille, Walter Duranty, Mr. and Mrs. Corliss Lamont, Mr. and Mrs. Osgood Field, Mr. and Mrs. Sherman Pratt, Mr. and Mrs. Maxwell Stuart of the Foreign Policy

Association, Mr. Jerome Davis of Yale, Mr. Julian Bryan, Elmer Rice, Leopold Stokowski, Martin Flavin, Dr. John M. Kingsbury, Dr. Frankwood Williams, Alexander Woolcott, Joseph Freeman, Charles Malamuth, Alexander Kaun, Max Eastman, W. L. Austin (of the Austin Construction Co., Cleveland), Senators Borah, Wheeler, Cutting and Barkley, and innumerable others, would merely ridicule a picture released by such a person on Russia." (A nice list of pro-Soviets.)

"I am afraid that if you do release the picture we shall find it necessary in the interests of truth and fairness and an Administration which wishes to recognize the Soviet Union to take such steps as we shall deem necessary and feasible to make clear to all movie-goers the kind of a movie author you have selected. You will readily realize that in a world on the brink of war with war feelings created by just such reports as Carveth Wells puts out, in which there is not one glimmer of truth, one cannot allow your studio to proceed without mobilizing every voice in denunciation, *opposition and boycott*. Very truly yours, Ella Winter."

Mr. Carveth Wells wrote to the chairman of the American Coalition of Patriotic Societies as follows:

"Dear Sir: "Having learned that you have organized a coalition of about one hundred Patriotic Societies, permit me, although a perfect stranger, to appeal to you as a fellow citizen for assistance in bringing to the attention of the American people, a concrete example of a Communist boycott, organized to prevent the presentation of an ordinary travel picture showing the people and scenery of Russia from Leningrad to the Turkish border.

"I am an author and lecturer and am not connected in any way with propaganda. For the last twenty years I have devoted my entire time to exploration in foreign countries, in order to secure pictures and general information which I present to the public in the form of illustrated lectures. Entertainment of an educational nature is my sole object, and I have not now nor have I ever had any political affiliations.

"So much interest was aroused by my description of Russia that I decided to have the motion pictures synchronized with my voice and distributed to the theatres of the United States, by Mr. Sol Lesser, of Principal Distributing Corporation, whose offices are in the RKO Building, Radio City, New York.

"The moment the news leaked out that I had prepared a Motion Picture entitled 'Russia Today,' which showed a true picture of the condition of Russia and the Russian people after fifteen years of the Great Experiment, The Friends of the Soviet Union, which I am ashamed to say is an American Institution with branches all over the United States, organized a protest, by requesting their various branches and individual members to write letters to Mr. Sol Lesser threatening to boycott all his pictures if he dared to distribute my picture.

"Here is an educational motion picture which has been shown before the National Geographical Society in Washington, and was actually taken for the Geographic Society of Chicago, yet, by means of a snowball threatening letter organized by Communists, such fear has been instilled in the heart of Mr. Sol Lesser, that he is afraid to release it to the Theatres.

"It is a good illustration of what a well organized and active minority can accomplish.

"I am most anxious to bring this matter before your Coalition and before as many other patriotic societies as possible, in the hope that I may interest them to organize a similar snowball of protests *against* this weakkneed submission to the demands of American Communists.

"For many years the theatre-going public has been forced to look at a whole series of Russian propaganda pictures, yet the moment a genuine picture of a purely Travel Nature is placed upon the market, the American Communist Party has succeeded at least temporarily, in having it banned.

"My picture 'Russia Today' has never been publicly shown. The fact that in their letters of protest they refer to the title as 'The Truth About Russia' clearly shows that the picture has been condemned without ever being seen.

"I should be most grateful to you for any suggestion you have to make as to my best course of action. "Faithfully yours, Carveth Wells."

The American Coalition of Patriotic Societies, 823 Albie Bldg., Wash., D.C., sent photostatic copies of these letters to officers of patriotic societies, stating:

"We trust your indignation will be sufficiently aroused to organize immediately among your friends a counter protest against the action of the Friends of the Soviet Union . . . urging the immediate release of Mr. Carveth Wells' film for the information of the public on conditions in Russia. Mr. Wells assures us that the film was censored and returned to him by agents of the Soviet Government before he left Russia at which time there was small probability that the American people would permit their government to loan taxpayers' money to a country which has been stripped of every marketable commodity and the mass of its population reduced to the verge of starvation and hopeless misery by a remorseless clique of political theorists. We make this appeal because it is obvious that this attack on the Carveth Wells film by the Friends of the Soviet Union is part of Communist propaganda for the recognition of Russia."

F.S.U. nat. hdqts. 80 E. 11th St., N.Y. City; Norman Tallentire, nat. organizer.

California branch, 129 West Third Street, Suite 415-416, Los Angeles, Cal.; Dr. Robt. Whitaker, chmn.; Delta Weinrich, vice chmn.; Dr. J. C. Coleman, educational director; Robt. Edwards, treas.; Clara Ward, sec.; M. Movshovitch, literature agent.

Nat. com. F.S.U. endorsing call for F.S.U. Convention, Jan. 26, 27, 28, 1934, N.Y. City:

Thos. R. Amlie, Roger Baldwin, Carleton Beals, Alfred M. Bingham, Frank Borich, "Bishop" W. M. Brown, Earl Browder, Julian Bryan, Anne Burlak, George S. Counts, Malcolm Cowley, Edw. Dahlberg, H. W. L. Dana, Floyd Dell, James W. Ford, Richard Farber, Wm. Z. Foster, Waldo Frank, Jos. Freeman, Ben Gold, Michael Gold, Lem Harris, Clarence Hathaway, Donald Henderson, Granville Hicks, John Haynes Holmes, Roy Hudson, Langston Hughes, Wm. N. Jones, Howard Kester, Mary Van Kleeck, Corliss Lamont, Margaret Lamont, Katherine Lewis, Robt. Morss Lovett, J. B. Matthews, John Meldon, Robt. Minor, Scott Nearing, A. Overgaard, Wm. Patterson, Philip Raymond, Jack Stachel, Maxwell Stewart, Genevieve Taggard, Justine Wise Tulin, Chas. R. Walker, Dr. Harry F. Ward, Louis Weinstock, Susan H. Woodruff, Albert Rhys Williams, Walter Wilson. ("Soviet Russia Today," 12/33.)

FRIENDSHIP TOURS

"A non-commercial cultural organization" conducting (1933) propaganda tours to Soviet Russia. Leaders: Phil Brown; F. Tredwell Smith (in Russia); Sponsoring Committee: Prof. Geo. S. Counts, Prof. Harry Ward, Prof. Harold O. Rugg, Prof. Goodwin Watson, Prof. Harrison Elliott, Prof. Reinhold Niebuhr, Dr. Addison T. Cutler. Hdqts. 261 Fifth Ave., N.Y. City. (Same address as Intourist, Soviet Govt. agency.)

FURNITURE WORKERS INDUSTRIAL UNION

Communist T.U.U.L. union with organizations at Grand Rapids, Jamestown, N.Y., Rockford, Ill., Chicago, etc.; 818 Broadway, N.Y. City.

G

GARLAND FUND

The AMERICAN FUND FOR PUBLIC SERVICE is popularly known as the "Garland Fund" or the "Free Love Fund" because it was founded by a radical, Chas. Garland of Mass., who served a term in the penitentiary for running a "Free Love Farm." Being an opponent of private ownership of property, he turned over his inheritance to form this fund in order to further the radical cause. The Fund's official report states that between 1922, when it was founded, and 1930, $1,378,000 was given away and $780,000 loaned. (The Fund is practically exhausted now.) To quote: "The Board of Directors of the Fund is a self perpetuating group, the directors serving for terms of three years each. The original directors were picked out as persons of diverse connections with radical, labor and liberal movements, who, despite philosophical differences, were practical-minded enough to deal harmoniously with immediate issues." These directors have been members of the I.W.W., Communist and Socialist parties, which are all basically aiming for the same ends—the abolition of the property right and the undermining and eventual overthrow of our present form of government—the differences between them being largely those of stress on certain tactics, such as use of violence or of parliamentary action, to gain control.

The Fund has been the life stream of the Red Revolutionary movement in the U.S., having sustained all the leading Communist, Socialist and I.W.W. activities. Samuel Gompers of the A.F. of L. wrote the Fund asking for money for a legitimate labor cause and was refused, Roger Baldwin of the Fund replying that: "We do not see our way clear to financing any enterprise except those definitely committed to a radical program . . . ", etc.

The original directors and officers were (from the Fund's report of July 31, 1923, "for the first year of operation"):

Roger N. Baldwin, Wm. Z. Foster, Lewis S. Gannett, Sidney Hillman, James Weldon Johnson (colored), Robt. Morss Lovett, Scott Nearing, Mary E. McDowell, Judah L. Magnes, Norman M. Thomas, Harry F. Ward, Morris L. Ernst, Walter Nelles.

The report of June 30, 1924, "for the second year," lists:

Scott Nearing, pres.; Robt. Morss Lovett, vice pres.; Roger N. Baldwin, sec.; Morris L. Ernst, treas.; Walter Nelles, counsel, and Eliz. Gurley Flynn, Wm. Z. Foster, Lewis S. Gannett, Clinton S. Golden, James Weldon Johnson, Freda Kirchwey, Norman M. Thomas, Leo Wolman, fellow directors.

The reports show that the directors changed about during the year in serving as officers. The report of Feb. 1929 (for the three years 1925-8) lists the same directorship with the exceptions that Communist Wm. Z. Foster, Robt. Morss Lovett and Leo Wolman are replaced by Communists Clarina Michelson, Benj. Gitlow and Robt. W. Dunn. The report of May 1931 (for 1928-30) lists same directors except for the omission of Eliz. Gurley Flynn. The 1932 officers (given in the statement of ownership of the Communist magazine "New Masses," which states that its owner and publisher is the Am. Fund for Pub. Service) were:

James Weldon Johnson, pres.; Robt. W. Dunn, sec.; Morris L. Ernst, treas.

1933 Officers are:

Roger Baldwin, pres.; Clinton S. Golden, vice pres.; Robt. W. Dunn, sec.; Morris Ernst, treas.; with Gannett, Gitlow, Johnson, Kirchwey, Michelson and Thomas fellow directors as before.

For Anarchist-Communist Activities

The inextricable interweaving of Red forces is shown not only in the personnel of the Fund's directorship but also in the organizations it has supported. Studying the Fund's reports is like studying the whole Red network. Socialists, Communists and I.W.W.'s intermingle in organizations, on committees and in practically all Red activities. One sees, for example, in the reports the sums of $500 and $500 donated to the anarchist-communist *Ferrer* or Modern School at Stelton, N.J., aided by Emma Goldman and Berkman. In 1925-6, $1125 and $875 were given to it. Wherever treason has lifted its head, it seems, the Fund has aided financially. When Wm. Z. Foster and other Communists were seized at Bridgman, Mich., with two barrels full of documentary evidence of their plans to overthrow the U.S. Govt., the *Labor Defense Council* (later I.L.D.) was formed to defend these criminals caught in their Moscow-directed conspiracy. The Fund lists: "To Labor Defense Council—for defense of Michigan criminal syndicalism cases $10,000," then "$3,000," then "$200." (Incidentally, treason is now practically unchallenged and quite in the open. Then traitors had to meet secretly.) Then, to its successor the *I.L.D.* Chicago "for substitution of bail in Michigan criminal syndicalism cases—$7,000," and again "$5,000," and "for legal fees in endeavoring to secure dismissal of Michigan criminal syndicalism cases $500"; also such enlightening items as: To I.L.D. (1) Chicago Office—for legal expenses in the cases of the Ziegler, Ill. miners, $2,000. (2) Pittsburgh Branch—for legal expenses in Pittsburgh sedition cases, $1,500. (3) Boston Branch—for legal expenses in Bimba blasphemy case, $500. (4) National Bail Fund for substitution of bail in deportation case, $1,000.

The *"Daily Worker,"* official Communist newspaper, received sums of $38,135, $1,200, $6,500, $3,900, $1,050 and $6,875, at different times.

The Fund's own Communist magazine, *"New Masses,"* received sums of $1,500, $30,000, $28,000, $3,000, $2,000 and $400.

The Communist N.Y. *"Workers School"* (to train leaders for the Communist Revolution in the U.S., so it states) received "for books for library—$859.25" and also for general expenses, $11,122 and $641.

International Publishers, the Communist publishing house, received "for promotion of Americanization of Labor by Robt. W. Dunn, $298.95," and for publication of fifteen Communist "International Pamphlets," $1,400 and $1,500.

Workers Library Publishers (Communist) received for publishing three pamphlets, $800.

The *Passaic, N.J. Communist strike* in 1926 was called the "first lesson in Revolution" and the Fund spent generously in supporting it. The committee formed for this purpose by Norman Thomas, the A.C.L.U. and L.I.D., called the *"Emergency Committee for Strikers Relief,"* received $1,520 in 1926, and, later, for Passaic and other activities, sums of $5,000 and $1,000. *The United Front Textile Committee,* Passaic, N.J., "for expenses of Mary Heaton Vorse for publicity work on textile strike" recd. $818. Other items are: "Passaic, N.J. strike relief, publicity and research—$25,318"; "bail underwritten—$45,000"; *"Wm. Jett Lauck,* for investigating textile industry Passaic, N. J., $4,500," also $500; *"I.L.D.*—for premiums on bail in Passaic, N.J. cases, $3,022," and other fees, $200.

Another Communist strike, well supported by the Fund, was the *Gastonia, N.C. strike,* where, to quote U.S. Report 2290, "there was a bloody conflict between the Communist-led textile workers and the police, in which the chief of police was shot and killed and two of his assistants wounded. Seven Communists were sentenced to long terms in prison, but jumped their bonds and went to Russia, where they presumably are today. The I.L.D. headed by J. Louis Engdahl, a well-known Communist, and the A.C.L.U. cooperated in the defense of the convicted strikers and assisted in securing the money for the bail bonds from the Garland Fund, which was forfeited." And so we see in the Fund's reports the items: *"I.L.D.*—$29,218" and *"I.L.D.*—for legal fees and expense in connection with Gastonia, N.C. cases," $15,000 and $5,475. The I.L.D. (N.Y. branch) received other sums, such as $2,850 and $2,000, for its general activities.

The Communist *"Young Workers League"* (now called Young Communist Lg.), at Superior, Wis. was graciously presented with $1,200; and its Chicago branch the same amount. These gifts are listed under "Education"—one may well imagine what sort.

The *Russian Reconstruction Farms* (Jan. 1926) recd. $3,000, then $1,015, and "for purchase of equipment in U.S.," $20,000.

The Communist (there is also an I.W.W. union of same name) *Agricultural Workers Industrial Union* recd. $3,000. The Communist *National Textile Workers Union* recd. $5,570 "for organizational work in the South," and $500 "to Local No. 2, New Bedford, Mass. for final payment on a lot in Fall River on which to hold meetings." The Communist *Marine Workers League,* N.Y., recd. "for books for their library—$599.87." The *House of the Masses* (Communist) in Detroit recd. $4,000.

In 1927 the Communist *A.A.A.I. Lg.,* then being organized all over the U.S., received a nice gift of $1,000—"for organization work during summer months," and in 1929-30, is listed "Anti-Imperialist League of the U.S., N.Y.C.—for preliminary expenses of reorganization—$500" (same organization).

The Communist *Trade Union Educational League,* of which Wm. Z. Foster was the head (now the T.U.U.L., and he is still the head), recd. at the Chicago branch "for publication of pamphlet on Company Unions by Robt. W. Dunn—$600"; the N.Y.C. branch recd. $900; etc.

The *Labor Research Assn.,* N.Y.C., a Communist subsidiary organized by Robt. W. Dunn, recd. "for secretarial assistance for Scott Nearing in connection with series of books on economic subjects—$1,000"; it also recd. $750.

"Novy Mir," the Russian Communist paper published in N.Y., recd. gifts and loans of $3,000, $500, etc.

The Communist *"Daily Worker Pub. Co."* recd. (1) For publication of one volume of the works of Lenin in English—$2,500; (2) For publication of ten volumes of the 'Little Red Library'—$1,875; (3) For the publication of Report of British Trade Union Delegation to Russia—$2,500, etc.

The Communistic *Vanguard Press* was started by the Fund itself and was a big favorite, receiving in one report alone $139,453 for capital, for books on Negro labor, and for "series of studies on Russia," for which other large sums were also appropriated.

To Communist *"Max Eastman,* Croton, N.Y.—for preparation and production of a historic film on the Russian Revolution, $2,500." (Loan.)

The *Federated Press,* regarded by Communists as their own press service, recd. generous aid; the first year, $15,640 (partly for salary of director Leland Olds), the second year, $12,640, the third year, $10,130, for the next three years, $26,441, and the next two years, $12,000.

For A.C.L.U. Activities

The *A.C.L.U.,* ever on the firing line in behalf of Red revolutionaries, recd. sums almost too numerous to list. These are representative: "A.C.L.U.,—for special campaign against criminal syndicalism law, $5,000"; "A.C.L.U.—for expenses in connection with *Tennessee Anti-Evolution case,* $500"; "A.C.L.U., N.Y.C.—June 5 and July 12, 1923—for an *investigation of reactionary organizations,* $1,972.50"; "A.C.L.U., Southern Cal. Branch, Los Angeles, Cal., Aug. 1, 1923—$1,000," (also other sums). The close connection between the A.C.L.U. and the Fund is shown by such items as these: "A.C.L.U., N.Y.C.—revolving loan fund for civil liberties cases administered by agreement between the Union and the Fund, $2,000"; "Emergency Case Fund, administered by the A.C.L.U.—$14,989" (1925-28); *"A.C.L.U. So. Cal. Branch*—for deficit incurred in campaign for release of *Mooney and Billings*—$800"; "A.C.L.U., special projects, $4,197" (1928-30); "A.C.L.U. Northern Cal. Branch, San Francisco, Cal. — $2,395.07"; A.C.L.U., N.Y.C. (1) For lawyers fees in connection with recovering of bail bond—$750. (2) For legal expenses in connection with Passaic, N.J. strike cases—$500; *"Pa. Civil Liberties Committee,* Harrisburg, Pa.—$500"; "A.C.L.U.—for free speech fight in West Va.—$1,000"; A.C.L.U. (1) For expenses of field organizer for definite work in civil liberties cases—$500; (2) For campaign against injunctions in labor disputes—$500; (3) For emergency case fund—$1,726.67 (1929-30); etc., etc., etc.

Criminals convicted of treason, sedition and Red revolutionary activities are always referred to sympathetically by the Reds as "political prisoners." The *International Committee for Political Prisoners,* formed by the A.C.L.U. to aid them, recd. $300 and $1,527.50 from the Fund.

Loyal aid to Communists is indicated in items like these:

"Walter Pollak and Carroll Weiss King, N.Y.C.—For fees and expenses in case of Emanuel Vatjauer, in the U.S. Supreme Court, held for deportation as a Communist—$1,900"; Isaac Schorr, N.Y.C.—Expenses in the case of Herbert Mahler and others, U.S. Supreme Court, ex-political prisoners held for deportation—$300."

As soon as the U.S. Govt. tries to protect its existence by jailing or deporting Reds, the Fund, the I.L.D., the A.C.L.U., and the whole army of Reds and their organizations are there to fight it. A united Red fight against Criminal Syndicalism laws in the States is now being waged in order that sedition shall not be punished.

For I.W.W. Activities

These donations to *I.W.W.* activities show a "unity of spirit" in the "class war": "General Defense Committee (of I.W.W.) San Francisco, Cal.—for fighting criminal syndicalism cases—$500" (1923); to Chicago branch—"for relief of released political prisoners, $1,250"; to Cal. branch—"$500"; "for payment and repairs on building, $6,500"; "for expenses in connection with Centralia case," $170 and $170; "To Chgo. Gen. Def. Com.—$20,007.79"; items of $10,475.68, $12,000 and $6,000 are listed to the *Equity Printing Co.* (owned by the I.W.W.).

Harry F. Ward, director of the Fund in 1922 and chmn. of the A.C.L.U., had shown his friendly spirit of cooperation with the defense of the I.W.W. murderers of four American Legion men at Centralia, Wash., by presiding over a meeting held at the Rand School, N.Y.C., Feb. 9, 1920, to raise money for their defense (Lusk Report). The Fund, later, donated to *"Centralia Publicity Committee*—For publicity in connection with release of Centralia prisoners —$250."

The Rand School, at which the I.W.W. defense meeting and so many other Red meetings have been held, must practically have been supported by the Fund, to judge by the contributions, sums of $5,000, $3,200, $400, $4,400, $7,200, $10,140, $16,116, $7,957.26, etc., being listed from time to time, and large sums to the *Rand Book Store* for publication of the *"Am. Labor Year Book"* (covering radical activities).

Brookwood Labor College, another Socialist institution, fared bountifully also at the Red feeding trough, receiving in one period (1928-30) $41,751 and in another (1925-28) $74,227.

The *National Association for the Advancement of Colored People* (N.A.A.C.P.) was well cared for with appropriations of $31,552 (1925-28), $7,365 in 1923-24, and a loan of $5,000 in 1929-30.

Significant items are these: *"Teachers Union,* N.Y.C." (1) "towards the campaign *for the repeal of Lusk Laws* $500"; (2) "For research and publicity work outside of regular activities, mimeograph machine, $3,172.50"; the Teachers Union also recd. $6,000 in a three-year period for "operating expenses"; the *"Minneapolis Federation of Teachers,* Mpls., Minn.—for legal expenses and publicity in connection with dismissal of two members—$250"; *"American Federation of Teachers* — $2,000"; and "The *New Student, N.Y.C.*— for traveling expenses of editors of college papers to conference—$333.06."

The *Manumit School* at Pawling, N.Y., which is directed by Nellie Seeds (wife of Communist Scott Nearing), recd. 1928-30, $5,000; and 1925-28, $10,907.

Communism-Socialism fights the Christian standards of marriage and morality. Ben Lindsey is looked upon evidently as an ally of this Red cause, since this item was voted to him: *"Ben B. Lindsey,* Denver, Colo.—For election contest in Denver, involving the issue of the Ku Klux Klan—$1,000" (1924-25 Report, April 22).

The *League for Mutual Aid* received for "Social Service for radicals" sums of $200, $450, $3,000, and $500.

The *Brooklyn, National* and *N.Y. Urban Leagues* recd. gifts and loans of $15,000, $1,000 and $500. One item was for the study of "relations of Negroes to trade unions."

The *American Birth Control League,* another movement used by Reds to break down the fear of sex relations outside of marriage and to generally loosen the marriage tie, recd. $10,400, $500, and "for salary and expenses of organizer—$2,000" (1928-30).

The Red agitation in behalf of Anarchist-Communist Mooney recd. hearty support from the Fund. The *"National Mooney-Billings Committee"* (1928-30) recd. "for publicity campaign for Mooney and Billings $1,000," and also $800. *"Mooney Molders Defense Committee*—for campaign for pardon of Mooney and Billings—$500"; *"N. Cal. Committee for Mooney and Billings*—$250"; *"Mooney Defense Committee* —$900" (also $100 and $100), etc.

Sacco and Vanzetti, the gentle Anarchist murderers and thieves who died yelling "Long Live Anarchy," recd. loving aid as well; "Provisional Committee for calling Sacco and Vanzetti conference, N.Y.C., expenses in connection with meeting—$1,000"; *"Sacco-Vanzetti Defense Committee*—$20,000" (loan), and gift of $2,500. Between 1925 and 1928, $11,000 was given to "Sacco-Vanzetti case."

Intellectual-Red papers and periodicals were evidently considered suitable agencies, for the *New Republic* (the Fund director, Robt. Morss Lovett, being an editor) recd. a loan of $1,000, "for book on 'The Supreme Court and Minimum Wage Legislation,' published by *National Consumers League";* The *World Tomorrow* (of Kirby Page) recd. "for general expenses—$3,000" (1925), $1,000 (1923), $2,000 (1924); and to *"Fellowship Press,* N.Y.C.—For operating expenses of the World Tomorrow, to Dec. 31, 1925, (May 27)—$3,000," etc.

The Socialist *New Leader* recd. large sums, as did *Labor Age* (organ of the Conf. Prog. Lab. Act.); one item was "For financing testimonial dinner to James Maurer—$250."

"For *Mr. Brophy's* salary as director," the *Pittsburgh Educational Forum and Labor College,* Pittsburgh, Pa., recd. $1,700.

The Conference for Progressive Labor Action recd. $5,266 at one time and also "for publication of a pamphlet $1,065.76." The *Committee on Coal and Giant Power* —"for completion of Mr. Raushenbush's research work and half budget of Committee under Prof. Bird—$5,266," and also $2,847, 1928-30. The New York Call, and Leader recd. $54,500; etc.

The reports are peppered with donations to the *L.I.D.*, which changed its name from "Intercollegiate Socialist Society" after the unsavory Socialist War record, in order not to frighten off prospective student members, but which now grows ever bolder and bolder in its talk of Red Revolution. That it was always considered a useful organization is shown by gifts of $6,400 the first year; $3,500 and $2,000 the second year "for field secretary's salary" and "for field secretary's traveling expenses, contingent upon raising their budget for the year"; between 1925 and 1928, $10,500 was given for "field secretary's salary"; also (1) "For study on Coal and Superpower by *H. Stephen Raushenbush*—$5,000." (2) "For survey of conditions in cotton mills in the South by *Paul Blanshard*—$700." (3) "For study on 'New Developments of Capitalism in the U.S.'—$600"; and many thousands for publication of pamphlets (to be found in student Y.M.C.A.'s such as at N.U., Evanston).

The *International Ladies Garment Workers* recd. a huge loan of $100,000 (in Communist-led strike of 1926) and also a loan of $25,000 for their Workers Center at Forest Park, Pa. Nor were their friends the *Amalgamated Textile Workers Union* forgotten, receiving thru L. Hollingsworth Wood and Albert De Silver (in strike of 1919) $850. The *Central Trades and Labor Council* recd. $2,000. The *Nat. Women's Trade Union Lg.*, Chgo. branch, recd. $1,147.33 and $629, and the N.Y. branch, $2,500, $2,500, and $913. The *Nat. Consumers Lg.* recd. $2,945.84, $1,000, etc. The *Cooperative League of America, N.Y.*, recd. $2,000 and $1,500. The *Northern States Cooperative League*, "For organization work in Minn., Wis., and Mich.," recd. $1,000. The *Cooperative Central Exchange*, Superior, Wis. recd. loans amounting to $10,000.

Commonwealth College, where the Internationale is sung with fervor, was handsomely provided for, being given $1,000 in 1924 and $23,580 in the next three-year period. After this Red sympathizers were called upon to take up its support by donations.

Pioneer Youth of America recd. $25,710, 1925-28, $6,227, 1928-30, and other sums.

W. E. B. Du Bois was paid $5,000 for services evidently considered valuable to the cause. "For expenses *Albert Coyle's* trip to Mexico $549.64"; "For expenses of trip to Pa. and W. Va. coal fields by *Louis Budenz*—$321.29." These last two items appear under Federated Press gifts for the year 1925-26. *Il Nuovo Mondo*, a daily paper, recd. $12,000, 1925-28, and was a mainstay in the Sacco-Vanzetti agitation.

"Am. Student Delgation to Russia, N.Y.C." cost $950, plus $350 for "organization." The item in the 1924 report, *"Investigation of Department of Justice 'spy system'*—$1,345," coincides nicely with the cessation of funds granted the Dept. of Justice the following year for investigation of radical activities and the Dept. is crippled today because of this lack.

For "Pacifism"

Truly the Red tentacles reach far. While opposing the mild, liberal, modern, so-called "Imperialism" of America, England and France, which has brought civilization to still barbarous lands, the Socialists and Communists strive to bring about a world imperialism on Russian lines in which absolute autocracy and force would rule. While talking "Peace," they work to weaken national defense and patriotic spirit in order that at the right moment a bloody revolution may put the "dictatorship of the proletariat" (in reality a dictatorship of combined intellectual and gutter Red revolutionaries) into power. Bearing in mind the Fund's policy to give only to enterprises "definitely committed to a radical program," the following donations to "Peace" causes are interesting:

"To a group of students at *Northwestern University* and *Garrett Biblical Institute*, Evanston, Ill.—April 9, 1924—for anti-militaristic movement — $497.41"; To *"Wyoming State Conference Methodist Church*, Laramie, Wyo.—for publication of literature against compulsory military training—$300" (1926); *"Fellowship of Youth for Peace*, N.Y.C.—for distribution of 1,100 copies of June number of 'World Tomorrow,' among Japanese students in America—$88" (now Fell. Recon.); *"Women's International League for Peace and Freedom*, N.Y.C.—For traveling expenses of speakers on imperialism to Senate Committee hearing and to Chicago conference, (Mar. 4th and May 22nd)—

$543.17" (1924-25); To *"W.I.L.P.F.,"* Wash, D.C., "For general expenses, 6 months (Oct. 22nd) $1,000"; To W.I.L. P.F., Wash., D.C., "For publication of monthly bulletin 'Pax'—$2,400" (1925-26); To W.I.L.P.F., "For publication of Monthly bulletin 'Pax'—$1,200" (1926-27); To W.I.L.P.F. — "For publication of monthly bulletin 'Pax'—$1,200" (1927-28); To *"Committee on Militarism in Education,* N.Y.C." (1) "For preparation and distribution of pamphlet on 'Military Training in Schools and Colleges in the U.S.'—$5,400" (Lane Pamphlet), and (2) "Toward general budget—$5,000" (1925-26); also "To Committee on Militarism in Education—for general expenses—$2,000" (1926-27).

For *"Studies of American Imperialism* (research and publication) — $27,956" (1925-28), is a staggering item indicating to what pains the Fund went to discredit America by propaganda representing the U.S. as "bullying" and "imperialistic." Red intellectuals hired to "research" must have been well pleased at this appropriation.

The Communist *Workers International Relief,* many radical "Labor" schools, periodicals, Pioneer Camps, and "Summer Schools for Workers in Industry," were financed; for the I.W.W.'s, "Wayne, Alberta, Canada—for relief to striking miners, $500"; and the *"Speakers Service Bureau"* recd. $12,500. Donations to the *Labor Bureau* were $1,107.24, $1,000, $381.07; to the *Bureau of Industrial Research,* N.Y. "for Mr. Raushenbush's studies on coal situation—$5,700"; *"Midland Empire Coop. Publishing Co.,* Billings, Mont.—for 4 Farmer-Labor papers—$1,500"; *"Oklahoma Leader,* Oklahoma City—$6,000"; *"Camp Tamiment,* Forest Park, Pa." recd. help; *"Trade Union Committee for organizing Negro Workers"* recd. $2,434 and $600.

"In order to get a complete picture of the enterprises in the labor and radical movements in the U.S., a survey was made jointly by Roger Baldwin and Stuart Chase . . . ", so a Fund report says (It covered them nicely it would seem); and "after being assured of the sound management of an enterprise, of the effectiveness of its directing personnel and the *significance of its objects,* the Fund has given or loaned without further questions."

GARLAND FUND COMMITTEE ON AMERICAN IMPERIALISM

Says the 1925 official report: "A number of research jobs which no enterprise was equipped to tackle were organized and financed by the Fund. Chief among these is a study of American imperialism under the direction of Prof. Harry Elmer Barnes of Smith College who heads an advisory committee composed of Prof. E. M. Borchard, Emanuel Celler, Prof. Paul H. Douglas, Robt. W. Dunn, Kenneth Durant, Prof. Edw. M. Earle, Ernest Gruening, Prof. Manly O. Hudson, Dr. Samuel Guy Inman, Basil M. Manly, Dr. Chas. Clayton Morrison, Kirby Page, Judge Otto Schoenrich, Henrik Shipstead, Edgar Speyer, Moorfield Storey, John F. Sinclair, Oswald Garrison Villard and Arthur Warner."

"Studies are now being made by American investigators in Cuba, Santo Domingo and Bolivia. . . . Two studies made last year under the auspices of the Fund have been published in book form. They are 'American Foreign Investments' by Robt. W. Dunn and 'Dollar Diplomacy' by Scott Nearing and Jos. Freeman. These studies are made under the direction of a committee of the Fund composed of Lewis S. Gannett, Chairman; Morris L. Ernst, James Weldon Johnson, Roger N. Baldwin and Scott Nearing." (See A.A.A.I. Lg., etc.)

GENERAL DEFENSE COMMITTEE

Legal defense association of the I.W.W. corresponding to the Communist I.L.D.; hdqts. 555 W. Lake St., Chicago.

GORKI AWARD

Given yearly by Maxim Gorki of Russia to American Communist authors who produce the best revolutionary literature of the year.

GREEN INTERNATIONAL

To quote from its own literature, it "Is a League of students from among the schools, colleges and universities of the world, intent on War Resistance. Aims: To direct, to encourage . . . systematic War Resistance. . . . To radicalize the cause of peace. . . . Symbol: The Green International Shirt will be the outward symbol of War Resistance—the visible expression of World Patriotism. . . . The Green International requires from its members a personal spiritual pledge to refuse to take part in or to support any kind of war either directly or indirectly."

It aims to enlist at least 2 per cent of all college students in the U.S. to affiliate with war resisting societies. The 2 per cent idea was advanced by Prof. Einstein in 193[illegible] (see "Who's Who" for his Communis[illegible] affiliations). The theory is that if 2 per cent of the population are organized as militant war resisters they can cripple their government in the prosecution of any war. At that time thousands of buttons bearing the insignia "2 per cent" were distributed by radical pacifist groups. The Green International is "Sponsored by Peace Patriots, War Resisters International, War Resisters League, Women's Peace Society, New History Society; Cooperating organizations: Committee on Militarism in Education; Fellowship of Reconciliation"; hdqts. 132 East 65th Street, N.Y. City. (See W. R. Intl. and W. R. Lg.).

GRIFFIN BILL COMMITTEE

Formed to uphold the radicals' Griffin Bill, backed by the A.C.L.U., which proposed admission of aliens without their taking an oath to bear arms in defense of the U.S. government. A letter signed by the nat. sec., Alfred Lief, asking that friends of the Griffin Bill come out to a Hearing Jan. 26, 1932, and saying "Our experience at the first Hearing of this Bill during the past session was that the patrioteers and militarists filled the room ahead of us, thus creating an atmosphere of hostility," lists on the letter head as national chairman of the Griffin Bill Committee, Lola Maverick Lloyd.

Chmn. N.Y. City committee, Elizabeth Black; chmn. Boston committee, Helen Tufts Bailie; chmn. Northampton committee, Elaine Goodale Eastman; chmn. Chgo. committee, Olive H. Rabe; National sponsors: Willis J. Abbott (Boston), Jane Addams, Emily Greene Balch, Harry Elmer Barnes, Mrs. Victor Berger, Alice Stone Blackwell, Roy E. Burt, Carrie Chapman Catt, Dr. Wm. C. Dennis (Pres. of Earlham College), John Dewey, Arthur Fisher, Dorothy Canfield Fisher (Arlington), Mrs. Caroline Foulke Urie (Yellow Springs, O.), Felix Frankfurter, Dr. Alice Hamilton, John Haynes Holmes, Fannie Hurst, Mercer G. Johnston, Harold D. Lasswell, Alfred Lief, Robt. Morss Lovett, James H. Maurer, Prof. Samuel E. Morison (Harvard U.), Agnes Nestor, Willy Pogany (Hollywood), Elmer Rice (N.Y.), James T. Shotwell (Columbia U.), Lillian D. Wald, Dr. Mary E. Woolley (Pres. Mt. Holyoke College), and about twenty others. Hdqts. 135 W. 79th St., N.Y. City, Alfred Lief.

H

HANDS OFF COMMITTEES

Various committees, such as the American Committee for Justice to China, American Committee for Fair Play to China, American Committee for Chinese Relief, and Hands Off China Committees, were formed under Communist inspiration to create propaganda against U.S. interference in China when Red revolutionaries were endangering American lives and property there.

The Kuomintang, or Nationalist Party of China, founded by Sun Yat Sen, were in full alliance with the Communist International and were at the height of their revolutionary activities between 1924 and 1927, with the Soviet agent Grusenberg, alias Borodin, as he was known when he visited Chicago and Hull House circles, acting as chief adviser of Chiang-Kai-Shek, the Kuomintang leader. Communists claim that the Kuomintang Party broke with them and started fighting Communists April 12, 1927. Kuomintang spokesmen place this date as much as two years later. However that may be, the Feb. 28, 1927 issue of the Third International publication, called "The Communist International," stated: "In order to mobilize all the reserves of the International Revolutionary Movement, it is necessary to carry out, with the speed commensurate with the exceptional importance of the matter, the united front under the slogan 'Hands Off China,' while, at the same time, the Communists' parties must act independently and employ all forms of mass revolutionary struggle."

The Marvin Data Sheets report: that Communist Manuel Gomez speaking at a meeting of the "Hands Off China Committee" in Chicago, May 8, 1927, said his organization, the Communist All-America Anti-Imperialist League, had formed 172 Hands Off China Committees in the United States and England; that Carl Haessler presided at this meeting and Jane Addams spoke, as did also Chandra Sena Gooneratne, "a Hindu U. of Chgo. student said to be an active propagandist in the U.S. for a revolution in India similar to the one going on in China"; Marvin adds that, counting the "Hands Off Nicaragua" (Nicaragua was then seething under Communist-supported Gen. Sandino) and "Hands Off Mexico" Committees formed for similar purposes, the total number of Communist-inspired "Hands Off" Committees organized then was probably around 250.

A full page advertisement in the World Tomorrow of Aug. 1925 said that Harry Ward and Paul Blanshard were then in Shanghai and had cabled a request asking for immediate funds to aid the Chinese Communist group then in charge of the Hankow government, saying there was little financial support from Russia and urging the stopping of "every effort to use American gunboats, American money and American men to fasten foreign imperialism on China." This cablegram was quoted with the appeal that contributions be sent to the Garland Fund to aid this cause; and the appeal was signed by Kirby Page, Robt. Morss Lovett and Rose Schneidermann.

The N.Y. Herald Tribune of April 27th, 1927 referred to Harry Ward as Chairman of the executive committee of the American Committee for Justice to China, the same article referring to "another plea for justice received by William Pickens of the Hands Off China Association from Earl Browder, American Communist editor, who went to China as a delegate to labor conference there and since Feb. 23 has been a guest of the Cantonese government."

A vivid description of the great communist Hands Off China mass meeting staged in Union Square, N.Y. City and quotation from the columns of space proudly given it in the communist Daily Worker are cited in Marvin Data Sheets, and the following committee listed:

Hands Off China Committee: Prof. John Dewey, Paul Jones, H. H. Broach, Rev. J. H. Holmes, Dr. James M. Yard, Louis Budenz, Rev. Edmund B. Chaffee, Rev. Chas. C. Webber, Lewis G. Gannett, Wm. Pickens, H. Lanson, chmn. Chinese Students Com. of Columbia. Speakers for their meeting, May 9, 1927 (printed in Daily Wkr.): Louis Budenz, L. Linson, Alex. Trachtenberg, D. Benjamin (Wkrs. Sch.), Richard B. Moore, L. Navarez (Anti-Imp. Lg.), S. D. Ogino, Jap. Wkrs. Alliance (Communist), Geo. Siskind, A. Rosemond, Haitian Patriotic Lg. (Communist), N. Napoli, Anti-Fascist Lg. (Communist), Rebecca Grecht, A. Markoff, Lena Cherbnenka, and Juliet Poyntz (all of Communist Party), Scott Nearing, Robt. W. Dunn, H. M. Wick (Daily Wkr.), Powers Hapgood. (Marvin Data Sheets, 28-29, May 11, 1927.)

HARLEM LIBERATOR

See Liberator.

HARLEM PROGRESSIVE YOUTH CLUB

Communist club; 1538 Madison Ave., N.Y. City.

HARLEM TENANTS LEAGUES

Communist Negro subsidiary groups. Richard B. Moore, director of the National Negro Dept. of the Communist Party, mailed out a report after the 1928 Communist Party Convention in N.Y. City saying: "The establishment of the Harlem Tenants Leagues is considered by the Central Executive Committee as an achievement in united front work among the Negroes. It is necessary to link up the problems of housing with the issues of unemployment, segregation, etc." (Marvin Data Sheets, 62-3.)

HOSPITAL WORKERS LEAGUE

Communist T.U.U.L. union.

HUMANISM

A new religion without God, without worship or prayer and without belief in a future life. The American Assn. for the Advancement of Atheism in its June 1930 report said: "However much Humanists for reasons of expediency shun the title 'Atheist,' they are godless. Consequently we welcome their aid in overthrowing Christianity and all other religions based on the supernatural."

The first Humanist Society of New York was founded by a New York preacher, Chas. Francis Potter, several years ago. A 1933 conference on Humanism of about 40 ministers and educators meeting in Chicago, signed the following resolutions said to have been drawn up originally by Prof. Roy Sellers of the U. of Michigan and made public by Rev. Raymond B. Bragg, Chicago Unitarian minister.

"Religious humanists regard the universe as self-existing and not created.

"Religion must formulate its hopes and plans in the light of the scientific spirit and method.

"The distinction between the sacred and the secular can no longer be maintained.

"Religious humanism considers the complete realization of human personality to be the end of a man's life, and seeks its development and fulfilment in the here and now.

"In place of the old attitudes involved in worship and prayer, the humanist finds his religious emotions exprest in a heightened sense of personal life and in a cooperative effort to promote social well-being.

"There will be no uniquely religious emotions and attitudes of the kind hitherto associated with belief in the supernatural. Man will learn to face the crises of life in terms of his knowledge of their naturalness and probability. Reasonable and manly attitudes will be fostered by education and supported custom.

"We assume that humanism will take the path of social and mental hygiene, and discourage sentimental and unreal hopes and wishful thinking.

"The goal of humanism is a free and universal society in which people voluntarily and intelligently cooperate for the common good.

"The time has come for wide-spread recognition of the radical changes in religious thoughts throughout the modern world. Science and economic change have disrupted the old beliefs.

"Religions the world over are under the necessity of coming to terms with new conditions created by a vastly increased knowledge and experience."

Signers and endorsers of the above Program include Prof. J. A. C. Fagginger Auer, Harvard

University; John Dewey; Prof. Robert Morss Lovett, University of Chicago; Chas. Francis Potter; Rabbi Jacob J. Weinstein, Advisor to Jewish students at Columbia University; Prof. Edwin Arthur Burtt, Cornell University; Prof. Frank Hankins, Smith College; Prof. A. Eustace Haydon, University of Chicago; Prof. Oliver L. Reiser, University of Pittsburgh; and Prof. Roy Wood Sellers, University of Michigan.

HUNGARIAN DRAMATIC CLUB (N.Y.)

Communist mass foreign language section cultural group.

HUNGARIAN PROLETARIAN WRITERS ASSN.

Section of communist Revolutionary Writers Federation.

HUNGARIAN SICK AND DEATH BENEFIT SOCIETY

Communist fraternal insurance foreign language organization.

HUNGARIAN WORKERS CLUB HUNGARIAN WORKERS HOME SOCIETY

Communist Hungarian mass organizations.

I

ICOR

Jewish Communist society helping the colonization of Biro Birdjan, the Jewish Soviet Socialist Republic in Russia; has branches in Brooklyn, New York City, Chicago, etc. Chicago hdqts. 3301 W. Roosevelt Road.

IL NUOVO MONDO NAT. COM.

The full title is "The American Committee for the Support of Il Nuovo Mondo." Il Nuovo Mondo was previously heavily financed by the Garland Fund (see). A letter in 1931 signed by Marguerite Tucker the secretary of the Committee said: "Il Nuovo Mondo is a pro-labor, anti-militarist and anti-fascist daily for the Italians living in this country. Without Il Nuovo Mondo the long Sacco-Vanzetti campaign could never have been carried on," and solicited funds to aid the campaign of Il Nuovo Mondo "to amend our immigration laws so that the right of asylum for political prisoners from other lands . . . may be assured." Radicals use the term "political prisoners" to indicate those jailed for revolutionary activities. Headquarters 81 East 10th Street, New York City.

Clinton S. Golden (of the Garland Fund), treas.; Marguerite Tucker, sec.; Nat. Com.: Morris Berman, Sarah Bernheim, Leroy Bowman, Paul F. Brissenden, Heywood Broun, Louis F. Budenz, Dr. Charles Fama, Dr. Ninon Firenze, Elizabeth Gilman, Arturo Giovannitti, Clinton S. Golden, Florence Curtis Hanson, John Haynes Holmes, Alexander Howat, Harry W. Laidler, Vito Marcantonio, James H. Maurer, Mrs. John F. Moors, A. J. Muste, Jacob Panken, J. Nevin Sayre, Joseph Schlossberg, Vida Scudder, A. I. Shiplacoff, Dr. M. Siragusa, Norman Thomas, Girolamo Valenti, Stephen S. Wise.

INDEPENDENT LABOUR PARTY OF GREAT BRITIAN

Ind. Lab. Party or I.L.P.

A left wing Socialist Party founded by Friedrich Engels, collaborator of Karl Marx, in 1893, aided by Marx' youngest daughter, "Tussy" (who disdained "bourgeois" marriage with Dr. Aveling, her "husband"), G. B. Shaw and others. The April 17, 1933 issue of the American communist Daily Worker quoted from the National Administrative Council of the Independent Labour Party recommendation "'to the party that its affiliation with the Labor and Socialist International (2nd International) should be terminated. . . . It takes the view that there is now no hope of the Labor and Socialist International becoming an effective instrument of revolutionary socialism,'" etc. Whether the I.L.P. will now join the Third International (Communist) remains to be seen. It has long been in close sympathy with Moscow and "took the lead in Pacifist agitation 'during the war'; its anti-recruiting meetings formed the nucleus out of which all Defeatist and Bolshevik movements developed." (From "Socialist Network" by Nesta Webster.) Among its past and present leaders are Ramsay MacDonald (recently expelled for cooperating with the present Coalition Government), Tom Mann (now Communist), Arthur Ponsonby, Chas. Trevelyan, H. N. Brailsford, Josiah Wedgewood, E. D. Morel, Philip Snowden, Pethwick Lawrence, A. Fenner Brockway (recent lecturer in the United States for the L.I.D.), etc. The I.L.P. program states: "The I.L.P. is a Socialist organization and has for its object the establishment of the Socialist Commonwealth." Mrs. Pethwick Lawrence was a co-worker with Jane Addams in the United States in forming the W.I.L.P.F. (see). Socialist Margaret Bondfield was the long time associate in the Labor Party movement of Ramsay MacDonald, who made her Britain's first woman Cabinet Minister in his 1929-31 Cabinet when he was I.L.P. Premier of England. She was not made a member of the Coalition government which followed. She took a prominent part with Jane Addams in the congress of the International Council of Women held July 16, 1933 in Chicago (see Ramsay MacDonald's activities as I.L.P. leader under "Who's Who," also "English Reds" for further information).

The Daily Worker, Oct. 4, 1933, reporting the arrival of Tom Mann, English Communist, said: "Responding to a question about the recent action of the I.L.P. of Great Britain in support of united front action with the Communist International, Mann said that 'the rank and file of the I.L.P. is more and more taking part in joint actions with the Communists—not gingerly, mind you, but heartily!' "

INDUSTRIAL WORKERS OF THE WORLD

I.W.W.

From 1905, when it was founded, until the advent of the Bolsheviks to power, after which many of its unions and leaders joined the Communist forces, the I.W.W. was the most formidable revolutionary organization in the United States. Only about 25,000 of the 100,000 membership remained in 1933, but new blood is now being recruited.

Among the Socialists and Anarchists who founded it or served as its early leaders were Eugene V. Debs, "Big Bill" Haywood, Wm. Z. Foster, Eliz. Gurley Flynn and her husband Carlo Tresca, "Mother" Jones, Ernest Untermann, etc. Wm. Z. Foster and "Big Bill" Haywood went over to the newly-formed Communist Party, which began assuming the more dominant role. However, the Garland Fund donated thousands of dollars to the I.W.W. and during the depression it has had a considerable revival, largely in the west.

As an Anarcho-Syndicalist organization its purpose is the organization of industrial workers into unions to war against employers by any and all means, including sabotage, burning of forests and wheat fields, murder and violence, and eventually, by means of the General Strike, to overthrow the government and present capitalist system of society. A 48-page I.W.W. booklet, sold in 1933, entitled "The General Strike," is entirely devoted to the subject of the General Strike as the I.W.W. revolutionary weapon. After the revolution the plan is to have no central government but only a government by unions.

Its organ "One Big Union Monthly" (Oct. 1920), describing its "Chart of Industrial Communism," stated: "Please note that this plan leaves no room for a political party which specializes in government and ruling other people. All power rests with the people organized in branches of the Industrial Unions. From production and distribution standpoint this means Industrial Communism. From Administration standpoint it means industrial democracy. Such is the program of the I.W.W." The Aug. 11, 1920 issue stated: "The I.W.W. views the accomplishments of the Soviet government of Russia with breathless interest and intense admiration. . . . The I.W.W. has always expelled members who were not true to the basic principles of the world revolution." In answer to Zinoviev's invitation to the I.W.W. to join the Third International, the I.W.W. moved: "That we endorse the Third International with reservations as follows: 'That we do not take any part whatever in parliamentary action and that we reserve the right to develop our own tactics according to conditions prevailing.' "

The few surviving leaders of the old I.W.W. are now free from prison and came from all sections of the United States to attend the I.W.W. convention held Sept. 29-30, 1933 at the Irving Plaza Hotel, N.Y. City. Among these were: James P. Thompson, leader of the pickets in the great 1912 textile strike at Lawrence, Mass.; James Price, once kidnaped and badly beaten during trouble in Kentucky mines; Arthur Boose, agricultural organizer; Monoldi from the metal mining districts of the west; F. Leigh Bearce, building trades organizer; Jack Walsh, marine organizer; and Ben Fletcher, Negro waterfront organizer in Phila. Herbert Mahler, who was among the group arrested after the explosion of the bomb in the Chicago post office and afterwards sent to Leavenworth Penitentiary with Thompson, Walsh and Price, gave an interview in Sept. 1933 at the new I.W.W. headquarters, 94 Fifth Ave., N.Y. City, on the I.W.W. present plans to build anew a militant aggressive organization on the old lines insisting now on a four-hour day and four-day week with no wage cuts for workers.

Official organs 1933: Industrial Worker (weekly newspaper in English), 555 W. Lake St., Chicago; Tie Vapauteen (Finnish monthly), Box 99, Duluth, Minn.; Industrialiste (Finnish daily newspaper), Box 3912, Sta. F.F., Cleveland, O.; Il Proletario (Italian weekly), Box 24, Sta. T, Brooklyn, N.Y.; Jedna Velka Unie (Czecho-Slovakian weekly), 11314 Revere Ave., S.E., Cleveland, O. I.W.W. main hdqts. 555 W. Lake St. and 1618 W. Madison St., Chicago; branches in England and Australia; legal defense society is called General Defense Committee (555 W. Lake St., Chicago); its unemployed organizations are "Unemployed Unions"; cooperates with Socialists, Anarchists and Communists in the revolutionary "united front" "class struggle."

INPRECORR

An abbreviation, in typical Soviet style, of "International Press Correspondence"; published under the latter title in pamphlet form and sold at Communist bookstores; published by the Communist International, originally in Vienna, then, until Hitler's regime, in Berlin, now in London; in four languages—German, French, Russian and English; contains articles by Communist leaders in various countries on revolutionary activities, speeches by Stalin, etc.; 31 Dudden Hill Lane, London, N.W. 10.

INTERCOLLEGIATE STUDENT COUNCIL

Of the League for Industrial Democracy (see).

INTERNATIONALS (1st, 2nd and 3rd)

The *1st International* was formed Sept. 28, 1864 in St. Martin's Hall, London, by a group of peaceful French syndicalists aiming to improve conditions of labor, joined by English members and the Karl Marx clique, which latter completely captured the organization. It was then known as the International Workingmen's Association. In 1869, the "Alliance Sociale Democratique," a secret society headed by the Russian anarchist Michael Bakunin was admitted to the International and here commenced the struggle for power which ended in Marx wrecking the International to get rid of these powerful anarchist rivals. In advocacy of the class war and militant atheism Marxists and Bakunists were one, but, while Marx stood for State Socialism, conquest of political power, that is the State, by the working classes, "nationalization of production and distribution of wealth" until all classes should become one and "bourgeois" desire for individualism should be eradicated, at which time (eternity, perhaps) State control would become unnecessary and the State political machine would then simply "wither away," Bakunin, in his own resumé of his program, advocated: "Abolition of the State in all its religious, juristic, political and social realizations; reorganization by the free initiative of free individuals in free groups"; and declared "I abominate Communism because it is a denial of freedom and I cannot understand anything human without freedom." In 1872 the Anarchists were expelled and the headquarters moved to New York, and four years later the 1st International expired completely.

2nd International: After a 13-year interval, during which there was no Socialist International, a Congress at Brussels, in 1889, founded the 2nd Intl. and set up an Intl. Socialist Bureau composed of three delegates from each of the Socialist or Labor Parties of the various countries represented. Altho Karl Marx had died in 1883, this 2nd Intl. was more purely Marxian than the 1st had ever been owing to the long educational agitation by his followers. By 1893 the 2nd Intl. had become completely Germanized (according to Adolphe Smith, Official Interpreter of the Congresses from the outset). Altho Congresses held in Brussels, 1891, Zurich, 1893, London, 1896, Paris, 1900, Amsterdam, 1904, Stuttgart, 1907, Copenhagen, 1910, Basle, 1912, each one developed increasing Socialist internationalism or "class solidarity" as opposed to patriotism, yet at the outbreak of the World War temporary disruption of the 2nd Intl. occurred because so many of its 12,000,000 members in 27 countries, with the exception of those in America and Italy, adhered to their countries instead of to their Socialist principles. While some in each country hindered and sabotaged their governments, yet because of the general weakening of internationalism, present day Communists refer to the 2nd Intl. as the "Yellow International."

After the war, conferences held Feb. 2, 1919 at Berne, in April, 1919 at Amsterdam, and at Lucerne, Aug. 2, 1919, revived the 2nd Intl., not however without violent dissension concerning leadership, tactics, cooperation with the Bolshevik Socialists, etc., these points causing splits in some national parties and a going-over en masse of others to the 3rd International, then being formed.

The 2nd Intl. has, in 1933, been crippled by Hitler's rise to power in Germany, which was its stronghold, and is looking to Spain and the U.S.A. as its future hope, the Rooseveltian regime being considered the groundwork for Socialism. There is also considerable agitation among Socialists for full affiliation with the Communist Intl. The Socialist and Labor International (see) is also the name of the 2nd Intl.

3rd (or Communist) International: Russia, having by its 1917 revolution been the first to achieve a Socialist government, is regarded as the "Fatherland" of Socialists everywhere. In Jan. 1919, the Soviet government, with the avowed purpose of placing itself at the head of the international Socialist movement sent out a call to the revolutionaries of the world to send dele-

International Committee

Romain Rolland
Henri Barbusse
Theodore Dreiser
Albert Einstein
Maxim Gorky
Heinrich Mann
Bernard Shaw
Madame Sun Yat-sen

American Committee

Theodore Dreiser, Hon. Chairman
Malcolm Cowley, Chairman
Oakley Johnson, Secretary
A. A. Heller, Treasurer

Sherwood Anderson
Newton Arvin
Roger Baldwin
Harry Elmer Barnes
Joseph R. Brodsky
Winifred Chappell
Joseph Cohen
Ida Dailes
H. W. L. Dana
John Dos Passos
W. E. B. Du Bois
Joseph Freeman
Michael Gold
Donald Henderson
Sidney Hook
Joshua Kunitz
Corliss Lamont
Lola Maverick Lloyd
Robert Morss Lovett
Pierre Loving
J. C. McFarland
Rev. R. Lester Mondale
Felix Morrow
Alla Nazimova
Scott Nearing
William Simons
Upton Sinclair
Lincoln Steffens
Leopold Stokowski
Belle G. Taub
Thornton Wilder
Ella Winter

Chicago Committee

Robt. Morss Lovett, Chairman
R. Lester Mondale, Vice-Chairman
Edith M. Lloyd, Secretary
Edward M. Winston, Treasurer
Miron A. Morrill, Publicity

Eugene Bechtold
Jessie Binford
Karl Borders
Alice Boynton
Percy H. Boynton
Sophanisba Breckenridge
Edwin R. Embree
Julia Felsenthal
John Fitzpatrick
Dr. S. B. Freehof
Charles W. Gilkey
Mrs. Alfred Hamburger
Carl Haessler
Mrs. Alfred Kohn
Blanche Lowenthal
Dr. Louis L. Mann
Harriet Monroe
Curtis W. Reese
Dr. H. M. Richter
Donald Slesinger
T. V. Smith
Lorado Taft
Graham Taylor
Jan Wittenber
James M. Yard

CHICAGO COMMITTEE FOR

STRUGGLE AGAINST WAR

CHICAGO, ILL.

HENRI BARBUSSE TO SPEAK

AGAINST WAR AND FASCISM !

Henri Barbusse, the noted French author, who is in America to attend the U.S. Congress Against War, now being held in New York, will speak at a mass meeting against War and Fascism at the Chicago Coliseum on Monday evening, October 23rd.

M. Barbusse is one of the organizers of the International Committee to Aid the Victims of German Fascism. His work against war, both in his novels, such as Under Fire, and his public activities, is internationally known. Last year he was Chairman of the Amsterdam Congress Against War.

A preliminary meeting is being called at the CITY CLUB, 315 Plymouth Court, on Thursday, October 5th at 4 p.m., to make plans for supporting the Barbusse mass meeting. All peace societies, and organizations interested in fighting German fascism, are urged to send representatives. Individuals are also invited to attend. Members of the Chicago Committee for Struggle Against War should by all means be present.

The visit of Henri Barbusse is a tremendously important event. To make the mass meeting a success it is necessary that every organization send delegates to this preliminary meeting.

Sincerely yours,

Robert Morss Lovett
Chairman

Dr. S. B. Freehof

Edith M. Lloyd
Secretary
7921 S.LaSalle

Facsimile of notice urging support of Communist Barbusse meeting, which was jointly sponsored by the Chicago Committee for Struggle Against War and the Chicago Committee of the communist National Committee to Aid Victims of German Fascism, Communist Barbusse being an international officer of both organizations. This Chicago Committee for S.A.W. was called to the platform to occupy seats of honor. John Fitzpatrick, president of the Chicago Federation of Labor, although a member, sidestepped an invitation to speak as a representative of the A.F. of L., according to "Anti-Fascist Action" (magazine of the Chgo. Com. of Nat. Com. to Aid Victims of German Fascism), which was sold at the meeting.

gates to Moscow, where, as a result, Mar. 2-6, 1919, 32 delegates representing 12 countries founded the 3rd International, or Komintern as it is sometimes called (from a combination of Russian words Kommunistitcheski Internazional). The platform proposed in the call (quoted in full in Lusk Report) included: "taking possession at once of the governmental power . . . in order to replace it by the apparatus of proletarian power. (4) The dictatorship of the proletariat should aim at the immediate expropriation of capitalism and the suppression of private property and its transfer to the proletarian state under Socialist administration of the working class. (5) In order to make the Socialist revolution secure, the disarming of the bourgeoisie and of its agents and the general arming of the proletariat are necessary." (Naturally, disarmament is backed by Communists everywhere for this purpose.) "(6) The fundamental condition of the state is the mass action of the proletariat going as far as open conflict with arms in hand against the governmental power of capitalism," etc. Sept. 8, 1919, a Manifesto was sent out urging all revolutionaries, whether I.W.W., Anarchist, or Socialist, to unite in forming a united Communist Party.

As a result of the formation and call of the 3rd International a division occurred in other Socialist revolutionary ranks. As parties the Norwegian Labour Party, Swedish Left Socialist Party, Hungarian Communist Party, Swiss Social Democratic Party, Italian Socialist Party, went over en masse to the 3rd International, while the American Socialist Party split, the Left wing forming the Communist Party on Sept. 1, 1919, in Chicago. The British, French, Belgian, Dutch and Swedish Parties and the German majority Socialists retained their allegiance to the 2nd International. Communist Parties were, however, then formed in all of these countries and the 3rd International or Comintern now controls parties operating in 57 countries.

INTL., AMERICAN AND CHICAGO COMMITTEES FOR STRUGGLE AGAINST WAR

Intl., Am., Chgo.,

Com. for S.A.W.

The communist Intl. League Against Imperialism's agencies for agitating against national defense in various countries and advocating sabotage, revolutionary defense of the Soviet Union, and the turning of "imperialist war into civil war" or Red revolution.

A letter sent out July 19, 1932 signed by Theodore Dreiser asking for funds to aid the communist-called World Congress Against War at Amsterdam, Aug. 20, 1932, listed on its letterhead as the Intl. Committee for the World Congress, the same committee now listed as the Intl. Committee for Struggle Against War on the letterhead (see facsimile) of the Chgo. Com. for Struggle Against War, which sent out a letter calling a meeting at the Chicago City Club, Oct. 5, 1933, to "make plans for supporting the Barbusse mass meeting," which was sponsored jointly with the Chicago Committee to Aid Victims of German Fascism (of the Communist W.I.R.).

At this Communist mass meeting at the Coliseum, called to honor Communist Henri Barbusse, only the Red flag was displayed and the International, song of Red revolution, sung. The Chicago Committee were called to the platform to occupy seats on the stage. Clayton C. Morrisson, editor of the "Christian (?) Century," presided and was cheered when he said that he was proud to stand shoulder to shoulder with Barbusse and that we would never have peace until our capitalistic system was abolished! Jos. Gardner of the Workers Ex-Service Men's League, Robt. Brown of the Metal Wkrs. Industrial Union (Communist), Jos. Freeman of communist "New Masses," and a representative of the Young Communist League spoke. Prof. H. W. L. Dana of Harvard, who greeted the audience as "Comrades" and said he was traveling around with Barbusse to translate his French speeches, collected money from the Communist organizations for the "cause." Mrs. J. Louis Engdahl, a Chicago Public School teacher, widow of the head of the communist I.L.D., donated $20.00. Communist resolutions were passed with thunderous unanimity and Barbusse was ushered in by a delegation of the Wkrs. Ex-Service Men's League, a Negro bearing the velvet banner. Barbusse is the founder of this organization, which teaches soldiers of all nations to turn their country's war into a bloody Red revolution.

International Committee for Struggle Against War:

(Same as Intl. Com. for World Congress Against War.)

Romain Rolland, Henri Barbusse (the honored Communist from France), Theodore Dreiser, Albert

Einstein, Maxim Gorky, Heinrich Mann, Bernard Shaw, Mme. Sun Yat Sen.

American Committee for Struggle Against War:

Theo. Dreiser, hon chmn.; Malcolm Cowley, chmn.; Oakley Johnson, sec.; A. A. Heller, treas.; Sherwood Anderson, Newton Arvin, Roger Baldwin, Harry Elmer Barnes, Jos. R. Brodsky, Winifred Chappell, Jos. Cohen, Ida Dailes, H. W. L. Dana, John Dos Passos, W. E. B. Du Bois, Jos. Freeman, Michael Gold, Donald Henderson, Sidney Hook, Joshua Kunitz, Corliss Lamont, Lola Maverick Lloyd, Robt. Morss Lovett, Pierre Loving, J. C. McFarland, Rev. R. Lester Mondale, Felix Morrow, Alla Nazimova, Scott Nearing, Wm. Simons, Upton Sinclair, Lincoln Steffens, Leopold Stokowski, Belle G. Taub, Thornton Wilder, Ella Winter.

Chicago Committee for Struggle Against War (which sponsored the Henri Barbusse Communist mass meeting and which lists on its letterhead these International, American, and Chicago Committees for Struggle Against War—see facsimile):

Robt. Morss Lovett, chmn.; R. Lester Mondale, vice chmn.; Edith M. Lloyd, sec.; Edw. M. Winston, treas.; Miron A. Morrill, publicity; Eugene Bechtold, Jessie Binford, Karl Borders, Alice Boynton, Percy H. Boynton, Sophonisba Breckenridge, Edwin R. Embree, Julia Felstenthal, John Fitzpatrick (Chgo. Fed. of Lab.), Dr. S. B. Freehof, Rev. Chas. W. Gilkey, Mrs. Alfred Hamburger, Carl Haessler, Mrs. Alfred Kohn, Blanche Lowenthal, Dr. Louis L. Mann, Harriet Monroe, Curtis W. Reese, Dr. H. M. Richter, Donald Slesinger, T. V. Smith, Lorado Taft, Graham Taylor, Jan Wittenber, James M. Yard.

The full memberships of the International and American Committees for Struggle Against War as listed by their Report and Manifesto may be found under "World Congress Against War."

INTERNATIONAL COMMITTEE FOR POLITICAL PRISONERS

Intl. Com. for Pol. Pris.

Formed by A.C.L.U. members to aid and raise money for "political prisoners," the term used by radicals to designate those jailed for seditious activities; recd. money from Garland Fund; sent an appeal in 1933 to the Chinese government in behalf of the Communist Chen Du Hsui which was signed by John Haynes Holmes, Oswald Garrison Villard, Arthur Garfield Hays, Roger N. Baldwin, Upton Sinclair, Lewis S. Gannett, Sherwood Anderson, Theodore Dreiser, Floyd Dell, Waldo Frank, Malcolm Cowley.

INTERNATIONAL LABOR DEFENSE

The American section of the Moscow-controlled communist International Red Aid, the Russian section being called M.O. P.R.; formed in Chicago, 1925; legally aids and propagandizes in behalf of Communist criminals arrested for revolutionary activities; has sections in 67 countries, 37 existing illegally; claims 9,000,000 members and an additional 1,600,000 in affiliated organizations (Am. Labor Year Book); continually cooperates with the American Civil Liberties Union on cases; now agitating race hatred with its money-making Scottsboro campaign (see under article "News").

INTERNATIONAL LADIES GARMENT WORKERS UNION

Intl. Ladies Garm. Wkrs. Un.

"The Amalgamated Clothing Workers, the International Ladies Garment Workers Union and the Cloth Hat, Cap and Millinery Workers Union. . . . And the Knit Goods Union. . . All of these organizations are in the control of leaders who are either open Socialists or open Communists. . . . The membership of these organizations is fully 90 per cent Socialist or Communist. Fully 75 per cent of the membership is foreign born, only a small proportion of this element having gained citizenship papers or even applied for such papers. Being firmly of the belief that through 'general strike' they can and will bring about the 'revolution' they expect soon to control and direct the government of the United States just as their brothers now control and direct the government of Russia. . . . They join with their communist brothers in the celebration of a 'red' May Day. . . . The Intl. Ladies Garm. Wkrs. recently (1927) called a strike in the city of New York. It was followed by rioting and general disorder. . . . The committee directing this strike was in the hands of open Communists" (Marvin Data Sheets, 28-18); The Lusk Report says of the Intl. Ladies Garm. Wkrs.: "The preamble of the constitution indicates that it is founded upon the principles of the class struggle; that it adopts the One Big Union idea and seeks to bring about the overthrow of the present system of society. . . . It is affiliated with the Workers Defense Union of which Eliz. Gurley Flynn is the leader, and with which F. G. Biedenkapp of the Metal Workers' Union is secretary. . . . This Union recognizes the need of educating its members in Economics, Sociology and other cultural subjects so that they may prepare to conduct and manage the industry if their program of seizure is carried out . . . began its educational work in 1914 in conjunction with the Rand

School. About 150 members of the Union were sent to the school. . . . It is closely affiliated with the Socialist Party of America"; its hdqts., 3 W. 16th St., New York City, David Dubinsky.

INTERNATIONAL LEAGUE AGAINST IMPERIALISM

See under All-America Anti-Imperialist League, its American branch.

INTERNATIONAL LEAGUE FOR WORKERS EDUCATION

Moscow's Communist organization controlling subsidiary societies such as the Russian Educational Society, etc. in various countries.

INTERNATIONAL LITERATURE

Organ of International Union of Revolutionary Writers (see).

INTERNATIONAL OF THE GODLESS

Communist anti-religious organization formed at Moscow 1931; the American section is the Proletarian Anti-Religious League (50 E. 13th St., N.Y. City). It is affiliated also with the World Union of Atheists and its American section, Union of Militant Atheists, which was organized by the American Association for the Advancement of Atheism.

INTERNATIONAL OF SEAMEN AND HARBOR WORKERS

Section of the Red International of Labor Unions (R.I.L.U.).

INTERNATIONAL OF TRANSPORTATION WORKERS

Section of Red International of Labor Unions (R.I.L.U.).

INTERNATIONAL PAMPHLETS

Series of official Communist propaganda pamphlets selling at 5c and 10c each; especially compiled for International Pamphlets (799 Broadway, New York), by Party authorities and published by the communist International Publishers; formerly aided by the Garland Fund; "On the Chain Gang," by John L. Spivak (printed serially also in the Daily Worker) is, for example, number 32; "The Church and the Workers" by Bennett Stevens (which sets forth the militant atheistic standpoint of Communism) is No. 15; "The Injunction Menace" by Charlotte Todes is No. 22, etc., etc. Among other writers are:

J. S. Allen, B. D. Amis, George Anstrom, Louis Berg, Grace Burnham, James Barnett, Donald Cameron, Elliot E. Cohen, Whittaker Chambers, Robt. L. Cruden, Robt. W. Dunn, R. Doonping, Bert Grant, Harry Gannes, Harold Ware, Maxim Gorki, Henry Hall, Grace Hutchins, Harry Haywood, Milton Howard, A. B. Magil, Felix Morrow, Joseph North, Vern Smith, Anna Louise Strong, N. Sparks, Ray Stewart, Wm. Siegel, Alexander Trachtenberg.

INTERNATIONAL PRESS CORRESPONDENCE

See under Inprecorr.

INTERNATIONAL PUBLISHERS

Official Soviet publishing house in the U.S. headed by Alexander Trachtenberg, long an active Communist executive; 381 Fourth Ave., N.Y.C.

INTERNATIONAL RED AID

World Moscow-directed organization of which M.O.P.R. is the Russian section, and International Labor Defense, the American section; gives legal aid and relief to Communist revolutionaries.

INTERNATIONAL SEAMEN'S CLUBS

Affiliated with the Intl. of Seamen and Harbor Workers and the communist Marine Workers Industrial Union.

INTERNATIONAL UNION OF THE REVOLUTIONARY THEATRE

Moscow's Communist organization, a Section of Agit-Prop, which controls Mid-European, Anglo-American, Latin-European, East Asiatic theatre commissions headed by Soviet propaganda theatre leaders who study the "problems of the revolutionary theatre"; has 419 affiliated Czecho-Slovakian groups with 10,000 members, an English section, Holland section and 232 groups in Germany; American sections are the League of Workers Theatres (see), the Proletarian Dramatic League, and affiliated groups; formerly called the International Workers Dramatic Union of Moscow; directs activities of Communist propaganda theatres, dance leagues and production of motion pictures.

INTERNATIONAL UNION OF REVOLUTIONARY WRITERS

(of the International Bureau of Revolutionary Literature).

Moscow's international Communist organization; the Revolutionary Writers Federation is the American branch (see); its 2nd World Conference, held Nov. 15, 1930 at Kharkov, Russia, commissioned the John Reed Club American delegation of writers to organize the Workers Cultural Federation (see); its official organ is "International Literature," which advertises itself as: "Literature of the World Revolution—devoted to the proletarian and revolutionary literature of all countries—the central organ of the International Union of Revolutionary Writers"; published every two months in Moscow in English, French, German, and Russian. Yearly subscription $1. "Send all subscriptions: Moscow, Central Post Office, Box 850." The Oct. 1933 issue, No. 4, gave as its International Advisory Board:

M. Anderson-Nexo, Henri Barbusse, J. R. Becher, Michael Gold, Maxim Gorki, A. Lunacharsky, A. Magil, Go Ma-jo, John Dos Passos, Ludwig Renn, Romain Rolland, A. Serafimovich, *Upton Sinclair*, Tokunaga Naossi, E. Weinert; Permanent Contributors (many countries listed): United States: Emjo Basshe, Walt Carmon, Jack Conroy, John Dos Passos, Theodore Dreiser, Fred Ellis, Ed. Falkowski, Joseph Freeman, Michael Gold, Horace Gregory, John Herrmann, Josephine Herbst, Langston Hughes, Joseph Kalar, Joshua Kunitz, Louis Lozowick, Norman Macleod, A. B. Magil, Myra Page, Upton Sinclair, Agnes Smedley, Herman Spector, Mary Heaton Vorse; Germany: Oskar Bauer, J. R. Becher, O. Biha, B. Brecht, W. Bredel, E. Ginkel, E. Glaeser, O. M. Graf, K. Gruenberg, A. Hotopp, E. E. Kosch, K. Klaeber, A. Kurella, H. Marchwitza, K. Neukranz, L. Renn, G. Ring, F. Rubiner, B. Scharrer, A. Seghers, L. Turek, E. Weinert, F. Weisskopf, K. Wittvogel; France: L. Aragon, H. Barbusse, J. Duclos, J. Freville, F. Jourdain, L. Moussinac, Romain Rolland, P. Vaillant-Couturier; England: Ch. Ashleigh, Bob Ellis, Harold Heslop; (staff changed but slightly from 1932).

INTERNATIONAL WORKERS AID

Communist; changed name about 1929 to Workers International Relief (see).

INTERNATIONAL WORKERS ORDER I.W.O.

Communist fraternal and agitational insurance society formed in 1930 by 7,000, mainly Jewish, members of the left wing of the Workmen's Circle. Now, after three years, it claims 34,000 members including branches of Hungarians, Slovaks, Ukrainians, Italians, Polish, Russians, Armenians, Spanish, Bulgarians, Greeks, Negroes and Americans; conducts Russian, Slovak, Ukrainian, and Jewish Communist language schools and about 130 elementary and high schools for children in order to counteract "capitalistic" and "nationalistic" public school influences. To quote: "In these schools the children are taught the various languages and are told about the struggle of the workers against their bosses. The children learn not only about the workers and their struggle but actually participate in demonstrations, mass meetings, etc. People send their children to these schools in order that they may learn the language taught there. Some parents, when they learn what is taught at the schools, are drawn into the branches of the "International Workers Order." (From 2nd I.W.O. Convention Program.) "Many workers from basic industries have been introduced to the revolutionary movement through the I.W.O.," said the Chgo. Workers Voice (Feb. 15, 1933).

I attended the I.W.O. Second Annual Convention held at the Chicago Coliseum, June 17, 1933. Fully 12,000 people were there. A children's chorus of 500, a mass pageant of 1,000, 700 delegates, and speakers Max Bedacht, Ben Gold, M. Olgin had been advertised. The usual printed signs about the Scottsboro boys, Mooney, disarmament (for America) and many Red flags were in evidence. Children were dressed in red. The Internationale was sung, holding right arms upraised with clenched fists. Loud applause greeted speakers when they referred to the coming Red revolution. Barefooted girl dancers dressed in red, representing the Communists, at the left of the stage pageant, were backed by grim bare-armed, shirt-sleeved "working" men with clenched fists. In the center a group of girls dressed in yellow represented the Socialists. At the right, "capitalist" girls in black decorated with silver dollar signs and backed by a priest with a cross, two plug-hatted "capitalists," and police, danced about until the Reds were joined by the Yellows and finally surged forward, struck the cross out of the priest's hands, drove out all the "Capitalists" and took possession of the stage sets representing banks, factories, hospitals, etc. This pageant was in four episodes. Wild applause greeted the riotous Red triumphs. When at the opening of one scene the priest was seen seated alone on a park bench, a mighty "boo" arose from the audience.

INTERNATIONAL WORKING MENS ASSOCIATION

Anarcho - syndicalist association with affiliated groups in 24 countries; headquarters in Berlin; its congress held in Madrid, 1931 "in greeting the overthrow of the Spanish monarchy, expressed great faith in the ability of the Confederacion Nacional del Trabajo, which claimed a membership of 600,000, to do its part in the final emancipation of the Spanish proletariat" (Am. Labor Year Book);

the Confederacion Nacional del Trobajo is its Spanish, and strongest, unit, with a membership of about a million and a half members claimed in 1933.

This anarchist-communist group was responsible for the overthrow of the Spanish government. Anarchist M. Olay of Chicago, in "Recovery Through Revolution," writes of the power of anarchist-communism in Spain. He himself takes part in the anarchist, I.W.W., Socialist, Communist "united front" activities. Advisory Associates, Nov. 8, 1933, report that the Intl. Workingmens Assn. has opened headquarters at 94 Fifth Ave., N.Y. City, and are to issue a special press service release giving information concerning Anarchist activities throughout the world, and comments that "Organized Anarchism is reestablishing itself in the United States once more." (See Free Society Group also.)

INTOURIST

Official Soviet government travel agency, with offices in England, Germany, France, Chicago, New York City (261 Fifth Ave.), etc. Has sole charge of all tourist travel in the U.S.S.R.; provides and trains the guides to show and tell tourists what they "should" see and hear; distributes "Soviet Travel," a monthly magazine containing the usual false propaganda articles and "staged" photographs; affiliated with "Open Road."

IRISH WORKERS CLUB

304 W. 58th St., N.Y. City; Communist Party club; recd. 200 copies weekly from Ireland of Irish Workers Voice "until Duffy's blue shirted heroes burned down Connolly House, the hdqts. of the Communist Party in Ireland; the group at home have had to forego regular publication for lack of funds." (Daily Worker, Nov. 8, 1933.)

IRON AND BRONZE WORKERS INDUSTRIAL UNION

A Communist T.U.U.L. union.

IZVESTIA

Official organ of the Soviet government or "All-Russian Central Executive Committee"; published in Moscow.

J

JACK LONDON CLUBS

A section of the communist Revolutionary Writers Federation; named in honor of Jack London, the revolutionary who was the first president of the Intercollegiate Socialist Society (now L.I.D.) and who said: "Few members of the capitalist class see the revolution. Most of them are too ignorant, and many are too afraid to see it. It is the same old story of every perishing ruling class in the world's history. Fat with power and possession, drunken with success and made soft by surfeit and by cessation of struggle, they are like drones clustered about the honey vats when the worker-bees spring upon them to end their rotund existence." The Newark, N.J. branch was forming "Hands Off Cuba" Committees in answer to the call of the A.A.A.I. Lg. (Daily Worker, Oct. 17, 1933.)

JAPANESE CULTURAL FEDERATION

Section of communist Revolutionary Writers Federation.

JEWELRY WORKERS INDUSTRIAL UNION

Communist T.U.U.L. union.

JEWISH WORKERS CLUBS OF AMERICA

Communist; N. I. Costrell, sec. Nat. Exec. Com.; I. Goldberg, sec. N.Y. City Com.; M. Strassburger, sec. Chicago City Com.; N. Korman, sec. Phila. City Com.; E. Kingston, sec. Detroit City Com.

The following clubs donated a half page advertisement to the 10th Anniversary edition of the Daily Worker, Jan. 6, 1934, expressing their wholehearted backing of its Communist revolutionary agitations saying "On with the struggle":

N.Y. City Clubs: Artef Workers Club, Bath. Beach Workers Club, Boro Park Workers Club, Bridge Plaza Workers Club, Brighton Beach Workers Club, Bronx Workers Club, Brownsville Workers Club, Brownsville Youth Center, Coney Island Workers Club, Downtown Workers Club, East N.Y. Workers Club, East Side Workers Club, Hinsdale Workers Club, Jackson Workers Club, Jerome Workers Club, Mapleton Workers Club, Middle Bronx Workers Club, New Lots Workers Club, Prospect Workers Club, Vegetarian Workers Club, Williamsburg Workers Club, Workers Self-Education Club, White Plains Workers Club, Zukunft Workers Club; Chicago: Hirsch Leckert Workers Club, North West Workers Club, West Side Workers Club, M. Winchevsky Workers Club; Philadelphia: Down Town Workers Club, Strawberry Mansion Workers Club; Detroit: Jewish Young Workers Club, Oakland Workers Club, West Side Workers Club; Boston: Dorchester Workers Club, Roxbury Workers Club; Baltimore Workers Club; Cleveland Workers Club; Los Angeles Workers Club; Minneapolis Workers Club; Newark Workers Club; New Brunswick Workers Club;

Paterson Workers Club; Rochester Workers Club; Toledo Workers Club; Wash., D.C.: Five Star Youth Club.

JEWISH WORKERS PARTY

(Poale Zion Left Wing)

Socialist, pro-communist, Zionist party; a supporting organization of the Nat. Com. to Aid Victims of German Fascism.

JOHN REED CLUBS

Communist Clubs named in honor of the so-called "first American Communist," John Reed. Affiliate of the Intl. Union of the Revolutionary Theatre. As a section of the communist International Union of Revolutionary Writers, the New York Club, 430 6th Ave., organized the Workers Cultural Federation (see) with which the John Reed branches are affiliated. There are now (1933) about 30 branches located in New York, Chicago, Detroit, Waukegan, Illinois, Madison, Wis., Chapel Hill, N.C., etc.

The formation of the New York branch was thus described by Communist Michael Gold ("New Masses," Jan. 1930 issue): "The John Reed Club was organized about two months ago here in New York. It is a small group of writers, artists, sculptors, musicians and dancers of revolutionary tendencies. . . . Several activities have begun. The artists arranged an exhibition at the Workers Co-operative House in the Bronx. About 35 pictures were hung. The exhibit will be shown for about 4 weeks. Over 300 workers came to the opening. There was a furious discussion led by Lozowick, Basshe, Gropper, Klein and others. . . . At the next meeting I shall propose the following:

"That every writer in the group attach himself to one of the industries. That he spend the next few years in and out of this industry, studying it from every angle, making himself an expert in it, so that when he writes of it he will write like an insider, not like a bourgeois intellectual observer. He will help on the publicity in strikes, etc. He will have his roots in something real. The old Fabians used to get together and write essays based on the books they had read. We will get close to the realities."

The Detroit branch publishes a monthly magazine, "The New Force," at 8224 Twelfth St., Detroit, Mich.; the Chicago branch, 1475 S. Michigan Ave., started publishing (June, 1933) a magazine, "Left Front," which issue announced that Speakers during the 1932-33 season "have included Malcolm Cowley, Eugene Bechtold, Waldo Frank, Robt. Morss Lovett, Dr. James M. Yard, Wm. Gebert, Robt. Minor, Leo Fisher, Carl Haessler, and Professors Harold Lasswell, Frederic Schuman, Louis Wirth, Lawrence Martin, Francis Heisler, Louis Gottschalk and Melville J. Herskovitz. . . . Members of the club have taken a leading part in the organization at the Workers' School, the Free Tom Mooney Conference, the Chicago Workers Theatre, the Committee for Struggle Against War, the Anti-Fascist United Front, the School for Workers' Children and the May First Demonstration. A year ago one of the Chicago Club members helped to organize the Milwaukee John Reed Club, and during the winter he also assisted in the forming of a John Reed Club at the University of Wisconsin at Madison."

Those listed as signing the John Reed Club protest against anti-Red propaganda (published in the N.Y. Times of May 19, 1930) are:

L. Adohmyan, Sherwood Anderson, Emjo Basshe, Helen Black, Prof. Franz Boas, Alter Brody, Samuel Brody, Fritz Brosins, Jacob Burck, David Burlink, Rev. R. B. Callahan, Walt Carmon, Ralph Cheyney, N. Cirovsky, Lydia Cinquegrana, Sarah N. Cleghorn, Ann Coles, Malcolm Cowley, Franz E. Daniel, Miriam A. DeFord, Adolf Dehn, Floyd Dell, L. A. DeSantes, Babette Deutsch, Carl Van Doren, John Dos Passos, Robert W. Dunn, Max Eastman, Charles Ellis, Fred Ellis, Ernestine Evans, Kenneth Fearing, Sara Bard Field, Waldo Frank, Harry Freeman, Al Frueh, Hugo Gellert, Michael Gold, Floyd S. Gove, C. Hartley Grattan, Horace Gregory, Wm. Gropper, Rose Gruening, Carl Haessler, E. Haldeman-Julius, M. Haldeman-Julius, Ruth Hale, Jack Hardy, Mina Harkavy, Prof. S. R. Harlow, Chas. Y. Harrison, Aline D. Hays, Arthur G. Hays, Lowell B. Hazzard, Josephine Herbst, John Hermann, Harold Hickerson, Grace Hutchins, Eitaro Ishigaki, Joseph Kaphan, Ellen A. Kennan, Rev. C. D. Ketcham, Rev. Frank Kingdon, I. Kittine, I. Klein, Alfred Kreymborg, Joshua Kunitz, Melvin P. Levy, Louis Lozowick, Grace Lumpkin, Norman Macleod, A. B. Magil, Jan Matulka, H. L. Mencken, Norma Millay, Harriet Monroe, Prof. Frank McLean, Scott Nearing, Alfred H. Neumann, Eugene Nigob, Joseph North, Harvey O'Connor, M. J. Olgin, Joseph Pass, Morris Pass, Nemo Piccoli, Harry A. Potamkin, John Cowper Powys, Juanita Preval, Walter Quirt, Burton Rascoe, Anton Refregier, Philip Reisman, Louis Ribak, Boardman Robinson, Anna Rochester, Anna Rosenberg, Julius Rosenthal, Martin Russak, Samuel Russak, David Saposs, E. A. Schachner, Theodore Scheel, Isidor Schneider, Evelyn Scott, Edwin Seaver, Edith Segal, Esther Shemitz, Wm. Siegel, Upton Sinclair, John Sloan, Otto Soglow, A. Solataroff, Walter Snow, Raphael Soyer, Herman Spector, Prof. J. M. Stalnaker, Genevieve Taggard, Eunice Tietjens, Carlo Tresca, Jim Tully, Louis Untermyer, Joseph Vogel, Keene Wallis, Frank Walts, Prof. R. E. Waxwell, Rev. C. C. Webber, G. F. Willison, Edmund Wilson, Jr., Adolf Wolff, Chas. E. S. Wood, Art Young, Stark Young, Avrahm Yarmolinsky, Wm. Zarach.

JOINT COMMITTEE ON UNEMPLOYMENT

A union of radical organizations headed by John Dewey. A letter was sent out by him Nov. 1931, urging individuals and representatives of organizations to come to a "Conference on The Unemployment Program for Congress" to be held Nov. 30, in Washington. The letterhead read as follows: The Joint Committee on Unemployment: 22 East 17th St., New York City. Washington Office: Room 39, Bliss Bldg., Washington, D.C. Council: Church League for Industrial Democracy, Wm. Spofford Director; Conference for Progressive Political Action, A. J. Muste, Director; Fellowship of Reconciliation, J. B. Matthews, Secretary; Labor Bureau, Inc., Alfred Bernheim, Director; League for Independent Political Action, Howard Y. Williams, Secretary; League for Industrial Democracy, Norman Thomas, Director; National Unemployment League, Darwin J. Meserole, President; Peoples Lobby, Benj. Marsh, Executive Sec.; Social Service Commission of the Central Conference of Rabbis, Rabbi Edward I. Israel; Social Service Commission of the Methodist Church, Winifred Chappell, Secretary; Workmen's Sick and Death Benefit Association, Wm. Spuhr, Secretary; Abraham Epstein, Executive Sec. American Assn. for Old Age Security; Hubert C. Herring, Exec. Sec. of the Dept. of Social Relations Congregational Education Society; Sidney Hillman, President of the Amalgamated Cloth. Workers of America; A. J. Kennedy, President of the Amalgamated Lithographers of America; Abraham Lefkowitz of the Teachers' Union; Emil Rieve, President of the American Federation of Full Fashioned Hosiery Workers (socialistic). The National Religion and Labor Foundation became a member 1933. The Jt. Com. on Unemp. Conference held March 18, 1933 was addressed by Father John A. Ryan, Jerome Davis, Rabbi Edw. Israel, all of the Foundation, and these addresses were broadcast by radio.

Officers: chmn., John Dewey; vice chmn.: Harriet Stanton Blatch, Mrs. Ethel Hyde, John Haynes Holmes, Bishop Francis J. McConnell, Father John A. Ryan, Norman Thomas, Stephen S. Wise; sec.-treas., Mary Fox; exec. com.: Alfred Bernheim, Abraham Epstein, Mary Fox, Sidney Goldstein, Benj. Mandel, Benj. Marsh, Darwin J. Meserole, Howard Y. Williams.

K

KENTUCKY MINERS DEFENSE AND RELIEF COMMITTEE

An I.W.W. Committee formed to defend 43 Harlan, Ky. miners arrested for Red agitation and terrorism; its letterhead gives its address as 1618 W. Madison St., Chgo. (I.W.W. hdqts.), and lists Hochrein, Carl Keller and Chas. C. Velsek, as chmn., sec. and treas.; Advisory Committee: Ralph Chaplin (I.W.W.), Robt. Morss Lovett, Norman B. Barr; and states that it is "Endorsed By": General Defense Committee (of I.W.W.); Proletarian Party (Communist); Socialist Party; Free Society Group (Anarchist); Socialist Youth League; Industrial Workers of the World; Arbeiter Kultur und Sport Kartell; Connolly Club.

L

LABOR AGE

Monthly official organ of the Conference for Progressive Labor Action, militant left wing Socialist labor organization; pres., A. J. Muste; editor, Louis Budenz; 128 E. 16th St., N.Y.C. Changed 1933 to weekly paper "Labor Action."

LABOR AND SOCIALIST INTERNATIONAL

The Socialist, or Second, International (see); its 1931 Congress met in Vienna with 742 delegates representing 37 parties in 29 countries. Emile Vandervelde was chairman.

LABOR BUREAU, INC.

Socialist statistical bureau analysing economic, labor developments from a Socialist viewpoint; located in New York with branches in Chicago and San Francisco; issues monthly bulletin "Facts for Workers"; is composed of Alfred and Sarah Bernheim, Stuart Chase, Kathryn Fenn, S. B. Lewin, Estelle Shrifte, George Soule and Norman Ware.

LABOR DEFENDER

Monthly organ of the communist International Labor Defense; editors: Wm. L. Patterson, Joseph North; assoc. eds.: Louis Coleman, Sasha Small; contrib. eds: Henri Barbusse, Jacob Burck, Whittaker Chambers, Robt. W. Dunn, John Dos Passos, Maxim Gorki, Eugene Gordon, Hugo Gellert, Josephine Herbst, Grace Hutchins, Melvin P. Levy, Esther Lowell, Joseph Pass, Paul Peters, Ludwig Renn, Lincoln Steffens, Chas. Rumford Walker, Walter Wilson; 80 E 11th St., Room 430, New York.

LABOR DEFENSE COUNCIL

Organized by the Communist Party Central Executive Committee in 1922, to raise

NATIONAL COMMITTEE

ROGER N. BALDWIN, New York City
NORMAN B. BARR, Chicago
Director Oliver Institute
DENNIS E. BATT, Detroit
Editor Detroit Labor News, O. O. Det. Fed. Labor
EUGENE J. BROCK,
Chairman Progressive Voters' League of Michigan
J. G. BROWN, Chicago
National Sec'y Farmer-Labor Party
ROBERT M. BUCK, Chicago
Editor New Majority, O. O. Chicago Fed. of Labor
JOHN C. CLAY, Chicago
Sec'y Teamsters Local Union 712
LENETTA M. COOPER, Chicago
R. D. CRAMER, Minneapolis
Editor of Min. Labor Review
EUGENE V. DEBS, Terre Haute
ELIZABETH GURLEY FLYNN, New York
JOHN C. FLORA, Chicago
JOHN HAYNES HOLMES, New York
MAX S. HAYES, Cleveland
FRANCIS FISHER KANE, Philadelphia
DR. JOHN A. LAPP, Chicago
Director National Catholic Welfare Council
MORITZ J. LOEB, Chicago
FRANCES C. LILLIE, Chicago
FATHER JOHN A. RYAN, Washington
Director National Catholic Welfare Council
JOHN T. TAYLOR, Detroit
HULET M. WELLS, Seattle
GEORGE P. WEST, San Francisco

LOCAL COMMITTEE

H. BERLIN,
Joint Board Dress and Waistmakers Union, I. L. G. W. U.
ELIZABETH GURLEY FLYNN,
HENRY R. LINVILLE,
HERMA BERMAN,
National Defense Committee
BROWNSTEIN,
Joint Board Furriers Union
BENJAMIN MANDEL,
Teachers Union
JULIUS LAZARD,
Bakers Union Local No. 164
LENA GOODMAN,
Ladies Waistmakers Union Local 25
S. E. BEARDSLEY,
Organizer International Jewelry Workers Union Local 1
M. WEINER,
Local 62, I. L. G. W. U.
M. OBERMEIER,
Hotel Workers Local of Amalg. Food Workers of America
LEO HAUFFBAUER,
Architect Ornamental Iron and Bronze Workers Union
MORRIS EDELSTEIN,
Fancy Leather Goods Workers Union
H. De FRANK,
United Auto., Aircraft and Vehicle Workers of A., Local 49

CO-OPERATING WITH COMMITTEE OF THE DEFENDANTS

EARL R. BROWDER, Chicago
WILLIAM F. DUNNE, New York City
WILLIAM FOSTER, Chicago
C. E. RUTHENBERG, Cleveland

NATIONAL OFFICERS

ROBERT M. BUCK, *Chairman*
EUGENE V. DEBS, *Vice-Chairman*
REV. JOHN A. RYAN, D.D., *Vice-Chairman*
MORITZ J. LOEB, *Secretary*
FRANCES C. LILLIE, *Treasurer*
WILLIAM Z. FOSTER, *Sec'y Defendant's Com.*

LABOR DEFENSE COUNCIL

FRANK P. WALSH, Chief Counsel for the Defendants

For the defense of the Michigan criminal syndicalist defendants prosecuted at the instance of the Federal Secret Service, in its drive against organized labor.

To carry on in connection with the legal defense a campaign against all infringement upon the right of free speech, free press and freedom of assemblage and all measures restricting the rights of the workers.

ROOM 434
80 EAST ELEVENTH STREET
New York City

National Secretary
WILLIAM Z. FOSTER

Telephone STUYVESANT 6616

April 6, 1923

Dear Friend:

The press has brought you information of the progress of the trial of the first of the so-called Michigan cases at St. Joseph. Every day it is becoming clearer that the issue in this trial is the right of free speech and free assemblage in America, as well as such due processes of law, as constitute the just basis of any democratic society. Mr. Frank P. Walsh, attorney for the defense, has stated clearly that the provisions of the Criminal Syndicalist Acts, under which Foster and his associates have been brought to trial, violate the Constitution of the state of Michigan and the Constitution of the United States. Evidence for this contention is fast becoming abundant.

A group of men and women met together peacefully to consider the business of their party organization, contemplating no acts of violence and cherishing no intent to promote or induce acts of violence, was itself treated with utmost violence by the officers of the law. If ever there was a trial involving persecution and tyranny, it is this one. It comes as the last echo of the disgraceful mania of governmental terrorism, which was one of the plagues of the war.

The defense of these men and women, now on trial, is an expensive one. Large sums of money must be raised to guarantee them justice. This money can come only from those who believe in the vindication of basic democratic rights in this country. We appeal to you to help us in this cause. Read the inclosed pamphlet giving the story of the case and then send your contribution in the inclosed envelope.

Sincerely yours,

Freda Kirchwey   Norman Thomas
John Nevin Sayre   Mary Heaton Vorse
Roger Baldwin   Percy Stickney Grant
Paxton Hibben   John Haynes Holmes

BS&AU 12646

MAKE CHECKS PAYABLE TO THE LABOR DEFENSE COUNCIL
Accounts audited by Stuart Chase, C.P.A.

Facsimile of circular letter sent out by the Labor Defense Council soliciting funds for the defense of Communists arrested at Bridgman, Mich. Signed by Freda Kirchwey, Norman Thomas, John Nevin Sayre, Mary Heaton Vorse, Roger Baldwin, Rev. Percy Stickney Grant, Paxton Hibben, Rev. John Haynes Holmes (see this "Who's Who" for their affiliations). The name of Father John A. Ryan of Washington appears conspicuously along with that of Wm. Z. Foster, the Communist leader, as fellow National Officers.

funds for the defense of Communists arrested in the Bridgman Raid (see); received huge sums from Garland Fund; became in 1925 the official Communist legal defense society, changing its name to International Labor Defense (see); a circular letter sent out April 6, 1923 (see facsimile) bore the following heading: "Labor Defense Council"—"For the defense of the Michigan criminal syndicalist defendants prosecuted at the instance of the Federal Secret Service in its drive against organized labor. To carry on in connection with the legal defense a campaign against all infringements upon the right of free speech, free press, and freedom of assemblage and all measures restricting the rights of workers—Room 434, 80 East 11th St., New York City—Frank P. Walsh, Chief Counsel for the Defendants—National Secretary, Wm. Z. Foster" (one of the Communist leaders arrested) "Telephone Stuyvesant 6616." The letter read in part:

"Dear Friend: The press has brought you information of the progress of the trial of the so-called Michigan cases at St. Joseph. Every day it becomes clearer that the issue in this trial is the right of free speech and free assemblage in America. . . . A group of men and women met together peacefully to consider the business of their party organization contemplating no acts of violence and cherishing no intent to promote or induce acts of violence, was itself treated with utmost violence by the officers of the law." (Author's note: This typical Red falsehood is daily refuted by the Communists' own spoken and written affirmations, for instance the following in the Marx "Communist Manifesto": "Communists disdain to conceal their views and aims. They openly declare that their ends can be attained only by the forcible overthrow of all existing conditions. Let the ruling classes tremble at a Communist revolution" (p. 44).) This letter, after soliciting funds, was signed "Sincerely yours, Freda Kirchwey, Norman Thomas, John Nevin Sayre, Mary Heaton Vorse, Roger Baldwin, Percy Stickney Grant, Paxton Hibben, John Haynes Holmes." (Their own signatures.) Printed on the side of the letterhead was:

"National Officers: Robert M. Buck, chairman; Eugene V. Debs, vice chairman; Rev. John A. Ryan, D.D., vice-chairman; Moritz J. Lieb, secretary; Frances C. Lillie, treasurer; Wm. Z. Foster, Sec. Defendants' Com.; Cooperating with Committe of the Defendants: Earl R. Browder, Chicago, Wm. F. Dunne, New York City, Wm. Foster, Chicago, C. E. Ruthenberg, Cleveland." National Committee: Roger N. Baldwin (A.C.L.U.); Norman B. Barr (Chicago, Director Olivet Institute); Dennis E. Batt (Proletarian Party, Detroit); Robt. M. Buck (editor "New Majority," Farmer-Labor Party); Eugene V. Debs (revolutionary Socialist Party leader); Eliz. Gurley Flynn (Workers Defense Union of N.Y.); Moritz J. Loeb (Civil Liberties Union and Communist Party); Eugene J. Brock (chmn. Progressive Voters' League of Michigan); John C. Clay (Sec. Teamsters' Local Union 712, Chgo.); Lenetta M. Cooper, Chgo.; John C. Flora, Chgo.; John Haynes Holmes, N.Y.; Max S. Hayes, Cleveland; Francis Fisher Kane, Phila.; Dr. John A. Lapp, Director National Catholic Welfare Council; John J. Taylor, Detroit; Hulet M. Wells, Seattle; Geo. P. West, San Francisco. N.Y. Local Committee: H. Berlin (Intl. Ladies Garm. Wkrs. U.), Eliz. Gurley Flynn, Henry R. Linville, Nerma Berman (Nat. Defense Com.); Brounstein (Jt. Bd. Furriers' Union); Benj. Mandel (Teachers Union), etc. Headquarters were also at 166 W. Washington St., Chicago.

"One of the first things done by the organization was the appointment of a publicity department to flood the daily newspapers of the country with propaganda for the movement. 'Press Releases' were issued and spread broadcast. Much of the material thus furnished was printed in reputable newspapers ignorant of the fact that they were printing appeals for a movement aimed at the overthrow of the country." (Whitney's "Reds in America," p. 174.) The Reds completely won this fight and the right apparently in Michigan to openly advocate violent overthrow of the U.S. Government when these cases were dismissed and about $100,000 bond money was returned in 1933 through the aid of Patrick H. O'Brien, A.C.L.U. attorney, elected Atty. General of Michigan in 1932.

LABOUR PARTY OF GREAT BRITAIN

A Marxian-Socialist Party ("Socialist Network" by Nesta Webster). "The conversion of the old pre-war Labour Party devoted to the interests of Labour—into the politically-run Socialist Party was effected by the unceasing propaganda and wire pulling of the Independent Labour Party, an organized group directed for years by Messrs. MacDonald and Snowden." . . . "In the (Labour) Party's printed campaign programme for the 1929 election —which was called 'Labour and the Nation' and put the Socialists in power—there was a foreword by Mr. Ramsay MacDonald saying 'The Labour Party, unlike other parties, is not concerned with patching the rents in a bad system, but with transforming Capitalism into Socialism'. . . . Many of those Labour Party members were Communists; but it has always been the policy of the Party at annual conferences to repudiate Communism in order to retain their black coat followers, while working hand in glove with individual Communists." ("The Patriot" of London, Oct. 5, 1933.)

LABOR RESEARCH ASSOCIATION

A Communist subsidiary; received money from Garland Fund; organized by Communist Robt. W. Dunn for linking organized labor to the Communist movement; prepares pamphlets for Intl. Pamphlets; collects material for use of Communist speakers, organizers, etc.; Chicago Labor Research is a branch; N.Y. hdqts. 80 E. 11th St., N.Y. City; issues five bulletins: Steel and Metal Notes; Mining Notes; Textile Notes; Economic Notes; NRA Notes; is organizing (1933-34) groups in principal cities and industrial centers.

LABOR SPORTS UNION

The official federation of hundreds of Communist labor sports organizations functioning all over the U.S.; American section of the Red Sports International; organ "The New Sport and Play," published at 813 Broadway, New York City; sponsored the Counter-Olympics Games held at University of Chicago Stagg Field, 1932, in opposition to the "capitalistic" Olympics held in Los Angeles.

LABOR TEMPLE (AND SCHOOL)

A settlement maintained by the Presbyterian Church; a center and meeting place for Communist unions and radical organizations; features radical lectures, such as the 1929 "New series of lectures by V. F. Calverton" (the Communist) on Freud and "The Sexual Motif as an Economic Corollary in Contemporary Literature," etc., announced with an appended commendation by Harry Elmer Barnes (vice pres., Freethinkers (atheist) Society); the 1932 lectures for industrial workers and "consultation and guidance in mental hygiene with 5 lectures in this connection: 'Substitute for Religion,' 'Biology of Sex' ", etc. The director is Edmund B. Chaffee, whose sympathies for Communism are clearly shown by the following example: Communist organizations commonly buy space in each other's periodicals to send "Greetings" as a "comradely" gesture and a financial contribution. The March 18, 1932 issue of the viciously revolutionary race-hate-inciting "Liberator," organ of the communist Lg. of Struggle for Negro Rights (see), carried nearly two pages of such advertisements headed "Greetings to the Liberator." Such communist organizations as the Daily Worker, Icor, I.L.D., T.U.U.L., W.I.R., Workers' School, Council of Working Class Women, and various Communist Unions and Party Sections contributed "Greetings," and among these appeared the "Greeting" of "Labor Temple, Edmund B. Chaffee, Director, 242 East 14th St., New York City." Dr. G. F. Beck is director of the School and radicals Harry A. Overstreet, Will Durant, E. C. Lindeman are its educational advisors. The communist Labor Sports Union held its 6th annual convention at the Labor Temple, Dec. 23, 24, 25, 1933.

LABOR UNITY

Official monthly organ of the communist Trade Union Unity League (T.U.U.L.), American section of the Red International of Trade Unions, Wm. Z. Foster, nat. sec.; editor, N. Honig; mgr., S. H. Krieger; 2 W. 15th St., New York City.

LANE PAMPHLET

A pamphlet by Socialist Winthrop D. Lane entitled "Military Training in Schools and Colleges of the United States"; $5,400 was paid to the Committee on Militarism in Education for its "preparation and distribution" by the red Garland Fund in 1926; it opposes military training for the defense of the U.S. government as does all Red pacifist literature; heading the list of signers endorsing it was Jane Addams; other endorsers were:

Will W. Alexander, Leslie Blanchard, Wm. E. Borah, Benjamin Brewster, John Brophy, Carrie Chapman Catt, Samuel Cavert, Francis E. Clarke, George A. Coe, Henry Sloane Coffin, Albert F. Coyle, John Dewey, Paul H. Douglas, W. E. B. Du Bois, Sherwood Eddy, Charles A. Ellwood, Zona Gale, Charles W. Gilkey, Thomas Q. Harrison, Harold A. Hatch, Stanley High, George Huddleston, Hannah Clothier Hull, James Weldon Johnson, Rufus M. Jones, Paul U. Kellogg, Wm. H. Kilpatrick, Robert M. LaFollette, Jr., Halford E. Luccock, Frederick Lynch, Henry N. MacCracken, Irving Maurer, James H. Maurer, Francis J. McConnell, Orie O. Miller, Charles Clayton Morrison, Samuel K. Mosiman, John M. Nelson, George W. Norris, Edward L. Parsons, Kirby Page, George Foster Peabody, David R. Porter, Francis B. Sayre, John Nevin Sayre, J. Henry Scattergood, Joseph Schlossberg, Charles M. Sheldon, Henrik Shipstead, Abba Hillel Silver, John F. Sinclair, William E. Sweet, Wilbur K. Thomas, Henry P. Van Dusen, Oswald G. Villard, Stephen S. Wise, Mary E. Woolley.

LAUNDRY WORKERS INDUSTRIAL UNION

Communist T.U.U.L. Union; Max Burland, sec.

LEAGUE AGAINST FASCISM

American section of the "Matteotti Fund," an international anti-Fascist group; formed 1933 by the National Executive Committee of the Socialist Party on direct request from German Socialist Party and Labor and Socialist International; purpose is "raising a large fund to help finance German Socialist activities against Hitlerism, and secondly, to carry on vigorous anti-Fascist propaganda in the United States."

The nat. chmn. is Daniel W. Hoan, Mayor of Milwaukee; treas., Morris Hillquit; exec. sec., Edw. Levinson; National Committee members: Devere Allen, Jos. Baskin, Fannia Cohn, Jerome Davis, Julius Gerber, Daniel W. Hoan, Leo Krzycki, Robt. Morss Lovett, Kirby Page, Jos. Schlossberg, John Sloan, Oswald Garrison Villard, Prof. Franz Boas, Harriet Stanton Blatch, Abraham Cahan, John Dewey, Morris Hillquit, Darlington Hoopes, E. C. Lindeman, Jasper McLevy, John C. Packard, Cong. F. H. Shoemaker, Norman Thomas, Lilith M. Wilson, Max Zaritsky, Edw. L. Israel, Albert S. Coolidge, David Dubinsky, Dorothy Detzer, Powers Hapgood, Paul Blanshard, Algernon Lee, James H. Maurer, Emil Rieve, Clarence Senior, B. C. Vladeck, Louis Waldman. Hdqts. 112 E. 19th St., N.Y. City.

LEAGUE FOR AMNESTY OF POLITICAL PRISONERS

See also Anarchist-Communism; "New York anarchist organization" (Lusk Report); formed in 1917, after anarchists Emma Goldman and Alexander Berkman were arrested, "To obtain the release of all political offenders"; this organization first popularized the title "political prisoners" now generally given by Reds to revolutionaries who are jailed for seditious activities; M. Eleanor Fitzgerald, said to have been one of Berkman's "loves," was sec. at that time.

The legal advisory board consisted of Isaac A. Hourwich (head of the statistical dept. of the Russian Soviet Bureau), Jessie Ashley, Theo. Schroeder,Harry Weinberger (counsel for Emma Goldman and Berkman) and Bolton Hall; gen. com.: Leonard D. Abbott, Lillian Brown-Olf, Dr. Frederick A. Blossom, Lucy Robins, Helen Keller, Eliz. Freeman, Prince Hopkins, Margaret Sanger, Rose Baron, Robt. Minor, Anna M. Sloan, Stella Comyn, Lincoln Steffens, Alexander Cohen, Roger N. Baldwin and Rose Strunsky. Offices were at 857 Broadway, N.Y. City.

LEAGUE FOR INDEPENDENT POLITICAL ACTION

L.I.P.A.

Socialist in officership and platform. Advocates: socialistic public ownership; "free speech for minority groups" (radicals call revolutionaries "minority groups"); repeal of the syndicalist and espionage laws (against sedition); Negro social equality; revision of the Constitution (!); complete disarmament for America and abolition of military training; that we "safeguard conscientious objectors" and admit aliens without any pledge of allegiance to serve the U.S. Govt. in time of war; urged recognition of the bloody, militaristic Soviet Government, which is frankly bent on attaining Socialist world power through causing world revolution. It opposes deportation or exclusion of alien "Reds" (American Labor Year Book). Howard Y. Williams, exec. sec.; John Dewey, chmn.; Paul H. Douglas and Anna Clothier Hull, vice chairmen; Oswald Garrison Villard, treas.; The Federated Press (Communists'), Sept. 7, 1929, release on the formation of the League named John Dewey as chmn., James Maurer, Zona Gale, Paul Douglas and W. E. B. DuBois as vice chmn. and Devere Allen, editor of "World Tomorrow," as chmn. of the exec. com. Kirby Page is supposed to have "inspired" its organization. Hdqts. 52 Vanderbilt Ave., N.Y. City. See Conf. for Prog. Pol. Action, its new line up.

LEAGUE FOR INDUSTRIAL DEMOCRACY

Militant Socialist; headed by Robt. Morss Lovett, active in Communist organizations; founded by the revolutionary Jack London in 1905 as the Intercollegiate Socialist Society; changed its name in 1921, after Socialism acquired a bad odor owing to the jailing of many Socialists during the war for seditious activities; heavily subsidized by Garland Fund; spreads Socialist-Communist propaganda and literature in colleges; operates chapters of its Intercollegiate Student Council in about 140 colleges, many under the guise of "Student Councils," "Social Problems," "Radical" or "Socialist" Clubs, etc.; in 1933 it claimed: "Last year the speakers corps of the L.I.D. reached almost every state in the union and spoke to some 175,000 people. Norman Thomas, Harry Laidler, Paul Blanshard, Paul Porter and Karl Borders reached about 60,000 students in 160 colleges and universities in 40 states. Likewise they spoke to about 100,000 people in non-college meetings. In addition to these speeches there were innumerable general meetings, political meetings, and radio broadcastings at which L. I. D. speakers appeared"; very closely interlocked by officership with the A.C.L.U.; prepares and widely distributes thousands of Communist and Socialist leaflets, and pamphlets; publishes four publications: "Disarm," "Unemployed," "Revolt" (now "Student

Outlook"), and "L.I.D."; issues a news service and fortnightly Norman Thomas editorial service to some 250 leading papers throughout the United States; has a national board of directors from twenty-three States composed mostly of leaders of over 300 other interlocked organizations; conducts student conferences on red revolutionary subjects; drills students in radicalism each summer at Camp Tamiment, Pa.; formed the Federation of Unemployed Workers Leagues of America all over the U.S., under joint Communist, Socialist, I.W.W., and Proletarian Party (Communist) control; sponsors the Emergency Committee for Strikers' Relief (see), which aids Communist-Socialist strikes; agitates: for government ownership (and against individual ownership) of all banking, transportation, insurance, communication, mining, agricultural and manufacturing enterprises, forests, and oil reserves; for socialization of land and other property, and for social, unemployment, sickness, old-age, and other State doles to the public; its slogan is "education towards a new social order based on production for use and not for profit" (of the individual), which is of course the Socialist-Communist tenet; joins the Communists in advocating disarmament of the so-called "capitalist state" and the arming of the proletarian state and endeavors to convince students and workers that this will bring about "prevention of war," claiming the "capitalists" use the armed forces to fight for markets, etc.—not mentioning how the Socialists use armed forces to rule the workers after the system they advocate has made them paupers and slaves (as in Russia); it calls on youth to "help put the War Department out of colleges by stamping out the R.O.T.C." and claims it enlisted 10,000 students in 1931, in 150 colleges, who signed petitions against military training (however, J. B. Matthews, prominent in Communist meetings and an editor of its "Student Outlook," says he "is not opposed to a war that will end capitalism"); it boasts that "student members of the L.I.D. have been in the thick of the miners' struggles in Harlan County, Ky., and in West Virginia" and in picketing and making "investigations of labor conditions," helping organization work of unions, and other radical agitation; it states of its literature: "These publications are widely used by college classes and labor, church and *Y.M.C.A. and Y.W.C.A.* groups."

Many of these pamphlets were paid for by the red Garland Fund. Pamphlets issued in 1929 dealing with such subjects as Public Ownership, Challenge of War, Dollars and World Peace, Dollar Diplomacy, Imperialism, Socialism, Communism, Christianity and the Social Crisis, Roads to Freedom, The State of Revolution, Soviet Russia, The Profit Motive, Economic Revolution, and Capitalist Control of the Press, were prepared by such radicals as Norman Thomas, Kirby Page, Scott Nearing (Communist) Bertrand Russell, Norman Angell, Harry Elmer Barnes, Morris Hillquit, Lewisohn, Stuart Chase, Harry F. Ward, Harry W. Laidler, Lenin (Communist), Robt. Dunn (Communist), Rex. G. Tugwell, Upton Sinclair, Prof. John Dewey, Jett Lauck (employed by Garland Fund), John Fitch, Prof. J. E. Kirkpatrick, Paul Blanshard, etc. (nearly all of whom are listed in this "Who's Who").

Of these pamphlets, "Roads to Freedom" by Harry Laidler (a "Syllabus for Discussion Groups") is possibly the most revolutionary of all. It urges these groups to use: The "Communist Manifesto" by Marx, "Socialism Utopian and Scientific" by Engels (Marx' collaborator), "State and Revolution" and "Soviets at Work" by Communist Lenin, "Dictatorship vs. Democracy," "State Capitalism in Russia," "Russia After Ten Years," and "New Worlds for Old" by Communist Trotsky. In "Roads to Freedom," Laidler takes up the study beginning with a section on "The Need for Change," then "The Socialist Society," "Utopian and Scientific Socialism," "Guild Socialism," "Cooperative Democracy," and "Single Tax."

The subject of the 1931 student conference (for the West) held at the University of Chicago was: "The Students in World Revolution." The Dec. 1931 national conference held at Union Theological Seminary, New York City, was entitled "Guiding the Revolution" and topics discussed were: "America in a State of Revolution," by Norman Thomas and Harry Laidler; "College Students in a Changing World," by Arnold Johnson (of the Union Theological Seminary, an A.C.L.U. representative jailed in Harlan, Ky. for criminal syndicalism), and a representative of the communist John Reed Club; "What Tactics Should Students Use" by Norman Thomas (who in 1933 was one of the "militant" Socialist Party executive committee members voting for immediate cooperation with the Communist Party—see Socialist Party). A "Forum of the Revolution" was held at Barnard College with Norman Thomas and others discussing plans for the supposedly inevitable revolution, and such topics as Birth Control. The students were asked to live like Communists in preparation for the general upheaval to come.

The first page of the L.I.D. "Student Outlook" for Feb. 1933 is headed "Wanted: Students With Guts" and says in part: "it is questionable whether the student who hasn't guts enough to get out on his college campus and hawk the Student Outlook will overcome his delicate scruples if the time comes to face tear gas and machine guns. The same sort of well-bred doubts and inertia that afflict one when saddled with the responsibility of escorting a petition or putting up posters will arise more urgently and subtly if the time should come to *refuse to go to war* or to picket the Chicago Tribune. . . . *If you have enlisted under the banners of Socialism you've got to carry the job through."* A special announcement on this page states: "With this issue 'Revolt' becomes the 'Student Outlook.' Students felt it was more important to sell our magazine and convince by its contents than to shout 'revolution' and have no one listen. *Persons who give us more than a glance will not mistake our colors."*

In a letter published in the Nation, Feb. 3, 1932, Paul Porter, L.I.D. organizer, valiantly defended the L.I.D. from the charge by a Nation correspondent (Mr. Allen) that the L.I.D. conference "Guiding the Revolution" was an "example of liberal futility" and retorts: "Had Mr. Allen attended the conference or secured a published report of the proceedings . . . he would have discovered (1) that the conference was not a talk-fest of liberals and (2) that the student participants were not wholly innocent of experience in the class struggle," and, after bragging about Arnold Johnson's "five weeks' jail residence" and other student activities "in the course of which more than one has been beaten by thugs" he says: "Unless Mr. Allen expects a revolution to be suddenly produced as a magician might whisk a rabbit from a silk topper, he will recognize the necessity for these humble beginnings. They are tasks in which even college students and college graduates and readers of the Nation may share. Paul Porter."

National Office: 112 East 19th St., New York City; Chicago Office: 20 West Jackson Blvd. 1932 Officers:

Pres. Robert Morss Lovett; vice-presidents: John Dewey, John Haynes Holmes, Vladimir Karapetoff, Florence Kelley, James H. Maurer, Alexander Meiklejohn, Mary R. Sanford, Vida D. Scudder, Helen Phelps Stokes; treas., Stuart Chase; exec. directors: Harry W. Laidler, Norman Thomas; field sec., Paul Porter; special lecturer, Paul Blanshard; exec. sec., Mary Fox; Sec. Chgo. Office, Karl Borders; Board of Directors: Forrest Bailey, Andrew Biemiller, Paul Blanshard, Leroy E. Bowman, McAllister Coleman, H. W. L. Dana, Elizabeth Dublin, Abraham Epstein, Frederick V. Field, Elizabeth Gilman, Hubert C. Herring, Jesse H. Holmes, Jessie Wallace Hughan, Nicholas Kelley, Broadus Mitchell, Reinhold Niebuhr, William Pickens, David Saposs, B. C. Vladeck, Bertha Poole Weyl, Howard Y. Williams. National Council: California—Ethelwyn Mills, Upton Sinclair; Colorado—Powers Hapgood; Connecticut—Jerome Davis; Dist. of Columbia—Mercer G. Johnston; Georgia—Mary Raoul Millis; Illinois—Catherine L. Bacon, Gilbert S. Cox, Paul H. Douglas, Paul Hutchinson, Harold Lasswell, Clarence Senior, James M. Yard; Indiana—William P. Hapgood; Iowa—Minnie E. Allen, Laetitia Moon Conrad; Kansas—John Ise; Maryland—Edward L. Israel; Massachusetts—Emma S. Dakin, Elizabeth G. Evans, Alfred Baker Lewis, George E. Roewer; Michigan—A. M. Todd; Minnesota—Sarah T. Colvin; Missouri—Joseph Myers; New Hampshire—James Mackaye; New Jersey—James W. Alexander; New York—Harriot Stanton Blatch, William E. Bohn, Louis B. Boudin, Paul F. Brissenden, Morris Ernst, Louise A. Floyd, Morris Hillquit, Frederic C. Howe, Darwin J. Meserole, William P. Montague, A. J. Muste, J. S. Potofsky, George D. Pratt, Jr., Evelyn Preston, H. S. Raushenbush, Nellie M. Seeds, George Soule, N. I. Stone, Caro Lloyd Strobell, David Rhys Williams, Helen Sumner Woodbury; North Carolina—Mary O. Cowper; Ohio—Isaac E. Ash, Alice P. Gannett, Paul Jones, Phil Ziegler; Pennsylvania—Emily F. Dawson, Maynard C. Krueger, Simon Libros, Agnes L. Tierney; South Carolina—Josiah Morse; South Dakota—Daniel J. Gage; Utah—James H. Wolfe; Wisconsin—Percy M. Dawson.

Chicago Chapter L.I.D.

Sponsors Chicago Emergency Committee for Strikers Relief, Chicago Workers Committee on Unemployment, etc. Chapter Officers:

President, Paul Hutchinson; vice-presidents: Lillian Herstein, Curtis Reese; rec. sec., Ethel Watson; treas., Frank McCulloch; exec. sec., Karl Borders; Executive Committee: Chapter Officers and Catherine Lillie Bacon, Aaron Director, Paul Douglas, Charles W. Gilkey, Meyer Halushka, Florence Jennison, John Lapp, Harold D. Lasswell, Hilda Lawrence, Sam Levin, U. M. McGuire, Fred Moore, Clarence Senior, Sarah B. Schaar, Ernest Fremont Tittle, Edward Winston, James Yard.

LEAGUE FOR MUTUAL AID

Designated by the Garland Fund, which aided it financially, as a "social service for radicals"; hdqts. N.Y. City.

LEAGUE FOR THE ORGANIZATION OF PROGRESS

A radical internationalist organization with hdqts. at Yellow Springs, Ohio, which is the seat of Antioch College. To quote the communistic Federated Press Labor's News of Jan. 17, 1931: "Pointing out that our national income is being cut at least $300,000,000 a month in wages alone as the result of unemployment, Max Senior in a political letter of the League for the Organization of Progress suggests the use of this sum in a revolving credit fund to Soviet Russia, to be used in purchasing American goods. . . . Senior believes that the establishment of the loan fund would relieve the tension now prevailing in Russia due to the constant necessity of meeting credit obligations and thus enable her 'to market her surplus in a more orderly fashion' " . . . etc. In a pamphlet entitled Notes of the League for the Organization of Progress, it states: "The following men of high distinction have agreed to serve on the Board:

"Devere Allen, editor, 'The World Tomorrow'; Seba Eldrige, University of Kansas; Irving Fisher, Yale University; William Floyd, editor, 'The Arbitrator'; Arthur N. Holcombe, head of the department of government, Harvard University; John Haynes Holmes, minister, Community Church, New York; Paul U. Kellogg, editor, 'The Survey'; Harry Laidler, executive director, League for Industrial Democracy; Daniel L. Marsh, president, Boston University; Arthur E. Morgan, president, Antioch College; Robert Morss Lovett, University of Chicago, editor, 'The New Republic'; Philip C. Nash, director, League of Nations Association; William Ogburn, University of Chicago; Frederick A. Ogg, University of Wisconsin, editor, 'American Political Science Review'; G. Bromley Oxnam, president, De Pauw University; P. B. Potter, University of Wisconsin; John H. Randall, president, World Unity Foundation; N. B. Reuter, University of Iowa; James Shotwell, Carnegie Endowment for International Peace; Edwin R. A. Seligman, Columbia University; E. A. Ross, University of Wisconsin; Charles F. Thwing, President Emeritus, Western Reserve University; Joseph P. Chamberlain, Columbia University; Quincy Wright, University of Chicago."

"Virtually every member listed as serving on the Board of the League has a considerable record of close affiliation and support of socialistic, communistic, international pacifist, pro-soviet activities." (Am. Vigilant Intelligence Fed. Report.)

LEAGUE OF NEIGHBORS

See Fellowship of Faiths.

LEAGUE OF STRUGGLE FOR NEGRO RIGHTS

Official Communist Negro subsidiary organization; organized originally in Chicago, Oct. 1925, as the American Negro Congress; changed name to its present one at St. Louis Congress, Nov. 16, 1930; official organ is the Weekly "Liberator," recently re-named "Harlem Liberator," which agitates race hatred and tries to make Negroes believe that the Communists are their only friends and that they must unite with tthe Communists "against the common enemy." For example, the Mar. 18, 1932, issue printed a huge caption "I Ain't Sayin' Sir to Any More White Men" over "A Story of Camp Hill," also much revolutionary agitation and lurid horror pictures of "abused" Negroes, and a poem entitled "Stop Foolin' Wit' Pray," which says in part:

"Your head 'tain no apple
For danglin' f'om a tree;
Your body no carcass
For barbecuin' on a spree.
"Stand on your feet,
Club gripped 'tween your hands;
Spill their blood too,
Show 'em yours is a man's."

Officers and Nat. Coun. elected at national convention held in Harlem, New York, Oct. 29, 1933 are:

Pres., Langston Hughes; Vice Presidents: James W. Ford, Mrs. Jessica Henderson, Wm. L. Patterson, Robert Minor, Benjamin Davis, Jr., Hose Hart; Gen. Sec., Richard B. Moore; Asst. Sec., Herman MacKawain; Finan. Sec., Esther Anderson; Record. Sec., Bernice Da Costa; Treas., Dr. Reuben S. Young; Dir. of Education and Culture, Louise Thompson; Dir. Defense Activities, Harold Williams; Dir. Bureau Intl. Relations, Chas. Alexander; Dir. Young People's Activities, Leonard Patterson; Dir. Activities Among Women, Williana Burroughs; Liberator Staff: Eugene Gordon, Maude White; Dir. Research, Tom Truesdale; Steve Kingston, Henry Shepard, Harry Haywood, Dr. Arnold Donawa, Rabbi Ben Goldstein, James Moore, Mrs. Mary Craik Speed, Bonita Williams, Hanou Chan, James Allen, Cyril Briggs, Wm. Fitzgerald, George Maddox.

National Council, *New York:* Eleanor Henderson, Agricult. Wkrs. Union; Jos. Brodsky, I.W.O.; Clarence Hathaway, Daily Worker; Myra Page, Writer; Wm. Z. Foster, T.U.U.L.; Robt. W. Dunn, Labor Research Assn.; Irving Potash, Needle Trades Wkrs. Indust. Un.; Henry Shepard, T.U.U.L. Coun., N.Y.; Louis Weinstock, A.F. of L.; Jos. Moore, Mechanic's Assn. of Harlem; B. D. Amis, Communist Party; Israel Amter, nat. com. Unemployed Councils; Peter Uffre, Tobacco Wkrs. of Harlem; Wm. F. Dunne, T.U.U.L.; Gladys Stoner, N.S.L. Com. on Negro Student Problems; Ben Goldstein, Nat. Com. Def. Pol. Pris.; Earl Browder, Communist Party; Ruth Ruben, N.S.L.; Samuel Patterson, Caribbean Union; Steve Kingston, Lg. Struggle Negro Rights; Harry Haywood, Communist Party; Bill Lawrence, I.L.D.; Leonard Patterson, Young Communist Lg.; Louis Coleman, I.L.D.; J. Adler, I.W.O.; James Toney, Lg. Struggle Negro Rights; Gil Green, Young Communist Lg.; Wm. Burdell, Lg. Struggle Negro Rights.

Southern Section: Al. Murphy, Alabama Sharecroppers Un.; Mrs. Mary Craik Speed, Montgomery, Ala.; Rev. J. A. Morten, Angelo Herndon Defense, Ala.; Jane Speed, I.L.D., Birmingham, Ala.; Mrs. Ada Wright and Mrs. Jamie Patterson, Scottsboro Mothers of Chattanooga, Tenn.; Atty. Peirson, Durham, N.C.; Anna Williams, Communist Party, Charlotte, N.C.; Bernard Ades, I.L.D., Baltimore, Md.; Gough McDaniels, High School Teacher, Baltimore, Md.; Robt. Hall, Nat. Farmers Com. Action, Wash., D.C.; Macey, New Orleans R.R. Worker; Manny Jackson, Longshoreman, Savannah, Ga.

Chicago: Herbert Newton, Communist Party; Claude Lightfoot, Lg. Struggle Negro Rights.
Pennsylvania: Dr. Patterson, Pitts. physician; Tom Myerscough, Nat. Miners Un., Pitts.; Henry Wickman, Marine Wkrs. Indust. Un., Phila.; Ben Carruthers, Communist Party, Pitts.
Detroit: Joe Billups, Lg. Struggle Negro Rights.
Minnesota: Alfred Tiala, nat. sec. United Farmers Lg., Mpls.
New England: Mrs. Cravath Simpson, Federation of Women's Clubs, Boston; Ann Burlak (Communist organizer).
California: Tom Mooney, San Quentin Penitentiary, Cal.; Lauren Miller, Journalist, Los Angeles, Cal.; Matt Crawford, San Francisco Nat. Scottsboro Com. Action.
Buffalo, N.Y.: Manning Johnson, Communist Party.
Missouri: A. W. Berry, Communist Party, Kansas City, Mo.; Carrie Smith, Nut Pickers Union, St. Louis, Mo.
Cleveland, O.: Arthur Murphy, Steel and Metal Wkrs. Indust. Un.
Hdqts. 50 E. 13th St., New York City.

LEAGUE OF WOMEN VOTERS

An organization formed by Carrie Chapman Catt, a co-worker with Jane Addams, to educate women to take part in political life. It serves a good purpose and is fair enough in presenting various sides of public questions to render the great majority of its innocent and non-radical members unaware that they are also fed radical propaganda in regular doses. It campaigned for the League of Nations, circulated the W.I.L.P.F. (Jane Addams') petition for total disarmament of the U.S. 1931, etc.; features many radical speakers. (See under W.I.L.P.F.)

LEAGUE OF WORKERS THEATRES

A league of Communist theatre groups; an American section of Moscow's International Union of the Revolutionary Theatre; formed April 16, 1932 (at Manhattan Lyceum, N.Y. City); official organ is "Workers Theatre," now called "New Theatre"; includes groups such as the Chicago Workers Theatre (see), Workers Laboratory Theatre, John Reed Club dramatic groups, German Prolet Buehne of Milwaukee, Nature Friends Dram. Group of Syracuse, Workers Experimental Theatre of St. Louis, Dramatic Council of Detroit, Harlem Progressive Youth Club Dram. Section, N.Y., and innumerable others.

It was formed, according to the report of its conference in the May, 1932 "Workers Theatre": "to spread the idea of the class struggle by raising funds for campaigns and for the revolutionary press and by recruiting workers into the revolutionary unions and mass organizations and especially to arouse workers for the defense of the Soviet Union against the coming imperialist attack. . . . Every worker's theatre group must realize that its existence is closely tied up with that of the entire revolutionary movement—that its aims are the same—that its slogans are the same. . . . It must win workers and farmers including those in the armed forces for the tactic of turning the coming imperialist war against the Soviet Union into a civil war against the imperialists." Greetings from the following groups were received at this conference:

International Bureau Theatrical Club, Moscow; Moscow Blue Blouse Theatre; Secretariat International Workers Dramatic Union; Workers Cultural Council of W.I.R. of Seattle, Wash.; Rebel Players, Los Angeles, Cal.; Writers Group of John Reed Club, N.Y. City; Workers International Relief (W.I.R.).

Its Eastern Regional conference was held Aug. 5-6, 1933 at the Nature Friends Camp at Midvale, N.J. Hdqts. 42 E. 12th St., N.Y. City.

(THE) LETTERS OF SACCO AND VANZETTI

A book published to help along the Communist agitation in favor of the two Anarchist-Communist murderers, who died yelling "Long Live Anarchy!" The book cover states: "This volume sponsored by the following International Committee:

"Benedetto Groce, John Dewey, Theodore Dreiser, Maxim Gorki, Horace M. Kallen, Sinclair Lewis, Romain Rolland, Bertrand Russell, H. G. Wells, Stefan Zweig."

LIBERATOR

A revolutionary paper formerly published at 34 Union Square, N.Y. City; founded before the Communist Party was formed in the U.S. (1919); second class mailing privileges were withheld by U.S. Postoffice Dept.; some of its Red editorials are reprinted in Lusk Report.

Editors were Max Eastman, Crystal Eastman and Floyd Dell; bus. mgr., Margaret Lane; contrib. eds.: Cornelia Barns, Howard Brubaker, Eugene V. Debs, Hugo Gellert, Arturo Giovannitti (of Il Nuovo Mondo Com.), Chas. T. Hallinan, Helen Keller, Robt. Minor, Boardman Robinson, Maurice Stern, Alexander Trachtenberg, Louis Untermyer, Clyde Weed and Art Young.

(Note the present day active Communists.) In 1920 it had a circulation of 50,000 and was supported by stockholders (who are listed in Lusk Report); recd. $500 from Garland Fund in 1923 (Communist Party-owned at that time.)

More recently the "Liberator" has been the name of the Negro Communist paper, official organ of the *League of Struggle for Negro Rights* (see).

LUMBER WORKERS INDUSTRIAL UNION

A Communist T.U.U.L. union.

M

MANUMIT SCHOOL

A Socialist School for "children of trade union workers" at Pawling, N.Y. conducted by Nellie Seeds Nearing, wife of Scott Nearing, the Communist leader; recd. about $15,000 from Garland Fund.

MARINE TRANSPORT WORKERS INDUSTRIAL UNION

I.W.W. union.

MARINE WORKERS INDUSTRIAL UNION

A communist T.U.U.L. union; the American section of the communist Intl. of Seamen and Harbor Workers; has been creating considerable trouble among the crews of American ships; official organ "Marine Workers Voice"; maintains Union hdqts. at: 140 Broad St., N.Y. City; 312 S. Second St., Phila.; 1629 Thames St., Baltimore; 7211 "L" Avenue, Houston; 239 Decatur St., New Orleans; 614 First St., Seattle; 191½ 3rd St., Portland, Ore.; 3064 E. 92nd St., South Chicago, Ill. Head is Roy Hudson, 61 Whitehall St., N.Y. City; formerly called Marine Wkrs. League.

MARY WARE DENNETT DEFENSE COMMITTTEE

M.W.D. Def. Com.

Mary Ware Dennett, a radical whose activities were exposed in the Lusk Report, wrote a sex pamphlet, "The Sex Side of Life," of such a nature that she was convicted of, and fined $300 for publishing obscene matter. A group of radicals leaped to her defense and, in 1930, formed this committee, carried her case to the Appellate Court, and a reversal was finally won. After this the pamphlet, "The Sex Side of Life," was flaunted more than ever. The Federal Council of Churches' Sex Pamphlet (see) lists it as "indispensable." The 4A recommends it in its 1930 Report among "Anti-Religious Books" sold by the 4A.

Committee chmn., John Dewey; vice chmn.: Henry Sloane Coffin, Kath. Bement Davis, Abel J. Gregg; treas., Corliss Lamont; sec., Forrest Bailey. Among committee members: Alice Stone Blackwell, Edwin M. Borchardt, Sophonisba P. Breckenridge, Paul H. Douglas, Sherwood Eddy, Fannie Hurst, Lewis Mumford, James Rorty, Jessie Taft, Miriam Van Waters, Goodwin Watson, Stephen S. Wise.

MASSES

Communist magazine; changed name in 1926 to New Masses (see).

MECHANICAL DENTISTS INDUSTRIAL UNION

Communist T.U.U.L. union.

MEDICAL WORKERS INDUSTRIAL UNION

Communist T.U.U.L. union.

MESSENGER

(Organ of Brotherhood of Sleeping Car Porters)

A radical publication for Negroes "looking toward their conversion to revolutionary radicalism. . . . It is committed to the principles of the Soviet government of Russia and to the proposition of organizing negroes for the class struggle. . . . A Philip Randolph and Chandler Owen," editors, have been "instructors in the Rand School" (Lusk Report). It received money from the Garland Fund; is now the official organ of the Brotherhood of Sleeping Car Porters, which was Communist-penetrated and also received $11,200, $4,000, $2,724.56, etc., from Garland Fund, and is now under Socialist control.

METAL WORKERS INDUSTRIAL UNION

Communist T.U.U.L. union; John Meldon, 611 Penn. Ave., Pittsburgh, Pa.; 35 East 19th St., N.Y. City., etc.

METHODIST FEDERATION FOR SOCIAL SERVICE

A radical social service organization cooperating with Socialist and Communist organizations; operates in the Methodist Church and disseminates its influence through the Federal Council, Y.M.C.A. and other church groups; has solicited funds for the Moscow-directed communist International Labor Defense in its Social Service Bulletins, and stated in the 1932 Bulletin No. 8: "The Federation has continued to cooperate with boards and agencies within our own church and with many groups outside the church *working definitely for a new social order*. Among these may be mentioned several departments of the Federal Council of Churches, the American Civil Liberties Union, the League for Industrial Democracy, Labor Research Assn., International Labor Defense, Committee on Militarism in Education, . . . We simply cannot be respectable." This was signed by Bishop Francis J. McConnell, pres., and Harry F. Ward, sec. (The Labor Research Assn. and I.L.D. are Communist organizations and the others, except the Federal Council of Churches, are red Garland Fund protegés). Winifred Chappell, co-editor and co-secretary with Ward, served on a Communist Party campaign committee and signed the manifesto endorsing the Communist platform, principles and revolutionary program in 1932 (see Communist P. G. for F. & F.). Harry Ward, who returned in 1932 from a year spent in Soviet Russia is the A.C.L.U. nat. chmn. and a former Garland Fund director. Bishop McConnell aided the Socialist 1932 campaign. G. Bromley Oxnam and E. F. Tittle (exec. sec. and chmn. of the nat. com. respectively) also have lively records for radicalism.

To quote from Bulletin No. 8, April 15, 1928: "Through the courtesy of the Federated Press" (Communists') "our members may receive the 'Labor Letter,' a weekly summary of labor news for $1.00, half of the regular price. An increasing number are availing themselves of this offer, thereby increasing their equipment for the basic task . . . the basic task—the securing of a Christian Social Order. . . . To this end every whit of our work is consciously and deliberately directed. . . . The Bulletin is used in many classrooms and as a source material for sermons, forum discussions, theses, etc. A few of the topics discussed during the quadrennium have been 'The Spy in Government and Industry'; 'Missions and Our Chinese Diplomacy' (data for several issues . . . were sent by the senior secretary while he was lecturing in the Orient; first hand material on China was also available to him in his capacity of chairman of the American Committee for Justice to China)." (Note: See Harry F. Ward and Hands Off Committees); "'Is Justice Breaking Down in the United States' (dealing with the Sacco-Vanzetti and Mooney and Billings cases. This issue was speedily exhausted); 'The New Red Hunt' (our close cooperation with the American Civil Liberties Union brings much first hand material in this field not otherwise easily available to our readers); 'The Present Coal Strike' (a second edition of this was ordered by the Emergency Committee for Miners' Relief). . . . As often as our treasury permits, we send some big pamphlet on a vital theme to our members. Laidler's 'Public Ownership' and Ward's 'Profit Motive' and a reprint of his address on 'Repression of Civil Liberties in the United States' . . . have been sent during this quadrennium as well as some leaflets and reprints. All members have received also the book 'An American Pilgrimage,' portions of the letters of Grace Scribner, selected and arranged by Winifred L. Chappell, foreword by Harry F. Ward. . . . Incidentally the Vanguard Press which published this book in its 50c series has sold over 600 copies. . . . W. L. Chappell spends a month at Epworth League and Y.W. teaching in summer and does occasional teaching and speaking during the winter, especially at Epworth League winter institutes and young people's groups. . . . Part of our regular work is the recommendation of speakers for church and other meetings. . . . We have frequent inquiries for book lists; we constantly recommend books. . . . Earlier efforts included not only much counselling with leaders in other denominations and groups like the Y.M. and Y.W.C.A. and speaking for many church and labor groups, but also the preparation of several curricular studies. These were widely used by the Epworth League, the Board of Sunday Schools, the Student Movement and others. We have reason to believe that these studies, supplemented by the social interpretation of the Sunday School Lesson for two years and the contribution of a page each month to the 'Adult Bible Class Monthly' have promoted social thinking in our own denomination and others. This policy of cooperation has been continued through this quadrennium. For instance: The secretaries are regular members of the Department of Social Service and Research and Education of the Federal Council of Churches, with a voice in those programs; we constantly use the resources of the Council. The office prepared eight articles for a handbook on social service for the Research Dept. Both secretaries contribute to Sunday School publications. Miss Chappell is on the Topics Committee of the Epworth League, helped to prepare the Social Service Manual, has written a chapter for the forthcoming social service text book and in other words counsels with that organization. . . . The special material on the Passaic Strike" (the Communist-led so-called "first lesson in revolution") "which was used in the Passaic number of the 'Christian Century' was collected by the office. The task was undertaken because of the bearing of that industrial struggle on a *Christian social order.* As this report goes to press, the Federation is joining with the Department of Social Relations of the Congregational Education Society in a conference of preachers to be held at Pittsburg, April 24 to 26th, to face up the coal crisis. . . . " "Soon after the organization of the Federation there sprang into existence in several annual conferences small voluntary groups of preachers who set themselves to support our program. . . . Most of the commissions function most actively at annual conference time. The presentation of statements on social issues on the conference floor, obtaining a place on the conference program for the social message . . . are typical activities. Several commissioners see that the message is presented at the district conferences. The Rock River commission cooperates closely with the Chicago Church Federation and has been interested in free speech, preachers' salaries, the Book Concern and organized labor. . . . The Colorado and Pittsburgh groups have concerned themselves with the coal strikes. . . . The Methodist Federation for Social Service is celebrating its twentieth anniversary. A national committee of 63, with Ernest F. Tittle as chairman and G. Bromley Oxnam as executive secretary, is sponsoring the celebration. The occasion is being used to promote church-wide discussion of such issues as war, property, labor, civil liberties." (Signed) "By Francis J. McConnell, president; Harry F. Ward, secretary." (Note the Vanguard Press above.) The 1933 Bulletins, as one ex-Communist Party executive remarked, "read like the Daily Worker, only more so."

Exec. Com.: F. J. McConnell, H. F. Rall, George Elliott, Herbert N. Shenton, Ralph B. Urmy; treas., Gilbert Q. LeSourd; secretaries: Harry F. Ward, Winifred L. Chappell; National Com.: E. F. Tittle, chmn., G. Bromley Oxnam, exec. sec., F. W. Adams, Springfield, Mass.; O. W. Auman, Chgo.; Ray Allen, Hornell, N.Y.; M. P. Burns, Phila.; L. H. Bugbee, Minneapolis; King D. Beach, Chgo.; Dan B. Brummitt, Chgo.; Stella W. Brummitt, Chgo.; Esther Bjornberg, Chgo.; F. O. Beck, Evanston; E. W. Blakeman, Berkeley, Cal.; W. C. Barclay, Chgo.; James C. Baker, Urbana, Ill.; Geo. A. Coe, Glendora, Cal.; R. E. Diffendorfer, N.Y.; Edw. T. Devine, Washington; D. F. Diefendorf, E. Orange, N.J.; E. P. Dennett, San Fran.; A. E. Day, Pitts.; F. C. Ebinger, Oak Park, Ill.; F. B. Fisher, India; R. W. Graham, Creston, Ia.; W. E. J. Gratz, Chgo.; W. M. Gilbert, Madison, N.J.; A. A. Heist, Denver; Paul Hutchinson, Chgo.; L. O. Hartman, Boston; H. S. Hamilton, Boise, Idaho; E. S. Hammond, Salem, Ore.; Isabelle Horton, Lake Bluff, Ill.; A. W. Harris, N.Y.; C. P. Hargraves, Chgo.; Frank Kingdon, Lansing, Mich.; Louisa Litzel, Vickery, O.; J. C. Lazenby, Milwaukee; J. W. Langdale, Brooklyn; H. E. Luccock, N.Y.; Jesse Lacklen, Billings, Mont.; G. S. Lackland, Meadville, Pa.; Amy Lewis, N.Y.; W. H. McMaster, Alliance, O.; Mary McDowell, Chgo.; H. H. Meyer, N.Y.; A. E. Monger, South Bend, Ind.; Edw. Laird Mills, Portland, Ore.; J. R. Magee, Seattle; O. H. McGill, Seattle; F. M. North, N.Y.; O. T. Olson, Baltimore; Earl Roadman, Mitchell, S.D.; W. J. Sherman, San Fran.; W. B. Spaulding, Billings, Mont.; C. D. Skinner, Tulsa, Okla.; W. L. Stidger, Kansas City; Robt. L. Tucker, Columbus; W. P. Thirkield, Chattanooga; Worth M. Tippy, N.Y.; L. K. Willman, Wilkes-Barre, Pa.; Herbert Welch, Korea; V. O. Ward, Minneapolis; James M. Yard, N.Y. (now Chgo.).

Executive Com. 1933:

Francis J. McConnell, Herbert N. Shenton, Ralph B. Urmy, Halford E. Luccock, Charles C. Webber, Robt. Leonard Tucker, Gilbert S. Cox. Officers: Pres., Bishop Francis J. McConnell; vice pres., Harris Franklin Rall; sec.-treas., Gilbert Q. LeSourd; secretaries, Harry F. Ward, Winifred L. Chappell.

Hdqts. 150 Fifth Ave., New York.

MEXICAN PROPAGANDA

In 1927 Elias Calles was the Communist-supported President of Mexico and American property in Mexico was to be seized. Soviet forces, aided by Communist agents from the U.S., were very active, and, lest the U.S. should intervene and spoil the Soviet plot to gain control of the Mexican government, the U.S. was flooded with "non-intervention" propaganda through the communist All-American Anti-Imperialist League echoed by such committees as the National Citizens Committee on Relations with Latin America, Non-Intervention Citizens Committee, Committee on Relations with Latin America, and about 250 Hands Off Mexico (Nicaragua and China) Committees. The Garland Fund at the same time spent thousands of dollars on "Anti-imperialism" work. The communist Daily Worker, Oct. 8, 1927, said: "The following telegram from the Communist Party of Mexico was received yesterday by the Daily Worker: 'Mexico City, Oct. 6, 1927: Reaction has launched revolt. We request agitation on behalf of the Mexican proletariat in its struggle *jointly with the government.* (Signed) Mexican Communist Party.'" The Daily Worker then went on to comment: "The foregoing telegram, in harmony with all reports from Mexico, is taken as indicating the policy of the Mexican Communist Party in the present crisis. . . . As against the present counter-revolutionary attempts of agents of U.S. oil speculators allied with the whole landlord and *clerical group* of reaction, . . . the Communist Party of Mexico calls upon the working class and peasantry to resort to arms in defense of the Calles government and urges the workers and farmers of the United States to support the Calles government against the counter-revolutionary reaction." Said Marvin (Data Sheet 25-6, Feb. 1, 1927): "It is probably true that the President of Mexico is . . . not a member of any Communist organization. . . . The fact remains however that the alleged constitution of Mexico is aimed to destroy both religion and the private property rights. The initial steps have been taken in both cases. The attack on the Catholic Church is more or less of a 'smoke screen' to hide the real issue. It was the belief of the advisors of those who put over the alleged present constitution that such an attack would bring to the support of Mexico all anti-Catholics in the United States. It has confused a great many. The pronounced anti-Catholic organizations have been swept almost bodily to the support of Mexico. When the final step was taken to deprive the Catholics of the liberties accorded them in the past the forces in Mexico directing this knew what was going on in Nicaragua. In fact they were directing them in Nicaragua as they were directing them in Mexico."

Sept. 1933 press reports stated that 300 churches were being closed in Mexico which would indicate that Red influences are still active there. Travel literature, 1934, states that any minister of the Gospel must secure special permission to enter Mexico.

MIDWEST WORKERS CULTURAL FEDERATION

Midwest section of the communist Workers Cultural Federation (see).

MILITANT LEFT WING MINERS OF AMERICA

New Red miners union founded Sept. 1933; bd. of admin.:

Walter Seacrist, Powers Hapgood, Tom Tippett, Dennis Shaw, Gerry Allard, Loren Norman, Wm. Truax, James White, Jo Angelo, Ricco Florini; Organ is "The Fighting Miner," first issue, Oct., 1933; editors, Loren Norman and Gerry Allard; bus. mgr., Irene Allard, wife of Gerry.

Box 202, Springfield, Illinois.

MILWAUKEE LEADER

Socialist Party newspaper; Victor Berger formerly editor.

MINE, OIL AND SMELTER WORKERS INDUSTRIAL UNION

Communist T.U.U.L. Union.

MOSCOW DAILY NEWS

Communist propaganda paper published in English in Moscow; M. M. Borodin, ed.; Anna Louise Strong (associate of Jane Addams), assoc. ed.

N

NATION, THE

"Advocate of revolutionary socialism" (Lusk Report); a weekly; founded by Oswald Garrison Villard.

Board of Editors: Ernest Gruening, Freda Kirchwey, Joseph Wood Krutch; Associate Editors: Mauritz A. Hallgren, Margaret Marshall, Dorothy Van Doren; Contributing Editor, Oswald Garrison Villard.

In 1933 Villard relinquished editorship of "The Nation," turning it over to Board of Editors, and became a contributing editor.

NATIONAL ADVISORY COUNCIL ON RADIO IN EDUCATION

Broadcasts over nation-wide network in cooperation with the left wing socialist League for Industrial Democracy, featuring radical speakers; recommends radical books.

Officers: Robert A. Millikan, pres.; Livingston Farrand, Meta Glass, Robert M. Hutchins (pres. of the Univ. of Chgo.), Walter Dill Scott, (pres. Northwestern U.), Michael I. Pupin, vice presidents; Ralph Hayes, treas. and chmn. bd.; Wm. J. Donovan, vice chmn. bd.; Levering Tyson, sec.-treas.; *Com. on Economics:* Harry W. Laidler, chmn.; Felix Morley, sec.; Wesley C. Mitchell, H. G. Moulton, E. G. Nourse, Rexford G. Tugwell; *League for Industrial Democracy Committee:* Harry W. Laidler, Wesley C. Mitchell, George Soule, Norman Thomas, Levering Tyson.

Hdqts.: 60 E. 42nd St., N.Y. City or L.I.D., 112 E. 19th St., N.Y. City.

NATIONAL ASSOCIATION FOR ADVANCEMENT OF COLORED PEOPLE

N.A.A.C.P.

Communists Wm. Z. Foster, Benj. Gitlow, Scott Nearing, Eliz. Gurley Flynn, Robt. W. Dunn, and their fellow Garland Fund directors, Norman Thomas, etc., were generous with appropriations of $31,552 (1925-28), $7,365 (1923-24), and $5,000 (1929-30) to the N.A.A.C.P.

The official Report of the Communist Party's 4th national convention stated that the Party had penetrated the N.A.A.C.P. Socialist Florence Kelley (formerly of Hull House), the personal friend of Engels and Lenin, with Jane Addams, a founder and "for twenty years a member of the board of directors," was very active in the N.A. A.C.P. The field secretary, Wm. Pickens, is a Socialist Party member, active as well in Communist affairs and organizations (see "Who's Who"). James Weldon Johnson, now and for years, an executive of the N.A.A.C.P. and also a Garland Fund director, has served at the same time in company with most of the Garland Fund directors on the national committee of the "Reds' aid society," the A.C.L.U. W. E. B. DuBois, another N.A.A.P.C. executive, is a Socialist and also member of Communist subsidiaries (A.S.C.R.R., A.A.A.I. Lg., etc.) and received money directly from the Garland Fund in 1928 for services. Clarence Darrow, John Haynes Holmes, Oswald G. Villard, and other executives, have similar affiliations.

The N.A.A.C.P. emulates the A.C.L.U. among Negroes. In fighting for "Negro rights" naturally it has won the friendship of many Negroes, themselves opposed to the Red movement, who believe it to be a purely altruistic agency without radical or political motivation.

An article, sarcastically entitled "Ever Sincerely, Walter White," in the communist I.L.D. magazine "Labor Defender," for Aug. 1933, is a typical exhibit of the quarrelsomeness and professional jealousy shown between the "family" of cooperating radicals and their organizations. To quote:

"Three months ago, pressed by its membership, the N.A.A.C.P., of which Walter White is Secretary, asked the I.L.D. for authorization to collect funds for the Scottsboro defense. This was granted but, finding that the agreement had been broken by the N.A.A.C.P., Wm. L. Patterson, Nat. Sec. of the I.L.D. wrote a letter on June 1, demanding that the funds be unconditionally turned over to the I.L.D."

Then follows a very sneering analysis of White's letter ending *"Ever sincerely, Walter White"*; then the article resumes:

"Wm. Patterson's reply shows how the N.A.A.C.P. in 1931 and 1932 collected $7,178.63 for the defense. The letter states: 'This is the most unprincipled case of robbery, known in the history of the struggle of the Negro masses.' . . . The difference between the legal 'defense' of the N.A.A.C.P. and the I.L.D. policy of the 'unity of mass action with legal defense' is then gone into after which Comrade Patterson mentions the 'distinguished white and Negro citizens' serving on the Executive Board of the N.A.A.C.P., such gentlemen as Lt. Col. J. E. Spingarn . . . Senator Capper of Kansas . . . Governor Herbert Lehmann of New York and Frank Murphy now governor of the Philippines, and Mayor of Detroit at the time of the Ford Massacre of March, 1932."

This is a sarcastic inference that Murphy is opposed to radicals, whereas one might point to his appointment by Pres. Roosevelt as Gov. of the Philippines, his praise by the A.C.L.U. (see), and the holding of Communist meetings in Detroit public schools while he was Mayor, as evidence to the contrary. At one meeting in a Public School, Detroit, the Communists held a mock trial and condemned Henry Ford to death, according to the Communist press. The article says Patterson's letter ended with:

"We call the membership of the N.A.A.C.P. . . . to join and build the Scottsboro Action Committees. . . . Step over the heads of your leadership. . . . Only mass pressure will free the Scottsboro boys."

A 1931 letterhead lists:

J. E. Spingarn as Pres.; Vice Presidents: Arthur Capper, Senator from Kansas, Bishop John A. Gregg, John Haynes Holmes, James Weldon Johnson, Arthur B. Spingarn, Oswald G. Villard; Executive Officers: Mary Ovington White, chmn. bd.; Walter White, sec.; Dr. W. E. B. DuBois, Robt. W. Bagnall, dir. of branches; Wm. Pickens, field sec.; Mrs. Daisy Lampkin, regional field sec.; Herbert J. Seligmann, dir. of publicity; Wm. T. Andrews, special legal asst.; National Legal Committee: Arthur B. Spingarn, chmn.; James Marshall, Herbert K. Stockton, Felix Frankfurter, Chas. H. Studin, Clarence Darrow, T. J. Nutter.

NATIONAL ASSOCIATION FOR CHILD DEVELOPMENT

The official name of the group directing the Pioneer Youth of America (see).

NATIONAL CATHOLIC WELFARE CONFERENCE

Cooperates with the Federal Council of Churches, Central Conference of American Rabbis, Catholic Association for International Peace, American Civil Liberties Union, etc.; dir. Social Action Dept., John A. Ryan of the A.C.L.U. (same position held by John A. Lapp, 1920-27).

NATIONAL CHILD LABOR COMMITTEE

Abolition of child labor is a worthy humanitarian cause, with which most kindly people are in sympathy, but the outstanding Socialists active on this committee, in accordance with Socialist principles, seek more than is apparent on the surface. They back all laws giving parents less and the State more and more control over children. Socialism aims at abolition of private ownership of children, and of Christian marriage, as well as of property rights. Complete State control of children, free abortions, and free love in Russia today, are the fulfillment of this Marxian Socialist dogma.

NATIONAL CITIZENS COMMITTEE ON RELATIONS WITH LATIN AMERICA

Nat. Citiz. Com. Rel. Lat. Am.

A committee echoing the communist A.A.A.I. Lg's. "Hands Off" propaganda; similar to the Non-Intervention Citizens Committee; formed in Wash., D.C., with hdqts. at the Peoples Legislative Service, in 1927, when the U.S. Govt. was having trouble with the Communist-supported Nicaraguans and Calles' Communist-supported Mexican Govt., which was intent on seizing American-owned property (and was persecuting religion in true Soviet style); it circulated the statement of the revolutionary Nicaraguan Governor whom the U.S. Govt. refused to recognize; and, said Marvin: it "is the organization which we are forced to opine sent Rev. Samuel Guy Inman" (of the Garland Fund Com. on American Imperialism (see)) "into Mexico for the purpose of manufacturing a little additional propaganda with which to flood the United States. John F. Moors of Boston, who is listed as president, in a recent statement said the committee . . . believed 'that our present Latin American policy as manifested in Nicaragua, Mexico, and elsewhere is in violation of every sound American tradition.' . . . The Honorary President of the Nat. Citiz. Com. is Senator George W. Norris of Nebraska who, just now, is being strongly touted as a candidate for President on a third ticket to be guided by the same Socialist-Liberal forces that guided the candidacy of LaFollette and Wheeler. Practically all of them were backers of the Socialist ticket — LaFollette and Wheeler — in 1924. . . . In view of the Communist agitation in connection with the Sacco-Vanzetti affair . . . the same names in many instances, will be found attached to petitions in favor of the two condemned murderers . . . a large percentage . . . are closely related with the Socialist Party." (Marvin Data Sheets, 25-12, 28-23, 34-15, 1927) "The complete list follows":

Hon. pres., Senator Geo. W. Norris; pres., John F. Moors, Mass.; sec., Mercer G. Johnson, Md.; treas., W. P. Neville, Wash., D.C.; hon. vice presidents: Mrs. Edw. P. Costigan, Colo.; Mrs. J. Borden Harriman, Wash., D.C.; Bishop Francis J. McConnell, Pa.; Cong. R. Walton Moore, Va.; Sen. David I. Walsh, Mass.; Wm. Allen White, Kans.; Rabbi Stephen S. Wise, N.Y.; Members: Dr. Felix Adler, N.Y.; Judge Geo. W. Anderson, Mass.; Mrs. Francis C. Axtell, Wash.; Hon. Newton D. Baker, O.; James H. Batten, Cal.; Judge Robt. W. Bingham, Ky.; Mrs. Emily Newell Blair, Mo.; Mrs. Harriet Stanton Blatch, N.Y.; Rev. W. Russell Bowie, N.Y.; Alfred Brandeis, Ky.; P. H. Callahan, Ky.; Wm. F. Cochran, Md.; Everett Colby, N.Y.; Pres. Ada A. Comstock, Mass.; Herbert Croly, N.Y.; Oscar K. Cushing, Cal.; Dr. Edw. P. Devine, Wash., D.C.; Prof. John Dewey, N.Y.; Prof. Wm. E. Dodd, Ill.; Judge Chas. A. Douglas, Wash., D.C.; Prof. Edw. Meade Earle, N.Y.; Mrs. Mary E. Fels, N.Y.; Prof. Irving Fisher, Conn.; Wm. Floyd, N.Y.; Mrs. J. Malcolm Forbes, Mass.; Sen. Lynn J. Frazier, N.D.; Zona Gale, Wis.; Dean V. C. Gildersleeve, N.Y.; Eliz. Gilman, Md.; J. W. Gitt, Pa.; Prof. Chas. W. Hackett, Tex.; Norman Hapgood, N.Y.; Arthur Garfield Hays, N.Y.; Morris Hillquit, N.Y.; Prof. Wm. E. Hocking, Mass.; Dr. Samuel Guy Inman, N.Y.; Will Irwin, N.Y.; Rabbi Edw. L. Israel, Md.; Cong. Meyer Jacobstein, N.Y.; W. D. Jamieson, Wash., D.C.; Edw. Keating, Wash., D.C.; Paul U. Kellogg, N.Y.; Mrs. Eliz. T. Kent, Cal.; Horace G. Knowles, N.Y.; Cong. O. J. Kvale, Minn.; Sen. Robt. M. LaFollette, Wis.; Cong. F. La Guardia, N.Y.; Geo. La Monte, N.J.; John A. Lapp, Ill.; Mrs. Henry Goddard Leach, N.Y.; Jos. Lee, Mass.; Hon. John Lind, Minn.; Pres. H. N. MacCracken, N.Y.; Judge Julian W. Mack, Ill.; Amy G. Maher, O.; Basil M. Manly, Wash., D.C.; Lowell Mellett, Wash., D.C.; Prof. S. E. Morison, Mass.; James H. Moyle, Utah; Pres. Wm. A. Neilson, Mass.; David K. Niles, Mass.; Mrs. Gordon Norrie, N.Y.; Sen. Gerald P. Nye, N.D.; John D. Pearmain, N.Y.; Prof. Bliss Perry, Mass.; Dr. Albert H. Putney, Wash., D.C.; Jackson H. Ralston, Cal.; Donald R. Richberg, Ill.; Dr. Wm. L. Robins, Wash., D.C.; Elmer E. Rogers, Wash., D.C.; Hon. Cato Sells, Tex.; Prof. Frederick Starr, Wash., D.C.; Moorfield Storey, Mass.; Prof. F. W. Taussig, Mass.; Norman Thomas, N.Y.; Hon. Huston Thompson, Colo.; Mrs. Eliz. Towne, Mass.; Oswald Garrison Villard, N.Y.; Hon. Carl S. Vrooman, Ill.; Henry A. Wallace, Ia.; Frank P. Walsh, N.Y.; Cong. Knud Wefald, Minn.; Sen. Burton K. Wheeler, Montana; Wm. Allen White, Kans.; Prof. Tyrell Williams, Mo.; Prof. A. P. Winston, Tex.; Pres. Mary E. Woolley, Mass.; Peter Witt, O.

NATIONAL COMMITTEE FOR THE DEFENSE OF POLITICAL PRISONERS

Nat. Com. Def. Pol. Pris.

Formed 1931 as an outgrowth of the communist Emergency Committee for Defense of Southern Political Prisoners —"political prisoners" being the radical term for those arrested for seditious revolutionary activities; communist intellectuals and sympathizers led by

Theo. Dreiser, chmn.; Lincoln Steffens, Sherwood Anderson, vice chmn.; John Dos Passos, treas.; Melvin P. Levy, sec.; Adelaide G. Walker, asst. sec.; com. members: Harry Elmer Barnes, William Rose Benet, Prof. Franz Boas, Lester Cohen, Eleanor Copenhaver, Malcolm Cowley, Bruce Crawford, Edward Dahlberg, Floyd Dell, Adolph Dehn, Edgar Fraley, Waldo Frank, Hugo Gellert, Lydia Gibson, Murray Godwin, Eugene Gordon, C. Hartley Grattan, Paul Green, Horace Gregory, Julius Heiman, Josephine Herbst, Langston Hughes, Grace Hutchins, Maxwell Hyde, Leon Kahn, Yereth Kahn, Alfred Kreymborg, Suzanne LaFollette, Pierre Loving, Louis Lozowick, George Maurer, Claude McKay, Edna St. Vincent Millay, Dr. Henry Neumann, Samuel Ornitz, Joseph Pass, Frank Palmer, Paul Peters, Burton Rascoe, Lola Ridge, James Rorty, Edwin Seaver, Upton Sinclair, Bernard J. Stern, Ruth Stout, William Monroe Trotter, Mary Heaton Vorse, Charles R. Walker, Webb Waldron, Eric Walrond, Walter Wilson, Ella Winter (Mrs. Lincoln Steffens), Carl Zigrosser, Marguerite Zorach, William Zorach.

Hdqts. Room 337 St. Denis Bldg., 11th and Broadway, N.Y. City. (Communist hdqts.)

The Daily Worker, Nov. 13, 1933, carried a picture of

"Members of delegation of Nat. Com. for Def. Pol. Pris. now in Tuscaloosa, Ala. . . . Members of the delegation are: Alfred H. Hirsch, secretary Nat. Com. for Def. Pol. Pris. (of N.Y.); Jessica Henderson, Boston, prominent in Sacco-Vanzetti defense; Howard Kester, Nashville, Tenn., Southern Secretary, Fellowship of Reconciliation; Bruce Crawford, Norton, Va., editor, Crawford's Weekly; Hollace Ransdell of Ky., investigator for A.C.L.U. in Scottsboro case; Grace Lumpkin of South Carolina, author 'To Make My Bread,' proletarian novel; Barbara Alexander of Savannah, Georgia, artist."

NATIONAL COMMITTEE ON LABOR INJUNCTIONS

Formed by A.C.L.U. 1932 to prevent employers who are harassed by radical strikers from obtaining injunctions prohibiting their activities. Chas. F. Amidon (former Judge), chmn.; Forrest Bailey, sec.

NATIONAL COMMITTEE TO AID STRIKING MINERS FIGHTING STARVATION

N.C. to A.S.M.F.S.

Formed to aid the communist National Miners Union operating in Pineville and Harlan County, Ky., 1931; an intellectual communistic group headed by

Communist John Dos Passos, chmn.; Hugo Gellert, sec.; Leon Kahn, treas.; com. members: Sherwood Anderson, Roger Baldwin, Polly Boyden, "Bishop" Wm. M. Brown, Horace B. Davis, Agnes De Lima, Floyd Dell, Babette Deutsch, H. W. L. Dana, Robert W. Dunn, Clifton P. Fadiman, Sarah Bard Field, Waldo Frank, Lydia Gibson, Eugene Gordon, Michael Gold, William Gropper, Charles Yale Harrison, Harold Hickerson, Sidney Hook, Grace Hutchins, Horace M. Kallen, Carol Weiss King, Corliss Lamont, Margaret Larkin, Melvin P. Levy, Jessie Lloyd, Robert Morss Lovett, Louis Lozowick, Paul Luttinger, M.D., Clarina Michelson, Elsie Reed Mitchell, M.D., Lewis Mumford, Liston M. Oak, Harvey O'Connor, Samuel Ornitz, Webster Powell, Harry Alan Potamkin, John Cowper Powys, Anna Rochester, Upton Sinclair, Lincoln Steffens, Bernard J. Stern, Marguerite Tucker, Genevieve Taggard, Mary Heaton Vorse, Alfred Wagenknecht, Charles K. Walker, Rev. Eliot White, Anita Whitney, Walter Wilson, Charles Erskine Scott Wood, and Carl Zigrosser.

Hdqts. 799 Broadway, N.Y. City (from letter appealing for funds, dated June 21, 1932, signed by Chas. R. Walker).

NATIONAL COMMITTEE TO AID VICTIMS OF GERMAN FASCISM

Nat. Com. to Aid Vic. G. Fascism.

Organized by communist Workers International Relief 1933, "affiliated membership 400,000" (Daily Wkr., 9/29/33).

National Officers: A. J. Muste, chmn.; Dr. Harry A. Warwick, vice chmn.; Alfred Wagenknecht, exec. sec.; J. B. Matthews, treas.; International officers: Lord Marley (Labor Party), London, England, chmn.; Prof. Francis Jourdain, Paris, France, sec.; *International Supporters:* England: Fenner Brockway (I.L.P.); Alice Neal (Coop. guild); Saklatvala (Communist Party); Jim Watson (Catholic Crusade); Havelock Ellis; E. Sylvia Pankhurst (Communist); France: Romain Rolland (Communist); Prof. Challaye; Henri Barbusse (Communist); Mme. Gabrielle Duchene (W.I.L.P.F. and communist Lg. against Imperialism); Mme. Wanner (W.I.L.P.F.); Czechoslovakia: Prof. Nejedly; Egon Erwin Kisch; C. Weiskopf; Franz Hoellering; Prof. Schalda; Holland: Regisseur Joris Ivans; Helene Ankersmith; Belgium: Henry Marteau and Karel Van Dooren; Germany: Prof. Albert Einstein, Ernst Toller, E. J. Gumbel, Hanns Eeisler, Arthur Holitscher, Willi Muenzenburg (intl. sec. of communist Intl. Lg. against Imperialism), Prof. Arthur Eddington, Prof. Levy, Hugh Walpole, Ellen Wilkinson, Edo Fimmen, Harry Pollitt, Count Michael Karolyi, Prof. Manoury, L. Levy-Bruehl, Paul Langevin, Charles Nicolle; *U.S.A. Supporters:* Harry Elmer Barnes, Konrad Bercovici, Roger Baldwin, Prof. Franz Boas, Robert C. Brooks, Stephen V. Benet, Heywood Broun, Leo Bulgakov, Malcolm Cowley, Dorothy Chertak, Ralph Cheyney, Prof. Merle Curti, Prof. Addison T. Cutler, Prof. Horace B. Davis, Will Durant, Robert W. Dunn, Edward Dahlberg, Olin Downes, Prof. H. W. L. Dana, Floyd Dell, Joseph Freeman, Donald Friede, Clifton Fadiman, Rabbi Benjamin Goldstein, Louis Golding, Mordecai Gorelik, Michael Gold, Granville Hicks, Max S. Hayes, Ali A. Hassan, Carl Haessler, Inez Haynes Irwin, Maxwell Hyde, Francis Fisher Kane, Carol Weiss King, Jerome Klein, J. A. Kittine, Joshua Kuntz, Eva Le Gallienne, Maxim-Lieber, Louis Lozowick, Corliss Lamont, Jessie Lloyd, Lola Maverick Lloyd, Prof. Robert Morss Lovett, Prof. R. M. Mac Iver, Dr. Lillian Milgrim, Rev. Lester Mondale, Henry Newman, Prof. Wm. L. Nunn, Harry Alan Potamkin, Dr. William J. Robinson, Burton Rascoe, Meyer Shapiro, Prof. Bernard J. Stern, Harry Slochower, W. R. Sassaman, Prof. Winifred Smith, George Soule, Prof. Margaret Schlauch, Lincoln Steffens, Otto Sattler, Lucia Trent, Ella Winter, Nathaniel Weyl, John Wexley.

Supporting organizations (listed on letterhead):

Workers International Relief (Communist); Conference for Progressive Labor Action (left wing Socialist, cooperates with Communists); International Labor Defense (Communist); Jewish Workers and People's National Committee Against Fascism and Pogroms in Germany; German National Anti-Fascist United Front; communist Intl. Workers Order; communist T.U.U.L.; Communist Party; Arbeiter Saengerbund of U.S.; Neue Volkszeitung; communist National Miners Union; communist Natur Freunde (Nature Friends); German Workers and Farmers Verband (Winnipeg, Canada); Socialist Jewish Workers Party (Left Paoli Zion); Amalgamated Food Workers; communist A.F. of L. Committee for Unemployment Insurance; communist Needle Trades Workers Industrial Union; communist Shoe Workers, and also Food Workers, Industrial Unions; Italian Anti-Fascist Committee of Action; Youth United Front Against German Fascism; Cultural United Front Against German Fascism; communist Finnish Workers Federation; Der Arbeiter; Kampf-Signal; German Workers Clubs; Arbeiter Turn und Sport Bund, U.S.A.; New York German Branch of Socialist Party; Elizabeth German Branch Socialist Party.

Hdqts. 75 Fifth Ave., Room 5, N.Y. City; Chicago Committee Hdqts. Room 310, 208 N. Wells St.

NATIONAL CONSUMERS LEAGUE

Nat. Cons. Lg.

A Garland-Fund-aided, Socialist-controlled organization founded in 1916 by Socialist Florence Kelley (formerly of Hull House, translator of Marx and Engels, and friend and correspondent of Engels and Lenin); organizes workers; issues "white lists" to blacklist firms not conforming to its program; ostensibly promotes consumption of union made goods, etc.

In 1931, Florence Kelley (now deceased) was gen. sec.; Dr. John R. Commons of Madison, Wis., pres.; and Jane Addams, Newton D. Baker, Mrs. Edw. P. Costigan, Alice Hamilton, John Haynes Holmes, Julia C. Lathrop, Henry R. Mussey, Mrs. Franklin D. Roosevelt, Mrs. M. R. Trumbull, etc., vice presidents; Mrs. J. Borden Harriman, chmn. of the bd.; hon. pres., John Graham Brooks; hon. vice pres., Irving Fisher; Jacob H. Hollander (John Hopkins), Frank L. McVey (U. of Ky.), Josiah Morse (U. of S. Car.), Wm. A. Neilson (Smith Coll.), Jessica B. Peixotto (U. of Cal.), Dean Roscoe Pound, Dr. John A. Ryan, E. R. A. Seligman (Columbia U.), Walter F. Wilcox (Cornell U.), A. B. Wolfe (Ohio State), Mary E. Woolley (Mt. Holyoke), etc. (listed on the letter head). Hdqts. 156 Fifth Ave., N.Y. City.

NATIONAL COUNCIL FOR PREVENTION OF WAR

N. C. for P. W.

Seymour Waldman, editor of the N.C. for P.W. "International Disarmament Notes," 1931-32, in October 1933 became head of the Washington bureau of the communist "Daily Worker." Has been called "a clearing house for Socialist-Communist pacifist propaganda"; formed Sept. 1921 under chairmanship of a Foreign Policy Assn. officer; its director, Frederick J. Libby, to quote Arthur Sears Henning, "has gained national notoriety for utterances widely regarded as unpatriotic and which were the cause of the board of education of the District of Columbia barring him from speaking in the Washington public schools. Libby is leading the movement for the abolition of military training in schools. . . . Libby was a prime mover in organizing the propaganda to deter the President from withdrawing recognition from the Calles government if American properties should be confiscated. . . . Libby has espoused the Calles side of the oil and alien land law controversy." (See Mexican Propaganda.) " . . . One of the common aims of the pacifist and radicals is to weaken the military preparedness of the United States for national defense. The most active pacifist organization is the National Council for Prevention of War which expends $85,000 a year as a clearing house for the peace work of 34 groups among which are the American Association of University Women, the American Farm Bureau Federation, the American Federation of Teachers, which fights military training of youth, the Fellowship of Reconciliation, the Foreign Policy Assn., the National Board of the Y.W.C.A., National Education Assn., National Women's Trade Union League, Women's International League for Peace and Freedom, National Consumers League, the W.C.T.U. and World Alliance for International Friendship Through the Churches. These component organizations of the National Council expend independently, partly or wholly on pacifist propaganda an aggregate of more than $500,000 a year. Other members of the Foreign Policy Association directorate who are also members of the directorate of the National Council for Prevention of War are Jane Addams, Katherine Ludington, Wm. Allen White, Bishop Francis J. McConnell, James G. McDonald and Bishop G. Ashton Oldham." (From Arthur Sears Henning's "Government by Propaganda.") Five of the cooperating organizations mentioned above are red Garland Fund protegés.

In 1927 it claimed to have sent out "more than 1,000,000 pieces of literature" to 13,600 newspapers, 75,000 ministers and others, against the President's naval program alone, to have voted a budget of $113,000 for 1928 and maintained a staff of 11 persons in the two offices in Washington and California with 7 stenographers, 14 clerks, and 3 "speakers in the fields." Hdqts. in 1932 were 532 Seventeenth Street, N.W., Washington, D.C.; branch offices in San Francisco, Portland, Ore., Louisville, Ky., Springfield, Mass., Des Moines, Ia.

Exec. sec., Frederick J. Libby; vice chairmen, Jane Addams, Rev. Peter Ainslie, Clement M. Biddle, Mrs. Louis D. Brandeis, Mrs. J. Borden Harriman, Will Irwin, John A. Lapp, Julia C. Lathrop, Katharine Ludington, Bishop Francis J. McConnell, James G. McDonald, Hugh S. Magill, Mrs. Lucia Ames Mead, Bishop G. Ashton Oldham, Mrs. Arthur Charles Watkins, and William Allen White; exec. bd.: T. Janney Brown, William F. Cochran, Edward T. Devine, Elizabeth Eastman, Mrs. J. Malcolm Forbes, Elisabeth Gilman, Mrs. J. Borden Harriman, Arthur E. Holder, Rabbi Edward L. Israel, Frederick J. Libby, Felix Morley, Rev. R. A. McGowan, Mrs. Sina M. Stanton, Richard R. Woop; assoc. secretaries: Mrs. Florence Brewer Boeckel, Eleanor D. Brannan, Gaylord W. Douglass, Mrs. Mary Flahaven, J. J. Handsaker, Thomas Que Harrison, Mrs. Laura Puffer Morgan, Jeannette Rankin, Dorothy Reed, Cynthia Smith, E. Guy Talbott, Jacob H. Taylor, Harry E. Terrell, Seymour B. Waldman, Arthur Charles Watkins, Mary Phillips Webster and Mary Ida Winder; office sec.: Mrs. Gladys K. Gould Mackenzie; treas.: T. Janney Brown.

Listed on the 1932 letterhead as "Participating Organizations" are:

Am. Assn. Univ. Women; Am. Fed. Tchrs.; Am. School Citizenship Lg.; Church of the Brethren Bd. of Relig. Ed.; C.M.E.; Fell. Recon.; Gen. Alliance Unitarian Women, Com. on Social Serv.; Gen. Conf. of Religious Soc. of Friends; Intl. New Thought Alliance; Nat. Bd. Y.W.C.A.; Nat. Coun. Jewish Women; Nat. Coun. Jewish Juniors; Nat. Edu. Assn.; Nat. Fed. of Temple Sisterhoods; Nat. Reform Assn.; Nat. Wom. Tr. Un. Lg.; Peace Assn. of Friends in Am.; Soc. to Eliminate Economic Causes of War; Woman's Missionary Un. of Friends in Am.; W.I.L.P.F.; Cooperating Organizations: Central Conf. of Am. Rabbis; Council of Women for Home Missions; Nat. Consumers Lg.; Intl. Soc. of Christian Endeavor; United Synagogue of Am.; Womens Lg. of the United Synagogue of Am.; World Peace Union.

NATIONAL COUNCIL FOR PROTECTION OF FOREIGN BORN WORKERS

Nat. Coun. for Prot. For. Bn. Wkrs.

A Communist subsidiary (U.S. Fish Report; also P. 77 of Report of Exec. Com. of Communist International, issued 1924); claims 270,000 members, staged mass demonstration when Congress convened Dec. 6, 1930; agitates against alien registration, deportation of alien Reds, etc. The N.Y. World, Oct. 16, 1927, stated:

"Jos. B. Dean, pres. of the Moving Picture Operators Union, is pres. of the National Council for Protection of Foreign Born Workers; Nina Samoradin is nat. sec., and among members of the board are James H. Maurer, pres. of the Pa. State Federation of Labor, Timothy Healey of the Steamfitters Union, W. E. Burghardt Du Bois, editor of the Crisis, Clarence Darrow, Albert F. Coyle, Robert Morss Lovett, Arthur Garfield Hays, and Fred Atkins Moore."

Henry T. Hunt was legal advisor. The Communist Daily Worker, Dec. 19, 1927 told of a conference of the N.Y. Council addressed by Robt. W. Dunn and Dr. Edmund B. Chaffee of the Labor Temple (of the Presbyterian Church). Marvin says the advisory board of the N.Y. Council was in 1927

"Composed of Adolph Blumfield, Louis F. Budenz, August Burkhardt (gen. sec. Amalgamated Food Workers), Stuart Chase, P. E. Cosgrove, Solon de Leon, Marion Finn Scott, G. E. Powers, Robt. H. Haskell, John Dos Passos, Joseph Freeman, Paxton Hibben, I. A. Kittine, Horace Liveright, Ludwig Lore, Scott Nearing, Chas. W. Wood, Arthur Calhoun, Rev. A. Wakefield Statin.

"All of the above are Communists or Socialists or closely allied with the Communist-Socialist movement in the United States. Both the Communists and Socialists openly state their purpose is to destroy the government of the U.S. . . . On Jan. 9, 1926 a luncheon conference in opposition" (to alien registration and deportation bills) "was held at Hotel Astor, N.Y. City. At this meeting the bills were denounced in no uncertain terms by Max J. Kohler, the prominent pacifist Sherwood Eddy, the Rev. Chas. K. Gilbert of the Federal Council of Churches and Florence F. Cassidy of the Y.W.C.A. of Bridgeport, Conn. A letter of denouncement from the Immigrants' Protective League of Chicago, upon whose directorate appear the names of Jane Addams, Prof. Ernst Freund, Julia C. Lathrop and other equally well-known radicals was read." (Marvin Data Sheets, 56-16 and 34-2.)

N.Y. officers and exec. com.:

Pres.: Joseph Dean; vice-pres.: Max Orlowsky, P. Pascual Cosgrove; sec.-treas.: Nina Samoradin; legal advisor: Henry T. Hunt; field sec.: Jeannette D. Pearl; Executive Committee: Timothy Healy, Max S. Hays, James Maurer, William Cohen, Fred Suiter, Percy Thomas, J. L. Studder, A. M. Allman, Carl Appel, Rebecca Grecht, A. G. Boorman, John Brahtin, J. R. Brodsky, August Burkhardt, E. G. Horacek, J. E. Lewandowski, J. Pede, John Sesesky, Anna Sevcik, Maurice Sugar, Paul J. Zoretich, W. E. B. Du Bois, Clarence Darrow, Albert F. Coyle, Robert Morss Lovett, Arthur Garfield Hays, Alice Stone Blackwell, Francis Fisher Kane, Fred Atkins Moore. (1930 Fish Report of Investigation of Communist Propaganda, Part 5, Vol. 4, p. 1321.)

NATIONAL COUNCIL ON FREEDOM FROM CENSORSHIP

Of the A.C.L.U.; to abolish censorship of obscene or seditious art, literature, and movies and for "freedom in schools and colleges"; fought in behalf of Corliss Lamont's Russian posters, held by authorities as seditious matter. Hdqts. 100 Fifth Ave., N.Y. City.

Chmn.: Hatcher Hughes; vice chairmen: Barrett H. Clark, Fannie Hurst, Elmer Rice; treas.: Harry Elmer Barnes; sec.: Gordon W. Moss; members: Helen Arthur, Bruce Bliven, Dr. Louise Stevens Bryant, Witter Bynner, James Branch Cabell, Henry Seidel Canby, Edward Childs Carpenter, Marc Connolly, Mrs. Mary Ware Dennett, Walter Pritchard Eaton, Morris L. Ernst, Rabbi Sidney E. Goldstein, Paul Green, Dr. Louis I. Harris, Arthur Garfield Hays, Theresa Helburn, B. W. Huebsch, Sidney Howard, Rupert Hughes, Inez Haynes Irwin, Dorothy Kenyon, Kenneth MacGowan, H. L. Mencken, Lewis Mumford, Henry Raymond Mussey, George Jean Nathan, Rabbi Louis I. Newman, Rev. Robert Norwood, Eugene O'Neill, Maxwell E. Perkins, Llewelyn Powys, Aaron J. Rosanoff, Robert E. Sherwood, Claire Sifton, Paul Sifton, Harry Weinberger, Stewart Edward White, Dr. Ira S. Wile, Harry Leon Wilson.

NATIONAL EDUCATION ASSOCIATION

Radical educational association which fostered the National Save Our Schools Committee; affiliated with N. C. for P. W.

NATIONAL FARMERS HOLIDAY ASSOCIATION

A supporting organization of the Communist-organized U.S. Congress Against War (see). Its leader, Milo Reno, is active in the radical Conference for Progressive Political Action (see).

NATIONAL MINERS UNION

Communist T.U.U.L. Union; hdqts. Frank Borich, 413 Fourth Ave., Pittsburgh, Pa.; responsible for violence in Ky., Pa., and Ohio mining districts; now agitating in New Mexico and Utah, claiming over 1,000 members in Utah, Carbon County district.

NATIONAL MOONEY-BILLINGS COMMITTEE

Aided financially by Garland Fund; formed by A.C.L.U. to aid the Communist agitation for release of Mooney and Billings, convicted of bombing the 1917 San Francisco Preparedness Day Parade, killing 10 and injuring 50 persons. Mooney was then an anarchist-communist labor agitator and with anarchist Alex. Berkman started and ran "The Blast," an anarchist paper. His letter to Stalin appears on the front page of the Communist Labor Defender for Nov. 1932. In it he says, *"My dear Comrade Stalin,"* and after rejoicing over the Fifteenth Anniversary of the Russian Proletarian Revolution, thanks Stalin

> "For the magnificent spirit of International working-class solidarity by the militant workers of Russia in defense of my fight for freedom, and for the freedom of all class war and political prisoners. Were it not for the Revolutionary workers of Petrograd led by our beloved comrade Lenin, in militant demonstrations before the American Embassy on April 25, 1917, I would not now be addressing these greetings to you. Thus my life was saved and my usefulness to the revolutionary working class prolonged. It is my hope that these revolutionary greetings to you and through you to the Toilers of the Soviet Union will be presented to you in person on the Fifteenth Anniversary of the Russian Revolution by my dear 84 year old mother, who will be in Moscow on Nov. 7th, 1932 in the continued interest of the working class fight for my freedom from the Dungeons of American Capitalist Imperialism. All hail to the Russian Revolution and the Dictatorship of the Proletariat. I'm for it hook, line and sinker, without equivocation or reservation. Please accept my warm personal regards and best wishes. I am, Comradely yours, Tom Mooney, 31921."

Committee Hdqts., 100 Fifth Ave., N.Y. City; Henry T. Hunt (Roosevelt appointee as gen. counsel PWA), chmn.; members:

Lemuel F. Parton, vice chmn.; Roger N. Baldwin, sec.; Harry Elmer Barnes, Alice Stone Blackwell, John Rogers Commons, Clarence Darrow, Jerome Davis, Edward T. Devine, John Dewey, Robert L. Duffus, Morris L. Ernst, Sara Bard Field, Glenn Frank, Gilson Gardner, Elizabeth Gilman, Norman Hapgood, Max S. Hayes, Arthur Garfield Hays, Morris Hillquit, Fannie Hurst, Inez Haynes Irwin, Philip LaFollette, Sinclair Lewis, Walter W. Liggett, Owen R. Lovejoy, Robert Morss Lovett, James H. Maurer, Alexander Meiklejohn, H. L. Mencken, Wesley C. Mitchell, Fremont Older, George D. Pratt, Jr., Roger William Riis, John A. Ryan, John Nevin Sayre, Alva W. Taylor, B. C. Vladeck, Stephen S. Wise, W. E. Woodward.

NATIONAL MOONEY COUNCIL OF ACTION

Formed 1933 by the Communist I.L.D. for the purpose of drawing radicals together in a "united front" under Communist leadership for the Mooney ballyhoo of hate against our "capitalist" government upon which Communism thrives. "Free Tom Mooney" has, with the Scottsboro case, been a money making agitation for the Communist Party and the excuse for countless riots, strikes, demonstrations and profitable collections, as was the Sacco-Vanzetti case, formerly. The "Free Tom Mooney Congress" called by the Communist I.L.D. met April 30—May 2, 1933, in Chgo., and passed the resolution: "Brother Mooney for 17 years now the symbol of the unity of working class martyrdom must now become the living symbol of the unity of the working class. . . . Just as the frame-up and imprisonment of Tom Mooney was connected with the preparations for the entry of this country into the world war, so now the continued imprisonment of Mooney and other victims of capitalist class justice . . . is the preparation of a second imperialist war by the capitalist nations and against the Union of Soviet Socialist Republics. . . . This council hereby establishes the National Tom Mooney Council of Action, a United Front for Workers Rights and the Rights of the Negro People. . . . The legal murder of the innocent Sacco and Vanzetti was a part of the price of disunity of the workers. . . . Mass pressure not the 'justice' of the courts is responsible for such victories as the working class has won."

"38 Chicago locals of the A.F. of L., 121 locals of other cities, 23 locals of the Progressive Miners of S. Ill., 82 independent and revolutionary unions affiliated with the T.U.U.L.—Delegates from the Communist Party, Socialist Party, League for Independent Political Action, Defense organizations, Young Communist League, Young People's Socialist League, Industrial Workers of the World, . . . " were represented by 1,200 delegates according to the

May 15th "Workers Voice" (Communist) and "Robert Minor, veteran comrade of Mooney . . . made the keynote address." Other speakers were: "W. L. Patterson of the I.L.D., A. J. Muste of the Lg. for Ind. Lab. Act., Clarence Hathaway and Bill Gebert of the Communist Party, Socialists, Trade Union men, delegates of the I.W.W. and of farmers groups. . . . Alex Fraser of Gillespie, militant leader of the Progressive Miners was elected as first chairman of the congress . . . the proposals of the I.W.W. delegation for an 'immediate' general strike and boycott of California products was rejected while at the same time the congress adopted all methods of mass struggles, including strikes, demonstrations, etc. for the Mooney defense. . . . A national Mooney Council of Action of 42 members was elected" which "will lead a fight 'for Workers Rights and Against Oppression of the Negro Masses.'"

Council members: C. A. Hathaway (Communist Party); Al. Renner (Proletarian Party, Detroit); Joshua Kunitz (Nat. Com. Def. Pol. Pris.); George Smerkin (Young People's Socialist Lg., Chgo.); James P. Cannon, Communist Lg. of Am. (Trotskyite); Frank Borich (communist Nat. Miners Union, Pitts.); James Eagan (Journeyman Plasterers, Pitts., Communist); Phil Van Gelder (Socialist Party, Phila.); Anthony Chuplis (A.F. of L. Gen. Mine Bd. U.M.W.A., Shenandoah, Pa.); John Metzger (communist Marine Workers Union, New Orleans); Ella Reeve Bloor (communist Nat. Farmers Com. for Action, Sioux City, Ia.); Chas. Crone (A.F. of L. Intl. Hod Carriers, Mpls., Minn.); Trent Longo (A.F. of L. Painters Union, Clev., O.); L. O. Puchot (A.F. of L. Bldg. Trades Coun., Des Moines, Ia.); Prof. Robert Morss Lovett (Am. Civil Liberties Union, Chgo.); James Kodl (Irish-Am. Labor Lg., Chgo., Communist sympathizer); Mrs. Sabina Burrell, Socialist, of Progressive Miners of America (P.M.A.) Ladies Auxiliary, Gillespie, Ill.; Pat Ansboury, P.M.A. and Communist Lg. of Am. (Trotskyite); L. Weinstock (Painters N.Y. and communist A.F. of L. Com. for Unemployment Insurance); L. B. Scott (A.F. of L. Tom Mooney Molders Def. Com., San Francisco, Cal.); Jack Clark (I.W.W., Chgo.); Chas. Blome (A.F. of L. Conf. Bd. of Molders Unions, St. Louis, Mo.); Emil Arnold (A.F. of L. Painters, Chgo.); D. Poindexter (Lg. Struggle Negro Rights—Communist); Jesse Taylor (A.F. of L. Bricklayers, Buffalo, N.Y.); M. Olay (Free Society Group of anarchists, Chgo.); Robert Minor (Communist Party); Wm. Patterson (communist I.L.D.); L. Hyman (communist Needle Trades Workers Indust. Union); Jack Kling (Young Communist Lg., Chgo.); Karl Lore, Socialist (Unemp. Citiz. Lg., Chgo.); Albert Hansen (Ky. Miners Defense Com. of I.W.W., Chgo.); A. J. Muste (Leftwing Socialist, Conf. Prog. Lab. Act., N.Y.); Roger Baldwin (A.C. L.U., N.Y.); Israel Amter (communist Unemployed Councils, N.Y.); Aileen Barnsdall (Mooney's personal appointee, Los Angeles); Arthur Scott (A.F. of L. Mooney Molders Def. Com., San Francisco); J. B. Matthews (Fellowship Reconciliation, N.Y.); Joe Weber (communist T.U.U.L.); John Werlik (A.F. of L. Metal Polishers Union, Chgo.); Jack Johnstone (communist T.U.U.L., Pitts.); Alex Fraser (removed from Socialist Party, Ill., exec. com. as a Communist, P.M.A., Gillespie, Ill.); A. Thorpe (Gen. Defense Com. of I.W.W., Chicago).

NATIONAL POPULAR GOVERNMENT LEAGUE

Nat. Pop. Govt. Lg.

A publicity bureau for the various organizations represented on its directorship, namely: the A.C.L.U., Socialist Party, L.I.D., Public Ownership League (its affiliate), the Peoples Legislative Service, and the Conference for Progressive Political Action. Judson King, now Pres. Roosevelt's Research Investigator for Tennessee Valley Authority, is its active director, although ex-Senator Robt. L. Owen is listed as president. Started in 1913, it has consistently advocated government ownership of the key industries of the nation in true Socialist style, as might be expected with seven officers of Carl Thompson's Public Ownership League at various times serving on its directing committee (Wm. H. Johnston, Carl S. Vrooman, Father John A. Ryan, John R. Haynes, James H. McGill, and the deceased Delos F. Wilcox and Wm. Kent), and also eight executives of the People's Legislative Service (Senator Geo. W. Norris, Wm. H. Johnston, J. H. McGill, Jackson Ralston, Prof. E. A. Ross, Edw. Keating, Father John A. Ryan, Wm. Kent). W. H. Johnston also called the Conference for Progressive Political Action (see) at Cleveland, July 4, 1924, which nominated LaFollette for President and gave impetus to the fashion of calling radicals "progressives."

The League conducts a Forum in Washington, circulates reprints of Congressional speeches attacking the utilities, and issues a bulletin service which it estimated, in 1927, reached through 125 library subscribers, the A.P. and Universal Press services, some 59,582,000 readers. It declared that it did not need to issue a newspaper since it could secure such wide publicity.

Among its pamphlets, it lists as "Valuable to Students and Libraries as Research Material": "'The Deportations Delirium of 1920,' by Hon. Louis F. Post. The true story of how the 'Red Raids' were brought about"; "'Report of the Twelve Lawyers on the Illegal Practices of the U.S. Department of Justice,' by Dean Roscoe Pound of Harvard University and others. An indictment of the illegal methods of Attorney General Palmer in his famous 'Red Raids' of 1920"; "'Official Hearings of Testimony Before the Senate Sub-Committee Which Investigated the Report of the Twelve Lawyers,' 788 pages"; also "Report of Senator Walsh Sustaining the Twelve Lawyers."

The "Report Upon the Illegal Practises of the U.S. Department of Justice" was issued May 27, 1920 by Judson King and signed by the twelve lawyers, who were: Felix Frankfurter, Ernst Freund, and David Wallerstein, all of the Red-aiding A.C.L.U. national committee; Jackson H. Ralston and Francis Fisher Kane of the A.C.L.U.; and Zechariah Chafee, Jr. of Harvard Law School, R. G. Brown, Judge Alfred Niles, Swinburn Hale, Frank P. Walsh, Dean Roscoe Pound (Harvard Law Sch.), and Tyrrell Williams.

This report was a bitter and untruthful attack upon the Department of Justice, charging wholesale arrests of Reds without warrants, cruelty to prisoners, forgery by agents to make out cases against "innocent" Reds, refusal to let prisoners communicate with friends, etc., etc. Of course the report took the usual sniping position of claiming that its authors were not themselves in favor of any radical doctrines (?), but were solely interested in upholding the law! The old, deliberately deceptive argument, that Attorney General Palmer's suppression had aided rather than harmed the Reds' revolutionary cause in America, was also used. (Then why did radicals protest suppression?) They bitterly attacked the use of Government funds to discover and deport revolutionary Anarchist and Communist agitators.

In reply, Attorney General Palmer sent a telegram to the Popular Govt. League signers, saying: "Some of the aliens themselves have since denied the very statements which your committee filed. Your apparent willingness to believe these statements made by alien anarchists when facing deportation in preference to the testimony of sworn officers of the Government, whose only motive is the performance of duty, *indicates some other desire on your part than just administration of the law*." (Emphasis mine.)

The N.Y. Times, June 2, 1920, quoted Palmer as saying of the lawyer-signers: "We find several of them appearing as counsel for Communist and Communist Labor Party members at deportation hearings. I have difficulty in reconciling their attitude with that of men sworn to uphold the Constitution of the United States."

But this Red campaign started by these men was continued. The Garland Fund appropriated funds and bemused Americans slept, stupefied by confusing propaganda, and all funds were, in 1925, stopped for anti-Red activities of the Department of Justice. Since that time, radicalism has made its phenomenal strides in the United States undisturbed by the Government.

One letterhead of the League lists:

Pres., Robt. L. Owen (U.S. Senator, Okla.); General Committee: Wm. Kent (Kentfield, Cal., Ex-Congressman); Dr. John R. Haynes (Los Angeles); Senator *Geo. W. Norris; J. H. McGill* (Valparaiso, Ind. manufacturer); E. A. Ross (Madison, Wis., Prof. Sociology, U. of Wis.); Harry A. Slattery (Wash., former sec. Nat. Conservation Assn.); *Jackson H. Ralston* (Wash., Atty.); director, Judson King, Wash.; Consulting Committee: Alice Stone Blackwell, Boston; Warren S. Blauvelt, Terre Haute; Lawrence G. Brooks (Boston, Atty.); Geo. H. Duncan (E. Jaffrey, N.H., Mem. State Legis.); Herman I. Ekern (Madison, Atty. Gen. Wis.); A. R. Hatton (Cleveland, Prof. Pol. Science, Western Reserve U.); A. N. Holcombe (Cambridge, Prof. of Govt. Harvard U.); Wm. H. Johnston (Wash., Pres. Intl. Machinists); *Edw. Keating* (Mg. Ed. "Labor," then official organ Conf. for Prog. Political Action); Edwin Markham, Staten Is., poet; Frank Morrison (Wash., sec. A.F. of L.); Chas. H. Porter (Cambridge, Mass., manufacturer); Alice Thatcher Post (Wash., former mg. ed. "The Public"); Louis F. Post (former Asst. Sec. of Labor); Herbert Quick (Berkeley Springs, W. Va., author); Chas. Edw. Russell (Wash., author); *Dr. John A. Ryan* (Wash., Prof. Industrial Ethics, Catholic Univ.); J. Allen Smith (Seattle, Prof. Pol. Science, U. of Wash.); Wm. S. U'Ren, Portland; Carl S. Vrooman (Bloomington, Ill., farmer, Ex-Sec. of Agriculture); Delos F. Wilcox (Grand Rapids, Mich., consulting franchise expert); *Mrs. Laura Williams* (director Progressive Education Assn.); H. H. Wilcox (Pittsburg manufacturer); J. A. Woodburn (Bloomington, Ind., Prof. History, U. of Ind.). There are a few minor changes 1933: Robt. Beecher Howell, U.S. Sen., Nebr., added; nine dropped (Owen, Kent, Blackwell, Blauvelt, Wilcox, Porter, L. F. Post, Quick, Russell).

Hdqts. 637 Munsey Bldg., Wash., D.C.

NATIONAL RAILROAD WORKERS INDUSTRIAL UNION

Communist T.U.U.L. Union; now called the "Railroad Brotherhoods Unity Committee" (see).

NATIONAL RELIGION AND LABOR FOUNDATION

Nat. R. & L. Found.

Organized by radicals, about 1932, to propagandize "the new social order" (Communism-Socialism) within Jewish, Catholic and Protestant churches. Its Bulletin, "Economic Justice," carries plain Red revolutionary propaganda; the Nov. 1932 issue (the first) printed a cartoon of Jesus by Art Young, the New Masses Communist cartoonist (see page 202); the Jan. 1933 issue said of this cartoon: "This cut has been in demand by the churches and is still available. The Editors"; the Jan. issue printed a typical atheist Soviet cartoon

ECONOMIC JUSTICE

REWARD

For Information Leading to the Apprehension of—

JESUS CHRIST

WANTED—For Sedition, Criminal Anarchy, Vagrancy, and Conspiring to Overthrow the Established Government.

Dresses poorly, *said* to be a carpenter by trade, ill-nourished, has visionary ideas, associates with common working people, the unemployed and bums. Alien—believed to be a Jew—ALIAS 'Prince of Peace,' 'Son of Man', 'Light of the World' &c. &c. *Professional Agitator*, Red beard, marks on hands and feet the result of injuries inflicted by an angry mob led by respectable citizens and legal authorities.

An Important City.

"The bulletin would have been worth the effort expanded in publishing it if it had contained nothing except the striking cartoon of Jesus by Art Young." A minister in a personal letter. (This cut has been in demand by the churches, and is still available. The Editors).

Ithaca, Nebraska.

"I find a conservative in religion is a conservative in social and economic attitudes." Walter E. Ulrich.

A Town in Illinois.

"I wanted to go into business and did. I have been continuously connected with an Agricultural Implement Manufacturing Company ever since, until very recently. I have for the last twenty years had the hope that at fifty years of age I could be somewhat free from 'private profit making' . . . . . In a sense I am responsible for the present situation.

Editors

Jerome Davis — George A. Douglas — Francis A. Henson

Book Editors

Edward L. Israel — John A. Ryan — Ernest F. Tittle

Corresponding Editors

Toyohiko Kagawa, Japan; Enkichi Kan, Japan; Yao Hsien-hui, China; Mahatma Gandhi, India; Max Yergan, South Africa; Andre Philip, France; H. L. Henriod, Switzerland; N. Stufkens, Holland; W. A. Visser 't Hooft, Geneva; Judah Magnes, Palestine; Robert Garric, France; Hans Stroh, Austria; Paul Piechowski, Germany; Anne Guthrie, South America; Julius Hecker, U. S. S. R.; Ralph Dwinnel, Egypt; Edwin Barker, England; Fritz Beck, Germany.

A few hundred priests, ministers, rabbis and leaders in the labor movement are acting as correspondents in the United States.

Subscriptions to the bulletin $0.50 for the eight monthly issues each year.

On the left is facsimile of the cartoon of Jesus by Art Young of the staff of Communist-atheist "New Masses" (from Nov. 1932 issue of "Economic Justice," Bulletin of the National Religion and Labor Foundation). On the right are facsimile excerpts (from Jan. 1933 issue of the Bulletin) showing (above) the editorial reference to and offer to distribute this revolutionary, blasphemous cartoon, and (below) the editorial staff.

(see page 100) ridiculing Christianity, representing Christ, unburdened, leading ahead workers with bowed backs crushed beneath the weight of a huge cross, while these workers are also harnessed to, and pulling, "Capitalism" represented as always by the Soviets as a fat man with a plug hat. The cartoon is a plea to throw off "Capitalism," the Cross, and Christ's leadership.

It prints propaganda such as that of Communist Robert Whitaker of Los Angeles (see), one of its correspondents and national committeemen who says in the same issue: "It is no longer a question of the need of a revolution; the question is as to the method of bringing the revolution to pass. . . . To this conclusion I have very definitely come: that there is little hope of making any considerable change in the psychology of the masses except as the sequence of *radical social action outside of respectable ranks;* that the work of revolt will have to be carried through in two sections, the first of these, the long-suffering and no longer quiescent disinherited and unemployed, who will respond to their desperation rather than to any well digested education, the second, a trained and disciplined group who will know how to function in a *Lenin-leadership* when the hour of opportunity comes. Consequently our concern is to build the understanding leadership for the crisis from those who need no longer the milk of infantile adaptations to their timidities and polite prejudices but are ready to talk business and digest the strong meat of *direct revolutionary preparation.*"

The April 1933 issue carries the following horrifying anouncement: "A new religious Brotherhood is in process of formation. The method which it intends to employ toward the accomplishment of its purpose is designed to fill two long felt wants in the radical movement and in the religious field. Robert R. Warner, the Brother Secretary of the Order, expresses its function: 'We place ourselves under the vows of poverty and obedience, plus a rule of life entailing purity—but not necessarily celibacy. Being a disciplined group, willing and anxious to enter into industrial disputes to take the posts of danger, we feel that there we can be of great benefit, since we will not feel the terror of the black list, the lock out, or other means of capitalist economic terrorization. Likewise in areas of class warfare we feel that the innate reverence of the average policeman for the religious habit will protect our own heads from his blows, and so, if we place ourselves in the place of greatest danger, we can also by that very act, protect the workers. On the other hand, we know many liberal and radical priests and ministers who are prevented from themselves preaching the 'social gospel' in understandable and plain terms for fear of losing their jobs; but who would not hesitate to permit an outside preacher to do so, rather would jump at the opportunity. . . . Address inquiries or send contributions to Robert R. Warner, Brothers Secretary, 27 Winthrop House, St. John's Road, Mass.'" The slogan of this issue was: "URGE RECOGNITION OF RUSSIA."

Says the Jan. issue: "We are glad to announce that Dr. Willard E. Uphaus . . . has joined the staff of the foundation on a part time basis. . . . Another addition to the staff is Arnold Johnson, recent graduate of Union Theological Seminary, who was in jail in Harlan, Kentucky, for a number of weeks on a charge of criminal syndicalism. Arnold Johnson will specialize in organizing the unemployed into Unemployed Citizens Leagues and for the purpose of making hunger marches and other demonstrations to dramatize the economic crisis. He is now working in Ohio." "Communism Is the Way" by James W. Ford, colored Communist, Vice Presidential candidate (running mate of Wm. Z. Foster) in 1932, appeared in the May-June issue.

Excerpts from the address of the pro-Soviet "Brain Trustee," Rex. Guy Tugwell, delivered before the American Economic Assn., 1932 and entitled "The Principle of Planning and the Institution of Laissez Faire," appeared in the Jan. 1933 issue. To quote: "Planning will necessarily become a function of the federal government; either that or the planning agency will supersede that government, which is why, of course, such a scheme will eventually be assimilated to the state rather than possess some of its powers without its responsibilities. Business will logically be required to disappear. This is not an overstatement for the sake of emphasis; it is literally meant. The essence of business is its free venture for profits in an unregulated economy. Planning implies guidance of capital uses . . . adjustment of production to consumption . . . the insurance of adequate buying capacity. . . . New industries will not just happen as the automobile industry did; they will have to be foreseen, to be argued for, or seem probably desirable features of the whole economy before they can be entered upon. . . . There is no denying that the contemporary situation in the United States has explosive possibilities. The future is becoming visible in Russia; the present is bitterly in contrast; politicians, theorists and vested interests seem to conspire ideally for the provocation to violence of a long patient people. No one can pretend to know how the release of this pressure is likely to come. Perhaps our statesmen will give way or be more or less gently removed from duty; perhaps our constitutions and statutes will be revised; perhaps our vested interests will submit to control without too violent resistance. It is difficult to believe that any of these will happen; it seems just as incredible that we may have a revolution. Yet the new kind of economic machinery we have in prospect cannot function in our present economy. The contemporary situation is one in which all the choices are hard; yet one of them has to be made." (Tugwell is now Asst. "Commissar" of Agriculture and leader of Roosevelt's Brain Trust.)

Lists of Red books which will be loaned to members for merely the cost of return postage are sent out. Rabbi Edw. L. Israel, Father John A. Ryan and Rev. E. F. Tittle are the "Book Editors" and list for such distribution: "The Little Lenin Library" (Communist); "Toward Soviet America" by Wm. Z. Foster (Moscow's U.S. Communist Party leader); "The Soviets Conquer Wheat" by Anna Louise Strong, Communist editor of the communist Moscow Daily News, a paper which, along with other Red periodicals, is also distributed by this book service; "The Necessity of Communism" by Middleton Murray; "The Road to Plenty" by Foster and Catchings; and other radical literature. How self-styled Christians expect to sow with atheist Communist enemies of Christianity and reap with Jesus Christ is hard to understand. The national conference of the Foundation was held July 21, 1933 at Jane Addams' Hull House.

Editors, besides the Book Editors mentioned above, are: Jerome Davis, Geo. A. Douglas, Francis A. Henson; Corresponding Editors: Toyohiko Kagawa, Japan; Enkichi Kan, Japan; Yao Hsien-hui, China; Mahatma Gandhi, India; Max Yergan, South Africa; Andre Philip, France; H. L. Henriod, Switzerland; N. Stufkens, Holland; W. A. Visser't Hooft, Geneva; Judah Magnes, Palestine; Robt. Garric, France; Hans Stroh, Austria; Paul Prechowski, Germany; Anne Guthrie, South America; Julius Hecker, U.S.S.R.; Ralph Dwinnel, Egypt; Edwin Barker, England; Fritz Beck, Germany. A few hundred priests, ministers, rabbis and leaders in the labor movement are acting as correspondents in the United States.

Subscriptions to the bulletin, $0.50 for the eight monthly issues each year. Hdqts. 304 Crown St., New Haven, Conn. Sends out leaflets for Common Sense Magazine, Christian Social Action Movement and Emergency Committee for Strikers' Relief; is member of Jt. Com. on Unemp.

Honorary Presidents: Sidney Hillman, pres. Amalg. Cloth. Wkrs. of Am.; J. E. Hagerty, pres. Catholic Conference on Industrial Problems; Francis J. McConnell, Bishop N.Y. Area, M.E. Church, and pres. Fed. Coun. Chs. 1929-32. Field secretaries are Arnold Johnson and Williard E. Uphaus; exec. secretaries, Geo. A. Douglas and Francis A. Henson; office sec., Helen-Louise Porter; National Committee: Grace Abbott, Jane Addams, Donald B. Aldrich, Roland H. Bainton, E. Wight Bakke, A. G. Baldwin, Bernard J. Bamberger, W. R. Barnhart, John C. Bennett, John C. Biddle, Dwight Bradley, Harvie Branscomb, Chas. R. Brown, Chas. S. Brown, J. F. Burke, Vincent Burns, S. Parkes Cadman, Robt. L. Calhoun, E. Fay Campbell, Edmund B. Chaffee, Elisabeth Christman, Wm. F. Cochran, Geo. A. Coe, Geo. S. Counts, Albert F. Coyle, James R. Cox, Abraham Cronbach, Ethel M. Davis, Gardiner M. Day, William Horace Day, Sherwood Eddy, Robert B. Eleazer, A. R. Elliott, Phillips Elliott, Harold Fey, Charles W. Gilkey, James Gordon Gilkey, Elisabeth Gilman, William E. Gilroy, Israel Goldstein, Herbert D. Graetz, Harold Gray, Ernest Graham Guthrie, Herman J. Hahn, Powers Hapgood, S. Ralph Harlow, Erdman Harris, Hornell Hart, A. A. Heist, Arthur E. Holt, John Hope, Walter M. Horton, Lawrence T. Hosie, Lynn Harold Hough, Allan A. Hunter, Paul Hutchinson, Cecelia I. Jeffrey, Paul Jones, Howard A. Kester, A. Roger Kratz, Maynard C. Krueger, George S. Lackland, Halford E. Luccock, Alex Lyall, Louis L. Mann, J. B. Matthews, Oscar E. Maurer, Jacob Mirviss, Darwin J. Meserole, Herbert A. Miller, Ethelwyn Mills, H. W. Morgan, Charles Clayton Morrison, Claud Nelson, Richard Niebuhr, Kelly O'Neall, G. Bromley Oxnam, Kirby Page, William Pickens, Arthur Pound, Helen E. Price, F. J. Schlink, Clarence Shedd, Guy Emery Shipler, E. B. Shultz, Tucker P. Smith, Edmund D. Soper, George Soule, T. Guthrie Speers, George Stewart, Alfred W. Swan, Ronald J. Tamblyn, Wellington H. Tinker, Ernest F. Tittle, Henry P. Van Dusen, H. J. Voorhis, John Warford, Wellman Warner, Luther A. Weigle, Robert Whitaker, Eliot White, Walter White, J. Stitt Wilson, L. Hollingsworth Wood, Winnifred Wygal; Executive Committee: Herman A. Brautigam, P. H. Callahan, Allan K. Chalmers, Eleanor Copenhaver, Jerome Davis, Sidney Goldstein, William P. Hapgood, Hubert C. Herring, John Haynes Holmes, Edward L. Israel, Berton E. Kile, John A. Lapp, Douglas C. Macintosh, A. J. Muste, Reinhold Niebuhr, Frank Olmstead, A. Phillip Randolph, Alva W. Taylor, Edward Thomas, Norman Thomas, Charles C. Webber, Stephen S. Wise.

NATIONAL SAVE OUR SCHOOLS COMMITTEE

Nat. Save Our Schs. Com.

Says the expert Francis Ralston Welsh of Phila.: "It is a red affair through and through, with possibly a very few respectable dupes. The evident object was to take patriotic teaching out of the schools and substitute propaganda more pleasing to Leftwing Socialists and Communists. It is the Communist-aiding American Civil

HONORARY PRESIDENTS

J. E. Hagerty, President Catholic Conference on Industrial Problems and Director, School of Social Administration, Ohio State University.

Sidney Hillman, President, Amalgamated Clothing Workers of America.

Francis J. McConnell, Bishop, New York Area, Methodist Episcopal Church, and President, 1929-33, Federal Council of the Churches of Christ in America.

NATIONAL RELIGION AND LABOR FOUNDATION

NON-SECTARIAN, NON-DENOMINATIONAL

304 CROWN STREET, NEW HAVEN, CONNECTICUT

TELEPHONE: 8-6667

Executive Secretaries
George A. Douglas
Francis A. Henson

Field Secretaries
Arnold Johnson
Willard E. Uphaus

NATIONAL COMMITTEE
Grace Abbott
Jane Addams
Donald B. Aldrich
Roland H. Bainton
E. Wight Bakke
A. G. Baldwin
Bernard J. Bamberger
W. E. Barnhart
John C. Bennett
John O. Biddle
Dwight Bradley
Harvie Branscomb
Charles R. Brown
Charles S. Brown
J. F. Burke
Vincent Burns
S. Parkes Cadman
Robert L. Calhoun
E. Fay Campbell
Edmund B. Chaffee
Elisabeth Christman
William F. Cochran
George A. Coe
George S. Counts
Albert F. Coyle
James R. Cox
Abraham Cronbach
Ethel M. Davis
Gardiner M. Day
William Horace Day
Sherwood Eddy
Robert B. Elsasser
A. R. Elliott
Phillips Elliott
Harold Fey
Charles W. Gilkey
James Gordon Gilkey
Elisabeth Gilman
William E. Gilroy
Israel Goldstein
Herbert D. Graets
Harold Gray
Ernest Graham Guthrie
Herman J. Hahn
Powers Hapgood
S. Ralph Harlow
Erdman Harris
Hornell Hart
A. A. Heist
Arthur E. Holt
John Hope
Walter M. Horton
Lawrence T. Hosie
Lynn Harold Hough
Allan A. Hunter
Paul Hutchinson
Cecelia I. Jeffrey
Paul Jones
Howard A. Kester
A. Roger Krats
Maynard C. Krueger
George S. Lackland
Halford E. Luccock
Alex Lyall
Louis L. Mann
J. B. Matthews
Oscar E. Maurer
Jacob Mirviss
Darwin J. Meserole
Herbert A. Miller
Ethelwyn Mills
H. W. Morgan
Charles Clayton Morrison
Claud Nelson
Richard Niebuhr
Kelly O'Neall
G. Bromley Oxnam
Kirby Page
William Pickens
Arthur Pound
Helen E. Price
F. J. Schlink
Clarence Shedd
Guy Emery Shipler
E. B. Shults
Tucker P. Smith
Edmund D. Soper
George Soule
T. Guthrie Speers
George Stewart
Alfred W. Swan
Ronald J. Tamblyn
Wellington H. Tinker
Ernest F. Tittle
Henry P. Van Dusen
H. J. Voorhis
John Warford
Wellman Warner
Luther A. Weigle
Robert Whitaker
Eliot White
Walter White
J. Stitt Wilson
L. Hollingsworth Wood
Winnifred Wygal

EXECUTIVE COMMITTEE
Herman A. Brautigam
P. H. Callahan
Allan K. Chalmers
Eleanor Copenhaver
Jerome Davis
Sidney Goldstein
William P. Hapgood
Hubert C. Herring
John Haynes Holmes
Edward L. Israel
Berton E. Kile
John A. Lapp
Douglas C. Macintosh
A. J. Muste
Reinhold Niebuhr
Frank Olmstead
A. Philip Randolph
Alva W. Taylor
Edward Thomas
Norman Thomas
Charles C. Webber
Stephen S. Wise

Office Secretary
Helen-Louise Porter

February 16, 1933.

Mr. John E. Waters,
Box 242,
Madison Wisconsin.

My dear Mr. Waters:

I regret that the Foundation is unable to help you carry forward the work you outline in your letter. We believe that the primary job today is one of achieving economic justice. We believe that this will require revolutionary changes in our social and economic order. Therefore, instead of attacking Soviet Russia , we are anxious to appreciate the contributions which it has made and, at the same time, build here in this section of the world an order that has all of the values of the one that is being created in the Soviet Union, without the sacrifice of other important values.

Very sincerely yours,

Francis A. Henson,
Economic Adviser.

Facsimile of letter significant of the pro-Soviet attitude of the National Religion and Labor Foundation. Letterhead contains names of officers, National Committee, etc.

Liberties Union crowd at work. Among members of the Nat. Save Our Schools Committee given out and released to the public in December 1928 are the following:"

Jane Addams, Prof. Wm. C. Bagley and Prof. Fred G. Bonsall (both of Teachers Coll. Columbia U.); Mrs. Mary C. Barker (then pres. of the radical Am. Fed. Tchrs.); Selma M. Borchardt; Prof. John Bremer of Harvard; Prof. Sterling G. Brinkley; A. S. Burrows of Seattle; Prof. Chas. Cooley (U. of Mich.); Prof. Geo. S. Counts; Prof. Wm. N. Connor; Mrs. Edw. P. Costigan; Mrs. Minnie Fisher Cunningham (New Waverly, Tex.); Jerome Davis; Edw. T. Devine; John Dewey; Paul H. Douglas; Prof. Edw. M. Earle (Columbia U.); Prof. Felix Frankfurter of Harvard; Wm. Floyd (editor of the radical "Arbitrator"); Eliz. Gilman; Mrs. J. Borden Harriman; Prof. Jos. K. Hart (U. of Wis.); Prof. Wm. E. Hocking of Harvard; Richard W. Hogue; Dean Chas. W. Hunt (Sch. of Edu., Cleveland); Jesse H. Holmes of Swarthmore; Mercer Green Johnson; Wm. H. Johnston ("former president of the Machinists' Union A.F. of L. and the man who stood in with the communist Otto Wangerin in trying to get up the 16 railroad brotherhoods"); Francis Fisher Kane; Edward Keating (editor of the radical paper "Labor"); Prof. Wm. Kilpatrick (Columbia U.); Prof. Wm. S. Knickerbocker (Univ. of the South, Sewanee); Mrs. Laura Underhill Kohn; John A. Lapp; Abraham Lefkowitz ("censored as a teacher in the N.Y. schools for his unpatriotic and untruthful utterances"); Henry R. Linville; Prof. Robt. Morss Lovett; Miss Amy Maher of Toledo; Basil Manly; Bishop Francis J. McConnell; Eliz. R. McCormick (Howe School, Superior, Wis.); Prof. Alex. Meikeljohn (U. of Wis.); Chas. Clayton Morrison; Prof. Josiah Morse (U. of S. Carolina); Prof. John R. Neal ("Neal Institute of Law and afterwards attorney for communists under the I.L.D. and A.C.L.U., who testified before the Fish Committee that exposed some of these people"); John J. Noonan; Prof. Herman Oliphant (Columbia U.); Prof. Ralph D. Owen (Temple U., Phila.); Evelyn Preston; Prof. John Herman Randall, Jr. (Columbia U.); W. T. Rawleigh (pres. of own company, Freeport, Ill.); Miss Florence Rood of St. Paul; Edw. A. Ross (U. of Wis.); Father John A. Ryan; Jos. H. Saunders (Supt. of Schools, Newport News, Va.); E. Schwartztrauber of Portland, Ore.; Prof. Edw. L. Sisson (Reed Coll., Portland, Ore.); Harry A. Slattery; Dr. Henry Lester Smith (U. of Indiana); Dr. Frederick Starr of Seattle; Prof. Alva W. Taylor (Vanderbilt U., Nashville); Dr. M. Carey Thomas (former pres. Bryn Mawr Coll.); Huston Thompson (former radical member of Federal Trade Commission); Oswald Garrison Villard; Frank P. Walsh; Henry A. Wallace (now Secretary of Agriculture); Wm. Allen White; Prof. Tyrell Williams (Law Sch., Washington U., St. Louis); Caroline S. Woodworth (prin. State Normal Sch., Castleton, Vt.); Mary E. Woolley.

NATIONAL STUDENT LEAGUE (AND STUDENT REVIEW)

N.S. Lg.

Communist High School and College student organization which, after getting under way early in 1932, spread like wildfire into about 150 schools and colleges, giving the L.I.D. strenuous competition; but like Communist and Socialist rival organizations everywhere these two co-operate in riot demonstrations, picketing, red student tours to agitate Kentucky miners, Mooney and Scottsboro agitations, red Hunger Marches, demonstrations in front of the Japanese consulates in Chicago and elsewhere "for the defense of the Chinese Soviets," in the Student World Congress Against War organized by the N.S. Lg., held at the U. of Chgo., etc., etc.; N.S. Lg. Students have been arrested in many places. Prof Donald Henderson, an organizer and its nat. exec. sec., when ousted from Columbia U., was tendered a riotous protest demonstration at which Rivera, Mexican Communist artist of Rockefeller "Radio City" fame, harangued the students. Henderson's wife, a Communist candidate, was arrested in a Negro red riot. The U. of Chgo. branch in 1933 published a paper called "Upsurge" at 1373 E. 57th St., near a Communist Party center located at 1505 Cable Court. U. of C. Profs. Robt. Morss Lovett and Fred L. Schuman are N.S. Lg. leaders (see "Who's Who") and the N.S. Lg. is a recognized U. of Chgo. student activity, defended by Pres. Hutchins (at Springfield Hearing May 1933) on the basis that Communism is allowed on the ballot of the State of Ill.; large N.S. Lg. mass meetings with Communist speakers and the N.S. Lg. Student Congress (see) are held in U. of Chgo. bldgs. The U. of Illinois branch, while not so powerful, has acquired a radical book shop, conducts forums, etc., the May 14, 1933, meeting being addressed at 109 Lincoln Hall by Jack Sher of the Communist I.L.D. The N.S. Lg. takes credit for strikes and demonstrations of thousands of Chicago school children; supported by the A.C.L.U., it fights any suppression of "academic freedom" for revolutionary Reds.

Its *Anti War Committees* have been formed in Crane Junior College, Northwestern U. (led by James M. Yard), and many other schools. The Northwestern branch shows Soviet movies and meets in Rev. Mondale's Unitarian Church, Mondale being on the nat. com. (see Intl., Am. and Chgo. Coms. for Struggle Against War).

The official organ is the "Student Review"; the staff and contributors are part of the Revolutionary Writers Federation; it agitates the whole revolutionary Communist program. Hdqts. 13 W. 17th St., N.Y.C.

Editorial bd.: Harry Magdoff, Herschel Pravdan, Nathaniel Weyl, Robt. Eastfield, Muriel Rukeyer, Mgr. Paul D. Lazare, and Ralph Glick.

Contrib. Editors: Sherwood Anderson; Jos. Budish (City Coll.); Gabriel Carritt (Oxford U.); Elliot Cohen; H. W. L. Dana; John Dos Passos; Theo. Draper (Brooklyn Coll.); Waldo Frank; Jos. Freeman; Leonard Gans (Wis. U.); Carl Geiser (Tenn. and Nash. Junior Colleges); A. Girschick (U.S.S.R. Correspondent); Michael Gold; Donald Henderson; Arthur S. Johnson (Wis. U.); Herbert Solow; Herbert Spence (Harvard U.); Edmund Stevens (Columbia U.); Geo. Perazick (U. of Cal.); Louise Preece (U. of Texas); James Rorty; Stanley Ryerson (Canadian correspondent).

In the Daily Worker, Sept. 28, 1932, a call was issued by the New Masses group begging financial support for the communist National Student League and praising its efforts. Signers of this call were listed as:

Sherwood Anderson, Newton Arvin, Roger Baldwin, Malcolm Cowley, H. W. L. Dana, Mark Van Doren, Theodore Dreiser, Max Eastman, Waldo Frank, Michael Gold, Oakley Johnson, Corliss Lamont, Scott Nearing, and John Dos Passos.

Contributions were directed to be sent to Nathan Solomon, treas. of the N.S. Lg., 13 W. 17th St., N.Y. City; hdqts. now 114 W. 14th St., N.Y. City.

NATIONAL TEXTILE WORKERS UNION

Communist T.U.U.L. Union; hdqts. M. Russak, 1755 Westminister St., Providence, R.I.

NATIONAL WOMEN'S TRADE UNION LEAGUE

Nat. Wom. Tr. Un. Lg.

An ultra radical A.F. of L. affiliate to which Mrs. F. D. Roosevelt announced that she donated her radio earnings and of which (according to a press report) she said she had been a member "for years." It is listed in the Lusk Report as "a Socialist organization favoring pacifism."

Whitney's "Reds in America" (p. 177) states that "In a document found at Bridgman at the time (1922) of the raid of the illegal convention of Communists was one on 'Work Among Women' in which it is set forth that: 'The interest of the working class demands the recruiting of women into the ranks of the proletariat fighting for communism.'" (Four categories of work were then defined.) "'The Woman's Trade Union League is at present jogging along. With the introduction of new blood it could be made a powerful weapon.'"

At any rate, the official reports of the Garland Fund, which I have, show that Communists Wm. Z. Foster, Scott Nearing, Benj. Gitlow (the first American Communist arrested during the war), Robt. W. Dunn, Eliz. Gurley Flynn (I.W.W.-Communist) and their fellow Fund directors (Norman Thomas, Harry Ward, Sidney Hillman, etc.) voted as a Board to donate to the "National Women's Trade Union League, Chicago, Ill.—April 11, 1923—for general budget for 1923, with special reference to training workers in the trade union movement, $2,500"; and (Report for year ending June 30, 1926) to the "National Women's Trade Union League, Chicago, Ill., $1,147.33" and to the "New York Women's Trade Union League, New York City—for salary of an organizer, $2,500"; and (Report for year ending June 30, 1927) to the "National Women's Trade Union League, Chicago—for educational work conditioned on raising an equal amount from trade union sources, $629." A notation also of $913 paid on conditional appropriations is listed on p. 8 of the 1924-5 report.

According to Whitney's "Reds in America," Mrs. Raymond Robins and Agnes Nestor, its executives, sponsored a parade for the release of "Big Bill" Haywood (who afterwards escaped to Russia), referred to by the Chicago Tribune at the time as an "anarchist parade." Its president, Rose Schneidermann (now a Roosevelt appointee to the NRA Labor Board) has resented, it is said, the nickname given her of "the Red Rose of Anarchy." She has a long record for radicalism.

According to the Am. Labor Year Book 1932, the Women's Trade Union League was aided by the Young People's Socialist League during the year; "The local units aided as usual in organization and strike activities"; conferences in Greensboro, N.C., Waukegan, Ill., Mt. Kisco, N.Y., on "Labor's Stake in Economic Planning" "included students and faculty members of colleges and high schools, government officials, social workers, members of unions, industrial workers, agricultural interests, housewives," etc.; the officers and executive board are:

Mrs. Raymond Robins, hon. pres.; Rose Schneiderman, pres.; Mathilda Lindsay, vice pres.; Eliz. Christman, sec.-treas.; Mary E. Dreier (sister of Mrs. Robins), Mary V. Halas, Irma Hochstein, Agnes Nestor, Ethel M. Smith, and Maud Schwartz.

The Progressive Labor World, Sept. 17, 1931 in an article headed "A Million Women Demand Arms Cuts" stated: "The Women's Trade Union League of N.Y. has started a campaign to get the signatures of at least 10,000 women on a petition for 'bold reduction of every variety of armament.' . . . The country-wide movement is under the auspices of the National Committee for the Cause and Cure of War which is headed by Carrie Chapman Catt. The Women's Trade Union League, an organization devoted to the interests of working women, has in its membership Mrs. Franklin D. Roosevelt, Mrs. Otto H. Kahn, Mrs. Ruth Baker Pratt, Mrs. Gerard Swope, Mrs. James Lees Laidlaw, Mrs. Frank Day Tuttle, Miss Lillian D. Wald, Mrs. Dwight W. Morrow, Mrs. Thos. W. Lamont, Mrs. Daniel O'Day, and other leaders who will aid in the circulation of the petition."

NATURE FRIENDS (NUDISTS)

Communist subsidiary; affiliated with communist Labor Sports Union; "organized in 21 countries with a world membership of 170,000 and 400 camps. The organization was founded in Vienna (1895) as a hiking club, but it has now widened its scope of activity to include workers' education and country camps. Most of the branches have music, photo and junior sections . . . in the United States it has 15 branches" (Am. Labor Year Book), with units in New York City, Brooklyn, Syracuse, Rochester, Newark, N.J., Paterson, Jersey City, Philadelphia, Allentown, Chicago, Milwaukee, Detroit, St. Louis, San Francisco, Oakland, Los Angeles, Cal., with camps at Midvale, N.J., Elka Park, Greene Co., N.Y., Boyerstown, Pa., Long Pond Road, Lima, N.Y., Crisman, Ind., Mill Valley, Cal., etc. Hdqts. N.E. District: 43 E. 84th St., N.Y.; Hdqts. West Coast: 143 Albion St., San Francisco.

NEEDLE TRADES WORKERS INDUSTRIAL UNION

Communist T.U.U.L. union; its fur section alone claims 11,400 members; leader of strikes in Chicago, N.Y. City, Bridgeport, Conn., Gloversville, N.Y., etc., in Sept. 1933; hdqts., Ben Gold, 131 W. 28th St., N.Y. City.

NEW DANCE GROUP

Communist; organized in N.Y.C., Feb. 26, 1932; "have worked hard at a repertoire of revolutionary dances and are now planning to present a whole program of them on their first anniversary at the Hecksher Theatre, N.Y.C., Sunday, Mar. 12, 1933. . . . Membership includes about 300 comrades—They have large sections of workers who meet to dance and talk every evening." ("Workers Theatre," Mar. 1933.)

NEW FRONTIER

Organ of Chicago Workers Committee on Unemployment (see).

NEW LEADER

Official Socialist Party organ.

NEW MASSES

A very revolutionary Communist monthly magazine owned and operated by the Garland Fund (American Fund for Public Service) directors of which (1933) are: Roger Baldwin, Robt. W. Dunn, Morris L. Ernst, Lewis S. Gannett, Benj. Gitlow, Clinton S. Golden, James Weldon Johnson, Freda Kirchwey, Clarina Michelson, and Norman Thomas. It started in 1910 as "The Masses," changed name to "New Masses," 1926; the Sept. 1931 issue announced: "After Sept. 3 the New Masses will be located at 63 West 15th Street, New York City. We leave a historic location, since our old address was also the address of the old Masses as far back as 1911. We go now to what we believe will be another historic location; the first American Revolutionary Center, in which we join hands with the John Reed Club of New York (with an Art gallery and Art School) and the new Workers Cultural Federation. We invite our readers to visit us at our new headquarters."

Editorial bd.: Robert Evans, Whittaker Chambers, Hugo Gellert, Michael Gold, Louis Lozowick, Moissaye J. Olgin; contributors: Phil Bard, Emjo Basshe, Jacob Burck, Whittaker Chambers, Robert Cruden, Jack Conroy, Adolph Dehn, Robert Dunn, John Dos Passos, Kenneth Fearing, Ed. Falkowski, Hugo Gellert, Eugene Gordon, Horace Gregory, Wm. Gropper, Chas. Yale Harrison, Wm. Hernandez, Langston Hughes, Jos. Kalar, I. Klein, Melvin P. Levy, Louis Lozowick, H. H. Lewis, Norman Macleod, A. B. Magil, Scott Nearing, Myra Page, Harry Alan Potamkin, Paul Peters, Walter Quirt, Louis Ribak, Anna Rochester, E. Merrill Root, James Rorty, Martin Russak, Esther Shemitz, Wm. Siegel, Upton Sinclair, Agnes Smedley, Otto Soglow, Herman Spector, Bennett Stevens, Joseph Vogel, Mary H. Vorse, Keene Wallis, Jim Waters, Art Young.

Becomes a weekly with an increased staff 1934.

"NEW REPUBLIC"

Weekly magazine; "advocate of revolutionary socialism" (Lusk Report); pres. Bruce Bliven; editors: Bruce Bliven, Malcolm Cowley, R. M. Lovett, Stark, Young; contrib. eds.: H. N. Brailsford, John Dewey, John T. Flynn, Waldo Frank, E. C. Lindeman, Lewis Mumford, Gilbert Seldes, Rex. G. Tugwell, and Leo Wolman; 421 W. 21st St., N.Y.C.

NEW SCHOOL FOR SOCIAL RESEARCH

Was "established by men who belong to the ranks of near-Bolshevik Intelligentsia, some of them being too radical in their views to remain on the faculty of Columbia U." (Lusk Report p. 1121); research institution fostering communistic-socialistic doctrines; instructors for 1932: Communist Moissaye J. Olgin, Sidney Hook, Horace M. Kallen, Harry Elmer Barnes, Mrs. Henry Goddard Leach (Agnes Brown

Leach), Harry A. Overstreet, Leo Wolman and Henry Cowell; 66 W. 12th St., N.Y. City.

NEW WORKERS SCHOOL

Of the Communist Party (Opposition); 1933 was being decorated by artist Diego Rivera; faculty includes: Benj. Gitlow, Jay Lovestone, Will Herzberg, Herbert Zam, Bertram Wolfe (director). Am. Lab. Year Book states it reported 410 students for 1931-2 and "arranged debates between Bertrand Russell and Jay Lovestone on 'Proletarian Dictatorship' and between Rev. Edmund B. Chaffee and Bertram Wolfe on 'Religion and Labor'"; organized 1929. Hdqts. 51 West 14th St., N.Y.C. (were 228 Second Ave.); branches in Philadelphia, Paterson, Passaic, etc.

NEW YORK SUITCASE THEATRE

Communist; organized by Workers Cultural Federation in 1931 at 63 W. 15th St., "to create a group of proficient actors who will travel with a minimum equipment and a repertory of working-class plays to be given before labor organizations"; its directors are Paul Peters, Whittaker Chambers, Langston Hughes and Jacob Burck.

NON-INTERVENTION CITIZENS COMMITTEE

Said Marvin (Daily Data Sheets 28-4 and 5, March 9, 1927): "The 'center' organization in the city of New York engaged in propaganda against the United States and in favor of the Socialist-Communist scheme to Sovietize Mexico and all Central American States is easily located in what is called the Non-Intervention Citizens Committee. Through the members of this committee the work ramifies into more than one hundred organizations some of them openly Socialistic and Communistic, while others are legitimate enough but appear to be in the hands of clever Adepts. . . . Those dominating and controlling as will be shown are Socialists or Communists. As such they believe our entire system is wrong and should be destroyed. They hold to the theory that any form of nationalism backed up by any form of patriotism should be destroyed. . . . The inspiration for this organization came from Moscow, via Mexico. Its object is to aid Moscow in Mexico. Because of its nature and purposes one is forced to ask the question: Who is doing the financing for the nation-wide propaganda scheme now being carried on in the interests of Mexico and its Socialist-Communist controlled bodies and against the foreign policies of the United States? . . . In the center or 'controlling group' of the Non-Intervention Citizens Committee we place the following: Jos. Schlossberg, B. C. Vladeck, Max Zuckerman, Rose Schneidermann, Stephen S. Wise, A. I. Shiplacoff, Oswald Garrison Villard, Fannia May Cohn, Lillian Wald, Morris Hillquit, A. J. Muste, A. Castro, Robt. Dunn, Louis Budenz, L. Hollingsworth Wood, August Claessens, Norman Thomas, John Nevin Sayre, Max Danish, S. E. Beardsley, J. Lieberman, John Haynes Holmes, Abraham Beckerman, Morris Ernst, J. M. Budish, Paul U. Kellogg. Here we have the dominating controlling and directing forces—26 out of the total of 75 names presented as making up the entire Nat. Citizens Committee.

"While we have not placed them as a part of the 'real center' of the Non-Intervention Citizens Committee there are a number on the general committee who are exceptionally active in working with one or more of the organizations . . . guided . . . by the true 'center.' We will not go into the connections of the others except to say that all have been more or less connected unto the pacifist movement in the United States" (Data Sheet 28-8).

Chmn., John Howard Melish; sec., Eleanor Brannon (N.Y. sec. W.I.L.P.F.); exec. com.: Fannia May Cohn (Intl. Ladies Garm. Wkrs. Un); Paul U. Kellogg (ed. Survey); Miss Gordon Norries (N.Y. Council for Intl. Cooperation to Prevent War); Mrs. Egerton Parsons (Am. Assn. Univ. Women); John Nevin Sayre (sec. Fell. Recon.); Norman Thomas (exec. sec. L.I.D., Socialist leader). Members: Ruth Morgan (Lg. Women Voters); *Mrs. Franklin D. Roosevelt* (vice chmn., N.Y. Womens Democratic State Committee); Lillian D. Wald (head of Henry St. Settlement, etc.); Mrs. Francis O. Affeld, Jr. (Am. Assn. Univ. Women); Mrs. Chas. Niel Edge; Mrs. Chas. R. Henderson; Mrs. Frank D. Tuttle; Mrs. F. Louis Slade of the Y.W.C.A.; Mrs. John Lewis Childs (chmn. Com. on Latin Relations of N.Y. State Fed. Womens Clubs); Mrs. John Ferguson (pres. Council of Women for Home Missions); Mrs. E. H. Silverthorn (Womens Board of Foreign Missions); Evelyn Preston; Mrs. Harriet B. Laidlaw; "Professors": James T. Shotwell, Edw. M. Earle, Le Roy Bowman (all of Columbia Univ.); "Business men": Raymond Fosdick, Harold A. Hatch, L. Hollingsworth Wood, George La Monte, Geo. Foster Peabody, Morris Ernst, Gould Harold; "Labor Leaders": Jos. Schlossberg, Adolph Held, B. C. Vladeck, A. J. Muste, S. E. Beardsley, Max Zuckerman, A. Castro, J. Liebermann, Morris Hillquit, Max Danish, August Claessens, Abraham Beckerman, A. I. Shiplacoff, J. M. Budish, Rose Schneidermann; "Writers": Kirby Page, Wm. Floyd, Rev. Halford E. Luccock, Rev. Isaac Landman, Guy Emery Shipler, Fleming H. Revell, Robt. W. Dunn, Edward Levinson, S. A. Dewitt, Margaret Shipman, Oswald Garrison Villard, Louis Budenz; "Clergy": Rev. Henry Sloane Coffin (pres. Union Theol. Sem.), Samuel M. Cavert (gen. sec. Fed. Coun. Chs.), S. Parkes Cadman (pres. Fed. Coun. Chs.), Samuel Guy Inman (of Nat. Citiz. Com. on Relations with Latin Am.), Karl Reiland, Ralph W. Sockman, W. Russell Bowie, John Haynes Holmes, John H. Lathrop, Rabbi Alexander Lyons, John W. Langdale, A. Lane Miller, S. M. Shoemaker, Henry Evertson Cobb, T. Guthrie Speers, Finis S. Idleman, W. T. Crocker, Minot Simons (pastor All Souls Unitarian Ch.), Felix Adler (pres. Ethical Culture Society), Rabbi Stephen S. Wise.

NON-PARTISAN COMMITTEE FOR LILLIAN HERSTEIN

Formed to aid the campaign of Lillian Herstein (See "Who's Who") as candidate in the 1932 election on the Farmer-Labor (Socialist) ticket. According to a letter to the Chicago Evening Post of Sept. 15, 1932 by Prof. Arthur E. Holt, 7800 signatures were obtained on a petition to have Lillian Herstein's name placed on the ballot and among the so-called "Civic Leaders" supporting her candidacy named by Holt were:

Anton J. Carlson (U. of C.); Edith Abbot, Sophonisba Breckenridge, Rev. W. R. Boddy, Mollie Ray Carroll, Dr. H. W. Cheney, Mr. and Mrs. Paul Douglas, Mrs. James A. Field, Mr. and Mrs. A. L. Foster, Mrs. Chas. W. Gilkey, Harry D. Gideonse, Anton Johannsen, A. Eustace Haydon, Rev. Douglas Horton, Rev. Blaine Kirkpatrick, Dr. John A. Lapp, Mary McDowell, Dr. Louis L. Mann, H. A. Millis, James Mullenbach, Letitia R. Myles, Mr. and Mrs. W. A. Roberts, S. D. Schwartz, Lorado Taft (father-in-law of Paul Douglas) and Rev. Norris L. Tibbetts.

NON-PARTISAN LEAGUE

"This was purely a Socialist movement, organized, directed and dominated, at all times, by those who had been prominent in the Socialist Party" (Marvin Data Sheet 81-27).

O

OFFICE WORKERS UNION

Communist T.U.U.L. union; hdqts. 799 Broadway, N.Y. City; its official organ "Office Worker" announced (Feb. 1933 issue): "O.W.U. meets every 2nd and 4th Thurs., 7 P.M., at Labor Temple, 14th St. and 2nd Ave., N.Y.C." (of Presbyterian Church). A Chicago branch was formed in the Kimball Bldg., Room 1430, on Aug. 18, 1933. Clyde Jenkins (alias Wade D. Rogers) the Chgo. exec. sec. has been arrested and his membership records seized by the police, 1934.

OPEN ROAD

Affiliate of communist Intourist (Soviet Govt. travel agency) and V.O.K.S. (see A.S.C.R.R., its Communist - subsidiary American branch); a propaganda travel bureau "primarily concerned with what happens to the traveler emotionally and intellectually . . . the first travel bureau to establish independent representation in the Soviet Union and has been the only one to maintain it constantly since," says its 1933 booklet; organizes summer schools abroad for American university students; arranges for travelers to meet the "right" Soviet representatives; I.S.H.A. or International Student Hospitality Association is its European collaborator; Carleton Washburne's praise of its I.S.H.A. guides, and Elmer Rice's and Louis Fischer's endorsement of its Russian service are printed in the 1933 booklet, which lists as its "American Advisory Committee":

Wm. Allan Neilson, chmn. (pres of A.S.C.R.R., the Communist-subsidiary, and of Smith College); Stephen P. Duggan and John Dewey (A.S.C.R.R. officers); Mary E. Woolley (pres. Mt. Holyoke Coll.); Glenn Frank (pres. U. of Wis.); Arthur E. Morgan (pres. Antioch Coll., Yellow Springs, O., birthplace of Lg. for Org. of Progress); Aurelia H. Reinhardt (pres. Mills Coll.); Henry Noble MacCracken (pres. Vassar Coll.); Ada L. Comstock (pres. Radcliffe Coll.); Lotus D. Coffmann (pres. U. of Minn.); Donald J. Cowling (pres. Carleton Coll., Minn. and member of 1928 delg. to Russia); Livingstone Farrand (pres. Cornell Coll.); Harry A. Garfield (pres. Williams Coll.); Meta Glass (pres. Sweet Briar Coll.); Hamilton Holt (pres. Rollins Coll., pacifist); Kerr D. Macmillan (pres. Wells Coll., N.Y.); Marion Edwards Park (pres. Bryn Mawr Coll.); Ellen F. Pendelton (pres. Wellesley Coll.); David Allan Robertson (pres. Goucher Coll.); Ray Lyman Wilbur; Harry D. Gideonse; etc. Eliot Pratt (A.C.L.U.) and Frederic V. Field (bd. dir. L.I.D., etc.) are members of the board of directors. Other officers and directors are: Sherman Pratt, pres.; Frank R. Pentlarge, vice pres.; Anita L. Pollitzer, sec.; Chas. Denby, Jr., treas.; John Rothschild, Jos. Barnes, Helen Everett, Raymond V. Ingersoll, Francis T. P. Plimpton, Robt. Proctor, and Mrs. Arthur G. Rotch, directors.

Among 1933 "Open Road" Russian tour conductors were:

Karl Borders; Colston E. Warne for L.I.D. tour (Amherst Coll. prof.); Lucy Textor (Vassar prof. and member John Dewey's 1928 delegation); Lord Marley of the red Ind. Lab. Party, who was barred from Japan; Edith Osbourne, W.I.L.P.F. tour; Maxwell Stewart, Foreign Policy Assn. economist, and his wife, "both former residents in Russia as teachers at Moscow Institute"; John Rothschild, director of Open Road; etc., etc.

Hdqts. 56 W. 45th St., N.Y. City.

P

PACKING HOUSE WORKERS INDUSTRIAL UNION

Communist T.U.U.L. union; M. Karson, Communist organizer at St. Paul and Mpls., reports, for example, that there are now 850 packing house workers organized in it there and that an independent union has been organized at Austin, Minn., by the Communists.

PAINTERS INDUSTRIAL UNION

Communist T.U.U.L. union.

PAN PACIFIC TRADE UNION SECRETARIAT

Oriental counterpart of the American Communist T.U.U.L.; for the organization and spread of Communist labor groups in the Orient; Hdqts. Shanghai, China. When Walter Noullens Ruegg, its sec., was arrested by the Chinese Govt. in 1932 charged with sedition, "a sharp protest was made by hundreds of Socialists and Liberals, including Prof. Albert Einstein and Senator Borah. . . . Shortly before the arrest, the Pan Pacific Trade Union Secretariat had issued denunciations of French rule in Indo-China and American imperialism in the Philippines" (Am. Lab. Year Book 1932).

"*Organization Conference*—With the backing of the trade union federations of New South Wales, China, France, and the Soviet Union, all affiliated with the Red International of Labor Unions, and the minority left wing movements in the United States, Great Britain, Java, Japan, Korea, and elsewhere, a conference was held in Hankow, China, May 19-26, 1927, and the Pan Pacific Trade Union Secretariat was established. An executive meeting followed in Shanghai, in February, 1928. Due to the refusal of Prime Minister Bruce to permit the meeting to be held in Australia, the next conference will take place in Vladivostok, Russia, starting August 1, 1929. After a sharp debate, the Australian trade union council voted at its last convention to continue affiliation.

"At the first organization conference in Hankow resolutions were adopted to maintain a struggle against the dangers of war in the Pacific, to oppose the imperialists in China, to demand self-determination for the peoples of the Pacific, to demand the removal of racial and national prejudices, and to promote international trade union unity."

(Am. Lab. Year Book 1929, p. 239.)

PAPER BAG WORKERS INDUSTRIAL UNION

Communist T.U.U.L. union.

PAXTON HIBBEN MEMORIAL HOSPITAL FUND

"To do honor to the Communist Paxton Hibben whose remains were taken by the Communists to Russia for burial" (Francis Ralston Welsh). Photo of Paxton Hibben decorating grave of John Reed in Moscow appears in Whitney's "Reds in America."

PEACE PATRIOTS

Radical A.C.L.U. - controlled "peace" society. According to its pamphlet "War Resistance" (by Wm. Floyd, its director; price 20c), which was distributed at the communist Student Congress Against War (see), the Peace Patriots' program (to quote): "includes the following activities: 1. Requesting universal total disarmament as the chief aim of the conference to be held in Geneva in Feb. 1932. 2. Encouraging membership in the War Resisters League or Fellowship of Reconciliation, repeating the request already made to President Hoover for recognition of exemptive status for their members in the next war. 3. Distributing '2 per cent' buttons to symbolize Einstein's idea that if 2 per cent of the people will not fight, governments will not declare war (6 buttons for 25 cents, 100 for $1.50, 500 for $6.00). There are no dues. Office expenses have been provided. . . . American men and women may join by signing the following declaration—Membership Declaration of Peace Patriots: Since our government has pledged itself never to resort to war for the solution of international controversies and has agreed to settle all disputes by pacific means, we express our loyalty to this principle by opposing all preparation for war. We condemn military training and conscription and demand universal disarmament."

Ironically enough, after Germany went anti-communist and anti-Einstein, Einstein urged preparations for war against Germany (in Patrie Humaine, a newspaper, in the form of a letter to Alfred Nahon, Belgian "war resister," reprinted in Chicago Tribune, Sept. 10, 1933), saying:

"There is in the center of Europe a state, Germany, which is publicly preparing for war by all means. In these conditions the Latin countries, above all France and Belgium are in great danger and *can only count on their preparedness*. . . . Imagine Belgium occupied by present-day Germany! It would undoubtedly be worse than 1914. . . . That is why I am telling you in the most direct fashion that if I were a Belgian *I would not refuse to do military service under the present circumstances,* but on the contrary I would accept it in full conscience with the feeling that I was contributing to save European civilization. This does not mean I am renouncing my former opinion. I desire nothing more than to see the moment return when refusal to do military service could be the means of an efficacious fight for the progress of humanity."

Listed "Peace Patriot Sponsors" are:

Roger N. Baldwin, Norman B. Barr, Edwin L. Clarke, Marguerite W. Clarke, Sarah N. Cleghorn, Mary Ware Dennett, Babette Deutsch, Kate Crane Gartz, C. H. Hamlin, Hornell Hart, Jesse H. Holmes, Paul Jones, Alfred Lief, Edwin D. Meade, Lucia Ames Meade, Henry Neumann, Kirby Page, Orville S. Poland, John Nevin Sayre, Vida D. Scudder, Geo. H. Spencer, Sidney Strong (father of Communist Anna Louise), Margaret Loring Thomas, Goodwin Watson, Eliot White, and Wm. Floyd (director).

Hdqts. 114 East 31st St., N.Y. City.

PEN AND HAMMER

Communist clubs; 114 W. 21st St., N.Y. City; Detroit Pen & Hammer Forum, 111 Forest West; etc.; section of Revolutionary

Writers Federation; Chicago club meets in Kimball Bldg.

PENNSYLVANIA COMMITTEE FOR TOTAL DISARMAMENT

Pa. Com. for Total Disarm.

A supporting organization of the communist-organized U.S. Congress Against War; affiliate of the Green International. Its letterhead slogan is: "Work for a Constitutional Amendment to make war and *preparedness* for war illegal for the United States." Its letter-questionnaire sent out to statesmen, Mar. 21, 1932, questioning their position on U.S. national defense states that the Pa. Com. for Total Disarm. "was formed two years ago to work for total world disarmament by *example* or by international agreement." Listed on this letterhead are the following:

Chmn., Wm. I. Hull, Swarthmore; assoc. chairman, Wm. Eves, 3rd (George School); vice chairmen: David W. Amram, Feasterville; Henry J. Cadbury, Haverford; Mrs. Walter Cope, Phila.; Rev. Wm. H. Fineshreiber, Phila.; Walter W. Haviland, Lansdowne; Leslie P. Hill, Cheyney; Jesse H. Holmes, Swarthmore; Darlington Hoopes, Reading; Maynard C. Krueger, Phila. (now U. of Chgo. Prof.); Mrs. Helen Martin, Harrisburg; Rev. Jos. Paul Morres, Ardmore; Vincent D. Nicholson, Phila.; Andrew G. Smith, Pitts.; Agnes L. Tierney, Phila.; Nathan P. Walton, New Garden; legislative chairman: Mary Winsor, Haverford; sec., Mrs. Stanley Carnell, Phila.; treas., Edw. N. Wright, Moylan; exec. sec., Sophia H. Dulles, Phila.; Council: John H. Arnett, M.D., Phila.; M. Georgina Biddle, Phila.; Andrew J. Biemiller, Phila.; E. Lewis Burnham, Berwyn; Mr. and Mrs. Henry H. Collins, 3rd, Phila.; Helen Crawley, Pitts.; Emily Dawson, Phila.; Rev. John M. De Chant, Phila.; Dorothea De Schweinitz, Phila.; Herbert W. Fitzroy, Jr., Phila.; Alex. Fleisher, Churchville; Mrs. John F. Folinsbee, New Hope; Mary K. Gibson, Wynnewood; Jessie Gray, Phila.; Allan G. Harper, Harrisburg; Wm. B. Harvey, West Town; Walter W. Hyde, Phila.; Mrs. E. E. Kiernan, Phila.; Mrs. Philip Kind, Jenkintown; Mrs. Spencer King, Pitts.; Rev. Paul S. Leinbach, Phila.; Mr. and Mrs. Simon Libros, Cynwyd; Ada F. Liveright, Phila.; Eliz. G. Marot, Phila.; Mary T. Mason, Phila.; Raymond E. Maxwell, Greensburg; Mrs. Mildred S. Olmstead, Moylan; Anna M. W. Pennypacker, Phila.; Clarence E. Pickett, Phila.; Edw. C. M. Richards, Pottsville; Florence L. Sansville, West Town; Arthur Shrigley, Lansdowne; Mrs. Samuel A. Shuman, Phila.; D. Owen Stevens, Pitts.; C. Seymour Thompson, Morton; Geo. L. Townsend, Pitts.; Geo. T. Underwood, Clearfield; Ernest N. Votaw, Media; J. Barnard Walton, Swarthmore; Rev. Ben F. Wilson, Erie; Chas. E. Wright, Dusquesne; Mrs. Sue C. Yerkes, Lansdowne.

PEOPLE'S COLLEGE

The "Yours for the Revolution" college in which Carl D. Thompson of the Public Ownership League of America played an active part. Six Socialists associated with him in this venture became affiliated with the Non-Partisan League (Geo. D. Brewer, Marion Wharton, Kate Richards O'Hare, Chas. Edw. Russell, John M. Work, Arthur Le Sueur). "The Peoples College—Fort Scott, Kansas, J. I. Sheppard, President—Eugene V. Debs, Chancellor—Arthur Le Sueur, Vice President—'To remain ignorant is to remain a slave' " was printed on the letterhead of a letter dated Jan. 12, 1916, addressed to Timothy Woodham, Fairdale, No. Dakota, which said:

"Dear Comrade: Answering yours of the 7th instant will say that we will hold all lessons and material until we hear from you again with another address. You are making first class work with the law study, and if you have the nerve to stick through with it I feel that you will strike many a valiant blow to the damned old capitalist system that makes it necessary for a man to worry about becoming unvagranted. At any rate, Comrade, you can rest assured now and for all time, that we are *Yours for the Revolution,* (signed) Arthur L. Le Sueur, Vice President."

The International Socialist Review, May 1915, advertising it, said:

"Study law in your own school and save money. We offer all that the capitalist schools offer you and something else they canot give. . . . Remember the Peoples College is the only school in the world owned and controlled by the working class. . . . On its controlling board are Caroline A. Lowe, George D. Brewer, Charles P. Steinmetz, Duncan P. McDonald, George Allen England, George R. Kirkpatrick, J. Stitt Wilson, John M. Work, Marion Wharton, Carl D. Thompson."

PEOPLE'S COUNCIL OF AMERICA

People's Coun.

According to its own literature and the Lusk Report, it was " 'modeled after the Council of Workmen's and Soldiers' Councils, the sovereign power of Russia today,' " whose "Proclamation to the People of the Whole World" appealing for Red revolution everywhere and saying "Proletarians of all countries unite! . . . Long live the international solidarity of the proletariat and its struggle for final victory" signed by the "Petrograd Council of Workers and Soldiers Deputies" was reprinted and widely distributed in the People's Council Bulletin of Aug. 17, 1917 with the note: "The original copy of this bulletin was smuggled over to this country." The Lusk Report says: "We have in Lochner's running footnotes in the People's Council Bulletin of Aug. 7, 1917 'proof of the altogether socialistic cooperation of these People's Councillors as well as a forecast of the Bolshevist revolution of Nov. 1917' "; a telegram sent March 3, 1918, signed by Lochner, Scott Nearing and James Maurer, to the "People's Commissars at Petrograd" said: "People's Council of America for democratic peace representing 300 radical groups in 42 states has consistently stood for Russian formula of no annexations, no indemnities, and self determination. We urge you to make no other terms."

"By 1917," says the Lusk Report, "the old peace strategy having worn rather thin, Lochner and his followers came more and more into the open with their revolutionary Socialism." People's Councils were formed all over the U.S. aided openly by the committee (Lola M. Lloyd, Carl Haessler, etc.), and quietly through private cooperation by Jane Addams (who recommended Norman Thomas, Rabbi Magnus for certain posts, etc.), and with Max Eastman, James H. Maurer, I.W.W.'s, and other radical speakers, holding mass meetings extensively, at which the Russian system was extolled and the American denounced. The U.S. was then at war. It is no wonder that Roger Baldwin became a little uneasy and advised typical Red camouflage in his letter of Aug. 21, 1917 to Lochner, saying: "1. Do steer away from making it look like a Socialist enterprise. Too many people have already gotten the idea that it is nine-tenths a Socialist movement. 2. Do get into the movement just as strong as possible the leaders in labor circles . . . not the radical Socialists. . . . Also bring to the front the farmers. . . . 3. I think it is an error to get the public thinking we are launching a political party at Minneapolis. To be sure we are launching a political movement but that is quite another matter from a political point. It is a mistake already to have tied up with the name of Mr. LaFollette fine as he is. . . . 4. We want to look like patriots in everything we do. We want to get a lot of good flags, talk a good deal about the Constitution and what our forefathers wanted to make of this country, and to show we are the folks that really stand for the spirit of our institutions." Lochner, answering (Aug. 24, 1917), agreed to all four points even to "I agree with you that we should keep proclaiming our loyalty and patriotism. I will see to it we have flags and similar paraphernalia."

When it was expected that anarchists Emma Goldman and Alex Berkman would be elected to the Council's Assembly (Morris Hillquit was their attorney), Lochner, from Minneapolis hdqts., wrote the People's Council's N.Y. hdqts.: "As for Berkman and Goldman, I do hope they will not be elected. Here people are awfully stirred up about the I.W.W. . . . but if in addition we have those two splendid fighters for liberty with us that may be too big a burden to carry. . . . Personally I have only the highest regard for the two." However, public opinion arose to such a pitch that Gov. Burnquist of Minnesota barred the People's Council from holding a meeting in that state because, if held, it might "result in bloodshed, rioting and loss of life" and could "have no other effect than that of aiding and abetting the enemies of this country." They held a convention in Chicago, Sept. 2, 1917, but were finally dispersed by order of the Gov. of Illinois.

A "Justice to Russia" bulletin (which I have seen) tells of a People's Council mass meeting addressed by John Haynes Holmes and others which passed the following resolution: "This mass meeting of citizens assembled in the Madison Square Garden this 25th day of May, 1919, congratulates the people of Russia upon having thus far maintained a successful revolution against the powers of reaction in the face of terrific obstacles interposed from within and without and sends greetings of sympathy and solidarity to the people of Russia and to the Federated Soviet Republics," etc. (It demanded: lifting the Russian blocade; that troops be recalled; that the American Govt. refuse to recognize counter revolution, etc.). Published by Peoples Print, 138 W. 13th St., N.Y.C.

Among names listed on the organizing committee of the People's Council we find:

Emily Greene Balch, Jos. D. Cannon, H. W. L. Dana, Eugene V. Debs, Mary Ware Dennett, Crystal and Max Eastman, Edmund C. Evans of Single Tax Society, P. Geliebter of Workmen's Circle, Morris Hillquit, Bishop Paul Jones, Algernon Lee, Rabbi Judah L. Magnes, James H. Maurer, Rev. Howard Melish, Scott Nearing, James O'Neal, Jacob Panken, Benj. Schlesinger, Jos. Schlossberg, Rose Schneidermann, Sidney Strong of Seattle, Mrs. Wm. I. Thomas (sec. Womens Peace Party, Chgo.), Irwin St. John Tucker, John D. Works (former U.S. Sen.), etc., etc. Officers: Louis Lochner, exec. sec.; Lella Fay Secor, org. sec.; Rebecca Shelley, finan. sec.; Eliz. Freeman, legislative; Wm. E. Williams, publicity; David Starr Jordan, treas.; etc., etc.

Jordan was paid by the Council for his activities, according to Lusk Report evidence, which also prints letters he wrote to Lochner of his work with "statesmen" in Washington, D.C., which he called his "Courses of instruction" and "university extension for statesmen," naming as his "pupils":

" 'Senators LaFollette, Norris, Johnson, Borah, Vardaman, Gronna, Smoot, Curtis, New. Representatives Kitchen, Huddleston, Crosser, Hilliard, Dill, Gordon, Little, Rankin, Randall, Dillon, Cooper (Wis.), Cooper (W. Va.), Bowers, Crampton, Mondell, Frear, Woods (Ia.), Lundeen, La Follette (an excellent man), Sisson, Slayden, Ragsdale, Mason, London. . . . ' ".

PEOPLE'S FREEDOM UNION

The 1920 successor of the infamous People's Council; cooperated with and occupied same premises with A.C.L.U. at 138 W. 13th St., N.Y. City. "The curious combination of so-called liberals, educators, writers, anarchists and revolutionary socialists, who bend their energies toward controlling public opinion through the medium of this association, is revealed by the following list of officers of the union and the members of the committee which is known as the Free Political Prisoners Committee. . . . it was this organization that sponsored a rather melodramatic demonstration on Christmas Day, parading on Fifth Ave., in N.Y. city, in single file, with touching banners, for the purpose of arousing sympathy for so-called political prisoners."

"John Lovejoy Elliott, chmn.; Arthur S. Leeds, treas.; Frances Witherspoon, exec. sec. Committee Members: Tracy D. Mygatt, sec.; Pauline Cahn, Evans Clark, Joe Coffin, Stella Daljord, Lottie Fishbein, Anna Fite Peck, M. E. Fitzgerald, Eliz. Gurley Flynn, Paul Furnas, Lewis Gannett, Gratia Goller, Ruth Gordon, Alfred Hayes, Helen Holman, Wilfred Humphries, Virginia Hyde, Harry W. Laidler, Gertrude U. Light, Winthrop D. Lane, Florence Lattimore, Alice E. Mauran, Therese Mayer, Donald McGraw, Leland Olds, Ida Rauh, Florence Rauh, Merrill Rogers, Jessica Smith, Evan Thomas, Norman Thomas, Pauline H. Turkel, Albert Rhys Williams, Jacob and Jules Wortsman." (Lusk Report, p. 1110.)

PEOPLE'S LEGISLATIVE SERVICE

A radical lobby supplying "facts and figures" to radicals in Congress, and promoting socialistic legislation for nationalization of all public utilities; closely affiliated with the Public Ownership League, National Popular Government League, League for Industrial Democracy, and Socialist Party; made a special drive for socialization of Muscle Shoals and Boulder Dam projects; organized Dec. 17, 1920, under the leadership of Robt. M. LaFollette, Socialists Basil Manly and Wm. H. Johnston; it called (Feb. 20-22, 1922) the Conference for Progressive Political Action (see) to "steal" party nominations and elections for radical candidates; Basil Manly, director, in the Sept. 1927 bulletin, under the heading "A Program for Progressives," in a call for unity of radical elements "to double or treble their forces in the next congress," said: "The nation-wide publicity devoted to the informal conferences which a few of the Progressive Senators held in Washington is a clear cut recognition of the power which the Progressives can wield during the coming year. . . . they can effectively control the course of legislation in the Senate. . . . with such a block to build upon it will then be time to consider how best to mobilize the voters so as to have a real voice in the election of a president in 1932." Manly has now been rewarded by appointment by Pres. Roosevelt as chairman of the Federal Power Commission, which controls the Muscle Shoals project, etc. and has broad powers affecting the public utility industry (and its "progress" toward socialization).

According to Robt. M. LaFollette's account (in June 1921, United Farmers Forum), it was organized with a legislative division, to keep watch of all pending legislation; a statistical division, to compile information for use of radical legislators; and a publicity division "To keep the people informed regarding pending legislation." On the first National Council which was then set up to direct the lobbying activities of the People's Legislative Service the following names, among others, appear:

Director, Basil M. Manly; chmn. exec. com., Robt. M. LaFollette; Wm. H. Johnston, sec.-treas.; nat. coun. members: Geo. W. Norris, David I. Walsh, Chas. F. Amidon (U.S. Dist. Ct.), J. F. Sinclair (mem. Congress), Jane Addams, Harriet Stanton Blatch, Wm. Bouck, Smith W. Brookhart, Mrs. Edw. P. Costigan (of Nat. Lg. Women Voters, wife of Colorado Sen.), Herbert Croly (ed. New Republic), Eliz. Glendower Evans, E. H. Fitzgerald (Broth. R. R. & Steamship Clerks), Rev. John Haynes Holmes, Frederic C. Howe (Roosevelt appointee), Florence Kelley, W. Jett Lauck, Owen R. Lovejoy, Prof. E. A. Ross of Madison, Wis., Robert Morss Lovett, James H. McGill of Valparaiso, Ind., Rabbi Judah L. Magnes, Anne Martin of Reno, Nev., J. P. Noonan, Jackson H. Ralston, Donald R. Richberg, Rev. John A. Ryan, John F. Sinclair, Prof. Thorstein Veblen, Oswald Garrison Villard, Frank P. Walsh, Wash., D.C., etc.

Publishes the "People's Business," edited by Basil Manly. Hdqts. 212 First St., Southeast, Washington, D.C.

PEOPLE'S LOBBY

Radical Socialist lobby; the red Garland Fund official reports of donations for 1925-26 lists: "People's Reconstruction League (now the People's Lobby), Washington, D.C.,—for general expenses, $1,000"; and for 1929-30, "People's Lobby, Washington, D.C.—for anti-imperialism work, conditioned on raising an equal amount, $1,800." The 1933 letterhead reads: "The People's Lobby—To Fight for the People—We Get and Give the Facts—63 Bliss Bldg. —35 Constitution Avenue—Lincoln 2748—Washington, D.C." A letter headlined "Kill the Sales Tax by Taxing Wealth" sent out May 19, 1933 to members stated in part: "The President has signed the

Costigan-LaFollette-Wagner Bill appropriating $500,000,000 for relief grants—for which we have been working for three years. Income redistribution through taxation is now our BIG JOB—Yours sincerely, Benjamin C. Marsh." It listed as "Officers":

John Dewey, pres.; Ethel Clyde, vice pres.; Henry T. Hunt, treas.; Benjamin C. Marsh, exec. sec. "Board of Directors": Harry W. Laidler and the officers. "Council": Oscar Ameringer, Harry Elmer Barnes, Paul Blanshard, Harriet Stanton Blatch, Leroy E. Bowman, Stuart Chase, Otto Cullman, Harry Pratt Fairchild, Kate Crane Gartz, Florence C. Hanson, Chas. H. Ingersoll, Edward L. Israel, F. C. Leubuscher, E. C. Lindeman, Broadus Mitchell, Francis J. McConnell, J. H. McGill, Jackson H. Ralston, S. A. Stockwell, Wm. S. U'Ren, and Oswald G. Villard.

PIONEER CAMPS

Are conducted for the Young Pioneers (Communist) by the communist Workers International Relief, and for the Pioneer Youths (Socialist) by the Nat. Assn. for Child Development, otherwise known as the Pioneer Youth of America (see).

PIONEER YOUTH OF AMERICA

A Socialist organization well aided by the red Garland Fund; formed 1924, "to provide camp and club activities for the children of workers"; corresponds to the Communist Party's "Young Pioneers"; during 1931, camps and groups were maintained in N.Y., Philadelphia and Baltimore, two camps in N.C., and "play schools for children of textile workers . . . in five southern mill towns . . . three conferences each year are held for the training of camp and club leaders" (Am. Labor Year Book). Among its organizers were:

James Maurer, Wm. H. Johnston, Henry Linville, A. J. Muste and Maude Schwartz, Socialists, and Morris Sigman, Abraham Baroff, Abraham Bronstein, Max Zuckerman, Jos. Schlossberg, Socialists born in Russia. Officers 1931 were: Walter Ludwig, exec. dir.; Thos. J. Curtis, pres.; Fannia M. Cohn and A. J. Muste, vice presidents; Eva A. Frank, treas.; E. C. Lindeman, exec. dir.; John Dewey, Florence Curtis Hanson, John Haynes Holmes, James Weldon Johnson, Wm. H. Kilpatrick, A. J. Muste, Wm. F. Ogburn, Rose Schneidermann, Norman Thomas, and Stephen S. Wise, advisors.

Hdqts. Walter Ludwig, 45 Astor Place, N.Y. City.

POLISH CHAMBER OF LABOR

To quote "The Communist," Sept. 1933 issue: "The newly organized Polish Chamber of Labor, which is a united front organization and which has already established a certain influence, is a good instrument with which to penetrate among the masses of workers. One of the outstanding tasks confronting the Party among the Polish Workers is to develop cadres and to orientate the entire work toward the major problem of organizing Polish workers into the T.U.U.L. and Communist Party."

POLISH WORKERS CLUBS

Communist Foreign Language Groups (see) in various cities.

PORTO RICAN ANTI-IMPERIALIST ASSN.

Section of the All-America Anti-Imperialist Lg. (now Anti-Imperialist League).

PRAVDA

Meaning "Truth"; the official organ of the Communist Party of Russia.

PRINTERS INDUSTRIAL UNION

Communist T.U.U.L. union.

PRISONERS AID SOCIETY

Of the communist International Labor Defense.

PRISONERS RELIEF FUND

Of the communist I.L.D.; "Organized under the Auspices of the International Labor Defense to Help Political Prisoners and Dependents—80 East 11th St., Room 338, New York City," says the letterhead of this organization. It solicits funds to provide $5 each month "to every political prisoner in the United States" and "To dependent families of prisoners the Fund attempts to send $20 a month." "Political prisoners" is the radical term for those prisoners who are jailed for revolutionary and seditious crimes. They are treated therefore as the honored martyrs of the Red Revolutionary movement by their sympathizers. The following names are listed on the letterhead, Dec. 1932:

Sherwood Anderson, chmn.; Edmund Wilson, treas.; Diana Rubin, sec.; Roger N. Baldwin, Silas Bent, Winifred Chappell, Elliot E. Cohen, Malcolm Cowley, Robt. Cruden, Horace B. Davis, Solon de Leon, John Dos Passos, Robt. W. Dunn, Sara Bard Field, Eliz. Gurley Flynn, Waldo Frank, Lydia Gibson, Michael Gold, Jack Hardy, Josephine Herbst, Walter Hinkle, Henry T. Hunt, Grace Hutchins, Oakley Johnson, Ellen Kennan, Margaret Larkin, Melvin P. Levy, Esther Lowell, Jessie Lloyd, Louis Lozowick, Helen Mallery, Clarina Michelson, Geo. Novak, Wm. L. Nunn, Harvey O'Connor, Frank Palmer, Paul Peters, Wm. Pickens, Hannah Pickering, Hollace Ransdell, Anna Rochester, Edward Royce, Adelaide M. Schilkind, Bernard J. Stern, Ruth Stout, Maurice Sugar, Belle Taube, Charlotte Todes, Marguerite Tucker, Jessie London Wakefield, Chas. R. Walker, Paul Wander, Arthur Warner, Anita Whitney, Walter Wilson, Chas. E. S. Wood.

"PROFESSIONAL PATRIOTS"

An A.C.L.U. publication. Its distribution was listed as "Work in Hand" for 1927 in the A.C.L.U. 1926 Report. The book was edited by Norman Hapgood, whose wife was then a director of the American Society for Cultural Relations with Russia, a Communist subsidiary. It ran serially in the communist Daily Worker (June 1927) as Communist pprpaganda. In it, Hapgood attempts to show that all outstanding patriotic societies which fight the A.C.L.U. and Communism are motivated in doing so by greedy commercialism or cowardice. The term "professional patriot" was eagerly taken up by the Reds and is now popularly used by them to scornfully describe anyone who opposes them.

The list of "Endorsers" of this book as printed therein is as follows:

Alice Stone Blackwell; Harry Elmer Barnes, Smith Coll.; Prof. Phillips Bradley, Amherst Coll.; Bishop Chauncy B. Brewster, Hartford, Conn.; John Graham Brooks, Cambridge, Mass.; John Brophy; Dr. Richard C. Cabot; Prof. F. A. Cleveland, Boston, Mass.; Prof. Francis W. Coker, Ohio State U.; Pres. Norman F. Coleman, Reed Coll.; Mrs. Edward P. Costigan; Herbert Croly; Prof. H. J. Davenport, Cornell U.; Prof. Jerome Davis, Yale U.; Edward T. Devine; Prof. John Dewey; Prof. R. C. Dexter, Skidmore Coll.; Prof. Paul H. Douglas, U. of Chgo.; Mary Dreier; W. E. B. Du Bois; Fred Eastman, Chgo.; Prof. H. A. Eaton, Syracuse U.; Sherwood Eddy; Prof. Thomas D. Eliot, Northwestern U.; John Lovejoy, N.Y.C.; Prof. C. A. Ellwood, U. of Missouri; Charles T. Ennis, Lyons, N.Y.; Prof. C. O. Fisher, Wesleyan U.; Rev. Harry Emerson Fosdick; Prof. Felix Frankfurter, Harvard Law School; Senator L. J. Frazier, Hoople, N. Dak.; Zona Gale; Prof. Karl F. Geiser, Oberlin O.; Prof. Max Handman, U. of Texas; Mrs. J. Borden Harriman; Prof. E. C. Hayes, U. of Ill.; Robert Herrick, York Village, Maine; Prof. A. N. Holcombe, Harvard U.; Congressman Geo. W. Huddleston, Birmingham, Ala.; Henry T. Hunt; Paul Hutchinson; Prof. L. H. Jenks, Rollins Coll.; Rev. Burris A. Jenkins, Kans. City, Mo.; Prof. David Starr Jordan, Stanford U.; Francis Fisher Kane; Paul Kellogg; Prof. W. S. Knickerbocker, U. of the South; Prof. Frank H. Knight, U. of Iowa; Congressman F. H. La Guardia; Prof. William Ellery Leonard, U. of Wis.; Dean William Draper Lewis, U. of Pa.; Prof. E. C. Lindeman; Judge Ben B. Lindsey; Prof. Robert Morss Lovett; Rev. Halford E. Luccock; Prof. C. C. Maxey, Whitman Coll.; Bishop Francis J. McConnell; Lucia Ames Mead; Prof. H. A. Miller, Ohio State U.; Prof. Underhill Moore, Columbia U. Law Sch.; Pres. William A. Neilson, Smith Coll.; Fremont Older, San Fran., Cal.; Prof. William A. Orton, Smith Coll.; Prof. Max C. Otto, Madison, Wis.; Prof. Harry A. Overstreet; Jessica B. Peixotto; James D. Phelan, San Fran., Cal.; Amos Pinchot; Prof. Louise Pound, Lincoln, Nebr.; Mrs. Raymond Robins and Raymond Robins, Chgo.; Prof. Edward A. Ross, U. of Wis.; Father John A. Ryan, Wash., D.C.; Dean William Scarlett, St. Louis, Mo.; Prof. Ferdinand Schevill, Chgo.; Prof. A. M. Schlesinger, Harvard U.; Prof. Nathaniel Schmidt, Cornell U.; Prof. Vida D. Scudder, Wellesley Coll.; John F. Sinclair, Mpls.; Dean M. Carey Thomas, Bryn Mawr, Pa.; Samuel Untermyer, N.Y.C.; Senator T. J. Walsh, Helena, Mont.; Prof. U. G. Weatherly, Indiana U.; Senator B. K. Wheeler, Butte, Mont.; William Allen White, Emporia, Kans.; Prof. J. M. Williams, Hobart Coll.; Peter Witt, Cleveland, O.; and H. B. Woolston, Seattle, Wash.

PROFINTERN

Russian abbreviation of Red International of Labor Unions (of which the T.U.U.L. is the American section).

PROGRESSIVE EDUCATION ASSOCIATION

Prog. Edu. Assn.

Hon. pres. John Dewey; Leroy Bowman, Arthur E. Morgan, Joshua Lieberman, Carleton Washburne, Harold Rugg, E. C. Lindeman, Alvin Johnson, and other radicals serve as directors and advisory board members.

Says Francis Ralston Welsh, Nov. 20, 1933: "We learn from yesterday's papers that the Progressive Education Association (Pink, yellow and red) is to hold a meeting on November 24th and 25th and that such people as Mrs. Franklin D. Roosevelt; Louis Montgomery Howe, the President's secretary; Norman Thomas, Socialist candidate, communist sympathizer and member of the A.C.L.U. national committee; William H. Kilpatrick of pink fame; Harry A. Overstreet, exposed in the Lusk Report on Revolutionary Radicalism; F. Ernest Johnson of the Federal Council of Churches and frequently exposed, and Reinhold Niebuhr, member of the openly communist National Council for the Protection of Foreign-Born Workers, are to be speakers. Mrs. Roosevelt will probably be in congenial company. Perhaps it will be even more congenial since Litvinoff's arrival."

"We have always claimed that the Progressive Education Assn., a competitor of the radical National Education Assn., was a radical left-wing teachers group. . . . The following special release just issued by the John Day Co., Inc., leaves but little doubt as to the actual pro-revolutionary character of the Prog. Ed. Assn." (From report of Advisory Associates.) Its manifesto is written by a committee and entitled "A Call to the Teachers of the Nation."

To quote from the declarations of this committee: "our society has come to the parting of the ways. It has entered a revolutionary epoch. It stands in the presence of momentous decision. It is already at war with itself. . . . If the teachers are to play a positive and creative role in building a better social order they will have to emancipate themselves completely from the domination of the business interests of the nation, cease cultivating the manners and associations of bankers and promotion agents . . . take up boldly the challenge of the present, recognize the corporate and inter-dependent character of the contemporary order and transfer the democratic tradition from individualistic to collectivist economic foundations. . . . This would involve the frank abandonment of the doctrines of 'laissez faire,' . . . and the wide adoption of the principle of social and economic planning. . . . First of all if the profession is to be a factor in the process of social reconstruction, its members must prepare to struggle co-operatively and valiantly for their rights and ideas. They must fight for tenure, for adequate compensation, for a voice in the formulation of educational policies; they must uphold the ancient doctrine of academic freedom . . . they must oppose every effort on the part of publishing houses, business interests, privileged classes and patriotic societies to prescribe the content of the curriculum" (note the opposition to patriotic societies). ". . . Consequently if the foregoing argument means anything it means that the progressive-minded teachers of the country must unite in a powerful organization, militantly devoted to the building of a better social order. . . . In the defense of its members against the ignorance of the masses and the malevolence of the privileged such an organization would have to be equipped with the material resources, the legal talent, and the trained intelligence necessary to wage successful warfare in the press, the courts, and the legislative chambers of the nation. To serve the teaching profession of the country in this way should be one of the major purposes of the Progressive Education Association." A list of recommended books by radicals such as Paul H. Douglas, Lincoln Steffens, Stuart Chase, etc. is then appended.

This manifesto is printed as John Day Pamphlet No. 30 (other pamphlets of the series include such radical authors and subjects as V. F. Calverton "On Revolution," Albert Einstein "The Fight Against War," Norman Thomas, Stuart Chase, Geo. S. Counts, etc.). Its full title is: *"A Call to the Teachers of the Nation:* by the Committee of the Progressive Education Association on Social and Economic Problems"; the author-committee-members listed are:

Geo. S. Counts, chairman; Merle E. Curti, Smith Coll. prof.; John S. Gambs, Teachers Coll. prof.; Sidney Hook, N.Y.U. prof.; Jesse H. Newlon, dir. Lincoln's School, Teachers Coll.; Chas. L. S. Easton, headmaster Staten Is. Acad.; Goodwin Watson, Teachers Coll. prof.; Willard W. Beatty, pres., and Frederick Redefer, exec. sec. of the Progressive Education Assn.

PROGRESSIVE MINERS OF AMERICA UNION

P.M.A. or Prog. Miners Un.

After ten years of constant agitation against the dictatorship of John L. Lewis, leader of the A.F. of L. United Mine Workers Union, led by the communist National Miners Union, the Communists in conjunction with the left wing Socialists (Conf. Prof. Lab. Act. under A. J. Muste) and the Communist League or "Trotskyites," effected a split and organized 46,000 Southern Ill. Miners in 1932 into this new P.M.A. union. Active in the formation were: Hugo Oehler (Communist League); Gerry Allard (a Communist Lg. "Trotskyite"), editor of the P.M.A. organ "The Progressive Miner" with Loren Norman (Trotskyite), assistant editor, and Scott Nearing (Communist), editorial writer; Pat Ansboury (Trotskyite), organizer; Tom Tippett, made educational director of the P.M.A. by the Conf. for Prof. Labor Action; etc. The communists have delegates at every P.M.A. conference to present Communist resolutions. Delegates from the P.M.A. attend Communist "united front" congresses. The "militancy" of the P.M.A. is highly praised by the Communist press. The P.M.A. communistic parade to Springfield in 1933, the murders, bombings, and disorders in S. Ill. since its formation which have necessitated the presence of the Ill. National Guard for long periods of time, the protests of the A.C.L.U. against the *interference* of the National Guard with these revolutionary activities, are all testimonials of its character. It remains to be seen which faction will finally emerge as its dominating one.

PROLETARIAN ANTI-RELIGIOUS LEAGUE

American section of the communist International of the Godless, formed in Moscow 1931; Kalmon Marmor, exec. sec., 50 E. 13th St. (and St. Denis Bldg.), N.Y. City; affiliated with the World Union of Atheists of the 4A.

PROLETARIAN DRAMATIC LEAGUE

One of the American sections of Moscow's communist International Union of the Revolutionary Theatre (see also Lg. of Wkrs. Theatres).

PROLETARIAN PARTY

A "highbrow" Communist party supporting the program of the Communist International altho not affiliated; "Proletarian News," its organ, said in May 1, 1932 issue: "The organization in America that is preparing the workers for the momentous act of self emancipation is the Proletarian Party"; the Feb. 15, 1932 issue: "We must spread the message of communism to all. Workers, Comrades, Friends support the Proletarian News. It is needed to instill class consciousness into the American workers, to organize them for the approaching conflict. Build for Communism in America!", and under the heading "God and the Holy Ghost in Russia" (same issue): "Things will never be the same again for religion in Russia. Since the workers came into power, the state no longer pays and protects the church for keeping the minds of the workers filled with superstition. On the contrary, religion is receiving the ridicule it so richly deserves as pointed out in the following from the magazine Time: 'Common in Soviet cartoons is a comical little old man, always accompanied by a comical little white bird. The little old man who has wings, flops awkwardly about, annoying Comrades who sometimes smack him with a fly swatter while the little white bird squawks in terror. The little old man is labeled "God," the little white bird "Holy Ghost" and both are kept constantly in Red cartoons by the zealous efforts of Comrade Emilian Yaroslavsky, Leader of the Godless!' It is gratifying to see this survival of man's primitive ignorance relegated to its proper place—the joke book and the museum. E. A." Edgar Anderson of the nat. com., is in charge of Chicago activities; C. Jilset is editor and Martin Larson, bus. mgr. of the paper; Lenin Memorial meetings are held; cooperates with Communists, Socialists, and I.W.W.'s in various joint activities such as the Mooney committee, Kentucky Miners Def. and Relief Com., U.S. Congress Against War, Karl Borders' C.W.C. on Unemp., Communist Party's Oct. 31, 1932 joint Chgo. Hunger March, etc.; conducts "Open," "Labor" or "Proletarian" forums and study classes in Chicago, Grand Rapids, Ann Arbor, Los Angeles, Rochester, Detroit, Cleveland, etc., frequently addressed by radical college professors; organizes unemployed into "Workers Leagues." Hdqts.: 2409 W. Chicago Ave., Chicago, Edgar Anderson; "Proletarian News" pub. same address.

PUBLIC OWNERSHIP LEAGUE OF AMERICA, THE

As Socialist Norman Thomas said: "To begin with, Socialists first seek key industries." This Socialist League, headed by Carl Thompson, former executive of the "Yours for the Revolution" People's College and Information Director (1912-16) of the Socialist Party, thus outlines its activities: "In the cities, the League works for municipal ownership; nationally it works for such immediate measures as the permanent public ownership of railroads, postalization of the telegraphs and telephones, conservation of natural resources and the like." In his Report of the League's work in 1924, he said " . . . the public ownership movement goes steadily forward step by step, point by point, from victory to victory. The action is not so spectacular, the victories not so notable, that they awaken nation wide interest . . . but they are the necessary steps . . . and as such are quite as essential as the others . . . and may ultimately prove to be the one sure approach to the *larger achievements.*" (Emphasis supplied.)

The Nov. 1933 issue of "Public Ownership," organ of the Public Ownership Lg. headlined the following:

"FATHER COUGHLIN FOR PUBLIC OWNERSHIP—Comes Out Baldly for Nationalization of Banks, Currency and Credit—Millions Hear Him."

The jubilant article beneath this headline states in part:

"Father Coughlin's heroic stand brings encouragement to those of us who have come to the same conclusions and who are urging the same remedy. Through his national hookup, Father Coughlin's addresses reach no less than ten millions of people in the United States, and by way of cables across the sea, reach many millions more in England and Continental Europe. This is an educational effort of *unparalleled extent and significance* and means much to the country. In the course of his address, he told his hearers that any who wished to have copies of his speeches could get them by merely addressing to him a request for them. *We rushed in our request,* and would certainly advise all of our readers to do the same. Address Rev. Chas. E. Coughlin, Box 150, Detroit, Mich."

In the light of what is now being done

in Washington, Carl D. Thompson's leaflet entitled "Are Socialists Practical," issued when he was director in the National Office of the Socialist Party, 1912-16, about 20 years ago, is interesting and prophetic. He said: "Some folks object to Socialism because they say—it's impractical—it won't work. We are going to answer that objection. As a matter of fact Socialists are the most practical people in the world today.

"First—they have actually succeeded in putting into the statute books of the various states 134 different laws. . . . A hundred and thirty-four measures of that kind, secured by the merest minority of representatives, is surely a good beginning. But it is only the beginning.

"The measures mentioned above are, after all, only the less important parts of the program of Socialism. They are such as the old party politicians thought they were compelled to pass, throwing them out as a sop to the growing Socialist sentiment in the country. They hope thereby to stop Socialism, not to advance it.

"We want no one to think these sops are Socialism. By no means. We want something more than sops. We want the whole soup. We are going to take all the sops they give and thereby gain strength to get the whole feed. . . . Fighting it out on this line will . . . *finally overthrow capitalism.* (Emphasis supplied.)

"States under the direction of this Socialist program, and finally the nation, will take over one after the other the public utilities, mines, railroads, power plants, telegraph and telephone systems, waterways, forests." (Communism.)

"The Socialists will push their campaigns. They will elect more representatives in the states where they already have them. They will win seats in new states. They will capture cities. Later they will control State Legislatures, and finally, the United States Congress and the *Supreme Court.* . . . Socialism will push the tendency to its logical conclusion. . . . Is not this a practical program? There is nothing else that IS practical." "Public Ownership," organ of the Pub. O. Lg., Feb. 1924 stated: "Five years ago we were a voice crying in the wilderness on this public ownership question. Today a chain of powerful daily papers, monthly and weekly journals reaching every section of the continent is carrying our story. . . . Ten students from one Chicago High School, the Crane Technical, called upon the League recently. They were all required to write a theme of 2,000 words on the subject."

Voters are deluged with public ownership propaganda during campaigns. "It is not unusual for the League to handle sometimes three or four lists of voters in towns and villages in a single day," says Thompson, and "Careful canvasses of Congress are made to supply them with information. Conferences are arranged with Congressmen and other public officials who are willing to give government ownership their attention." And yet Thompson says the League is *non-political!*

Rejoicing over Wisconsin State legislation manipulated by the League is expressed in the 1928-29 Report and Thompson calls particular attention to their economical system of reaching every voter in a community with public ownership literature under Senator Norris' frank! Cooperation of the Methodist Federation for Social Service and the Debs Memorial Radio station (WEVD, station of the 4A Atheist Society), is reported, as might be expected.

National office: 127 N. Dearborn St., Room 1439, Chicago.

1933 Secretary and leader, Carl D. Thompson; treas., Chas. H. Ingersoll; pres., Willis J. Spaulding; vice presidents: W. T. Rawleigh, J. D. Ross, John R. Haynes, Robt. M. LaFollette, Jr., Charles Edward Russell, E. F. Scattergood, D. B. Robertson, L. E. Sheppard, Rudolph Spreckels, William T. Evjue, M. C. Parsons, Arthur P. Davis, Lynn J. Frazier, C. H. Foster, John A. Ryan, E. H. Fitzgerald, A. Emil Davies, Theo. F. Thieme, Amos Pinchot, Bishop F. J. McConnell, S. A. Stockwell, E. J. Manion, C. C. Dill, Homer T. Bone, Chas. W. Ward, William Madgett, Edward P. Costigan, Gov. Floyd B. Olson, Thos. R. Amlie. Executive Committee: William H. Holly, chairman; Otto Cullman, James H. McGill, Fay Lewis, Edward F. Dunne, Grace F. Peter, Wiley W. Mills, S. J. Konenkamp, David Rosenheim, Margaret Haley, Ralph U. Thompson, John J. Walt, James H. Andrews, Clarence Darrow, George A. Schilling, R. E. McDonnell.

In 1920 the officers were Carl D. Thompson, as ever, secretary; Albert M. Todd, pres.; Chas. H. Ingersoll, treas.; vice presidents: Jane Addams, Frank P. Walsh, Warren S. Stone, Chas. Zueblin, David J. Lewis, Hon. Lynn J. Frazier, Amos Pinchot, Carl S. Vrooman, Glenn E. Plumb, Delos F. Wilcox, Frederic C. Howe, Timothy Shea, Wm. Lemke. Executive Board: Otto Cullman, Dr. G. H. Sherman, James H. McGill, Willis J. Spaulding, Duncan MacDonald, Fay Lewis, Chas. K. Mohler, Ed. V. de La Grange, Edw. F. Dunne, Harriet T. Treadwell, Austin P. Haines, Grace F. Peter, Wm. Rodriguez, Wiley W. Mills, S. J. Konenkamp.

R

RAILROAD BROTHERHOODS UNITY COMMITTEE

Formerly National Railroad Workers Industrial Union, a communist T.U.U.L. union; the Chicago branch organ is "Railroad Unity News," pub. at 2003 N. California Ave., C. A. Adams, chmn.

RAILROAD WORKERS INDUSTRIAL LEAGUE

Communist T.U.U.L. union; hdqts. Otto Wangerin, 717 East 63rd St., Chicago.

RAND SCHOOL OF SOCIAL SCIENCE

A Socialist training school for labor agitators formerly heavily supported by the Garland Fund (see) and owned by the American Socialist Society, which was convicted under the Espionage act in 1919 and fined $3,000 for "feloniously obstructing enlistment service of the U.S." and for publishing and distributing a pamphlet "The Great Madness" by Scott Nearing, a regular instructor there. Among other regular instructors were H. W. L. Dana, Alex. Trachtenberg, Louis P. Lochner, Norman Thomas, D. P. Berenberg, Algernon Lee, Herman Epstein, Ludwig Lore, etc. Evidence produced in the Lusk Report illustrates its teachings namely: class hate; to "Take Over the State"; to fight government defense; work for U.S. disarmament; class consciousness; red agitation of all kinds.

"In the Rand Book Store, run in conjunction with the Rand School itself, and which contributes toward the support of the school, are found works dealing not only with Socialism and extreme radical thought, but a large number of books on sex problems, and a section of the book store is devoted solely to the subject of sex. These sex books are sold to boys and girls of immature age, and one of these books, entitled 'Love and Marriage' by Marie C. Stopes, was sold to a young lad of fifteen. Some portions of the book are of an extremely lascivious and indecent character." (Lusk Report.)

It publishes the American Labor Year Book (of radical activities), which states that in 1932 it had 231 students, that its lecturers included John Dewey, Marc Connolly, Jos. Schlossberg, George Soule, Hendrik Van Loon, John B. Watson, Anita Block, etc. and names: Algernon Lee as pres. of the staff; W. E. Born as educational director; Nathan Fine as dir. of research dept., which publishes the Am. Labor Year Book; and Anna Bercovitz as exec. dir.

At a meeting held Apr. 27, 1933 attended by some 400 Socialists and sympathizers, pledges were made for a fund of $17,000 to save the school from loss of its quarters, "Peoples House." Among those pledging support were John Dewey, Ex-Congressman La Guardia, Norman Thomas, John Haynes Holmes, and Morris Hillquit. An appeal was sent out asking for funds signed by the above and also by Upton Sinclair, Paul Douglas, Gilbert Seldes, Wm. H. Kilpatrick, Stuart Chase, Oswald Garrison Villard, Chas. A. Beard, Wm. P. Montague, Clarence Senior, Heywood Broun, Helen Keller, Margaret I. Lamont, Fanny Hurst, Hendrik Willem Van Loon, Eliz. Gilman, Jerome Davis, Broadus Mitchell, Elmer Rice, Michael Strange. The appeal stated: "We join with John Dewey in saying: 'It would be a calamity to intelligent untrammeled thought and speech everywhere . . . all sincere friends of sound adult education MUST JOIN IN KEEPING THE RAND SCHOOL DOORS OPEN.'" ("The Nation," July 5, 1933.)

Hdqts. 7 East 15th St., N.Y. City.

REBEL PLAYERS

Of Los Angeles, etc.; Communist dramatic group affiliated with the League of Workers Theatres (the American section of the Intl. Union of the Revolutionary Theatre).

RECEPTION BANQUET COMMITTEE FOR FORD

Recep. Banq. Com. for Ford.

As announced by the Communist Chicago paper, "Workers Voice," Oct. 15, 1932: The Communist Party and a "non-partisan" committee sponsored a reception banquet for "white and negro workers and intellectuals" in honor of James W. Ford, colored Communist Vice Presidential candidate held Thursday, Oct. 18, 1932, 10 P.M. at Alvin Hall, 51st St. and Michigan Ave., Chicago. The committee was composed of:

Lucius Harper (mg. ed. Chicago Defender), chmn.; Frank Hamilton, sec.; I.L.D. atty. Albert Goldman, treas.; Prof. Frederick L. Schuman, U. of C.; Rev. Raymond Bragg (sec. Western Unitarian Conf.); Mrs. Bragg; Thomas McKenna (A.C.L.U. exec. sec.); Perry O. Thompson (editor Chicago Review); Rev. O. F. Peterson (pres. of Phylanx Club); Miss Thelma McWater; Dr. James W. McCaskill; Dr. Homer Cooper; Geo. W. Clark; John Williamson (Party functionary); Mrs. Blanche Cole Lowenthal (social worker); Carl Haessler of the Communist Workers School.

RECEPTION COMMITTEE FOR SOVIET FLYERS

Recep. Com. Soviet Flyers.

A committee formed by the communist Friends of the Soviet Union (F.S.U.) to welcome and raise funds for the Soviet flyers who, in September 1929, flew from Moscow to New York (photographing landing fields and gathering other military information on their way). A letter sent out on stationery headed "Reception Committee for Soviet Flyers—Auspices of the Friends of the Soviet Union—175 Fifth Ave., Room 304, New York" said in part: "To commemorate this first Moscow-New York flight, we want to present these flyers with a present. We want to give them something that they can take back to the workers and peasants of Russia to help them in their economic and agricultural upbuilding. . . . During the famine days, appeals for help from the Soviet Union met with splendid response. Those days are now over. Now we are helping the Soviet Union to build its new society. The money you send will be devoted to this one end, and this only, to buy tractors and trucks to be given to the Soviet airmen for the Russian people." Members of the committee listed on this letterhead are:

S. Alexanderson, Jack Baker, Roger N. Baldwin, Forrest Bailey, Louis B. Boudin, J. M. Budish, Heywood Broun, Louis F. Budenz, Ralph E. Blount, H. Bank, S. W. Barnett, A. Brenner, Nathan Beilas, Carl Brodsky, Joseph R. Brodsky, Mike Belcastro, A. Basskoff, Paul Brissenden, David Burlind, Dr. Frank Hurburt Booth, Stuart Chase, Ann Coles, E. Calligan, Sonia Chaikin, Bertha Crawford, Chas. H. Calvin, S. Citvet, K. M. Chen, Harry W. L. Dana, Margaret DeSilver, Anna N. Davis, Horace B. Davis, W. E. B. Du Bois, Robert Dunn, Jerome Davis, Solon DeLeon, Virginia Ellen, J. Evans, A. Freidenferd, Hilja Frilund, A. Fox, Lewis S. Gannett, Dorothy Gary, F. Geschlecht, M. Grener, Milton Goodman, Dr. A. L. Goldwater, Dr. I. B. Goodman, Pauline Gorbaty, F. Goodstone, Mike Gold, Arthur Garfield Hays, Ellen Hayes, Dr. Alice Hamilton, Henry T. Hunt, Grace Hutchins, Y. Hsu, T. Hoyos, Anna J. Haines, John Haynes Holmes, Timothy Healy, Paul Jones, Dr. Oakley Johnson, William Johnson, I. A. Kittine, Alfred Kreymborg, Walter Kowolsky, Bertha Kaleva, M. Kniazewich, Dr. Horace M. Kallen, Jacob Kepecs, N. Kotlenko, Esther Lowell, Lola Maverick Lloyd, Walter Landauer, L. Landy, Geo. Laitsch, Irma Lee, M. Lurie, Ernest Lundeen, M. Maichalowski, Darwin J. Meserole, Frank Mozer, Margaret A. Marsh, Roy Mezara, J. Miller, D'Arcy Milliken, John Morelly, G. Mink, M. Malyk, Dr. A. Markoff, Dr. J. Mindel, James Mo, P. Mueller, S. Merz, Chas. Musil, Scott Nearing, Dr. Per Nelson, A. Olken, Harvey O'Connor, M. Olgin, Frank L. Palmer, Alex Pappas, Henry W. Pinkham, Leon Pruscika, M. Piser, Rose Paul, J. Pearl, Ruth H. Pearson, F. Piskothy, M. Pittkoff, J. S. Joyntz, Dr. L. M. Powell, Anna Rochester, Gilbert E. Roc, J. F. Romese, William Ross, S. B. Russack, Edith Rudquist, J. Rappoport, M. Rosenblatt, J. Reed, Dr. Karl Sandberg, Freda Sahud, Dr. Moses Sahud, Art Shields, Dr. David Saletan, A. Trachtenberg, H. Silverman, A. W. Sevtrino, E. R. Stout, J. Stillman, Carlo Tresca, Ben Thomas, N. Turlewich, Mary Heaton Vorse, Arthur Warner, A. Wagenknecht, Lillian Wald, E. Wickstrom, J. B. Collings Woods, Helen Yaskevich, M. Zibel, John Zatko; Jessie Lloyd, sec.; Jacques Buitenkant, treas.

The Committee was revived in 1933 to raise funds for the Soviet flyers, returning this time without their plane, the money to be donated to buy machinery for Russia.

RECONCILIATION TRIPS

Are "group visits" of the Fellowship of Reconciliation under the direction of Clarence V. Howell, who urged support of the Communist Party and announced he was voting Communist in the 1932 election (Christian Century, Sept. 21, 1932). According to Howell's definition of the Trips: "The Purpose: is to reconcile group to group—as well as person to person. . . . The Method: . . . to bring quarrelling persons or anti-pathetic groups face to face at the point of conflict under cordial auspices. So we conduct nordic blondes, many southerners, into the heart of Negro Harlem. . . . We conduct the same kind of trips to thirty other groups. Reconciliation trips are now being conducted in New York, Chicago, Milwaukee, Syracuse and Boston."

"Cooperating Educators" see that College young people are formed into groups and taken to Communist, Socialist, and I.W.W. headquarters, where they are given propaganda lectures. They listen to sex lectures and participate in sex discussions. The trips are made attractive by taking the young people to unusual places to dine, such as "Black and Tan" joints, "Dill Pickle Clubs," or those having fantastic or foreign customs. Revolutionary songs are sung and the idea advanced that the trips are venturesome educational larks and not propaganda tours.

Of course the propaganda of Communism is the reconciliation of all religions into no-religion and all varying moral laws into no-moral law.

The Chicago Herald and Examiner (N. Shore edition, Oct. 9, 1933) described one trip taken by Northwestern Students and others led by Frank Orman Beck which visited Socialist Party headquarters and included a round-table symposium at Hull House, and to quote: "The highlight of the trip was a visit to the West Side Workers' Forum at 338 S. Halsted St., headquarters of Unemployed Council C 1—The tourists were greeted by the militant words of the 'Internationale' lustily intoned by more than 300 Communist sympathizers who had gathered for the regular Saturday night discussion meeting." This was followed by a question box period at the Communist headquarters.

Each week (in spite of complaints) the "Daily Northwestern," college paper (Evanston, Ill.), makes announcements of these Reconciliation Trips conducted by Frank Orman Beck (I have also seen the announcements on Tittle's M.E. Church bulletin board). A front-page column (Nov. 15, 1929) devoted to describing one trip promised "The tour will leave the Public Health Institute, 159 N. Dearborn St., Chicago, at 9 o'clock Saturday morning. The first trip of inspection will be through the largest venereal disease clinic in the world," etc.

To quote from the printed program of another tour headed "Love, Sex, Marriage, and the Family," Saturday, July 12, 1930: "There has been too great a tendency to regard this aspect of life as something dangerous. The trip is an honest facing of facts, hoping thereby to make some contribution to a positive and constructive ideal of the place of love and sex in life."

"Northwestern University, 8:15 A.M. Leave Davis St. 'L.' Chicago University, 8:15 A.M. Leave Reynolds Club. . . . 2 P.M. Clinic of the American Social Hygiene Assn. and the American Birth Control League. 'Sex and Health' will be presented by Rachelle S. Yarros, M.D. (General discussion and inspection of the clinic.) 4 P.M. 'Companionate Marriage,' a round table discussion, 6 P.M. Stroll by the Oak St. Beach, the city's most popular playground through area where 'the night club is the thing . . . land of the new Hedonism." (An atheist term) " . . . 8:15 P.M. 'What Is There About Life Man Should Not Know,' Lee Alexander Stone, M.D. . . . general discussion and summary. 9:30 P.M. Dill Pickle Club, No. 18 Tooker Alley. . . . Frank Orman Beck, director, 2000 Sheridan Rd., Evanston, Ill. Russel de Long, assistant."

A poster for a New York trip (Mar. 21, 1931), "For Everybody," headlines for its program: "Margaret Sanger, Dr. Eugene L. Swan on 'Love Art,' Dr. Eliot White on 'Companionate Marriage'; 3:30 P.M. Love art which depicts the Art of Love where goodness and beauty meet in uplifting ecstacy . . . 6:30 P.M. Ceylon India dinner . . . 7:15 P.M. Psychologist on 'What Is Love?' . . . 9:15 General symposium. Books to read": (a list of sex books by V. F. Calverton, Judge Ben. Lindsey, Margaret Sanger is given.) "Conducted by Clarence V. Howell, N.Y."

Another program for a tour, "Especially arranged by Prof. LeRoy Bowman for his class in Columbia U. and for all who care to go," features "Frank Olmstead, friend of Judge Lindsey on 'Companionate Marriage' and V. F. Calverton on 'Changes in Sex Attitudes Versus Monogamy" (Jan. 13, 1931). Sex books by Calverton (the Marxist), Judge Lindsey and Margaret Sanger are listed for preparatory reading.

Another poster program, headed "Visit Anarchists, Communists, Socialists, Rochdale Cooperative, I.W.W.'s. How profound the ignorance of most people on what the radical really believes," lists on its program: "2:15 P.M. 'What the Anarchists Believe and How They Have Helped Modern Education,' 219 Second Ave.—by Harry Kelly, an Anarchist. Answers to questions. 3:15 P.M. Leave. Walk west to 26-28 Union Square, Workers Party Hdqts. (communist). 3:30 P.M. 'What the Communists Believe and How They Propose to Achieve Their Ends' by Comrade Biedenkapp. Answers to questions. 4:45 P.M. West to Rand School of Social Science, 7 E. 15th St. 5 P.M. 'What Socialists Would Do With the City, State, Nation and World' by August Claessens, executive secretary Socialist Party, Local New York. Answers to questions. 6:45 P.M. Dinner Rochdale Cooperative Restaurant . . . others Russian Restaurants (Russian Balalaika orchestra). 8:30 'Their Preamble—The Basis on Which the I.W.W. Organized Unskilled and Skilled Workers Whom Others Had Failed to Organize,' 31 Coentis Slip—by Fellow Worker Leigh H. Bearce. Answers to questions. This will be followed for those who can remain, with a chance to meet the I.W.W. 10 P.M. Leave for home. Directors Clarence V. Howell, Ida Oatley Howell, Marvin H. Shore. For everyone who cares to attend. Expenses 75c for each trip . . . Add cost of dinner.—Pay on trip. Reconciliation Trips, 229 W. 48th St., N.Y."

Director Howell in a release listing programs said: "All trips, except four, this year in New York City were sponsored by professors or other groups." He lists: "'Love, New Sex Ideals,' 'Conflict of Cultures' sponsored by LeRoy E. Bowman; 'New Religions (sometimes called Cults)' by Arthur L. Swift; 'Radical Labor Headquarters' by Jerome Davis; 'Atheist,' 'Dope, drink,' 'Union Labor,' 'Social Settlement,' etc. by Wm. M. Gilbert; 'Negro, Harlem and Radical Headquarters' by Lyford P. Edwards of St. Stephens College (see); five trips each summer for Summer Conference at Union Theological Seminary; New Riverside Church High School Dept., also Guild trips,'" etc., etc. Y.W.C.A. and Y.M.C.A. branches frequently sponsor and advertise trips.

The Reconciliation Trips letterhead lists as its "Committee":

Prof. LeRoy E. Bowman of Columbia U., chmn.; Julia Pettee, 85 Bedford St., treas.; Edmund B. Chaffee; Winifred L. Chappell (of the Communist P. G. for F. and F. campaign committee); Frederick B. Newell; Arthur L. Swift of Union Theol. Sem.; Frederick M. Thrasher of New York U.; C. Everett Wagner; Chas. C. Webber; and "Cooperating Educators": Harrison S. Elliott, Daniel J. Fleming, Robt. Ernest Hume, *Harry F. Ward,* Gaylord S. White, for Union Theol. Sem.; Jerome Davis, for Yale Divinity School; Sarah E. D. Sturges, for National School, Y.W.C.A.; Walter W. Pettit for N.Y. School of Social Work; Chas. Homer Boynton for General Theol. Sem; Sidney E. Goldstein and Stephen S. Wise for Jewish Institute of Religion; Thos. C. Blaisdell, LeRoy E. Bowman, Henry R. Seager for Columbia U.; Clarence G. Dittmer, Louis R. Spriggs, Frederick M. Thrasher for New York U.; Eliz. F. Baker, Mabel Foote Weeks for Barnard Coll.; Arthur Dickson for Coll. of City of N.Y.; Paul M. Limbert for Franklin and Marshall Coll.; Twila Lytton Cavert (wife of Samuel McCrea Cavert) for Sarah Lawrence Coll.; S. Ralph Harlow for Smith Coll.; Adelaide T. Case, John L. Childs, Daniel H. Kulp, Sarah L. Patrick, F. Tredwell Smith for Teachers Coll.; Wm. M. Gilbert for Drew Theol. Sem.

"RECOVERY THROUGH REVOLUTION"

This is the title of a 1933 book, "A Symposium edited by Samuel Schmaulhausen," on the "revolutionary trends in all major countries," by writers who favor a Red revolution of violence.

Editor Schmaulhausen (p. 476) says: "We, the people, must recover from Capitalism, a disease that has wasted and undermined our lives. Recovery through revolution! That's the road of sanity in our insane social order. . . . Life and creation belong henceforth to Communism."

He also says (p. 468): "I have long maintained that if the Communists in Soviet Russia had never done anything else of great moment than to undo the evil power of the church . . . they would deserve in ensuing centuries of light and liberation the immortal thanks and affection of their mortal fellow men. . . . From a psychiatric point of view religion is a compound neurosis; it specializes in teaching men and women to feel inferior . . . ; not only that but to feel ashamed of their sexual impulses. . . . If the modern mind and our civilized emotions are to be saved . . . the *very first task of a new social order is to eliminate the church completely from among man's institutions.*" Speaking of liberty, he says (p. 471): "A proletarian revolution . . . must revoke this liberty which is so precious to the classes pursuing profit and prestige. . . . Class consciousness is the newer and deeper type of fraternity. Comradeship in Communism . . . attained by means of socialization of the State and the communization of cultural and human relations."

Robert Briffault, of England, another contributor, tells (p. 486) that promiscuity, nudism, sex expression is a revolt against the Dictatorship of the Bourgeoisie with its present Christian tabus concerning sex, family and marriage, but that the way to abolish these tabus is to abolish the Dictatorship of the Bourgeoisie by a violent Red Revolution.

Says he (p. 494): "To argue with a Christian, a business man, a senator, an old lady of independent means, or an influential university pundit is puerile. . . . *The only instruments of persuasion relevant to the case are lethal weapons.* Force is the only argument. *Those who cannot be persuaded must perforce be liquidated.* The social revolution . . . cannot be effected without a considerable liquidation of irrationalists. . . . Failure of gentle intellectuals to perceive that necessity is one of the most pathetic effects of their failure to apprehend the Marxian keythought. . . . "

V. F. Calverton, the Sex and Communist author, says on p. 390: "It is only by revolution that that realization" (of Communism) "can be translated into action. It is no little task that confronts us and it behooves us to gather up all our energies and dedicate all our strength to its achievement."

Other contributors are: Maxmilian Olay, Anarchist-Communist: Prof. Robt. Morss Lovett of Chicago; John Gunther, Chicago Daily News correspondent; H. N. Brailsford, G. D. H. Cole, Harold J. Laski, of England; Lewis Corey; Louis Fischer, since 1922 principally in Russia; Ludwig Lore; Max Nomad; Walter Polakov; Sachio Oka, Japanese Red; Chi-Chen Wang, Chinese lecturer at Columbia U. since 1929; Herman Simpson, former teacher City College, N.Y.; Gaetano Salvemini, barred from Italy, but visiting professor at Yale 1932, Harvard 1930; Edwin D. Schoonmaker, former college professor; Arnold Roller, the pen name of the author of "Anti-militarist syndicalist pamphlets on Direct Action and the Revolutionary General Strike . . . has so far been in 35 countries and 8 jails. . . . He has traveled through all Caribbean and most South American countries to get acquainted with the background and the men behind the revolutionary movements in these regions. . . . He was also a translator, smuggler, hod carrier and even lecturer." (Contributor to "The Nation," "New Masses," etc.)

RED INTERNATIONAL OF LABOR UNIONS (R.I.L.U. Magazine)

R.I.L.U.

The Profintern's international federation of communist Moscow-directed unions; the Trade Union Unity League (formerly known as the Trade Union Educational League, then and now headed by Wm. Z. Foster) is the American section; Confederation Generale du Travail Unitaire is the French section; founded in England in 1921 led by Tom Mann; its magazine, "R.I. L.U." published at 59 Cromer St., London W.C.1, is sold at all Communist bookstores.

RED SPORTS INTERNATIONAL

Moscow's international Communist sports organization of which the Labor Sports Union is the American section; called the second line of defense of the Soviet Union by U.S.S.R. Commissar of Army and Navy—Voroshilov. Conducted a Spartakiade (sports contest) at Moscow 1933 attended by delegates from all over the world.

REPEAL COMMITTEE

A San Francisco A.C.L.U. and communist I.L.D. committee working for repeal of syndicalism laws (against sedition).

RETAIL CLERKS INDUSTRIAL UNION

Communist T.U.U.L. union.

REVOLUTIONARY WRITERS FEDERATION

American section of Moscow's communist "International Union of Revolutionary Writers" (of the International Bureau of Revolutionary Literature); it formed the Workers Cultural Federation (see); it includes the John Reed Club Writers Group, Proletpen, Hungarian Proletarian Writers and Worker-Correspondents Assn., Japanese Cultural Federation, Finnish Cultural Federation, Lithuanian Literary Dramatic Group, Jack London Club, Pen and Hammer, Student Review (New Masses, Ap. 1933); American author members who served on the 1933 staff of the International Union of Revolutionary Writers issuing its organ "Intl. Literature" include:

Upton Sinclair, Michael Gold, A. Magil, John Dos Passos, Emjo Basshe, Walter Carmon, Theodore Dreiser, Fred Ellis, Ed. Falkowski, Jos. Freeman, Josephine Herbst, Langston Hughes, Joseph Kalar, Joshua Kunitz, Louis Lozowick, Norman Macleod, Myra Page, Horace Gregory, Agnes Smedley, Mary Heaton Vorse, Jack Conroy, John Herrmann, Herman Spector; in 1932: Whittaker Chambers, Charles Yale Harrison, Melvin P. Levy, Harry Alan Potamkin, K. Wallace.

Issues a monthly "Literary Service" edited by Keene Wallis of the John Reed Club, beginning Aug. 1932. Typical of the efforts of these writers is this sacrilegious poem by Langston Hughes, Negro poet:

"GOODBYE CHRIST"

"Listen, Christ,
You did alright in your day, I reckon—
But that day's gone now.
They ghosted you up a swell story too,
Called it Bible—
But its dead now.
The popes and the preachers 've
Made too much money from it.
They've sold you to too many

"Kings, generals, robbers and killers—
Even to the Czar and the Cossacks,
Even to Rockefeller's church,
Even to THE SATURDAY EVENING POST.
You ain't no good no more.
They've pawned you
Till you've done wore out.

"Goodbye,
Christ Jesus Lord God Jehova,
Beat it on away from here now.
Make way for a new guy with no religion at all—
A real guy named
Marx Communist Lenin Peasant Stalin Worker *ME*—

"I said, *ME!*

"Go Ahead on now,
You're getting in the way of things, Lord.
And please take Saint Ghandi with you when you go,
And Saint Pope Pius,
And Saint Aimie McPherson,
And big black Saint Becton
Of the Consecrated Dime.
And step on the gas, Christ!
Move!
Don't be so slow about movin'!
The world is mine from now on—
And nobody's gonna sell ME
To a king, or a general,
Or a millionaire."

RUBBER WORKERS INDUSTRIAL UNION

Communist T.U.U.L. union.

RUSSIAN-AMERICAN INDUSTRIAL CORPORATION

Prior to 1924 a circular sent out by the communist Friends of Soviet Russia (Whitney's "Reds in Am.") read: "The Friends of Soviet Russia, Local New York, has just opened a joint campaign for the Russian-American Industrial Corporation and the Children's Homes in Soviet Russia. The corporation, formed recently in the Amalgamated, has for its purpose the promotion of industrial activity in Russia by raising sufficient capital to start large factories. A million dollars is needed for the initial capital, and thousands have already purchased stock, which sells at $10 a share. Every worker who wishes to see Soviet Russia prosper must lend his financial assistance to this project." Sidney Hillman of the Amalgamated Clothing Workers headed this organization. Lenin, Eugene V. Debs, Jane Addams, P. Steinmetz, Congressman LaGuardia, etc., were listed as stockholders.

RUSSIAN COOPERATIVE ASSOCIATION

One of the communist Russian language mass organizations; see Foreign Language Groups.

RUSSIAN MUTUAL AID SOCIETY

Official Russian language Communist fraternal insurance group.

RUSSIAN RECONSTRUCTION FARMS

Formed to aid and finance "teaching Russian peasants machine methods in agriculture . . . located in the Caucausus and is under American management . . . without the Fund's aid the first year it would not have gotten under way," says the red Garland Fund's official report listing its donations of $20,000, the purchase of $10,000 stock and a gift of $3,000 "for purchase of equipment in the United States —Jan. 20, 1926."

Says Francis Ralston Welsh: "This organization was under contract with the Communist government and its funds aided the Communist objects. It was gotten up and controlled by the American Civil Liberties Union crowd and almost all the officers and advisory board were members of that crowd." Taken from its official pamphlet soliciting funds put out in 1925 are the following names:

Officers: Horace W. Truesdell, pres.; Dr. Gregory Spragnell, vice-pres.; Stuart Chase, treas.; A. A. Heller, sec.; J. B. Collings Woods, auditor; W. Mills Hinkle, counsel; Harold A. Ware, mgr. in Russia; Donald Stephens, mgr. in America; Lucy Branham, field sec.; and Jessica Smith, exec. sec. Advisory board: Jane Addams, Roger N. Baldwin, Alice Stone Blackwell, Susan Brandeis, Prof. Sophonisba Breckinridge, Horace J. Bridges, Prof. Arthur W. Calhoun, C. N. Carver, Clarence Darrow, Anna N. Davis, Prof. Jerome Davis, Mary Dreier, Sherwood Eddy, Zona Gale, Dr. Alice Hamilton, Rev. L. O. Hartman, Arthur Garfield Hays, Prof. O. P. Hedrick, Stanley High, Hilda P. Holme, Prof. Jesse H. Holmes, Rev. John Haynes Holmes, J. A. H. Hopkins, Charles H. Ingersoll, Marietta Johnson, Rufus Jones, David Starr Jordan, Mabel Hyde Kittredge, Mary Knoblauch, Owen R. Lovejoy, Robert Morss Lovett, Dr. Charles Clayton Morrison, Prof. Henry R. Mussey, Dr. Henry Neumann, Mrs. Gordon Norrie, LeRoy Peterson, Walter W. Pettit, Roscoe Pound, I. J. Sherman, Rev. George Stewart, Dr. Gregory Stragnell, Graham R. Taylor, Seth Sprague Terry, Jr., Norman Thomas, Wilbur K. Thomas, C. A. Tupper, Allen Wardwell, Dean R. L. Watts, Edward C. Wentworth, and Mary E. Woolley.

S

SACCO-VANZETTI NATIONAL LEAGUE

Sacco-V. Nat. Lg.

Formed to aid the Communist agitation in behalf of Nicolai Sacco and Bartolomeo Vanzetti, the anarchist-communists convicted of the murder of a paymaster and theft of $15,000 at Braintree, Mass. The red Garland Fund contributed thousands of dollars for this cause, to committees and to Il Nuovo Mondo, a newspaper. In 1927 the case was finally carried to the Supreme Court and Moscow-instigated demonstrations of Reds were held all over the world, falsely using the argument that this conviction was a "frame up" of our "capitalistic government" against the innocent downtrodden Red "working class" (just as the Scottsboro and Mooney cases are now being used), thus inciting hatred of our government and revolutionary sentiment. When executed, finally, these murderers died yelling "Long live anarchy!" The home of a Judge in the case who ruled against them was recently bombed, according to press reports, by their sympathizers.

A letter sent out by the Sacco-Vanzetti Nat. Lg., May 1928, signed by Robt. Morss Lovett, listed on its letterhead the following names:

Executive Committee: Robt. Morss Lovett, chmn.; Eliz. Glendower Evans and Robt. L. Hale, vice chmn.; B. W. Huebsch, treas.; Leonard D. Abbott, Forrest Bailey, Paul F. Brissenden, Stuart Chase, Michael A. Cohn, John Lovejoy Elliott, Morris L. Ernst, Norman Hapgood, Jessica Henderson, John Haynes Holmes, Karl Llewellyn, Arthur Warner; exec. sec., Hollace Ransdell; "National Committee (To Date)": Jane Addams, Egmont Ahrens, Ruth Ahrens, Devere Allen, Dudley Babcock, Corinne Bacon, Warren Worth Bailey, Ella Reeve Bloor, Edmund B. Chaffee, Ralph Cheyney, Susan S. Codman, Felix S. Cohen, Morris R. Cohen, Algernon Coleman, John Collier, Helen Gray Cone, Clarence Darrow, Anna N. Davis, Floyd Dell, John Dewey, Smith O. Dexter,

Wm. E. Dixon, John Dos Passos, Paul H. Douglas, Betty Dublin, Will Durant, Louise A. Elsworth, John F. Finerty, Gilson Gardner, Karl F. Geiser, Eliz. Gilman, Frank A. Hamilton, Mildred F. Harnack, Eliz. S. Harrison, Margaret Hatfield, Mrs. H. C. Herring, Elsie Hillsmith, Paul J. Himmelreich, Hector M. Holmes, Henry T. Hunt, Louisa C. James, Heath Jones, Bishop Paul Jones, Alex. Kadison, Francis Fisher Kane, Wm. S. Kennedy, Natalie B. Kimber, A. H. Klocke, Frank H. Knight, Jos. Wood Krutch, F. H. LaGuardia, Harry W. Laidler, Wm. Ellery Leonard, Horace Liveright, Frank A. Manny, Jeannette Marks, Margaret Marshall, George Mischke, Dorothy I. Mulgrave, A. J. Muste, F. S. Onderdonk, Eugene O'Neill, John Orth, C. E. Parsons, Wm. L. Patterson, Helen Peabody, Eliz. G. Peckham, Caroline H. Pemberton, Henry W. Pinkam, Allan Rathburn, Mabel L. Rees, A. K. Rogers, John Nevin Sayre, J. Salwyn Schapiro, Samuel D. Schmaulhausen, P. M. Schubert, Vida D. Scudder, C. W. Shumway, Claire C. Simmonds, Upton Sinclair, Garland Smith, May Stanley, Eliz. Stuyvesant, Geo. Sutherland, Genevieve Taggart, Geo. L. Teele, Norman Thomas, Lucia Trent, John Veldhuis, Oswald Garrison Villard, Ernest Waldstein, Arthur L. Weatherly, Harry Weinberger, Jos. Weinrebe, Howard Y. Williams, Laura C. Williams, Milton Wittler, Arthur Evans Wood, Amy Woods, Mary E. Woolley.

Hdqts. 104 Fifth Ave., N.Y.C.

SAN FRANCISCO WORKERS SCHOOL

A communist Workers School (see) "sponsored by Lincoln Steffens, Langston Hughes," etc., opened Dec. 4, 1933; temporary address, 624 Golden Gate Ave. (Daily Worker, Dec. 2, 1933.)

SCANDINAVIAN WORKERS CLUBS

Communist mass Foreign Language Groups (see).

SCOTTSBORO COMMITTEES OF ACTION

Several hundred local Committees in cities all over the United States had already been formed by the communist I.L.D. in May 1933. Their purpose is to stir up race and class hatred and distrust of our form of government among Negroes and to show them that "class solidarity" with the revolutionary Communists against the "boss class" of whites is their only hope of justice and equality.

"The National Scottsboro Committee of Action is a united front body supporting the fight of the International Labor Defense for the Scottsboro Boys and the enforcement of civil rights for Negroes," said the communist Daily Worker, May 12, 1933, in describing a meeting of 4,500 persons held at Rockland Palace, N.Y. City, the night before to greet the Scottsboro committees' marchers (to Pres. Roosevelt). Richard B. Moore, colored Communist organizer, Ruby Bates, and others succeeded in stirring up a hysteria of class hatred, evidently, in this audience. " 'Strikes for the enforcement of the Bill' " (for Negro rights) " 'and freedom of the Scottsboro Boys must be brought into existence,' declared Moore.... A most impressive part of the meeting was when Moore declared 'We know who the rapists of America are.' The audience broke into a tremendous ovation that lasted over three minutes and women shouted 'Tell the truth brother. You're on the right way.' Moore received an ovation when he exposed the white ruling class as rapists and oppressors also of white women workers."

The Chicago Scottsboro Action Committee, which is headed by Prof. Robt. Morss Lovett of the U. of Chgo., staged an interracial dance at the colored "Savoy Ballroom" (South Parkway near 47th St., Chgo.), Aug. 19th, 1933, arranged under the name of "Freedom Ball" and supported by various intellectual Communist-Socialist sympathizing radical educators, ministers, etc. The national executive committee of the National Scottsboro Committee of Action as printed in the Daily Worker, May 3, 1933 is as follows:

Roger Baldwin, A.C.L.U.; J. B. Matthews, Fell. Recon.; A. Clayton Powell, Abyssinian Baptist Church; James W. Ford, T.U.U.L.; Shelton Hale Bishop, St. Phillips Church; Wm. L. Patterson, I.L.D.; Edward Welsh, Harlem Interracial Forum; John Henry Hammond, Jr., Nat. Com. Def. Pol. Pris.; W. C. Handy, hon. chmn. of former Scottsboro United Defense Com.; Harry Haywood, Communist Party of Am.; Heywood Broun, N.Y. World-Telegram; Cyril Briggs, editor "Liberator"; A. J. Muste, Conf. for Prog. Lab. Act.; Maude White, T.U.U.L. council; Bishop Collins, Episcopal Synod; Joshua Kunitz, exec. sec. Nat. Com. Def. Pol. Pris.; Sophie Epstein, Women's Council; John Goldber, Conf. for Prog. Lab. Act.; Sam. C. Patterson, Caribbean Union and Grand Order of Odd Fellows; Wm. Fitzgerald, I.L.D. (Harlem division); Mrs. Adelaide Blackwell, Eureka Temple of Elks Women; Cyril Phillip, Students Literary Assn.; Mary D. James, Supreme Coun. of Moses; Grace Campbell, Professional Wkrs. Lg.; Herman Osborne, Nat. Students Lg.; John J. Ballam, I.L.D.; G. B. Maddox, Williamsbridge Scottsboro Action Com.; Mrs. C. J. West; Sidney Spencer, Young Communist Lg.; J. Dalmus Steele, Elks; Jos. Moore, Mechanics Assn.; Herman W. Mackwain, Lg. Struggle for Negro Rights; Paul Petters, John Reed Club; Louise Thompson, sec. of former Scottsboro Unity Def. Com.; Frank Palmer, Fed. Press; Wm. N. Jones, Baltimore Afro-American; Matthews Crawford, Jr., Scottsboro Com. in San Francisco; Loren Miller, editor of Cal. Eagle, Los Angeles; Eugene Gordon, Boston Post; J. B. Blayton, Atlanta, Ga. Negro Chamber Commerce; Benj. J. Davis, Jr., Atlanta Com. for Defense of Angelo Herndon; Rev. J. W. Broun, Mother Zion Church; Rev. R. M. Bolden, First Emanuel Ch.; Wm. M. Kelley, Amsterdam News; Dr. Thos. S. Harten, Holy Trinity Baptist Ch., Brooklyn; Dr. L. H. King, St. Marks Ch.; Channing H. Tobias, Y.M.C.A., a representative of Corona Scottsboro Com.; Richard Warner; Samuel Mitchell; H. I. Thomas; Seward L. Virgil.

SCOTTSBORO UNITY DEFENSE COMMITTEE

Preceded the present Scottsboro Committees of Action (see).

SHARECROPPERS UNION

Cotton pickers' communist T.U.U.L. union; affiliated with the League of Struggle for Negro Rights; organized largely in Alabama; membership in 1933, about 5,000.

SHOE AND LEATHER WORKERS INDUSTRIAL UNION

Communist T.U.U.L. union; Fred Biedenkapp (see "Who's Who") nat. sec.; its 10-day amalgamation convention held in Boston, Dec. 1933, succeeded in uniting 70,000 shoe workers under the banner of a new union, the United Shoe Workers Union, under Communist leadership. (Daily Worker, Dec. 23, 1933); a celebration meeting held in N.Y. City was addressed by Rose Wortis of the T.U.U.L. and by Biedenkapp, over a telephone broadcasting arrangement.

SLOVAK WORKERS SOCIETY

Communist fraternal mass Foreign Language Groups (see).

SMALL HOME AND LAND OWNERS ASSOCIATION

A communist-conceived organization which has been successful in Detroit and Cleveland; a unit being organized in Pittsburg was to be addressed Sept. 1, 1933 by Cleveland organizers. Communists certainly do not care whether small home owners lose their property or not, for wherever they gain control they intend, as in Russia, to take it away from private owners anyway, but they use any pretext whatever to stir up strife.

SOCIALIST-LABOR PARTY

Left-wing openly revolutionary Socialist party; publishes Hungarian, South Slavonian, Bulgarian, Greek papers, and the English paper "Weekly People." John P. Quinn, nat. organizer; hdqts. Arnold Petersen, 45 Rose St., N.Y.C.

SOCIALIST PARTY

See under general articles, Socialist Party and the New Deal, etc., also under Internationals (2nd), and Socialist and Labor International. 1933 Socialist Party National Executive Committee: Norman Thomas, Albert Sprague Coolidge, Powers Hapgood, Darlington Hoopes, Leo. M. Krzycki, Morris Hillquit, James D. Graham, Daniel W. Hoan, Jasper McLevy, John L. Packard, Lilith M. Wilson.

SOUTHERN LEAGUE FOR PEOPLES RIGHTS

Organized in 1933 at Atlanta, Ga.; stands for unlimited "free speech," academic freedom, social and racial equality, etc. Sherwood Anderson was elected chmn., Bruce Crawford, vice chmn., Vann Woodward, exec. sec. and Jessie B. Blayton, treas.

SOVIET AMERICAN SECURITIES CORPORATION

Organized Dec. 1932 to sell in the U.S.A. a ten million dollar issue of Soviet government bonds to finance the second Five Year Plan. A 1933 Chgo. Daily News article stated that the organization was being investigated for a possible violation of the Security Act of 1933. It is reported that thousands of dollars worth of these bonds have already been sold—many to American workers. Incorporators were:

Miles Sherover of Greenwich, Conn. (former Consulting Engineer for Soviet Govt.); Osmund Fraenkel of Greenwich, Conn. (an attorney for the communist I.L.D., who has been active in the Scottsboro and other Communist cases in the South); Arthur Fisher of Winnetka, Ill. (pres. of the A.C.L.U. Chgo. Committee and a director of the Amalgamated Bank, Chgo.)

The communist Daily Worker, July 27, 1933, featured a huge advertisement of this Corporation and its Soviet bonds.

SOVIET RUSSIA TODAY

Magazine of communist Friends of the Soviet Union; published monthly; 80 E. 11th St., N.Y.C.; ed. bd.: A. A. Heller, Cyril Lambkin, Liston M. Oak.

SOVIET TRAVEL

Intourist (Soviet govt. travel agency) magazine; pub. at 261 Fifth Ave., N.Y.

SOVIET UNION INFORMATION BUREAU

Until recognition, the unofficial embassy of the Soviet govt. in the U.S.; headed by Boris Skvirsky; 1637 Mass. Ave., N.W., Wash., D.C.; publishes "Soviet Union Review" and recommends books favorable to the U.S.S.R.

SOVIET UNION REVIEW

Publication of Soviet Union Information Bureau.

SOVKINO

Soviet government official motion picture organization which produces revolutionary propaganda films shown all over the world. Serge Eisenstein, one of its Moscow staff, was recently engaged by Hollywood producers. Upton Sinclair and Kate Crane Gartz aided and financed his Mexican picture, according to the latter's letter published in New Republic, Sept. 6, 1933.

SPARK, THE

Official organ of the communist Student League of Canada.

SPORT AND PLAY, NEW

Monthly magazine of the communist Labor Sports Union; 813 Broadway, N.Y.C.

STEEL AND METAL WORKERS INDUSTRIAL UNION

Communist T.U.U.L. union; claimed 14,600 members in 1933 with 2,000 in Buffalo district, 820 in the Chicago district, 3,100 in the Pittsburg district, 450 in the St. Louis district, and 2,400 in the N.Y. district; led strikes (Sept. 1933) in St. Louis, N.Y. City, Chicago, Indiana Harbor, Buffalo, N.Y., McKee's Rocks, Pa.

STELTON SCHOOL

At Stelton, N.J.; see under "Anarchism."

ST. STEPHENS COLLEGE

See Union Theological Seminary.

STUDENT CONGRESS AGAINST WAR (AT U. OF CHICAGO)

Student Cong. Ag. War.

In opening the Congress, Jos. Cohen, who had been a student delegate of the communist National Student League to the World Congress Against War at Amsterdam, said: "This Congress was called by the National Committee at the suggestion of the World Congress Against War in Amsterdam" (see).

Professors Robt. Morss Lovett, Frederick L. Schuman and Harry D. Gideonse were official faculty sponsors of this Student Congress, which was held at the University of Chicago, Mandel Hall, Dec. 27-29, 1932, with the sanction, necessarily, of Pres. Hutchins.

According to the official printed program of the Congress, speakers and leaders of its discussion groups were: Earl Browder, nat. sec. of the Communist Party of the U.S.A. (who attends the more important Communist functions); Scott Nearing, a Communist leader; Jos. Freeman, Communist editor of New Masses and co-author with Scott Nearing of "Dollar Diplomacy"; J. B. Matthews of the Fell Recon.; Upton Close; Jane Addams (speaker with Scott Nearing and J. B. Matthews, Dec. 28, afternoon session); and a few others. It stated also: "Arrangements are being made to house the delegates on or near the campus." Dec. 27th was given to registering the delegates at Mandel Hall.

According to the Advisory Associates stenographic report of the session, the following events occurred:

Joe Weber and Joe Jurich, Communist Party functionaries, were officially present; Ben Gray of Cleveland and Jack Kling of Chicago, both of the Young Communist League, and communist I.L.D. atty. Vladimir Janowicz and his wife, were also present. The sessions averaged about 600 delegates present and a gallery of from 50 to 300 visitors.

The chairman first read greetings sent by sympathizers. Among these was a message from Communist Theodore Dreiser saying: "This is the most significant step towards peace since the Russian Revolution." This message also called upon the youth in capitalist countries to convince members of existing armed forces that their real enemies were at home—that it is the capitalist system and those enemies, who are driving people to poverty and death. A message from Rev. Henry Sloane Coffin, president of Union Theological Seminary, started: "Every Christian should be heart and soul against war. I heartily endorse the Student Congress Against War." Corliss Lamont and Jos. Freeman sent "Revolutionary Greetings."

Jos. Cohen in his "Keynote Address" urged that the "Manifesto" of the Amsterdam W.C.A.W. be studied by every delegate of this Congress. He asserted that "the importance of this Congress lay in the action that would be taken for the future, in the fight against the R.O.T.C. and C.M.T.C., and other war institutions."

Earl Browder (nat. sec. Communist Party) was greeted with a burst of applause. He said that Communism, while opposing imperialist war was not opposed to civil war, which was the only way to overthrow capitalist imperialism and stop imperialist war; and that the only answer to the war dangers in schools was the National Student League (Communist); that the student of today must tear down tradition and fight for the abolition of the private ownership system; that in Russia and throughout the world Communists advocate birth control and allow only those physically fit to bring children into the world the same as manufacturing is limited to the needs of the nation; and that anyone really working against war must unite with the Communist Party for the overthrow of capitalism. Following Browder's address was a question period in which the question was asked "Can Communist students strike against the R.O.T.C.?", to which Browder replied: "The Communist Party energetically supports any movement designed to fight the R.O.T.C. Every student should join in a united front against the damn menace."

J. B. Matthews said the pacifists have always been a failure because they were one war behind; that in the next war they must be organized in a united front to march on the seat of authority where war is declared, and that in order to do this we must be organized and prepared to overthrow any government that attempts to plunge us into war for any cause whatever; that even if capitalism could outlaw war, pacifists would still have a social duty to perform, as there can be no peace in the world for the workers as long as this parasitical bloodsucking system has the world in its grip. He also lauded Jane Addams and Scott Nearing for their war time work.

Jane Addams spoke next and said she stood with Gandhi in his policy of non-violence. (He unfortunately incites such violence in others that he has to be jailed continually.)

Communist Scott Nearing, who spoke next, said that war is the central political function of modern capitalist states, that the only way to peace was through a new social order based on production for use and not for profit, and that the producers must organize to take away the social and economic machinery from the gang of profiteers now in power. "We call it seizure of power" he said. He said that the Amsterdam Congress advocated strikes in munition plants, fraternization among troops of opposing armies, refusal to transport war materials, and organization of nuclei in armed forces to spread revolutionary ideals. Concluding, he said the day would come when organized groups would settle all differences over green-top tables and say "Down with Capitalism and up with the Soviet Union."

An evening discussion of Group No. 1 was led by J. B. Matthews and Mac Gordon and delegates from Toledo, Syracuse, John Hopkins U., N.Y. City, etc. told of their efforts to smash the R.O.T.C. A delegate from Columbia stated: "If a college is in the Soviet Union, a military unit should be an integral part of the institution's life but not so in the United States." At Syracuse, it was explained, the pacifist clergymen among the alumni body were played upon to work against military training in the schools. This was highly recommended for a line of strategy in Church schools. Mac Gordon summarized the discussion by saying that "the most important thing is not whether I take it or not" (military training), "but to break up the corps entirely by propagandizing against it and to fight against the National Guard, C.M.T.C. and American Legion."

Discussion Group No. 2 was led by Communist Eugene Bechtold, instructor in the communist Chicago "Workers School" of revolution. Recommendations were: "Present a petition to Congress refusing to support militarism in any form. In case of war, the students must call a strike in all industry and agriculture. But we must now join the R.O.T.C., C.M.T.C., Army and Navy so we can bore from within to cause its downfall. We changed from the Feudal system to the Monarchy and from the Monarchies to the Capitalist system, of which the United States is the bastard child. The Communist party calls on all the workers and students of the United States to overthrow this government and set up a Communist state."

The morning session of Thursday, Dec. 29, opened with the reading of a "Revolutionary Greeting" from the communist "Chicago Workers School." The first speaker was Donald Henderson, nat. sec. of the communist National Student League. He said the R.O.T.C. must be penetrated and the cadets convinced that they were merely being trained for cannon fodder and that the students must also fight against the economic system and demand that the money for military training be given for educational purposes instead. A Hyde Park High School delegate stated that teachers let girls talk to classes for five or ten minutes to get delegates to the Congress. C. Jones, colored graduate of Columbia and student of a "Wilkins College" in Chicago, advocated boring from within and made a vicious attack on Christianity which was received with great applause. A woman delegate from Antioch College, Yellow Springs, Ohio, made a viciously revolutionary talk urging the entire system of profit be done away with and that a revolution was the only way out. A delegate from Milwaukee State Teachers College attacked the National Guard and military expenses and said his campus was too liberal to support any R.O.T.C. unit. Jos. Cohen presented resolutions on recognition of Russia, Student Fight Against Militarism in High Schools and Colleges, etc.

Communist literature was distributed including: Student Review (of N.S. Lg.); the Communist International's "Struggle Against Imperialist War and the Task of the Communists"; "Is the American Intellectual?" by Maxim Gorki; "A Warless World" by Scott Nearing; "Stop Munitions" by C. Bulazel, pub. by R.I.L.U.; W.C.A.W. pamphlet pub. by its Am. Com. for Struggle Against War; Moscow Daily News; Lenin's "The Threatening Catastrophe and How to Fight It"; "Socialism and War" by G. Zinoviev and V. I. Lenin; Intl. Publishers Catalogue; "The Soviets Fight for Disarmament" by A. Lunacharsky; Anti-Imperialist Review; "Another World War" by Scott Nearing; "The World Crisis and War Danger" by N. Rudolph, printed in Russia; etc.

Also distributed were: "Program 1931-1932, *Women's International League for Peace and Freedom*"; "Out of a Job—Why?" by *Women's International League for Peace and Freedom* (headed by Jane Addams); Application Blank of *"Green International, a World Movement for the Higher Patriotism"*; Prospectus of *Green International;* "What Is War Resistance" by Jessie Wallace Hughan, issued by *War Resisters Lg.*, 171 W. 12th St., N.Y. City; "War Resistance" by Wm. Floyd, dir. *Peace Patriots,* issued by Arbitrator Press, 114 E. 31 St., N.Y. City.

The "National Committee for the Student Congress Against War" was formed by members of the American Committee for Struggle Against War (of the World Congress Against War at Amsterdam) in conjunction with the communist National Student League. All of these committees and Congresses are under the control and direction of Moscow's Intl. Lg. Against Imperialism and its leaders. A comparison will show that certain leaders serve on the various committees.

The Nat. Com. for the Student Congress Against War as printed on the official program is as follows:

Sherwood Anderson, Henri Barbusse, Eleanor Copenhaver (Y.W.C.A.), George S. Counts, Leo Gallagher (I.L.D.), Donald Henderson, H. W. L. Dana, Corliss Lamont, J. B. Matthews, Herman J. Muller, Scott Nearing, Margaret Schlauch, Frederick L. Schuman, Thos. Woody, Robt. Morss Lovett; Students: Edmund Stevens of the N.S. Lg., chmn., Columbia U., N.Y.; Dora Zucker, sec., Coll. City of N.Y.; Margaret Bailey, treas., N.Y. Univ.; Gregory Bardacke, Syracuse Coll., Mass.; Jos. Cohen, Brooklyn Coll., N.Y.; Edwin L. Diggs, Lambuth Coll., Tenn.; Henry Forblade, Commonwealth Coll., Ark.; Carl Geiser, Tenn. Coll., Ohio; Edw. Hartshorne, Jr., Harvard U., Mass.; Richard Lake, State U., Mont.; George Perazich, U. of Cal.; Eugene Schaffarman, U. of Mich.; Norman Spitzer, Cornell U., N.Y.; Nathaniel Weyl, Columbia U., N.Y.; Ira Latimer, LeMoyne Coll., Memphis, Tenn.

STUDENT LEAGUE

See National Student League (Communist).

STUDENT OUTLOOK

Organ of socialist League for Industrial Democracy (see); pub. by its "Intercollegiate Student Council"; changed name from "Revolt"; previously called Intercollegiate Socialist Review; 112 E. 19th St., N.Y.C.

STUDENT REVIEW

Organ of communist National Student League (see); staff and contributors affiliated with Revolutionary Writers Federation.

SUIT CASE AND BAG WORKERS UNION

Now the Pocketbook section of the Shoe and Leather Workers Industrial Union, a communist T.U.U.L. union; under Fred Biedenkapp.

"SURVEY"

And "Survey Graphic"; intellectual socialistic publications; Paul U. Kellogg, editor; evidence concerning its favorable attitude toward the I.W.W., its "apologetic attitude toward extreme radical activities," its articles "to encourage the demand for the release of so-called 'political prisoners' like Debs and Kate Richards O'Hare," is printed in the Lusk Report, also that it received $13,000 yearly from the Russell Sage Foundation; Edward T. Devine, Graham Taylor, Jane Addams, Jos. K. Hart, Haven Emerson, M.D., Robt. W. Bruere, Joanna C. Colcord, are contributing editors and Mary Ross, Beulah Amidon, Leon Whipple, John Palmer Gavit, Loula D. Lasker, Florence Loeb Kellogg, and Gertrude Springer, assoc. editors (1933); Arthur Kellogg is mg. ed.; Lucius R. Eastman is pres., Julian W. Mack, Joseph P. Chamberlain, John Palmer Gavit are vice presidents, Ann Reed Brenner is sec., and Arthur Kellogg treas. of Survey Associates, Inc., the publishers: bd. dir.: Jane Addams, Eleanor R. Belmont, Jacob Billikopf, Alexander M. Bing, Jos. P. Chamberlain, Francis G. Curtis, Lucius R. Eastman, Felix Frankfurter, Nicholas Kelley, John A. Kingbury, Agnes Brown Leach, Adele Rosenwald Levy, J. Noel Macy, Rita Wallach Morgenthau, Edw. L. Ryerson, Jr., Richard B. Scandrett, Jr., Harold H. Swift, Lillian D. Wald, 112 E. 19th St., N.Y.C.

SYNDICALISM

Means: "The ownership and operation of each industry by the workers in that industry—the political state to be abolished." Anarchists, Communists, I.W.W.'s, and Socialists are all in some degree syndicalists; all favor the abolition of the present political state. Hence laws passed against seditious, revolutionary activities aimed at the overthrow of the state have come to be called "syndicalism" laws, the name being derived from the foreign name for labor unions or "syndicates."

T

TASS (CABLE SERVICE)

Official Soviet cable service; has office with the Federated Press in Washington, D.C.

TAXI WORKERS UNION

Communist T.U.U.L. union.

TEACHERS UNION

Radical-pacifist, anti-national-defense, pro-Soviet Teachers Union of N.Y. City; received from the red Garland Fund "towards the educational campaign for the repeal of Lusk Laws, $500," also $6,000 and $3,172.50 for "operating expenses" and "research and publicity work outside of regular activities." (The Lusk Laws were anti-sedition laws recommended by the Lusk Committee of the N.Y. State Legislature.) Henry R. Linville is president. He is also pres. of the radical American Federation of Teachers.

TEXTILE WORKERS INDUSTRIAL UNION, NATIONAL

Communist T.U.U.L. union.

TOBACCO WORKERS INDUSTRIAL UNION

A communist T.U.U.L. union; primarily organized around Tampa, Fla.; agitated strikes involving more than 9,000 workers in cigar industry there in 1933; the Communist Labor Defender, Aug. 1933, exults over the freeing of all Tampa prisoners by the communist I.L.D.; conducted general strike affecting 40 shops and 4,000 workers, in N.Y. City, Aug. 1933, from hdqts. at 350 E. 31st St., N.Y. City.

TRADE UNION EDUCATIONAL LEAGUE

Organized Nov. 1920; reorganized as the Trade Union Unity League at Cleveland, Aug. 1929; headed then and now by Communist Wm. Z. Foster; it specialized in "boring from within" other unions while the present organization in addition organizes Red Unions; received $900 from Garland Fund, 1925-26.

TRADE UNION UNITY LEAGUE T.U.U.L.

Communist federation of labor; American section of the Profintern or Red International of Labor Unions directed by Moscow; a federation of Communist labor unions directing and spreading the Red trade union movement and also directing Communist members who have bored from within A.F. of L. unions to gain control; organizes the communist Unemployed Councils; membership 1933 is 89,700; organized at Cleveland, Aug. 1929; succeeded the Trade Union Educational League, which specialized on "boring from within" regular unions; Wm. Z. Foster is nat. sec. and was also head of the former Trade Union Educational League; official organ is "Labor Unity"; hdqts. 2 W. 15th St., N.Y. City.

TRANSPORTATION WORKERS LEAGUE

A communist T.U.U.L. union; also the American section of the International of Transportation Workers.

TUNNEL WORKERS INDUSTRIAL UNION

Communist T.U.U.L. union.

U

UKRAINIAN PROLETARIAN WRITERS AND WORKER-CORRESPONDENTS ASSOCIATION

Section of communist Revolutionary Writers Federation.

UKRAINIAN WOMENS TOILERS ASSOCIATION

UKRAINIAN WORKERS CLUBS

Communist Foreign Language Groups (see).

UNEMPLOYED COUNCILS

Communist Party organizations for agitating the unemployed; organized July 4, 1930 at a Chicago Congress of Communist District Organizers; is a section of the T.U.U.L.; is controlled by "Party fractions" and officerships (as are Foreign Language Groups); nat. sec. Israel Amter; Cook County, Ill. sec., Karl Lockner; Chicago has 71 city branches and local quarters; Ill. State hdqts. 2401 W. Roosevelt Road; Cook Co. organ is "The Chicago

Hunger Fighter"; agitates in 36 States, each State having State as well as local hdqts.; nat. hdqts. N.Y. City.

UNEMPLOYED ORGANIZATIONS

In order to distinguish the unemployed groups of one Party from those of another:

Unemployed Councils are groups of the Communist Party.

Workers Leagues are those of the Proletarian Party (Communist).

Unemployed Unions are those of the I.W.W.

Unemployed Citizens Leagues, often called *Unemployed Leagues,* are those of the Conference for Progressive Labor Action (left-wing, militant, Socialist, Communist-cooperating organization led by A. J. Muste).

Associations of Unemployed are those of the Communist Party (Opposition) led by Jay Lovestone.

(*National*) *Federation of Unemployed Workers Leagues* is the Communist-I.W.W. dominated united front of all groups, organized by Karl Borders.

Workers Committees on Unemployment (of N.Y., Chicago, etc.) are Borders' L.I.D. Socialist groups cooperating with all of the others.

UNION OF EAST AND WEST

See Fellowship of Faiths.

UNION THEOLOGICAL SEMINARY (AND ST. STEPHENS COLLEGE)

The notable number of ministerial graduates and instructors of Union Theological Seminary who are also active agitators in the Red Socialist-Communist movement have helped, no doubt, to popularize its nickname "The Red Seminary." The L.I.D. conference "Guiding the Revolution" held there Dec. 1931, the activities of men like Karl Borders, Harry Ward, Reinhold Niebuhr, Arnold Johnson (arrested for criminal syndicalism), the Seminary's advertised recommendation of a filthy sex book for the Eugenics Publishing Co. (fellow publishers of the atheist Freethought Press), etc., etc., help this reputation along.

The Lusk Report (p. 1115) states: "There are two dangerous centers of Revolutionary Socialist teaching of a university type in ecclesiastical institutions. One is the Union Theological Seminary of New York, where Christian Ethics are taught by Dr. Harry F. Ward; the other is St. Stephens College at Annandale, N.Y., where the president is the Rev. Iddings-Bell, and the professor of economics the Socialist, Dr. Edwards. . . .

"Dr. Ward is the author of 'The New Social Order,' in which he shows a decided sympathy for Socialist social forms and is friendly to Bolshevism in Russia. . . . He characterized the cognate I.W.W. 'philosophy' as the most ideal and practical philosophy since the days of Jesus Christ, and as expressing the ideas of Christ much more closely than any church of the present day.

" . . . He is chairman of the American Civil Liberties Union which champions the I.W.W., and presided over the I.W.W. meeting of Feb. 9, 1920, held at the Rand School, to raise money for the defense of the I.W.W. murderers of the four members of the American Legion at Centralia.

" . . . The pro-Bolshevik articles which Dr. Ward contributed to 'The Social Service Bulletin' of the Methodist Federation for Social Service were considered particularly objectionable because the Bulletin was circulated not only by the Methodist Church but by the Congregational, Northern Baptist and other organizations. They called attention to Dr. Ward's text books circulated by the Graded Sunday School Syndicate. Dr. Ward is also connected with the Y.M.C.A., the Y.W.C.A. and the Inter-Church World Movement.

" . . . Such specialists in Bolshevism as Lieutenant Klieforth and Wm. English Walling have characterized Dr. Ward's statements as downright falsehoods or distorted facts, and as a kind of Bolshevism far worse than the Bolshevism of Russia.

"The same attempt to swing existing educational institutions to the support of the atheism and materialism of the I.W.W. and Bolshevism is shown in the movement in the Episcopal Church of which the nominal leader is the Rev. Bernard Iddings Bell. He is at the head of St. Stephens College at Annandale. . . . The head of the department of economics is the Rev. Lyford P. Edwards, an able expositor of Socialism and member of the Socialist Party. He gives courses at the college on the I.W.W., on Syndicalism, Socialism and Bolshevism. As a Socialist . . . he teaches these movements to the young Episcopalians sympathetically.

"What the President, Dr. Bell himself, thinks, can be judged from his book, 'Right and Wrong after the War.' He here bases the whole history and character of civilization on what he calls the two great 'Urges,' the Hunger Urge and the Sex Urge. He accepts, in other words, the lowest form of the Karl Marx materialistic conception of history, in which there is absolutely no place for God in the evolution of the universe. Logically this is inescapable atheism. As a corollary he states two fundamental articles of faith: (1) that private property should be absolutely abolished and (2) that interest on invested property, rents, savings, etc. is robbery. He also condemns, as the Bolsheviki do, the present institution of the family, which he regards as a purely sexual relation, except insofar as it subserves the raising of the young.

"In a sermon delivered on May 23, 1920, in the Cathedral of St. John the Divine, Dr. Bell announced his sympathy with the revolutionary element of labor which demands the abolishing of the wage system and the communistic assumption of control."

UNITED CONFERENCE FOR PROGRESSIVE POLITICAL ACTION

See under Conference for Progressive Political Action.

UNITED COUNCILS OF WORKING CLASS HOUSEWIVES

UNITED COUNCILS OF WORKING CLASS WOMEN

American sections of the Womens Communist International; very active in preventing evictions, in unemployed demonstrations, in picketing and, in 1932, led strikes in N.Y., Chicago, etc., to compel reduction of price of bread; the official organ is "The Working Woman," "published monthly by the Central Committee of the Communist Party U.S.A. Section of the Communist International, Fifty East 13th St., N.Y. City" (price 50c year). The following groups bought space in the May 1933 issue to send "Revolutionary Greetings to the Workers of the Soviet Union":

Nairjosta, Waukegan, Ill.; Scandinavian Working Women's Council of Cleveland; Womens Councils of Elmwood, Ill. and of Albany Park, Chicago; Council No. 3 Chicago; Lithuanian Working Womens Alliance branch No. 17, Detroit; Branch No. 130; Ukrainian Working Women Red Star of Dearborn, Mich.; Armenian Working Women, Detroit; Womens Council of Stamford, Conn.; Fitchburg Womens Club and Secretariat, Fitchburg, Mass.

UNITED FARMERS LEAGUE

(and Communist Farm Movement)

Communist Party organization; formerly known as the United Farmers Educational League. To quote: "As to making the U.F.L. a mere propaganda organization I want to say we have purposely taken the word 'educational' from the name of the United Farmers Educational League, to indicate that we now abandon our propaganda stage among the farmers and now enter into actual struggles. . . . " "The leadership in the . . . revolution itself, must go to the city proletariat as the really conscious, revolutionary class by virtue of the fact that the city proletarians are so situated, socially and economically, that they can gain control of, and dominate the institutions which are of decisive importance when it is a question of seizing and holding power. Obviously the farmers are not so situated. . . . However the city proletariat must diligently seek the masses of poor farmers as an ally in the Revolution, and the consummation of such an alliance, is a necessary prerequisite for a *successful Revolution in America*. The revolutionary city industrial workers, guided and led by the Communist Party, cannot seize and hold power without such an alliance."

"What is the function of the United Farmers League? The Party has set up the U.F.L. and its official organ the United Farmer, as a means of reaching the poor farmers with the revolutionary message, as an aid to the Party . . . not in any passive or extraneous sense, but quite actively, and as a means of actual struggle and combat with the capitalists and the capitalist authorities."

"The U.F.L. is not and will not be a 'dead' organization. That the poor farmers will actually do something for themselves . . . is proved by what took place in a small town in Wisconsin recently, where the farmers objected to the high taxes foisted upon them, and took physical action against the tax collectors, and also by an incident in Arkansas, where a group of farmers, who were starving, helped themselves to foodstuffs by stealing it openly." "Yes, the poor farmers will fight. Just try them out and see!" (From Alfred Knutson's Communist Party treatise "Function of the Revolutionary U.F.L.")

The Communist farmer movement has been growing by leaps and bounds. In the Western States such as Colorado, California, etc., where there are large numbers of Japanese, Mexican and Filipino laborers in the fruit and vegetable areas, the communist Agricultural Workers Industrial Union of the T.U.U.L. has been operating successfully. December 7-10, 1932 at Washington, D.C. the communist-controlled Farmers National Relief Conference under the leadership of Lem Harris formed a *National Farmers Committee for Action.*

NATIONAL FARMERS COMMITTEE FOR ACTION

Typical Red resolutions were adopted demanding: recognition of Russia; Negro equality; unlimited "free speech" and rights to parade; elimination of all appropriations for national defense; "Hands Off" Haiti, China, Philippines, or wherever revolutionary activities endanger American holdings. To quote: "No American investor in foreign lands should have any claim on our government for the protection of his property."

Lem Harris' executive committee was composed of John Marshall (Ohio Communist executive); Fred Chase, New Hampshire Communist leader; Lew Bentzley, for whom the Young Pioneers sawed wood (see United Farmers Protective Assn.); and Philip Smith of New Hope, Pa., close associate of Bentzley. The organization voted to maintain a permanent office at 1622 H St., N.W., Washington, D.C. and to publish the Farmers National Weekly as its official organ with Robt. H. Hall as editor (now combined with United Farmers Lg. organ).

Others elected on the National Committee were:

Chmn., A. O. Rosenberg, vice pres. Nebr. State Holiday Assn.; L. B. Stein, Connecticut Valley Farmers; George Keith, communist United Farmers Lg. of Idaho; Geo. C. Wright of Iowa; W. M. Hobby, Mass. Farmers Lg.; Booker T. Thurman, Keystone Club of Negro Farmers, Mich.; George Casper, communist United Farmers Lg. of Mich.; James Flower, Wadena Committee of Action, Minn.; Andrew Oja, Farmers Union Local 165; Andrew Dahlsten, Nebraska Farmers Holiday Assn. (Madison County Plan) (referred to in communist Henry Puro's article as a leftwing Red organization); Stephen Negroescu, West New Jersey Dairy Union; A. Salo, Spencer Cooperative Society, New York; Andrew Omholt, Farm Holiday Assn., N.D.; Paul Dale, Finnish Farmers Club, Oregon; A. Meyer, Farm Holiday Assn., S.D.; P. E. Rhinehart, Va.; Ralph Nelson, communist United Farmers Lg., Wash.; J. Hetts, communist United Farmers Lg., Wis.; Fred C. Strong, Wyo. Holiday Assn.

This National Farmers Committee, a subsidiary of the United Farmers League, formed State groups. The Iowa group, for example, under the leadership of "Mother" Ella Reeve Bloor, veteran Communist agitator, proceeded to stir up violence around Sioux City. The State groups penetrated the Farmers Holiday Association groups that had been organized by Milo Reno (himself active in the radical Conference for Progressive Political Action movement) and seized control of them by placing Communist leaders at the head. Some time ago (summer 1933) when it was claimed that the combined membership of the three groups numbered 92,000 with 68,000 of this number in the Farmers National Committee for Action, Advisory Associates Bulletin stated:

"The conservative farmers' organizations, such as the American Farm Bureau Federation, have consistently refused to recognize or admit the spread of Communist influence in agricultural districts and therefore have been of little service in exposing or opposing the advance of Communism. 92,000 farmers under Communist revolutionary leadership is a lot of farmers. Unite this force with the Communist industrial workers and there develops a picture that should be startling to even the most apathetic citizen."

I attended one of the sessions of the Farmers Second National Conference held at the Chicago Coliseum, Nov. 17, 1933. The Internationale was sung and the usual Communist banners decorated the hall. Israel Amter and Ella Reeve Bloor of the Communist Party central committee spoke. Over 700 delegates from 36 states representing organizations with *130,885* members were in attendance and a total audience of about 3,000 people.

Ella Reeve Bloor, the clever old agitator introduced as having occupied many a jail, said: "Last year we stood for a *moratorium* on mortgages. This year we have unanimously voted for *cancellation* of all mortgages. Next year we will be so strong we will seize the power and will *confiscate* the rich property holders lands!" For this she was cheered vociferously. She told how in certain towns the relief authorities had refused relief to farmers who drove automobiles and how she and her crowd had forced them not only to give relief but to buy gasoline for the cars. More cheers. Her entire talk was a popularly received incitement to violence.

I glanced around at this crowd of colored and white people of the cheering audience with their fur-collared, silk-lined coats, good shoes and overcoats and with them mentally contrasted the many Russians whom I had seen carrying their shoes when it rained in order to save them, who wear rags about their heads, the best of them, and I thought of the pitiful millions in Russia now being deliberately mercilessly liquidated by starvation on the theory that they are "bourgeois" class enemies of their heartless atheist Communist government.

Two delegates from one state who are acquaintances of mine told me of the wire sent by the conference to Moscow expressing solidarity of the American farmers with the workers (poor slaves) of Soviet Russia and of the reply of gratification received back from Moscow. Communist Party organizers held firm control of every session and it was apparent, they said, that every act, every resolution, had been cut and dried in advance for the delegates by these trained Party organizers.

A parody to be sung to the tune of "My Country 'Tis of Thee," entitled "Greed's Country 'Tis of Thee," was dedicated to the Conference by the communist United Farmers League and was in part as follows:

* * * * * *

Bosses of slavery,
Graft, crime and charity,
Prepare for tours!
Our hearts with rapture thrill
To know that home and hill
Field, stock, crop and mill
Will not be yours!
Etc., etc.

Another song dedicated to the Conference by the same author is entitled "Before the Revolution," sung to the tune of "Yankee Doodle."

Nat. hdqts. United Farmers Lg., 1629 Linden Ave., Minneapolis, Minn.; nat. sec., Alfred Tiala; official organ "Producers News," "published Friday of each week at Plentywood, Montana, by the Peoples Publishing Co., Inc."; Eric Bert, ed.; L. M. Lerner, acting ed.; Chas. E. Taylor, mg. ed.; Hans Rasmussen, bus. mgr.; Jan. 1934 combined with National Farmers Committee of Action "Farmers National Weekly" with hdqts. at 1510 W. 18th St., Chicago.

Farmers' National Committee for Action Affiliated Organizations (calling Second Conference):

Alabama: Alabama Farmers' Protective Assn.; Cullman County Debt Holiday Assn.; Share Croppers' Un.; *Arkansas:* Farmers' Protective Assn. of Arkansas; Hugh Gore, Route 2, Mena, State sec.; *California:* United Farmers' League, Carl Patterson, 2546 Inyo St., Fresno, State sec.; *Colorado:* Farm Holiday Assn. of San Juan Basin, Enoch Hardaway, Dove Creek, sec.; *Connecticut:* United Farmers of Windham County, Aino Koskinen, Box 100, Brooklyn, sec.; *Florida:* Farmers' Protective Assn. of Pasco County, Victor Eikeland, Route 1, Zephyrhills, sec.; Farmers' and Farm Workers' Lg.; *Illinois:* Westville Branch, Small Home and Land Owners' Lg., John F. Sloan, 114 Illinois St., Westville, sec.; *Iowa:* Iowa Regional Committee for Action, E. R. Bloor, 1117 McDonald St., Sioux City, sec.; *Kentucky:* Kentucky Farmers' Local Committee for Action, No. 1; C. W. Button, Hibernia, sec.; *Michigan:* Michigan Farmers' League, Clyde U. Smith, Route 1, Beulah, sec.; *Minnesota:* United Farmers' League, James Flower, 1629 Linden Ave., Minneapolis, State sec., Alfred Tiala, 1629 Linden Ave., Minneapolis, National sec.; Minnesota State Youth Committee for Action, Matt Hill, Box 318, Virginia, sec.; *Montana:* United Farmers' League, Rodney Salisbury, Plentywood, State sec.; *Nebraska:* Holiday Assn. of Nebraska (Madison County Plan), J. J. Schefcik, Alliance, pres.; *New Jersey:* New Jersey Farmers' Protective Assn., Harry W. Springer, 3rd and Park Aves., Vineland, pres.; West New Jersey Farmers' Dairy Un., John F. Buggeln, Jutland, sec.; *North Dakota:* North Dakota State Committee for Action, Ashbel Ingerson, Flaxton, sec.; United Farmers' Lg., P. J. Barrett, Sanish, State sec.; *Ohio:* Ohio Farmers' Lg., John W. Marshall, Route 1, Leetonia, sec.; *Oklahoma:* Oklahoma Farm Debt Holiday Assn., Local No. 1, John Phillips, Tuttle, sec.; Oklahoma Farm Debt Holiday Assn., Local No. 3, W. I. Cecil, Blanchard, sec.; Farmers' Organization of Red Hill, J. M. Weeks, Route 1, Newalla, sec.; Atowah Farmers' Committee for Action, F. W. Avants, Route 1, Noble, sec.; Cole Farmers' Committee for Action, E. S. Easley, Route 2, Blanchard, sec.; *Oregon:* Oregon State Committee for Action, Paul Dale, Knappa, sec.; Farmers' Protective Assn. of Oregon; *Pennsylvania:* United Farmers' Protective Assn., Lewis Bentzley, Route 3, Perkasie, pres.; Philadelphia Regional Committee for Action, Lillian Gales, care of Bentzley, Route 3, Perkasie, sec.; Farmers' Protective Assn., H. H. Hawbaker, Greencastle, sec.; *South Dakota:* South Dakota State Committee for Action, E. L. Bolland, Pierpont, sec.; United Farmers' Lg., Julius Walstead, Sisseton, State sec.; *Texas:* Texas Farmers' Protective Assn., Ralph Gillespie, Route 2, Center, sec.; Texas Farm Debt Holiday Assn., Ben Lauderdale, R.F.D., Breckenridge, sec.; *Washington:* Washington State Committee for Action, Ralph Nelson, Route 1, Sedro-Woolley, sec., Casey Boskaljon, Route 1, Box 269, Eatonville, State sec.; *Wisconsin:* United Farmers' Lg., John Hetts, Colby, State sec.; *Wyoming:* Stockman-Farmers' Holiday & Protective Assn., Mack Smith, Yoder, sec.

UNITED FARMERS PROTECTIVE ASSOCIATION

Of the communist United Farmers League; exec. sec., Alfred Miller, Dublin, Pa.; pres., Lewis C. Bentzley. The organ "Organized Farmer" is printed as part of the Farmers National Weekly of the Farmers National Committee of Action. The Nov. 10th, 1933, issue tells how the communist Young Pioneers chopped wood for Bentzley when he was sick recently as an "act of solidarity."

UNITED WORKERS COOPERATIVE ASSOCIATION

Jewish Communist society operating Camp Nitgedaiget (see).

U.S. CONGRESS AGAINST WAR

No one can doubt the cooperation between "pacifists" and revolutionaries after reading a list of committee members and supporting organizations of this Congress (2,700 delegates from 35 states).

See "World Congress Against War" for an idea of these Congresses organized and controlled by Moscow's communist Intl. League Against Imperialism, also for the personnel of its American Committee for Struggle Against War, the headquarters (104 Fifth Ave., N.Y.C.) and organizer of this U.S. Congress Against War held in N.Y. City, Sept. 29-Oct. 2, 1933.

The communist Daily Worker, Sept. 29, 1933, described the greeting planned for Henri Barbusse, French Communist docking that day, coming to address the Congress, and said: "The principal speakers at the opening session will include, besides Barbusse, *Devere Allen* of the *War Resisters League; Earl Browder,* General Secretary, Communist Party; Dr. Alfons Goldschmidt, exiled German professor; *William Pickens,* field secretary Nat. Assn. for the Advancement of Colored People; Prof. *Reinhold Niebuhr,* and others. The same speakers will speak at both opening meetings" (Mecca Temple and St. Nicholas Arena). Communist Donald Henderson and J. B. Matthews of the "pacifist" Fellowship of Reconciliation were scheduled as the two chairmen. To again quote: "More than 115 national organizations, with a combined membership of about 800,000, have endorsed the Congress, including the People's Lobby with *John Dewey* as president. . . . " "Five delegates have been elected by the Pennsylvania branch of the Women's International League for *Peace* and Freedom, of which Jane Addams is honorary international chairman." (Emphasis supplied.)

The Daily Worker, Sept. 30, 1933 reported overflow crowds at both halls, 2,500 delegates present, and told something of the speeches of Communist Henri Barbusse, A. J. Muste, and Communist Earl Browder.

Barbusse's formal message through the Daily Worker, Sept. 30, "to all American workers of hand and brain" was: "I urge them to join as one man in a movement to which the *revolutionaries* of all European countries have already pledged their adherence—the struggle to the death against Fascism and *imperialist* war."

Previously, one of the headline speakers coming to address this Congress, Tom Mann, a notorious veteran English Communist agitator, had been delayed by the U.S. State Dept. in entering the U.S., but vigorous protests from Communist, Socialist, "Pacifist" groups, and the Red-aiding American Civil Liberties Union, caused the bar to be lifted and Mann to be granted a special visa to enter the United States to give speeches "protesting against war" and favoring bloody revolution. Communists Barbusse and Mann were booked to address a series of Communist mass meetings following the Congress (Chicago, Oct. 23, etc.).

Its call to "every organization to form a united front," sent out in leaflet form, listed its "Members of the Arrangements Committee for the U.S. Congress Against War" as follows:

Donald Henderson, exec. dir. Am. Com. for Struggle Against War; Mrs. Annie E. Gray, dir. Women's Peace Society; J. B. Matthews, exec. sec. Fell. Recon.; Roger Baldwin, exec. dir. A.C. L.U.; F. E. Bearce, Marine Workers Unemployed Union I.W.W.; Herbert Benjamin, nat. organizer Nat. Com. Unemployed Councils; Leroy Bowman, N.Y. Chapter, L.I.D.; A. Davis, sec. A.F. of L. Trade Union Com. for Unemp. Insur.; Anna N. Davis, treas. War Resisters Lg.; James W. Ford, Communist T.U.U.L.; Wm. Z. Foster, chmn. Communist Party U.S.A.; Mary Fox, exec. sec. L.I.D.; Carl Geiser, nat. sec. Youth Section, Amer. Com. for Struggle Against War; Julius Gerber, exec. sec., N.Y.C. Socialist Party; Dr. Israel Goldstein, chmn. Social Justice Section Rabbinical Assembly of Am.; Gilbert Green, nat. sec. Young Communist Lg.; Powers Hapgood, nat. exec. com. Lg. Against Fascism; J. B. S. Hardman, ed. "The Advance," Amalg. Cloth. Wkrs. of Am.; Lem Harris, nat. sec. Farmers Nat. Com. for Action; Clarence Hathaway, ed. Daily Worker; John Herling, Emer. Com. Strik. Rel.; Harold Hickerson, Wkrs. Ex-Service Men's Lg.; Roy Hudson, nat. sec. Marine Wkrs. Indust. Un.; Mrs. Addie Waite Hunton, hon. pres. Intl. Coun. of Women of Darker Races; Abraham Kaufman, exec. sec. War Resisters Lg.; Dr. Harry Laidler, dir. L.I.D.; Edw. Levinson, pub. dir. Socialist Party of Am.; Aaron Levinstein, N.Y. sec. Young Peoples Socialist Lg.; Lola Maverick Lloyd, Women's Peace Society; Richard Lovelace, nat. treas. Vet. National Rank and File Com.; Robt. Morss Lovett, pres. L.I.D.; Robt. Minor, cent. exec. com. Communist Party; A. J. Muste, nat. chmn. Conf. Prog. Lab. Act.; Ray Newton, sec. Peace Section, Amer. Friends Serv. Com.; Albert G. Sellers, nat. treas. Bonus Expeditionary Forces Rank and File Com.; Upton Sinclair, Am. Com. for Struggle Against War; Tucker P. Smith, Brookwood Lab. Coll.; Chas. Solomon, Socialist Party; Jack Stachel, acting sec. T.U.U.L.; Norman Thomas, nat. exec. com. Socialist Party; Louise Thompson, I.L.D.; Wm. R. Truax, pres. Ohio Unemp. Lg.; Gus Tyler, Young Peoples Socialist Lg.; Howard Y. Williams, exec. sec. L.I.P.A.; Alfred Wagenknecht, exec. sec. Nat. Com. to Aid Victims of German Fascism.

"Supporting Organizations":

Am. Com. for Struggle Against War*; A.F. of L. Trade Un. Com. for Unemp. Ins.*; Anti-Imperialist Lg. of the U.S.*; Bonus Expeditionary Forces Rank and File of Am.*; Committees on Militarism in Education; Communist Party of U.S.A.*; Conf. for Prog. Lab. Act.; Farmers Nat. Com. of Action*; Farmers Union Cooperative Marketing Assn.; Fell. Recon.; Finnish Workers Fed.*; Friends of the Soviet Union*; Icor*; Intercollegiate Council, L.I.D.; Intl. Com. for Political Prisoners; Intl. Lab. Defense*; Intl. Wkrs. Order*; John Reed Clubs of the U.S.*; Labor Sports Union*; L.I.D.; Lg. of Professional Groups for Foster and Ford*; Lg. Struggle for Negro Rights*; Marine Wkrs. Indust. Un.*; Marine Transport Ind. Un. I.W.W.; Nat. Com. to Aid Victims of German Fascism*; Nat. Farmers Holiday Assn.; Nat. Lithuanian Youth Fed.*; Nat. Miners Union*; Nat. Student Com. for Struggle Against War*; Nat. Student Lg.*; Needle Trades Wkrs. Indust. U.*; Ohio Unemployed Lg.; Pa. Com. for Total Disarmament; Socialist Party of Am.; Steel and Metal Wkrs. Indust. Union*; T.U.U.L.*; Unemp. Councils Nat. Com.*; United Farmers Lg.*; United Farmers Protective Assn.*; Veterans Nat. Rank and File Com.*; War Resisters

Lg.; Wkrs. and Farmers Cooperative Unity Alliance*; Wkrs. Ex-Service Men's Lg.*; Wkrs. Intl. Relief*; World Peaceways, Inc.; Women's Peace Society; Wkrs. Unemp. Union, I.W.W.; Young Communist Lg.*; Young Pioneers of Am.*; Youth Section Am. Com. for Struggle Against War.*

Formed Am. Lg. Against War and Fascism (see).

*Communist or Communist-controlled organizations. Note the cooperation of "peace" societies.

UTILITY CONSUMERS AND INVESTORS LEAGUE (OF ILLINOIS)

A Socialist-controlled organization attacking the public utilities of Illinois in order to break down public confidence in private ownership of utilities. Its Bulletin issued Feb. 1933 states that its "Officials, Directors, Advisory Committee" are as follows:

Prof. Paul H. Douglas, Chicago, pres.; Senator Thos. P. Gunning, Princeton, vice pres.; James H. Andrews, Kewanee; Dr. Edward Bowe, Jacksonville; E. A. Bronson, Evanston; Prof. A. R. Hatton, Evanston; Harold L. Ickes, Chicago; Isaac Kuhn, Champaign; Mrs. B. F. Langworthy, Winnetka; Dr. Louis L. Mann, Chicago; A. D. McLarty, Urbana; W. T. Rawleigh, Freeport; Carl Vrooman, Bloomington; Karl Eitel, Chicago; Amelia Sears, Chicago; John Fitzpatrick, Chicago; Leo Heller, Chicago; Prof. Chas. E. Merriam, Chicago; H. R. Mohat, Freeport; Mrs. Laura K. Pollak, Highland Park; Donald R. Richberg, Chicago; Alfred K. Stern, Chicago.

(Of these Harold Ickes, Paul H. Douglas, A. K. Stern, James H. Andrews, and Donald Richberg are among Roosevelt appointees). Hdqts. Room 1820, 77 W. Washington St., Chicago.

V

VANGUARD PRESS

Founded and financed with $139,453 (1925-8) by the red Garland Fund; dedicated to the publication of revolutionary, "class-struggle," Communist-Socialist literature; 80 Fifth Ave., N.Y. City.

VOKS

Soviet govt. organization describing itself in 1933 Communist Soviet periodicals as the "Society for Cultural Relations with Foreign Countries" (the American branch is A.S.C.R.R.) and stating that it "1. Gives information in foreign countries on all questions of Soviet construction and Soviet culture. . . . 2. Interchanges publications on science, literature and art with all countries in the world. 3. Organizes exhibitions of science and art in foreign countries. 4. Helps foreign artists and scientific workers coming to the U.S.S.R. and sends Soviet workers in art and science abroad. 5. Carries on cultural work with foreigners arriving in the U.S.S.R. 6. Arranges meetings and lectures . . . in the U.S.S.R. and abroad. 7. Publishes . . . many publications in three languages (English, German and French)." Hdqts. V.O.K.S., Moscow 69, Trubnikooski Pereulok, 17.

W

WAR RESISTERS INTERNATIONAL

W.R. Intl.

Plainly called "a communist organization" by "The Patriot" (Boswell Pub. Co., London, Aug. 31, 1933 issue); the initiator of the War Resisters International Council (see below), of which it is a part; held its first international conference at Bilthoven, Holland, 1921; its International Conference at Sonntagsberg, Austria, as reported in the War Resister, Oct. 1928 issue, regretted "the absence of friends from Moscow," while the conference discussions centered around "War Resistance and Revolution," and the report said "The discussion of War Resistance and Revolution revealed the deep sympathy of those present with all those who struggle for a new social order, and the recognition that we, the members of the War Resisters International, have to be within this struggle." Delegates from the International Fellowship of Reconcilation, International Anti-Militarist Bureau, International Co-operative Movement, Friends Committee for International Service, International Bahai Movement, World League of Catholic Youth, International Movement for Christian Communism, among whom were Free Thinkers, Liberals, Socialists, and Anarchists, composed this conference.

Among the sections of the W.R. Intl. are the Union of Anarcho-Socialists of Austria, the Womens Intl. League (for Peace and Freedom) of Australia and Ireland, the Fellowship of Reconciliation, Women's Peace Society, Women's Peace Union, The Movement for Christian Communism, the Young Anti-Militarists, the Holland Union of Religious Anarcho-Communists, the Nat. Peace Council, etc. (three of them openly anarchistic-communistic organizations).

The beliefs and objectives of the War Resisters International are officially admitted ("War Resistance a Practical Policy," p. 7) in part as follows: "Out of the present chaos the War Resisters International believes a new social order can and will be established. . . . It believes these changes may be accomplished by revolutionary uprisings. . . . Every war resister desires to take part in the struggle confident in the ultimate triumph of the forces which make for a new social order." And p. 22: "We have made representations to the various governments. . . . These representations are not sent direct from the International, but in this we have always had the willing help of men of eminence, such as Prof. Einstein."

The "Statement of Principles" of the War Resisters International declares against "wars to preserve the existing order of society," but concerning "wars on behalf of the oppressed proletariat, whether for its liberation or defense" says: "To refuse to take up arms for this purpose, is most difficult. (1) Because the proletarian regime, and even more the enraged masses, in time of revolution, would regard as a traitor any one who would refuse to support the new order, by force. (2) Because our instinctive love for the suffering and the oppressed would tempt us to use violence on their behalf." In other words, open resistance to defense of existing governments is urged, while the idea is advanced that it would be considered traitorous to refuse to support revolutionaries in overthrowing these governments. "And this is called 'pacifism' not 'communism'!", says the National Republic, April, 1933, issue.

Einstein, whose communistic work is regarded so highly by Moscow, is a War Resisters International leader, and the founder of its Einstein War Resisters Fund. He asks that contributions to the Fund be sent to the War Resisters International headquarters, at Middlesex, England, to aid militant war resisters who get into trouble with their governments. He is also author of the "2 per cent" slogan which agitates that if only two per cent of the population will militantly refuse all war service in defense of their government, the jails will not be large enough to hold them all, and they can effectively cripple their government in the prosecution of any war. Lenin's slogan "Turn an imperialist war into a civil war in all countries!" is along the same line, only Lenin frankly termed this Red Revolution, not pacifism. After Hitler's anti-communist regime came into power, Einstein recommended war against Germany.

WAR RESISTERS INTERNATIONAL COUNCIL

W.R. Intl. Coun.

Initiated by the War Resisters International, and composed of the War Resisters International and its sections, of the Friends Service Council and the Friends Peace Committee, The Woman's International League for Peace and Freedom, International Fellowship of Reconciliation, International Womens Cooperative Guild, International Anti-Militarist Bureau, Syndicalist International, International Union of Anti-Militarist Ministers and Clergymen. These, according to the War Resisters International bulletins, are international Anti-Militarist organizations, having their first meetings in Holland, and all the movements are linked together *"working for the supercession of capitalism and imperialism, by the establishment of a new social and international order, based on the principle of cooperation for the common good."* (War Resister, August 1927 issue, p. 6).

The international chairman of the War Resisters International Council is A. Fenner Brockway, who is also national chairman of the very red Independent Labour Party of Great Britain. He said, in a recent issue of the International War Resister, concerning the supposed present breakdown of capitalism, that this crisis is "likely to make the government rock" and that "It is the duty of Socialists to speed the rocking, until it brings down, not only the government, but the system of which the government is an expression." He toured the United States in 1932, under League for Industrial Democracy auspices. (See Independent Labour Party.)

WAR RESISTERS LEAGUE

W.R. Lg.

American affiliate of the War Resisters International (see); Einstein became its honorary chairman in Feb. 1933; its organ is the Socialist-Pacifist magazine "The World Tomorrow," so well financed by the communistic Garland Fund; the League sent out a so-called "Peace Letter to the President of the United States" around Armistice Day, announcing the peacetime treason, which in wartime would become actual treason, that its members "declared deliberate intention to refuse to support war measures or to render war service," in case our government should resort to arms; it sent out a questionnaire asking in part "is it necessary to change the economic system before we get rid of war?" with the answer "No, we must attack both problems at once" (D.A.R. bulletins 1930-1); the slacker pledge required for enrollment in this league is:

"I declare it to be my intention never to take part in war, offensive or defensive, international or civil, whether it be by bearing arms, making or handling munitions, voluntarily subscribing to war loans, or using my labor for the purpose of setting others free for war service."

(1933) Albert Einstein, hon. chmn.; Devere Allen, chmn.; exec. com.: Devere Allen, Edmund B. Chaffee, Frank Olmstead, Sidney E. Goldstein, chmn.; Beatrice Greenfield and Jessie Wallace Hughan, secretaries; Anna N. Davis, treas.; Abraham Kaufman, asst. treas.; Ellen Chater, Mrs. J. Sergeant Cram, Kedar N. Das Gupta, Anna N. Davis, Dorothy Detzer, Mary Fox, Annie E. Gray, Jessie Wallace Hughan, Edwin C. Johnson, Leon Rosser Land, Frados Langer Lazarus, Mary B. Orr, John Nevin Sayre, Mirza Ahmad Sohrab, Tucker P. Smith. *National Committee:* Roy E. Burt, Kath. Duffield, Adelaide Case, Allan Chalmers, Bernard Clausen, Bruce Curry, Edwin Fairley, Wm. Floyd, Eliz. Gilman, Alvin C. Goddard, Francis Henson, Clarence V. Howell, Evelyn West Hughan, Edw. L. Israel, Paul Jones, John Howland Lathrop, Paul Limbert, Darwin J. Meserole, Francis J. McConnell, Henry Neumann, Harry A. Overstreet, Kirby Page, Edw. C. M. Richards, Clarence Senior, Olivia Dunbar Lawrence, Truda J. Weil, Lydia G. Wentworth, Wayne White, Mary Winsor, Winnifred Wygal, Hdqts.; Devere Allen, 40 W. 68th St., N.Y. City.

WOMEN'S COUNCIL

A term used for United Council of Working Class Women (see).

WOMEN'S INTERNATIONAL LEAGUE FOR PEACE AND FREEDOM W.I.L.P.F.

Formed, and headed continuously as international president, by Jane Addams. Communists Wm. Z. Foster, Scott Nearing, Benj. Gitlow, Eliz. Gurley Flynn and their close associates, Robt. Morss Lovett (who lives at Hull House), Roger N. Baldwin, Sidney Hillman, Morris L. Ernst, Lewis S. Gannett, Clinton S. Golden, Freda Kirchwey, Norman Thomas, and James Weldon Johnson, etc., the Board of Directors of the Garland Fund, voted to this approved "peace" and "total disarmament" society, which also agitated for recognition of Soviet Russia, the following sums: (1924-25 Report, page 22) "Women's International League for Peace and Freedom, New York City. For traveling expenses of speakers on imperialism to Senate Committee hearing and to Chicago conference, (Mar. 4th and May 22nd) $543.17"; (same Report, p. 33) "For general expenses, 6 months (Oct. 22nd) $1,000"; (1925-26 Report, p. 12) "For publication of monthly bulletin 'Pax' $2,400"; (1926-27 Report, p. 28) "For publication of monthly bulletin 'Pax' $1,200"; (1927-28 Report, p. 37) "For publication of monthly bulletin 'Pax' $1,200."

How many people reading these loving peace and total disarmament "Peace" bulletins and hearing the anti-imperialist "Peace" speakers on the "Pax Special" realized that Moscow's Communist leaders for bloody revolution helped to vote funds to pay for both? Jane Addams, in plaintive and characteristically dulcet style, says in her book, "Second Twenty Years at Hull House" (p. 173) concerning the W.I.L.P.F. Congress held in Wash., D.C., 1924: "We found the newspapers, the patriotic societies and the military making a charge against us of 'internationalism' as if that in itself were altogether damaging. . . . The Congress of the W.I.L. was followed by a two week summer school in Chicago, where no difficulties were encountered, although some arose in connection with a private car, the Pax Special which carried twenty-five of the delegates to and from Chicago, making an opportunity for them to be heard in many cities of the United States and Canada. On the journey westward in certain of the cities meetings and receptions were cancelled because of propaganda based not only on misunderstandings but on deliberate misrepresentation which had first made itself felt in Washington."

The "Woman Patriot," May 1, 1922, states: "Frequent changes of name as advised by Nicolai Lenin are resorted to by the International feminist-pacifist bloc as often as necessary, but the entire movement originates with the International Woman's Suffrage Alliance. The work is divided up like an army's artillery, cavalry and infantry into three mobile divisions: the political under Mrs. Catt and her International Woman Suffrage Alliance and League of Women Voters. The pacifist under Miss Jane Addams and her W.I.L.P.F. The industrial under Mrs. Raymond Robins and her International League of Working Women and Womens Trade Union League" (also Garland Fund-supported). "The three branches are employed precisely as a wise general would engage artillery, cavalry or infantry; using all three together whenever necessary, each one alone for special objectives."

Said Whitney's "Reds in America" in 1924, p. 181: "That the W.I.L.P.F. is closely aligned with the Third International in interest and objective is clearly shown in an advertisement which recently appeared in the 'World Tomorrow' and cited by the 'Woman Patriot' in which it is stated that Miss Jane Addams of Hull

House, Chicago, is listed as a stockholder in the Russian-American Industrial Corporation (Sidney Hillman) along with Nicolai Lenin, Eugene V. Debs, Charles P. Steinmetz and Congressman La Guardia. The Woman Patriot also quotes the Federated Press Bulletin as stating that Anna Louise Strong, for many years Moscow correspondent of the Federated Press, and for the official American Communist organ 'The Worker,' expects to fill numerous lecture engagements during the winter and can be reached at Hull House, No. 800 S. Halsted St., Chicago, Ill."

The International Entente against the Third International (hdqts. Geneva, Switzerland), in a 1932 report on Communist activities, said of India: its "North west frontier is infested by the Red Shirts of Abdul Gafar, a revolutionary organization in relations with Moscow and which also appears to be similarly connected with the Hindu National Congress. It has no doubt been remarked that Mahatma Gandhi recalled in haste by this Congress, nevertheless found time to pay a visit to Romain Rolland and to speak at Geneva under the auspices of the Women's International League for Peace and Freedom . . . the secretary-general of the French section of the W.I.L.P.F." (which recently published an appeal to all Frenchmen to defend the U.S.S.R. against its enemies), "Mme. Duchene, is at the same time a member of the executive committee of the Anti-Imperialist League directed by the German Communist Muenzenberg."

The W.I.L.P.F. was formed in 1915 at The Hague after "peace" agitations in the United States led by Jane Addams, Socialist Louis P. Lochner (afterward head of the Communists' Federated Press), Rosika Schwimmer (mem. radical Nat. Coun. of 15 governing Hungary 1918-19, under communist-aiding Count M. Karolyi), and Mrs. Pethwick Lawrence, a British radical. Jane Addams sailed with Lochner and Sophonisba P. Breckenridge, April 1915, for The Hague where they joined Rosika Schwimmer and delegates from 18 countries and formed there the Women's International Committee for Permanent Peace, since 1919 called the W.I.L.P.F. Jane Addams became and has remained its international president.

The British section, Oct. 1, 1915, took the name of Women's International League. They ran a Peace Crusade organized by Mrs. Helen Crawfurd (later a member of the British Communist Party) and also supported the notorious Moscow-inspired Leeds Conference of June 3, 1917, which congratulated the people of Russia on the success of their revolution and appointed a committee to set up Soviets in England which would cause a revolution that would end war. (See "English Reds.") Mrs. Pethwick Lawrence was honorary secretary of the British section and the executive committee included Miss Margaret Bondfield (who spoke in 1933 in Chicago at the Intl. Council of Women with Jane Addams; a member of the very Red Ind. Labor Party and 1917 Club "combining Pacifism with definitely revolutionary aims"); Maud Royden of the same 1917 Club; Mrs. Philip Snowden (wife of Ind. Labour Party leader and a radical); Mrs. Despard (of the Communist W.I.R. British section), etc.

Francis Ralston Welsh in a published report refers to the W.I.L.P.F. as "virtually a feminine branch of the A.C.L.U.," Jane Addams, Sophonisba P. Breckenridge, Mrs. Henry Goddard Leach, Eliz. Glendower Evans, Kate Crane Gratz, having served with Communists Wm. Z. Foster, Scott Nearing, Robt. W. Dunn, Eliz. Gurley Flynn and Max Eastman, etc. on the nat. com. of the A.C.L.U., as well as in active W.I.L.P.F. positions, and many other W.I.L.P.F. leaders such as Fanny Bixby Spencer, Miss Mary Winsor, Miss Sophia Dulles, etc., having served on local A.C.L.U. committees. He says: "Some members of the W.I.L.P.F. have been members and promoters of openly Communist organizations" (Charlotte Anita Whitney, who was aided by Jane Addams, being one). "The communist Daily Worker of July 1, 1923 lists the W.I.L.P.F. as one of the organizations that cooperated with the Communists in organizing the so-called Farmer Labor Party, a radical organization gotten up by the American Civil Liberties Union crowd. They sent a delegation to Washington" (Jan. 1920) "to protest against deportation 'of those designated as Reds.'" He refers to the W.I.L.P.F.'s nickname as "Women's International League for Civil War and Communism" on account of its tendencies. Marvin, in "Ye Shall Know the Truth," states: "In December, 1922, the fourth international conference was held at The Hague, Miss Addams, among others from the United States, attending. Among other resolutions adopted was one 'in regard to the release of the American political prisoners before Christmas.' It will be noted that in this matter of so-called 'political prisoners,' as in practically all other matters the W.I.L.P.F.

adopted the same position as the Communists and Socialists."

Madeleine Z. Doty, wife of Roger Baldwin (director of both Garland Fund and American Civil Liberties Union), for a long time was international secretary of the W.I.L.P.F., with hdqts. at Geneva, Switzerland, and is still editor of its bulletin "Pax."

The W.I.L.P.F., which in 1930 claimed sections in 26 countries and a total membership of 50,000 members, is a section of the War Resisters International Council, which is "working for the supercession of capitalism and imperialism by the establishment of a new social and international order" (War Resister, Feb. 1927). The Vienna W.I.L.P.F. congress recommended that "they support law looking to the gradual abolition of property privileges," which is simply Communism (Wash., D.C., April 1923 release of W.I.L.P.F. on its "Program and International Aims").

The 1931 W.I.L.P.F. letterhead lists:

Meta Berger (widow of the revolutionary Victor Berger) as chmn. of Publicity; Mildred Scott Olmstead (wife of Allen S.), Organization; Amy Woods, Literature; Dorothy Detzer, Legislative; Addie W. Hunton, Inter-Racial; Clara S. Laddey, Finance; Helen Everett of Madison, Wis., Education; pres., Emily Greene Balch; chmn., Hanna Clothier Hull; treas., Florence G. Taussig; asst. treas., Juliet C. Patten; rec. sec., Margaret Loring Thomas; regional director Pacific Coast states, Anne Martin; exec. sec. Dorothy Detzer; *Chairmen of State Branches:* Margaret Long, Colo.; Ethelwyn Mills, Cal.; Gertrude Scott Straub, Hawaii; Alice Boynton, Ill.; Lena C. Van Bibber, Md.; Martha Helen Elliott, Mass.; Lillian Holt, Mich.; Maud C. Stockwell, Minn.; Amelia B. Moorfield, Wis.; Lucy J. M. Taylor, N.M.; Grace Hoffman White, N.Y.; Emily B. Harvey, Pa.; National Board: the officers, chmn. of standing committees, state chmn., and Zonia Baber, Ill.; Katherine D. Blake, N.Y.; Zona Gale, Wis.; Kathleen McGraw Hendrie, Mich.; Alice Marion Holmes, Mass.; Bessie Kind, Pa.; Lucy Biddle Lewis, Pa.; Kathleen Jennison Lowrie, Mich.; Emma Guffey Miller, Pa.; Esther Morton Smith, D.C.; Lillian D. Wald, N.Y.; Carrie S. Weyl, Pa.; Jane Addams, Honorary International President.

WOMEN'S PEACE PARTY

Cooperated during the war with the Socialist Party in the Emergency Peace Federation (1917) and with the American Union Against Militarism, whose Civil Liberties Bureaus defending radicals calling themselves "conscientious objectors" became the American Civil Liberties Union ("Red-aid Society"). A letter from Rosika Schwimmer to Louis Lochner on Women's Peace Party stationery is reproduced in the Lusk Report. Jane Addams was nat. chmn.; Mrs. Amos Pinchot, chmn. N.Y. City branch; Mrs. Louis D. Brandeis, a vice chmn.; Carrie Chapman Catt was a leader, as was Mrs. Henry Villard; other active workers were: Eliz. Glendower Evans, Lucia Ames Mead, Crystal Eastman, Mrs. James Warbasse, Madeleine Doty, Mary Austin, Mrs. Frederic Howe, Mrs. Florence Kelley, Mary Shaw, Lillian D. Wald, Anna Strunsky Walling, Margaret Lane, Agnes Brown Leach, etc., etc. (Lusk Report).

WOMEN'S PEACE SOCIETY

See "Who's Who" for affiliations of Annie E. Gray, its exec. sec. "Founded by the late Fanny Garrison Villard" (mother of the radical Oswald Garrison Villard); a radical pacifist "International Non-Resistant Organization" claiming members "in every state in the U.S.A. and in Austria, Canada, Cuba, England, France, Ireland, Mexico, Sweden, Switzerland and Turkey"; affiliated with the ultra-radical War Resisters International (see), which is "working for the supercession of capitalism and imperialism by the establishment of a new social and international order." (War Resister, Aug. 1927, p. 6). Annie E. Gray is sec. and a speaker for such Communist meetings as the U.S. Congress Against War (see), World Congress of Youth (see), etc. (Daily Worker, Sept. 15, Oct. 2, 1933). She says: "Our method is educational through such channels as the radio; the publication of a News Letter and other literature, which is distributed by mail and at indoor and outdoor meetings on appropriate occasions such as Good Will Day, Memorial Day, Armistice Day, etc. and throughout the summer, thereby reaching great masses of people who could not otherwise be reached." Its membership pledge is: "I declare it to be my intention never to aid in or sanction war, offensive or defensive, international or civil, in any way, whether by making or handling munitions, subscribing to war loans, using my labor for the purpose of setting others free for war service, helping by money or work any relief organization which supports or condones war." Hdqts. 20 Vesey St., New York City. Supporting organization communist U.S. Cong. Ag. War.

WOMEN'S PEACE UNION

Affiliated with the radical War Resisters International (see), which is presided over by the very red Ind. Labour Party leader, Fenner Brockway; a sponsor of the Green International; organized 1920; circulates leaflets attacking the Boy Scouts as "militaristic" and ridiculing the Star Spangled Banner. One called "Militarism" by Fannie Bixby Spencer says: "If you or I salute the flag or stand up to the tune of that barbaric war whoop called the Star Spangled Banner, we are complying with the demands of militarism, sinister mental militarism which is driving us headlong into another World War for the magnificent destruction of civilization." Another pamphlet called "Idols" is circulated, which says of the U.S. flag: "Upon every rostrum, pulpit and altar in the land this fetish is given the place of honor. This idol which stands for the glorification of war, hate, violence, the fostering of nationalism, which represents all that is contrary to the laws of God, is openly worshipped in the house of God. . . . It is an important part of the present curriculum of the public schools that the children be forced daily to bow to and worship the idol," etc.

With Jane Addams' W.I.L.P.F., Fellowship of Reconciliation, and War Resisters League, it formed a Fenner Brockway Luncheon Committee which invited a large audience to welcome him in Wash., D.C. Its skillful organizers send representatives to War Resisters meetings in the United States and abroad where suggestions are offered looking toward the "establishment of a new social and international order." Claims a "nation-wide membership." Hdqts. 4 Stone St., N.Y. City.

WORKERS AND FARMERS COOPERATIVE UNITY ALLIANCE

Section of the communist T.U.U.L.; official publication Workers and Farmers Cooperative Bulletin, Box 571, Superior, Wis.

WORKERS CULTURAL FEDERATION

(of at least 130 Societies)

Wkrs. Cult. Fed.

Amalgamation of Communist revolutionary cultural groups; slogan is "Toward an American Revolution"; Midwest Workers Cultural Federation is a section; formed by the John Reed Club delegates to the 2nd Conference of the International Union (or Assn.) of Revolutionary Writers, held at Kharkov, Russia, Nov. 15, 1930. They were given their instructions to form, on their return to the U.S.A., a national organization of revolutionary writers and artists (Daily Worker, Dec. 6, 1930). These delegates were:

Fred Ellis, Michael Gold, Wm. Gropper, Joshua Kunitz, A. B. Magil, Harry Alan Potamkin. Accordingly, a conference held in N.Y. City, June 14, 1931 formed the Workers Cultural Federation and elected as Honorary Presidium: Maxim Gorki, and N. Krupskaya (Lenin's widow) of the U.S.S.R.; Ludwig Renn of Germany; Henri Barbusse of France; Tomas of Hungary; Lo Hsun of China; and Theodore Dreiser, John Dos Passos, Upton Sinclair, Wm. Z. Foster of the United States. An active presidium was elected also consisting of: Wm. Gropper, Alex. Trachtenberg, R. B. Glassford, Michael Gold, K. Marmor, J. Shafer, A. B. Magil, Harry Alan Potamkin, T. H. Li (Chinese Communist held for deportation).

Hdqts. were established at 63 W. 15th St., N.Y. City with the John Reed Club and New Masses magazine, called by the New Masses "the first American revolutionary center."

A cablegram from Moscow was read at this conference saying in part: "International Union Revolutionary Writers Welcomes Launching of Federation Workers Cultural Organizations America Stop. . . . Before Federation Stands Task of Creating Proletarian Culture in Womb of Capitalist System Stop Launching Federation Is Most Signicant Event in History American Revolutionary Culture," etc.

Groups represented consisted of 19 dramatic, 12 literary, 2 Esperanto, 31 educational, 6 sports, 10 large choral societies, 8 instrumental music societies, 2 photo and film groups and 40 miscellaneous organizations as follows: (Note: "W.C." stands for "Workers' Club" and "I.W.O." for "International Workers Order.")

"A.I.D.L.D.; Aida Chorus; American Culture Center; Arbeiterbund; Artef; A.S.D.S.D.; B.B. W. C.; B.G.T.W.O.; Boro Park W.C.; Bronx Hungarian W.C.; Brownsville Youth Center; Chelsea Open Forum; Chernishisky Society; Chorus Pirmyn; Clove Dramatic Club; Co-operative Colony; Council of Working Class Women; Cuban W.C.; Daily Worker Worker's Correspondents; D.T.W. Club; E.N.Y.W.C.; East Side W.C.; Educational W.L.; Elore Hungarian Dramatic Club; Estonian W.C.; Federation of Workers Choruses; Finnish W.C.; Flatbush Forum of Ethiopian Culture; Food Workers Industrial Union; Freemont W.C.; Freiheit Gesang Verein; Freiheit Mandolin Orchestra; Friedrich Engels I.W.O.; Golden's Bridge Co-operative Colony; Hal Shal; Harlem School; Harlem Women's Educational Club; Hungarian Writers Group; Hungarian Literature Group; Hungarian Singing Society; Hungarian Workers Correspondents; Hungarian Workers Home; Hungarian Workingmen's Sick Benefit Educational Federation; Icor; Italian Worker's Center; Ivan Frank Society; City Committee I.W.O.; Br. No. 3 I.W.O. School; Br. 146; Br. 91; Br. 521; Br. 10; Br. 11; I.W.O. Children's School; Br. 37; I.W.O. Youth Section; Br. 122; Br. 91, 22, 116, 137, 127, 215; I.W.O. School 14; National Executive of I.W.O. Schools; Jack London Club; Jewish Children High School I.W.O.; Jewish Workers University; Jewish Workers Musical Alliance; John Reed Club; Jugoslav W.C.; Russian Children's School; Labor Research Assn.; Labor Sports Union; League of Struggle for Negro Rights; Lithuanian Assn.; Lithuanian Literature Society; Lithuanian Physical Culture; Lithuanian Workers' Literary Society; Lithuanian Working Woman; Lyra; Mapleton W.C.; M.B.O.S.Z.; Middle Bronx W.C.; Serp i Molot; Momarts; Natur

Freunde; New Negro Art Theatre; New Pioneer; N.Y. Br. of Chinese Anti-Imperialists; N.T.M.N. Brass Band; Peasant Society; Proletart; Prolet Buhne; Proletcult Progressive Russian School; Proletpen; Prospect W.C.; Rebel Poets; Red Dancers; Red Spark A.C.; Russian N.M.M.S.; Russian Proletarian Art School; Russian Prolet Writers; R.U.W. Ch. Col.; Scandinavian W.C.; School 12; School 7; Sietyno Chorus; Social Problems Club N.Y. Univ.; Ukr. W.C.; Spanish W.C.; Spartacus A.C.; Student's League; Syras Chorus; Thule; Tietynos; T.U.U.L.; Ukrainian Labor Club; Ukrainian Toilers of A.; Ukrainian E.W.S.; Ukrainian Women's Club; Unemployed Council Mad. Sq. Br.; Un. W. Club, Harlem; Vanguard Community Center; Will Work Club; W.I.R.: Brass Band, Symphony Orchestra, Co-op House, English Chorus, Scouts; World Cinema League; W. C. Brighton Beach; W.C. Bronx; W.C. Brooklyn; Workers School; Workers Defense Club; Workers Esperanto Group; Workers Film and Photo League; Workers Gymnastic and Sport Alliance; Workers Lab. Theatre; Workers Music School; Workers Youth Club; Working Women Br. I; Young Finlanders Society; Young Pioneers Orchestra; Y.W.A.D. Club; N.M. Orchestra; Lettish W.C.

WORKERS DANCE LEAGUE

Affiliate of the communist Proletarian Dramatic Assn. of Am.

WORKER'S EX-SERVICE MEN'S LEAGUE

Communist; agitates Bonus Marches to Washington and hatred of the American government among American veterans; it masks itself as "Veterans Provisional Liaison Committees," "Veterans Expeditionary Forces," etc., etc. in order that loyal veterans may not readily realize they are being agitated to become traitors to the flag they fought for. It has largely taken over the work of the communist Defense Corps in protecting Communist speakers from the police, etc.

WORKERS 'FILM AND PHOTO LEAGUE

A section of the communist Workers International Relief; secures photos for the Communist Party of U.S.A.

WORKERS INTERNATIONAL RELIEF W.I.R.

Communist propaganda relief organization ministering to Red strikers, hunger marchers, etc.; recd. money from Garland Fund; its June 1933 letterhead says "Organized Ten Years—18 Million Members Internationally—25 Million Dollars Collected for Workers Relief" and states it is leading campaigns of "Protest and relief in behalf of victims of German Fascism . . . and the struggle for immediate urgent demands in all localities. . . . Relief to Help Win the Struggles of Striking and Unemployed Workers on the Basis of Solidarity—Not Charity" (see its Nat. Com. to Aid Victims of German Fascism); is American section of Moscow's International Red Aid; runs Young Pioneer Camps (see) all over the U.S.; formed Workers Laboratory Theatre, etc.; its eighth congress held in Berlin, Oct. 9-15, 1931, had "several hundred delegates from about 40 countries present including a number representing Socialist, anarchist, pacifist and similar organizations" (Am. Labor Year Book); U.S. section is headed by Communist, atheist "Bishop" Wm. Montgomery Brown, author of anti-religious books for children; in 1929 in soliciting subscriptions it sent out under the heading "Workers International Relief Camp Dept." a facsimile of Albert Einstein's endorsement written in his own hand writing, in German, with the following translation: "All honor to the Workers International Relief (Internazionale Arbeiter Hilfe) for the work it has done! All hand and brain workers should realize the importance of this organization and seek to strengthen it. A. Einstein." Below this was added: "Theodore Dreiser endorses W.I.R. Camps for Workers children. Henri Barbusse endorses the W.I.R." and then the typically deceptive Red statement: "Non Political, Non Sectarian, Non Partisan, but Always for the Workers. Rose Pastor Stokes, National Camp Director, One Union Square, New York City." Einstein is a member of other Communist organizations. A letter head of the "Workers International Relief, Department of Cultural Activities, Childrens Camp Department, 949 Broadway, Room 512, New York" lists:

"Bishop" Wm. M. Brown as nat. chmn.; Ludwig Landy, exec. sec.; Emjo Basshe, director; "Endorsed by Henri Barbusse, Theodore Dreiser, Prof. Albert Einstein, Upton Sinclair"; "National Committee: Arthur Bodanski, Heywood Broun, John Dos Passos, Wm. Gropper, Harold Hickerson, Serge Koussevitsky, Eva LeGallienne, Louis Lozowick, Kenneth MacGowan, Clarina Michelson, Eugene Nigob, Harry Alan Potamkin, Leopold Stokowski, Edmund Wilson."

WORKERS LABORATORY THEATRE (WORKERS THEATRE SCHOOL) (WORKERS THEATRE MAGAZINE)

The Workers Laboratory Theatre of the communist Workers International Relief (Agit-Prop section) formed in 1933 a Workers Theatre school to teach dramatic art, voice training, etc. to performers in Communist dramatics (also a Puppet group and children's Agit-Prop troupe); it organized the Workers Theatre magazine, name changed Aug. 1933 to New Theatre, organ of the communist League of Workers Theatres; N.Y. hdqts. 42 E. 12th St.

The Chicago branch of the Workers Laboratory Theatre meets 1932-33 at Abraham Lincoln Center. To quote the Daily Worker, Oct. 27, 1933: "The Theatre Council of the Midwest Workers Cultural Federation sponsors the Workers Laboratory Theatre School, which opened Oct. 25, at Lincoln Center, 700 E. Oakwood Blvd. The school offers three courses to workers and students who are interested: "1. History and Principles of the Marxian Theatre, led by Leon Hess every Monday evening. 2. Stage Technique, Voice Diction, led by Louise Hamburger, every Wednesday evening. 3. Working Class Playwriting, led by Bill Andrews, every Friday evening.

"The entire work of this school will be directed toward writing, rehearsing and producing effective revolutionary plays to be presented before working class audiences. The use of a fine stage at Lincoln Center is one of the features of the school. Anyone interested in taking these courses is urged to register at once by sending name and address to Workers Laboratory Theatre, 700 East Oakwood Blvd., Chicago."

How the Communist revolutionaries must chuckle at the capitalistic "saps" who provide them with this stage and meeting place!

WORKERS LIBRARY PUBLISHERS

Communist Party publishers; 50 E. 13th St., P.O. Box 148, Sta. D, New York City; rec'd. money from Garland Fund; publishes Party pamphlets by Max Bedacht, Alex. Bittleman, Lloyd Brown, Earl Browder, Sam Don, Dave Doran, Wm. F. Dunne, Harrison George, George Padmore, Helen Stassova, Walter Trumbull, Sadie Van Veen, Israel Amter, etc.

WORKERS MUSIC LEAGUE

Recently formed American section of the International Music Bureau of Moscow (Communist). "Under the management of Frances Strauss this outfit staged a Workers Music Olympiad in the auditorium of City College of N.Y., May 21, 1933. Proletarian music of the United States and Russia was featured on the program." (Advisory Associates.)

WORKERS PHILATELIC SOCIETY

Communist stamp collectors society.

WORKERS SCHOOLS (N.Y., CHICAGO, ETC.)

Communist schools to train leaders for the revolutionary overthrow of the U.S. government (Permitted to exist and flourish in defiance of sedition laws through the negligence of American citizens who, perhaps, will awaken and blame their own laxity only when approaching fascism or Communism knocks on their very own doors). On the stationery of the main and governing New York School (which rec'd over $12,000 from the Garland Fund) appears the quotation from Lenin: "Without revolutionary theory there can be no revolutionary practise." (Hence the Red howls for "free speech"). The Am. Labor Year Book states it had 1,063 students for the fall term of 1931 (the Communist press reported 1,600 for the fall of 1932) and that: "The School has established Sections in the various parts of Greater New York. It also guides the educational work of many unions, workers' clubs and fraternal organizations. It conducts a correspondence course in the Fundamentals of Communism, with students in all parts of the United States, Canada, Mexico, Australia and elsewhere. The school holds a Forum every Sunday night where, it is claimed, there is an average attendance between 500 and 600. It also supervises the activities of its branches in Chicago, San Francisco, Detroit, Cleveland, Baltimore, Philadelphia, Boston, Kansas City, St. Paul, Minneapolis and other cities. In addition it has a full time training group, the students of which are sent by the unions and party divisions for intensive preparation for work in the movement. The executive committee of the Workers School consists of R. Baker, Max Bedacht, Wm. Z. Foster, M. James, A. Markoff, G. Siskind, Alexander Trachtenberg and W. W. Weinstone." Esperanto, as well as Russian, English and Spanish, is taught. Hdqts. 35 East 12th St., N.Y.C.

Chicago Workers School, located at 2822 S. Michigan Ave., states that it is affiliated with the N.Y. School and its Fall 1932-33 announcement contained the following: "The Chicago Workers School is the central school of the revolutionary working class organizations of the middle west. Its object is to train leaders for the growing mass struggles against the capitalist offensive and for the *revolutionary way out* of the crisis of capitalism." The slogan is "Training for the Class Struggle." D. E. Earley was listed as director, Lydia Beidel, sec. Advisory Committee: Lydia Beidel, Wm. E. Browder, D. E. Earley, Romania Ferguson, Albert Goldman, Carl Haessler (also a teacher there), Vladimir R. Janowicz. Among Courses listed were: Principles of Communism; Strike Strategy and Tactics (by Joe Weber); Principles of Communist Organization; Marxism-Leninism; Colonial and Negro Problems . . . "Deals specifically with the rise of the oppressed Negro in the U.S. and colonial revolutions against imperialist rule"; Problems of Youth, "Designed to train young and adult workers for the organization of revolutionary youth"; Dialectic Materialism (anti-religion); Practical Labor Journalism (by Carl Haessler); Labor Research; "Workers' Children's Art School will hold classes for children from the ages of 10 to 15 at the school every Saturday afternoon from 1 to 5. Music, dancing, drawing, writing and other arts and crafts will be offered. Instructors Topchevsky, Weed, Skolnick, Morris, etc."

The Fall 1933-34 announcement lists as "Executive Committee: Beatrice Shields, director; Dena Van Heck, sec.; D. E. Earley, A. Feinglass, Walter Lamson, Claude Lightfoot, Eugene Bechtold, J. Taugner, Herbert Newton," and "Representatives of Workers Organizations." An interesting course on "Labor Defense" is added teaching "The role of the governmental forces, legislation, police, stool pigeons . . . use of injunctions and criminal syndicalists laws . . . tactics of defense in arrests and trials, the use of attorneys, witnesses and self defense, prisoners relief"; also "Tactics in the Reformist Unions" (boring within A.F. of L. unions). Has four branches 1934-35.

WORKERS TRAINING SCHOOL

Conducted 1933 at Chicago City Club by Karl Borders' Chicago Workers' Committee on Unemployment (see) to train Socialist agitators and organizers, with Maynard C. Krueger, militant Socialist, teaching "New Economics for Old"; Lillian Herstein, Socialist and member of Communist subsidiary organizations, teaching "The Class Struggle in American History"; W. B. Waltmire teaching "How to Organize," etc.

WORKMEN'S CIRCLE

Socialist fraternal insurance society; primarily Jewish; participates in Red strikes, May Day demonstrations, Socialist Party campaigns, labor agitations, "peace" meetings, etc.; its left-wing formed the communist I.W.O.; left-wing activities in 1932 were being led by Communist Party (Majority), "Lovestoneites"; Young Circle League, its Youth section, with 90 clubs and 1,800 members, studies such subjects (a month to a subject) as "Russia, Civil Liberties, Strikes," etc.; maintains over 100 schools for children, where they are taught to read and write Yiddish; owns 5 camps, one near Pawling, N.Y., costing $500,000; has over 10,000 women members in 79 branches, 700 branches with about 75,000 members in the U.S. and Canada; contributed in 1931 over $63,000 to Rand School, Brookwood Labor College, Victor Berger Nat. Foundation, League for Industrial Democracy, etc.; Elias Lieberman, chmn.; Jack Zukerman, sec.; J. L. Alfos, nat. dir. of Young Circle Lg.; N. Chanin, chmn.; F. Epstein, vice chmn.; Dr. L. Hendrin, treas.; J. Baskin, gen. sec.; P. Geliebter, edu. dir. of Workmen's Circle; hdqts. 175 E. Broadway, N.Y.C.; the anarchist Free Society Forum is held at one of its Chicago schools (1241 N. Cal. Ave.).

WORLD CONGRESS AGAINST WAR

One of the Congresses Against War (against imperialist, but favoring Red civil war), organized and controlled by Moscow's Intl. League Against Imperialism (see) and held at Amsterdam, Aug. 27-29, 1932. The same leaders have since organized the Student Congress Against War (U. of Chgo., Dec. 1932); World Congress of Youth Against War (Paris 1933); U.S. Congress Against War (Sept. 29-Oct. 2, 1933, N.Y. City); a Congress barred from Shanghai, 1933, Anti-War Committees in schools and colleges, Intl., Am. and Chicago Committees for Struggle Against War, Am. Lg. Against War and Fascism, etc.

An idea of all of these Congresses may be gained from the report of the Amsterdam Congress published in pamphlet form by the American Committee for Struggle Against War (104 Fifth Ave., Room 1811, N.Y. City) with commendatory forewords by Scott Nearing and Lola Maverick Lloyd (saying "True pacifists are rebels," etc.).

To quote: "It was a Congress initiated by the eloquent appeal of intellectuals of international fame, Romain Rolland and Henri Barbusse, to arouse the people of the world against . . . specifically the danger of an attack on the Soviet Union. They sent forth a call to action; it was taken up by like-minded men and women in various countries, such as Maxim Gorki,

Bertrand Russell, Heinrich Mann, Albert Einstein, Michael Karolyi, Martin Anderson Nexo, Mme. Sun Yat Sen, Theodore Dreiser, and Upton Sinclair. Geneva . . . Paris, London and Brussels refused to harbor such an assemblage." Of the 2,196 delegates from 27 countries, "there were 1,041 without party allegiance, 830 Communists, 291 Social Democrats, 24 Left Socialists and 10 of the Communist Opposition."

"The Russian delegation had been barred by the Dutch government, but the banner of greeting sent by its chairman, Maxim Gorki, was received with thunderous applause. . . . When Henri Barbusse rose to address the delegates he was visibly moved . . . Barbusse pleaded for unity of all elements . . . the workers of hand and of brain in the common cause. The need for unity was also stressed by Romain Rolland in the message he sent to the opening session of the Congress ... he drove home the point ... this was to be a militant Congress. . . . A Belgian striking miner told dramatically how the month before, when the army was called out and ordered to fire on the striking miners, the soldiers refused to obey. Equally impressive was a German marine transport worker who urged that the fight be carried on, not only in the munitions industries, but in all key industries. He pledged the active support of his union in preventing the transport of munitions.

"Len Wincott described the Invergordon strike in the British navy last year" (Communist) ... "Mrs. Wright, mother of two of the negro boys condemned to death at Scottsboro, was received with a memorable ovation when she arose to greet the Congress. . . . Prof. H. W. L. Dana briefly described the mass unemployment and hunger in America and the consequent unrest the ruling class attempts to sidetrack through war. He urged a concrete program including such steps as protest strikes in munitions factories against the manufacture of munitions, refusal to transport munitions or troops and continual *struggle against the capitalist system,* which is the chief cause of war." (He was barred from England because of his radicalism, the press reported.) . . . "there were 291 members of the Socialist Party present. . . . Two were French Socialist members of the Châmber of Deputies, Hamon and Poupy; another was Nicole, editor of 'Travail,' a Swiss Socialist paper." (Nicole, named as an emissary of Moscow by foreign press reports, was convicted (June 3, 1933, Chgo. Tribune) of having caused a bloody riot, Nov. 9, 1932, in Geneva, which cost the lives of 13 and injured 70). "These Socialists as a group passed a resolution in which they stated 'We decide to work zealously within our respective organizations to win them over to the united front against war and for the *defense of the Russian Revolution.*'" (Nicole got busy very soon evidently.) "Spontaneous cheering broke out when Sen Katayama, veteran Japanese revolutionary leader, came forward to make his speech," saying, "'don't forget that you, by handling such shipments'" (arms and munitions for Japan) "'are helping to murder your fellow workers and to attack the Soviet Union which is the *guarantee of your hopes for socialism.*' . . . Patel, picturesque white bearded Indian nationalist, denounced British imperialism for its brutal oppression of the Indian masses . . . Cachin, a leading French Communist . . . was vigorously applauded when he presented a program of action: 'Penetrate the armed forces; win over workers and peasants in the factories and fields.'"

"The most stirring, breath taking demonstration occurred towards the end of the last session, in honor of an unexpected speaker whose name we shall never know. The chairman stepped forward, and in an electrically vibrant voice he cried out: 'Comrades! I have an extraordinarily important announcement to make! The sailors of the *Italian warship* now in the harbor of Amsterdam have heard of this Congress, and one of them has come to bring you greetings from his comrades! . . . But first let me warn you: take no pictures! This boy's life is doomed if his picture gets into the hands of the police. And now I present him to you—a *nameless sailor* of the Italian fleet!' Instantly the Congress was on its feet as one man, and the 'International' rang out from thousands of throats. And there mounted the rostrum ... a sun bronzed sailor in the dazzling white uniform of the Italian navy. He gazed at the audience calmly until the singing was over, then just as calmly but with full consciousness of what he was doing, he spoke for ten minutes in Italian. He described the absolutism of the Fascist dictatorship which, he said, makes revolution the only possible means of change. . . . Nevertheless there are small groups in the army and navy who are *preparing for the only possible resistance* when the crucial moment comes. The speaker concluded: 'Abbasso il Fascismo! Viva la rivoluzione soziale!' (Down with Fascism! Long live the social revolution!) The appearance of the sailor symbolized the courageous, determined character of the Congress."

To quote from Romain Rolland's declaration "read at the opening of the Congress by Mme. Duchene" of Jane Addams' W.I.L.P.F. (as he was ill): "We French have especially to hold in check—until we can smash them—our money and business powers, our great barons of industry who are the secret or proved masters of politics." He suggested the sabotage of "armament factories and the means of transportation . . . *at decisive moments.*"

Among pledges assumed in the "Manifesto of the Congress" were these: "We pledge ourselves to dedicate ourselves with all our resources to our immediate and pressing tasks, taking our stand: against armaments, against war preparations and for that reason *against the imperialist powers that rule us;* against the campaign of propaganda and slander aimed at the Soviet Union, the country of Socialist construction *which we will not allow to be touched;* for the effective support of the Japanese workers who have raised the standard of struggle against their own imperialist government."

The *Intl. Com.* for Struggle Against War (as listed) includes:

Theo. Dreiser, John Dos Passos, Upton Sinclair, Prof. H. W. L. Dana, Sherwood Anderson, Frank Borich, Ella Reeve Bloor, Jos. Gardner, Emanuel Levin, Wm. Simons (A.A.A.I. Lg.), Malcolm Cowley, Sonia Kaross, the American members, and Henri Barbusse, (Intl. Chmn.), Romain Rolland, Marcel Cachin, Georges Poupy, Albert Einstein, Heinrich Mann, Clara Zetkin, Hugo Graef, Havelock Ellis, Bertrand Russell, Tom Mann, Martin Anderson Nexo, Karin Michaelis, Maxim Gorki, Michael Karolyi, Leon Nicole, General Sandino, Sen Katayama, Saklatvala, Mme. Sun Yat Sen.

A smaller Intl. Bureau within the above includes as American members Wm. Simons and H. W. L. Dana.

The American Committee for Struggle Against War (as listed) includes:

Theo. Dreiser, hon. chmn.; Malcolm Cowley, chmn.; Dr. Oakley Johnson, sec.; A. A. Heller, treas. and Sherwood Anderson, Newton Arvin, Roger Baldwin, Harry Elmer Barnes, Ella Reeve Bloor, Franz Boas, Edwin M. Borchard, Frank Borich, Jos. R. Brodsky, Winifred Chappell, Jos. Cohen, Ida Dailes, H. W. L. Dana, John Dos Passos, W. E. B. Du Bois, Julia Ellsworth Ford, Jos. Freeman, Lillian Furness, Jos. Gardner, Kate Crane Gartz, Michael Gold, Jos. Gollomb, Eugene Gordon, Louis Grudin, Robert Hall, Ali H. Hassan, Donald Henderson, Harold Hickerson, Sidney Hook, Morris Kamman, Sonia Kaross, Joshua Kunitz, Corliss Lamont, Emanuel Levin, E. C. Lindeman, Lola Maverick Lloyd, Robt. Morss Lovett, Pierre Loving, J. C. McFarland, Rev. R. Lester Mondale, Felix Morrow, Alla Nazimova, Scott Nearing, Dr. Henry Neumann, Rabbi Henry M. Rosenthal, Jos. G. Roth, Edward Royce, James Humphrey Sheldon, W. R. Sassaman, Margaret Schlauch, Wm. Simons, Upton Sinclair, Lincoln Steffens, Samuel J. Stember, Bernard J. Stern, Leopold Stokowski, Maurice Sugar, Belle G. Taub, Charlotte Todes, Lillian D. Wald, Lloyd Westlake, Thornton Wilder, Ella Winter.

The smaller 1933 "International, American, and Chicago Committees for Struggle Against War" are listed under that title in this book.

American delegates to the Amsterdam Congress were:

Henry G. Alsberg, Sherwood Anderson, Jos. Brodsky, N. Buchwald, Stella Buchwald, Jos. Cohen, Prof. H.W.L. Dana, Leon Dennenberg, Lillian Furness, Jos. Gardner, Eliz. Gilman, Dr. Israel Goldstein, Minna Harkavy, Karl Herrmann, Vivienne Hochman, Sonia Kaross, Lola Maverick Lloyd, J. C. McFarland, Clara Meltzer, Scott Nearing, J. G. Roth, I. Schendi, Prof. Margaret Schlauch, John Scott, Wm. Simons, Samuel Stember, Bernhard J. Stern, Maurice Sugar, Belle G. Taub, Charlotte Todes, Lloyd Westlake, Dorothy Detzer, Samuel W. Eiges, Henry George (Waukegan, Ill.).

WORLD CONGRESS OF YOUTH AGAINST WAR AND FASCISM

Held in Paris, France, Aug. 5-6-7, 1933; organized by the Intl. and American Committees for Struggle Against War controlled by Moscow's communist Intl. Lg. Against Imperialism leaders, who organized the World Congress Against War at Amsterdam and its successors.

The send off of three *"peace"* delegates and the spirit of these *"pacifists"* was graphically described by the communist Daily Worker, Sept. 15, 1933, as follows: "Down the full length of 14th St. to the Cunard Steamship Line, marched 500 workers Wednesday night at 11 P.M. behind three flowing *red flags* in a send-off demonstration to the three young workers leaving for the Paris World Youth Congress Against War and Fascism. . . . The resounding *militant music* of the Red Front Band played the *fighting songs* of *revolutionary* workers engaged in the struggle against wars and bosses' oppression in the form of NRA. Workers watched the parade amazed at the rythmic shouting of the whole line 'Hands Off Cuba,' 'Fight Against Imperialist War' . . . six policemen attempted to arrest Leonard Patterson, Negro Young Communist League member, while he was making an extraordinary appeal for funds at Union Square. . . . *One cop was clipped on the jaw* by a worker, the others were quickly surrounded by an *angry, screaming crowd,* and for a moment it looked like the police would start clubbing. The police, however, realizing the *furious militancy of the crowd,* immediately released Patterson. A few minutes later the group of 200 arrived from the open air meeting they had been forced to hold at 15th St. and Irving Place when the war authorities refused a permit for a mass *demonstration* inside the Washington Irving High School. Speakers at this meeting included Abraham Kaufman of the War *Resister's League* and Annie Gray of the *Women's Peace Society.*" "When the line of marchers approached 13th Ave., on which the piers are located, the band started playing the *Internationale,* and *500 fists were raised to the day when the revolutionary workers will take possession of the waterfront* and smash shipments of ammunition. . . . Carl Geiser, National Organizer of the United States Anti-War Congress, and a member of the Workers Ex-Service Men's League" (Communist) "quickly jumped up on top of a delivery car and addressed the marchers. Three rousing cheers were given the delegates Clemence Strauss, Phil Rosengarten, and Toiva Oja. . . . Then with the drums thumping out the *Internationale* to the accompaniment of lusty voices the workers bade farewell to the delegates and marched back." (Emphasis supplied.)

A copy of the leaflet entitled "To the Youth of America—A Call for Action Against War and Fascism" issued by the American Committee for this Congress is before me. It urges penetration of the armed forces, C.M.T.C., R.O.T.C., steel and chemical plants, Conservation Camps, transportation industries, National Guard, and "Wherever Youth Meets," for distribution of this "Call" and for propagandizing disloyal activities against these very organizatons for which the youths are working.

One page is devoted to the endorsers and their endorsements of this Congress and lists as "Supporters of Call" the following:

American Committee for Struggle Against War (hdqts. of the committee issuing the "Call"); Anti-Imperialist League, Youth Section (Communist); Fellowship of Reconciliation; Green International; International Workers Order, Youth Section (Communist); Labor Sports Union (Communist); National Lithuanian Youth Federation (Communist); National Student Committee: Negro Student Problems (Communist); National Student Committee for Struggle Against War (Communist); National Student League (Communist); Nature Freunde (Communist); Needle Trades Workers Industrial Union, Youth Section (Communist); W. Walter Ludwig, secretary of Pioneer Youth of America (Socialist); Edwin C. Johnson, secretary of the Committee on Militarism in Education (Garland Fund-aided); War Resisters League; Young Communist League; Young Pioneers (Communist).

Carl Geiser, of the communist Wkrs. Ex-Service Men's Lg., was listed as secretary of the American Committee arranging this Congress, and Abraham Kaufman, of the War Resisters Lg., as treasurer, and the hdqts. as 104 Fifth Ave., N.Y. City. (Hdqts. of Am. Com. for Struggle Against War.)

WORLD PEACEWAYS

Another "peace" society formed 1931; endorsed by radicals of all hues; successor to World Peace Posters; supporting organization communist U.S. Cong. Ag. War; "Disarm or Be Destroyed! That's about what it boils down to" is its challenge in appealing for funds. Hdqts. 31 Union Square, N.Y. City; 1933 letterhead gives as "Endorsers Committee":

Dr. Jos. H. Apple, Prof. Franz Boaz, Chas. Corbett, Dr. Geo. S. Counts, Dr. Donald J. Cowling, Dr. John D. Finlayson, Rev. Walter Getty, Dr. Sidney Goldstein, Rev. Sidney Gulick, D.D., Horace W. Hardy, Dr. S. Ralph Harlow, Dr. Lynn Harold Hough, Mary Hobson Jones, Mrs. Rebecca Kohut, Mrs. Henry Goddard Leach, James G. McDonald, Philip C. Nash, Ray Newton, Rev. Reinhold Niebuhr, Prof. Harry Allen Overstreet, John Nevin Sayre, Tucker P. Smith; "Organizing Committee on Peace Advertising": Bruce Barton, Bennett Chapple, Jos. Deutsch, Mrs. Theresa Mayer Durlach, Herbert S. Houston, Frank W. Nye, Frank L. Palmer, Pres. Walter Dill Scott of Northwestern Univ., Tucker P. Smith, Crosby B. Spinney; "Executive Committee": Chmn., Mrs. Theresa Mayer Durlach; treas., Frank W. Nye; sec., Mrs. Dorothy Siegel; members: Roswell P. Barnes, E. Harrison Eudy, Dr. Alvin C. Goddard, Prof. Carlton J. H. Hayes, Clifton D. Jackson, Frederick C. Libby, and Mrs. Estelle M. Sternberger.

WORLD TOMORROW

Socialist publication founded by Norman Thomas; mouthpiece of the radical-pacifist War Resisters League; rec'd. thousands of dollars from the red Garland Fund. The N.Y. State Lusk Report (p. 1129) says, concerning John Haynes Holmes and other communistic ministers: "An insidious anti-religious campaign is being carried on by these men and their colleagues in such reviews as 'The World Tomorrow' (New York) and 'Unity' (Chicago)." (See under Abraham Lincoln Center "Unity.") Devere Allen and Reinhold Niebuhr were prominent at communist U.S. Congress Against War (see).

Hdqts. 52 Vanderbilt Ave., N.Y. City; editors:

Kirby Page, Devere Allen, Reinhold Niebuhr, Paul H. Douglas (of the "Brain Trust"); assoc. editors: H. N. Brailsford, Geo. A. Coe, Halford E. Luccock, H. C. Engelbrecht; contrib. eds.: John Bennett, Sherwood Eddy, John Haynes Holmes, Samuel Guy Inman, Edward L. Israel, Paul Jones, A. Albert MacLeod, Patrick Murphy Malin, Francis J. McConnell, Rhoda E. McCulloch, Helen Grace Murray, A. J. Muste, H. Richard Niebuhr, William Pickens, Maxwell S. Stewart, Norman Thomas; pres., John Nevin Sayre; sec., Dorothy Detzer; treas., Henry P. Van Dusen.

WRITERS PROTEST COMMITTEE

Affiliated with the Revolutionary Writers Federation.

Y

YOUNG CIRCLE CLUBS

Workmen's Circle youth section.

YOUNG COMMUNIST LEAGUE

Y.C. Lg.

Originally Young Workers League; rec'd. money from Garland Fund (Chicago branch, $1,200; Superior, Wis., $2,000); youth section of Communist Party; American section of Moscow's Young Communist International; for young Communists, 16 to 22 years of age; especially charged with subversive work in the armed forces; official organ is "The Young Worker" (P.O. Box 28, Sta. D, N.Y.C.; 60c for 6 mo.). The message of the 9th Plenum of the Exec. Com. of the Young Communist International (Apr. 1, 1933 issue, Young Worker), after praising the U.S.S.R., said in part: "Their brothers who are not as yet released from the oppression of the boss class sharply watch all the maneuvers of the enemy, consolidating their united militant front for the defense of the Soviet Union. And if the enemy will dare to raise its bloody claws against the fatherland of the proletariat of the whole world, in all the capitalist countries of the world a wall of iron defense of the U.S.S.R. will grow up and millions of young revolutionists will defend it. Long live the U.S.S.R., the first country of Socialism! Long live the Comintern, the leader of the world workers revolution! Long live the Young Communist International! Long live the unity of the young workers and toilers in the struggle against the bourgeoisie!"

YOUNG PEOPLES SOCIALIST LEAGUE

Y.P.S.L.

Youth section of Socialist Party and affiliated with Socialist Youth International (hdqts. were Berlin); has about 90 branches in U.S.; members participate in militant Red strike activities; aided Intl. Ladies Garment Workers, Amalgamated Cloth. Workers, Women's Trade Union League in 1932 (Am. Labor Year Book); takes part in Communist Anti-War, Mooney, May Day, etc. united front activities; George Smerkin, its nat. sec., who spoke at the Communist Mooney meeting, May 1, 1933, said the Y.P.S.L. was with the Communist Party not only in the Mooney and Scottsboro matters but until the very end to help put over the Revolution! His delegation was cheered as it entered the Chicago Stadium bearing a large red banner just like the Communists' with "Y.P.S.L." on it. Exec. com.: Julius Uniansky, nat. chmn.; Winston Dancis (N.Y.); Lester Shulman (Mass.); John Hall (Mass.); Eugene McStroul (Wis.); Pearl Greenberg (Ill.); Max Wohl (Ohio).

YOUNG PIONEERS OF AMERICA

Communist organization for boys and girls 8 to 15 years of age, who may graduate from it into the Young Communist League and then at 23 into the Communist Party proper; modeled after the Boy Scout movement but passionately antagonistic to it. To quote the U.S. Fish Report: "Many Young Pioneer summer camps conducted by the Workers International Relief have sprung up in various sections of the United States since 1925 at which time there were 2 camps. In 1929 the number had increased to 20 located in 8 different states. New York State predominates with 5 such camps all teaching hatred of God, of our form of government and of the American flag. In New York state alone over 15,000 young communists are turned out each year from these camps, trained to promote class hatred and to urge the destruction of all American ideals and traditions. . . . There is no Federal law prohibiting such camps teaching disloyalty and practically treason to thousands of healthy and bright young future Americans. . . . During their attendance at these summer camps these children are educated in the principles and tenets of communism; anti-patriotic and anti-religious instructions are stressed and they are taught hatred and contempt for the American government, American institutions and all religions. They render no respect or allegiance to the American flag—the Stars and Stripes—and it is never displayed. In fact they are taught not to salute the flag or to pledge allegiance to it. They are, however taught to reverence the red flag of communism and world revolution and to formally pledge allegiance to it. The red flag is displayed in the conduct of the daily camp programs. Admission of children to these camps is not restricted to those whose parents are communists. An effort is made to draw into the camps children of working people, both white and Negroes, who are non-communist, with the hope of making them converts and through them influence other children and their parents."

In Chicago, 1933, under the name of "Shule" there were ten Young Pioneer training schools located as follows: 3308 Crystal St.; 2653 W. Division St.; 3507 Lawrence Ave.; 1228 S. Lawndale Ave.; 3313 Armitage Ave.; 1209 S. Karlov Ave.; 1224 S. Albany Ave.; 1124 W. 59th St.; 2052 W. Division St.; 1554 S. Homan Ave. In the Chicago Communist May Day parade, 1933, about 500 Young Pioneers marched carrying Red flags and singing revolutionary songs.

The official organ is the "New Pioneer," which publishes the most vicious class-hate, revolutionary propaganda. A child's poem praised as "among the best" printed in the Nov. 1932 issue is characteristic—to quote: "We'll organize and fight the boss for cutting father's pay; Hey, fellow workers, to Hell with the bosses we say!"

Under the heading "A Grand New Science Book," the Feb. 1933 issue says: "Once there was a young man who made his living by telling the workers fairy tales about how the world was created. . . That is what all ministers and priests make their living by doing and this young man was a minister. He preached in the Episcopal Church. But as he grew older he came to see how false this preaching was. . . . He began to show the workers how the churches had always taught what was not true. . . . For that he was thrown out of the church. . . . Now he has written a grand book especially for workers children. . . . And how different it all is from the dull, mistaken stuff they teach us in school and church—no hocus pocus about spirits that don't exist, no comments to be 'loyal' to the employers and their government and let them keep on robbing us. Quite the opposite. Every page tears to tatters some pet idea that the bosses try to make the teachers try to force into our heads. . . . The name of the book? O! Yes—it is Science and History for Boys and Girls by Wm. Montgomery Brown." (Atheist Communist deposed Episcopal Bishop and head of Workers International Relief.)

"New Pioneer" is pub. at 50 E. 13th St., N.Y.C. Editorial board:

Everett Burns, Bert Grant, William Gropper, Gertrude Haessler, V. Jerome, Harry Potamkin, J. Preval, Bernard Reines, Ernest Reymer, Sasha Small; Editors: Helen Kay, Wm. Siegel; mgr., Anna Cornblath. Contributing editors: Mary Adams, Phil Bard, Max Bedacht, "Bishop" Wm. Brown, Julia Davis, Marion Davis, Robert Dunn, Wm. Z. Foster, Lydia Gibson, Hugo Gellert, Mike Gold, Maxim Gorki, Al Harris, Grace Hutchins, Harry Kaplan, M. Kirkland, Melvin Levy, Grace Lumpkin, Marya Morrow, Myra Page, John Dos Passos, Abel Plenn, Walter Quirt, Hannah Rile, John C. Rogers, Ruth Shaw, Dr. Slatkin, Otto Soglow, Sadie Van Veen, Jos. Vogel, Ryan Walker, Waly, Wex, John Worth.

Y.M.C.A. AND Y.W.C.A.

A speaker for the Young Communist League drew attention at the Chicago Coliseum Communist mass meeting for Barbusse, Oct. 23, 1933, to the placards placed around the walls announcing their "Preliminary Youth Conference Against War, Wednesday, Nov. 1st, Y.M.C.A. Central College, 19 South La Salle St., Room 360." The Communist press records *many* similar incidents.

While exposures in the press of communistic activities of the Y.M.C.A. in Asia and Europe and of dynamite found in the Y.M.C.A. and complicity of Y.M.C.A. officials in Cuba, and the prevalence of League for Industrial Democracy Socialist-Communist literature and influence in student Y.M.C.A. college branches, arouse comment from time to time, it is still generally supposed that the "C" in Y.W.C.A. and Y.M.C.A. stands for "Christian," not "Communist."

The publications of the Y.W.C.A. National Board would seem to make this a question. The Camp Gray (Saugatuck, Mich.) Conferences for Y.W.C.A. *leaders*, held each summer for consecutive groups, in 1932 used their own song sheet with the official Communist revolutionary song "The Internationale" (four verses) and "Solidarity Forever," the I.W.W. song by Ralph Chaplin who served five years in the penitentiary for sedition. The latter is sung to the tune of "Battle Hymn of the Republic" at Communist meetings. The next year (1933) they printed a Conference book and entitled it "Solidarity—'For the Union Makes Us Strong'" (from words of Chaplin's I.W.W. song). They included the entire Industrial Song Sheet of 17 songs of the Y.W.C.A. National Board and added, besides, the following Communist songs:

COMINTERN

From Russia victorious
The Workers October,
Comes storming reaction's
Regime the world over.
We're coming with Lenin
For Bolshevik work,
From London, Havana, Berlin and New
York.

Rise up fields and workshops,
Come out workers, farmers;
To battle march onward,
March on world stormers
Eyes sharp on your guns,
Red banners unfurled;
Advance proletarians to conquer the world.

RED MARCHING SONG

* * * * * * *

Hear our voices, hear our marching,
Hear how they make the despots quake!
We are treading rapidly
The mountain paths to victory!
Etc., etc.

ARISE YOU WORKERS

Arise you workers, fling to the breeze
The scarlet banner, the scarlet banner,
Arise you workers, fling to the breeze
The scarlet banner triumphantly.

Chorus

Wave scarlet banner triumphantly,
Wave scarlet banner triumphantly,
Wave scarlet banner triumphantly,
For Communism and Liberty!
Etc., etc.

This conference book, "Solidarity," thanks Miss Annetta Dieckmann, Chicago Y.W.C.A. secretary, for having secured the use of this camp for summer conferences since 1925. She is also listed as a group leader, and Sonya S. Forthal (said to be wife of Dr. J. G. Spiesman of 222 N. Oak Park Ave., Oak Park, Ill.) as leader of Political Action. The pro-Soviet talk on Russia of Lucy Carner, "Executive of Industrial Department on National Board since 1924," is also summarized in it.

The Industrial Song Sheet used in this conference book is also issued separately by the Y.W.C.A. National Board. It includes but two verses of the Communist "Internationale." But one of the two chosen is the *anti-religious one:*

THE INTERNATIONALE

We want no condescending saviors,
To rule us from a judgement hall,
We workers ask not for their favors;
Let us consult for all.

* * * * * *

Refrain:

'Tis the final conflict
Let each stand in his place
The International Party
Shall be the human race.
Etc.

The Communists sing it with the difference of one word: "The International *Soviet* shall be the human race."

"Solidarity Forever," by Ralph Chaplin, is included, as is the Communist song "The Advancing Proletaire," which expresses anything but the Christian spirit:

We are coming unforgiving
And the earth resounds our tread.
Bone and sinew of the living,
Spirit of the rebel dead,
You who sow'd the wind of sorrow
Now the whirlwind you must dare,
As you face upon the morrow
The advancing Proletaire.

"I'm Labor" is No. 10, a very good class-hate selection:

I'm very humble, I'm Labor.
I rarely grumble, I'm Labor.
In summer heat and winter gale,
I pack a load or swing a flail;
But some one else rakes in the kale,
I'm Labor (All: He's Labor)

* * * * * *

From birth to death my life is spent
In hovel shack or tenement;
But still some landlord gets the rent,
I'm Labor! (All: He's Labor!)
I have no say, I'm Labor.
I just obey, I'm Labor.
I slaved through years of hate and war
Or spilled my own or my brother's gore
But did I know what the shootin's for?
I'm Labor (All: He's Labor).
Etc., etc.

"Nations Come and Join Us" and "We Shall Be Free," Socialist Party songs, the communist Russian "Work Song," "Over All the Lands" by Communist Anna Louise Strong, *"Song of the Workers"* ("Men who toil like hosses, Will you serve the bosses, And bow down to heels of steel?" etc.), are included. Also "Comrades Join the Mustering Forces":

Comrades join the mustering forces;
Lift your eyes from work and hear
High above the grind and rattle
The *Internationale* sounding strong and clear.
Etc.

All of the 17 songs are somewhat similar with the exception of two Negro spirituals. These two are the *only* songs that mention the word "God" and *not one* song in the book alludes to Christ in any way.

The "Program Exchange" issued by the "Laboratory Division, National Board Y.W.C.A., 600 Lexington Ave., New York, additional copies 25 cents from the Woman's Press," says (p. 4):

"Someone has said 'the excuse for being of Association Music is its relation to program.' How then are labor songs tied into workers education in the Y.W.C.A.? . . .

"Such songs as 'Solidarity Forever,' *'Song of the Workers'* " (Men who toil like hosses, etc.), "from the Vagabond King, and local adaptations of the 'Song of the Flame' are similarly excellent devices *for arousing class consciousness* through participation. (Emphasis supplied.)

"So many groups are becoming interested in Russia that the *'Internationale'* with its stirring call to action and world brotherhood can be used increasingly. This song offers immediate discussion material for *communism and socialism,* internationalism, etc. . . . Many so-called 'Red' songs can be altered a bit by groups studying Russia to fit the various stages of *social awareness* of the groups."

(p. 13): "The Friends of Soviet Russia" (Communist) "offer us exhibits of pictures on work life among the Soviets. They will prepare special exhibits for groups studying special subjects. There is no charge except postage. They suggest that clubs use their magazine 'Soviet Russia Today' for pictures and facts. Subscriptions are $1.00 a year. If clubs sell 5 or more subscriptions they may make 25 cents on each subscription. Address 80 East 11th St., New York." (Communist hdqts.)

"The League for Industrial Democracy, 112 East 19th St., New York, has the best bibliography we have seen. It deals with Social Reconstruction and covers biography and drama as well as general fiction and economics. Order it for *advanced* girls, for committees and for setting up conferences. Price 5 cents." (The Socialist L.I.D. is closely associated with the Y.M.C.A. and Y.W.C.A.).

"A new interest in public ownership" of public utilities with "study and action in this field", on p. 10 (Socialism), and "more knowledge about free dental, lung and heart clinics, about *birth control,* about how to learn to dance", on p. 2, and "music and worship groups united in writing a new grace that should express *new social thinking uninhibited by the traditional feeling of personal religion* attached to the old hymn tunes", on p. 5, are suggested.

An ex-Communist tells me that Eleanor Copenhaver, National Industrial Secretary of the Y.W.C.A., has recently married Sherwood Anderson, prominent Communist worker. There should be a thorough investigation made of the whole personnel and program of the Y.W.C.A. and either a change of name or a change of National Board policy made. Why should *Christians* support those who "wave scarlet banner triumphantly for Communism and Liberty"? (See page 338.)

YOUTH CRUSADE FOR DISARMAMENT AND WORLD PEACE

Sponsored by Fellowship of Reconciliation (see).

(Abbreviations of organizations named in "Who's Who" are explained in the Index.)

admin.	administration	finan.	financial
advis.	advisory	gen.	general
agt.	agent	govt.	government
Am.	American	grad.	graduate
Amb.	Ambassador	hdqts.	headquarters
anniv.	anniversary	hon.	honorary
apptd.	appointed	indust.	industrial
assn.	association	instr.	instructor
assoc.	associate	intl.	international
asst.	assistant	lab.	labor
atty.	attorney	lect.	lecturer
bd.	board	lg.	league
bet.	between	mag.	magazine
br.	branch	mem.	member
bus.	business	mg.	managing
camp.	campaign	mgr.	manager
cand.	candidate	nat.	national
cent.	central	org.	organizer or organization
ch.	church	perm.	permanent
chmn.	chairman	pet.	petition
citiz.	citizens	pres.	president
coll.	college	prof.	professor
com.	committee	pub.	public
commr.	commissioner	publ.	publicity or publication
conf.	conference	recep.	reception
contrib.	contributing / contributor / contribution	recog.	recognition
		reg.	regular
coop.	cooperative	rep.	representative
corres.	correspondent	sch.	school
coun.	council	sec.	secretary
delg.	delegate or delegation	sect.	section
dept.	department	soc.	social or society
dir.	director	spkr.	speaker
dist.	district	tchr.	teacher
ed.	editor	theol.	theology
edu.	education or educational	treas.	treasurer
edtl.	editorial	U.	University
endors.	endorser	un.	union
exec.	executive	wkrs.	workers
fed.	federation	yr.	year

EXPLAINING SOME "RED" TERMS

"Proletariat": the poorest class of society; those who own no savings, property, business, insurance, or other investment, and hire no labor.

"Bourgeoisie": small property, investment, or business-owning class.

"Exploiters": all who collect profit from investments, rent, or labor of others. All bourgeoisie are "exploiters" and all proletarians are "exploited".

"Class consciousness": the sense of being "exploited" and eager for the "class struggle".

"Class war" or *"Class struggle":* the struggle of the proletariat to set up a dictatorship over the bourgeoisie, first by strikes, "daily struggles" against employers, landlords, and bourgeois governmental authorities leading to revolution, seizure of governmental power, then the subjugation of the bourgeoisie by force or "liquidation". After 16 years the class war is still going on in Russia, to purge it from bourgeois "class enemies".

"Class enemy": one who hinders the proletariat in any way from carrying out its program of dictatorship.

"Liquidate": to get rid of. It may mean getting rid of bourgeois ideas by education, but more frequently in Russia it means getting rid of persons by shooting, exile, or by "giving them the wolf card", that is, disenfranchising them by refusing them food, housing, or job cards without which, the government being the sole landlord, employer, and store keeper, the victim is turned out to wander and finally die of starvation. Millions were thus liquidated in 1933 as "class enemies".

"Cadres": leaders forming a skeleton military organization capable of engineering revolutionary uprising. All Communist Party members who are promising material as military officers are trained either by enlistment in National Guard and other "bourgeois" organizations, there to act as traitors at the moment of uprising, or by the Red Front League affiliated with the Young Communist League (see Red Army in U. S. A.) and other "workers defense" organizations.

"Left wing": the most radical or extreme element in any organization. A "leftist" is one of the left wing.

"Right wing": the most moderate or conservative element in any organization.

"Centrists": those occupying a position between left and right wings.

"Reactionary" or *"Rightist":* tending toward the conservative and away from the radical.

"Collectivize": to take private property and put it under collective management and ownership. Farmers in Russia give up their homes, stock, and tools to be used as part of a collective farm upon which they work as employees and receive such share of the proceeds as the Party and farm authorities give them.

"Capitalism": the system of government which defends private ownership of business and property.

"Socialism": collectivized or State ownership of property, business, employment, means of production; the opposite from private ownership; its slogan: "Production for use and not for profit."

"Worker": a Communist is always a "worker". Non-Communists are always "exploiters" in Communist literature. Supposedly only Communists "work".

"Classless society": the objective of Socialism-Communism; the State owned and controlled society under which all receive an equal income, the "profit motive" being replaced by punishment: "He who does not work does not eat," etc.

"New Social Order" and *"Cooperative Commonwealth":* Socialism-Communism.

SUPPLEMENT TO THIRD PRINTING, JULY 1934

ANGLO-AMERICAN INSTITUTE OF THE FIRST MOSCOW UNIVERSITY

A communist summer school in Moscow conducted in conjunction with American educators; to quote its announcements: "The ANGLO-AMERICAN INSTITUTE will offer at the First Moscow University, during the summer of 1934, a variety of courses to serve as a means of furthering cultural contacts between American, English and Russian teachers and students." "All instruction is in English, under the direction of a faculty of Soviet professors and specialists, with an advisory staff of American instructors. Moscow University certifies academic credit for foreign students."; director: I. V. Sollins; Nat. Advis. Coun.: W. W. Charters, Dir. Bur. of Edu. Research, Ohio State U.; Harry Woodburn Chase, Chancellor N. Y. U.; George S. Counts, Prof. Edu. Tchrs. Coll., Columbia U.; John Dewey, Prof. Emeritus of Phil., Columbia U.; Stephen Duggan, Dir. Inst. Intl. Edu.; Hallie F. Flanagan, Prof. Engl., Vassar Coll.; Frank P. Graham, Pres. U. of N. C.; Robert M. Hutchins, Pres., U. of Chgo.; Charles H. Judd, Dean Sch. Edu., U. of Chgo.; I. L. Kandel, Prof. of Edu., Tchrs. Coll., Columbia U.; Robert L. Kelly, Sec. Assoc. of Amer. Coll.; John A. Kingsbury, Sec. Milbank Mem. Fund; Susan M. Kingsbury, Prof. of Soc. Econ. and Soc. Research, Bryn Mawr Coll.; Paul Klapper, Dean Sch. of Edu., Coll. City of N. Y.; Charles R. Mann, Dir. Am. Coun. on Edu.; Edward R. Murrow, Asst. Dir. Inst. of International Edu.; William Allan Neilson, Pres. Smith Coll.; Howard W. Odum, Prof. of Soc. and Dir. Sch. of Pub. Welfare, U. of N. C.; William F. Russell, Dean Tchrs. Coll., Columbia U.; H. W. Tyler, Gen. Sec. Am. Assn. of U. Profs.; Ernest H. Wilkins, Pres. Oberlin Coll.; John W. Withers, Dean Sch. of Edu., N. Y. U.; Thomas Woody, Prof. of Hist. of Edu., U. of Pa.; Harvey W. Zorbaugh, Dir. Clinic for the Soc. Adj. of Gifted Children, N. Y. U.

OFFICERS

President
WILLIS J. SPAULDING

Honorary President
ALBERT M. TODD

Executive Committee
WILLIAM H. HOLLY, CHAIRMAN
OTTO CULLMAN
JAMES H. MCGILL
FAY LEWIS
EDWARD F. DUNNE
GRACE F. PETER
WILEY W. MILLS
S. J. KONENKAMP
DAVID ROSENHEIM
MARGARET HALEY
RALPH U. THOMPSON
JOHN J. WALT
JAMES. H. ANDREWS
CLARENCE DARROW
GEORGE A. SCHILLING
R. E. MCDONNELL

Secretary
CARL D. THOMPSON

Treasurer
CHARLES H. INGERSOLL

For the Protection and Promotion of our Municipal and Public Utilities and Natural Resources

The Public Ownership League of America

NATIONAL OFFICE
127 N. DEARBORN ST. ROOM 1439
CHICAGO, ILL.
PHONE DEARBORN 8133

Vice-Presidents
W. T. RAWLEIGH
J. D. ROSS
JOHN R. HAYNES
ROBERT M. LA FOLLETTE, JR.
CHARLES EDWARD RUSSELL
E. F. SCATTERGOOD
D. B. ROBERTSON
J. F. CHRISTY
L. E. SHEPPARD
RUDOLPH SPRECKELS
WILLIAM T. EVJUE
M. C. PARSONS
ROBERT B. HOWELL
ARTHUR P. DAVIS
LYNN J. FRAZIER
C. H. FOSTER
JOHN A. RYAN
E. H. FITZGERALD
A. EMIL DAVIES
THEO. F. THIEME
AMOS PINCHOT
BISHOP F. J. MCCONNELL
S. A. STOCKWELL
E. J. MANION
C. C. DILL
HOMER T. BONE
CHAS W. WARD
WILLIAM MADGETT
EDWARD P. COSTIGAN
GOV. FLOYD B. OLSON
HON. THOS. R. AMLIE

June 26, 1933.

In Re: Appointment of Regional Directors Under National Industrial Recovery Act.

Second Message to Members and Friends of The Public Ownership League:

Since writing you last Wednesday, June 21st, I have had a long distance conversation with Harold Ickes, Secretary of the Interior, and learn that matters have been held in abeyance and plans somewhat changed.

Mr. Ickes tells me that there will be no regional directors. The state directors will be appointed by the President.

He also suggests that we send direct to him any protests that we may have against the appointment of men that are being proposed for state directors and also any suggestions as to the men that we think ought to be appointed. So address your protests and your nominations and suggestions direct to Harold Ickes, Secretary of the Interior, Washington, D. C.

Let us know of your action and we will support and cooperate with you in every possible way.

Cordially yours,

Carl D Thompson

Carl D. Thompson, Secretary

CDT:MB

Facsimile of significant letter sent out to "Members and Friends" by socialist Public Ownership League. Reveals close ties with Secretary Ickes. See "Who's Who" for signer of the letter, Carl D. Thompson, and other League leaders listed on letterhead.

PART III

"WHO'S WHO"

WHO IS WHO IN RADICALISM?

The Communist-Socialist-Anarchist-I.W.W. teaching is that the Red revolutionary movement is the Marxian "class struggle" of the proletariat, or poorest class, against the "bourgeoisie", or small-property-owning and tradesman class, in an effort to dispossess and create a "dictatorship of the proletariat" over the "bourgeoisie". It is amusing to hear this preached at a great Red meeting filled with several thousand well dressed "bourgeoisie" and to see, as I have, the numerous fine cars, including a Rolls-Royce, draw up to the door after such a meeting.

The Red movement is a *revolutionary,* not a class, movement. Its strongest *opponents* are neither scented, sleeping capitalists nor the shiftless bums, but the great working class of ambitious, self respecting, common-sense Americans who have no desire to be proletarians, glorified or otherwise. Radical forces are drawn from all classes, from the dumbest type of "proletarian" bum who anticipates revolution as a diverting opportunity to vent his envy and hatred by looting and murder, all the way to the befogged capitalist type with "suicidal tendencies" who helps finance the Red movement and whose sons acquire their warped theories from Red capitalist-supported college professors, and the idealistic sincere humanitarian tvpe who believes the Red road is the right road and who beckons others to follow him over the precipice into Bolshevism believing it is for the good of humanity.

Probably few leaders become really great unless they do believe sincerely in their cause. Even Lenin when he ordered the torture and murder of millions of dissenting Russians and ended freedom for the rest of the population probably believed the end justified the means. Idealistic Reds may dislike the deception, camouflage, "boring from within", false fronts, and ruthlessness characteristic of the Red movement, yet consider these tactics necessary and justifiable. Dupes are enlisted in every Red organization. Sincere Pacifists make excellent material, for, while all Pacifists are not Reds, all Reds are militant Pacifists and all Pacifists are used directly or indirectly to further the Red scheme of breaking down patriotic spirit and national defense which are major hindrances to Red revolution, internationalism and "the new social order".

We may believe in the altruism and personal sincerity of the intellectual radical leader, admire his learning or personal charm, just as we believe in the sincere religious devotion of the Hindu who, according to his religion, offers his baby girls for vile sex degradation and physical injury, jabs nails into himself, and offers bloody human sacrifices to his god "Kali", but we need not follow either. Neither sincerity nor ignorance mitigates the effects of their acts upon their followers and victims. On an old tombstone was carved:

"As you are now, so once was I;
As I am now, so you will be.
Prepare for death and follow me!"

But, underneath, a wag had scribbled:

"To follow you I am not bent,
Unless you say *which way* you went!"

Americans now living in a fog of radical propaganda created by "Pinks", "Yellows" and "Reds" of all hues and shades of opinion need to know *"which way"* leaders, writers, lecturers, and public officials are going so that they may be free to decide whether or not they are "bent" to follow them.

The fact that some of those working for one phase of the Red movement may disapprove of other of its component parts does not lessen the assistance given to the whole.

Various grades and types of radical organizations have been provided to enlist those of all sorts of interests and of all shades of "pinkness". Those who will go "just so far" and no farther toward Red revolution are led along until, like pupils, they often move up a grade from time to time. Just as the stockyards utilize "all but the squeal", the Red movement utilizes all possible persons in the service of its "united front". Even the discontented Reds who leave the main Communist Party in anger or disgrace are gathered up by the smaller "opposition" Communist parties whose leaders fight in print and fraternize in private. There they work for the cause as before.

The Reds and their friends the "Liberals" or pinks, who so violently clamor for the unlimited right of "free speech" for Reds, to agitate violent revolution and confiscation of property, and to fling abuse at religion, our form of government and its defenders, bitterly object to the slightest free speech on the part of their opponents, and are fond of vilifying and suing for libel those who comment unfavorably upon their activities. They not only endeavor to silence opposition by suits, intimidation and boycott threats, but also by confusing and lulling to sleep the non-radical American public. Intellectual radical leaders are constantly "pooh-poohing" in public the very existence of a Red revolutionary movement, so that they themselves may be unopposed while working for its success. An alert and hostile public is a formidable force to combat. "Better that those who would oppose us sleep," says the radical. "Better wake up", says the patriot, for only a minority of any nation guides its destiny.

THIS "WHO'S WHO"

Lists one or more of the affiliations of about 1,300 persons who are or have been members of Communist, Anarchist, Socialist, I.W.W. or Pacifist-controlled organizations, and who, thru these memberships, knowingly or unknowingly, have contributed in some measure to one or more phases of the Red movement in the United States. Both list and data are incomplete. To make either complete would be an impossibility.

The full names of organizations which have been abbreviated in this "Who's Who" may be found both in the Index and at the head of the descriptive matter concerning them under the section in this book on "Organizations", which is alphabetically arranged. Most of the organizations and publications referred to in the "Who's Who" are identified or described in the section on Organizations.

To find out what "N. S. Lg.", for example, means and is, one might either turn first to the Index to find that "N. S. Lg." is the abbreviation for "National Student League" and then turn to the section on Organizations to read the data concerning it, or look directly among the Organizations, beginning with the letter "N", for the abbreviation "N. S. Lg." listed side by side with the full title "National Student League", heading the descriptive matter concerning it. Abbreviations of words, such as "nat.", "com.", "coun.", etc., are explained separately.

Names and information in this "Who's Who" have been taken principally from the official literature and letterheads of the organizations mentioned; from the radicals' own "American Labor Year Book" and "American Labor Who's Who"; from the Report of the Joint Legislative Committee of the State of New York Investigating Seditious Activities (called the Lusk Report) based upon documentary evidence; from U. S. Report 2290 of the Special Committee of the House of Representatives to Investigate Communist Activities in the United States headed by the Hon. Hamilton Fish; from literature and data sheets of Mr. Fred Marvin, national secretary of the American Coalition of Patriotic Societies, N. Y. City; from reports by Mr. Francis Ralston Welsh of Philadelphia, attorney, long a patriotic research authority on subversive activities; from the documentary files of the Advisory Associates, Chicago; from data furnished by the Better America Federation of California; and from other reliable sources.

Mention in this Who's Who will be regarded by those who are proud of their affiliations as a badge of honor, by those ashamed of them as a black list.

A

ABBOTT, EDITH: sister of Grace; dean Sch. Social Serv. Adm. of U. of Chgo. since 1924; sec. Immigrants' Prot. Lg. Chgo.; co-author with Sophonisba Breckenridge and co-editor Soc. Serv. Review; Non-Partz. Com. Lillian Herstein.

ABBOTT, GRACE: Chief U. S. Children's Bureau, Wash., D. C.; resident Hull House, Chgo. 1908-15; dir. Immigrants' Prot. Lg. 1908-17; nat. com. Nat. R. & L. Found. 1933; listed by Devere Allen as one of 24 leading Am. radicals.

ABBOTT, LEONARD D.: born England; ed. staff Encyc. Soc. Sciences since 1929; a founder of Intercollegiate Socialist Soc., now L.I.D.; a founder of Rand School and of Ferrer Colony and Ferrer School (anarchist) at Stelton, N. J.; author of "Francisco Ferrer, His Life, Work and Martyrdom" (executed Spanish anarchist); active in behalf of Sacco and Vanzetti; Freethinkers Ingersoll Com. 1933.

ABERN, MARTIN: born Rumania; was mem. cent. exec. com. Workers' Party and nat. exec. com. Young Wkrs' Lg.; now on nat. com. Communist Lg. of Am.

ADAMS, C. A., chmn. communist R. R. Brotherhoods Unity Com.

ADAMS, LÉONIE: Communist Lg. P. G. for F. & F. 1932; poetess.

ADDAMS, JANE: Was active during the war in organizing "peace" societies with Socialists Louis P. Lochner and Rosika

Schwimmer. (Lochner, then an alleged German agent, in 1919 helped organize the communists' Federated Press and became European director and manager of the Berlin office, used by the Communist International of Moscow as its propaganda agency. Rosika Schwimmer was Minister to Switzerland and mem. radical Nat. Coun. of 15 governing Hungary 1918-19, under communist-aiding Count M. Karolyi, who delivered Hungary to Bela Kun Communist terror regime.) J. Addams was nat. chmn. Woman's Peace Party, 1914. (A letter on the Party's stationery from Rosika Schwimmer to Lochner, showing its activities, is reproduced in the Lusk Report p. 973). The Emergency Peace Federation, 1914-15, and renewed 1917, was organized by Lochner, Rosika Schwimmer, and J. Addams. In the National Peace Federation, 1915, J. Addams was vice pres. and Lochner, secy. April 13, 1915, J. Addams, Sophonisba P. Breckenridge, and Lochner sailed together for The Hague. Lochner acted as J. Addams' special secretary (A postcard signed by all three is reproduced in the Lusk Report). They joined Rosika Schwimmer at The Hague and formed there the Woman's International Committee for Permanent Peace, since 1919 called the Woman's International League for Peace and Freedom (financially aided by the Garland Fund). Lochner, J. Addams and others from the congress then lectured in Germany. The Ford Peace Ship party, which sailed Dec. 4, 1915, was organized by Rosika Schwimmer, with Lochner gen. secy. and J. Addams a delegate, but because of illness J. Addams' place was taken by Emily Balch. Lochner remained a year in Germany, returning early in 1917 to organize with Rosika Schwimmer and J. Addams the renewed Emergency Peace Federation, composed of Socialists, radicals, pacifists, and pro-Germans, which functioned against America while we were at war, and also the First American Conference for Democracy and Terms of Peace, which sent out a call for a meeting to be held at Madison Square Garden, N. Y. C., May 30-31, 1917, after we had been at war nearly two months. The foreword to the call said in part:

"Such an organization was rendered doubly necessary by the revolution in Russia. . . . They (the American people) wanted to make known to this free Russian people that the feelings of those who dwell in the United States were not truly expressed by the war like, undemocratic action of the official government that was elected to represent them. They wanted to show that they stood solidly behind the Russian democracy and are ready to work with them until the autocracy of the entire world is overthrown." (Note that the United States Government is now being called autocratic, capitalistic, militaristic, and imperialistic by those seeking to destroy it.)

J. Addams was vice chmn. of the American Neutral Conference Committee, 1916, and an active organizer of the American League to Limit Armaments, 1914, which formed the Union Against Militarism with Civil Liberties Bureaus, used during the war to give legal aid and encouragement to anti-Americans and radical revolutionaries who called themselves "conscientious objectors." The outgrowth of these Civil Liberties Bureaus was their separate establishment in 1917. The name was changed in 1920 to the American Civil Liberties Union. J. Addams was a founder-member and served on its national committee for ten years along with Communists Wm. Z. Foster, Scott Nearing, Robt. W. Dunn, Elizabeth G. Flynn, and Max Eastman, working then as now to defend and keep from punishment, jail, or deportation those Socialist, Communist, and I.W.W. agitators who seek to overthrow the U.S. Government. Another outgrowth of these pacifist activities was the formation in the U. S. by Norman Thomas, aided by J. Addams, Harry F. Ward, Emily Balch, and others, of the Fellowship of Reconciliation, a slacker-pacifist, pro-Soviet organization spreading, then and now, entering-wedge communistic propaganda; spkr. at its Youth for Peace Institute (Feb. 26, 1926, at U. of Chgo.) with Eugene Debs and Communist Robert Minor.

J. Addams was a stockholder in Sidney Hillman's Russian-American Industrial Corporation along with Nicolai Lenin, Congressman LaGuardia, and Eugene V. Debs ("Reds in America" by Whitney); chmn. of American Relief for Russian Women and Children; on advis. bd. of Russian Reconstruction Farms for propaganda and financial aid of Soviet Russia, with Norman Thomas, Roger Baldwin, etc.; kept the records of anti-American organizations being raided during the war safe for them at Hull House (See her books "Twenty Years at Hull House"); is head of Hull House, a home and meeting place for radicals then and now; was exposed in Senate investigation 1919; member of the socialistic National Consumers League promoted by Socialist Florence Kelley, translator of Marx and Engels and a former resident of

Hull House; signed foreword of Lane Pamphlet (financed by communistic Garland Fund); aided "Hands Off China" communist propaganda affairs; mem. of socialistic Public Ownership League of America; mem. advisory council Chicago Forum, 1928, which features Red speakers; vice chmn. National Council for the Reduction of Armaments (Russia's not mentioned); mem. of the radical Immigrants' Protective League, with headquarters at Hull House; on advisory committee and active in Sacco-Vanzetti National League, a Communist agitation; Hull House windows featured placards in behalf of these two Red murderers; was contributing editor of the "New Republic," "an advocate of revolutionary socialism" (Lusk Report); on American Committee on Information about Russia, 1928, which spread misinformation and Communist propaganda; mem. American Association for Labor Legislation; vice chmn. National Council for the Prevention of War, 1932; supported Communist Charlotte Ann Whitney, who was convicted under the California State Syndicalism Law; a sponsor, with Carrie Chapman Catt, of lecture tour of Countess Karolyi, wife of the communistic President of Hungary who turned Hungary over to the Bela Kun Communist regime of terror in 1919; director Survey Associates; on National Save Our Schools Committee (organized to take patriotic propaganda out of school books); on Debs Memorial Radio Station Committee; director of National Assn. for the Advancement of Colored People, supported by communistic Garland Fund; on national committee of the World Court Committee; on advisory council of the National and director of the Chicago branch of the American Society for Cultural Relations with Russia (A.S.C.R.R.), a Communist subsidiary (U. S. Report 2290); mem. Committee on Militarism in Education Ill., supported by Garland Fund; mem. People's Legislative Service; Foreign Policy Assn.; vice pres. of the socialistic American Assn. for Old Age Security; vice pres. Berger National Foundation, 1931 (Berger, Socialist Congressman from Wis. at one time refused seat in Congress, advocated violent revolution); speaker at the communist Student Congress Against War (at U. of Chgo., Dec. 28, 1932) with Scott Nearing, Communist leader. (The Congress was endorsed by U. of Chgo. Prof. Robert Morss Lovett, who lives at Hull House and is a leader of the communist National Student League at the U. of Chgo.); 1933 hon. pres. Fellowship of Faiths com. of 300; opposed Baker Bills (to penalize seditious teachings in colleges) at Legislative Hearing, Chgo., May 29, 1933; nat. com. Nat. Religion and Labor Foundation, 1933, the ultra radical organization which held its national conference at Hull House July 21, 1933; gave interview in behalf of the Communists' pet agitation, the "Scottsboro Boys," published in Chgo. Daily News, Feb. 25, 1933; communist Chicago Scottsboro Committee of Action meeting held at Hull House, Sept. 6, 1933, was addressed by the "communist convert" Ruby Bates now lecturing for the I.L.D.; listed as a subversive by Ill. American Legion report 1933, also by Congressional Exposure of Radicals (see); see also article "Jane Addams" in this book and the Garland Fund aided Women's Intl. Lg. for Peace and Freedom, of which she is intl. pres.; the communist Chicago Workers Theatre Feb. 1934 play was presented at Hull House.

AINSLIE, REV. PETER: vice chmn. N. C. for P. W.; Peace Patriots; Fed. Coun. of Chs.; nat. coun. Berger Nat. Found.; ed. bd. Encyc. Britannica; "stood four-square against the war," said he would rather be shot by his Govt. than by the enemy ("World Tomorrow," Aug. 1933); Baltimore, Md.

ALBERTSON, WILLIAM: Communist Party functionary; organizer Food Wkrs. Indust. Un.

ALDRICH, DONALD B.: N. Y. C. Episc. minister; nat. com. Nat. R. & L. Found.

ALEXANDER, GROSS W.: com. Chr. Soc. Act. M.; Fresno, Cal.

ALEXANDER, JAMES W.: nat. coun. L. I. D. for New Jersey.

ALLARD, GERRY: formerly cent. exec. com. Communist Party; next a Trotskyite (Communist Lg.); grad. N. Y. C. Workers' Sch.; Prog. Miners Un. and until recently ed. of its official organ.; ed. Militant Left Wing Miners organ 1934.

ALLEN, DEVERE: Socialist; Am. com. of W.C.A.W.; vice chmn. W. R. Lg. 1930-1; nat. advis. com. Sacco-V. Nat. Lg.; Lg. for Mut. Aid; bd. dir. L. I. D.; vice chmn. L. I. P. A.; Fell. Recon.; ed. "World Tomorrow"; N. Y. bd. of Lg. for Org. Progress 1931; assoc. ed. "The Nation"; nat. com. Lg. Against Fascism, 1933; spkr. for communist U. S. Cong. Ag. War; nat. coun. Berger Nat. Found.

ALLEN, JAMES S.: Communist; writer for Intl. Pamphlets; ed. "Southern Worker" 1933; Lg. Strugg. Negro Rts.

ALLEN, MINNIE E.: nat. coun. L.I.D. for Iowa.

ALLEN, ROBERT S.: dir. L.I.P.A.

ALLINSON, BRENT DOW: co-worker with Stanley High in Youth Movement; was field sec. radical Nat. Student Forum; mem. com. W.R.Lg.; co-worker with Norman Thomas, Jane Addams and Louis Lochner in First Am. Conf. for Democ. (see Addams); served two years in Leavenworth Pen. for evading draft; home Ravinia, Ill.; A.S.C.R.R. Com. 1934.

ALSBERG, HENRY G.: writer; Intl. Com. for Pol. Pris.; Am. delg. to W.C. A.W. at Amsterdam.

AMERINGER, OSCAR: militant Socialist Party organizer; was Socialist cand., Wis.; ed. Am. Guardian, Okla. City; indicted under U. S. Sedition Law during war; Com. on Coal & Giant P.; coun. People's Lobby; nat. coun. Berger Nat. Found.

AMIDON, BEULAH: daughter of Chas. F.; was mem. bd. dir. nat. A.C.L.U.

AMIDON, CHAS. F.: nat. com. A.C. L.U.; former N. D. Federal judge; heads Nat. Com. on Labor Injunctions; People's Legis. Serv.; home now Cal.

AMIS, B. D.: mem. cent. com. Communist Party, dist. org. Cleveland Dist. 6 (in 1933); writer for Intl. Pamphlets; Lg. Strugg. Negro Rts.

AMLIE, THOS. R.: radical Wis. Congressman; chmn. Conf. Prog. Pol. Act. 1933; vice pres. Pub. O. Lg. of Am.; nat. com. F.S.U.

AMRON, PHIL.: Communist Party functionary.

AMTER, ISRAEL: exec. com. Communist Intl. 1923-4; now mem. cent. com. Communist Party; pamphlets published in Russia; nat. sec. communist Unemployed Coun.; six months in jail 1930; Lg. Strugg. Negro Rts.; home N. Y.

ANDERSON, DOUGLAS: exec. com. Chr. Soc. Act. M.; Illiopolis, Ill.; Socialist P.

ANDERSON, EDGAR: nat. com. Proletarian Party (Communist).

ANDERSON, GEO. WESTON: Federal Judge, Boston; nat. com. A.C.L.U. 1932; trustee World Peace Found.; Am. Assn. Lab. Legis.; Lusk Report tells of his activity in preparing A.C.L.U. pamphlet for the I.W.W.

ANDERSON, SHERWOOD: writer; Communist Lg. P. G. for F. & F. 1932; Am. com. W.C.A.W. and Amsterdam delg.; Am. Com. for S.A.W.; A.C.L.U.; John Reed Club; contrib. "New Masses" (author of "Let's Have More Criminal Syndicalism" in Feb. 1932 issue) and "Student Review" of communist N.S.Lg., which he supports; sponsor Chgo. Wkrs. Theatre 1933; N.C. to A.S.M.F.S.; Pris. Rel. Fund (I.L.D.); Nat. Com. Def. Pol. Pris.; Intl. Com. Pol. Pris. 1933.

ANGELL, NORMAN: see English Reds and Ind. Labour Party; British N.C. for P.W.

ANSTROM, GEORGE: Communist; writer for Intl. Pamphlets.

ARONBERG, PHILLIP: mem. cent. com. Communist Party.

ARVIN, NEWTON: Prof. Smith College; Socialist 1928; Communist Lg. P. G. for F. & F. 1932; supporter N. S. Lg.; Am.com. W.C.A.W.; contrib."New Masses"; Am. Com. for S.A.W.

ASCHER, HELEN: exec. bd. A.C.L.U. Chgo. Com.

ASCHER, ROBT. E.: ed. "New Frontier," organ of C.W.C. on Unemp. (Borders'); assoc. ed. L.I.D. "Revolt" and "Student Outlook"; Socialist.

ASH, ISAAC E.: Ohio U.; nat. com. L.I.D. for Ohio; educators' Com. for Thomas, 1928.

AUMAN, LESTER: Chr. Soc. Act. M.; Jamaica, N. Y.

AUMAN, ORRIN W.: Meth. minister; C.M.E. Ill.; Chr. Soc. Act. M. 1932; Meth. Fed. for Soc. Serv.

B

BABER, ZONIA: C.M.E. Ill.; nat. bd. and com. on Russian recog. of W.I.L.P.F.; A.A.A.I. Lg. Chgo. branch, 1928.

BABCOCK, FRED'K.: U. of Chgo.; A.C.L.U. Chgo. Com.

BACON, CATHERINE L.: nat. coun. L.I.D. for Ill.

BAILEY, FORREST: dir. nat. A.C.L. U.; sec. (A.C.L.U.) Com. on Academic Freedom; bd. dir. L.I.D.; nat. coun. Berger Nat. Found.; Sacco-V. Nat. Lg.; treas. Emer. Com. Strik. Rel. 1928; sec. M.W.D. Def. Com.; Recep. Com. Soviet Flyers; Freethinkers Ingersoll Com. 1933; deceased.

BAINTON, ROLAND H.: nat. com. Nat. R.&L. Found.

BAKER, NEWTON D.: Nat. Citiz. Com. on Rel. Lat. Am. 1927; a "Communist-Recommended Author"; vice pres. Fell. Faiths nat. com. of 300; vice pres. with Mrs. F. D. Roosevelt, Jane Addams, etc., of Nat. Cons. Lg.

BAKER, RUDOLPH: cent. com. Communist Party; N.Y.C. Wkrs. Sch.

BALCH, EMILY GREENE: former Wellesley Prof.; infamous People's Coun.; Civ. Lib. Bureau; W.I.L.P.F. (pres. U.S. section and mem. intl. exec. com. 1933); Fell. Recon.; Cong. Exp. Radicals; ed.

staff "The Nation"; Emer. Peace Fed.; Am. Neut. Conf. Com. (see Jane Addams); Ford Peace Party; Griffin Bill sponsor; nat. coun. Berger Nat. Found.

BALDWIN, A. G.: nat. com. Nat. R. & L. Found.

BALDWIN, ROGER: dir. nat. A.C.L. U.; Garland Fund. dir.; former I.W.W.; former assoc. Berkman anarchist gang; in anarchist Berkman's Lg. for Amn. of Pol. Pris.; war time anti-Govt. "peace" worker (see infamous People's Council for letter to Lochner); served Federal prison sentence 1918-19; Am. Lg. to Limit. Arm.; Labor Def. Coun. 1923; Russ. Reconst. Farms, 1925; bd. Pris. Rel. Fund (of I.L.D.); nat. com. Intl. Wkrs. Aid, 1927 (now W.I.R.); nat. com. W.I.R. 1928; delg. with Communist Gomez to World Cong. Against Imperialism (Communist), Brussels, 1927; wife is Madeleine Z. Doty, intl. sec. and ed. of organ ("Pax") of W.I.L.P.F.; Cong. Exp. of Radicals; Emer. Com. Strik. Rel. 1930; N.C. to A.S.M.F.S. 1932; com. U.S. Cong. Ag. War; Am. com. W.C.A.W. 1933; a "Communist-Recommended Author"; supporter of communist N.S.Lg.; speaker at Communist meetings; Peace Patriots; Recep. Com. Soviet Flyers; Am. Com. for S.A.W.; Freethinkers Ingersoll Com.; Nat. Mooney-Billings Com.; Nat. Mooney Coun. of Action, 1933; Nat. Scottsboro Com. of Action, 1933; Am. Neut. Conf. Com.; Intl. Com. Pol. Pris. 1933; nat. com. A.A.A.I. Lg. 1928; chmn. Lg. for Mutual Aid, 1920-25; indicted for participation in American work of Kuzbas Indust. Colony, Siberia, 1923 (Am. Labor Who's Who), indictment dismissed; Nat. Com. to Aid Vic. G. Fascism; nat. com. F.S.U. 1933.

BALLAM, JOHN J.: cent. com. Communist Party; Nat. Scottsboro Com. of Act.; I.L.D.; organizer Nat. Text. Wkrs. Un.

BAMBERGER, BERNARD J.: nat. com. Nat. R. & L. Found.

BARBUSSE, HENRI: French Communist; chmn. intl. com. W.C.A.W.; organized Ex-Serv. Men's Intl. (Communist) to "make war on war" by Red revolution (Am. section is Workers' Ex-Serv. Men's Lg.); Student Cong. Ag. War; Intl. Com. for S.A.W.; heads Anti-Imperialist Lg. of France (Am. section is A.A.A.I. Lg.); joined staff of "L'Humanité," French Communist daily, immediately after the war; delg. to U.S. Cong. Ag. War, Sept. 1933, N.Y.C.; hon. mem. Wkrs. Cult. Fed. of U.S.; endorser of Am. W.I.R.; French corres. "New Masses" 1933; Nat. Com. to Aid Vic. G. Fascism.

BARCLAY, WADE CRAWFORD: M.E. minister; now M.E. Ch. official, Chgo. hdqts.; also lecturer Garrett Bibl. Inst., Evanston, Ill.; exec. com. Chr. Soc. Act. M.

BARNES, HARRY ELMER: former Smith Coll. Prof.; now Scripps-Howard Pub. columnist; nat. com. and bd. of dir. A.C.L.U.; Nat. Com. Def. Pol. Pris. 1932; nat. com. W.C.A.W.; Peace Patriots; coun. People's Lobby; Nat. Mooney-Billings Com.; hon. vice pres. Freethinkers of America (Atheist); treas. Nat. Coun. on Freedom from Censorship; headed Garland Fund Com. on American Imperialism; instr. New Sch. Social Research, 1932; Griffin Bill sponsor; Freethinkers Ingersoll Com. 1933; Am. Com. for S.A.W.; Nat. Com. to Aid Vic. G. Fascism.

BARNES, ROSWELL P.: exec. bd. C.M.E.; Com. for Thomas, 1929; exec. com. World Peaceways, 1932.

BARNETT, JAMES: Communist; writer for Intl. Pamphlets.

BARNHART, W. R.: nat. com. Nat. R. & L. Found.

BARON, ROSE: Communist Party functionary; anarchist Berkman's Lg. for Amn. of Pol. Pris. 1917; sec. Sacco-V. Emer. Com. 1927.

BARR, REV. NORMAN B.: Presbyterian minister; founder and pastor Olivet Inst. Ch. and supt. Olivet Inst., Chgo.; was on nat. com. Labor Def. Coun. (now I.L.D.) 1923, formed for defense of Bridgman Communists; L.I.D.; C.M.E.; Chgo. Forum Coun.; advis. com. C.W.C. on Unemp. (Borders); Fell. Faiths; Peace Patriots; five Olivet trustees said to have resigned because of Barr's radical, unpatriotic utterances (Chgo. Tribune, Oct. 14, 1927); debater for Chgo. Atheist Forum, Dec. 3, 1933 and Feb. 18, 1934.

BASKIN, JOSEPH: Jewish Socialist; born Russia; gen. sec. Workmen's Circle (see); active revol. agitator while student; nat. coun. Berger Nat. Found.; N.Y.C.

BASS, NATHAN: Communist Party functionary.

BASSHE, EMJO: Communist; Communist Lg. P. G. for F. & F. 1932; sec. cultural dept. and dir. W.I.R.; in charge Young Pioneer Camps; contrib. ed. "New Masses"; John Reed Club; Intl. Union Revol. Writers; perm. contrib. Intl. Lit.; Revol. Writers' Fed.

BAYLY, MILTON D.: M.E. minister; sec. Chgo. Meth. Preachers Meeting which sent out resolutions signed by him (June 13, 1932) berating the American Vigilant Intelligence Federation for exposing the Red activities of M.E. ministers and protesting that such organizations "menace the constitutional rights of free speech" (the battle cry of all Reds).

BEALS, CARLETON: author of section of "Recovery Through Revolution" (see) 1933; speaker for A.A.A.I. Lg. at New Sch. for Social Research, N.Y.C., with Communists Robt. W. Dunn, Waldo Frank, and Manuel Gomez (Nov. 3, 1933); A.A.A.I. Lg. ("Govt. by Propaganda" by A. S. Henning); nat. com. F.S.U. 1933.

BEARCE, F. E.: Marine Wkrs. Transport Un. (I.W.W.); Unemp. Un. (I.W.W.); U. S. Cong. Ag. War.

BEARD, CHAS. A.: Coll. Prof.; supporter Rand Sch. 1933; prominent author.

BEARDSLEY, JOHN: chmn. So. Cal. A.C.L.U. Com.

BEARDSLEY, SAMUEL ELI: active Socialist; former mem. Socialist Party nat. com.; Socialist cand. periodically since 1912; instr. Rand Sch. 1915-18; Labor Def. Coun. 1923; Non-Intervention Citiz. Com. 1927; N.Y.C.

BEBEL, AUGUST: deceased German Socialist leader; author of books on Socialism; pupil of Marx.

BECHTOLD, EUGENE: Communist; mem. advis. com. and teacher Workers' School, Chgo.; arrested Bridgman raid, 1922; Chgo. Com. for S.A.W.

BECK, FRANK ORMAN: M.E. minister; C.M.E.; Fell. Faiths; Prof. Garrett Biblical Inst.; Fell. Recon. leader of Reconciliation Trips; Meth. Fed. for Soc. Serv.; Chgo. Forum Coun.

BECK, DR. G. F.: Dir. radical Labor Temple, N.Y.C. (of Presb. Ch.).

BECKER, MAURICE: Communist Lg. P. G. for F. & F. 1932.

BECKERMAN, ABRAHAM: Socialist; bus. agt. Amalg. Cloth. Wkrs. of Am.; Non-Intervention Citiz. Com. 1927; N.Y.

BEDACHT, MAX: Communist writer and agitator; nat. sec. I.W.O. (Communist); one of ten prin. U.S. Communist leaders; Wkrs. Sch. N.Y.C.

BEIDEL, LYDIA (ALIAS BENNETT): Communist agitator; advis. com. Workers' Sch., Chgo. 1932; former pub. sch. teacher; police record; F.S.U. delg. Russia; expelled from Communist Party, 1933; now conducting Marxian Sch. with Albert Goldman for Communist Lg. Struggle; Room 1916—205 W. Wacker Drive, Chicago.

BEIDENKAPP, FRED: see Biedenkapp.

BELL, REV. BERNARD IDDINGS: Pres. St. Stephens Coll. (Episc.); was on exec. com. Ch. Socialist Lg.; his views quoted in Lusk Report; see under Union Theol. Sem.; listed in Communist Daily Worker, Jan. 31, 1933, as signer of Fell. Recon. petition for Russian recog.

BENET, WM. ROSE: author; Nat. Com. Def. Pol. Pris.; Emer. Com. So. Pol. Pris.; N.Y.C.

BENJAMIN, HERBERT: cent. com. Communist Party; nat. org. Unemployed Councils (Communist); U.S. Cong. Ag. War.

BENNETT, JOHN C.: nat. com. Nat. R. & L. Found.

BENNETT, MARGARET B.: exec. bd. A.C.L.U. Chgo. Com.; atty.

BENSON, JEAN: membership sec. L.I.D.

BENTALL, DAVID J.: sec. dist. cent. com. Communist Party, Chgo. (dist. no. 8); official I.L.D. atty.

BERENBERG, DAVID PAUL: Socialist; mgr. Rand Sch. 1918-21; also teacher Rand Sch.; reinstatement in N.Y.C. pub. sch. system opposed by patriotic forces, 1923; Teachers' Union.

BERG, LOUIS: Communist; writer for Intl. Pamphlets.

BERGER, META: widow of Victor; nat. publicity chmn. W.I.L.P.F.; Berger Nat. Found.; regent U. of Wis.; Griffin Bill sponsor.

BERGER, VICTOR L.: deceased; Socialist Congressman from Wis.; indicted and convicted for violating Espionage Act, 1919; tho re-elected, was denied seat by Congress; mem. nat. exec. com. Socialist Party; exec. com. Socialist Intl.; agnostic; Fell. Recon.; praised by Zinoviev, the Russian Commissar; advocate of "direct action" or violent revolution; ed. Milwaukee Leader (Socialist); in the course of speech at Socialist Party Nat. Convention in 1908, Berger said: "I have heard it pleaded that the only salvation for the proletariat of America is direct action; that the ballot box is simply a humbug. Now I don't doubt that in the last analysis we must shoot and when it comes to shooting, Wisconsin will be there. We always make good"; on July 31, 1909, in the Milwaukee "Social Democratic Herald," Berger said: "No one will claim that I am given to the reciting of 'revolutionary' phrases. On the contrary, I am known to be a 'constructive' Socialist. However, . . . it is easy to predict that the safety and hope of this country will finally lie in one direction only—that of a violent and bloody revolution. Therefore, I say, each of the 500,000 Socialist voters and of the 2,000,000 workingmen who instinctively incline our way, should, besides doing much reading and still more thinking, also have a good rifle and the necessary rounds of ammunition in his home and be prepared to back up his ballot with his bullets if necessary." (Lusk Report).

BERKMAN, ALEXANDER: Am. Anarchist-Communist; deported to Russia with Emma Goldman; had served in prison for shooting and stabbing Frick, steel magnate, as a protest against capitalism ("Living My Life" by Emma G.).

BERMAN, MORRIS: Jewish Socialist; born Russia; Il Nuovo Mondo Nat. Com.; nat. coun. Berger Nat. Found.; bd. dir. "New Leader" (N.Y.C.); active strike agitator; arbitrator for Intl. Ladies Garm. Wkrs. Un.; Conf. Prog. Pol. Act. 1924.

BERNHEIM, ALFRED: exec. com. Jt. Com. on Unemp.; Conf. Prog. Pol. Act.; artists' and writers' Com. for Thomas, 1929; staff Labor Bureau, Inc. since 1920; N.Y.C.

BERNHEIM, SARAH: Il Nuovo Mondo Nat. Com.; educators' Com. for Thomas, 1929; Labor Bureau, Inc. staff.

BIDDLE, CLEMENT M.: vice chmn. N.C. for P.W.

BIDDLE, JOHN C.: nat. com. Nat. R. & L. Found.

BIDDLE, WM. C.: treas. Fell. Recon.

BIEDENKAPP (OR BEIDENKAPP), FRED: Communist leader; nat. sec. communist Shoe and Leather Wkrs. Indust. Un.; nat. com. I.L.D.; former nat. sec. Intl. Wkrs. Aid (now W.I.R.); alternate men. cent. exec. com. Communist Party, 1927; long police record cited in Report of U.S. Fish Com., Vol. 1, Part 3. For instance, the following on Page 115 (testimony of Mr. Charles G. Wood, Commissioner of Conciliation, U.S. Dept. of Labor, July 16, 1930): "Beidenkapp was one of the men indicted in Massachusetts. He is still under indictment. Governor Allen tried to have him extradited to Massachusetts, but Beidenkapp resisted it, and Governor Roosevelt protected him, denied the jurisdiction of Massachusetts; and Beidenkapp was kept in New York to cause all the trouble in the shoe industry."

BIELOWSKI, JOHN: A.A.A.I. Lg. Chgo. 1928; A.F. of L. Carpenter's Local 1367.

BIEMILLER, ANDREW J.: nat. bd. dir. L.I.D.; exec. sec. Phila. Chap. L.I.D.; Pa. Com. for Total Disarmament; U. of Pa.

BIEMILLER, HANNAH M.: asst. sec. L.I.D. for Pa.

BIGELOW, HERBERT S.: minister; nat. com. A.C.L.U.; Fed. Coun. Chs.; vice pres. A.A. for O.A.S.; lecturer Brookwood Lab. College 1932; Conf. Prog. Pol. Act.; nat. coun. Berger Nat. Found.

BIMBA, ANTHONY: cent. com. Communist Party; sued for blasphemy in Mass. and defended by Garland Fund, 4A., and A.C.L.U.

BINFORD, JESSIE F.: exec. bd. A.C. L.U. Chgo. Com.; lives at Hull House; dir. Juvenile Prot. Assn.; Chgo. Forum Coun.; petitioned Police Comm. Allman for permit for the Communist Hunger March on March 4, 1933 (with Curtis Reese and Thos. McKenna of A.C.L.U.); C.W.C. on Unemp.; Chgo. Com. for S.A.W.

BINGHAM, ALFRED: son of ex-Sen. Hiram of Conn.; ed. ultra-radical magazine "Common Sense"; exec. sec. Conf. Prog. Pol. Act. 1933; Eastern sec. L.I.P.A. 1933; nat. com. F.S.U.; Farmer-Labor Political Fed.; N.Y.C.

BINKLEY, W. G.: Communist Party functionary.

BITTLEMAN, ALEXANDER: cent. com. Communist Party; one of ten principal U. S. Communist leaders.

BLACKWELL, ALICE STONE: daughter of Lucy Stone; ed. of women's magazines; exec. com. Nat. Coun. Prot. For. Born Wkrs.; active in Am. Friends of Russian Freedom; Nat. Mooney-Billings Com.; Lg. of Women Voters (hon. pres. Mass. br.); M.W.D. Def. Com.; nat. com. I.L.D.; LaFollette elector, 1924; Griffin Bill sponsor; Mass. A.C.L.U. Com.; Russ. Reconst. Farms; Nat. Pop. Govt. Lg.; officer communistic Commonwealth Coll.; home Boston.

BLAKEMAN, E. W.: M.E. minister; now dir. Wesley Found. at U. of Mich.; Meth. Fed. for Soc. Serv.; Fell. Recon.; com. Chr. Soc. Act. M.; Ann Arbor, Mich.

BLAND, RICHARD C.: sec. St. Louis A.C.L.U. Com.

BLANSHARD, PAUL: bd. dir. and lecturer L.I.D.; active Socialist 15 yrs.; La Guardia backer; gen. org. and edu. dir. Amalg. Cloth. Wkrs. 1920-3; mem. Loc. 1200 Amalg. Cloth. Wkrs.; gen. org. Amalg. Textile Wkrs. 1919-20; mem. Anti-Enlistment Lg. 1915; was pastor Maverick Church, Boston, Mass.; sought slacker pledges from his congregation; graduate Union Theol. Sem.; has been arrested in strikes; joined with Harry Ward in cabled request from Shanghai for immediate funds to aid Communist Chinese group then in charge of Hankow govt.; cablegram stated there was little financial aid from Russia and urged the stopping of "every effort to use American gunboats, money and men to fasten foreign imperialism on China" (this cablegram quoted in ad. in "World Tomorrow" Aug. 1925, which asked contributions to Garland Fund to aid this cause, the appeal being signed by Kirby Page, Robert Morss Lovett, and Rose Schneidermann); described Fish Report as mostly hokum, saying we were in no danger of a Communist revolution here (Des Moines Trib. Jan. 20, 1931); coun. People's Lobby; Emer. Com. Strik. Rel. 1933; Fed. Unemp. Wkrs. Lgs. of N.Y.C.; contrib. "The Nation"; nat. com. Lg. Against Fascism, 1933; member Mayor La Guardia's cabinet Jan. 1934.

BLATCH, HARRIOT STANTON: writer, lecturer; Socialist; exec. com. Fabian Society, London, 1890; nat. com. A.A. A.I. Lg. 1928; exec. Wom. Tr. Un. Lg.; Peace Patriots; nat. coun. L.I.D. for N.Y.; Emer. Com. Strik. Rel.; vice chmn. Jt. Com. on Unemp.; Conf. Prog. Pol. Act.; People's Legis. Serv.; Nat. Citiz. Com. on Rel. Lat. Am. 1927; coun. People's Lobby; nat. com. Lg. Against Fascism, 1933; Freethinkers Ingersoll Com. 1933; home N.Y.C.

BLEWITT, WM.: nat. com. A.A.A.I. Lg. 1928.

BLIVEN, BRUCE: pres. and ed. "New Republic"; dir. and chmn. finance com. For. Pol. Assn.; Nat. Coun. on Freedom from Censorship of A.C.L.U.; N.Y.C.

BLOCK, JOHN S.: Socialist Party executive; radical labor lawyer; Am. Assn. Lab. Legis.; L.I.D.; People's Legis. Serv.; nat. coun. Berger Nat. Found.; N.Y.C.

BLOOMFIELD, SIDNEY: Communist Party functionary.

BLOOR, ELLA REEVE: called "Mother Bloor"; cent. com. Communist Party; Communist lecturer; org. for Communist Party and United Farmers' Lg.; her son, Karl Marx Reeve, on ed. staff of Communist Daily Worker since 1923; intl. and Am. com. W.C.A.W.; Sacco-V. Nat. Lg.; Nat. Mooney Coun. of Act. 1933; Nat. Farmers Com. for Act., Sioux City, Ia., 1933.

BOAS, FRANZ: Prof. Columbia U.; advis. coun. A.S.C.R.R.; nat. com. W.C. A.W.; praised by 1927 4A Report for his atheism; John Reed Club, N.Y.C.; Nat. Com. for Def. Pol. Pris. 1932; endors. World Peaceways 1932; nat. com. Lg. Against Fascism, 1933; Nat. Com. to Aid Vic. G. Fascism.

BODANZKY, ARTUR: N.Y.C. orchestra conductor; nat. com. communist W.I.R.; condr. Metro. Opera Co. since 1915 and of Society of Friends of Music since 1916; Austrian.

BOECKEL, MRS. FLORENCE: radical pacifist; asst. sec. N.C. for P.W.

BOHN, WILLIAM E.: nat. coun. L.I.D. for N.Y.; lecturer; edu. dir. Rand Sch. 1932.

BONDFIELD, MARGARET: English tr. un. official; see "English Reds," Labour Party, and Ind. Labour Party; org. British W.I.L.P.F.; 1917 Club, "combining pacifism with definitely revolutionary aims"; speaker with Jane Addams, Chgo. 1933.

BOOKSTABER, REV. PHILIP DAVID: chmn. Pa. A.C.L.U. Com.

BOOTS, RALPH S.: chmn. Pitts. A.C. L.U. Com.

BORAH, WM. E.: U.S. Senator from Idaho; radical; pro-Soviet; his letter said to be worth more than a passport in Russia; has asked A.C.L.U. to draw up Bills for him; the minutes of an A.C.L.U. executive committee meeting, October 3, 1921, record that Borah asked, thru Albert de Silver (A.C.L.U. and treas. of I.W.W. Defense Fund), that Bills repealing title 12 of the Espionage Act, under which postal authorities censored the mail, be drafted, also that amendments eliminating the words "tending to murder, arson and assassination" from a section of the obscenity statute be drafted. The minutes of the following meeting on Oct. 10th show that deSilver reported the two Bills had been prepared and forwarded to the Senator. The minutes of the April 17, 1922, meeting read: "The material for Senator Borah has been submitted to him and it is expected he will make his speech to the Senate in a comparatively few days." (Whitney's "Reds in America"); with Einstein and others protested execution of Communist agitators Mr. and Mrs. Ruegg in China, 1932 (see Ruegg); protested (1926) landing of U.S. marines in Nicaragua to protect American citizens and property from Communist-directed revolutionaries who were against religion and the property right (with Senators Dill, Wheeler, and Heflin); documents seized in Bridgman raid on Communists record that Pogany, Moscow's envoy, favored Communist backing of Borah for President; ardent advocate of Soviet recognition; speaker for For. Pol. Assn.; endorser Lane Pamphlet.

BORCHARD, EDWIN M.: nat. com. A.C.L.U.; nat. com. W.C.A.W.; Prof. Yale U. Law School; mem. Garland Fund Com. on Am. Imperialism; M.W.D. Def. Com.

BORCHARDT, SELMA M.: advis. ed. of The American Teacher; vice pres. Am. Fed. of Teachers; Wom. Tr. Un. Lg.; N.C. for P.W.; Nat. Save Our Schs. Com.; home Wash.

BORDERS, KARL: chmn. exec. bd. A.C. L.U. Chgo. Com.; exec. sec. Chgo. Chap.

and western dir. L.I.D.; chmn. exec. com. A.S.C.R.R. Chgo. branch; tour conductor for Open Road; chmn. C.W.C. on Unemp.; was chmn. Federation of Unemp. Wkrs. Lgs., (see); biog. data concerning him which appeared in the announcement Bulletin of The Chicago Teke (Vol. 14, No. 11—October 1932), before which org. Borders spoke on Oct. 11, 1932, contained the following: "Graduate of Union Theological Seminary. For five years Director of a Social settlement in Chicago's Russian District. Then to Russia with the Quaker's Relief Organization in 1922." (For which Communist Robt. W. Dunn was then publicity director in Russia.) "Field Director of this group for 6 months. He won such high recognition that the Soviet authorities made him *Educational Director of North Caucasus District for two years. Since then he has returned every summer to act as tourist guide for the Russian Government.* More recently Assistant Head Resident of Chicago Commons Settlements. Now, lecturer in Social Service Administration School, University of Chicago" (emphasis supplied); cand. for Cook Co. Commissioner (Ill.), Farmer-Labor ticket 1932; sponsor Berger Nat. Found. dinner 1931; a "Communist-Recommended Author"; Chgo. Com. for S.A.W.; sec.-treas. Chgo. Emer. Com. Strik. Rel.; Fell. Faiths spkr. Chgo. 1933; Roosevelt appointee 1934 as research investigator for Nat. Relief Admn.

BORICH, FRANK: Communist Party functionary; nat. sec. communist Nat. Miners' Un.; intl. and Am. com. W.C.A.W. 1932; Feb. 22, 1932, Daily Worker announced he had been arrested the past year and the A.C.L.U. was fighting against his deportation; Nat. Mooney Coun. of Act. 1933; nat. com. F.S.U. 1933; released against recommendation of local Dept. of Labor Inspectors by Secy. Frances Perkins 1934.

BOUCK, WILLIAM MORLEY: Communist sympathizer; expelled by nat. body of Wash. Grange for radicalism, 1920; org. Western Prog. Farmers; delg. Farmer-Labor P. conv. May 17, 1924; nom. for Vice Pres. at this conv.; withdrew in favor La Follette; People's Legis. Serv.; officer Commonwealth College; nat. com. I.L.D. 1928.

BOUDIN, LOUIS B.: Socialist; lawyer; born in Russia; nat. coun. L.I.D. for N.Y.; delg. United Hebrew Trades; author "The Theoretical System of Karl Marx," etc.; Recep. Com. Soviet Flyers.

BOURKE-WHITE, MARGARET: a "Communist-Recommended Author"; pub. book of photos of Russia; signer pet. for Russ. recog.

BOWEN, W. C.: chmn. exec. com. Fell. Recon.

BOWIE, REV. W. RUSSELL: minister, Grace Episc. Ch. N.Y. since 1923; Nat. Citiz. Com. on Rel. Lat. Am. 1927; nat. coun. C.M.E.; Ch. Emer. Com. Strik. Rel.; Fed. Coun. Chs.; mem. bd. dir. Union Theol. Sem. and lecturer; mem. bd. dir. Vassar Coll. Attacked Am. Legion lobby at Wash. as a "sinister and deadly cancer upon the body of American life" (Chgo. Tribune March 19, 1934).

BOWMAN, LEROY E.: nat. bd. dir. L.I.D.; chmn. com. on Recon. Trips, N.Y.; dir. extension work Child Study Assn.; Prof. Columbia U.; sec. educators' Com. for Thomas 1928; Il Nuovo Mondo Nat. Com.; Non-Intervention Citiz. Com. 1927; com. U.S. Cong. Ag. War; coun. People's Lobby; Conf. Prog. Pol. Act. 1933-4.

BOYD, JAMES M.: asst. treas. Fell. Recon.

BOYNTON, ALICE: chmn. Ill. br. W.I. L.P.F.; Chgo. Emer. Com. Strik. Relief; picketer at strike at 711 W. Lake St. Chgo. with Lola M. Lloyd, etc. (Daily News, July 18, 1933); Chgo. Com. for S.A.W.; Illinois C.M.E.; A.S.C.R.R. Com. 1934.

BOYNTON, MELBOURNE P.: minister Woodlawn Bapt. Ch., Chgo.; A.C.L.U. Chgo. Com.

BOYNTON, PERCY H.: U. of Chgo. Prof.; A.C.L.U. Chgo. Com.; Chgo. Com. for S.A.W. 1933.

BOZURICH, P.: Communist Party functionary.

BRAGG, RAYMOND B.: minister; sec. Western Unitarian Conf.; exec. bd. A.C. L.U. Chgo. Com.; Reception Banquet Com. for Ford, Negro Communist Vice Pres. cand., Oct. 1932 (Mrs. Bragg also a member); active in investigating Melrose Park riots; speaker for communist F.S.U. Feb. 19, 1933; one of editors of Humanist magazine of the "new religion without God"; leader of Soviet tour 1933; contrib. ed. A. Lincoln Center "Unity."

BRAILSFORD, HENRY N.: prominent British Socialist; British branch A.S.C.R.R.; Ind. Labour Party.

BRANDEIS, MRS. LOUIS D.: vice chmn. N.C. for P.W.; was vice chmn. under Jane Addams of Women's Peace Party; consistent financial supporter with husband, radical U.S. Supreme Ct. Justice Brandeis, of communistic Commonwealth Coll.; one daughter, Susan, on Emer. Com. Strik. Rel. 1933, and Russ. Reconst. Farms, 1925; another daughter, "Miss" Elizabeth Brandeis, is Mrs. Paul A. Raushenbush (spkr. W.I. L.P.F.) (Milw. Leader, 11/3/33).

BRANHAM, LUCY: sec. A.S.C.R.R.; was field sec. for Russian Reconstruction Farms; signer of Sacco-V. petition; campaigned for Am. Friends for Russian Relief 1922; mem. Am. Fed. of Teachers; Communist sympathizer.

BRANNON, ELEANOR D.: Socialist; asst. sec. N.C. for P.W. (exec. bd. 1932); Non-Intervention Citiz. Com. 1927; Com. for Thomas 1929; N.Y. sec. W.I.L.P.F. 1927.

BRECKENRIDGE, SOPHONISBA P.: U. of Chgo. Prof.; A.C.L.U. Chgo. Com.; W.I.L.P.F.; C.M.E.; associate of Jane Addams and Lochner (see Addams); C.W.C. on Unemp. 1933; Russ. Reconst. Farms 1925; M.W.D. Def. Com.; Congressional Exposure Radicals; Chgo. Com. for S.A.W.; Roosevelt admn. delg. to Montevideo Conf. 11/33; A.S.C.R.R. Com. 1934.

BRESHKOVSKY, CATHERINE: Russian revolutionary propagandist; called "The Little Grandmother of the Russian Revolution."

BRIGGS, CYRIL: Communist Party functionary; colored; Lg. Strugg. Negro Rts.; editor "Liberator" (Harlem).

BRISSENDEN, PAUL F.: nat. coun. L.I.D. for N.Y.; Prof. Columbia U.; exec. com. Sacco-V. Nat. Lg. 1928; exec. com. L.I.P.A. 1931; Com. for Thomas 1929; Il Nuovo Mondo Nat. Com.; Recep. Com. Soviet Flyers; Conf. Prog. Pol. Act. 1934.

BROCKWAY, A. FENNER: English Left Wing Socialist; jailed during War; nat. chmn. Independent Labour Party of Great Britain (see); toured America, 1932, under L.I.D. auspices; intl. chmn. W.R. Intl. Council (see); delg. to communist W.C.A.W., Amsterdam, 1932, and to All-India Nat. Congress (Communist influenced); intl. com. of Nat. Com. to Aid Vic. G. Fascism; delg. communist Lg. Against Imperialism, Brussels, 1927.

BRODSKY, CARL: Communist Party functionary; Recep. Com. Soviet Flyers.

BRODSKY, JOSEPH R.: Communist Party lawyer; I.W.O.; Friends Soviet Russia; in London Arcos raid, found listed as U.S. representative to receive gold from Communist International; exec. com. Nat. Coun. Prot. For. Born Wkrs.; Recep. Com. Soviet Flyers; Am. delg. W.C.A.W. (Amsterdam); Am. Com. for S.A.W.; Lg. Strugg. Negro Rts.; N.Y.C.

BROOKHART, SMITH WILDMAN: former U.S. Senator from Iowa; radical Repub.; Roosevelt appointee as For. Trade Admin.; favored recog. Soviet Russia; mem. Farmers' Union; People's Legis. Serv.; speaker Fell. Faiths Chgo. 1933; debated with Cong. Hamilton Fish, 1932, taking the Red side; spkr. Pub. O. Lg. of Am. 1933; went to Russia with Burton K. Wheeler, 1923; listed in radicals' "Labor Who's Who" as having made investigation cooperative movement in 15 countries; attended cooperative congresses, Edinburgh and Chgo.

BROPHY, JOHN A.: Communists' cand. for pres. of United Mine Workers in 1927 against John L. Lewis; Pa. com. of Conf. Prog. Pol. Act.; first Am. Tr. Un. Delg. to Russia; vice pres. Pub. O. Lg. of Am.; nat. com. C.M.E.; nat. com. A.A.A.I. Lg. 1928; endorser "Professional Patriots" and Lane Pamphlet.

BROUN, HEYWOOD: N.Y. World-Telegram newspaper man; resigned from Socialist Party recently, saying, it was reported, that it was not radical enough for him; Rand School; wife, Ruth Hale of Lucy Stone Lg., went to Boston to help stage last-minute Sacco-V. protest meeting (N.Y. Post, Aug. 10, 1927); ousted as columnist for N.Y. World because of friction over his abuse of the authorities in the Sacco-V. matter; at once engaged by radical "Nation"; principal speaker at Level Club, N.Y.C., "Blacklist" party of speakers barred by D.A.R. as subversives, May 9, 1928. James Weldon Johnson, colored radical, was master of ceremonies and mock trial for revocation of D.A.R. charter was held, Norman Thomas being the Judge and Arthur Garfield Hays, one of the attorneys; nat. com. W.I.R., 1929; nat. com. W.R. Lg. 1930-31; L.I.D. (cand. bd. dir., April 1931); Recep. Com. Soviet Flyers; Fed. Unemp. Wkrs. Lgs. N.Y. 1933; contrib. "New Masses," 1933; Nat. Scottsboro Com. of Action, 1933; Emer. Com. Strike. Rel. 1933; Il Nuovo Mondo Nat. Com.; supporter Rand Sch. 1933; nat. coun. Berger Nat. Found.; Nat. Com. to Aid Vic. G. Fascism; pres. and org. Am. Newspaper Guild, 1933; Conf. Prog. Pol. Act. 1933-4; Roosevelt appointee, Theatrical Code authority, 1933.

BROWDER, EARL R.: sec. Communist Party U.S.A.; delg. Intl. Red Unions; sentenced to two years Leavenworth Pen. 1917; leader and speaker Student Cong. Ag. War at U. of Chgo., Dec. 27-29, 1932; one of ten prin. U.S. Communist leaders; nat. exec. bd. T.U.U.L.; Lg. Strugg. Negro Rts.; nat. com. F.S.U.; former sec. Pan Pacific Tr. Un. Secretariat.

BROWDER, WM. C.: sec. of Communist I.L.D.; com. of Communist Party, Dist. 8; "New Masses" staff, 1933.

BROWN, ROBT. (BOB): org. communist Steel and Metal Wkrs. Indust. Un.; Chgo.

BROWN, "BISHOP" WM. MONTGOMERY: unfrocked by Episcopal Church for heresy, 1924; Communist; author of anti-religious atheist Communist books, particularly for children (see Young Pioneers); nat. sec. W.I.R.; speaker Fell. Faiths, Chgo. 1933; in a letter sent broadcast 1933, he said: "In these days of my heresy, I am trying to make more members for the Communist Party than any of its propagandists, and two facts are encouraging me to hope for success: (1) there is the encouraging fact that I have long been receiving letters giving me credit for making revolutionists of their writers, and (2) there is the encouraging fact that the demand for my heretical literature is greater than that for the orthodox . . . ."; lecturer for 4A, 1926-7 (1927 4A Report); edtl. bd. "New Pioneer"; A.A.A.I. Lg. nat. com.; N.C. to A.S.M.F.S.; nat. com. F.S.U. 1933; Episc. Ch. considering his application for reinstatement to Hse. of Bishops (Chgo. Daily News, 3-3-34).

BRUBAKER, HOWARD: Socialist; writer; Communist sympathizer; A.C.L.U.; L.I.D.; contrib. ed. "Masses," "Liberator," 1913-24.

BRUERE, ROBT. W.: Com. on Coal and Giant Power; lecturer at Rand School, 1908-9; assoc. ed. Survey (1933); brother of Henry Bruere, a Roosevelt advisor; listed in Lusk Report as mem. of I.W.W. defense com. and aid in preparing I.W.W. pamphlet; L.I.D.

BRYAN, JULIAN: lecturer on Russia; nat. com. communist F.S.U. 1933; tour conductor to Russia for Open Road, 1933, Intourist 1934; one of Hindus party 1930.

BRYANT, LOUISE: Lusk report cites her cablegram with Lincoln Steffens, as part of Anarchist group, to Lenin and Trotsky 1918; she married John Reed, the "first American Communist," then W. C. Bullitt (Roosevelt appointee as Amb. to Soviet Russia, 1933).

BUDENZ, LOUIS F.: left wing Socialist; professional labor agitator; lecturer; Recep. Com. Soviet Flyers; Non-Intervention Citiz. Com. 1927; nat. com. and publicity dir. A.C.L.U. 1920; sec. N.J. Conf. for Prog. Pol. Act. 1924; nat. com. A.A.A.I. Lg. 1928; Il Nuovo Mondo Nat. Com.; Brookwood Labor College 1932; Nat. Coun. Prot. For. Born Wkrs.; ed. "Labor Age," organ of Conf. Prog. Lab. Act.; Conf. Prog. Lab. Act. strike leader.

BUDISH, JACOB M.: Socialist; born in Russia; Bryn Mawr Coll. summer school for wkrs. in industry; Non-Intervention Citiz. Com. 1927; co-author of book with George Soule; Workmen's Circle; cent. com. Farmer-Lab. Party; Cloth Hat, Cap and Millinery Workers Union; City Coll., N.Y.C.; expenses to Pa. and West Va. coal fields paid by Garland Fund ($321.29) 1926.

BUDISH, JOSEPH: student, City College of N.Y.; contrib. ed. "Student Review" of N.S. Lg. 1933.

BULLITT, WM. C.: Philadelphia radical; mem. Ford Peace Party; married Louise Bryant Reed, widow of John Reed (outstanding Am. Communist), 1923; special mission to Russia 1919; chief advisor of U. S. State dept. under Pres. Roosevelt, 1933; said to have resigned from State dept. under Pres. Wilson's administration because of refusal to recognize Russia; see under Anarchist-Communism; first U.S. Amb. to Bolshevik Russia, 1933 (see "Roosevelt Appointees"); Jewish press exults over his mother being Jewish.

BURCK, JACOB: Communist; artist; staff cartoonist Daily Wkr.; "New Masses" staff, 1933.

BURD, PHIL: Communist Party functionary.

BURGESS, ERNEST W.: U. of Chgo. Prof.; signer petition Russ. recog.; 1933 contrib. to Commonwealth Coll.; sister Roberta, pro-Soviet lecturer; was mem. Hindus Party in Russia; lecturer; Roosevelt AAA advisor; author of "Function of Socialization in Social Evolution"; spkr. A.S.C.R.R. Chgo. 1933; F.S.U. spkr. Chgo. Feb. 18, 1934.

BURKE, FIELDING: Communist Lg. P. G. for F. & F. 1932.

BURNSHAW, STANLEY: Communist poet and author; "New Masses" staff, 1933.

BURT, ROY E.: Socialist; M. E. minister; cand. Governor Ill., Socialist ticket, 1932; Young People's Dept., Board Education, Methodist Church; sponsor Griffin Bill; Chgo. Emer. Com. Strik. Rel.; Chr. Soc. Act. M.; active in Danville, Gastonia, Marion, N.C., strikes, "free speech" fights, etc.; arrested for picketing Tribune plant, Chgo., 1932; mem. Ill. exec. com. of Socialist Party, 1933; nat. com. W.R. Lg.

BURTON, WM.: A.S.C.R.R. Chgo. exec. com.

BYRON, CURTISS A. L.: nat. sec. Ch.

Socialist Lg.; contrib. radical Am. Labor Year Book.

C

CABOT, RICHARD C.: nat. com. A.C.L.U.

CACHIN, MARCEL: sec. French Communist Party; intl. com. W.C.A.W.

CADMAN, S. PARKES: nat. com. Nat. R. & L. Found., 1933; radio spkr. and former pres. Fed. Coun. Chs.; Non-Intervention Citiz. Com. 1927.

CAHAN, ABRAHAM: ed. Jewish Daily Forward; Socialist; Russian Jew; participated in Russian revolutionary movement; nat. com. Lg. against Fascism; nat. coun. Berger Nat. Found.; calls Pres. Roosevelt a socialist (by his actions).

CALDWELL, ERSKINE: Communist writer; Communist Lg. P. G. for F. & F. 1932; "New Masses" staff, 1933.

CALHOUN, ARTHUR WALLACE: nat. com. A.A.A.I. Lg. 1928; instr. communist Wkrs. Sch. 1928; Am. Fed. of Teachers; was instr. Brookwood Labor Coll. and Rand School; lecturer Wom. Tr. Un. Lg.; exposed in Lusk Report; Nat. Coun. Prot. For. Born Wkrs.

CALHOUN, ROBT. L.: nat. com. Nat. R. & L. Found.

CALLAHAN, PATRICK H.: exec. com. Nat. R. & L. Found. 1933; Cath. Assn. for Intl. Peace; developed Ryan-Callahan labor plan; Catholic Indust. Conf.; Catholic Press Assn., Louisville, Ky.; vice chmn. Fell. Faiths com. 300, speaker at its Parliament, Chgo. 1933; World Peaceways.

CALVERTON, V. F.: ed. Modern Monthly; Communist; book com. A.S.C. R.R.; writer and lecturer on sex and Marxism; endorsed by Harry Elmer Barnes for lectures in Labor Temple lecture series on sex topics, 1929; financial contrib. to communistic Commonwealth Coll.; Recon. Trip sex lecturer; author of "For Revolution" (John Day Co. Pamphlet No. 15); co-author of "Recovery Through Revolution" (see); mem. Am. Com. for Help to the Imprisoned and Deported Bolsheviks; contrib. Trotskyite "Militant," 12/31/32.

CAMERON, DONALD: Communist writer for Intl. Pamphlets.

CAMPBELL, EDMUND D.: Wash., D.C., counsel nat. A.C.L.U.

CAMPBELL, E. FAY: nat. com. Nat. R. & L. Found.

CANNON, JAMES P.: nat. sec. Communist League of America; exec. com. Communist Intl. 1922; Nat. Mooney Coun. of Action, 1933; former sec. I.L.D.

CANNON, JOS. D.: nat. com. A.C.L.U. 1922; infamous People's Coun.; exec. Socialist Party; steel and mine strike leader; arrested in Philadelphia at a street meeting; Congressional Exposure Radicals; N.Y.C.

CANTER, HARRY: Boston Communist Party functionary; frequent Communist cand.; convicted 1929 criminal libel charging Gov. Fuller guilty of murder Sacco and Vanz.; served 1 yr. hard labor Deer Island Pen; Feb. 1934, org. Taxi Wkrs. Un., N.Y.C.

CANTWELL, ROBERT: Communist Lg. P. G. for F. & F. 1932.

CARLSON, ANTON J.: Prof. U. of Chgo.; A.C.L.U. Chgo. Com.; Non Partz. Com. Lillian Herstein; leader Am. Lg. Ag. War and Fascism rally 3-1-34.

CARLSON, A. OLIVER: former Prof. U. of Chgo.; a founder and nat. sec. Young Communist Lg.; delg. to Communist 3rd. Intl.; teacher Commonwealth College, 1933; alias Connelly, Edwards.

CARMON, STELLA: sec. Office Wkrs. Un. (Communist).

CARMON, WALTER: Communist; Intl. Union Revol. Writers; Revol. Writers Fed.; editor of annual "Red Cartoons," 1928; perm. contrib. Intl. Lit.; mg. ed. "New Masses," 1931; assoc. ed. "Anvil," communist poetry magazine; John Reed Club.

CASE, ADELAIDE T.: vice chmn. Fell. Recon.; Tchrs. Coll. Columbia U.; on com. for Recon. Trips; Com. for Thomas 1929; W.R. Lg.

CASE, HAROLD C.: minister M.E. ch., Glencoe, Ill.; Chr. Soc. Act. M.; invited Communist to address group of his church members; Communist-Socialist sympathizer.

CAVERT, INEZ: C.M.E. exec. bd.

CAVERT, SAMUEL McCREA: grad. and former teacher Union Theol. Sem.; gen. sec. Fed. Coun. Chs.; ed. Fed. Coun. (official) Bulletin; C.M.E.; cooperates with A.C.L.U.; endorser Lane Pamphlet; Non-Intervention Citiz. Com. 1927; mem. "conference convened by Federal Council of Churches" which wrote Fed. Coun. Sex Pamphlet (see); wife, Twila Lytton Cavert, on Recon. Trips com. for Sarah Lawrence Coll.

CHAFEE, ZECHARIAH, JR.: Prof. Harvard U.; Fell. Recon. Pet. Russ. Recog.; Nat. Pop. Govt. Lg. (charges against Dept. Justice).

CHAFFEE, REV. EDMUND B.: head of Labor Institute (N.Y. Presbytery), a very radical institution; Emer. Com. Strik. Rel. 1927-33; Com. for Total Disarmament

Now; Fell. Recon. Trips; Sacco-V. Nat. Lg.; exec. com. W.R. Lg.; listed in Am. Lab. Yr. Bk. as debater at communist New Workers' School, N.Y.C., 1931-32; Nat. R. & L. Found. 1933; vice chmn. Fell. Recon. 1932; edtl. contrib. A. Lincoln Center "Unity."

CHALMERS, ALLAN K.: minister of Broadway Tabernacle, N.Y. City; Nat. R. & L. Found. exec. com.; nat. com. W.R. Lg.; preached sermon on Scottsboro Case (N.Y. Times, May 1, 1933).

CHALMERS, W. ELLISON: Prof. U. of Wis.; sec. Wis. U. A.C.L.U. Com.; former instr. Ec., U. of Pitts.; was sec. Pitts. A.C.L.U. Com. 1929; arrested Kenosha, Wis. at Communist meeting, Oct. 1930, with Frank Palmer, Lydia Beidel, and Nat Ross; fined $10.00 (Milw. Journal, Nov. 1, 1930, and Kenosha News, Dec. 5, 1930).

CHAMBERLAIN, JOS. P.: Prof. Columbia U.; Lg. for Org. Progress; vice pres. Survey Associates; For. Pol. Assn. Chmn.

CHAMBERLAIN, WM. H.: Russian corres. for Christian Science Monitor; with Walter Duranty and Louis Fischer honored by Soviet Govt. in recog. of his services as corres. there (Chgo. Trib. 10/1/32); "Communist-Recommended Author"; returned in Dec. 1932, after 10 yrs. in Russia; author of "Soviet Russia," "The Soviet Planned Economic Order," etc.

CHAMBERS, WHITTAKER: Communist; writer for Intl. Pamphlets; "Labor Defender"; Intl. Union Revol. Writers; perm. contrib. Intl. Lit.; "New Masses"; N.Y. Suit Case Theatre; Revol. Writers Fed.

CHAPLIN, RALPH HOSEA: I.W.W. poet; bd. dir. Chas. H. Kerr Publ. Co. 1908-13; Leavenworth Pen. 1918-23 (for sedition); author "Bars and Shadows," pub. by Mrs. Scott Nearing; dir. I.W.W. Gen. Def. Com. 1923-4; speaker at Communist Mooney meeting May 1, 1933, Chgo.; sponsor Berger Nat. Found. dinner 1931.

CHAPPELL, WINIFRED L.: Communist Lg. P. G. for F. & F. 1932; Prisoners' Relief Fund of communist I.L.D.; co-ed. with Harry F. Ward of Bulletin of Meth. Fed. for Soc. Serv.; Am. com. W.C.A.W.; petitioner for Communist Hunger Marchers, Wash. 1932; com. Recon. Trips of Fell. Recon.; mem. coun. Jt. Com. on Unemployment (representing Social Service Commission of Meth. Ch., of which she is sec.); L.I.D.; Com. on Church and Social Service of Fed. Coun. Chs.; Am. Com. for S.A.W.; Ch. Emer. Com. for Strik. Rel.; spkr. with Communists Earl Browder, James W. Ford, at Labor Temple Auditorium, 14th & 2nd Ave., N.Y.C., Sept. 18, 1933, to "protest against the Japanese conquest of N. China, and its threat against the Soviet Union" (Daily Worker, Sept. 16, 1933).

CHASE, STUART: treas. L.I.D.; advis. coun. A.S.C.R.R.; Garland Fund accountant; auditor Labor Defense Council; former associate of Berkman anarchist gang; was treas. Russian Reconst. Farms; on staff Rand School; Recep. Com. Soviet Flyers; Emer. Com. Strik. Rel. 1927-33; speaker for communistic Labor Institute Forum; Sacco-V. Nat. Lg.; coun. People's Lobby; exec. com. Nat. Coun. Prot. For. Born Wkrs. (Communist); author with Communist Robt. W. Dunn, Rexford Guy Tugwell, Carleton Washburne, etc., of the communistic propaganda book "Soviet Russia in the Second Decade" of First Am. Tr. Un. Delg. to Russia; articles in "New Republic," "Labor Age," "The Nation," and "World Tomorrow"; Com. on Coal and Giant P.; "Communist-Recommended Author"; vice pres. Berger Nat. Found.; Conf. Prog. Pol. Act. 1934.

CHEYNEY, RALPH: wife Lucia Trent; both poetry eds. A. Lincoln Center "Unity"; John Reed Club; co-editor with Communist Jack Conroy of Moberly, Mo., of "Rebel" poetry, "Unrest"; Nat. Com. to Aid Vic. G. Fascism 1933; nat. advis. com. Sacco-V. Nat. Lg.; sec. artists' and writers' com. for Tom Mooney, 1933; contrib. to "New Humanist," magazine of Humanism.

CHIANG KAI-SHEK: see Mme. Sun Yat Sen, also "Hands Off" Committees.

CHRISTMAN, ELIZ.: sec.-treas. Nat. Wom. Tr. Un. Lg.; attended Brookwood Labor Coll. 1924; Lg. Women Voters; home Chgo.; nat. com. Nat. R. & L. Found. 1933; Roosevelt appointee to code authority, leather and glove industry, 1934.

CLAESSENS, AUGUST: instr. Rand School; Socialist lecturer; sec. Socialist Party 1927; Non-Intervention Citiz. Com. 1927; elected Socialist mem. N.Y. Legislature, but expelled for sedition; some of his statements which resulted in his expulsion follow: "As international Socialists, we are revolutionary, and let it be clearly understood that we are out to overthrow the entire capitalist system"; "Now, thank goodness, Socialists are not only working along political lines. If we thought for a minute it was merely a dream on our part, a great political controversy until we had a majority of men elected, and then by merely that majority, declare the resolution, if any of you smoke that pipe-dream, if that is the quality of opium you are puffing now, give it up, give it up." (from speech made at celebration of second anniversary of establishment of Communism in Russia); "There is little difference between the Socialist Party and the Communists. We want to get to the same place, but we are travelling different routes." (from address at Bronxville Labor Lyceum as reported in N.Y. Call); and he declared that "the great mass of the American people were brutal, bestial and inferior to the Russian comrades of the Socialists." (from speech at Park View Palace, N.Y.C., November 1919); mem. edtl. staff of Socialist Party "New Leader" and making lecture tour of 24 states (1934) in its behalf.

CLARK, EVANS: exec. com. L.I.D.; Rand School; newspaper man, N.Y. Times; wife Freda Kirchwey (see).

CLINE, PAUL: Communist Party org.; police record; former school teacher, Chgo.; now Communist Party section organizer, Wash., D.C.

CLOSE, UPTON: real name Josef Washington Hall; Soviet sympathizer; advocate Russian recog.; dismissed from U. of Wash. for radicalism; associate of Sun Yat Sen, who introduced Communism into China (see Mme. Sun Yat Sen); speaker on Oriental subjects; conducts tours to Russia and China; speaker at Student Cong. Ag. War at U. of Chgo., 1932; advisor to Chinese students during student revolution, 1919.

COCHRAN, WM. F.: Socialist; formerly exec. com. A.C.L.U.; exec. bd. N.C. for P.W.; exec. com. Church Socialist Lg.; Nat. R. & L. Found., 1933; Nat. Citiz. Com. Rel. Lat. Am. 1927; Md.

CODMAN, JOHN S.: nat. com. A.C.L.U., 1932; chmn. Mass. A.C.L.U. Com. 1922-33.

COE, ALBERT BUCKNER: minister First Cong. Ch., Oak Park, Ill.; chmn. West Side Fell. of Faiths; sponsors radical Forums in his church, featuring Communist and Socialist speakers.

COE, GEORGE A.: chmn. exec. bd. C. M.E. 1930; nat. com. Meth. Fed. for Soc. Serv.; Com. for Thomas, 1928; Am. Fed. of Teachers; assoc. ed. "World Tomorrow," 1932; Prof. Relig. Edu. at Teachers' Coll., Columbia U.; co-author of pamphlet with John Dewey, Paul Porter, Sherwood Eddy, and J. Stitt Wilson; Nat. R. & L. Found. 1933; endors. Lane Pamphlet; Conf. Prog. Pol. Act. 1934.

COFFIN, HENRY SLOANE: minister; pres. Union Theological Seminary (see), often referred to as the "Red Seminary"; Fed. Coun. Chs.; vice chmn. M.W.D. Def. Com.; Non-Intervention Citiz. Com. 1927; petitioned for Sacco and V. Aug. 22, 1927; Com. for Thomas, 1929; signer Fell. Recon. Pet. Russ. Recog. 1932; endors. Lane Pamphlet; sent greetings to communist Student Cong. Against War.

COHEN, ELLIOT E.: Communist; writer for Intl. Pamphlets; finance chmn. I.L.D. 1932; bd. Pris. Rel. Fund, I.L.D.; contrib. ed. communist "Steel Review."

COHEN, JOS. E.: Socialist; assoc. ed. New Leader (Soc.); Am. delg. W.C.A.W. (Amsterdam); Am. Com. for S.A.W.; N.Y.C.

COHEN, LESTER: Communist Lg. P. G. for F. & F. 1932; poet, journalist; Nat. Com. for Def. Pol. Pris. 1932.

COHN, FANNIA MARIA: born in Russia; vice pres. Pioneer Youth of Am. 1931; vice pres. Intl. Ladies Garm. Wkrs. Un. and longtime leader of its strikes (its 1926 strike led by Communists rec'd $100,000 from Garland Fund); nat. com. Lg. Against Fascism; Non-Intervention Citiz. Com. 1927; Fed. Unemp. Wkrs. Lgs. of N.Y.C. 1933.

COIT, ELIZ. C.: sec. N.Y. City A.C.L.U. Com.

COLE, G. H. D.: see "English Reds"; British Society for Cultural Relations with Russia (British branch A.S.C.R.R.); Fabian Society.

COLEMAN, McALLISTER: A.C.L.U.; vice pres. L.I.D. for N.Y., nat. bd. dir.; Socialist; author of pamphlet against Lusk com.; corres. "Illinois Miner"; contrib. ed. "Disarm" (L.I.D.); New Leader; Emer. Com. Strik. Rel.; Com. on Coal and Giant P.

COLLINS, MR. AND MRS. HENRY H.: Pa. Com. for Total Disarm.

COLMAN, LOUIS V.: Communist Lg. P. G. for F. & F. 1932; publ. chmn. I.L.D. 1932; Lg. Strugg. Negro Rts.

COLVIN, SARAH T.: nat. coun. L.I.D. for Minnesota.

COMMONS, JOHN ROGERS: Prof. Economics U. of Wis.; Nat. Mooney-Billings Com.; pres. Nat. Cons. Lg. since 1923; author of radical books on social and labor subjects; vice pres. Am. Assn. for O.A.S., 1931; nat. com. Nat. World Ct. Com. 1931; signer Fell. Recon. Pet. Russ. Recog. 1932; finan. contrib. Commonwealth Coll. May, 1933.

COMPERE, RALPH: minister Peoples Church of West Allis, Wis.; mem. Socialist Party city central com. of Milw.; delg. to communist F.S.U. Convention, Jan. 26, 1934; had Liston Oak, Communist ed. F.S.U. mag. speak in his church (Daily Wkr. Jan. 6, 1934).

COMSTOCK, ADA L.: Nat. Citiz. Com. Rel. Lat. Am. 1927; Open Road, 1933; signer pet. for Russ. Recog. (Women's committee); pres. Radcliffe Coll.; Mass.

COMSTOCK, ALZADA: Prof. Ec. Mt. Holyoke Coll.; signer letter May, 1933 to Pres. Roosevelt for Soviet recog.; a "Communist-Recommended Author"; First Am. Tr. Un. Delg. Russia.

CONNELLY, MARC.: Emer. Com. Strik. Rel. 1933; Nat. Coun. on Freedom from Censorship of A.C.L.U.; lect. Rand Sch. 1931-2.

CONNER, ROSS: exec. com. Chr. Soc. Act. M.; Whitewater, Wis.

CONRAD, LAETITIA MOON: Prof. Grinnell Coll., Iowa; nat. coun. L.I.D. for Iowa; Com. for Thomas, 1928.

CONROY, JACK: Communist writer; middle west staff corr. "New Masses," 1933.

COOK, CARA: faculty mem. Brookwood Lab. Coll. 1932.

COOLIDGE, ALBERT SPRAGUE: nat. exec. com. Socialist Party; nat. com. Lg. Against Fascism.

COOPER, COL. HUGH L.: N.Y. engineer who has received huge fees from Soviet Govt. for supervising building of Dnieperstroy dam and power project; urged U.S. S.R. recog.; pro-Soviet; a "Communist-Recommended Author"; pres. American Russian Chamber of Commerce.

COPE, MRS. WALTER: See Francis Fisher Kane.

COPENHAVER, ELEANOR: N.C. to A.S.M.F.S.; exec. com. Nat. R. & L. Found. 1933; Nat. Com. Def. Pol. Pris.; Ch. Emer. Com. Rel. Tex. Strik., 1930; nat. com. for Student Cong. Ag. War, 1932; Nat. Industrial Sec. of Y.W.C.A. (see).

COREY, LEWIS: Communist Lg. P. G. for F. & F. 1932; says in "New Masses," May, 1933: "Struggle against Fascism must proceed on all fronts led by the revolutionary, the communist workers . . . to work!"

COSTIGAN, SEN. EDW. P.: radical U.S. Senator from Colorado; vice pres. Pub. O. Lg.; Colo. Com. Lg. Nations.

COSTIGAN, MRS. EDW. P.: wife of Sen. from Colo.; hon. vice pres. Nat. Citiz. Com. on Rel. Lat. Am. 1927; Nat. Save Our Schs. Com.; endors. "Professional Patriots"; Lg. Women Voters; People's Legis. Serv.; vice pres. Nat. Cons. Lg., 1931.

COUNTS, GEO. S.: lecturer for F.S.U.; endorsers com. World Peaceways; Teachers' Coll. Columbia U.; mem. "joint technical staff of the First Am. Trade Un. Delg. to Russia" (not recog. by A. F. of L. because of its communistic character) with Communist Robt. W. Dunn, Carleton Washburne, Arthur Fisher, Paul Douglas, etc.; author of section on "Education in Soviet Russia" in book "Soviet Russia in the Second Decade," written by said joint technical staff; translator from Russian and writer of eulogistic preface of Ilin's communist "New Russia's Primer"; Student Cong. Ag. War; advis. com. Highland Park Folk School (Socialist), Monteagle, Tenn.; sent greetings commemorating the Soviet 15th anniv. of the Oct. Revolution in "Soviet Russia Today" (Jan. 1933); was ed. of "The New Education in Soviet Republic" by Communist Albert P. Pinkovitch; Nat. R. & L. Found. 1933; Prog. Edu. Assn. and chmn. of its com. issuing revolutionary manifesto; Nat. Save Our Schools Com.

COWELL, HENRY: Communist Lg. P. G. for F. & F. 1932; New School for Social Research.

COWLEY, MALCOLM: Communist Lg. P. G. for F. & F. 1932; Pris. Rel. Fund (I.L.D.); supporter N.S. Lg.; Scottsboro Unity Def. Com.; sec. Am. com. W.C.A.W.; ed. "New Republic"; Nat. Com. Def. Pol. Pris. 1932; chmn. Am. Com. for S.A.W.; Emer. Com. So. Pol. Pris.; Intl. Com. for Pol. Pris. 1933; John Reed Club; sponsor Chgo. Wkrs. Theatre, 1933; Nat. Com. to Aid Vic. G. Fascism; nat. com. F.S.U.

COWLING, DONALD J.: pres. Carleton Coll., Minn.; Open Road; mem. 1928 delg. to Russia; endors. World Peaceways; Minn. State exec. com. Y.M.C.A.

COWPER, MARY O.: nat. coun. L.I.D. for North Carolina.

COX, REV. GILBERT S.: M.E. minister, formerly of Columbus, O., now of South Bend, Ind.; nat. coun. L.I.D.; chmn. exec. com. Chr. Soc. Act. M.; Ill. C.M.E.; exec. com. Meth. Fed. for Soc. Serv. 1933.

COX, FATHER JAMES R.: Catholic priest; Pittsburgh A.C.L.U. Com.; leader of a Hunger March delegation to Wash.; Nat. R. & L. Found. 1933.

COYLE, ALBERT F.: nat. coun. C.M.E.; expenses to Mexico paid by Garland Fund, 1926 ($549.64); was dir. All Am. Cooperative Commission; dir. sec. Cleveland Cooperative Coal Co.; county and state exec. com. (Ohio) Conf. for Prog. Pol. Act.; regular Federated Press contributor; exec. bd. Fed. Press, 1923; Rand School lecturer; officer Commonwealth College; more or less reg. contrib. "Daily Worker"; speaks Russian; was imprisoned for several months in Russia; John L. Lewis denounced him from floor of A. F.

of L. Convention at Detroit, 1926, and accused him of being a Communist and a henchman of Wm. Z. Foster; Lewis read a letter which he admitted had been obtained from an agent of his in which Coyle spoke of starting a new Communist paper amongst the miners financed by "wealthy friends," which was to be used to support John Brophy, who also is Communist supported; Nat. R. & L. Found. nat. com. 1933; Nat. Coun. Prot. For. Born Wkrs.; First Am. Tr. Un. Delg. Russia; A.A.A.I. Lg. 1927; endors. Lane Pamphlet.

CRAM, MRS. J. SARGENT: sister of Mrs. Gifford Pinchot; gave anarchists Berkman and Tom Mooney $500 to start their anarchist paper "The Blast" and contrib. $25 to Berkman's Lg. for Amn. of Pol. Pris.; her relations with anarchists and Communists exposed in a Congressional investigation; nat. coun. C.M.E.; exec. com. W.R. Lg.

CRANE, JACOB L.: city planner; pro-Soviet; engaged in work for U.S.S.R. 1931; sponsor Chgo. Workers Theatre (Communist); Roosevelt appointee as TVA associate 1933.

CRAWFORD, BRUCE: Communist Lg. P. G. for F. & F. 1932; Nat. Com. Def. Pol. Pris. (Dreiser); endorsed W.I.R. letter for Hunger Marchers, 1932; ed. Crawford's Weekly, Norton, Va.; shot in Harlan, Ky., strike area 1931; Southern Lg. for People's Rights, 1933.

CRICHTON, KYLE S.: Communist Lg. P. G. for F. & F.; ed. Scribners Mag. 1933; mem. citiz. com. to investigate conditions in fur industry, which reported in favor of communist Needle Tr. Wkrs. Indust. Un., Sept., 1933; endors. Intl. Lit. (organ of Intl. Un. Revol. Writers).

CROLY, HERBERT: ed. "New Republic"; People's Legis. Serv.; Emer. Com. Strik. Rel. 1930; endors. "Professional Patriots"; Nat. Citiz. Com. Rel. Lat. Am. 1927.

CROMBACH, ABRAHAM: Nat. R. & L. Found. nat. com.; contrib. I.L.D. 1928; Cinc., O.

CROUCH, PAUL: Communist; served prison term for trying to introduce Communism into U.S. armed forces in Hawaii while in the U.S. army; rewarded by Moscow for his treasonable work with title "Prof. of Military Sciences and Tactics for the Communist Party of the World, U.S. branch"; sec. A.A.A.I. Lg.; Communist campaign com. 1928; arrested Wash. D.C., Nov. 1928 for demonst. before War Dept. for release of Leavenworth prisoner; in charge military training in all Communist schools in U.S.; see also Walter Trumbull; arrested Sept. 1933 at Helper, Utah for "criminal syndicalism."

CRUDEN, ROBT. L.: Communist; writer for Intl. Pamphlets; "New Masses"; Pris. Rel. Fund (of I.L.D.).

CULLEN, COUNTEE: Negro poet; Communist; chmn. Foster-Ford Campaign for Equal Negro Rights; Communist Lg. P. G. for F. & F. 1932.

CUNNEA, WM. A.: Chicago Socialist; Farmer-Labor cand.; endorsed by L.I.P.A.; Communist sympathizer; sponsor Berger Nat. Found. dinner, 1931; dir. Amalg. Tr. & Savings Bk., Chgo.; appealed to State's Atty. Swanson for 7 Communists held on sedition charges, in the interest of "free speech," 1929 (one was C. A. Hathaway).

CURTIS, THOS. J.: pres. Pioneer Youth of Am.

D

DAHLBERG, EDW.: among first Americans arrested by Nazis for communistic activities and expelled from Germany; nat. com. F.S.U.; Communist Lg. P. G. for F. & F.; Revol. Writers Fed.; N.Y. John Reed Club; Nat. Com. Def. Pol. Pris.; Nat. Com. to Aid Vic. G. Fascism.

DAILES, IDA: Communist; Am. Com. for S.A.W. 1933; instr. in Principles of Communism, N.Y. Wkrs. Sch., 1932-33; org. Chgo. branch Am. com. for W.C.A.W. 1932; treas. Am. Lg. Ag. War and Fascism.

DAKIN, EMMA S.: nat. coun. L.I.D. for Mass.

DALLET, JOE: Communist Party functionary; Youngstown dist. org. Steel & Metal Wkrs. Indust. Un.; police record in Pa., Ohio and Chgo., where he was T.U.U.L. org.; former Fed. Press corres.

DAMON, ANNA: Communist Party cent. com.; head of women's division of Party.

DANA, H. W. L.: Prof. Harvard U.; Communist Lg. P. G. for F. & F. 1932; barred from England, 1932; bd. dir. L.I.D.; intl. and Am. com. W.C.A.W.; Am. delg. W.C.A.W. (Amsterdam); Student Cong. Ag. War (U. of Chgo.); "Student Review" of N. S. Lg.; Fell. Recon.; Recep. Com. Soviet Flyers 1929; N.C. to A.S.M.F.S.; Rand School lecturer since 1920; Brookwood Labor Coll.; New School Social Research; infamous People's Council; nat. com. F.S.U. and contrib. to F.S.U. magazine; John Reed Club, N.Y.C. 1930; traveled with Henri Barbusse, Oct. 1933, to translate his French speeches; Oct. 23, 1933, Chgo. collected money for Communist cause at Coliseum meeting and greeted the Reds as their comrade; Am. Com. for S.A.W.; Cong. Exp. Radicals; Nat. Com. to Aid Vic. G. Fascism.

DANISH, MAX D.: born in Russia; Socialist; exec. com. L.I.D.; with Intl. Ladies Garm. Wkrs. Un. since 1909; "Labor Age"; Pioneer Youth of Am.; Emer. Com. Strik. Rel. 1933; Non-Intervention Citiz. Com. 1927.

DARCY, SAM: Communist Party org. Dist. No. 13, Cal.; author of Communist pamphlets.

DARROW, CLARENCE: Attorney; nat. com. A.C.L.U.; nat. com. A.A.A.I. Lg. 1926-7-8; Nat. Mooney-Billings Com.; exec. com. Nat. Coun. Prot. For. Born Wkrs. (Communist) 1930; nat. com. I.L.D. (Communist) 1928-9-30; N.A.A.C.P.; hon. vice pres. Freethinkers Soc. of America (Atheist); dir. communist A.S.C.R.R. Chgo.; pres. Berger Nat. Found. 1931; Fell. Faiths, Chgo. 1932-3; Russ. Reconst. Farms 1925; vice pres. Pub. O. Lg. 1933; Freethinkers Ingersoll Com., 1933; Sacco-V. Nat. Lg.; Roosevelt appointee, chmn. NRA review bd. 1934.

DAS GUPTA, KEDAR N.: exec. com. W.R. Lg.; Fell. Faiths exec.

DAUCHY, SAMUEL: A.C.L.U. Chgo.

DAVIS, ANNA N.: Russ. Reconst. Farms, 1925; Emer. Com. Strik. Rel. 1927-33; treas. W. R. Lg. 1933; U.S. Cong. Ag. War com.; Recep. Com. Soviet Flyers; sec. treas. New England A.C.L.U. Com. 1922; Sacco-V. Nat. Lg. 1928; Com. for Thomas, 1929; treas. Am. Lg. Ag. War and Fascism, 1934.

DAVIS, ETHEL M.: nat. com. Nat. R. & L. Found. 1933.

DAVIS, HORACE B.: Communist; Fed. Press corres.; N.C. to A.S.M.F.S.; Dreiser Com. on Coal; Pris. Rel. Fund (of I.L.D.); Recep. Com. Soviet Flyers; Nat. Com. to Aid Vic G. Fascism; was S.W. U., Tenn., Prof. of Ec., 1930; arrested, Memphis, Tenn., June 6, 1930, for Communist activities; told to leave town, resigned from U.; author book "Labor and Steel"; Labor Research; now N.Y.C.

DAVIS, JEROME: Socialist; Prof. Yale Divinity School; pro-Soviet lecturer; nat. coun. L.I.D. for Conn.; grad. Union Theol. Sem.; mem. Social Serv. Commns. of Congl. Chs. and Fed. Coun. Chs.; translated constitution of Communist Party of Russia; C.M.E.; Recon. Trips; exec. com. Fed. Unemp. Lgs. of Am. (Borders); Recep. Com. Soviet Flyers; Nat. Mooney-Billings Com.; Peace Patriots; his "Studies of Soviet Russia" published by communistic Vanguard Press; was on Nat. Save Our Schools Com.; dir. A.S.C.R.R.; nat. coun. Berger Nat. Found.; mem. technical staff of First Am. Tr. Un. Delg. to Russia, denied recog. by A. F. of L. because of communistic character, and writer of two chapters ("The Communist Party" and "The Nature of the Russian Government") in its book, "Soviet Russia in the Second Decade"; carried credentials from Sen. Borah ("better than a passport in Russia"); endorser "Professional Patriots"; Fell. Recon. Pet. Russian Recog. 1932; Ch. Emer. Com. Rel. Tex. Strik.; Russ. Reconst. Farms, 1925; exec. com. Nat. R. & L. Found. 1933; investigated conditions in Russia with Edward A. Filene, 1927; nat. com. Lg. Against Fascism, 1933; Conf. Prog. Pol. Act. 1934.

DAWSON, EMILY F.: nat. coun. L.I.D. for Pa.; Pa. Com. Total Disarm., 1932.

DAWSON, PERCY M.: advis. in Alex. Meiklejohn's ultra radical Experimental Coll. at U. of Wis. 1927-9; edtl. contrib. A. Lincoln Center "Unity," 1933; nat. coun. L.I.D. for Wis.; Com. for Thomas, 1928.

DAY, GARDINER M.: nat. com. Nat. R. & L. Found. 1933.

DAY, WM. HORACE: nat. com. Nat. R. & L. Found. 1933; minister; pastor United Congl. Ch., Bridgeport, Conn., since 1917.

DEAN, VERA MICHELES: writer of pro-Soviet For. Pol. Assn. pamphlets; "Communist-Recommended Author."

DEBS, EUGENE V.: deceased; Socialist speaker and organizer; infamous People's Coun.; a founder in 1905 of the I.W.W.; sentenced to Atlanta Pen. 1919; he said: "For the cause of international revolution I would gladly sacrifice everything I possess; I would go to jail again; yes, I would even go to the gallows for this cause." (N.Y. Call, Socialist paper, Mar. 9, 1923); at a Socialist rally in Cleveland Mar. 12, 1919, he said: "With every drop of blood in my veins I despise their laws and I will defy them. . . . I am going to speak to you as a Socialist, as a Revolutionist, and as a Bolshevist, if you please." (Lusk Report, p. 555.); in Socialist N.Y. Call, issue of Aug. 6, 1919, he said: "The Socialist Party stands fearlessly and uncompromisingly for the overthrow of the labor-robbing, war-breeding and crime-inciting capitalist system."; in the issue of Oct. 18, 1919, he said: "My attitude has not changed one whit since I came to prison. I will make no promises of any kind or nature to obtain my freedom. I want to come out as Liebknecht came out. The proletariat of Germany shook the empire of Germany to its foundations, and the beasts of Berlin readily found it convenient to unlock the barred doors."; he was nominated for President by the Socialist Party while in jail. The official bulletin of the Socialist Party for June 1, 1920, contains Debs' speech of acceptance upon notification of his nomination in which he said: "Before serving time here, I made a series of addresses supporting the Russian Revolution, which I consider the greatest single achievement in all history. I still am a Bolshevik. I am fighting for the same thing here they are fighting for there. I regret that the Convention did not see its way clear to affiliate with the 3rd International without qualification." (Lusk Report, p. 1782); was praised by Lenin (see Lusk Report); was on Labor Defense Council (now I.L.D.) 1923, for defense of Bridgman Communists; Russ. Am. Indust. Corp.; Cong. Exp. Radicals.

DECKER, RICHARD: com. Chr. Soc. Act. M.; Auburn, Wash.

DE FORD, MIRIAM ALLEN: Communist Lg. P. G. for F. & F. 1932; corres. Fed. Press; John Reed Club.

DEHN, ADOLPH: Communist Lg. P. G. for F. & F. 1932; contrib. ed. "New Masses"; Nat. Com. Def. Pol. Pris.; John Reed Club; thanked by communist China Forum (May, 1932) for use of his communist cartoon.

DE LEON, SOLON: Socialist; A.C.L.U.; exec. com. L.I.D.; former I.W.W.; Am. Fed. of Teachers; Intl. Ladies Garm. Wkrs. Un.; Lg. Mut. Aid; Pioneer Youth of Am.; Am. Assn. Lab. Legis.; Pris. Rel. Fund. (I.L.D.); Recep. Com. Soviet Flyers; Nat. Coun. Prot. For. Born Wkrs.; N.Y.

DE LIMA, AGNES: N.C. to A.S.M.F.S.; financial contrib. to I.L.D.

DELL, FLOYD: vice pres. A.S.C.R.R.; nat. com. Sacco-V. Nat. Lg. 1928; Nat. Com. Def. Pol. Pris. (Dreiser); contrib. to communistic Commonwealth College; assoc. ed. "Masses" 1914-17; assoc. ed. "Liberator" 1918-24; indicted with other eds. of "Masses" for propaganda activities, 1918; N.C. to A.S.M.F.S.; Nat. Citiz. Com. for Sacco and V. (Boston Post, Aug. 21, 1927); Intl. Com. for Pol. Pris. 1933; John Reed Club; Nat. Com. to Aid Vic. G. Fascism; nat. com. F.S.U.

DENNETT, MARY WARE: writer of sex pamphlet "The Sex Side of Life"; convicted of writing obscene matter and fined $300 by N.Y. court; M.W.D. Def. Com. was formed, case was carried to appellate court, and a dismissal was won; Nat. Coun. on Freedom from Censorship; org. of infamous People's Coun. during War; her un-American wartime activities exposed in Lusk Report; Peace Patriots.

DE SILVER, ALBERT: was dir. A.C.L.U.; treas. I.W.W. Def. Fund; "Liberator" stockholder.

DE SILVER, MARGARET: Emer. Com. Strik. Rel. 1933; Recep. Com. Soviet Flyers.

DETZER, DOROTHY: exec. sec. W.I.L.P.F. for U.S.; exec. com. W.R. Lg.; sec. "World Tomorrow"; contrib. to "Disarm" (L.I.D. publication); nat. com. Lg. Against Fascism; Am. delg. W.C.A.W. (Amsterdam); Conf. Prog. Pol. Act. 1934; home Wash., D.C.

DEUTSCH, BABETTE: N.C. to A.S.M.F.S.; Peace Patriots; endors. W.I.R. letter for Hunger Marchers.

DE VALERA, EAMON: Pres. Irish Free State; in "World Tomorrow," 2/15/33, H. N. Brailsford refers to his party as professing "Christian Communism"; Socialistic.

DEVINE, REV. EDWARD T.: Prof. Columbia U.; exec. bd. N.C. for P.W.; endors. "Professional Patriots"; Nat. Mooney-Billings Com. 1929; Fed. Coun. Chs.; nat. com. Meth. Fed. for Soc. Serv. 1928; Nat. World Ct. Com.; vice pres. A.A. for O.A.S.; attacks deportation; Nat. Citiz. Com. Rel. Lat. Am. 1927; assoc. ed. "Survey"; Nat. Save Our Schs. Com.; Conf. Prog. Pol. Act. 1934.

DEWEY, JOHN: Prof. Columbia U.; nat. com. A.C.L.U.; nat. vice pres. L.I.D.; chmn. exec. com. L.I.P.A.; vice pres. A.S.C.R.R. and on its Delegation to Russia com. 1928; nat. com. Sacco-V. Nat. Lg.; on nat. com. sponsoring "Letters of Sacco-V." (to inflame the popular mind); endorser of "Professional Patriots"; contrib. "New Republic"; Nat. Citiz. Com. on Rel. with Latin Am.; denounced by Matthew Woll of A. F. of L. as a teacher of Communism; was vice chmn. Nat. Save Our Schools Com.; was mem. 1918 Defense Com. for I.W.W.; Peace Patriots; People's Lobby; Nat. Mooney-Billings Com.; chmn. M.W.D. Def. Com.; head of Jt. Com. on Unemp.; advis. of Pioneer Youth of Am.; signer Fell. Recon. Pet. Russ. Recog. 1932; Humanist, 1933; Open Road, 1933; a "Communist-Recommended Author"; vice pres. Berger Nat. Found.; Griffin Bill sponsor; vice pres. Fell. Faiths; Conf. Prog. Pol. Act. 1933, chmn. com. on action; nat. com. Lg. Against Fascism, 1933; Freethinkers Ingersoll Com. 1933; pres. People's Lobby; lecturer and supporter,

Rand School, 1932; endors. communist U.S. Cong. Ag. War 1933; endors. Lane Pamphlet; ed. Prog. Edu. Assn. organ.

DIAMOND, HILDA R.: Emer. Com. Strik. Rel. Chgo.; advis. coun. C.W.C. on Unemp.

DIECKMANN, ANNETTA: Chgo. Y. W.C.A. (see) exec.; exec. com. C.W.C. on Unemp.; Non-Partz. Com. Lillian Herstein; chmn. of scholarship com. for Bryn Mawr Summer Sch. for Workers; C.W.A. Cook County bd. Roosevelt appointee; cand. for Cook County commr. on Newton Jenkins' "Prog. Rep." ticket, April 1934.

DIEFFENBACH, ALBERT C.: chmn. for Boston, Fellowship of Faiths "Threefold Movement"; edtl. contrib. A. Lincoln Center "Unity"; Griffin Bill sponsor.

DILL, C. C.: radical U.S. Senator from Wash.; vice pres. Pub. O. Lg. 1933.

DILLARD, JAMES H.: nat. com. A.C. L.U.; nat. coun. C.M.E.; home Charlottesville, Va.

DIRBA, C.: Communist Party cent. com.

DIRECTOR, AARON: U. of Chgo. Prof.; Chgo. L.I.D.; C.W.C. on Unemp.; author "Economics of Technocracy," Chgo. U. pamphlet edited by Harry Gideonse; conducted Open Road Tours to Russia; mem. Jt. Com. on Unemp. of Illinois.

DODD, WILLIAM E.: Prof. U. of Chgo.; A.C.L.U. Chgo. Com.; Chgo. Forum Council; Nat. Citiz. Com. Rel. Lat. Am. 1927; now Roosevelt appointee Amb. to Germany.

DOMINGO, THEO.: author; colored; Communist sympathizer; mem. Negro Delg. to Russia to study Communism, 1932, under dir. Harold Williams (Negro Communist); Am. com. W.C.A.W.

DON, SAM: Communist Party functionary; exec. com. N.Y. Workers Sch.; nat. Agit-prop. dir., Communist Party; an asst. ed. Daily Wkr.

DOONPING, R.: writer for Intl. Pamphlets; Communist; educational chairman, I.L.D. 1932; Instr. N.Y. Wkrs. Sch. 1930; says his first connection with the Communist Party was made at the U. of Chgo.

DOS PASSOS, JOHN: Communist; presidium Wkrs. Cultural Fed.; nat. com. W.I.R.; winner Gorki award 1932; Intl. Union Revol. Writers; chmn. N.C. to A.S. M.F.S.; treas. Emer. Com. for So. Pol. Pris. 1930; contrib. ed. "New Masses," "Student Review," "New Pioneer," and "Soviet Russia Today" (all Communist) and Common Sense Magazine; Emer. Com. Strik. Rel. 1928; nat. com. W.C.A.W.; treas. Nat. Com. Def. Pol. Pris.; mem. bd. Pris. Rel. Fund (I.L.D.); with Hunger Marchers in Wash., D.C., Dec. 1932; Sacco-V. Nat. Lg.; was arrested in connection with Sacco-V. case; Communist Lg. P. G. for F. & F. 1932; John Reed Club; Nat. Coun. Prot. For. Born Wkrs.; Revol. Writers Fed.; supporter N.S. Lg.; Am. Com. for S.A.W.

DOTY, MADELINE Z.: wife of Roger Baldwin; 1925-27 intl. sec. W.I.L.P.F., Geneva, Switz.; ed. of its Bulletin "Pax" since 1925; was in Jane Addams' Women's Peace Party.

DOUGHTY, HOWARD N. JR.: Communist Lg. P. G. for F. & F.

DOUGLAS, PAUL H.: Prof. U. of Chgo.; A.C.L.U. Chgo. Com.; exec. com. Chgo. L.I.D.; nat. coun. L.I.D.; vice chmn. L.I.P.A.; M.W.D. Def. Com.; 1931 chmn. Chgo. branch A.S.C.R.R.; Sacco-V. Nat. Lg. 1928; signer of A.C.L.U. petition for Sacco and V., May, 1927; advis. com. C.W.C. on Unemp. (Borders); Am. Friends Service Com., Chgo.; Am. Com. for Inf. about Russia; Non-Partz. Com. Lillian Herstein, 1932; ed. "World Tomorrow"; mem. Garland Fund Com. on American Imperialism; pres. Util. Cons. and Inv. Lg.; Peace Assn. of Friends in America; Fell. for Chr. Soc. Order, now Fell. Recon.; Chgo. Forum Council; mem. of technical staff of Communist-organized First Am. Tr. Un. Delg. to Russia, repudiated by A. F. of L., and author of three chapters ("Labor Legislation and Social Insurance," "Wages and the Material Condition of the Industrial Workers," and "The Consumers' Cooperative Movement") and co-author with Communist Robt. W. Dunn of another chapter ("The Trade Union Movement") in its book, "Soviet Russia in the Second Decade"; head of Thomas and Maurer Socialist campaign com. 1932; now Roosevelt appointee as asst. to U.S. Labor Bd.; presided at Conf. Prog. Pol. Act. 1933; nat. coun. Berger Nat. Found.; mem. Socialist Party; Nat. Save Our Schs. Com.; endorser "Professional Patriots"; appealed for funds for Rand Sch. 1933; endorser Lane Pamphlet; Conf. Prog. Pol. Act. camp. com. 1934.

DOUGLASS, GAYLORD W.: assoc. sec. N.C. for P.W.

DREIFUSS, A.: sec. Cook Co. Socialist Party; Emer. Com. Strik. Rel.; C.W.C. on Unemp.; Socialist cand. for Sec. of State, 1932; Jt. Com. on Unemp. Conf., Illinois.

DREIER, MARY E.: Russ. Reconst. Farms, 1925; pres. Wom. Tr. Un. Lg. 1906-15, now mem. exec. com.; mem. nat. bd. Y.W.C.A.; sister, Mrs. Raymond Robins; Ch. Emer. Com. Rel. Tex. Strik.; Emer.

Com. Strik. Rel., 1933; endors. "Professional Patriots."

DREISER, THEODORE: author; Communist; Communist Lg. P. G. for F. & F. 1932; endorser "Letters Sacco and Vanzetti"; head of Nat. Com. Def. Pol. Pris.; Dreiser Com. on Coal; intl. com. and Am. com. W.C.A.W.; Intl. Union of Revol. Writers (hdqtrs. Moscow); author of articles urging break-down of moral sex standards; threatened with prosecution for adultery in Ky., 1932, while agitating miners (the famous "toothpick case"); perm. contrib. Intl. Lit.; Revol. Writers Fed.; Intl. Com. for S.A.W.; Intl. Com. for Pol. Pris. 1933; presidium Wkrs. Cult. Fed.; endorser W.I.R.; supporter N.S. Lg.

DUBLIN, ELIZABETH: bd. dir. L.I.D.; nat. com. Sacco-V. Nat. Lg. 1928.

DUBOIS, W. E. BURGHARDT: Socialist; Negro; nat. coun. Berger Nat. Found.; book com. A.S.C.R.R.; Am. com. W.C.A. W.; N.A.A.C.P.; nat. com. A.A.A.I. Lg. 1928; ed. "Crisis"; Recep. Com. Soviet Flyers; Communist sympathizer; received money from Garland Fund in 1928; Nat. Coun. Prot. For. Born Wkrs., exec. com. 1930; vice chmn. L.I.P.A.; endorser "Professional Patriots"; Am. Com. for S.A.W.; endors. Lane Pamphlet.

DUCHENE, MME. GABRIELLE: French W.I.L.P.F. exec.; communist Lg. Ag. Imperialism; see World Cong. Ag. War; intl. com. of Nat. Com. to Aid Vic. G. Fascism.

DUEL, HENRY: Chgo. A.A.A.I. Lg.; arrangements com. banquet Meyer Halushka, 1929; contrib. Commonwealth Coll. 1933; Chgo. L.I.D.

DUGGAN, STEPHEN P.: Prof. Coll. City of New York; vice pres. A.S.C.R.R. and on its Com. on Delg. to Russia; nat. com. Foreign Pol. Assn.; For. Lang. Inf. Serv.; signer Fell. Recon. Pet. Russ. Recog. 1932; bd. trustees World Peace Found.; Intl. Inst. of Edu.; Nat. World Ct. Com.

DULLES, SOPHIA: former sec. A.C.L. U., Phila. branch; sec. W.I.L.P.F., Phila.; exec. sec. Pa. Com. Total Disarm.

DUNCAN, THOS. M.: Socialist; was State Senator; former bus. mgr. of Socialist Milwaukee Leader (Victor Berger's); was Mayor Hoan's sec.; later was Gov. Philip LaFollette's sec. and "resigned" from Socialist Party when political pressure was brought on LaFollette for openly linking his admn. to Socialist Party.

DUNN, ROBERT W.: very prominent Communist; reputed mem. Communist Party cent. com.; nat. com. A.C.L.U., bd. dir. 1933; L.I.D.; dir. Garland Fund; publicity dir. in Russia of the Am. Friends Service Com. 1921-3; publicity agt. Russian-Am. Indust. Corp. 1923; acting dir. A.C.L.U. June-Oct. 1923; author A.C.L.U. pamphlets; organizer and head of Labor Research Assn.; nat. com. I.L.D.; nat. com. A.A.A.I. Lg. 1928; Recep. Com. Soviet Flyers; chmn. Pris. Rel. Fund, 1931; John Reed Club; "Labor Defender," 1931; "New Pioneer"; N.C. to A.S.M.F.S.; Lg. for Mut. Aid; Research Dept. Rand School; Garland Fund Com. on Am. Imperialism; Non-Intervention Citiz. Com. 1927; gen. org. Amalg. Textile Wkrs. 1921; mem. of "technical staff" of First Am. Tr. Un. Delg. to Russia, repudiated by A. F. of L.; editor and co-author with Paul H. Douglas of a chapter ("The Trade Union Movement") in its book, "Soviet Russia in the Second Decade"; writer for Intl. Pamphlets; Nat. Com. to Aid Vic. G. Fascism; Lg. Strugg. Negro Rts.

DUNNE, VINCENT: nat. com. Communist Lg. of Am.

DUNNE, WM. F.: mem. cent. com. Communist Party; ex-I.W.W.; sentenced June 3, 1927, to thirty days in workhouse and fined $500 as ed. of Communist Daily Worker, for printing obscene poem written by David Goronefsky, alias Gordon (protegé of Zona Gale), called "America," which likened America to a prostitute; nat. com. A.A.A.I. Lg. 1928; "New Masses" staff, 1933; Lg. Strugg. Negro Rts.; T.U.U. L.; I.L.D.; etc.

DURANT, WM. JAMES: Socialist; dir. Labor Temple School, N.Y.C.; Nat. Com. to Aid Vic. G. Fascism.

DURLACH, THERESE MAYER: People's Freedom Union, 1920; World Peaceways, 1933.

E

EARLE, EDWIN MEADE: Prof. Columbia U.; Nat. Citiz. Com. Rel. Lat. Am. 1927; Non-Intervention Citiz. Com.; A.S. C.R.R.; Garland Fund Com. on Am. Imperialism; Nat. Save Our Schs. Com.

EARLY, D. E.: Communist Party functionary; instr. Chgo. and S. Chgo. Wkrs. Schs.

EASTMAN, CRYSTAL: was ed. with brother Max, of "Liberator"; infamous People's Coun.; Women's Peace Party of Jane Addams.

EASTMAN, MAX: Communist; an A.C. L.U. founder; brother of Crystal; writer; translator of Trotsky; advis. com. F.S. Russia; ed. "Masses" 1913-17; "Liberator" 1918-22; divorced 1922; married Eliena Krylenko of Moscow 1924; home N.Y.; spkr. for People's Coun. during War; Congressional Exposure Radicals; supporter N. S. Lg.; John Reed Club.

EDDY, SHERWOOD: Socialist; nat. com. A.C.L.U.; L.I.P.A.; M.W.D. Def. Com.; formerly Asiatic sec. Y.M.C.A. (see); very pro-Soviet; conductor of carefully selected parties to U.S.S.R.; nat. coun. C.M. E.; recommends in "Toward a New Economic Society" (by Eddy and Page) reading communist Daily Worker; speaker for Nat. Coun. Prot. For. Born Wkrs. Jan. 9, 1926, when he denounced Bills for registration and deportation of alien Communists; Fell. Recon.; recommends in "Religion and Social Justice" Margaret Sanger's sex book on birth control, "Happiness in Marriage," formerly barred by P.O. Dept.; Emer. Com. Strik. Rel. 1933; nat. com. Nat. R. & L. Found. 1933; assoc. ed. "World Tomorrow"; nat. coun. Berger Nat. Found.; endors. "Professional Patriots"; Russ. Reconst. Farms, 1925; endors. Lane Pamphlet; Conf. Prog. Pol. Act. camp. com. 1934.

EDLOFF, ELTIAN: sec. L.I.D., Detroit.

EDWARDS, REV. LYFORD P.: Socialist; dean of Episc. St. Stephens Coll. (see under Union Theol. Sem.); leader of Recon. Trips. to radical hdqts.

EINSTEIN, ALBERT: "pacifist"; Better Am. Fed. Bulletin, March, 1933, reproduced photo of Einstein as one of participants in Communist congress of the 3rd Intl. at Moscow, 1929; endorser of the communist W.I.R. (see); intl. com. W.C. A.W.; founder Einstein Fund of W.R. Intl.; a leader of World Congress of the communist Anti-Imperialist Lg. July, 1929, at Frankfort on Main (see reproduction of photograph in Hadley's "T.N.T."); author of the 2% slacker slogan, a theory that 2% of the population who are militant war resisters can cripple their govt. in any war; preaches militant resistance to all armies except Soviet Russia's; daughter married to Russian; his much press-agented Relativity theory is supposedly beyond intelligence of almost everyone except himself; endorser of atheist book "If I Were God" by Robinson (see "Freethought Press"); protested execution of Mr. and Mrs. Ruegg, Communists of Pan Pacific Tr. Un. Secretariat in China, 1932; became hon. chmn. W.R. Lg. in America, Feb. 1933; in "Patrie Humaine" 1933, advised military preparations against Germany (see Peace Patriots); Intl. Com. for S.A.W. 1933 with Maxim Gorki and other leading Communists; Freethinkers Ingersoll Com. 1933; after exposure, and confiscation of his property in Germany, as a Communist, this "smart" man now claims (British press) that he did not "understand" his activities all these years were for Communist organizations; Pres. Roosevelt's over-night White House guest 1/24/34; Nat. Com. to Aid Vic. G. Fascism, of the communist W.I.R., 1933; called grotesque art of Communist Diego Rivera "gift to world" Feb. 1934.

ELEAZER, ROBT. B.: nat. com. Nat. R. & L. Found.; Atlanta, Ga. editor; prominent M.E. Church layman; trustee Clark U.

ELLIOTT, JOHN LOVEJOY: tchr. and social wkr.; Com. for Thomas, 1929; chmn. People's Freedom Union; Sacco-V. Nat. Lg.; chmn. in 1919 of N.Y. Bureau Legal Advice, with Ella Reeve Bloor, Fola La Follette, Chas. Recht, etc.; Emer. Com. Strik. Rel.; a leader of Ethical Culture Society; Freethinkers Ingersoll Com. 1933; Cong. Exp. Radicals; N.Y. City.

ELLIS, FRED: Communist; John Reed Club; delg. to Russia to Intl. Union of Revol. Writers, 1930; helped form Wkrs. Cult. Fed.; perm. contrib. Intl. Lit.; Revol. Writers Fed.; Daily Wkr. cartoonist.

ELLIS, HAVELOCK: English communistic sexologist; intl. com. W.C.A.W.; Freethinkers Ingersoll Com. 1933; Nat. Com. to Aid Vic. G. Fascism.

EMBREE, EDWIN R.: Chgo. Com. for S.A.W. 1933; vice pres. Rockefeller Found. 1927; pres. Rosenwald Fund.

EMERSON, HAVEN: M.D.; advis. coun. A.S.C.R.R.; contrib. ed. "Survey," 1933; medical branch Com. for Thomas, 1929; N.Y.

ENGDAHL, J. LOUIS: one of ten leading Am. Communist executives; I.L.D.; Daily Worker; etc.; traveled with Scottsboro mothers through Europe 1932, propagandizing; died in Moscow, 1932; wife is Chgo. public sch. tchr. (Von Humboldt Sch.) and contrib. $20 to Communist cause, Oct. 23, 1933.

EPSTEIN, ABRAHAM: bd. dir. L.I.D.; exec. sec. A.A. for O.A.S.; exec. com. Jt. Com. on Unemp. 1931.

ERNST, MORRIS L.: counsel for nat. A.C.L.U.; nat. coun. L.I.D. for N.Y.; Am. Assn. Lab. Legis.; dir. Garland Fund; L.I. P.A.; Emer. Com. Strik. Rel. 1927-33; People's Lobby; Nat. Mooney-Billings Com.; Nat. Coun. on Freedom from Censorship; atty., mem. firm Greenebaum, Wolff and Ernst, N.Y.C.; Com. on Coal & Giant P.; Fed. Unemp. Wkrs. Lgs. N.Y. (Borders) 1933; Non-Intervention Citiz. Com. 1927; co-author with Wm. Seagle of sex book, "A Study of Obscenity and the Censor," recommended by the atheist Freethought Club and listed in the catalogue of

Freethought Press Assn.; nat. bd. directors A.C.L.U. 1933; Sacco-V. Nat. Lg.; nat. coun. Berger Nat. Found.; Conf. Prog. Pol. Act. 1934.

EVANS, ELIZ. GLENDOWER: nat. com. A.C.L.U.; nat. coun. L.I.D. for Mass.; vice chmn., Sacco-V. Nat. Lg.; Emer. Com. Strik. Rel.; prominent mem. W.I.L.P.F.; People's Legis. Serv.; was in Women's Peace Party; home Boston.

EVANS, ERNESTINE: dir. A.S.C.R.R. and book com.; a "Communist-Recommended Author"; John Reed Club.

EVJUE, WM. T.: founder and ed. Wis. Capital Times, Madison, Wis., La Follette socialistic newspaper; vice pres. Pub. O. Lg.; Berger Nat. Found.

F

FADIMAN, CLIFTON R.: Communist; N.C. to A.S.M.F.S.; Nat. Com. to Aid Vic. G. Fascism; endors. W.I.R. letter for "Hunger Marchers"; author (New Masses, 1932) "How I Came to Communism."

FALKOWSKI, ED.: Communist; Intl. Union Revol. Writers; perm. contrib. Intl. Lit.; "New Masses"; Revol. Writers Fed.; Fed. Press corres.; Moscow Daily News corres.; now in Moscow.

FEINGLASS, ABE: org. fur section communist Needle Trades Wkrs. Indust. Un. of Chgo.

FEINSTONE, MORRIS: Socialist; sec.-treas. United Hebrew Trades; Pioneer Youth of Am.

FELSTENTHAL, JULIA: Chgo. Com. for S.A.W. 1933; Immigrants' Prot. Lg. (hdqtrs. Hull House); Chgo. com. of Am. Lg. Ag. War and Fascism and its delg. Feb. 1934, to protest to Austrian Consulate against anti-Red activities in Austria.

FIELD, BEN.: Communist journalist, specializing on farm situation; "New Masses" staff, 1933.

FIELD, FREDERIC VANDERBILT: of the capitalistic family; pres. Open Road, 1933; bd. dir. L.I.D.; Emer. Com. Strik. Rel.; contrib. to Commonwealth Coll., May 1933.

FIELD, SARA BARD: N.C. to A.S. M.F.S.; Nat. Mooney-Billings Com.; Pris. Rel. Fund (of I.L.D.); John Reed Club; endors. W.I.R. letter "Hunger Marchers"; advis. bd. Woman's Peace Society, 1928; Congressional com. of Woman's Peace Union, 1928-9; Los Gatos, Cal.

FILENE, EDWARD A.: see "Roosevelt Appointees"; socialistic; founder and pres. of Twentieth Century Fund, which financed NRA organization until Congress voted funds; Am. Russian Chamber of Commerce; For. Pol. Assn.; gen. advis. coun. Am. Assn. Lab. Legis.; organized and financed European "peace awards"; Boston merchant; "investigated" Russia with Jerome Davis 1927.

FINCKE, HELEN HAMLIN: Socialist; co-dir. and founder Manumit School, Pawling, N.Y.; a founder Brookwood Labor Coll.; Pioneer Youth of Am.; L.I.P.A.; Am. Fed. of Teachers.

FINCKE, WM. MANN: Socialist; Presb. minister; co-dir. and founder of Manumit School; a founder Brookwood Labor Coll.; dir. Labor Temple, Presb. Church, N.Y.C., 1918-9; L.I.P.A.; Am. Fed. of Teachers; participated in behalf of "free speech" in Duquesne, Pa. steel strike and was jailed, 1919.

FINE, NATHAN: Socialist; born Russia; Rand School since 1923 (research dept., which pub. Am. Labor Yr. Bk.); an org. Farmer-Labor Party; delg. Conf. Prog. Pol. Act. 1924.

FINERTY, JOHN F.: nat. com. A.C.L. U.; Sacco-V. Nat. Lg.

FISCHER, LOUIS: "Communist-Recommended Author"; his book "Oil Imperialism" pub. by Intl. Pub. and financed by Garland Fund ($1,000 in 1926); Am. corres. in Moscow for "The Nation," 1933; was "one of three newspaper men honored by Soviet Govt. marking 10 yrs. in Russia" (Chgo. Tribune, Oct. 1, 1932), other two being Walter Duranty and Wm. H. Chamberlain.

FISHER, ARTHUR: pres. A.C.L.U. Chgo. Com.; C.W.C. on Unemp.; incorp. of Soviet Am. Securities Corp.; advis. com. Amalg. Trust & Sav. Bk., Chgo.; exec. com. A.S.C.R.R., Chgo.; Griffin Bill sponsor; Illinois C.M.E.; Chgo. Forum Coun. 1928; associate of Jane Addams, Lochner, Eastman, Nearing, etc. in wartime "peace" activities exposed in Lusk Report; mem. technical staff of First Am. Tr. Un. Delg. to Russia, repudiated by A. F. of L. as communistic, and author of chapter "Foreign Concessions in Russia" in its propaganda book "Soviet Russia in the Second Decade"; A.A.A.I. Lg. Chgo. branch; sponsor Berger Nat. Found. dinner, 1931.

FISHER, IRVING: Prof. Yale U.; Nat. Citiz. Com. Rel. Lat. Am. 1927; nat. com. A.C.L.U. 1927 (Marvin); Lg. for Org. Progress, 1931; hon. vice pres. Nat. Cons. Lg.; Peace Patriots; Am. Neut. Conf. Com.; backer Fell. Faiths movement (Chgo. Daily News, 6/17/33).

FITZPATRICK, JOHN: pres. Chgo. Federation of Labor since 1906; Chgo. Com. for Struggle Against War, 1933, which put over Communist Barbusse mass meeting; Util. Cons. and Inv. Lg.; active in Tom Mooney defense; one of leaders in steel strike, on exec. com. with Wm. Z. Foster, in 1919; org. Ill. and Nat. Farmer-Labor parties; active in work for "amnesty of political prisoners"; former pres. Pub. O. Lg.; Roosevelt appointee on Chicago labor board of NRA, 1933.

FLEISHER, DR. ALEXANDER: sec. Nat. Com. on Labor Injunction of A.C.L. U.; Phila.

FLOYD, LOUISE A.: nat. coun. L.I.D. for N.Y.; Emer. Com. Strik. Rel.; Com. for Thomas, 1929; home N.Y.C.

FLOYD, WM.: ed. radical "Arbitrator," publication of Peace Patriots; Nat. Citiz. Com. Rel. Lat. Am. 1927; Non-Intervention Citiz. Com. 1927; in "Arbitrator," gives A.C.L.U. a monthly page (1932-3); Lg. for Org. Progress 1931; Nat. Save Our Schs. Com.; dir. Peace Patriots; nat. com. W.R. Lg.; Com. Total Disarm. 1931; artists' and writers' Com. for Thomas, 1929; Griffin Bill sponsor; N.Y.

FLYNN, ELIZ. GURLEY: Communist; former I.W.W.; nat. com. A.C.L.U.; dir. Garland Fund; wife of Carlo Tresca (anarchist-communist jailed after alleged felonious assault on a young school girl, whose parents shot, but did not kill, him. W.I.L. P.F. and A.C.L.U. members appealed for him, misrepresenting the facts); arrested many times in I.W.W. fights and at Phila. Sacco-V. meeting; active in Paterson and Lawrence textile strikes; author "Sabotage," suppressed during war; advis. com. Friends Soviet Russia, now F.S.U.; Pris. Rel. Fund (of I.L.D.); Cong. Exp. Radicals; People's Freedom Union, 1920; Labor Defense Coun. 1923 (for Bridgman Communists); nat. com. Intl. Wkrs. Aid 1927 (now W.I.R.); Emer. Com. Strik. Rel.; nat. chmn. I.L.D. 1928.

FORBES, MRS. J. MALCOLM: exec. bd. N.C. for P.W.; exec. bd. C.M.E.; Nat. Citiz. Com. on Rel. Lat. Am. 1927.

FORD, JAMES W.: Negro Communist; cand. for Vice Pres. 1932, with Wm. Z. Foster; Lg. Strugg. Negro Rts.; dismissed from Chgo. P.O. 1928 for Red activities; delg. to Red Intl. Labor Union Congress in Moscow, 1928; dir. Negro Bureau of the T.U.U.L.; org. and first sec. Intl. Tr. Un. Cong. of Negro Wkrs.; one of ten principal Am. Communist leaders; nat. exec. bd. T.U.U.L.; U.S. Cong. Ag. War com.

FOSDICK, HARRY EMERSON: Baptist minister; now pastor of Rockefeller's Riverside Drive Ch. in N.Y.C.; endors. "Professional Patriots"; Prof. Pract. Theol. Union Theol. Sem. since 1915; his books on religion very "liberal" and highly recommended by Socialists and other radicals (see 4A); pro-Soviet; signer Fell. Recon. Pet. Russ. Recog. 1932; signed A.C.L.U. petition to Gov. Fuller of Mass. asking clemency for Sacco and V. (N.Y. City Press, May 13, 1927); also signed ministers' commutation petition in behalf Sacco and V. (Boston Post, Aug. 22, 1927); persuaded Ruby Bates to testify in behalf of Scottsboro rapists and deny her previous story according to 1933 press reports; referred to in Communist anti-religious Intl. Pamphlet No. 15 as a "Christian Socialist" and "Rockefeller's pet preacher."

FOSTER, H. E.: chmn. Seattle A.C.L.U. Com.

FOSTER, WM. Z.: leading Am. Communist executive; Stalin's own mouthpiece in U.S.; Communist cand. for Pres. 1932; A.C.L.U. nat. com. until 1930; Garland Fund dir.; nat. com. A.A.A.I. Lg. 1928; head of (nat. sec) T.U.U.L.; jailed several times; presidium Wkrs. Cult. Fed.; U.S. Cong. Ag. War; Wkrs. Sch. N.Y.C.; Lg. Strugg. Negro Rts.; nat. com. F.S.U.; etc.

FOX, RABBI GEORGE: South Shore Temple, Chgo.; announced contemplated raising of $200,000 fund, to be sent to Russia for the new Jewish Soviet State of Biro Birdjan in U.S.S.R. (Chgo. Daily News, Feb. 17, 1932) (see I.C.O.R.).

FOX, MARY: exec. sec. L.I.D.; dir. Labor Chatauqua agitating in W. Va. 1931; sec.-treas. Jt. Com. Unemp.; advis. bd. "Revolt" 1932 (name changed to "Student Outlook," Feb. 1933); N.Y. Chap. L.I.D.; U.S. Cong. Ag. War com.; exec. com. W.R. Lg.

FRALEY, EDGARD: Nat. Com. Def. Pol. Pris.

FRANK, GLENN: pres. U. of Wis.; vice pres. A.A. for O.A.S.; Nat. Mooney-Billings Com. (of A.C.L.U.); vice pres. Berger Nat. Found. 1931; gave hon. degree to Harry F. Ward (see article "Glenn Frank"); Maurice Hindus dedicated book to him; Open Road, 1933; vice pres. Fell. Faiths nat. com. of 300.

FRANK, WALDO: Communist; Communist P. G. for F. & F. 1932; nat. bd. dir. A.C.L.U. 1933; John Reed Club; Scottsboro Unity Def. Com.; "Student Review"; contrib. ed. "Soviet Russia Today"; Pris. Rel. Fund; in "How I Came to Communism" (New Masses, Sept. 1932), he says: "The revolution tomorrow must be prepared today. Otherwise it may come too late to save mankind from the destruction of capitalistic war or still worse, from the moral syphilis of capitalistic peace."; N.C. to A.S.M.F.S.; Nat. Com. Def. Pol. Pris. 1932; speaker for the Chgo. Assn. for Child Study, Palmer House, Dec. 10, 1932; Intl. Com. for Pol. Pris. 1933; New Sch. Social Research 1931; contrib. ed. "New Republic"; sponsor Chgo. Wkrs. Theatre; Emer. Com. So. Pol. Pris.; supporter N.S. Lg.; "New Masses" staff, 1933; nat. com. F.S.U.

FRANK, WALTER: bd. dir. and nat. com. A.C.L.U.; Emer. Com. Strik. Rel.; Com. for Thomas, 1929; Fed. Unemp. Wkrs. Lgs. N.Y., 1933; Com. on Cultural Rel. Latin Am.; Conf. Prog. Pol. Act. 1934.

FRANKFELD, PHIL: former Communist leader in Chgo.; police record in Chgo. and Pitts.; mem. Party cent. com. Dist. No. 5 at Pitts. and sec. of city com. of Unemployed Coun. of Pitts.

FRANKFURTER, FELIX: Prof. Harvard Law School; nat. com. A.C.L.U.; Mass. A.C.L.U. Com.; Griffin Bill sponsor; severely condemned when counsel in Mooney case by Pres. Theodore Roosevelt for "an attitude which seems to me to be fundamentally that of Trotsky and the other Bolshevik leaders in Russia" (letter in Whitney's "Reds in America"); filed charges against the U.S. Dept. of Justice for its activities against Communists with Nat. Pop. Govt. Lg.; Nat. Save Our Schs. Com.; nat. legal com. N.A.A.C.P.; endors. "Professional Patriots"; said to have recommended Jerome Frank as Roosevelt appointee and to be an insider with the White House "brain trust."

FRASER, ALEX: Prog. Miners Un., Gillespie, Ill.; Nat. Mooney Com. Act.; pres. Gillespie Unemployed Council; removed from state com. Socialist Party, Aug. 1933, (Daily Wkr. 8/2/33) as a Communist; delg. Free Tom Mooney Congress, Chgo., 1933.

FRAZIER, L. J.: U.S. Senator, N.D.; radical Rep.; author of Frazier Amendment (see); officer of communistic Commonwealth College; Nat. Citiz. Com. on Rel. Latin Am. 1927; vice pres. Pub. O. Lg. since 1920; endors. "Professional Patriots."

FREEHOF, S. B.: Rabbi; Chgo. Com. for S.A.W. and spkr. for the communist Barbusse meeting, Oct. 23, 1933, which it sponsored; Chgo. com. Fell. Faiths; speakers bureau of Adult Edu. Council.

FREEMAN, JOS.: Communist; A.A.A.I. Lg. nat. com.; Intl. Un. Revol. Writers; perm. contrib. Intl. Lit.; Revol. Writers Fed.; art com. A.S.C.R.R.; nat. com. W.C. A.W.; W.I.R. 1927; publicity dir. A.C.L.U. since 1924; born Ukrainia; staff "Am. Hebrew," 1922; staff "Liberator," 1922; co-author with Scott Nearing of "American Imperialism"; contrib. ed. "Student Review" (of communist N.S. Lg.); ed. communist "New Masses"; spkr. Student Cong. Ag. War at U. of Chgo.; Nat. Coun. Prot. For. Born Wkrs.; Am. Com. for S.A.W.; Nat. Com. to Aid Vic. G. Fascism; nat. com. F.S.U.

FREUD, SIGMUND: sex psychoanalyst; says "Religious ideas are illusions," etc. (1927 4A Report); author of "The Future of Illusion"; Austrian prof.; supporter W. C.A.W. (Moscow News, Aug. 30, 1932).

FREUND, ERNST: Prof. U. of Chgo.; nat. com. A.C.L.U.; exec. bd. A.C.L.U. Chgo. Com.; For. Lang. Inf. Serv.; Am. Assn. Lab. Legis.; Nat. Pop. Govt. Lg. (charges against Dept. Justice).

FRIEDMAN, HERBERT J.: exec. bd. A.C.L.U. Chgo. Com.; Fell. Faiths; head of Municipal Voters Lg., Chgo.; atty. for Jane Addams; Valhabai Patel of India his house guest 1932 (see article "Who Are They?"); pres. Chgo. Forum Coun. 1928 and dir. Adult Edu. Coun., its successor; sponsor Berger Nat. Found. dinner, 1931.

FROST, WINIFRED: sec. exec. com. C.W.C. on Unemp. 1932; signer of call for Continental Congress for Economic Reconstruction (of Workers and Farmers).

FRUEH, ALFRED: Communist Lg. P. G. for F. & F.; John Reed Club.

FRUNZE, MICHAILOV: U.S.S.R.; was pres. Military Council U.S.S.R.

FUNKE, ADA H.: sec. Phila. A.C.L.U. Com.

FURNESS, MARGARET: A.C.L.U. Chgo. Com.

G

GAGE, DANIEL J.: nat. coun. L.I.D. for S. D.

GALE, ZONA: endors. "Professional Patriots"; author; advis. com. A.S.C.R.R.; vice chmn. L.I.P.A.; nat. com. A.C.L.U.; nat. coun. Berger Nat. Found.; former U. of Wis. Regent; sponsor and donor of scholarships to David Goronefsky, alias Gordon, Communist jailed for writing obscene poem called "America" in Daily Worker (see article "Glenn Frank"), and to Fred Bassett Blair, Communist cand. for Gov. Wis. 1932; nat. bd. W.I.L.P.F. 1931; endors. Lane Pamphlet; nat. coun. C.M.E.; Nat. Citiz. Com. on Rel. Latin Am. 1927; Russ. Reconst. Farms, 1925; edtl. contrib. A. Lincoln Center "Unity," 1933; Conf. Prog. Pol. Act. campaign com. 1934.

GALLAGHER, LEO: I.L.D. atty.; endorsed by Communist Party and Theo.

Dreiser, he rec'd 69,800 votes in 1933 Los A. election for municipal judge; active defense atty. in Mooney case; ousted from S.W. Law Sch., Los A. for radicalism; Student Cong. Ag. War; campaigner for repeal of Cal. Criminal Syndicalism law—leader of Communist protest delegation in Los A.; cand. for Los A. Bd. of Education; sent by I.L.D. to Germany to defend Communists charged with burning German Reichstag; mem. of Intl. Investigating Committee investigating Reichstag fire; jailed and ousted from Germany 1934.

GANDHI, MAHATMA: Leader of the Indian Nationalist movement, subsidized by Moscow as a first step in freeing India from England in order to Sovietize it; spoke under auspices of W.I.L.P.F. at Geneva, Switz.; conferred with Romaine Rolland, French Communist; corres. of the Nat. R. & L. Found. 1933; see also article "Who Are They?"

GANNES, HARRY: on staff communist Daily Worker; chmn. Anti-Imperialist Lg. Delg. to Cuba, 1933; speaker for N. S. Lg. in N.Y.; A.A.A.I. Lg. 1928; cent. com. Communist Party; writer for Intl. Pamphlets.

GANNETT, ALICE P.: nat. coun. L.I.D. for Ohio.

GANNETT, LEWIS S.: dir. Garland Fund; People's Lobby; nat. com. A.A.A.I. Lg. 1928; Recep. Com. Soviet Flyers; ed. "Nation" 1927; Socialist; Intl. Com. Pol. Pris. 1933; book reviewer for N.Y. Herald-Tribune.

GARDNER, JOE: Wkrs. Ex-Service Men's Lg.; Am. delg. W.C.A.W. (Amsterdam).

GARDOS, EMIL: Communist Party cent. com.; sec. Hungarian Buro of cent. com. Communist Party; citizenship revoked and deportation proceedings started 1934.

GARLIN, SENDER: one of ten most prominent Am. Communist Party leaders; writer for Daily Worker.

GARTZ, KATE CRANE: nat. com. A.C.L.U.; nat. com. W.C.A.W.; prominent Los A. W.I.L.P.F.; was on nat. com. Intl. Wkrs. Aid 1927 (now W.I.R.); nat. com. W.I.R. 1928; stockholder in "Liberator"; purchased advertising space in Daily Worker May Day, 1928, to greet her Communist friends; advis. com. and coun. People's Lobby; furnished bail for Communist Yetta Stromberg; contributor to communistic Commonwealth Coll., to I.L.D. (Communist), and to Young Workers Communist League summer school, 1929; close friend of Upton Sinclair and aided Soviet film director, Eisenstein; Peace Patriots; sister of R. T. Crane of firm of Crane Co. (plumbing supplies).

GEBERT, BILL: dist. org. Communist Party, Dist. No. 8 (Chgo); former org. Nat. Miners Un. (S. Ill.).

GEER, OWEN M.: sec. Chr. Soc. Act. M.; teacher at Chgo. Sch. of Socialism, 1933 ("New Frontier," Mar. 22, 1933); made investigation in coal fields of Ill. and reported favorably to radical miners (May 19, 1933, "Prog. Miner"); vice chmn. communist Am. Lg. Ag. War and Fascism Chgo. 1934; Meth. Ch. hdqts., 740 Rush St., Chgo.

GEISER, CARL: Communist; sec. of com. arranging World Cong. of Youth Ag. War and Fascism; arrang. com. U.S. Cong. Ag. War; contrib. ed. "Student Review" of N.S. Lg.; spkr. Student Cong. Ag. War, and mem. nat. com.; delg. of N.S. Lg. to Montevideo Cong. Ag. War; org. Pitts. Com. Strugg. Ag. War, June, 1933; made tour org. chapters N.S. Lg., May 1933.

GELLERT, HUGO: Communist; painter and cartoonist; assoc. ed. "Liberator"; staff "New Masses"; Nat. Com. Def. Pol. Pris.; "New Pioneer"; "Labor Defender"; "Soviet Russia Today"; sec. N.C. to A.S.M.F.S.; born Hungary; John Reed Club.

GEORGE, HARRISON: cent. com. Communist Party U.S.; I.L.D.; former ed. Daily Worker; former I.W.W.

GERBER, JULIUS: exec. sec. Socialist Party of N.Y.C.; U.S. Cong. Ag. War; nat. com. Lg. Against Fascism.

GERSH, E. B.: org. communist Needle Trades Wkrs. Indust. Un., Chgo.

GERSON, SI: Communist Party functionary; Labor Sports Union; pres. Bronx County (N.Y.) Amateur League (Communist); editor of Labor Sports Union organ ("Sport and Play").

GESSNER, ROBT.: sec. A.C.L.U. com. on Indian Civil Rights.

GIBSON, LYDIA: Communist; artist; edtl. bd. "New Pioneer"; Nat. Com. Def. Pol. Pris.; N.C. to A.S.M.F.S.; Pris. Rel. Fund (I.L.D.) 1927; wife of Robt. Minor; with Hunger Marchers, 1932, in Wash.; contrib. ed. "Liberator," 1922.

GIDEONSE, HARRY D.: U. of Chgo. Prof.; Open Road, 1933; faculty endorser of Student Cong. Ag. War at U. of Chgo.; was prominent in Youth Movement; said "the spirit of the movement was one of freedom, and would not tolerate the bonds and shackles of a rigid organization but they realized the present social system was deficient . . . this was being changed with the ideas students had as to marriage, that they felt a continuance of marital relations between people who are no longer congenial as merely prostitution," etc. (Marvin's "Ye Shall Know the Truth"); faculty mem. of Am. Friends Serv. Com. 1932; Non Partz. Com. Lillian Herstein; ed. of Aaron Director's "Economics of Technocracy."

GILKEY, REV. CHAS. W.: Dean of Rel. Edu. and Prof. U. of Chgo.; until recently pastor Hyde Pk. Bapt. Ch., Chgo.; now pastor U. of Chgo. chapel; exec. bd. A.C.L.U. Chgo. Com.; chmn. Emer. Com. Strik. Rel.; exec. com. L.I.D., Chgo.; endorsing com. Am. Friends Serv. Com.; endorser Lane Pamphlet; signer of petition for Sacco and V., Aug. 22, 1927; Fell. Faiths, chmn. for South Side; Illinois C.M. E.; Chgo. Forum Coun.; signer Fell. Recon. Pet. Russ. Recog. 1932; Nat. R. & L. Found. 1933; wife, Y.W.C.A. executive; Non Partz. Com. Lillian Herstein; Chgo. Com. for S.A.W. which staged communist Barbusse mass meeting 1933; sponsor Berger Nat. Found. dinner '31; A.S.C.R.R. Com. '34.

GILKEY, JAMES GORDON: minister; brother of Chas. W.; nat. com. Nat. R. & L. Found. 1933.

GILMAN, ELIZ.: Socialist; bd. dir. L.I.D.; sec. A.C.L.U. Md. Com. 1925 (Baltimore); exec. bd. N.C. for P.W.; Peace Patriots; Nat. Mooney-Billings Com.; Nat. Citiz. Com. on Rel. Lat. Am. 1927; Il Nuovo Mondo Nat. Com.; exec. com. A.A. for O.A.S.; delg. to W.C.A.W. 1932; Fell. Recon.; financial contrib. to Commonwealth Coll.; Nat. R. & L. Found. 1933; Emer. Com. Strik. Rel. 1933; Nat. Save Our Schs. Com.; supporter Rand Sch. 1933; nat. com. W.R. Lg.; Sacco-V. Nat. Lg.; vice pres. Berger Nat. Found. 1932.

GILROY, WM. E.: editor "The Congregationalist" since 1922; Nat. R. & L. Found. nat. com. 1933; Griffin Bill sponsor; Boston, Mass.

GITLOW, BENJ.: dir. Garland Fund, 1926-33; first Am. Communist imprisoned 1919 (for articles in "Revolutionary Age"); a leader with Jay Lovestone of the Communist Party (Opposition) since 1930.

GLOTZER, ALBERT: nat. com. Communist Lg. of Am.

GODDARD, ALVIN C.: nat. com. W.R. Lg.; treas. C.M.E. 1930; exec. com. World Peaceways, 1932.

GODWIN, MURRAY: Communist Lg. P. G. for F. & F.; Nat. Com. Def. Pol. Pris.; has contributed to "New Republic," "New Freeman" (Haldeman-Julius), "New Masses"; N.Y. City.

GOLD, BEN: Communist; Needle Tr. Wkrs. Indust. Un. nat. sec.; A.A.A.I. Lg. nat. com.; nat. com. F.S.U. 1934.

GOLD, MICHAEL: Communist; writer for Communist publications; Am. com. W.C.A.W.; Intl. Union Revol. Writers; "New Masses" staff, 1933; perm. contrib. Intl. Lit.; Revol. Writers Fed.; N.C. to A.S.M.F.S.; Pris. Rel. Fund; financial contrib. Commonwealth Coll.; sponsor Chgo. Wkrs. Theatre, 1933; Recep. Com. Soviet Flyers; supporter N.S. Lg.; Am. Com. for S.A.W.; John Reed Club; Nat. Com. to Aid Vic. G. Fascism; nat. com. F.S.U. 1934.

GOLDEN, CLINTON STRONG: dir. Garland Fund; Brookwood Labor Coll.; org. Amalg. Cloth. Wkrs. of Am.; treas. Il Nuovo Mondo Nat. Com.; Com. on Coal and Giant P.

GOLDMAN, ALBERT: Communist; I.L.D. atty.; sponsor Chgo. Wkrs. Theatre, 1933; expelled from Communist Party, 1933; now conducting a Chgo. Marxian school for the Communist Lg. of Struggle with Lydia Beidel.

GOLDMAN, EMMA: Anarchist-Communist; free love exponent; helped found Ferrer anarchist School, supported by Garland Fund; her book "Living My Life" tells of her intimate relations with Berkman, Ben Reitman, and many other men, and of her former devotion to the Soviet regime, which turned to hatred after she was deported to Russia; tells also of her escape to France; extended amnesty by Pres. Roosevelt, Dec. 1933, and has returned to U.S.A.

GOLDSTEIN, BEN: Rabbi; Nat. Com. Def. Pol. Pris.; nat. coun. communist Lg. Strugg. Negro Rts.; ousted from Synagogue, Birmingham, Ala. for radicalism, (Apr. 18, 1933 Daily Worker); chmn. Citiz. Scottsboro Aid Com. of Birmingham; now in N.Y. City; mem. Nat. Com. to Aid Vic. G. Fascism; mem. Citizens Com. to investigate N.Y. City fur industry, which reported in favor of communist Needle Tr. Wkrs. Indust. Un.

GOLDSTEIN, ISRAEL: Rabbi; nat. com. Nat. R. & L. Found.; exec. com. Fell. Faiths, Union East and West, Lg. Neighbors; chmn. com. on social justice, Rabbinical Assembly of Jewish Theol. Sem.; N.Y. City; com. U.S. Cong. Ag. War; Am. delg. W.C.A.W. (Amsterdam); mem. N.Y. citiz. com. investigating fur workers riots reporting in favor of communist Needle Tr. Wkrs. Indust. Un., July 1933; mem. governing council of Zionist organizations of America (Daily Wkr. 12/7/33); spkr. for Am. Lg. Ag. War and Fascism, with John Strachey (Communist) and Fenner Brockway, N.Y., Dec. 8, 1933.

GOLDSTEIN, SIDNEY E.: Rabbi; Jewish Inst. Religion; chmn. exec. com. W.R. Lg.; exec. com. Nat. R. & L. Found. 1933; Nat. Coun. on Freedom from Censorship of A.C.L.U.; Recon. Trips; World Peaceways; exec. com. Jt. Com. on Unemp.; clergymen's branch Com. for Thomas, 1929; attended Rosika Schwimmer reception for Einstein, March 19, 1933.

GOMEZ, MANUEL: right name is Chas. F. Phillips; Communist agitator; former Columbia U. student; draft resister, fined $500 by U.S. Govt.; a founder and head (sec.) Am. section of Anti-Imperialist Lg. (A.A.A.I. Lg.) 1927; carried on Communist agitation in Mexico in 1920; delg. with Roger Baldwin to communist World Congress Against Imperialism at Brussels 1927; contributor to "New Masses," 1933.

GORDON, EUGENE: Negro; Communist; Communist P. G. for F. & F. 1932; "New Masses" staff, 1933; Nat. Com. Def. Pol. Pris.; nat. com. W.C.A.W.; mem. Negro Delg. to Russia to study Communism; Scottsboro Unity Def. Com.; exec. bd. John Reed Club, Boston; "Labor Defender"; N.C. to A.S.M.F.S.; Scottsboro Com. of Action; Lg. Strugg. Negro Rts.; "Liberator" staff.

GORKI, MAXIM: One of world's leading Communists; U.S.S.R.; revolutionary writer; donor of Gorki Awards to best Communist revol. authors in U.S.; intl. com. W.C.A.W.; Intl. Com. for Struggle Ag. War; hon. mem. presidium Wkrs. Cult. Fed. of U.S.; writer Intl. Pamphlets; endors. "Letters of Sacco and Vanz."; "New Pioneer" edtl. bd.

GRAETZ, HERBERT D.: nat. com. Nat. R. & L. Found. 1933.

GRAHAM, JAMES D.: nat. exec. com. Socialist Party 1933.

GRANT, BERT: Communist writer for Intl. Pamphlets; edtl. bd. "New Pioneer."

GRATTAN, C. HARTLEY: Nat. Com. Def. Pol. Pris.; John Reed Club; contrib. Common Sense Magazine.

GRAY, ANNIE E.: dir. Wom. Peace Soc.; U.S. Cong. Ag. War com.; spkr. World Youth Cong. Ag. War and Fascism (see); exec. com. W.R. Lg.; Am. Lg. Ag. War and Fascism, with Earl Browder and other Communist Party leaders; social service branch Com. for Thomas, 1929; Griffin Bill sponsor.

GRAY, HAROLD: nat. com. Nat. R. & L. Found. 1933.

GRECHT, REBECCA: Communist Party org., Dist. 14, Newark, N.J.; exec. com. Nat. Coun. Prot. For. Born Wkrs. 1930.

GREEN, GILBERT: Communist Party cent. com.; nat. sec. Young Communist Lg.; Lg. Strugg. Negro Rts.; arrangements com. U.S. Cong. Ag. War.

GREEN, PAUL: Nat. Com. Def. Pol. Pris.; Nat. Coun. on Freedom from Censorship of A.C.L.U.

GREGORY, HORACE: Communist Lg. P. G. for F. & F.; Nat. Com. Def. Pol. Pris.; John Reed Club; contrib. to "New Masses," "New Freeman," "New Republic," "The Nation" (Daily Wkr., Feb. 28, 1933).

GRIFFIN, ANTHONY J.: N.Y. Congressman; author of the Griffin Bill (see); backed by radical pacifists, A.C.L.U., etc.; he announced Oct. 1933 that he anticipated the removal of the question "Will You Bear Arms?" from the naturalization questionnaire of the Dept. of Labor (presumably, since Frances Perkins is Sec. of Labor).

GROPPER, WM.: Communist; John Reed Club; staff cartoonist "Freiheit"; nat. com. W.I.R.; N.C. to A.S.M.F.S.; delg. Intl. Union Rev. Writers, 1930; helped form Wkrs. Cult. Fed.; staff "New Masses"; "New Pioneer."

GROSE, REV. WILBUR D.: organizer of Ill. C.M.E.; Wesley Found.

GRUDIN, LOUIS: Communist Lg. P. G. for F. & F. 1932; Am. com. W.C.A.W.

GRUENING, ERNEST: ed. "Nation"; Garland Fund Com. on Am. Imperialism.

GUTHRIE, ANN: C.M.E. Ill.; exec. sec. Chgo. Y.W.C.A.; Fell. Christ. Soc. Order; W.I.L.P.F.; delg. with Soph. P. Breckenridge to Montevideo Pan American Conf. Nov. 1933.

GUTHRIE, ERNEST GRAHAM: gen. dir. Chgo. Congregational Un. since 1926; nat. com. Nat. R. & L. Found. 1933.

GUYNN, CHAS.: communist Nat. Miners Union organizer in Pa. and N.M.; police record.

H

HACKER, CARL: Communist Party functionary; now District No. 5 (Pittsburg) I.L.D. organizer.

HAESSLER, CARL: staff "Left Front," Chgo. John Reed Club magazine; John Reed Club; A.C.L.U. Chgo. Com.; Communist lecturer; teacher and a director of the official Communist Party Dist. No. 8 Chgo. Workers School, 2822 S. Mich. Ave.; mgr. Fed. Press since 1922; Am. Com. on Inf. about Russia; instigator of Red riot and spokesman for its gen. strike com. while imprisoned in Leavenworth Pen., then transferred to Alcatraz prison (on an island in San Francisco Bay), 1918-20;

Recep. Banquet Com. for Ford (Negro Communist Vice Pres. cand.) 1932; lecturer Brookwood Labor Coll. 1932; home Ravinia, Ill.; Typographical Union 16; People's Council during war; Chgo. Com. for S.A.W. 1933; dir. "Institute for Mortuary Research," which, with the Fed. Press, A.C. L.U. Chgo. Com., and Chgo. Com. for S.A.W., has hdqts. in his office, 611—160 N. La Salle St., Chgo.; Nat. Com. to Aid Vic. G. Fascism; see article "Red Ravinia."

HAESSLER, GERTRUDE: Communist Party functionary; sister of Carl; writer for the Party Organizer; arrested leading Communist delg. to White House, Thanksgiving Day, 1932; edtl. bd. of "New Pioneer"; expert on Communist shop papers.

HAGERTY, J. E.: pres. Catholic Conf. on Industrial Problems and Dir. Sch. Soc. Admn., Ohio State U.; hon. pres. Nat. R. & L. Found. 1933; Catholic Assn. Intl. Peace; Columbus, O.

HAHN, HERMAN J.: nat. com. Nat. R. & L. Found.; cand. for Congress on Socialist ticket, 1932, from N.Y.; endorsed by L.I.P.A.; organizer Buffalo, N.Y. Unemployed Lg.; mem. exec. com. Erie County Continental Congress for Ec. Reconst.; cand. mayor Buffalo, Soc. ticket, Oct. 1933; exec. com. Buffalo Socialist Party; barred from radio for radicalism (Fed. Press clip sheet, 12/5/33).

HALDEMAN-JULIUS, E.: bd. dir. 4A; ed. "Am. Freeman" and "Militant Atheist"; one of his publications suppressed by P.O. Dept.; pub. Haldeman-J. Quarterly, also Monthly, and Little Blue Books, birth control and atheist books; financial contrib. Commonwealth Coll.; Freethinkers Ingersoll Com. 1933; "Communist-Recommended Author"; John Reed Club; his Little Blue Books on Socialism recommended by (Methodist) Chr. Soc. Act. M.; prefixed "Haldeman" to surname after marriage to Marcet Haldeman; now having marital split.

HALE, ROBT. L.: Com. on Coal and Giant P.; vice chmn. Sacco-V. Nat. Lg.

HALL, FLORENCE SLOCUM: L.I.D.; Fell. Recon.; Ill. Lg. Women Voters; Socialist; teacher; Chgo.

HALL, HENRY: Communist writer Intl. Pamphlets; I.L.D.; N.Y. City.

HALL, OTTO: Negro organizer for Communist Party; cand. for assembly, borough of Manhattan, 1933; instr. in N.Y. Wkrs. Sch. (Communist), 1930.

HALL, ROBERT: former head of communist N.S. Lg., Columbia U.; a leader of student delg. to Ky., 1932; Am. com. W.C. A.W.; Lg. Strugg. Negro Rts.; ed. Farmers Nat. Weekly (Communist) 1933.

HALLGREN, MAURITZ A.: ed. "Nation"; sponsor of Henri Barbusse appearance in Wash. (Wash. Star, 10/7/33) under auspices Wash. Com. for Strugg. Ag. War.

HALLOWELL, CHARLOTTE RUDYARD: Socialist; N.Y.C.; Nat. Cons. Lg.; For. Pol. Assn.; W.I.L.P.F.; assoc. ed. "New Republic" 1914-16.

HALONEN, YRJO: Communist; born Finland; trade repres. in U.S. of Karelian Soviet Republic 1922-3; Superior, Wis. (see Central Cooperative Wholesale, with which he is affiliated).

HALUSHKA, MEYER: exec. com. L.I. D., Chgo.; teacher John Marshall High Sch., Chgo.; Socialist cand. Ill. 1932; instr. Chgo. Sch. of Socialism 1933; sponsor Berger Nat. Found. dinner, 1931.

HAMBURGER, LOUISE LOEB (MRS. ALFRED): L.I.D.; W.I.L.P.F.; Lg. Wom. Voters; Chgo. Woman's Club; Socialist; Emer. Com. Strik. Rel., Chgo.; Chgo. Com. for S.A.W.; teacher at communist Wkrs. Laboratory Theatre School at A. Lincoln Center, 1933-4 (stage technique and voice diction).

HAMILTON, ALICE: A.C.L.U. Chgo. Com.; Recep. Com. Soviet Flyers, 1929; Griffin Bill sponsor; W.I.L.P.F.; Russ. Reconst. Farms; aided Sacco-V. agitation; vice pres. Nat. Cons. Lg. 1931; with Rosika Schwimmer-Jane Addams party to Hague Cong. 1915; appealed for Carlo Tresca, anarchist; com. Paxton Hibben Memorial Hosp. Fund; Intl. Com. for Pol. Pris.; gen. advis. com. Am. Assn. Labor Legis.; Pres. Hoover's Com. on Soc. Trends 1932, which made radical report; exposed in U.S. Fish Report (unabridged edition); "She wrote the Better America Federation not to send its bulletins to her as she was not in sympathy with its work" (Welsh).

HAMMERSMARK, SAM: dist. com. Communist Party, Dist. No. 8; Chgo. sec. I.W.O.; mgr. Communist "Workers' Bookstore," 2019 W. Division St., Chgo.; born Norway; studied for ministry, 1889-93.

HANKINS, FRANK H.: Smith Coll. Prof.; distributor of sex questionnaire; Humanist; ed. bd. "Birth Control Review."

HANSEN, HARRY: A.S.C.R.R.; columnist.

HANSON, FLORENCE CURTIS: A.C. L.U. Chgo. Com.; sec.-treas. Am. Fed. of Teachers and exec. ed. of its organ "The Am. Teacher"; Am. Com. on Inf. about Russia; advis. Pioneer Youth of Am.; coun. People's Lobby; Il Nuovo Mondo

Nat. Com.; Socialist cand. 1932; W.I.L. P.F.; nat. coun. Berger Nat. Found.; Lg. of Women Voters; contrib. to "The Nation."

HAPGOOD, NORMAN: nat. com. A.C. L.U.; author of anti-patriotic "Professional Patriots," which ran serially in communist Daily Worker; Nat. Mooney-Billings Com.; Sacco-V. Nat. Lg.; Nat. Citiz. Com. on Rel. Lat. Am. 1927.

HAPGOOD, MRS. NORMAN: exec. com. and dir. A.S.C.R.R.; nat. bd. W.I.L. P.F.; appealed to Pres. Hoover for Russian recog.

HAPGOOD, POWERS: nat. exec. com. Socialist Party; nat. com. A.C.L.U.; nat. coun. L.I.D. for Colorado; writer; coal miner and union org.; son of Wm. P.; sec. Sacco-V. Def. Com. 1927; he and wife arrested several times staging demonstrations; Nat. R. & L. Found. 1933; Emer. Com. Strik. Rel. 1933; U.S. Cong. Ag. War; nat. exec. sec. Lg. Ag. Fascism.

HAPGOOD, WM. P.: nat. coun. L.I.D. for Indiana; pres. of Columbia Conserve Co. (Socialist); treas. and exec. com. Nat. R. & L. Found. 1933; Fell. Faiths speaker Chgo. 1933; Conf. Prog. Pol. Act. 1934; see article "Capitalism, Hewer and 'Chiseler' of American Greatness."

HARDMAN, J. B. S.: ed. "The Advance," organ of Amalg. Cloth. Wkrs.; U.S. Cong. Ag. War; contrib. Common Sense magazine; expelled from Communist Party, 1922 (Communist, Sept. 1933); edtl. bd. "Labor Action", organ of Conf. Prog. Lab. Act. 1933.

HARFIELD, ABE: org. Buffalo, N.Y. Dist. of Communist Party.

HARLOW, S. RALPH: Prof. Relig. Ethics, Smith Coll., since 1923; mem. John Reed Club; W.R. Lg.; Reconciliation Trips "cooperating educator"; lecturer for L.I.D.; nat. com. Nat. R. & L. Found. 1933; chmn. soc. serv. com. Congl. Ch. N.E. Region; mem. com. Fed. Coun. Chs.; Fell. Recon.; L.I.D.; World Peaceways.

HARPER, ALLAN G.: State sec. and organizer A.C.L.U. for Pa.; Harrisburg; defended Frank Borich (nat. sec. communist Nat. Miners Un.) against deportation, Feb. 1933.

HARPER, SOL: Negro Communist leader formerly of Chgo.; mem. Wkrs. Ex-Service Men's Lg. N.Y. City; active in communist Unemployed Hunger March, 1932; leader and speaker in Harlem Dist., N.Y. City.

HARRIMAN, MRS. J. BORDEN: advis. com. A.S.C.R.R.; For. Lang. Inf. Serv.; nat. com. Justice to China (Communist inspired); endorser "Professional Patriots"; Nat. Citiz. Com. on Rel. Lat. Am.; Am. Com. Fair Play to China (communistic); aided Sacco-V. agitation; now vice chmn. N.C. for P.W.; W.I.L.P.F.; chmn. bd. dir. Nat. Cons. Lg.; Nat. Sav. Our Schs. Com.; advocate of Russian recog. 1933.

HARRIS, ERDMAN: nat. com. Nat. R. & L. Found. 1933.

HARRIS, LEM: nat. sec. communist Farmers Nat. Com. for Action; U.S. Cong. Ag. War; nat. com. F.S.U. 1933; worked Rostov combine factory, Russia, 1930; grad. Harvard U.; contrib. Moscow News, 1930.

HARRISON, CHAS. YALE: Communist Party functionary; disciplined 1933; N.C. to A.S.M.F.S.; Intl. Un. Revol. Writers; perm. contrib. Intl. Lit.; Revol. Writers Fed.; John Reed Club.

HARRISON, THOS. Q.: assoc. sec. N.C. for P.W.; "Youth Movement" leader; field sec. youth section, Fell. Recon. 1927; at U. of Chgo. (Feb. 26, 1926), advocated "study to bring discredit and ridicule on the military and the fetish of the flag."; endors. Lane Pamphlet.

HART, HORNELL: nat. com. Nat. R. & L. Found.; Pres. Hoover's Com. on Social Trends, which made radical report; prof. Bryn Mawr Coll. since 1924; Peace Patriots.

HATHAWAY, CLARENCE ALBERT: former dist. org. Communist Party, Dist. No. 8 (Chgo.) and Dist No. 2 (New York); Farmers Nat. Com. of Action; chmn. Foster-Ford Camp. Com. 1932; ed. Daily Worker; nat. exec. bd. T.U.U.L.; U.S. Cong. Ag. War; Lg. Strugg. Negro Rts.; nat. com. F.S.U.; cent. com. of Communist Party.

HATTON, A. R.: Prof. Northwestern U., formerly Western Reserve U., Cleveland; Nat. Pop. Govt. Lg.; presided June, 1933, at joint A.C.L.U., L.I.D. meeting, Evanston, Ill.; dir. Util. Cons. and Inv. Lg. (Paul Douglas').

HAWKINS, ISAIAH: colored; miner; relief chairman, Pa., Ohio, W. Va., Ky. Miners Relief Com., 1931; Nat. Miners Un. organizer in Pa.; Communist.

HAYDON, A. EUSTACE: U. of Chgo. Prof.; A.C.L.U. Chgo. Com.; Chgo. com. Fell. Faiths; ed. bd. A. Lincoln Center "Unity"; endorser, together with all Communist organizations, of Janowicz, Communist cand. for Ald. 5th Ward, Chgo., Feb. 1933; endorser of Humanism; sponsor Chgo. Wkrs. Theatre, 1933; Non Partz. Com. Lillian Herstein; nat. coun. Berger Nat. Found.

HAYES, CARLTON J. H.: Columbia U. Prof.; nat. coun. C.M.E.; dir. For. Pol. Assn.; Am. Assn. Labor Legis.; exposed in Lusk Report as mem. Civil Liberties Bureau I.W.W. defense committee (advertising in "New Republic" 6/22/18 for financial aid for 110 arrested I.W.W.'s); at a meeting of the C.M.E., he is reported to have sneered at patriotic observances and at respect for Old Glory and the Liberty Bell, which he called the "religion of nationalism" and the "cult for worship of the flag," which caused publicity. Capt. George L. Darte at that time described Hayes as one who raises the red flag in time of peace, and the white flag in time of war (Welsh); wife signed Am. Wom. Com. for Recog. Russia petition 1933; Catholic Assn. for Intl. Peace, Com. on Nat. Attitudes.

HAYES, ELLEN: formerly Prof. Wellesley Coll.; Socialist cand. for Mass. Sec. of State, 1912; A.C.L.U. Mass. Com.; nat. com. Intl. Workers Aid 1928 (now W.I.R.); hon. vice pres. Freethinkers of America (atheist) 1928; A.A.A.I. Lg. conf. 1927; Recep. Com. Soviet Flyers; nat. com. I.L.D. 1928.

HAYES, MAX S.: exec. com. Nat. Coun. Prot. For. Born Wkrs. 1930; Labor Def. Coun. 1923; Intl. Wkrs. Aid 1926 (now W.I.R.); nat. com. W.I.R. 1928; was ed. "Cleveland Citizen"; nominee Farmer-Labor Party, 1920, for Vice Pres.; Intl. Typographical Union since 1884; A. F. of L. conventions delg. from Central Labor Council of Cleveland and his union for 30 yrs.; wired his endorsement of communist F.S.U. convention (of Jan. 26-7-8, 1934) and called upon all trade unionists to support the convention and send delegates (Daily Worker, 1/3/34); Nat. Com. to Aid Vic. G. Fascism, 1933; Nat. Mooney-Billings Com.; spkr. F.S.U. mass meeting, 12/17/33.

HAYNES, JOHN R.: vice pres. 1933, Pub. O. Lg.; Nat. Popl. Govt. Lg.

HAYS, ARTHUR GARFIELD: Jewish lawyer; a nat. dir. A.C.L.U.; counsel for nat. A.C.L.U.; dir. A.S.C.R.R.; Nat. Citiz. Com. on Rel. Lat. Am. 1927; nat. com. A.A.A.I. Lg. 1928; Nat. Mooney-Billings Com.; Nat. Coun. on Freedom from Censorship; Com. on Coal and Giant P.; Fed. Unemp. Wkrs. Lgs. N.Y. (Borders) 1933; contrib. to "The Nation"; Emer. Com. Strik. Rel. 1933; John Reed Club; Freethinkers Ingersoll Com. 1933; nat. coun. Berger Nat. Found.; Intl. Com. Pol. Pris. 1933; Russ. Reconst. Farms; Nat. Coun. Prot. For. Born Wkrs., exec. com.; Recep. Com. Soviet Flyers; was N.Y. state chmn. "Progressive" Party 1924.

HAYWOOD, HARRY: very active Negro Communist organizer; writer Intl. Pamphlets; exec. bd. Lg. Strugg. Negro Rights, 1933; contrib. Daily Worker.

HAYWOOD, WM. D. (BIG BILL): former I.W.W. leader; lecturer for Moscow's communist Intl. Red. Aid (European section of I.L.D.); convicted under Espionage Act 1918; released on bail pending trial for murder 1920; escaped to Russia; see Mrs. Raymond Robins; was head Am. Kuzbas Colony, Siberia; was assoc. ed. "Intl. Socialist Review"; died in Russia.

HAZLITT, HENRY: bd. eds. "The Nation"; edtl. com. L.I.D. (for 100 best Socialist books for libraries); contrib. "Common Sense."

HEALEY, TIMOTHY: Steamfitters Un.; exec. com. Nat. Coun. Prot. For. Born Wkrs. 1930; Recep. Com. Soviet Flyers.

HECKER, JULIUS F.: has lived in Moscow last 12 yrs.; "Communist-Recommended Author"; 1933 corres. of Nat. R. & L. Found.; "he is now employed in the Soviet Education Dept.; certainly not to teach religion" ("Militant Atheist," Sept. 1933); lectured before British affiliate of A.S.C.R.R. (July 1933 British-Russ. Gazette); author of books on Russia pub. by Vanguard Press.

HEIST, A. A.: nat. com. Meth. Fed. for Soc. Serv.; nat. com. Nat. R. & L. Found.; pastor Grace Community Ch., Denver, Colo.; church used as Communist-I.W.W. meeting place during coal strike, 1927-8; associated with Frank L. Palmer.

HELLER, A. A.: Communist; treas. Am. com. W.C.A.W.; treas. Am. Com. for S.A.W.; ed. "Soviet Russia Today"; contrib. ed. Daily Worker; Russ. Reconst. Farms, 1925.

HENDERSON, ARTHUR: British statesman; a leader of the (Marxian Socialist) Labour Party of Great Britain, since 1911, and of disarmament conferences; British Nat. Council for Prevention of War.

HENDERSON, DONALD: Communist; ousted 1933 as Prof. of Economics, Columbia U. (see Rex G. Tugwell); Am. com. W.C.A.W.; nat. sec. N.S. Lg. and contrib. ed. "Student Review"; exec. dir. Am. Com. for Strugg. Ag. War; U.S. Cong. Ag. War; Student Cong. Ag. War; sec. Am. Lg. Ag. War and Fascism, 1933; nat. com. F.S.U.; sec. Agricultural Workers Indust. Un.

HENDERSON, ELEANOR: wife of Donald; Communist cand. for Cong. N.Y. 1932; arrested Oct. 1932 in colored demonstration and sentenced to ten days in jail;

Lg. Strugg. Negro Rts.; Agricult. Wkrs. Indust. Un. functionary.

HENRY, EDWARD E.: sec. Seattle A.C. L.U. Com.

HENSHAW, ESTHER (MRS. H. R.): Emer. Com. Strik. Rel., Chgo.; advis. coun. C.W.C. on Unemp.

HENSON, FRANCIS A.: Yale Prof.; exec. sec. Nat. R. & L. Found. and editor of its bulletin, 1933; mem. state exec. com. and a State auditor of Socialist Party of Conn.; Am. Fed. of Tchrs.; cand. for bd. dir. L.I.D. 1933; delg. Cleveland Trade Un. Conf. (Communist) Aug. 26, 1933; nat. com. W.R. Lg.; Com. for Thomas, 1929; org. Brotherhood of Edison Employees (Conf. for Prog. Lab. Act. controlled); contrib. "World Tomorrow," and "Soviet Russia Today" (March 1933); Fellowship of Socialist Christians; signer of telegram to Wash., D.C. churches asking aid for Communist Hunger Marchers while in Washington; delg. to Nat. R. & L. Found. conf. at Hull House (see article "Jane Addams"); sympathetic observer, strike of communist Needle Tr. Wkrs. Ind. Un., Chgo., 1933; appointed as joint sec. with Donald Henderson (Communist) of communist Am. Lg. Ag. War and Fascism, Dec. 1933; Revol. Pol. Com. (See p. 337.)

HERBST, JOSEPHINE: Communist; "New Masses" staff, 1933; "Labor Defender"; Nat. Com. Def. Pol. Pris.; Emer. Com. So. Pol. Pris.; Intl. Un. Revol. Writers; perm. contrib. Intl. Lit.; Pris. Rel. Fund (I.L.D.); Revol. Writers Fed.; John Reed Club.

HERLING, JOHN: publications sec. L.I. D.; circ. mgr. "Unemployed" (an L.I.D. organ); Fed. Press corres.; exec. sec. Emer. Com. Strik. Rel. N.W.F.S. Text. Strikers; Com. for Thomas 1929; advis. bd. "Revolt" (L.I.D. organ); Emer. Com. Strik. Rel. 1933, exec. sec.; U.S. Cong. Ag. War com.

HERMAN, JULIUS: Nat. Com. Def. Pol. Pris.

HERMAN, SAM: Y.C. Lg. org. in Kenosha, Wis. strike, 1928; mem. Chgo. br. A.A. A.I. Lg. 1928; Communist Party functionary.

HERMANN, JOHN: Communist Lg. P. G. for F. & F.; contrib. ed. "Left," a Communist magazine, 1931; Revol. Writers Fed.; Nat. Com. Def. Pol. Pris. com., holding hearings for farmers woes on evictions (Aug. 2, 1933 Daily Wkr.); with Hunger Marchers, Dec. 1932; John Reed Club.

HERRING, REV. HUBERT C.: minister; grad. Union Theol. Sem.; nat. com. A.C.L.U.; bd. dir. L.I.D.; exec. sec. Congl. Dept. of Social Relations since 1924; Nat. Citiz. Com. for Sacco and V. 1927; dir. Seminar on Relations with Mexico, which held sessions in Mexico City 1926-7-8-9; dir. Com. on Cult. Rel. with Lat. Am. since 1928; mem. coun. Jt. Com. on Unemp. (Dewey); Com. for Thomas 1929; exec. com. Nat. R. & L. Found. 1933; Socialist; Ch. Emer. Com. Rel. Tex. Strik.; brother of John W.

HERRING, REV. JOHN W.: Congl. minister; exec. sec. L.I.P.A.; dir. midwest and nat. coun. C.M.E.; Fed. Coun. Chs. and exec. sec. of its Com. on Good-will bet. Jews and Christians 1924-8; org. of metropolitan councils of Adult Edu. since 1924; Conf. Prog. Pol. Act. 1934; contrib. to A. Lincoln Center "Unity," "B'nai B'rith News," and "Christian Century"; brother of Hubert C.

HERRIOT, M. EDOUARD: of France; gave pro-Soviet report on Russia, 1933; Freethinkers Ingersoll Com. 1933; mem. radical Socialist cabinet.

HERSKOVITS, MELVILLE J.: Prof. Anthropology Northwestern U.; John Reed Club spkr.; backer of Proletarian Arts Ball of I.L.D.; spkr. John Reed Club banquet for Henri Barbusse, Oct. 21, 1933, at Chgo. Womans Club, with Jane Addams and Communists Bill Gebert, Herbert Newton, etc.

HERSTEIN, LILLIAN: A.C.L.U. Chgo. Com.; sponsor Berger Nat. Found. dinner, 1931; teacher Crane Jr. Coll.; Farmer-Labor Cand. 1932; Socialist; sec.-treas. Am. Com. on Inf. about Russia; Am. Fed. of Teachers; nat. com. A.A.A.I. Lg. 1928; Chgo. Emer. Com. Strik. Rel.; vice pres. Chgo. L.I.D.; exec. com. Chgo. A.S.C.R.R.; teacher of Workers Training School, 1933; exec. bd. Chgo. Fed. of Labor.

HIBBEN, PAXTON: deceased; Emer. Com. Strik. Rel.; Nat. Com. Prot. For. Born Wkrs. 1927; Lab. Def. Coun. 1923; A.A.A.I. Lg. nat. com. 1928; bd. dir. L.I.D. 1927; conducted Am. drive for Russian Red Cross (of Soviet Govt.) funds; Friends Soviet Russia; his photo decorating grave of John Reed appears in Whitney's "Reds in America"; Paxton Hibben Mem. Hosp. Fund Com. formed in his honor after ashes taken to Russia for burial by Communists.

HIBBEN, SHEILA: Emer. Com. So. Pol. Pris.; signer of letter to Rockefeller protesting against dismissal of Communist Diego Rivera.

HICKERSON, HAROLD: nat. com. W. C.A.W.; N.C. to A.S.M.F.S.; nat. com. W. I.R. 1929; U.S. Cong. Ag. War; Communist; executive of Wkrs. Ex-Service Men's Lg.; John Reed Club; N.Y.; Revol. Writers Fed.; A.A.A.I. Lg. protest delg. Wash. ("Upsurge," Sept. 1933).

HICKS, GRANVILLE: Communist; Prof. Rensselaer Poly. Inst., Troy, N.Y.; Communist Lg. P. G. for F. & F.; author "How I came to Communism" (New Masses, Sept. 1932); contrib. "Soviet Russia Today"; Nat. Com. to Aid Vic. G. Fascism; chmn. open hearings on farming evictions at Hilltown, Pa. of Nat. Com. Def. Pol. Pris., Aug. 1933; book reviewer, Daily Worker; nat. com. F.S.U., 1933; "New Masses" staff, 1933.

HIGH, STANLEY: grad. in theology; mem. M.E. Mission to China 1919-20; Russ. Reconst. Farms, 1925; Youth Movement Leader; Fed. Coun. Chs.; For. Pol. Assn.; C.M.E.; co-worker with Brent Dow Allinson; author of the slogan "Go to Leavenworth rather than fight," and yet fought in World War as 2nd Lieut. in aviation corps; said, "I am not so sure but that the atheism in Russia is a step in the right direction. . . . We have lost faith in the church that is servile to the Government." (N.D. City Journal, Oct. 17, 1924); proponent of intermixing of races; referred to Fell. Recon. (youth branch) and Pioneer Youth of Am. as centers of Youth Movement; endorser Lane Pamphlet; former editor of Christian Herald; contrib. "World Tomorrow"; bd. dir. and exec. com. World Peaceways, 1933.

HILLMAN, SIDNEY: dir. Garland Fund 1922-3; was on Def. Com. of I.W.W.; pres. Amalg. Cloth, Wkrs. of Am. from org. 1914; pres. and org. Russian-Am. Indust. Corp. from 1922 on; chmn. bd. Amalg. Bank of New York; dir. Amalg. Tr. & Sav. Bank, Chgo. since 1922; Lg. Mutual Aid; author "Reconstruction of Russia and the Task of Labor"; hon. pres. Nat. R. & L. Found. 1933; Lithuanian Jew; mem. coun. Jt. Com. on Unemp.; builder cooperative houses, N.Y.C.; Berger Nat. Found.; Conf. Prog. Pol. Act. campaign com. 1934; Roosevelt appointee to Labor Advis. Bd. of N.R. A. 1933.

HILLQUIT, MORRIS: real name Misca Hilkowicz; born Russia; Socialist leader; from 1904 intl. bureau Socialist Party (see "Socialist Party" for his speech on split bet. Socialists and Communists); was atty. for Alex. Berkman, anarchist; anti-Govt. "peace" worker during War; organizer of infamous People's Council and Am. Lg. to Limit Armaments; Emer. Peace Fed.; head of legal dept., Soviet Bureau in U.S., 1919; nat. com. A.C.L.U.; nat. coun. L.I.D. for N.Y.; Nat. Mooney-Billings Com.; Fell. Recon.; nat. com. World Ct. Com.; Non-Intervention Citiz. Com. 1927; Nat. Citiz. Com. on Rel. Lat. Am. 1927; nat. com. Conf. Prog. Pol. Act. 1922-25; Berger Nat. Found. 1931; lecturer Rand Sch.; chmn. nat. exec. com. of Socialist Party since 1900; Fed. Unemp. Wkrs. Lgs. N.Y.C., 1933; died Oct. 1933; Pres. Roosevelt sent condolences.

HILLS, R. O.: com. Chr. Soc. Act. M.; Casper, Wyo.

HILLYER, MARY W.: lecturer L.I.D.; assoc. ed. of "Revolt" of L.I.D.; see p. 337.

HINDUS, MAURICE: author whose Soviet propaganda books about Russia are recommended by official Soviet agencies; he is allowed to re-visit Russia each year; his book "Broken Earth" ran serially in the communist Daily Worker; he dedicated his "Red Bread" to Glenn Frank, U. of Wis. pres.

HOAN, DANIEL: Mayor of Milwaukee; nat. exec. com. Socialist Party; nat. chmn. Lg. Against Fascism; Berger Nat. Found.

HOLCOMBE, ARTHUR N.: head dept. govt. Harvard U.; Lg. for Org. Progress, 1931; Nat. Pop. Govt. Lg.; endors. "Professional Patriots"; signer, Fell. Recon. Pet. Russ. Recog. 1932.

HOLLY, WM. H.: lawyer; former law partner of Wiley W. Mills and Clarence Darrow; vice pres. A.C.L.U. Chgo. Com.; chmn. communist A.A.A.I. Lg. 1928; Am. Com. on Inf. about Russia; Chgo. Fell. Faiths; Chgo. Forum Coun. 1928; chmn. exec. com. Pub. Ownership Lg. of Am.; mem. coun. Northwestern U. Settlement; dir. City Club, Chgo.; atty. for Nat. Wom. Tr. Un. Lg. and Am. Fed. of Teachers; co-author (with Communist Harry Gannes) of pamphlet on Criminal Syndicalism; dir. Single Tax Lg. 1933; Chgo. Emer. Com. Strik. Rel.; sponsor Berger Nat. Found. dinner, 1931; apptd. Federal Dist. Judge by Pres. Roosevelt Dec. 1933; was permanent chmn. Hands Off China Com. Chgo. (communist Daily Wkr. 6/16/27); Labor Defender, communist I.L. D. organ (Oct. 1926, p. 184), listed under "cash receipts for August 1926" the following: "13920 William H. Holly, Chicago, Ill., $10.00."; A.S.C.R.R. Com. 1934.

HOLMES, JESSE H.: Prof. Hist. of Relig. and Phil., Swarthmore Coll. since 1900; bd. dir. L.I.D.; Russ. Reconst. Farms, 1925; exec. com. L.I.P.A.; Socialist cand. Pa. 1932; Pa. Com. Total Disarm.; active wkr. Society of Friends, especially in Sun. sch. work; commr. for Am. Friends relief work in Europe, 1920; edtl. contrib. A. Lincoln Center "Unity," 1933; Peace Patriots; Nat. Save Our Schs. Com.; speaker Fell. Faiths, 1933; vice chmn. A.C.L.U. Pa. branch; Conf. Prog. Pol. Act. 1934.

HOLMES, JOHN HAYNES: nat. bd. dir. A.C.L.U. and acting chmn. during Ward's absence, 1932; former Unitarian minister, became "independent" in 1919; pastor of Ch. of the Messiah, New York, since 1907 (now called The Community Church); Lusk report says he "changed the name of his so-called church from Church of the Messiah to Community Church as an outward mark of his change of heart from Christianity to Communism"; dir. Am. Un. Against Militarism 1917-9; vice pres. N.A.A.C.P.; nat. coun. Pioneer Youth of Am.; contrib. ed. "World Tomorrow," N.Y., and ed. "Unity," A. Lincoln Center, Chgo. (Lusk report says of Holmes and others: "an insidious anti-religious campaign is being carried on by these men and their colleagues in such reviews as the 'World Tomorrow' (N.Y.) and 'Unity' (Chgo.)"); endorser of atheist Jos. Lewis pamphlet "Atheism" (see Freethought Press); Fell. Recon.; Am. Lg. to Limit Arm.; Emer. Peace Fed.; Emer. Com. Strik. Rel.; Recep. Com. Soviet Flyers; vice chmn. Jt. Com. on Unemp.; Labor Def. Coun. 1923 (now I.L.D.), defending Communists arrested at Bridgman, Mich.; Nat. World Ct. Com.; exec. com. Nat. Sacco-V. Lg.; chmn. exec. com. W.R. Lg.; his church a meeting place for Communist N.S. Lg. and I.L.D.; sister sec. of Boston W.I.L.P.F.; Griffin Bill sponsor; Il Nuovo Mondo Nat. Com.; Lg. for Org. Prog.; Fed. Unemp. Wkrs. Lgs. N.Y. (Borders) 1933; Non-Intervention Citiz. Com. 1927; Nat. R. & L. Found. exec. com. 1933; Teachers' Union; lecturer Rand Sch.; contrib. ed. "Labor Age"; an officer of communistic Commonwealth Coll.; nat. vice pres. L.I.D.; Freethinkers Ingersoll Com. 1933; Russ Reconst. Farms, 1925; nat. coun. Berger Nat. Found.; vice pres. with Jane Addams, Mrs. F. D. Roosevelt, etc., of Nat. Cons. Lg., 1931; Cong. Exp. Radicals; Intl. Com. Pol. Pris. 1933; nat. com. F.S.U. 1934.

HOLT, ARTHUR E.: Congl. minister; now Prof. of Social Ethics, Chgo. Theol. Sem. and U. of Chgo. Div. Sch.; nat. sec. of soc. edu. Congl. Chs.; Y.M.C.A. and Y.W.C.A. consultant on foreign work 1929-30; nat. com. Nat. R. & L. Found. 1933; People's Legis. Serv.; advis. com. C.W.C. on Unemp. (Borders); Non-Partz. Com. Lillian Herstein 1932; chmn. milk com. of City Club and agitator among farmers preceding the Jan. 1934 Chgo. milk strike.

HOLT, HAMILTON: pres. Rollins Coll.; Open Road, 1933; pacifist; toured U.S. speaking for Lg. to Enforce Peace.

HOOK, SIDNEY: Prof. N.Y.U.; Communist Lg. P. G. for F. & F. 1932; nat. com. W.C.A.W.; speaker at N.S. Lg. Conf. at Community Church (John Haynes Holmes') N.Y. 1932; N.C. to A.S.M.F.S.; contrib. "New Masses"; instr. New Sch. for Social Research; Prog. Edu. Assn. and an author of its revolutionary manifesto; Am. Com. for S.A.W.

HOOPES, DARLINGTON: Socialist Party nat. exec. com.; nat. com. W.R. Lg. 1931; vice chmn. Pa. Com. Total Disarm.; home Reading, Pa.; nat. com. Lg. Against Fascism 1933; mem. Penn. State Legis.

HOPE, JOHN: Pres. Atlanta U.; nat. com. Nat. R. & L. Found. 1933; signer Fell. Recon. Pet. Russ. Recog. 1932.

HOPKINS, J. A. H.: Cong. Exp. Radicals; Russ. Reconst. Farms. 1925; Emer. Com. Strik. Rel. 1933; mem. com. of arrangements Nat. Farmer-Labor Party convention.

HORTON, WALTER M.: Union Theol. Sem. grad. and former prof.; L.I.P.A.; Prof. Theol., Oberlin Grad. Sch. of Theol., since 1926; nat. com. Nat. R. & L. Found. 1933; Oberlin, O.

HOSIE, LAWRENCE T.: nat. com. Nat. R. & L. Found.

HOUGH, LYNN HAROLD: pres. Northwestern U., 1919-20; prof. Drew Theol. Sem. since 1930; contrib. ed. "Christian Century"; nat. com. Nat. R. & L. Found. 1933; endors. World Peaceways; attacked military training in letter of Detroit Coun. of Churches, Jan. 1927; March 1928, suggested D.A.R. be called Daughters of the Ku Klux Klan.

HOWARD, MILTON: Communist writer Intl. Pamphlets; book reviewer for "The Communist"; Revol. Writers Fed.; contrib. to Daily Worker, Labor Unity.

HOWARD, SIDNEY: Communist; A.S. C.R.R.; Nat. Coun. on Freedom from Censorship; Communist Lg. P. G. for F. & F.; pres. communist Film Forum, N.Y. City; Pulitzer Prize, 1925; spends much time in Hollywood, Cal.; A.C.L.U.

HOWAT, ALEX: A.A.A.I. Lg. nat. com. 1928; Il Nuovo Mondo Nat. Com.; former officer United Mine Wkrs. Un. in Kansas.

HOWE, FREDERIC C.: lawyer; formerly Prof. of Law; nat. com. A.C.L.U.; nat. coun. L.I.D. for N.Y.; Conf. Prog. Pol. Act.; former corres. Fed. Press; People's Legis. Serv.; Def. Com. I.W.W.; bd. dir. Cooperative Lg. of Am.; Socialist; communist sympathizer; was Commr. of

Immigration, Port of N.Y., under Pres. Wilson and resigned following Cong. investigation because of his "unauthorized release of alien radicals held for deportation" (Record 66th Cong. pp. 1522-3); Freethinkers Ingersoll Com.; wife in Jane Addams' Women's Peace Party; Cong. Exp. Radicals; Single Tax Lg. 1896-1925; La Follette supporter; nat. coun. Berger Nat. Found.; Roosevelt appointee as chmn. Consumers' Bd. of AAA.

HOWE, QUINCY: nat. bd. dir. A.C.L.U. 1933.

HOWELL, CLARENCE V.: minister; co-dir. with Ida Oatley Howell of Fell. Recon. Trips, N.Y.; Emer. Com. Strik. Rel.; Com. for Thomas 1929; dir. Harlem Forums, N.Y.; announced he was supporting Communist campaign 1932 (Christian Century, Sept. 21, 1932), saying "I plan to vote Communist"; nat. com. W.R. Lg.

HUDSON, MANLY O.: Prof. Harvard Law Sch.; nat. coun. C.M.E. 1930; Garland Fund Com. on Am. Imperialism; trustee World Peace Found.; Lg. of Nations propagandist.

HUDSON, ROY: Communist; nat. sec. communist Marine Wkrs. Indust. Un. 1933; U.S. Cong. Ag. War; contrib. ed. "Soviet Russia Today"; communist Cleveland Tr. Un. Conf., Aug. 1933; nat. com. F.S.U. 1933.

HUEBSCH, B. W.: bd. dir. and treas. nat. A.C.L.U.; mem. Ford Peace Party; Socialist; Am. Neut. Conf. Com.; Nat. Coun. on Freedom from Censorship; treas. Sacco-V. Nat. Lg.; Com. for Thomas 1929; ed. "Freeman"; Cong. Exp. Radicals.

HUGHAN, JESSIE WALLACE: Socialist; formerly Eng. teacher N.Y.C. high schs.; head of coop. annex, Textile High Sch., N.Y.C. since 1928; teacher of econ., Rand Sch. 1910-21; frequent Socialist cand. for major office; bd. dir. L.I.D. since 1909; sec. W.R. Lg. since foundation; exec. com. Fell. Recon. 1923; vice chmn. Women's Peace Soc.; W.R. Intl.; author of books on Socialism; Com. for Thomas 1929.

HUGHES, HATCHER: asst. prof. English, U. of N. C. since 1922; address: Men's Faculty Club, Columbia U.; chmn. Nat. Coun. on Freedom from Censorship of A.C.L.U.

HUGHES, LANGSTON: Negro Communist author; Communist Lg. P. G. for F. & F. 1932; mem. Negro Delg. to Russia to study Communism 1932; Nat. Com. Def. Pol. Pris.; Scottsboro Unity Def. Com.; staff "New Masses"; sponsor San Francisco Wkrs. Sch. 1933; Intl. Un. Revol. Writers; perm. contrib. Intl. Lit.; Revol. Writers Fed.; Wkrs. Cultural Fed. (communist); lectured at U. of N.C. 1932; deported from Japan, 1933; Lg. Strugg. Negro Rts.; nat. com. F.S.U. 1934.

HUISWOOD, OTTO: Communist Negro leader; contrib. to "The Communist"; chmn. Negro Tr. Un. Com. of the R.I.L.U.

HULL, MRS. HANNA CLOTHIER: vice chmn. L.I.P.A.; chmn. nat. bd. W.I.L.P.F., 1933; nat. coun. C.M.E.; Emer. Peace Fed.; war time "peace" worker; endorser Lane Pamphlet; Conf. Prog. Pol. Act. camp. com. 1934.

HULL, WM. I.: prof. Swarthmore Coll. since 1904; Rand School; Cong. Exp. Radicals; trustee Church Peace Union; wife is Hannah Clothier Hull; spkr. at Oct. 1933 jt. Fell. Recon. and W.I.L.P.F., Swarthmore conference; chmn. Pa. Com. Total Disarm.

HUME, REV. THEODORE C.: pastor of New Eng. Congl. Ch., Chgo., which is meeting place for C.W.C. on Unemp. (Borders); speaker at radical meeting in church Oct. 21, 1932; radical Forum conducted in church 1932; Communist took charge of "Hunger March" meeting held in church Oct. 20, 1932; studied at Union Theol. Sem.; for three years a student at Oxford U.; led debate in behalf of pacifists at meeting of Northwestern U. Chapter of L.I.D., held on campus Mar. 23, 1933, at which students by vote of 68 to 17 adopted slacker resolution declaring that they would not "under any circumstances take part in international war to defend the Constitution of the United States." (Chgo. Herald-Examiner, Mar. 24, 1933).

HUNT, HENRY T.: an ex-mayor of Cincinnati, active in Red Passaic strike; Nat. Coun. Prot. For. Born Wkrs. since 1927; nat. sec. Nat. Mooney-Billings Com. of A.C.L.U.; Pris. Relief Fund of I.L.D. 1932; Sacco-V. Nat. Lg. 1928; treas. People's Lobby, 1933; endors. "Professional Patriots"; Recep. Com. Soviet Flyers; Emer. Peace Fed.; Fell. Recon.; Jt. Com. on Unemp.; Roosevelt appointee as Gen. Counsel Fed. Emer. Admin. Public Wks. 1933.

HUNTER. ALLAN A.: pastor Mt. Hollywood Community Ch., Los A., Cal. since 1926; nat. com. Nat. R. & L. Found. 1933; one of com. of seven calling on Mayor of Los A. to protest against attacks on Communists (Daily Wkr., Oct. 13, 1931).

HUNTON, MRS. ADDIE WAITE: hon. pres. Intl. Coun. of Women of Darker Races; com. U.S. Cong. Ag. War; nat.

chmn. Inter-Racial com. W.I.L.P.F.; Brooklyn, N.Y.

HURST, FANNIE: author; Freethinkers Ingersoll Com. 1933; Griffin Bill sponsor; M.W.D. Def. Com.; Nat. Coun. Freedom from Censorship of A.C.L.U.; Nat. Mooney-Billings Com.; supporter Rand Sch., 1933; nat. coun. Berger Nat. Found.; W.I.L.P.F.; artists' and writers' Com. for Thomas, 1929; Conf. Prog. Pol. Act. campaign com. 1934; advis. coun. for Independent Com. for Recog. Russ., March, 1933; Communist Ella Winter signs herself as "sec. to Fanny Hurst" in Jewish "Sentinel," Dec. 28, 1933.

HUTCHINS, GRACE: Communist; writer for Intl. Pamphlets; mem. coun. and exec. com. Fell. Recon. from 1921; sec. Fellowship Press from 1924; Pris. Rel. Fund (I.L.D.); staff Labor Research Assn.; Recep. Com. Soviet Flyers; N.C. to A.S.M. F.S.; contrib. ed. "Labor Defender" and "New Pioneer"; teacher in Wuchang, China, 1912-6; Nat. Com. Def. of Pol. Pris. 1932; John Reed Club.

HUTCHINS, ROBT. MAYNARD: see "Roosevelt Appointees"; pres. U. of Chgo.; teacher of course including Marxism and Leninism, and defender of Communism as a recognized U. of Chgo. student activity, on the ground that the Party is allowed on the ballot; opponent of Baker anti-sedition Bills at Springfield, 1933; endorser of Roosevelt's "Brain Trust" of radicals; spkr. with Norman Thomas and Mordecai Ezekiel, Oct. 30, 1933, at radical Hirsch Center Forum; signer of testimonial to Einstein (Standard Club, Chgo., March 1933); N.A.A.C.P. Chgo.; vice chmn. Nat. Coun. on Radio in Education; signed published appeal for Sacco-V.; Com. on Cultural Rel. Lat. Am. A Chgo. Daily News headline (3/17/34) said, "Hutchins Put on Moscow Board," referring to his appointment to the National Advisory Council of the Anglo-American Institute, "which will operate a school at Moscow University this summer."

HUTCHINSON, PAUL: minister; grad. Garrett Biblical Inst.; mg. ed. radical "Christian Century" since 1924; A.C.L.U. Chgo. Com.; pres. Chgo. Chapter and nat. coun. L.I.D.; Chr. Soc. Act. M. 1932 exec. com.; author "World Revolution and Religion" 1931, published by official Methodist Abingdon Press; advis. com. C.W.C. on Unemp. (Borders) 1932; was treas. Chgo. "Hands Off China" Com. of the A.A.A.I. Lg. 1927; nat. com. Nat. R. & L. Found. 1933; Chgo. Emer. Com. Strik. Rel.; endors. "Professional Patriots"; sponsor Berger Nat. Found. dinner, 1931; home Winnetka, Ill.

HYDE, MAXWELL: endors. Communist platform and candidates (Daily Wkr., Sept. 14, 1932); Nat. Com. Def. Pol. Pris.; Nat. Com. to Aid Vic. G. Fascism.

HYMAN, LOUIS: Communist Party central com.; chmn. Needle Tr. Wkrs. Indust. Un.; Nat. Mooney Coun. Act.; delg. to Russia, 1932; mem. bd. of I.C.O.R.

I

ICKES, HAROLD L.: radical Republican; now socialistic Democrat; Pres. Roosevelt's Secy. of Int.; dir. Util. Cons. and Inv. Lg.; Pub. O. Lg. of Am.; A.C.L.U. supporter; Chgo. Forum Council (pres. 1926-7); spkr. Chgo. Feb. 24, 1934, under Ill. Lg. Wom. Voters auspices, attacking "individualism" and upholding socialistic "New Deal" policies; wife Repub. mem. Ill. Legis.; home Winnetka, Ill.

INMAN, SAMUEL GUY: Nat. Citiz. Com. Rel. Lat. Am. 1927; Non-Intervention Citiz. Com. 1927; Garland Fund Com. on Am. Imperialism; contrib. ed. "World Tomorrow."

IRWIN, JOHN C.: exec. com. Chr. Soc. Act. M.; Meth. Ch. hdqts., Chgo.

IRWIN, WILL: vice chmn. N.C. for P. W.; Nat. Citiz. Com. on Rel. Lat. Am. 1927; wife Inez Haynes Irwin on Nat. Mooney-Billings Com.

ISE, JOHN: U. of Kans.; nat. coun. L.I.D. for Kansas; writer L.I.D. pamphlets.

ISRAEL, EDW. L.: Rabbi; nat. coun. L.I.D. for Maryland; exec. bd. N.C. for P.W.; exec. com. and book editor Nat. R. & L. Found. 1933-4; mem. coun. Jt. Com. on Unemp.; chmn. Social Service Commission of Central Conference of Rabbis and ed. of its Bulletin; Nat. Citiz. Com. Rel. Lat. Am. 1927; nat. com. Lg. Against Fascism, 1933; People's Lobby coun.; contrib. ed. "World Tomorrow"; nat. com. W.R. Lg.; nat. coun. Berger Nat. Found.; A.A. for O.A.S.; L.I.P.A.; Conf. Prog. Pol. Act. camp. com. 1934.

J

JACKSON, A. L.: A.C.L.U. Chgo. Com.

JANOWICZ, VLADIMIR R.: Communist; advis. com. Chgo. Wkrs. School, 1932 (for teaching revolution); harangued Melrose Park rioters 1932; Communist cand. Ald. 5th Ward, Chgo., 1933 and endorsed by Robt. Morss Lovett, A. Eustace Haydon, Martin Sprengling, and F. L. Schuman, all U. of Chgo. professors, and by all Chgo. Communist organizations; org. sec. T.U. U.L. 1933.

JAQUES, AGNES I.: A.S.C.R.R. Chgo. branch exec. com.; leader Intourist tour U.S.S.R. 1933.

JEFFREY, CECELIA I.: nat. com. Nat. R. & L. Found.

JENKINS, CLYDE (ALIAS WADE D. ROGERS): exec. sec. communist Office Wkrs. Un., Chgo.; arrested 1933-4.

JENKINS, NEWTON: lawyer; Chgo.; a LaFollette "Progressive Republican" (socialistic); given chief credit for Pres. Roosevelt's appointment of Wm. H. Holly to Federal Bench; sponsor of 1931 dinner of Berger Nat. Found.; editor "Broadcaster," official organ "Progressive Republican" Movement of U.S.A. printed at Marissa, Ill. (by the same presses that print the "Progressive Miner," organ of the radical Progressive Miners Union); closely allied with Secy. Ickes; sponsoring complete Cook County ticket, April 1934 primary, including Annetta Dieckmann and Wiley W. Mills (see "Who's Who").

JENNISON, FLORENCE: exec. com. L. I.D.; advis. com. C.W.C. on Unemp.

JENSON, PETER: chmn. System Fed. 130; Com. on Inf. about Russia; A.A.A.I. Lg. Chgo.; pres. Machinist Lodge 492 of A. F. of L.

JESMER, S.: treas. A.S.C.R.R., Chgo.; vice pres. Amalg. T. & S. Bank, Chgo.

JOHANSSEN, ANTON: bus. agt. Chgo. Carpenters Dist. Coun.; gen. org. Amalg. Cloth. Wkrs. of Am. 1919-22; canvassed U.S. in defense of dynamiters McNamara and Tom Mooney, and others; contrib. to "Workers' Voice" (Chgo. Communist paper); sold I.L.D. coupons to aid Communists arrested in Chgo. for seditious activities; born Germany.

JOHNS, ORRICK: Communist Lg. P. G. for F. & F.; author poem, "They are Ours," New Masses, Dec. 1932; tchr. Current Literature, Wkrs. School (Western Wkr. Jan. 2, 1933); spkr. at Stockton, Cal. meeting for repeal of criminal syndicalism law.

JOHNSON, ARNOLD: divinity student at Union Theol. Sem. N.Y.C.; arrested and jailed, while representing the A.C.L.U., with Jessie Wakefield of the Communist I.L.D., on criminal syndicalism charges at Harlan, Ky., 1932; corres. Fed. Press; now on staff of Nat. R. & L. Found., "organizing the unemployed into Unemployed Citizens Leagues and for the purpose of making hunger marches. . . . He is now working in Ohio." (from "Economic Justice," official bulletin of Nat. R. & L. Found., Feb. 1933); speaker at L.I.D. conference; delg. Cleveland Tr. Un. Conf. (communist) 1933.

JOHNSON, EDWIN C.: exec. com. W.R. Lg.; sec. C.M.E.; signer call for World Cong. Youth Ag. War and Fascism; an organizer of a special committee for defense of expelled radicals at City Coll. of N.Y.

JOHNSON, JAMES WELDON: colored; nat. com. A.C.L.U.; sec. N.A.A.C.P.; dir. Garland Fund; L.I.P.A.; C.M.E., nat. coun.; advisor Pioneer Youth of America; endors. Lane Pamphlet; home N.Y.

JOHNSON, MERCER G.: nat. coun. L.I.D. for Wash., D.C.; Griffin Bill sponsor; Nat. Save Our Schs. Com.

JOHNSON, OAKLEY: Prof. City Coll. of N.Y. dismissed recently; sec. Am. Com. for S.A.W.; exec. sec. John Reed Club (Communist); sec. Am. com. W.C.A.W.; Recep. Com. Soviet Flyers; Pris. Rel. Fund (I.L.D.); with "Hunger Marchers," Wash., 1932; supporter N.S. Lg.

JOHNSTON, WM. H.: Socialist; pres. Intl. Assn. Machinists since 1911; lecturer Rand Sch.; nat. coun. L.I.D.; sec.-treas. People's Legis. Serv.; exec. com. A.C.L.U.; chmn. orig. Conf. Prog. Pol. Act.; accused of saying he "sees great advantages in the establishment of a Soviet Govt. in the U.S." (Whitney's "Reds in America").

JOHNSTONE, JACK: Communist Party Dist. No. 5 org. and mem. Party cent. com.; Pittsburg; Nat. Mooney Coun. of Action, 1933.

JONES, PAUL: Student pastor, Antioch Coll.; nat. coun. L.I.D. for Ohio; sec. Fell. Recon. from 1920 on; chmn. Recon. Trips from 1923 on; resigned under pressure as Prot. Episc. Bishop of Utah, 1918, because of radical pacifism; contrib. ed. "World Tomorrow"; org. infamous People's Coun.; Peace Patriots; Emer. Peace Fed.; Socialist; Communist sympathizer; was first pres. of the Church Socialist Lg. (1911) and the field sec. of the Lg.; active in conf. of A.A.A.I. Lg. (Daily Worker, Dec. 14, 1926); Nat. Citiz. Com. for Sacco and V. 1927; spoke at Communist Sacco-V. meeting and used language inciting to violence (N.Y. Times, April 17, 1927); signed Sacco-V. telegram to Pres. (Boston Post, Aug. 21, 1927); Hands Off China Com. 1927; Non Intervention Citiz. Com. 1927; aided I.W. W.'s in efforts to raise funds for striking Colo. miners 1927-28; has spoken frequently at Communist meetings; Emer. Com. Strik. Rel. 1933; nat. com. Nat. R. & L. Found. 1933; Recep. Com. Soviet Flyers; nat. coun. Berger Nat. Found.; Peace Patriots; nat. com. W.R. Lg.; seat in Episc. Hse. of Bishops reported restored (Chgo. Daily News, 3/3/34).

JONES, WILLIAM N.: Communist Lg. P. G. for F. & F.; Negro; mg. ed. "Baltimore Afro-American"; chmn. Baltimore Scottsboro Action Com.; nat. com. F.S.U. 1933.

JOSEPHSON, MATTHEW: Communist Lg. P. G. for F. & F. 1932; speaker for Foster-Ford Independent Com., 1932 Communist campaign.

JURICH, JOE: sub-organizer communist T.U.U.L.; Chgo. organizer Steel and Metal Wkrs. Indust. Un.

K

KAHN, LEON: treas. N.C. to A.S.M.F. S.; Nat. Com. Def. Pol. Pris.

KAHN, YERETH: Nat. Com. Def. Pol. Pris.

KALAR, JOS.: communist Intl. Un. Revol. Writers; perm. contrib. Intl. Lit.; New Masses; Revol. Writers Fed.; contrib. ed. communist "Left" magazine of Davenport, Iowa; assoc. ed. "Anvil," communist magazine; contrib. ed. "Left Front," Chgo. John Reed Club publication, 1933.

KALININ, MICHAEL IVANOVITCH: Pres. of U.S.S.R. since 1923.

KALLEN, HORACE M.: A.S.C.R.R. book com.; Recep. Com. Soviet Flyers; N.C. to A.S.M.F.S.; active in behalf Sacco and V.; New Sch. Social Research; contrib. "New Masses"; endorser "Letters Sacco and Vanzetti."

KAMMAN, MORRIS: Am. com. W.C. A.W.; edu. dir. I.L.D. N.Y. Dist. No. 2; Communist.

KANE, FRANCIS FISHER: active in A.C.L.U.; Labor Def. Coun. (I.L.D.), 1923; exec. com. Nat. Com. Prot. For. Born Wkrs.; Sacco-V. Nat. Lg.; defended Communist May Day rioters, Phila. 1932; his sister, Mrs. Walter Cope (Eliza Middleton), contrib. to Communist causes and active in W.I.L.P.F.; Nat. Pop. Govt. Lg. charges against Dept. of Justice; Nat. Save Our Schs. Com.; Nat. Com. to Aid Vic. G. Fascism.

KANTER, FRANK: mem. Chgo. exec. com. F.S.U., org. of Douglas Pk. branch.

KAPLAN, MORDECAI: Rabbi; Am. com. W.C.A.W.

KAPLAN, NAT: Communist Party dist. org. of Dist. No. 1, Boston, 1931; nat. org. Nat. Textile Wkrs. Un. (communist) 1933

KARAPETOFF, VLADIMIR: Socialist; Prof. Cornell U.; vice pres. L.I.D. since 1924; Com. for Thomas 1928; born Leningrad, Russia; author of many articles on Socialism; nat. coun. Berger Nat. Found.; apptd. Lieut. Commander U.S. Naval Reserve 1933, under Roosevelt admin.

KAROLYI, COUNT MICHAEL: Hungarian communist sympathizer; intl. com. W.C.A.W.; when Pres. Hungarian Republic, turned over govt. to Lenin's Communist leader, Bela Kun (Cohen), Mar. 20, 1919; 132 days of Red Terror, confiscation and torture and murder of bourgeoise, nuns, etc., followed; mem. Anti-Horthy Lg.; Nat. Com. to Aid Vic G. Fascism 1933.

KATAYAMA, J. SEN: Japanese Communist; exec. com. Communist Intl.; repres. of Communist Parties in the East; founder of Japanese Socialist Assn. 1897; founder of weekly Socialist journal "Le Kodo Sejai" (The Labor World); forced to leave Japan, came to U.S.; delg. Intl. Socialist Cong. 1904; joined Communist Party 1920; delg. Berlin Socialist Unity Conf. 1922; delg. and speaker at W.C.A.W., Amsterdam, Aug. 1932; home Moscow; died there 1933.

KAUFMAN, ABRAHAM: exec. sec. W. R. Lg.; U.S. Cong. Ag. War; spkr. World Youth Cong. sendoff and treas. of arrangements com.

KAUN, ALEXANDER: advis. coun. A. S.C.R.R.

KAYE, MARTIN: ed. organ of communist A.A.A.I. Lg., "Upsurge"; mem. unit 24, section 15, Communist Party District 2, N.Y. City; author of communist pamphlet "Who Fights for a Free Cuba?"

KEATING, EDW.: Nat. Citiz. Com. Rel. Lat. Am. 1927; Cath. Assn. Intl. Peace, 1933; People's Legis. Serv.; Nat. Pop. Govt. Lg.; mg. ed. "Labor," formerly the official organ of Conf. Prog. Pol. Act., now of R.R. Labor Unions; Nat. Save Our Schs. Com.

KELLEY, FLORENCE (WISCHNEWETSKY): Socialist; wife of a Russian; deceased; Emer. Com. Strik. Rel.; was a founder and pres. Inter-Coll. Socialist Soc. (now L.I.D.); vice pres. L.I.D.; gen. sec. and leading spirit Nat. Cons. Lg.; bd. dir. Nat. Child Labor Com. 1904-20; bd. dir. N.A.A.C.P.; mem. Nat. Wom. Tr. Un. Lg.; translator of Marx and Engels and personal friend of the latter; resident at Hull House, Chgo., 1891-9; pres. Henry St. Settlement, N.Y.C.; correspondent of Lenin; People's Legis. Serv.; Cong. Exp. Radicals; her correspondence with Engels collected by his friend Sorge (head of U.S. Socialist movement then), who placed it in N.Y. Public Library.

KELLEY, NICHOLAS: son of Florence; bd. dir. L.I.D. 1932; treas. A.A. for O.A.S. 1931; Emer. Com. Strik. Rel. 1933.

KELLOGG, PAUL U.: ed. "Survey"; exec. com. For. Pol. Assn.; Fell. Recon.; endors. Lane Pamphlet; exec. com. Civil

Liberties Bureau; Am. Neut. Conf. Com.; active "peace" worker during war with Lochner, Jane Addams, etc.; Emer. Com. Strik. Rel.; Nat. World Ct. Com.; Com. for Thomas 1929; exec. com. Non Intervention Citiz. Com. 1927; Nat. Citiz. Com. on Rel. Lat. Am. 1927; bd. Lg. for Org. Progress 1931; nat. coun. Berger Nat. Found.; L.I.D.

KENNEDY, J. C.: Brookwood Lab. Coll. faculty mem.; Socialist; cand. for dir. L.I.D. 1931; contrib. to "Labor Age," official organ Conf. Prog. Labor Act. 1931; resigned Jan. 1933 from exec. com. Conf. Prog. Lab. Act.; former sec. Farmer-Labor Party of Washington; former instr. Economics, U. of Chgo.

KENYON, DOROTHY: nat. bd. dir. A.C.L.U.; chmn. N.Y. A.C.L.U. Com. (100—5th Ave.); mem. Nat. Coun. on Freedom from Censorship, 1931; exec. com. M.W.D. Def. Com.; Com. for Thomas, 1929; signer of resolution for Recog. of Russia, of the Am. Women's Com. for Russian Recog.

KESTER, HOWARD A.: Nashville, Tenn.; So. sec. of Fell. Recon.; nat. com. Nat. R. & L. Found. 1933; Nat. Com. Def. Pol. Pris. (see); Highlander Folk School (Socialist) at Monteagle, Tenn.; nat. com. F.S.U. and signer of convention call, Dec. 1933; spkr. at Citizens Scottsboro Aid Com. meeting, Birmingham, Tenn., April 1933.

KILE, BERTON E.: exec. com. Nat. R. & L. Found.

KILPATRICK, WM. H.: Prof. Teachers Coll. Columbia U.; nat. coun. Pioneer Youth of Am.; appealed for funds for Rand Sch. 1933; chmn. A.C.L.U. Committee on Academic Freedom; signer Fell. Recon. Pet. Russ. Recog. 1932; spkr. with Norman Thomas, Reinhold Niebuhr, Mrs. F. D. Roosevelt, at Progressive Edu. Conf., Nov. 1933; spkr. L.I.P.A. radio broadcasts; contrib. "Education Worker" (Dec. 1932 issue), organ of communist Education Wkrs. Lg.; endors. Lane Pamphlet; his books "Education and the Social Crisis" and "Educational Frontier" recommended in L.I.D. booklist of 100 books for radicals 1933.

KING, CAROL WEISS: communist I.L. D. atty.; author monthly law bulletins for A.C.L.U. 1923-5; N.C. to A.S.M.F.S.; atty. for Garland Fund; one of women petitioners for communist Hunger Marchers, Wash., D.C., 1932; Nat. Com. to Aid Vic. G. Fascism.

KING, JUDSON: Roosevelt Appointee as Research Investigator, Tenn. Valley Authority; dir. Nat. Pop. Govt. Lg. (see), which issued attack on Dept. of Justice for jailing Reds.

KINGSBURY, SUSAN: Prof. Bryn Mawr Coll.; advis. com. A.S.C.R.R.; hon. vice pres. Nat. Cons. Lg.

KINGSLEY, REV. HAROLD O.: C.W. C. on Unemp.; minister Ch. Good Shepherd, Chgo.; spkr. at Tittle's Church, Jan. 17, 1934.

KIRCHWEY, FREDA (MRS. EVANS CLARK): daughter of Geo. W.; dir. Garland Fund; wartime "peace" worker; Inter-Coll. Socialist Soc. (now L.I.D.); ed. bd. "Nation" since 1918; nat. com. A.A.A.I. Lg. 1928; Fed. Unemp. Wkrs. Lgs. N.Y.C. (Borders) 1933; Emer. Com. Strik. Rel. 1933; Labor Defense Council 1923 for defense of Bridgman Communists.

KIRCHWEY, GEO. W.: nat. com. A.C. L.U.; Socialist; associate of Lochner in wartime "peace" activities; vice chmn. Neut. Conf. Com.

KIRKPATRICK, BLAINE E.: minister; exec. com. Chr. Soc. Act. M.; Meth. Ch. Chgo. hdqts.; Non-Partz. Com. Lillian Herstein.

KITTINE, I. A.: Nat. Coun. Prot. For. Born Wkrs.; Recep. Com. Soviet Flyers; John Reed Club; Nat. Com. to Aid Vic. G. Fascism.

KLING, JACK: Chgo. dist. org. Young Communist League; Nat. Mooney Coun. Act.

KNIGHT, FRANK H.: U. of Chgo. Prof.; speaker for communist N.S. Lg. at U. of Chgo. (see Chgo. Tribune Nov. 3, 1932, for speech eulogizing Communism and telling why he accepts it, also terming the Bible a monstrosity); Sacco-V. Nat. Lg. 1928; endors. "Professional Patriots."

KNUTSON, ALFRED: alias Frank Brown; dist. org. Communist Party; Non-Partisan Lg. 1916-18, Bismarck, N.D.; sec. United Farmers Edu. Lg.; organizer England, Ark., food riots.

KOCH, LUCIEN: dir. Commonwealth Coll. 1933; former teacher in Meiklejohn's radical Experimental college of U. of Wis.; signer Fell. Recon. Pet. Russ. Recog.

KOERNER, RAY: sec. Boilermakers Union 626; Com. on Inf. About Russia; Chgo. A.A.A.I. Lg.

KOHN, MRS. ALFRED: Emer. Com. Strik. Rel. Chgo.; Chgo. Com. for S.A.W.

KOHN, ESTHER L.: A.C.L.U. Chgo. Com.

KOHN, LUCILLE: left wing Socialist; "Musteite" faculty mem. Brookwood Lab. Coll. 1932; cand. dir. L.I.D. 1931; Com. for Thomas, 1929; corres. Labor Action School of the Conf. for Prog. Lab. Act. 1933.

KOLLONTAY, ALEXANDRA: now representing U.S.S.R. in Sweden; took part in 1917 Russian Revolution; was U.S.S.R. commissar; exec. com. Communist Intl.; Soviet Ambassador to Mexico, Norway, etc.; author; "the world's greatest exponent of free love, the nationalization of children and the abolition of Christianity—arrested in Russia, Germany and Sweden for her Communistic activities" (Marvin Data Sheets, 25-2).

KONENKAMP, S. J.: La Follette "Prog. Repub."; sponsor dinner of Berger Nat. Found.; vice pres. Pub. O. Lg. of Am.; Chgo. attorney.

KOUSSEVITSKY, SERGEI: nat. com. W.I.R.; Boston symphony orchestra conductor since 1924; born Russia.

KRATZ, A. ROGER: nat. com. Nat. R. & L. Found.

KREYMBORG, ALFRED: Communist Lg. P. G. for F. & F. 1932; Emer. Com. So. Pol. Pris.; Recep. Com. Soviet Flyers; Nat. Com. Def. Pol. Pris. (Dreiser); New Sch. for Social Research; John Reed Club.

KRUEGER, MAYNARD C.: Prof. Economics at U. of Chgo. since fall of 1932; Wkrs. Training Sch., Chgo.; nat. coun. L.I.D.; vice chmn. Pa. Com. for Total Disarm. 1932; Chgo. organizer Thomas campaign committees 1932; close assoc. of Powers Hapgood and Norman Thomas; Nat. R. & L. Found. 1933; delg. 2nd Intl. Paris 1933, where he advocated arming proletariat according to press reports; teacher Marxian Economics at Chgo. Sch. of Socialism, 1933; reported to be suing Chgo. Tribune for its "free speech" in editorially referring to him as a "jackass."

KRUPSKAYA, NADOSHDA: Moscow, U.S.S.R.; widow of Lenin; head of Intl. Secretariat of Communist Intl.; hon. mem. Wkrs. Cult. Fed. of United States.

KRUTCH, JOS. WOOD: bd. ed. "The Nation"; A.S.C.R.R. book com.; Sacco-V. Nat. Lg.; Roosevelt N.R.A. appointee, Theatrical Code authority.

KRZYCKI, LEO: nat. exec. com. Socialist Party; nat. com. Lg. Against Fascism; nat. coun. Berger Nat. Found.; gen. exec. bd. Amalg. Cloth. Wkrs. of Am. since 1922; Wis. State sec. Socialist Party, 1933; org. of Needle Trades Socialist groups, leader Reading strike, July 1933 of needle workers; replaced Morris Hillquit as nat. chmn. Socialist Party; delegated in 1930 by 24 Socialist, Polish, and Labor orgs. to visit European countries to study labor legislation.

KUN, BELA: real name Cohen; intimate of Lenin; sent back to Budapest by Lenin with Russian money, to agitate; on Mar. 20, 1919, became Communist dictator over Hungary; twenty of his thirty-two Commissars were, like himself, Jewish; inaugurated Red Terror, confiscating, torturing, and executing; in 132 days, spent entire notes reserve (two milliard kronen) of Austria-Hungarian Bank, Budapest.

KUNITZ, JOSHUA: Communist; Intl. Un. Revol. Writers and delg. 1930; perm. contrib. Intl. Lit.; Revol. Writers Fed.; A.S.C.R.R. book com.; contrib. ed. "Soviet Russia Today"; was one of "first international brigade of writers sent out as literary shock troops thru Russia"; Am. com. W.C.A.W.; Nat. Mooney Coun. of Action 1933; speaker for F.S.U.; John Reed Club, N.Y.C.; Scottsboro Com. of Act. 1933; exec. sec. Nat. Com. Def. Pol. Pris. 1933; helped form Wkrs. Cult. Fed.; Am. Com. for S.A.W.; "New Masses" staff, 1933; Nat. Com. to Aid Vic. G. Fascism.

L

LACKLAND, GEO. S.: nat. com. Nat. R. & L. Found.; nat. com. Meth. Fed. for Soc. Serv. 1928; Meadville, Pa.

LA FOLLETTE, FOLA: A.S.C.R.R. book com.; Bureau of Legal Advice, N.Y. 1919, with communists Ella Reeve Bloor, Chas. Recht, etc.

LA FOLLETTE, PHILIP F.: Socialistic; pro-Soviet; ex-Gov. of Wis.; vice pres. Pub. Ownership Lg. of Am.; Nat. Mooney-Billings Com. (of the A.C.L.U.); Fell. Faiths spkr. Chgo. 1933.

LA FOLLETTE, ROBERT M.: deceased; organized People's Legis. Serv.; aided infamous People's Council; a founder and leader of Socialistic "Progressive Republican" movement backed by Socialist Party.

LA FOLLETTE, ROBERT M. JR.: radical Republican; U.S. Senator from Wis.; Socialistic; pro-Soviet; vice pres. Pub. Ownership Lg. of Am.; Nat. Citiz. Com. Rel. Lat. Am. 1927; endors. Lane Pamphlet.

LA FOLLETTE, SUZANNE: Nat. Com. Def. Pol. Pris. 1932; Emer. Com. So. Pol. Pris.

LA GUARDIA, FIORELLO: born N.Y. C., of Italian-Jewish parentage; La Follette-Socialist Repub. Congressman from N.Y., 1932; endors. "Professional Patriots"; Russian-American Indust. Corp. with Jane Addams, Debs, Lenin, etc.; supporter Rand Sch. 1933; nat. com. Sacco-V. Nat. Lg.; Nat. Citiz. Com. on Rel. Lat. Am. 1927; lawyer for Amalg. Cloth. Wkrs. 1925; ran for Congress on Socialist ticket, 1924; see article "New Deal and Roosevelt Appointees"; appointed Paul Blanshard and A. A. Berle to his mayoralty cabinet after election as Mayor of N.Y. City with support of A. A. Berle and other Roosevelt leaders; Carlo Tresca claims him as old associate (N.Y. Trib., 1/21/34); Conf. Prog. Pol. Act. campaign com. 1934 and one of those issuing its call in 1933.

LAIDLER, HARRY W.: Socialist; exec. dir. L.I.D. since 1910; Rand School since 1923; author numerous Socialist books; exec. com. L.I.P.A.; Civil Liberties Bureau; Fell. Recon.; contrib. ed. New Leader; nat. advis. com. Sacco-V. Nat. Lg.; Il Nuovo Mondo Nat. Com.; Com. on Coal and Giant P.; dir. L.I.D. tour to Russia 1931; bd. Lg. for Org. Prog. 1931; U.S. Cong. Ag. War com.; dir. People's Lobby; nat. coun. Berger Nat. Found.; mem. Soc. Serv. Commn. Fed. Coun. Chs. since 1924; People's Freedom Union, 1920; Nat. Advis. Coun. on Radio in Edu. 1934.

LAMBKIN, CYRIL: Communist; born Russia; mgr. House of the Masses, Detroit; nat. sec. F.S.U. 1933; formerly with Amtorg Trading Corp.; arrested in Bridgman, Mich. raid, 1922.

LAMONT, CORLISS: Prof.; son of Thos. W. Lamont (partner in Morgan Banking House); speaker for Freethinkers (atheist) Society 1932; Am. nat. com. W. C.A.W.; treas. M.W.D. Def. Com. 1930; Emer. Com. Strik. Rel.; Com. for Thomas 1929; contrib. "Soviet Russia Today" (official pub. F.S.U.); endorser communist N.S. Lg.; nat. com. Student Cong. Ag. War (U. of Chgo.); contrib. "New Masses"; speaker F.S.U.; in reviewing a Communist pamphlet by Bennett Stevens, "The Church and the Workers," he said: "It will take a long time to completely liquidate the church—the task cannot be undertaken too soon or too energetically."; his wife one of petitioners for Communist Hunger Marchers, Wash. D.C. 1932; nat. bd. dir. A.C.L.U., 1933; N.C. to A.S. M.F. S.; Am. Com. for S.A.W.; parents directors of For. Pol. Assn.; Nat. Com. to Aid Vic. G. Fascism; nat. com. F.S.U. 1934; Conf. Prog. Pol. Act. camp. com. 1934.

LAMSON, WARREN: Chmn. Cook Co. Ill. communist Unemp. Councils; Chgo. Wkrs. Sch.; nat. com. Fed. Unemp. Wkrs. Lgs. of Am.

LAND, REV. LEON ROSSER: Emer. Com. Strik. Rel.; exec. com. W.R. Lg.; leader radical Bronx Free Forum, N.Y. City; cand. dir. L.I.D. 1931; leader radical pastors' march to demand relief for unemployed from Mayor O'Brien, June, 1933.

LAND, YETTA: Communist Party functionary; I.L.D. Atty. Cleveland.

LANDY, LUDWIG: Communist; exec. sec. W.I.R. 1929; Recep. Com. Soviet Flyers.

LANE, WINTHROP D.: Socialist; author of "Lane Pamphlet" against military training, financed by Garland Fund thru the C.M.E. and widely distributed by Fell. Recon., L.I.D., A.C.L.U., W.I.L.P.F. and to some extent by Fed. Coun. Chs.; author of pamphlet circulated by A.C.L.U. telling of his activities in United Mine Workers violent terroristic strikes in W. Va.; amnesty com. of People's Freedom Union, 1920; Inter-Coll. Socialist Soc. (now L.I.D.).

LANGWORTHY, MRS. B. F.: W.I.L. P.F.; Util. Inv. & Cons. Lg.; Chgo. Forum Coun.; Lg. Women Voters; Woman's City Club; Fell. Faiths, Chgo. com.; sister-in-law of Mrs. Salmon O. Levinson; Com. for Human Rts. Against Naziism (Levinson chmn.).

LANSBURY, GEORGE: English Socialist; Independent Labour Party, mem. Parliament; served two prison terms; author of "What I Saw in Russia"; vice pres. W.I.R. 1923; N.C. for P.W. of England.

LAPP, JOHN A.: former Prof. Marquette U., Milw., Wis.; A.A.A.I. Lg., Chgo. 1928; dir. social act. dept. Nat. Catholic Welfare Coun. 1920-27; nat. com. A.C.L. U.; A.C.L.U. Chgo. Com.; chmn. Com. on Inf. about Russia; former pres. Nat. Conf. Social Work; vice chmn. N.C. for P.W.; exec. com. L.I.P.A.; vice pres. A.A. for O.A.S.; Labor Def. Coun. 1923 (I.L.D.); advis. com. C.W.C. on Unemp. (Borders); Nat. Citiz. Com. on Rel. Lat. Am. 1927; exec. com. Nat. R. & L. Found. 1933; active in behalf of Sacco and V.; vice pres. Fell. Faiths nat. com. 300; Nat. Save Our Schs. Com.; nat. coun. Berger Nat. Found.; Non Partz. Com. Lillian Herstein; exec. com. Chgo. L.I.D.; Roosevelt N.R.A. appointee; mem. several coms. of Cath. Assn. for Intl. Peace, 1933; Conf. Prog. Pol. Act. campaign com. 1934.

LARKIN, MARGARET: Communist; N.C. to A.S.M.F.S.; contrib. to "The Communist"; bd. Pris. Rel. Fund of I.L.D.; endors. W.I.R. Hunger March letter, 1932; contrib. Inprecorr, Dec. 15, 1932; sec. communist Film Forum.

LASSWELL, HAROLD D.: U. of Chgo. Prof.; A.C.L.U. Chgo. Com.; lecturer at Chgo. Workers School (Communist) 1932; exec. com. Chgo. L.I.D.; Griffin Bill sponsor; nat. coun. L.I.D.; wrote scurrilous attack on Nationalism and flag in "Christian

Advocate," Feb. 10, 1927; sponsor Chgo. Wkrs. Theatre, 1933; spkr. Am. Friends' Religious Forum, 1933.

LATHROP, REV. CHAS. N.: minister of Prot. Episc. Ch.; formerly Dean; exec. sec. Dept. of Chr. Soc. Serv. of Nat. Coun. Prot. Episc. Ch. since 1920; made typical Socialistic class-hate speech at A.C.L.U. meeting in N.Y.C., at which Harry F. Ward presided, June 9, 1927; expressed sympathy for Communists arrested in the Bridgman (Mich.) raid, and falsely referred to first Christians as "communists"—likened Communists Foster, Ruthenberg, and the others to Saint Peter, Saint John, and the other Apostles; said "I want to take my stand on the basic right for anybody in the United States to be a communist who wishes to be one." (Whitney's "Reds in America").

LATHROP, REV. JOHN HOWLAND: Unitarian minister; Fed. Coun. of Chs.; dir. Nat. Cons. Lg.; Nat. World Ct. Com.; Non-Intervention Citiz. Com.; signer of appeal for Sacco and V. (N.Y. Times, Aug. 22, 1927); Com. for Thomas 1929; nat. com. W.R. Lg.; home Brooklyn, N.Y.

LATHROP, JULIA C.: deceased; nat. com. A.C.L.U.; advis. com. A.S.C.R.R.; bd. trustees For. Lang. Inf. Serv.; N.C. for P.W.; vice pres. Nat. Cons. Lg.; W.I. L.P.F.; one of Jane Addams' Hull House group; Lg. of Women Voters; dir. Immigrants' Prot. Lg.; on com. to aid Mrs. Kalinin, wife of Soviet Pres., when she sought to enter U.S. for agitational tour in 1923.

LAUCK, WM. JETT: economist; employed by Garland Fund; author of radical pamphlets used by L.I.D. and other radical agencies; labor arbitrator; People's Legis. Serv.; Wash., D.C.

LAWRENCE, GLENFORD: com. chmn. C.W.C. on Unemp.; Emer. Com. Strik. Rel., Chgo.; mem. bd. "New Frontier," organ of C.W.C. on Unemp.; mg. com. Chgo. Forum Council; dir. men's work Chgo. Commons (Graham Taylor) since 1917; pastor Tabernacle Congl. Ch. Chgo. since 1917; Conf. Prog. Pol. Act.; Am. Assn. for Adult Edu.; World Assn. for Adult Edu.; Conf. Prog. Lab. Act.; studied Union Theol. Sem.; F.E.R.A. Wkrs. Edu. 1934.

LAWRENCE, HILDA HOWARD: exec. com. Chgo. chap. L.I.D.; Emer. Com. Strik. Rel., Chgo.

LEACH, AGNES BROWN (MRS. HENRY GODDARD): nat. com. A.C.L.U. 1932; was in Jane Addams' Woman's Peace Party; Civil Liberties Bureau; exec. com. A.A. for O.A.S.; endorser World Peaceways 1932; W.I.L.P.F.; New Sch. Social Research, 1932; Cong. Exp. Radicals; Nat. Citiz. Com. Rel. Lat. Am. 1927; nat. coun. For. Pol. Assn.

LEE, ALGERNON: infamous People's Council; pres. Rand School; Socialist Party nat. exec. com.; nat. com. Lg. Against Fascism.

LEFKOWITZ, ABRAHAM: born Hungary; A.C.L.U.; Am. Fed. of Teachers; co-ed. "N.Y. Teacher," since 1922; Socialist; dir. Nat. Urban Lg.; Brookwood Labor Coll.; Pioneer Youth of Am.; ed. "Am. Teacher"; Wom. Tr. Un. Lg.; mem. coun. Jt. Com. on Unemp.; chmn. Mooney Conf. 1931; Com. for Thomas, 1929; Nat. Save Our Schs. Com.; denied promotion in N.Y. Schools because of radicalism 1926; Conf. Prog. Pol. Act. camp. com. '34; home N.Y.

LE GALLIENNE, EVA: actress; advis. com. A.S.C.R.R.; nat. com. W.I.R.; Nat. Com. to Aid Vic. G. Fascism.

LEHMAN, LLOYD W.: exec. bd. A.C. L.U. Chgo. Com. 1933 (exec. sec. 1932); lives at Hull House, Chgo.; sponsor Berger Nat. Found. dinner, 1931; atty.

LEIGHTON, FREDERIC W.: A.C.L.U. Chgo. Com.

LEISERSON, WM. MORRIS: born Russia; Prof. Economics Antioch Coll. since 1925; chmn. bd. of arb. men's clothing industry, Chgo. from 1923; Conf. Prog. Pol. Act.; nat. coun. Berger Nat. Found.; Roosevelt appointee, 1933, as sec. National Labor Board; author of chapter on "Socialist Theory and the Class Struggle" in Laidler-Thomas book "The Socialism of Our Times"; contrib. to L.I.D. pub. "The Unemployed"; speaker at Brookwood Labor Coll. 1926; head O. State Commn. on Unemp. 1932; chosen as arbitrator of socialist Conserve Co. (see article "Capitalism, etc.").

LENIN, NICOLAI (ULANOV VLADIMIR ILYITCH): died Jan. 21, 1924, of syphilis; Russian Bolshevik revolutionary leader; overthrew the Kerensky Govt. Nov. 7, 1917 (October, according to Russian calendar; hence the term "October" is used by Communists for "revolution"); wife's name Nadoshda Krupskaya.

LEONARD, WM. ELLERY: Prof. U. of Wis.; defender of "free love" students there; Sacco-V. Nat. Lg.; Am. com. W.C. A.W.; endors. "Professional Patriots."

LE SUEUR, ARTHUR: lawyer, educator; nat. com. A.C.L.U. 1920-33; was vice pres. of "Yours for the revolution" People's Coll. 1916; Non-Partiz. Lg.; war time "peace" worker.

LEVIN, SAMUEL: Socialist; sponsor

Berger Nat. Found. dinner, 1931; born Russia; gen. exec. bd. and jt. Chgo. bd. Amal. Cloth. Wkrs. of Am.; exec. com. L.I.D. Chgo.; C.W.C. on Unemp.; bd. dir. Amal. Tr. & Sav. Bank, Chgo.; Chgo. Emer. Com. Strik. Rel.; A.S.C.R.R. Com. '34.

LEVINE, EMANUEL: Communist Party functionary; exec. of Wkrs. Ex-Serv. Men's Lg.; leader of bonus march to Wash., D.C. 1932.

LEVINSON, DAVID: prominent communist I.L.D. atty. who was in Moscow, June, 1933, and from there invited Arthur G. Hays, Paul Cravath, and Felix Frankfurter, to go to Germany to defend German Communist leaders on trial for firing the Reichstag (July 26, 1933); defended Communists arrested in Wilmington, Del. 1932; barred by Nazis from participating in trial; now lecturing on Reichstag trial.

LEVINSON, EDW.: publicity dir. Socialist Party; edtl. staff socialist New Leader from 1924 on; Workmen's Circle; author of "The Facts about La Follette and Wheeler," campaign handbook, 1924; formerly on New York Call, Socialist paper; Non-Intervention Citiz. Com. 1927; com. U. S. Cong. Ag. War; cand. dir. L.I.D. 1931; exec. com. N.Y. City L.I.D.; exec. sec. Lg. Against Fascism; contrib. Milwaukee Leader; delg. Labor and Socialist International, Paris, 1933; author "Russia in Recent Years."

LEVINSON, SALMON O.: pres. and trustee Abraham Lincoln Center (Communist meeting place), Chgo.; chmn. Am. Com. for Outlawry of War; trustee Northwestern U. Settlement; Nat. World Ct. Com.; Chgo. Forum Coun.; wife pres. bd. dir. A. Lincoln Center "Unity"; chmn. Com. for Human Rts. Against Naziism 1934.

LEVY, MELVIN P.: Communist; "Labor Defender"; N.C. to A.S.M.F.S.; sec. Nat. Com. Def. Pol. Pris.; Intl. Un. Revol. Writers; perm. contrib. Intl. Lit.; New Masses; Pris. Rel. Fund (I.L.D.); Revol. Writers Fed.; "New Pioneer"; John Reed Club.

LEWIS, ALFRED BAKER: nat. coun. L.I.D. for Mass.; State organizer Socialist Party, Mass.

LEWIS, JOSEPH: the "atheists' 'pope' "; pres. Freethinkers of America (atheist); aided and represented in his taxpayer's suit to prevent Bible reading and other religious exercises in N.Y.C. public schools by the A.C.L.U.; author of "The Bible Unmasked" and other irreligious, blasphemous books; is proud of his biography entitled "Joseph Lewis: Enemy of God," written by Arthur H. Howland, once a Methodist minister (see Freethought Press Assn.); is called "the most aggressive and effective leader of irreligion in America today" by Prof. Harry Elmer Barnes (hon. vice pres. Freethinkers of Am.).

LEWIS, LENA MORROW: Socialist Party nat. organizer, Los Angeles, Cal.

LEWIS, MARX: Socialist; was Victor Berger's sec.; Fed. Press corres.; exec. dir. Berger Nat. Found. 1932; A.A.A.I. Lg. 1926.

LEWIS, SINCLAIR: Socialist; propaganda author; A.S.C.R.R. book com.; Nat. Mooney-Billings Com.; endorser "Letters Sacco and Vanz."; (see 4A comment on his atheism).

LIBBY, REV. FREDERICK J.: Congl. minister until war time, then turned Quaker; exec. sec. N.C. for P.W.; nat. coun. C.M.E.; Nat. World Ct. Com.; World Peaceways; was barred from speaking in public schools of Wash. D.C.; associated with Soc. of Friends in reconstruction and relief work in France 1918-9, as European commr. Apr.-Dec. 1920, and in Phila. office 1921; Seymour Waldman his editor 1932 (head of communist Daily Wkr. Wash. bureau, 1933).

LIBROS, SIMON: nat. coun. L.I.D. (Cynwyd, Pa.); Pa. Com. for Total Disarm.

LIBROS, MRS. SIMON: Pa. Com. for Total Disarm.

LIDDELL, HOWARD SCOTT: advis. com. A.S.C.R.R.

LIEBERMAN, JOSHUA: exec. sec. Pioneer Youth of Am.; Socialist Party executive; bus. agt. Knit Goods Wkrs. Union, 1918-9; Non-Intervention Citiz. Com. 1927; N.Y.

LIEBKNECHT, KARL: German Communist; given 4-yr. sentence during war; in 1919, led Spartacus Communist revolution under Lenin, with Rosa Luxemburg, which threatened Sovietization of Germany for two weeks; both Liebknecht and Rosa L. killed in their uprising in Berlin, Jan. 15, 1919; factories were seized and bloody uprisings occurred in Dusseldorf, Hamburg, Berlin, etc.; Communist Party hdqts. in Berlin was named Liebknecht House until Hitler abolished it.

LIEF, ALFRED: nat. sec. Griffin Bill Com.; Peace Patriots; attended Rosika Schwimmer's reception for Albert Einstein, 1933; N.Y.

LIFSCHITS, DORA: Communist Party functionary.

LIGHTFOOT, CLAUDE: Chgo.; sec. communist Lg. Strugg. Negro Rts.; section org. section 7, Communist Party, Chgo.; colored.

LINDEMAN, E. C.: advis. com. A.S.C. R.R.; Am. com. W.C.A.W.; contrib. ed. "New Republic"; exec. bd. C.M.E.; Am. Fed. Teachers; bd. dir. People's Lobby; bd. dir. Prog. Edu. Assn.; Emer. Com. Strik. Rel.; New Sch. for Social Research lecturer; chmn. nat. com. Pioneer Youth of Am. 1931; signer Fell. Recon. Pet. Russ. Recog. 1932; nat. com. Lg. Against Fascism, 1933; Labor Temple Sch. advisor; exec. com. Am. Assn. for Adult Edu.; Teachers Union of N.Y.; trustee Nat. Child Labor Com.; Conf. Prog. Pol. Act. 1934.

LINDSEY, JUDGE BEN B.: author sex companionate marriage book; Garland Fund aided (see); endors. "Professional Patriots"; disbarred.

LINVILLE, HENRY R.: nat. com. A.C. L.U.; Labor Def. Coun.; pres. Am. Fed. Teachers; on ed. advis. bd. of "The Am. Teacher"; Socialist; Communist sympathizer; Emer. Com. Strik. Rel. 1933; pres. Teachers Union of N.Y.; Nat. Save Our Schs. Com.; nat. coun. Berger Nat. Found.; org. and chmn. admn. com. Pioneer Youth of Am.; vice chmn. bd. dir. Manumit Sch., Pawling, N.Y.

LIPMAN, JACOB G.: advis. coun. A.S. C.R.R.

LITTELL, ROBT.: advis. coun. A.S.C. R.R.; contrib. to "New Republic."

LITVINOV, MAXIM: "peace" delegate of U.S.S.R. to disarmament conferences; after bank robbery at Tiflis, planned by Stalin and Litvinov to secure money for revolutionary overthrow of Govt. of Russia, 1907 (50 killed and injured), was sought by police as Litvinov, alias Wallach, alias Harrison; author of letter of "revolutionary instruction" to Soviet agents in Great Britain resulting in Arcos Raid and severing of diplomatic relations; real name Meyer Moisevitch Wallach, alias Buckman, alias Finklestein; see under "English Reds," Leeds Conference.

LIUKKU, JACOB: sec. of communistic Cooperative Trading Co., Waukegan, Ill., since 1919; born Finland.

LIVERIGHT, HORACE B.: dir. A.S.C. R.R.; nat. com. Sacco-V. Nat. Lg.; Nat. Coun. Prot. For. Born Wkrs. (communist); Boni & Liveright Pub. Co.; "Successful in fight *against* Justice Ford's Clean Books Bill before N.Y. Assembly, 1924. Contribr. on censorship, sex freedom, also speaker and debater on same subjects." (Who's Who in Am.); "Jewish religion."

LLOYD, EDITH M.: sec. Chgo. Com. for Struggle Against War, 1933.

LLOYD, JESSIE: wife of communist Fed. Press corres. Harvey O'Connor; daughter of Wm. Bross and Lola Maverick Lloyd; N.C. to A.S.M.F.S.; Pris. Rel. Fund of I.L.D.; sec. Recep. Com. Soviet Flyers; corres. for Moscow Daily News, 1932; Nat. Com. to Aid Vic. G. Fascism.

LLOYD, LOLA MAVERICK: divorced wife of convicted Communist Wm. Bross Lloyd; on Ford Peace Ship; active in People's Council; Am. com. and delg. to W.C. A.W. 1932; Woman's Peace Soc.; active W.I.L.P.F.; organized delegation to meet "Comrade" Einstein at train when he passed thru Chgo., 1931; Emer. Com. Strik. Rel. Chgo.; Griffin Bill sponsor; U.S. Cong. Ag. War; Recep. Com. Soviet Flyers; Am. Com. for S.A.W.; Jessie, her daughter; Nat. Com. to Aid Vic. G. Fascism; home Winnetka, Ill.

LOCHNER, LOUIS P.: see Jane Addams; exec. sec. infamous People's Council, etc.; Cong. Exp. Radicals.

LOCKE, ALAIN: colored; A.S.C.R.R.; Prof. Philosophy, Howard U.; N.S. Lg. Com. on Negro Student Problems.

LOCKNER, KARL: Communist; sec. Cook County Unemployed Councils, Ill.; grad. U. of Wis. in chemical engineering; police record; chmn. Fed. of Unemp. Org. of Cook Co. 1933; former org. Y.C. Lg.

LORE, KARL: Socialist; Unemp. Citiz. Lgs., Chgo.; Nat. Mooney Coun. Act.

LORE, LUDWIG: former I.W.W., also Communist; has held many offices in Socialist Party; sentenced with Communists in 1919; ed. N.Y. Volkszeitung; Chgo. and N.Y.; Nat. Coun. Prot. For. Born Wkrs.

LOVEJOY, DR. A. O.: chmn. Maryland Civil Lib. Com., Inc., of A.C.L.U., 1932; contrib. to "Nation"; Prof. Philosophy, Johns Hopkins U.

LOVEJOY, OWEN REED: former M.E. and Congl. Minister; Russ. Reconst. Farms, 1925; Am. Assn. Labor Legis.; People's Legis. Serv.; Nat. Parent-Teacher Assn.; gen. sec. Nat. Child Labor Com.; Nat. Mooney-Billings Com.; Cong. Exp. Radicals; nat. coun. Berger Nat. Found.; Fla. and N.Y.

LOVELACE, RICHARD: Communist; nat. treas. Vet. Nat. Rank and File Com.; U.S. Cong. Ag. War; Oregon cand. for Cong. 1932 on Communist ticket; regional organizer of Wkrs. Ex-Serv. Men's Lg., Portland, Ore.; head Veterans Liason Com. (of Communist Party); spkr. July 4, 1933, for Socialist local Continental Congress at Wash., D.C.; mem. group protesting ban on Tom Mann, Aug. 1933.

LOVESTONE, JAY: former nat. sec. Communist Party, U.S.A.; mem. Communist Intl.; now leader Communist Party (Opposition).

LOVETT, ROBERT MORSS: U. of Chgo. Prof.; exec. bd. A.C.L.U. Chgo. Com.; nat. com. A.C.L.U.; dir. and one of four incorporators of Garland Fund; leader of communist N.S. Lg. at U. of C. 1932; Russ. Reconst. Farms, 1925; endorser Communist Janowicz, cand. for Ald. 5th Ward, Chgo., 1933; L.I.P.A.; nat. com. C.M.E.; nat. pres. L.I.D.; nat. com. A.A.A.I. Lg.; N.C. to A.S.M.F.S.; Am. com. W.C.A.W. and nat. com. Student Cong. Ag. War (U. of Chgo.); chmn. exec. com. Sacco-V. Nat. Lg.; assoc. ed. "New Republic"; advis. com. Ky. Miners Def. and Rel. Com. of Chgo. (I.W.W.); Nat. Mooney-Billings Com.; was pres. of communists' Fed.PressLg., when organized in 1922; Fair Play to China; Debs Memorial Radio Fund Com.; India Freedom Found.; Am. Com. on Inf. about Russia; chmn. Chgo. Emer. Com. Strik. Rel.; Nat. Mooney Coun. of Action, 1933; arrested with picketers at strike of communist Needle Trades Wkrs. Ind. Un., June 29, 1933; Humanist; exec. com. Nat. Coun. Prot. For. Born Wkrs. 1927-1930; endors. "Professional Patriots"; Cong. Exp. Radicals; Am. Com. for S.A.W.; July 26, 1933 Advisory Associates Bulletin said: "When 'Comrade' Lovett was up for trial he used the old Communist tactics of demanding a jury trial. We have checked up on the trial and find some peculiar circumstances. He was tried in the jury court, but there was no jury trial. Judge Gutknecht, the judge of the Boys' Court, was brought down to the jury court and turned both Lovett and McKenna loose and cautioned the State's Attorney not to try to file further charges against the two for inciting to riot. Lovett brought with him to court, probably as character witnesses, Jerome Davis, Soviet sympathizing Yale professor, Henry P. Chandler, former president and 'liberalizer' of the Chicago Union League Club, Annetta Dieckmann, industrial secretary of the Y.W.C.A., Morris Topchevsky, artist of the communist John Reed Club, and others."; sponsor communist Chgo. Wkrs. Theatre, 1933; com. U.S. Cong. Ag. War; Griffin Bill sponsor; nat. com. Lg. Against Fascism, 1933; Nat. Save Our Schs. Com.; People's Legis. Serv.; nat. coun. Berger Nat. Found.; chmn. Chgo. Forum Coun.; bd. Lg. for Org. Progress 1931; Emer. Com. Strik. Rel. 1933; see Hands Off Committees; lives at Hull House, Chgo.; Nat. Com. to Aid Vic. G. Fascism.; nat. com. F.S.U. 1934; Conf. Prog. Pol. Act. camp. com. 1934.

LOVING, PIERRE: Nat. Com. Def. Pol. Pris.; Am. Com. for S.A.W.; endors. W.I.R. letter for Hunger Marchers, 1932.

LOWENTHAL, BLANCHE (MRS. FRED): Chgo. Com. for Struggle Against War; Recep. Com. for Ford (Communist); resigned from Chgo. A.C.L.U. Com. because it did not endorse the communist Tom Mooney Conference, May 1, 1933; employed in Addison Street, Chicago, relief station, and dismissed, charged with being a communist agent (Daily News, Nov. 25, 1933); Chgo. Forum Coun., 1933; mem. communist Office Wkrs. Union; reinstated as relief worker, Jan. 1934, on plea of radical social agencies and workers.

LOWENTHAL, MRS. JUDITH: Emer. Com. Strik. Rel.; C.W.C. on Unemp.

LOZOWICK, LOUIS: Communist; Communist Lg. P. G. for F. & F. 1932; artist; nat. com. W.I.R.; Pris. Rel. Fund (I.L.D.); ed. bd. "New Masses"; elected intl. sec. John Reed Clubs at convention held at A. Lincoln Center, Chgo., 1932; contrib. F.S.U. "Soviet Russia Today"; Nat. Com. Def. Pol. Pris. (Dreiser); N.C. to A.S.M.F.S.; Intl. Un. Revol. Writers; perm. contrib. Intl. Lit.; Revol. Writers Fed.; Nat. Com. to Aid Vic. G. Fascism.

LUCCOCK, HALFORD E.: M.E. minister; grad. Union Theol. Sem.; Prof. Yale U. Div. Sch.; Fed. Coun. Chs.; Non-Intervention Citiz. Com. 1927; nat. coun. C.M. E.; favored Russian recog.; wrote "The Christian Crusade for World Democracy"; Nat. R. & L. Found. 1933; assoc. ed. "World Tomorrow"; endors. "Professional Patriots"; exec. com. Meth. Fed. for Soc. Serv.; endors. Lane Pamphlet.

LUDINGTON, KATHERINE: vice chmn. N.C. for P.W.

LUDWIG, WALTER: former student pastor at Athens, O.; exec. dir. Pioneer Youth of Am.; asst. treas. Fell. Recon.

LUMPKIN, GRACE: Communist Lg. P. G. for F. & F. 1932; recd. Gorki Award to communist authors 1932; endorser W.I. R. letter for "Hunger Marchers" 1932; contrib. ed. "New Pioneer"; contrib. "Working Woman" (Communist); John Reed Club; Nat. Com. Def. Pol. Pris.

LUNACHARSKY, ANATOL V.: Commissar of Education, U.S.S.R.; his "Workers' Reader and Declaimer" a blood-curdling collection of revolutionary poems; died 1933.

LUNDEEN, ERNEST: Farmer-Labor Congressman, Minn.; com. on action Conf. Prog. Pol. Act. 1933; Recep. Com. Soviet

Flyers; was endorsed by L.I.P.A.; hi Red speech May 8, 1933 in House on "civil liberties," right of revolution, hatred for wealthy (printed by U.S. printing plant) adopted by Continental Cong. for Ec. Reconst. as its "Declaration of Independence"; Conf. Prog. Pol. Act. camp. com. 1934. Introduced "Workers' Unemployment and Social Insurance Bill" (H. R. 7598), actively backed by all Communist organizations.

LUTTINGER, PAUL: M.D.; writer of Daily Worker medical column; N.C. to A.S.M.F.S.; prof. bacteriology; Communist.

LYALL, ALEX: nat. com. Nat. R. & L. Found.

LYONS, EUGENE: A.S.C.R.R. book com.; United Press corres.; author of "Life and Death of Sacco and Vanzetti"; contrib. "Nation"; former N.Y. corres. for Tass (official Soviet Govt. News Agency).

M

MacCRACKEN, HENRY NOBLE: pres. Vassar Coll. where communistic Experimental Theatre is conducted by Hallie Flanagan; Nat. Citiz. Com. Rel. Lat. Am. 1927; Open Road, 1933; endors. Lane Pamphlet.

MacDONALD, J. RAMSAY: leader of English "Independent Labour Party" (Socialist); Prime Minister of England; expelled and repudiated by Labour Party, 1931, for his supposed "whitened" attitude in cooperating with new "National Govt." and resistance to Labour P. demands, which he called "Bolshevism gone wild"; act. sec. 2nd International (Socialist) 1920-2; author of numerous books on Socialism; Boswell Ptg. & Pub. Co. of London, in "Potted Biographies," states that during the War "The Berliner Tageblatt said, 'Among those who systematically combat the English policy, Ramsay MacDonald occupies first place." (his writings were circulated in Germany); quoting further from Potted Biog.: "A Nonconformist minister of Leicester wrote in local paper August 1915: 'You insult this nation, His Majesty the King, and his Minister by your words. . . . You have no moral right to enjoy liberty and protection under the British flag, or sleep another night defended by the lifeblood of British men.' In June, 1917, MacDonald, assisted by Snowden, Smillie, Ammon, Anderson, Roden Buxton, Mrs. Despard, Mrs. Snowden, and many East End Jews, held a conference at Leeds, and agreed to the formation of Workmen's and Soldiers' Councils, on Russian lines, to end the war by outbreak of a revolution which would paralyse our military operations." . . . "He was appointed to the committee for acting and *creating thirteen soviets.*" . . . "As leader of the I.L.P. he was fully committed to the permanent policy which has corrupted trade unionism, and is that *there shall be no amicable relation between Labour and Capitalism short of the total abolition of the Capitalist system.*" . . . "In 1925 delegates from Moscow were in England arranging with members of the Trades Union Congress for strikes which might develop into revolution; and on 1 May, 1926, the great General Strike was declared at a meeting of trade union leaders, when MacDonald said: 'We (the Socialist Party) are there in the battle with you, taking our share uncomplainingly until the end has come and right and justice has been done.' He and J. H. Thomas then joined in singing 'The Red Flag'; and he became a coopted member of the Strike Committee, which was later charged in a Cabinet paper with 'having held a pistol at the head of Constitutional Government.'" (see also "Independent Labour Party").

MacGOWAN, KENNETH: nat. com. W. I.R.; Nat. Coun. on Freedom from Censorship; M.W.D. Def. Com. 1930.

MACINTOSH, DOUGLAS C.: Canadian; Prof. Theol. Yale U. since 1916; chmn. Dept. Religion, Yale Grad. Sch.; exec. com. Nat. R. & L. Found. 1933; "pacifist"; backed by radicals, a test case was pushed in behalf of his admission to U.S. citizenship without promising to bear arms in defense of this government in case of war; he was denied citizenship by a 5 to 4 vote of the U.S. Supreme Court.

MACKAYE, JAMES: nat. coun. L.I.D. for New Hampshire.

MACLEOD, NORMAN: Communist; Intl. Un. Revol. Writers; perm. contrib. Intl. Lit.; "New Masses"; Revol. Writers Fed.; John Reed Club; contrib. ed. "Left Front," 1933.

MAGIL, A. B.: Communist; writer Intl. Pamphlets; John Reed Club; delg. Intl. Union Revol. Writers, 1930; helped form Wkrs. Cult. Fed.; perm. contrib. Intl. Lit.; Revol. Writers Fed.; contrib. ed. "New Masses," 1931; contrib. ed. "Soviet Russia Today," 1932; ed. "Michigan Worker," official wkly. organ of Communist Pty., Dist. No. 7; instr. N.Y. Wkrs. Sch., 1930.

MAGNES, JUDAH LEON: Rabbi; nat. com. A.C.L.U.; Emer. Peace Fed. 1917; org. of infamous People's Coun.; dir. Garland Fund; Fell. Recon.; now Chancellor of Hebrew U. in Palestine, where he also acts as corres. for the Nat. R. & L. Found.

1933; People's Legis. Serv.; Cong. Exp. Radicals.

MAHONEY, WM.: Mayor St. Paul; Socialist; Conf. Prog. Pol. Act. 1933; exec. com. L.I.P.A., 1931; nat. com. L.I.D.; sec. Anti-War Lg. 1917; helped organize National Farmer-Labor Party; nat. com. A.A. A.I. Lg. 1928; spkr. Pub. O. Lg. conv., Chgo. Sept. 28-Oct. 1, 1933.

MALIN, PATRICK MURPHY: C.M.E. exec. bd.; contrib. ed. "World Tomorrow"; Com. for Thomas 1929; spkr. Y.M.C.A. Conf. (N.Y. Times, 2/4/33).

MANLY, BASIL M.: Socialist; dir. People's Legis. Serv. 1921-7; was on I.W.W. Defense Com.; Conf. Prog. Pol. Act.; mem. Garland Fund Com. on Am. Imperialism; was contrib. ed. of Inter-Coll. Socialist Society organ; 1933 appointed mem. Fed. Power Commission by Pres. Roosevelt; Nat. Save Our Schools Com.; author of publications distrib. by Rand Sch.; Nat. Citiz. Com. Rel. Lat. Am. 1927.

MANN, HEINRICH: German Red; intl. com. W.C.A.W.; Intl. Com. for S.A.W.

MANN, LOUIS L.: Rabbi of Sinai Temple, Chgo., and U. of Chgo. Prof.; A.C.L.U. Chgo. Com.; Chgo. Forum Coun.; Chgo. Emer. Com. Strik. Rel.; N.A.A.C.P.; Util. Cons. and Inv. Lg. 1932; Non-Partz. Com. Lillian Herstein 1932; Am. Com. for Outlawry of War (S. O. Levinson); advis. coun. Am. Birth Control Lg.; Eugenics Commn. of U.S.; vice chmn. Chgo. Fell. Faiths; Nat. R. & L. Found. 1933; conducts radical Hirsch Center Forum; edtl. contrib. A. Lincoln Center "Unity"; exec. bd. Cent. Conf. Am. Rabbis and on its commn. on social justice; Chgo. Com. for S.A.W.

MARGOLD, NATHAN: chmn. A.C.L.U. Com. on Indian Civil Rights.

MARKOFF, DR. A.: Communist Party central com. member; N.Y. Wkrs. School; Recep. Com. Soviet Flyers.

MARLEY, LORD: Ind. Lab. Party British whip; tour conductor 1933 for "Open Road" to Russia; delg. to communist Cong. against War, Shanghai 1933; refused permission to land in Japan; intl. officer of Nat. Com. to Aid Vic. German Fascism 1933.

MARRIOTT, REV. VICTOR: C.W.C. on Unemp. adv. com.

MARSH, BENJ. C.: born Bulgaria; exec. com. Conf. Prog. Pol. Act.; exec. com. Jt. Com. on Unemp.; exec. sec. People's Lobby; a sponsor of Barbusse's Wash. appearance (Wash. Star 10/7/33); speaker, Fell. Faiths, Chgo. 1933; "was a prominent supporter Non-Partizan Lg.; toured the Pacific Northwest in 1921 in the Fall seeking to collect money to prevent the recall of Frazier as gov. of N. Dakota." (Marvin Data Sheets, 12-5); nat. coun. Berger Nat. Found.; sec. N.Y. Lg. for Unemp.; home now Wash., D.C.

MARTELL, C. J.: A.A.A.I. Lg. Chgo.; Chgo. Watch and Clockmakers' Union.

MARTIN, ANNE H.: former Prof. U. of Nevada; prominent in woman's suffrage movement; nat. com. A.C.L.U.; western regional dir. W.I.L.P.F., U.S. section; Com. for Thomas 1929; People's Legis. Serv.; home Reno, Nev., and Carmel-by-the-Sea, Cal. (winter).

MARX, KARL: German Jew; born 1818; descendant of long line of Rabbis; real name Mordechia; a lifelong grief to his parents because of his violent temper, notoriety, domineering nature, poverty, wretchedness and "disregard for everything decent" (J. Spargo, "Karl Marx, His Life and Work"); saturated at college with Hegelian atheism and its motto, "Whatever exists is worth destroying"; his reputation as an aggressive atheist and violent rebel thwarted his efforts to secure a Prussian governmental or academic post after leaving college and he became the more enraged at all those more prosperous than himself; in 1842 became editor of the Rheinisch Zeitung, which was suppressed by the Govt. 1843; he then moved to Paris where he associated with anarchist Michael Bakunin, Friederich Engels, and imbibed French socialism from Proudhon; expelled from France, Jan. 1845, he moved to Brussels where he labored for three years to organize an international communist league to carry through an immediate bloody revolution, for which league he and Engels wrote the Communist Manifesto (1848); he participated in the French and German revolutionary disturbances of 1848; banished from Cologne, June, 1849, from France, July, 1849, he then went to England where he lived in extreme destitution until his capitalistic friend, Engels, gave him a dole of £350 a year (out of the proceeds, according to his own theory of "value," of the robbery of Lancashire workingmen). During his 34 years in England, he read, wrote, organized and controlled the First International, and quarrelled with his fellow revolutionaries (particulars concerning fourteen embittered brawls are given by Spargo); died May 5, 1883, after about 15 yrs. of ill health.

MATES, DAVE: 1933 Communist org. in Calumet dist. of Chgo.; formerly sec. Unemp. Councils of Cook County.

MATHES, MRS. G. M.: A.C.L.U. Chgo.

Com.; Chgo. W.I.L.P.F.; Chgo. Fell. Faiths; pres. Christian Citizenship Coun.

MATTHEWS, J. B.: exec. sec. Fell. Recon.; circulator of Fell. Recon. petition for recog. of bloody Soviet Russia (humorously) "in the interests of peace"; said to be sympathetically close to Moscow; has been annual visitor to Russia for past five years; presided at Student Congress against War; chmn. Am. Lg. Ag. War and Fascism; communist Anti-Imperialist Lg. Delg. to Cuba, 1933; U.S. Cong. Against War; treas. Nat. Com. to Aid Vic. G. Fascism; assoc. ed. "Student Outlook" (formerly "Revolt") of L.I.D.; Nat. R. & L. Found. 1933; mem. coun. Jt. Com. on Unemp.; speaker at Communist Mooney meeting May 1, 1933, Chgo. and applauded when he inferred he might soon change from the Socialist to the Communist Party; Nat. Scottsboro Com. of Action 1933; nat. com. F.S.U. 1934; ousted as sec. Fell. Recon. because of too open support of "Class Struggle," 1934.

MAURER, GEO.: Nat. Com. Def. Pol. Pris.

MAURER, JAMES H.: left wing Socialist; vice chmn. nat. com. A.C.L.U.; vice pres. L.I.D.; nat. coun. C.M.E.; nat. com. A.A.A.I. Lg. 1928; vice pres. A.A. for O.A.S.; mem. Am. Commn. on Conditions in Ireland, 1920; Nat. Mooney-Billings Com.; Fell. Recon.; Il Nuovo Mondo Nat. Com.; Conf. Prog. Pol. Act. nat. com. 1922; Labor Age Pub. Co.; dir. Brookwood Labor Coll.; Griffin Bill sponsor; with Scott Nearing and Lochner sent cablegram to Soviet Commissars at Petrograd, Mar. 3, 1918 (Lusk Report); Emer. Peace Fed.; war-time "peace" worker; mem. First Am. Trade Un. Delg. to Russia, 1927, which was repudiated by the A. F. of L. because of its communistic nature; Socialist cand. for Vice Pres. 1932; Am. Birth Control Lg.; exec. com. Nat. Coun. Prot. For. Born Wkrs. 1930; spkr. for infamous People's Coun. during war; pres. Pa. State F. of L. since 1912; nat. com. Lg. Against Fascism; vice pres. Berger Nat. Found.; org. Pioneer Youth of Am.; endors. Lane Pamphlet; vice chmn. L.I.P.A.

MAURER, OSCAR E.: pastor Center Ch., New Haven, Conn., since 1909; nat. com. Nat. R. & L. Found. 1933; dir. Congl. Home Boards; exec. com. Am. Missionary Assn.

McAFEE, JOS. ERNEST: dir. for John Haynes Holmes' church of "community service" since 1924; Union Theol. Sem.; edtl. contrib. A. Lincoln Center "Unity."

McCONNELL, FRANCIS J.: M.E. Bishop; close associate of Harry F. Ward; mem. A.C.L.U.; pres. Meth. Fed. for Soc. Serv.; in its Bulletin No. 8 for 1932, he and Ward signed the statement that they were cooperating with the Communist I.L.D., Labor Research, C.M.E., L.I.D., Fell. Recon., and A.C.L.U., "agencies working definitely for a new social order" (see Winifred Chappell, co-ed. with Ward of Meth. Fed. for Soc. Serv. Bulletin); on Socialist campaign committees in 1929 and 1932; C.M.E.; Nat. Citiz. Com. on Rel. Lat. Am. 1927; endorser Lane Pamphlet; signer A.C.L.U. petition for Sacco and V. May 1927; Emer. Com. Strik. Rel. (N.W.F.S.T. Strik.) 1930; pres. A.A. for O.A.S. 1931; vice chmn. Jt. Com. on Unemp.; nat. com. Nat. World Ct. Com.; contrib. ed. "World Tomorrow"; Fed. Unemp. Wkrs. Lgs. N.Y. City (Borders); pres. Fed. Coun. Chs. 1932; hon. pres. Nat. R. & L. Found. 1933; Emer. Com. Strik. Rel. 1933; chmn. Fell. Faiths com. 300 (1933); vice pres. Pub. O. Lg.; Nat. Save Our Schs. Com.; vice chmn. N.C. for P.W.; coun. People's Lobby; For. Pol. Assn. nat. coun.; endors. "Professional Patriots"; L.I.D. spkr. 1933-4; home N.Y.C.

McCULLOCH, CATHARINE WAUGH (MRS. FRANK HATHORN): A.C.L.U. Chgo. Com.; W.I.L.P.F.; Lg. of Women Voters; mem. bd. Chgo. Ch. Fed.; mem. bd. Chgo. Commons; chmn. Chgo. branch Com. on Cult. Rel. Lat. Am.; presided at A.C.L.U. meeting at Rev. Tittle's Ch. (Carl Haessler spkr.) (see article "News"); home Evanston, Ill.; A.S.C.R.R. Com. 1934.

McCULLOCH, FRANK W.: son of Cath. W.; treas. L.I.D. Chgo. Chapter; treas. C.W.C. on Unemp. (Borders); spkr. Chgo. A.S.C.R.R. Nov. 1933.

McDONALD, JAMES G.: formerly Coll. Prof.; chmn. bd. For. Pol. Assn. since 1919; vice chmn. N.C. for P.W.; World Peaceways; Commn. on Intl. Justice and Goodwill of Fed. Coun. Chs.; advis. coun. Lg. of Nations Assn.; speaker Labor Institute Forum 1927-8; as Lg. of Nations representative, aiding Jews exiled by Hitler 1933-4.

McDONALD, LEONIDES: colored; cand. for Gov. of Ill. Communist Party, 1932; then Sergeant Ill. Nat. Guard. (Who permits those pledged to overthrow our Govt. to join, or remain in, its armed forces?)

McDOWELL, MARY E.: dir. and head U. of Chgo. Settlement since 1893; dir. Garland Fund, July 19, 1922-May 7, 1924; nat. com. A.C.L.U.; N.C. for P.W.; C.M.E., Ill.; Debs Memorial Radio Fund Com.; vice pres. Ill. Wom. Tr. Un. Lg.; Am. Com. on Inf. about Russia; Chgo. Forum Coun.; Non-Partz. Com. Lillian Herstein 1932;

Chgo. com. Fell. Faiths; endors. com. of Am. Friends Serv. Com., Chgo. branch; nat. com. Meth. Fed. for Soc. Serv.; chmn. Com. on Intl. Cooperation for Prev. of War; chmn. com. Ill. Lg. of Women Voters; Peace Patriots; exec. Chgo. br. N.A.A.C.P.; dir. Immigrants' Prot. Lg.; sponsor communist Chgo. Wkrs. Theatre, 1933; spkr. Fell. Faiths, Chgo. 1933; sponsor Berger Nat. Found. dinner, 1931.

McFARLAND, J. C.: Communist; Am. Com. for S.A.W.; delg. from Marine Wkrs. Indust. Un. to World Cong. Ag. War (Amsterdam).

McGEE, CLYDE: A.C.L.U. Chgo. Com.; vice chmn. Com. on Cult. Rel. Lat. Am., Chgo. branch.

McGILL, J. H.: vice pres. Pub. O. Lg. of Am.; Nat. Pop. Govt. Lg.; People's Legis. Serv.; People's Lobby, bd. dir.; Com. on Coal and Giant P.

McGOWAN, REV. RICHARD A.: exec. bd. N.C. for P.W.; chmn. Lat.-Am. com. of Catholic Assn. Intl. Peace; Nat. Cath. Welfare Conf.; A.C.L.U. aid at hearing on admitting alien pacifist MacIntosh to citizenship (A.C.L.U. Report, 1931-2).

McGUIRE, REV. U. M.: Baptist minister; ed. of "The Baptist"; exec. com. Chgo. L.I.D.; Fell. Recon.; Pub. O. Lg.; Emer. Com. Strik. Rel., Chgo.; exec. com. C.W.C. on Unemp. (Borders); Socialist cand. for Clerk Supreme Ct., 1932.

McKAY, CLAUDE: Nat. Com. Def. Pol. Pris.; ed. "Liberator," 1922.

McKENNA, THOS. M.: exec. sec. A.C. L.U. Chgo Com.; a busy spectator at Communist riots and court witness for rioters; beaten up at Melrose Park, Ill., 1932, for his communistic activities; speaker at communist Lg. Strugg. Negro Rts. meeting, Feb. 26, 1933; Recep. Banquet Com. for Ford, 1932; arrested June 29, 1933 at communist strike (with Lovett) and at other riots (Jan. 27, 1934, etc.).

McLEVY, JASPER: nat. exec. com. Socialist Party; nat. com. Lg. Ag. Fascism; elected mayor of Bridgeport, Conn. Nov. 1933; Roosevelt admirer.

McVEY, DAVID: C.W.C. on Unemp.; Farmer-Labor Party.

MEAD, MRS. LUCIA AMES: vice chmn. N.C. for P.W.; Peace Patriots; Emer. Peace Fed.; active in Lg. of Nations movement; endors. "Professional Patriots"; was in Jane Addams' Women's Peace Party; husband is Edwin D., ex-dir. World Peace Found.; nat. coun. Berger Nat. Found.; W.I.L.P.F.; A.A.A.I. Lg. 1926.

MEIKLEJOHN, ALEX.: Prof. U. of Wis.; nat. com. A.C.L.U.; vice pres. L.I.D.; nat. coun. C.M.E.; Nat. Mooney-Billings Com.; Nat. Citiz. Com. for Sacco and V.; signed telegram to Pres. in behalf of Sacco and V. (Boston Post, Aug. 21, 1927); Nat. Save Our Schs. Com.; nat. coun. Berger Nat. Found.; founder and director of the experimental college at U. of Wis. which was called the "Guinea Pig" College, was very communistic in character, and after two years was dropped; Conf. Prog. Pol. Act. camp. com. 1934.

MEIKLEJOHN, KENNETH: son of Alex.; student at U. of Wis.; exec. bd. L.I. D.; U. of Wis. Com. for Thomas, 1932; Student Com. to Investigate Mining Conditions (L.I.D. and N.S. Lg.).

MEITZEN, ERNEST R.: Communist org. of farmer movement; nat. com. United Farmers' Lg.; I.L.D.; officer Commonwealth Coll.; home S.D.

MELDON, JOHN: very active Communist; nat. sec. Steel and Metal Wkrs. Indust. Un. (Communist); cand. for Pittsburg City Council on Communist ticket, 1933; nat. com. F.S.U. 1933.

MELISH, REV. JOHN HOWARD: Prot. Episc. minister; Socialist; an org. of infamous revolutionary People's Council during the War, exposed in Lusk Report; sec.-treas. Ch. Socialist Lg.; Jt. Commn. on Soc. Serv. of Episc. Ch.; Emer. Com. Strik. Rel.; Ch. Emer. Com. for Rel. Textile Strikers 1930; bd. dir. "World Tomorrow"; Fed. Unemp. Wkrs. Lgs. N.Y. (Borders) 1933; chmn. Non-Intervention Citiz. Com. 1927; home Brooklyn, N.Y.

MELMS, EDMUND T.: Milwaukee Socialist Party executive.

MENCKEN, H. L.: Nat. Mooney-Billings Com. and Nat. Coun. on Freedom from Censorship (both of A.C.L.U.); John Reed Club; contrib. ed. "Nation" 1932.

MERRIAM, CHAS. E.: U. of Chgo. Prof.; nat. A.S.C.R.R. book com.; dir. Chgo. A.S.C.R.R. branch; advis. com. Chgo. Forum Coun.; signer of A.C.L.U. appeal for Sacco and V., May 1927; bd. Util. Cons. and Inv. Lg.; Pres. Hoover's Com. on Social Trends 1932; in U. of Chgo. "Daily Maroon" May 17, 1933, he referred to the proposed Baker Bills to prevent teaching of sedition in Illinois schools as "another 'monkey law' of the type that made Tenn. a laughing stock"; with Harry Elmer Barnes author of "Recent Times"; sponsor Berger Nat. Found. dinner 1931.

MESEROLE, DARWIN J.: nat. coun. L.I.D. for N.Y.; Emer. Com. Strik. Rel. 1927-33; pres. Nat. Unemp. Lg.; nat. com. W.R. Lg.; Recep. Com. Soviet Flyers 1929;

exec. com. Jt. Com. on Unemp.; Com. for Thomas 1929; Nat. R. & L. Found. 1933; atty.; nat. coun. Berger Nat. Found.

MICHELES, VERA: see Vera Micheles Dean.

MICHELSON, CLARINA: Communist; N.C. to A.S.M.F.S.; nat. com. W.I.R.; Emer. Com. Strik. Rel. 1928 (exec. sec. 1927); Garland Fund director; Pris. Rel. Fund (I.L.D.); nat. com. I.L.D. 1928.

MICHELSON, HERMAN: Communist; formerly Sunday ed. New York World; "New Masses" staff, 1933.

MILLAY, EDNA ST. VINCENT: Nat. Com. Def. Pol. Pris.; artists' and writers' Com. for Thomas, 1929; Scottsboro Unity Def. Com.; picketed State House of Mass. in Boston in 1927 in protest against death verdict against Communist murderers Sacco and Vanzetti.

MILLER, HERBERT ADOLPHUS: formerly Prof. Ohio State U., dismissed 1932 because of his support of the Indian Nationalist movement, negro equality, and opposition to military training, all of which are also supported by Communists (Am. Labor Year Book 1932); Fed. Unemp. Wkrs. Lgs. N.Y. (Borders) 1933; Nat. R. & L. Found. 1933; advis. com. A.S.C.R.R.; endors. "Professional Patriots."

MILLER, MAURICE: regional chmn. Chgo., communist Wkrs. Ex-Service Men's Lg.

MILLIS, MARY RAOUL: nat. coun. L. I.D. for Georgia; Emer. Com. Strik. Rel. 1933.

MILLS, ETHELWYN: local com. communist Nat. Coun. Prot. For. Born Wkrs.; nat. coun. L.I.D. for Cal. (with Upton Sinclair); Cal. chmn. W.I.L.P.F. 1931; sec. Fell. Recon. Los Angeles, 1925; Nat. R. & L. Found. 1933; sec. Carl D. Thompson's speaking tour for Pub. O. Lg. 1933; sec. Los A. br. A.C.L.U. 1931; contrib. ed. "Open Forum," publication of A.C.L.U., 1927-31; spkr. Mooney-Billings mass meeting Feb. 22, 1930; referred to in Lusk Report as a Socialist.

MILLS, WILEY W.: lawyer; Ald. 37th Ward, Chgo. until 1933; A.C.L.U. Chgo. Com.; Chgo. com. Emer. Com. Strik. Rel.; bd. dir. People's Lobby; vice pres. Pub. O. Lg. of Am.; Newton Jenkins' "Prog. Rep." cand. for County Judge, April 1934; if he wins, the entire election machinery of Chicago and Cook County will be in radical hands.

MILNER, LUCILLE: nat. bd. dir. and research sec. nat. A.C.L.U.

MINER, THEO.: com. Chr. Soc. Act. M.; Saltsburg, Pa.; author of article in "World Tomorrow," Aug. 1933, "Pittsburgh Methodists Turn Left."

MINERICH, TONY: state sec. communist Unemployed Councils of Ill.; sec. Pa. Miners' Relief, 1928; spkr. at Russian Revol. Anniv. meeting, St. Louis, 1932; arrested in Jersey City, N.J. for disorderly conduct (Daily Worker, 10/17/33); former org. Nat. Miners Un. in Pa.

MINK, GEO.: Communist Party cent. com.; sec. Marine Wkrs. Indust. Un.

MINOR, ROBT.: very prominent Am. Communist; writer; cartoonist; cent. exec. com. Communist Party U.S.; indicted Bridgman, Mich. 1922; spread Bolshevism in U.S. Army in Europe; nat. com. I.L.D. 1928; F.S. Russia; an ed. Daily Worker 1928, arrested for publishing obscene poem "America" by Zona Gale's protegé David Gordon, alias Goronefsky; served six months in jail in 1930 for riot activity; "Labor Defender" 1931; speaker at Lenin Memorial mtg. Chgo., Jan. 21, 1933; formerly a leader of the Berkman anarchist gang; principal speaker at Communist May Day Mooney meeting, Chgo. 1933; Nat. Mooney Coun. Act. 1933; U.S. Cong. Ag. War; Lg. Strugg. Negro Rts.; nat. com. F.S.U. 1934.

MIRVISS, JACOB: nat. com. Nat. R. & L. Found. 1933.

MITCHELL, BROADUS: bd. dir. L.I. D.; bd. dir. People's Lobby; A.C.L.U.; supporter Rand Sch. 1933; Prof. Johns Hopkins U.

MITCHELL, ELSIE REED: M.D.; N. C. to A.S.M.F.S.; pro-Soviet; has traveled extensively in Soviet Union, together with Helen Calista Wilson, who is employed by the Soviet Govt. in literary work (N.Y. Tel. 10/30/33); spkr. for Recon. Trips at Labor Temple 1931.

MITCHELL, WESLEY C.: Prof. Columbia U.; dir. New Sch. for Social Research; A.S.C.R.R. book com.; Emer. Com. Strik. Rel. 1927-33; Nat. Mooney-Billings Com.; Com. for Thomas, 1929; Pres. Hoover's Com. on Social Trends, 1932, which made radical report; advis. coun. Am. Assn. Lab. Legis.; Advis. Coun. on Radio in Edu. 1934; lecturer at Rand Sch.; signed an appeal for Chinese Communists; listed in Lusk Report as stockholder in "Liberator."

MONDALE, R. LESTER: minister of Unitarian Church, Evanston, Ill.; A.C.L.U. Chgo. Com.; Am. nat. com. W.C.A.W.; his church regular meeting place for communist I.L.D. and N.S. Lg.; features revolutionary articles in church paper; lecturer at McGregor, Iowa, June 15-20, 1932 on:

"Religion Joins the Revolution," "What My Communist and Socialist Friends Are Doing and Saying," "The Revolt of the 'Tinted Races' (The White Man Steps Down, the Gandhis Up)," and "Revolution Just Around the Corner (What Causes, Helps and Consummates Revolution)," under the auspices of the Iowa Unitarian Assn.'s ninth annual Young People's Institute of Liberal Religion; speaker at communist John Reed Club, Chgo. Apr. 30, 1933, on "Democracy Becomes Plutocracy and Patriots become Racketeers"; Am. Com. for S.A.W. and chmn. Chgo. com. for S.A.W.; John Reed Club; A.S.C.R.R.Com.'34. see article "Jail or Asylum for Me."

MONROE, HARRIET: Chgo. Com. for Struggle Against War; John Reed Club.

MONTAGUE, WILLIAM P.: nat. coun. L.I.D. for N.Y.

MOON, PARKER T.: Prof. Columbia U.; For. Pol. Assn.; Cath. Assn. for Intl. Peace; his book "Imperialism and World Politics," part of study course for socialist L.I.D., 1927-8, along with books by Communists and Socialists.

MOONEY, THOS.: Anarchist-Communist; labor agitator; now imprisoned in San Quentin (Cal.) Pen. for bombing the San Francisco Preparedness Day Parade, July 22, 1916, with W. K. Billings, killing ten and injuring fifty persons; trying to free him is a Communist agitation and fruitful source of income; see Nat. Mooney-Billings Com. for his letter to Stalin; a letter signed by Bob Parker, org. of the Y.P.S.L. of Cleveland, O., written to Geo. Smirkin, reproduced in Daily Worker, Sept. 12, 1933, says that Clarence Senior stated: "Tom Mooney was expelled from the English speaking branch of the Socialist Party of San F. in 1913 for the very same thing for which he is now in jail, for the advocacy of dynamiting. He later joined the Hungarian branch. In spite of this, the Socialist Party has and will struggle for the release of Mooney"; Lg. Strugg. Negro Rts. 1933.

MOORE, FRED ATKINS: was Universalist minister; exec. dir. Chgo. Forum (and Adult Edu.) Coun. since 1925; A.C.L.U. Chgo. Com.; exec. com. Chgo. L.I.D.; Fell. Faiths; Nat. Coun. Prot. For. Born Wkrs. exec. com. 1927-31; home Oak Park, Ill., where he conducts radical Community forum in public high sch. featuring Communist-Socialist spkrs.

MOORE, JOHN W.: mem. Socialist Party; chmn. administration com. Fed. Coun. Chs.; minister.

MOORE, RICHARD B.: Communist Party functionary; colored; as delg. repr. Am. Negro Labor Congress, went with Wm. Pickens and Roger Baldwin to Anti-Imp. Lg. at Brussels (Daily Worker, Mar. 9, 1927); gen. sec. Lg. Strugg. Negro Rts.; field org. I.L.D. 1933.

MOORE, UNDERHILL: Prof. Yale U. since 1930; dir. A.S.C.R.R.; endorser of Hapgood's "Professional Patriots"; mem. of A.C.L.U. Com. of 100 (in behalf of dismissed radical teachers).

MOORS, JOHN F.: sec. Nat. Citiz. Com. on Rel. Lat. Am. 1927; Griffin Bill sponsor 1932.

MOORS, MRS. JOHN F.: nat. coun. C. M.E.; Il Nuovo Mondo Nat. Com.

MORGAN, ARTHUR E.: Roosevelt appointee as chmn. bd. Tenn. Valley Authority; pres. Antioch Coll., Yellow Springs, O.; Open Road, 1933; nat. coun. C.M.E.; Fell. Recon. Pet. Russ. Recog.; Lg. for Org. Progress; spkr. Pub. O. Lg. conv. Chgo. 1933; bd. dir. Prog. Edu. Assn.

MORGAN, H. W.: nat. com. Nat. R. & L. Found. 1933.

MORGAN, MRS. LAURA PUFFER: assoc. sec. N.C. for P.W.; exec. com. World Ct. Com. 1931.

MORLEY, FELIX: exec. bd. N.C. for P.W.

MORRISON, CHAS. CLAYTON: Prof. and lecturer Chgo. Theol. Sem.; Russ. Reconst. Farms. 1925; ed. ultra radical "Christian Century" since 1908; A.C.L.U. Chgo. Com.; C.M.E. Ill.; Chgo. Forum Coun.; with Sherwood Eddy delg. to Russia, 1926; nat. com. World Ct. Com.; petitioned for Sacco and V. Aug. 22, 1927; endorser Lane Pamphlet; Garland Fund Com. on Am. Imperialism; nat. com. Nat. R. & L. Found. 1933; presided at communist mass meeting for Henri Barbusse, Oct. 23, 1933, and I heard him say that he was proud to stand shoulder to shoulder with Barbusse and that we would never have peace until our capitalistic system was abolished; Nat. Save Our Schs. Com.; chmn. Chgo. gen. com. Fell. Faiths.

MORROW, FELIX: Communist; Am. com. W.C.A.W.; contrib. ed. "New Masses" and "Student Review"; writer for Intl. Pamphlets; arrested South Orange, N.J., 1932, for inciting to riot; Communist Lg. P. G. for F. & F.; Am. Com. for S.A.W.

MORSE, JOSIAH: nat. coun. L.I.D. for S.C.; vice pres. Nat. Cons. Lg.; chmn. Univ. Commn. on Race Questions; Prof. U. of S.C.; Nat. Save Our Schs. Com.

MORTON, MILES: alias Mike Morton, alias Kane, alias Daniels; Chgo. Hunger

Marchers column to Wash., 1932; org. Steel and Metal Workers Indust. Un. for Calumet dist. Chgo.

MOSHEVITZ, DR.: Communist Party cent. com.

MOSS, GORDON W.: sec. Nat. Coun. on Freedom from Censorship of A.C.L.U.

MUENZENBERG, WILLI: German Communist; intl. sec. W.I.R.; exec. com. Communist Intl.; intl. com. W.C.A.W.; head of Anti-Imperialist Lg.; intl. com. Nat. Com. to Aid Vic. G. Fascism.

MULLENBACH, JAMES: labor arbitrator for Amalg. Cloth. Wkrs. of Am.; lecturer Chgo. Theol. Sem.; associated with L.I.D.; advis. coun. C.W.C. on Unemp. (Borders), which staged "Hunger March" with Communists, Oct. 31, 1932; on Gov. Emmerson's Relief Commn.; Chgo. Forum Coun.; Fell. Faiths Chgo. Com.; Chgo. Emer. Com. Strik. Relief; Non-Partz. Com. Lillian Herstein; endors. com. Am. Friends Serv. Com. of Chgo.; formerly associated with Graham Taylor at Chgo. Commons; Roosevelt appointee as Labor Arbitrator for Industry, Chgo. area.

MUMFORD, LEWIS: N.C. to A.S.M.F.S.; Nat. Coun. on Freedom from Censorship of A.C.L.U.; M.W.D. Def. Com. 1930; author of article "The Day Before the Revolution" in "Student Outlook" Feb. 1933; spkr. at forum of revolution at Barnard Coll. 1932; contrib. to radical intellectual magazine "Contempo" and signer of protest letter against dismissal of Diego Rivera, Communist artist painting mural at Rockefeller Center.

MURPHY, FRANK: former Mayor Detroit praised by A.C.L.U.; vice pres. Fell. Faiths; Roosevelt appointee as gov. of Philippines; spkr. at Detroit Mooney Def. Conf. (Detroit Leader, 2/11/33); exec. bd. N.A.A.C.P.

MURPHY, J. PRENTICE: chmn. Phila. A.C.L.U. Com.; M.W.D. Def. Com. 1930.

MUSSEY, HENRY R.: nat. com. A.C.L.U.; Nat. Coun. on Freedom from Censorship of A.C.L.U.; Com. for Thomas, 1929; edtl. contrib. A. Lincoln Center "Unity," 1933; Russ. Reconst. Farms, 1925; vice pres. Nat. Cons. Lg. 1931, with Mrs. F. D. Roosevelt, Jane Addams, etc.

MUSTE, ABRAHAM J.: head of Conf. Prog. Lab. Action and new Am. Wkrs. Party; nat. com. A.C.L.U.; nat. coun. L.I.D. for N.Y.; until 1933 pres. Brookwood Labor Coll.; exec. bd. Fell. Recon.; vice pres. Pioneer Youth of Am.; vice pres. Am. Fed. of Teachers; L.I.P.A.; nat. coun. C.M.E.; Sacco-V. Nat. Lg.; W.R. Lg.; Il Nuovo Mondo nat. com.; sec. Amalg. Textile Wkrs.; strike leader; formerly a minister; ed. "Labor Age"; Non-Intervention Citiz. Com. 1927; exec. com. Nat. R. & L. Found. 1933; U.S. Cong. Ag. War; mem. coun. Jt. Com. on Unemp.; Nat. Scottsboro Com. of Action 1933; spkr. communist U.S. Cong. Ag. War; contrib. ed. "World Tomorrow"; chmn. Nat. Com. to Aid Vic. G. Fascism (of communist W.I.R.) 1933; revolutionary Socialist; very militant.

MYERS, REV. JAMES: sec. Ch. Emer. Com. Rel. Tex. Strik.; indust. and field sec. Fed. Coun. Chs. "Commn. on Ch. and Soc. Serv."; A.C.L.U. mem.; "The Progressive Miner" (Union's paper) Jan. 6, 1933, acknowledged $100 donation from him as sec. of Ch. Emer. Com. (to aid strikers).

MYERS, JOSEPH: nat. coun. L.I.D. for Mo.

MYERSCOUGH, TOM: Communist Party functionary; Lg. Strugg. Negro Rts.; pres. Nat. Miners Un.; jailed many times in Pa.

N

NAZIMOVA, ALLA: Am. com. W.C.A.W.; contrib. "Soviet Russia Today" (official organ F.S.U.); Am. Com. for S.A.W. 1933.

NEARING, NELLIE SEEDS: wife of Scott; nat. coun. L.I.D. for N.Y.; Fell. Recon.; Am. Fed. of Teachers; Pioneer Youth of Am.; Lg. for Mut. Aid; head of Manumit Sch., Pawling, N.Y. 1932.

NEARING, SCOTT: very prominent Communist; was wartime "peace" worker; chmn. of infamous People's Coun. 1917-8; indicted in 1918 under Espionage Act for writing of pamphlet "The Great Madness," the American Socialist Society (which maintains and operates Rand Sch. of Social Science) being convicted and fined $3,000 for its publication, circulation, and distribution; Garland Fund dir. from beginning; founder and on nat. com. A.C.L.U. until 1930; dismissed from U. of Pa. and U. of Toledo for Communist teachings; lecturer Rand Sch. of Soc. Sc.; nat. com. I.L.D. 1928; nat. com. W.I.R. 1928; nat. com. A.A.A.I. Lg.; Am. Fed. of Teachers; European corres. Fed. Press 1931; nat. coun. Fell. Recon. 1927; Emer. Com. So. Pol. Pris.; Recep. Com. Soviet Flyers; Am. com. and delg. to W.C.A.W.; nat. com. Student Cong. Ag. War and speaker with Jane Addams at its Congress at the U. of Chgo., Dec. 1932; contrib. to "The Communist," "Soviet Russia Today," and "Labor Unity" (organ of T.U.U.L.); writer of editorials for "Progressive Miner" (organ of Prog. Miners of Am.); 1933 lecturer for F.S.U. and for benefit Workers School, Chgo.; financial contrib. Commonwealth Coll.; sponsor Chgo. Wkrs. Theatre, 1933; Nat. Coun. Prot. For. Born Wkrs.; supporter N.S. Lg.; Am. Com. for S.A.W.; John Reed Club; Cong. Exp. of Radicals; nat. com. F.S.U. 1934; home Ridgewood, N.J.

NEILSON, WILLIAM ALLAN: born Scotland; pres. Smith Coll. (see Hadley's "Sinister Shadows" for Smith Coll. "sex questionnaire"); pres. A.S.C.R.R.; vice pres. A.A. for O.A.S.; nat. coun. For. Pol. Assn.; endorser "Professional Patriots"; signer of petition to free Sacco and V., the Anarchist-Communist murderers; was on nat. com. Nat. Citiz. Com. on Rel. Lat. Am.; hon. vice pres. Nat. Cons. Lg.; signer Fell. Recon. Pet. Russ. Recog. 1932; pres. Open Road advis. com. 1933; see p. 255.

NELLES, WALTER: nat. com. A.C.L.U.; atty. for Garland Fund; ed. Law & Freedom Bulletins for A.C.L.U.; counsel for Scott Nearing, Max Eastman, etc., when prosecuted under charges of criminal anarchy and sedition.

NELSON, CLAUD: nat. com. Nat. R. & L. Found. 1933.

NELSON, WALTER M.: Chmn. Detroit branch A.C.L.U.

NESSIN, SAM: Communist; instr. Wkrs. Sch. in Tr. Un. Strategy and Tactics; T.U.U.L. org.; exec. com. Unemp. Coun. of N.Y.; nat. com. I.L.D. 1930.

NESTOR, AGNES: vice pres. of Nat. and pres. Chgo. Wom. Tr. Un. Lg.; Bryn Mawr Summer Sch. for Workers in Industry; advis. bd. Chgo. Forum Coun.; Griffin Bill sponsor 1932; Woman's City Club, Chgo.; see also Mrs. Raymond Robins; sponsor Berger Nat. Found. dinner, 1931; backed Wm. H. Holly for Federal judge.

NEUMANN, HENRY: Am. com. W.C.A.W.; Emer. Com. Strik. Rel. 1927-33; exec. com. L.I.P.A. 1931; exec. com. W.R. Lg. 1931; Nat. Com. Def. Pol. Pris. (Dreiser); Com. for Thomas 1929; vice pres. Lincoln Settlement for Colored People, Brooklyn; Russ. Reconst. Farms, 1925; Peace Patriots; Freethinkers Ingersoll Com. 1933; nat. coun. Berger Nat. Found.; Conf. Prog. Pol. Action camp. com. 1934.

NEUMANN, MRS. HENRY: Woman's Peace Society, 1928; Com. for Thomas 1929.

NEWELL, J. PIERCE: M.E. minister, formerly of Park Ridge, now of Rockford, Ill.; L.I.D.; Chr. Soc. Act. M. 1933 exec. com.; sponsor Berger Nat. Found. dinner 1931.

NEWHOFF, ANDREW: sec. communist I.L.D.; instr. Chgo. Wkrs. Sch. in labor defense, fall term 1933.

NEWTON, HERBERT (ALIAS GILMER BRADY): colored; Ill. Communist cand. 1932; under sedition charges Atlanta, Ga.; an org. of N.S. Lg. at U. of Chgo. and reported to have majored there in Sociology; Agitprop dir. Communist Party, Dist. No. 8; was org. of Cleveland Lg. Strugg. Negro Rts.; lecturer for M.O.P.R. (Russian sec. of I.L.D.) in Russia 1929; editor Chgo. "Workers Voice," 1933; org. Packinghouse Wkrs. Indust. Un., Chgo., 1934.

NEWTON, RAY: sec. Peace Section of Am. Friends Serv. Com.; U.S. Cong. Ag. War; nat. com. War Resisters Lg. 1930-31; endorsers com. World Peaceways.

NICHOL, REV. D. M.: C.W.C. on Unemp. 1933.

NICOLE, LEON: Swiss Socialist; intl. com. W.C.A.W.; ed. radical newspaper and mem. Cantonal govt.; denounced by newspapers as emissary of Moscow and responsible for Red riot in Geneva, Switz., Nov. 9, 1932, in which eleven were killed and seventy wounded; convicted June 3, 1933.

NIEBUHR, REINHOLD: Prof. Union Theol. Sem. since 1928; bd. dir. L.I.D.; L.I.P.A.; chmn. Fell. Recon.; was sec. Fell. Chr. Social Order (now Fell. Recon.); nat. coun. C.M.E.; Fed. Coun. Chs.; Ald. cand. N.Y.C. on Socialist ticket; endors. com. World Peaceways; signer Fell. Recon. Pet. Russ. Recog. 1932; ed. "World Tomorrow"; contrib. ed. "Christian Century"; exec. com. Nat. R. & L. Found. 1933; author of "Moral Man and Immoral Society," which aims to show that we must have violent revolution to achieve Socialism and is praised by Communist publications as an exposition of true Marxism, according to Communist standards; the "Christian Century Pulpit," pub. for ministers only by the "Christian Century," Feb. 1933, stated in a review of the above book: "I recommend the book . . . Thus Dr. Niebuhr, though long a pacifist leader, goes over to the school of Karl Marx, accepts the class struggle as inevitable and justified, and offers us in this book his conception of the function of religion in such a world struggle."; spkr. for communist U.S. Cong. Ag. War; Emer. Com. Strik. Rel. 1933; Nat. Coun. Prot. For. Born Wkrs. (communist) Detroit br. 1928; nat. coun. Berger Nat. Found.; Conf. Prog. Pol. Act. camp. com. 1934.

NIEBUHR, RICHARD: Prof. Philos. Religion Eden Theol. Sem. since 1927;

brother of Reinhold; nat. com. Nat. R. & L. Found. 1933; Webster Groves, Mo.

NIGOB, EUGENE: pianist for Communist meetings; John Reed Club; nat. com. W.I.R. (1929).

NILES, DAVID K.: sec. Mass. A.C.L.U. Com.

NOE, A. C.: exec. com. A.S.C.R.R., Chgo.

NOONAN, JOHN J.: People's Legis. Serv.; Nat. Save Our Schs. Com.

NORMAN, LOREN: Communist Lg. ("Trotskyite"); Prog. Miners Un. and reg. contrib. "Progressive Miner"; ed. with Jerry Allard of "The Fighting Miner," official organ of the Militant Left Wing Miners of America.

NORRIES, MRS. GORDON: N.Y. Coun. for Intl. Coop. to Prevent War; Non-Intervention Citiz. Com. 1927; Russ. Reconst. Farms, 1925; Emer. Com. Strik. Rel. 1927.

NORRIS, GEO. W.: radical U.S. Senator from Nebraska; Com. on Coal and Giant P.; was hon. pres. Nat. Citiz. Com. on Rel. Lat. Am. 1927; nat. coun. People's Legis. Serv.; Nat. Pop. Govt. Lg.; endors. Lane Pamphlet.

NORTH, JOS.: communist writer for Intl. Pamphlets; John Reed Club; former ed. "Labor Defender"; "New Masses" staff, 1933.

NUNN, WM. L.: nat. bd. dir. A.C.L.U.; Pris. Rel. Fund of I.L.D.; contrib. to Fed. Press Clip Sheet Service; Prof., formerly of U. of Pitts., now of Dana Coll., N.Y.C.; Nat. Com. to Aid Vic. G. Fascism.

NYE, GERALD P.: radical Rep.; U.S. Sen. from N.D.; Nat. Citiz. Com. Rel. Lat. Am. 1927; spkr. at Mooney protest meeting, Wash., D.C., 1/25/32.

NYGARD, EMIL: Communist; elected Mayor of Crosby, Minn., a town of 4,000 people, Dec. 6, 1932 (first Communist mayor elected in U.S.); defeated for re-election, 1933.

O

OAK, LISTON M.: N.C. to A.S.M.F.S.; Communist editor of "Soviet Russia Today" (F.S.U. organ); Soviet propaganda spkr. Dec. 3, 1933 in People's Ch., West Allis, Wis. (pastor is pro-Soviet Ralph M. Compere, who was active in Milk Strike).

O'BRIEN, PATRICK H.: chmn. legal advis. com. A.C.L.U. Detroit branch; instrumental in securing injunction against the alien registration law which is being made permanent; elected Atty. General of Mich., Nov. 1932; 1933, dismissed Bridgman Raid criminal syndicalism charges against Wm. Z. Foster and other Communists, freeing for use of Communist Party thousands of dollars of bond money held by the State.

O'CONNOR, HARVEY: a communist Federated Press Corres.; author "Mellon's Millions"; N.C. to A.S.M.F.S.; bd. Pris. Rel. Fund (I.L.D); spkr. communist United Front Conf., 805 James St., Pittsburgh, Pa., Oct. 15, 1933; Recep. Com. Soviet Flyers; corres. "New Masses," 1933; arrested in Pittsburgh; John Reed Club; husband of Jessie Lloyd, daughter of Lola Maverick Lloyd and Wm. Bross Lloyd.

OEHLER, HUGO: nat. com. Communist Lg. Am.; Progressive Miners Union, 1933; former mem. cent. com. Communist Party, U.S.A.; nat. com. A.A.A.I. Lg., 1928.

OGBURN, WM. F.: Prof. U. of Chgo., formerly Columbia U.; advis. Pioneer Youth of Am.; bd. Lg. for Org. Prog. 1931; mem. Com. of 100 (org. by A.C.L.U.) to aid teachers dismissed in N.Y. as unpatriotic and disloyal; a speaker at Sacco-V. meeting held in Paris; mem. Pres. Hoover's Com. on Social Trends, which made radical report.

O'HARE, KATE RICHARDS: with husband and W. E. Zeuch, founded Commonwealth Coll. at Mena, Ark.; convicted under sedition law and served fourteen months in Mo. State Pen.; was Socialist Party lecturer and I.W.W. exec.; led children's crusade to Wash., D.C., 1922, in behalf of "Amnesty for Political Prisoners"; was teacher Commonwealth Coll. until recently; Cong. Exp. Radicals.

OHL, HENRY: Pres. Wis. Fed. Labor (A. F. of L. affiliate); com. on action of Conf. Prog. Pol. Act. 1933.

OLAY, MAXMILLIAN: Free Society Group (anarchists), Chgo.; Nat. Mooney Coun. of Action, 1933; contrib. "Recovery Through Revolution"; born Oviedo, Spain 1893; active in movement since childhood in Spain, Cuba, and U.S.A.

OLDER, FREMONT: newspaper ed. San Fran., Cal.; vice chmn. nat. A.C.L.U.; Nat. Mooney-Billings Com.; active in Mooney agitation; Nat. Citiz. Com. for Sacco and V. 1927; endors. "Professional Patriots."

OLGIN, MOISSAYE J.: Jewish, born Russia; exec. com. Communist Party U.S.; ed. communist Daily Freiheit (see "Freiheits"); contrib. ed. "Soviet Russia Today"; writer for Communist magazines; instr. New Sch. for Social Research, 1932; exec. com. N.Y. Wkrs. Sch.; Recep. Com. Soviet Flyers; John Reed Club; head of Jewish section, Communist Party.

OLMSTED, ALLEN S.: represented A.C.L.U. before House Immigration Com.

advocating admission of alien anarchists and Communists, regardless of their seditious beliefs and utterances; wife active in W.I.L.P.F.; For. Pol. Assn.

OLMSTEAD, FRANK: exec. com. Nat. R. & L. Found.; nat. coun. C.M.E.; nat. com. War Resisters Lg., 1930, exec. com. 1931; coll. sec. of Y.M.C.A., scheduled to speak at Tom Mann meeting, N.Y.C. (Daily Wkr. 10/11/33).

OLMSTED, MILDRED S.: Pa. Com. Total Disarm.; chmn. organization W.I.L. P.F.

OLSON, FLOYD B.: Farmer-Labor Party Gov. of Minn.; vice pres. Pub. O. Lg.; threatened confiscation of wealth in Minn. and hoped present system of govt. would go "right down into hell" (Lit. Digest 4/29/33); endorsed by L.I.P.A.

O'NEAL, JAMES: Socialist Party wkr.; ed. New Leader (official organ of Socialist Party); author "Militant Socialism," etc.; infamous People's Coun.

O'NEALL, KELLY: nat. com. Nat. R. & L. Found. 1933.

ORNITZ, SAMUEL: author; with Metro-Goldwyn-Mayer Studio, Culver City, Cal., since 1929; claims to be an atheist; Communist Lg. P. G. for F. & F. 1932; N.C. to A.S.M.F.S.; Nat. Com. Def. Pol. Pris. 1932; contrib. ed. "New Masses."

OROZCO, JOSE CLEMENTE: Communist; Mexican fresco painter; "New Masses" staff, 1933.

OSBY, LAURA: Lg. Strugg. Negro Rts.; Communist Party functionary; cand. for Ald. 20th Ward, Chgo. 1933; participant unemp. demonstration (Daily Worker, 3/6/33); colored.

OTTO, MAX C.: Prof. Phil., U. of Wis.; atheist; edtl. contrib. A. Lincoln Center "Unity," 1933; endors. "Professional Patriots"; his arguments for atheism are printed in "Is There a God?" pub. by (Herbert L.) Willett Clark & Co. (publishing affiliate of "Christian Century").

OVERGAARD, ANDREW: Communist; sec. T.U.U.L. council of N.Y.; nat. com. F.S.U.; instr. N.Y.C. Wkrs. Sch.

OVERSTREET, HARRY A.: Prof. at City Coll. of N.Y. since 1911; lecturer New Sch. for Soc. Research since 1924; wartime "peace" worker, cooperating with Lochner, Harry F. Ward, Norman Thomas, etc.; exposed in Lusk Report; nat. vice chmn. C.M.E.; endors. World Peaceways; signer of Fell. Recon. Petition Russ. Recog. 1932; John Reed Club, N.Y.C. 1930; Labor Temple Sch.; endors. "Professional Patriots"; nat. com. W.R. Lg.; Freethinkers Ingersoll Com. 1933; Cong. Exp. Radicals.

OXNAM, G. BROMLEY: pres. De Pauw U. since 1928; was Prof. at U. of So. Cal. 1919-23 and pastor of M.E. Church of All Nations, Los A.; was active exec. of A.C.L.U., So. Cal. branch, and very active in advocacy of repeal of Cal. criminal syndicalism laws; mem. People's Edu. Lg. (of Communists, Anarchists, I.W. W.'s, etc.); member "The Internationale" (extreme radical group led by Fanny Bixby Spencer); Federated Farmer-Labor Party; committeeman Meth. Fed. for Soc. Serv. and its exec. sec. 1928; abolished compulsory military training at De Pauw soon after he became president, urging its abolition entirely 1934; Nat. R. & L. Found. nat. com. 1933; signer Fell. Recon. Pet. Russ. Recog.; Lg. for Org. Progress; sec. World Peace Commn., M.E. Ch. 1932; see also under article "Who Are They?"

P

PACE, JOHN: Communist organizer and "General" of the Bonus March to Wash. 1932; was arrested in Detroit, and given 60 days imprisonment. He had demanded a welfare check of $6.00 and refused to work for it, arguing that he was too busy organizing another Communist march (Nat. Republic, Mar. 1933).

PACKARD, JOHN L.: nat. exec. com. Socialist Party; nat. com. Lg. Against Fascism.

PAGE, KIRBY: formerly minister and evangelist; now ed. "World Tomorrow"; Socialist; Commn. on Intl. Justice and Goodwill of Fed. Coun. Chs.; Garland Fund Com. on Am. Imperialism; was chmn. exec. com. Fell. for Chr. Social Order (now Fell. Recon.); vice chmn. Fell. Recon.; Non-Intervention Citiz. Com. 1927; "inspiration" of L.I.P.A.; nat. coun. C.M.E.; Peace Patriots; collaborator with Sherwood Eddy; contrib. to "Disarm" (of L.I.D.); pro-Soviet; author of infamous "slacker oath"; signer, with Robt. Morss Lovett and Rose Schneiderman, of ad. in "World Tomorrow" for Aug. 1925 asking for contributions to Garland Fund for use in aiding Chinese Communists; endorser Lane Pamphlet; in "Toward New Economic Society" (by Eddy and Page), recommends reading of Daily Worker (Communist); financial contrib. Commonwealth Coll.; Nat. R. & L. Found. 1933; nat. com. Lg. Against Fascism, 1933; nat. com. W.R. Lg.; nat. coun. Berger Nat. Found.; leader with Sherwood Eddy of delegation to Russia in 1926.

PAGE, MYRA: Communist writer; contrib. ed. "New Masses," "New Pioneer";

Intl. Union Revol. Writers; perm. contrib. Intl. Lit.; Lg. Strugg. Negro Rts.; "New Masses"; Revol. Writers Fed.; "New Pioneer."

PALMER, ALBERT W.: Congl. minister; Pres. and Prof. Chgo. Theol. Sem.; C.M.E. Ill.; signer Fell. Recon. Pet. Russ. Recog. 1932; introduced radical Sunday Evening Forum in First Cong. Church of Oak Park.

PALMER, FRANK LA VERNE: Communist supporter; nat. bd. dir. A.C.L.U. 1933; former ed. "Colorado Labor Advocate"; lecturer Brookwood Labor Coll. 1932; Nat. Com. Def. Pol. Pris. 1932; contrib. Daily Worker; field sec. A.C.L.U. Chgo. Com. 1930; mgr. Eastern bureau Fed. Press; speaker for various Communist groups; arrested many times in riots, etc.; he wrote in Communist "Labor Unity," Mar. 1928: "You will have to move fast to catch me between jails. However, I have written a little something for Labor Unity. This was a great strike. Fraternally, Frank Palmer."; mem. First. Am. Tr. Un. Delg. to Russia, 1927, which was repudiated by A. F. of L. because of communistic character; Pris. Rel. Fund (I.L.D.) 1932; Dreiser Com. on Coal; Scottsboro Com. of Action; exec. bd. Federated Press, 1927; Recep. Com. Soviet Flyers.

PANKEN, JACOB: Jewish Socialist; born Russia; Judge, N.Y.C., 1917; exec. com. infamous People's Coun. 1917; org. Intl. Ladies Garm. Wkrs. Un.; Il. Nuovo Mondo Nat. Com.; delg. 2nd Intl. 1933, Paris, where the Am. delegation was most revolutionary of all, according to press reports; nat. coun. Berger Nat. Found.; Cong. Exp. Radicals.

PANKHURST, ESTELLE SYLVIA: English suffragist imprisoned fifteen times (twelve hunger strikes) for woman's suffrage, anti-war, and Communist activities; founder Montessori School Nursery; org. British Communist Party; Nat. Com. to Aid Vic. G. Fascism 1933.

PARK, MARION: Pres. Bryn Mawr Coll.; Open Road; nat. coun. C.M.E.; Fell. Recon. Pet. Russ. Recog.

PARK, ROBERT EZRA: Prof. U. of Chgo.; edu. work among Negroes 1905-14; dir. Race Rel. Surv. of Pac. Coast 1923-5; A.C.L.U. Chgo. Com.

PARKER, JULIA S. O'CONNOR: nat. com. A.C.L.U.

PARSONS, MRS. EDGERTON: Am. Assn. Univ. Women; Non-Intervention Citiz. Com. 1927; Griffin Bill sponsor 1932; attended Rosika Schwimmer's recep. for Einstein, 3/16/33; endorser's com. World Peaceways.

PARSONS, EDW. LAMBE: Prot. Episc. Bishop of Cal.; also lecturer; active pacifist; nat. coun. C.M.E.; Nat. Mooney-Billings Com.; endors. Lane Pamphlet; campaign com. Conf. Prog. Pol. Action, 1933; home San Francisco.

PASS, JOSEPH: Communist; "Labor Defender"; Nat. Com. Def. Pol. Pris. 1931; John Reed Club; bd. Pris. Rel. Fund (I.L.D.).

PASTERNAK, N.: Communist; instr. Wkrs. Sch. N.Y. on "Principles of Communism."

PATTERSON, ERNEST M.: Prof. U. of Pa.; dir. A.S.C.R.R.; pres. Acad. Pol. and Soc. Science; For. Pol. Assn.; Fell. Recon. Pet. Russ. Recog.

PATTERSON, WM. L.: colored; nat. sec. communist I.L.D.; Nat. Scottsboro Com. of Action; Nat. Mooney Coun. of Action; cent. com. Communist Party; Sacco-V. Nat. Lg.; nat. com. F.S.U. 1934.

PEARL, RAYMOND: A.S.C.R.R.; biologist Johns Hopkins U.

PEIXOTTO, JESSICA B.: U. of Cal.; Nat. Cons. Lg.; endors. "Professional Patriots"; advis. coun. For. Lang. Inf. Serv. 1931.

PENDLETON, ELLEN F.: Pres. Wellesley Coll.; Open Road 1933; Fell. Recon. Pet. Russ. Recog.; favors embargo on arms shipments.

PERILLA, JACK: Communist Party cent. com.; writer for "Party Organizer," Jan. 1932; former circulation mgr. of Daily Wkr.

PETERS, PAUL: Communist; "Labor Defender"; "New Masses"; N.Y. Suitcase Theatre; Pris. Rel. Fund (I.L.D.); Nat. Com. Def. Pol. Pris. 1931; John Reed Club; Scottsboro Com. of Act.

PETERSON, ARNOLD: nat. sec. Socialist-Labor Party.

PETTIS, ASHLEY: pianist formerly of Eastman Sch. Music; Communist; "New Masses" staff 1933; F.S.U.; John Reed Club spkr.; a "Communist-Recommended Author."

PETTIT, WALTER W.: Russ. Reconst. Farms, 1925; A.S.C.R.R. advis. com. and book com.; Prof. N.Y. Sch. Social Work; cooperating educator Recon. Trips. N.Y.

PICKENS, WILLIAM: colored; formerly coll. prof.; nat. com. communist I.L.D. 1928; field sec. N.A.A.C.P. since Feb. 1920; nat. com. A.C.L.U.; bd. dir. L.I.D.; nat. com. A.A.A.I. Lg. 1928; Pris. Rel. Fund (I.L.D.) 1928-33; at one time regular contrib. of articles to Daily Worker; his book

"Bursting Bonds" was pub. by Gosidat Pub. Hse. (Communist), at Moscow, 1923; contrib. ed. "World Tomorrow"; Nat. R. & L. Found. 1933; rec'd diploma from British Esperanto Assn. 1906; Hands Off China Com.; advertised as speaker at joint N.A. A.C.P. and I.L.D. meeting, Waukegan, Ill., May 29, 1933; delg. to A.A.A.I. Lg. congress at Brussels, 1927, and at Frankfort, Germany, 1929; fellow vice chmn. with Earl Browder (sec. Communist Party) of the Am. Lg. Ag. War and Fascism, 1933.

PINCHOT, AMOS R. E.: nat. com. A.C. L.U.; nat. coun. Berger Nat. Found.; Emer. Com. Strik. Rel.; endors. "Professional Patriots"; nat. bd. dir. A.C.L.U. 1933; vice pres. Pub. O. Lg. of Am.; Cong. Exp. Radicals; home N.Y. City; brother Gifford is Gov. of Pa.

PISER, M.: nat. org. communist Furniture Wkrs. Indust. Un.; Recep. Com. Soviet Flyers, 1929.

POINDEXTER, D.: Communist Party functionary; exec. of Lg. Strugg. Negro Rts.; Nat. Mooney Coun. Act. 1933; Chgo. police record; cand. for Cong. on Communist ticket, 1932; chmn. Wash. Park Forum, 1933; under indictment on criminal charges for rioting at relief station, 1933.

POLLAK, KATH.: N.Y. Socialist Party; faculty mem. Brookwood Lab. Coll., 1932; Conf. Prog. Lab. Act.; cand. for dir. L.I. D.; mem. exec. com. Illinois division Cong. of Farmers and Workers for Ec. Reconstr.

POLLAK, WALTER H.: N.Y. I.L.D. lawyer, active in Scottsboro case; fin. contrib. to I.L.D. 1928; dir. For. Pol. Assn.

POLLETTI, W. CHAS.: nat. bd. dir. A. C.L.U. 1933.

PORTER, PAUL: mem. Socialist Party; field sec. and lecturer of L.I.D. (see); assoc. ed. "Revolt" (L.I.D.), now "Student Outlook"; tour conductor Russia, 1931.

PORTER, R. B.: com. Chr. Soc. Act. M.; Eugene, Ore.

POST, ALICE THACHER: editor; vice pres. A.A.A.I. Lg.; Peace Patriots; delg. Women's Intl. Cong., The Hague, 1915; Women's Peace Party; W.I.L.P.F.; home Washington, D. C.; widow of Louis F.

POST, LOUIS F.: former Asst. Sec. Labor; Nat. Pop. Govt. Lg. and author of its "Deportations Delirium of 1920" attacking Dept. of Justice for deporting anarchists and Communists; wife Alice Thacher; deceased.

POTAMKIN, HARRY ALAN: Communist; Intl. Un. Revol. Writers, etc.; deceased 1933.

POTASH, JOE: Communist Party functionary; N.Y. sec. Needle Tr. Wkrs. Indust. Un.

POTOFSKY, J. S.: nat. coun. L.I.D. for N.Y.

POTTER, CHAS. FRANCIS: a founder of "Humanism"; Freethinkers Ingersoll Com. 1933.

POUND, ARTHUR: nat. com. Nat. R. & L. Found. 1933.

POUND, ROSCOE: Dean Harvard Law School; contributed to I.L.D. funds for Scottsboro boys (Daily Wkr. 4/22/33); Fell. Faiths speaker Chgo. 1933; nat. coun. For. Pol. Assn.; Nat. Pop. Govt. Lg.; Nat. Cons. Lg.

POWELL, WEBSTER: N.C. to A.S.M. F.S. 1931; educators' Com. for Thomas 1929.

POWERS, GEO.: Communist Party functionary; Communist cand. for judge, N.Y. City; sec. Steel & Metal Wkrs. Indust. Un., N.Y. City; mem. Anti-Imperialist Lg. delg. to Cuba, 1933.

POWYS, JOHN COWPER: N.C. to A. S.M.F.S.; John Reed Club; novelist, lecturer and critic.

POYNTZ, JULIET STEWART: one of ten principal Communist leaders in U.S.; formerly Prof. Hunter Coll.; now nat. org. for Women's Division of Communist Party; returned from Moscow, 1931; Am. Assn. Lab. Legis.; Russ. Reconst. Farms, 1925; Recep. Com. Soviet Flyers; nat. com. I.L.D. 1928; dir. Bureau Labor Research, Rand. Sch.; very revolutionary.

PRATT, CAROLINE: Emer. Com. Strik. Rel.

PRATT, ELIOT: nat. bd. dir. A.C.L.U. 1933; Open Road.

PRATT, GEORGE D. JR.: nat. coun. L.I.D. for N.Y.; Emer. Com. Strik. Rel. 1933; Nat. Mooney-Billings Com.

PRESTON, EVELYN: nat. coun. L.I.D. for N.Y.; Emer. Com. Strik. Rel. 1927; Non-Intervention Citiz. Com. 1927; Nat. Save Our Schs. Com.; Com. on Coal & Giant P.; ed. com. L.I.D. (N.Y. Trib. 7/11/33).

PRICE, HELEN E.: nat. com. Nat. R. & L. Found. 1933.

PURO, HENRY: mem. cent. com. Communist Party; head Agrarian com. of Communist Party.

R

RADAMSKY, SERGEI: A.S.C.R.R.; popular singer at Communist functions.

RALSTON, JACKSON H.: lawyer; lecturer at Stanford U.; pres. bd. commnrs. (Hyattsville, Md.) which first applied Single Tax system of taxation, 1892; Peace Patriots; People's Lobby; Nat. Mooney-Billings Com.; vice pres. Am. Peace Soc.; Nat. Citiz. Com. Rel. Lat. Am. 1927; People's Legis. Serv.; A.C.L.U.; Nat. Pop. Govt. Lg. (charges against Dept. of Justice); home Palo Alto, Cal.

RAND, BARBARA: wife of Joe Dallett; former Fed. Press corres.; active in Communist work in Chgo. 1930-31.

RANDOLPH, A. PHILIP: ed. "Messenger"; pres. Bro. of Sleeping Car Porters; exec. com. Nat. R. & L. Found. 1933; former Rand Sch. lecturer; listed as "Negro agitator" in Lusk Report; signer of call for Cont. Cong. for Ec. Reconst. 1933; cand. for dir. L.I.D.; active in behalf of Tom Mooney; Tchrs. Un.; Socialist.

RANKIN, JEANNETTE: former Congresswoman from Mont.; nat. com. A.C.L.U.; nat. coun. Berger Nat. Found.; assoc. sec. N.C. for P.W.; Wom. Peace Union 1929; lobbyist against National Defense legislation; her People's Coun. affiliation exposed in Lusk Report.

RANSDELL, HOLLACE: of Ky.; Pris. Rel. Fund (I.L.D.); investigator for A.C.L.U. in Scottsboro Case; Nat. Com. Def. Pol. Pris.; exec. sec. Sacco-V. Nat. Lg. 1928.

RAPPORT, S.: Communist Party cent. com.

RASCOE, BURTON: Nat. Com. Def. Pol. Pris.; Emer. Com. So. Pol. Pris.; John Reed Club.

RASNICK, DR.: Communist; Doctor, Pittsburgh, Pa.; advertiser in Daily Wkr.

RAUSHENBUSH, H. STEPHEN: Socialist; nat. coun. L.I.D. for N.Y.; sec. Com. on Coal and Giant P.; staff mem. Bureau Indust. Research N.Y.; Emer. Com. Strik. Rel. 1927-33; formerly indust. advisor to Gov. Pinchot; com. on action Conf. Prog. Pol. Act. 1933; announced formation of Pa. Security Lg. (Fed. Press Clip. Sheet 1/10/33); reviewed Communist play "Peace on Earth" most favorably (Daily Worker, 12/5/33).

RAUSHENBUSH, PAUL: Socialist; Prof. U. of Wis.; financial contrib. Commonwealth Coll.; wife Eliz. Brandeis spkr. for W.I.L.P.F. (Milw. Leader 11/3/33).

RAWLEIGH, W. T.: pres. of firm of that name, Freeport, Ill.; vice pres. Pub. O. Lg. of Am.; Nat. Save Our Schs. Com.; advis. com. Util. Cons. and Inv. Lg.

RAYMOND, HARRY: Communist Party functionary; served 6 mos. in jail in 1930 with Foster, Minor, etc. for inciting riot; was org. Metal Wkrs. Indust. Un. 1930.

RAYMOND, PHILIP: Detroit Communist leader; nat. com. F.S.U., 1933; sec. communist Auto Wkrs. Un.; cand. on Communist ticket for city council, 1933; police record.

RECHT, CHAS. S.: "legal representative of Soviet Govt. in this country" (see Am. Anti-Bible Society); Cong. Exp. Radicals; finan. contrib. to "Soviet Russia Today" (S.R.T. Oct. 1932); official Soviet atty.

REDEFER, FREDERICK: exec. sec. Prog. Edu. Assn. and an author of its revolutionary manifesto; bd. ed. of its organ.

REED, DOROTHY: assoc. sec. N.C. for P.W.

REED, JOHN: deceased; buried in Kremlin, Moscow; an org. of Am. Communist Party; Communist "John Reed Clubs" named after him; returned from Russia as "consul general" for the Soviet regime; indicted for criminal anarchy in N.Y.; wife Louise Bryant Reed, who later married Wm. C. Bullitt, of special Russian mission (1919) fame and now Am. Amb. to Soviet Russia; was Am. newspaper correspondent.

REESE, CHAS.: org. communist Labor Sports Union; Chgo.

REESE, CURTIS W.: "Humanist" minister of All Souls Unit. Ch., Chgo.; mem. bd. and dean Abraham Lincoln Center, Chgo.; mem. bd. Unity Pub. Co., pub. of radical mag. "Unity," of which he is assoc. ed.; exec. bd. A.C.L.U. Chgo. Com.; Chgo. Emer. Com. Strik. Rel.; vice pres. L.I.D., Chgo. chapter; Chgo. com. Fell. Faiths; Chgo. Forum Coun.; City Club, Chgo.; A. Lincoln Center is meeting place of Workers' Laboratory Theatre, I.L.D., Unemp. Coun., and John Reed Club (all Communist); a convention of the latter was held there in May 1932; Communist notices fill the bulletin boards; endorser communist Counter-Olympics Com. (for independent Communist sports Olympic) 1932; sponsor of communist Chgo. Workers' Theatre, Mar. 1933; Freethinkers Ingersoll Com. 1933; Chgo. Com. for S.A.W.; presided at John Reed Club dinner for Barbusse at Chgo. Woman's Club (10/17/33 Daily News).

REEVE, KARL MARX (ALIAS PRICE): Communist Party org.; son of Ella Reeve Bloor; on ed. staff Daily Wkr. since 1923; now Communist Party section org. at Omaha, Neb.

REITMAN, BEN: See Free Society Group, also Emma Goldman.

RENN, LUDWIG: German Communist; "Labor Defender"; Intl. Union Revol. Writers; presidium Wkrs. Cult. Fed.; sentenced to 30 months imprisonment for revolutionary activities, Leipzig, Germany, 1/16/34; real name Arnold Friedrich Vieth von Golsserau.

RENO, MILO: leader Farm Holiday Assn.; nat. coun. Berger Nat. Found.; Conf. Prog. Pol. Act. 1933.

RENZI, MODERATO: exec. com. C.W. C. on Unemp. (Borders) 1933.

REYNOLDS, WM.: Communist Party functionary; police record in Detroit; writer for "Party Organizer"; cand. for Gov. of Mich. 1932; pres. of Unemp. Councils, Detroit.

RIBAK, LOUIS: communist "New Masses"; John Reed Club.

RICE, ELMER: nat. bd. dir. A.C.L.U. 1933; author of play "We, the People," an argument for revolution, given Apr. 29, 1933, at People's Playhouse, Chgo. as a benefit for the L.I.D.; Griffin Bill sponsor; endors. Open Road; Nat. Coun. Freedom from Censorship of A.C.L.U.; supporter Rand Sch. 1933; spkr. at election campaign dinner for Foster and Ford, N.Y. City, Oct. 1932.

RICE, WM. G.: Prof.; chmn. Wis. U. A.C.L.U. Com.; mem. com. to welcome Norman Thomas to Madison (Madison Capitol Times, 9/22/32); praised Thomas for Pres. Club at U. of Wis. ("Daily Cardinal," 9/23/32).

RICHARDS, EDW. C.: Socialist; L.I. D. speaker; exec. com. W.R. Lg.; Peace Patriots; coun. Pa. Com. for Total Disarm.; home Pottsville, Pa.

RICHBERG, DONALD R.: socialistic Chgo. lawyer; Com. on Coal & Giant P. of L.I.D.; Util. Cons. & Inv. Lg.; Nat. Citiz. Com. Rel. Lat. Am. 1927; Conf. Prof. Pol. Act. and chmn. Resolutions Com., 1924; sponsor and speaker, Berger Nat. Found. dinner 1931; contrib. to "New Republic"; Emer. Com. Strik. Rel., Chgo.; People's Legis. Serv.; Roosevelt appointee as General Legal Advisor, N.R.A. 1933.

RICHTER, H. M.: Chgo. surgeon and mem. Am. Medical Assn.; financial contrib. Daily Worker; Chgo. Com. for Strugg. Ag. War; Recep. Banquet com. for Ford (Negro Communist cand.) 1932.

RICHTER, KURT: A.S.C.R.R. and mem. of its com. on delg. to Russia.

RIDGE, LOLA: Nat. Com. Def. Pol. Pris.; Emer. Com. So. Pol. Pris.

RIEVE, EMIL: pres. Am. Fed. of Full Fashioned Hosiery Wkrs.; coun. Jt. Com. on Unemp.; nat. com. Lg. Against Fascism; vice chmn. exec. com. L.I.P.A.; signer of call for Cont. Cong. for Ec. Reconst.; spkr. U.S. Cong. Ag. War (Daily Wkr. 9/28/33).

RIIS, ROGER WILLIAM: nat. bd. dir. A.C.L.U. 1933; Nat. Mooney-Billings Com.

RITTER, HARRY O.: com. Chr. Soc. Act. M.; St. Louis, Mo.

RIVERA, DIEGO: former mem. cent. exec. com. Communist Party of Mexico and delg. to 1929 Anti-Imperialist World Congress, Frankfort on Main; hired by Rockefeller to decorate Rockefeller Center, N.Y.; decorated Communist Party (Opp.) New Workers School (N.Y.C.), 1933; came to U.S. on advice of Moscow friends as propagandist for the proletariat and revolution ("New Republic," May 24, 1933); disciplined by Communist Party of Mexico for accepting post as head of the National Art School "at a time when that same govt. was hounding the Party"; 1933 backed by "New Masses," John Reed Club, etc. in his fight against Rockefeller.

ROBINS, MARGARET DREIER: wife of Raymond Robins; pres. Nat. Wom. Tr. Un. Lg. 1907-22, hon. pres. since 1922, and now chmn. of its Intl. Com. on America's Relations with the Orient; one time pres. of N.Y. and Chgo. branches; Am. Assn. Lab. Legis.; Lg. Women Voters; with Agnes Nestor, organized agitative parade in Chgo. to stimulate public interest in release of Big Bill Haywood, I.W.W. leader on trial for murder, called by Chgo. Tribune an "anarchist parade" (Haywood was released on bail and escaped to Russia); endors. "Professional Patriots."

ROBINS, RAYMOND: pro-Soviet; advocated recognition; Chgo. Forum Coun.; endors. "Professional Patriots"; Com. for Human Rights Ag. Naziism 1934; photo featured in Intourist News No. 1 (summer 1933), which said: "He was in Moscow during the revolution as commander of the Red Cross. He was the first to make authentic reports to the U.S. on the successes of the new Soviet Govt. His work in Moscow brought him into personal contact with Lenin and other Soviet leaders, many of whom he intends to renew acquaintance with this summer."; Hon. David R. Francis, U.S. Amb. to Russia, who exposed him when testifying before a Senate Com. on Soviet Russia in 1917 wrote that Col. Robins was then "persona grata" to the Bolsheviks; Andrea Kalpaschnikoff, in his book, "A Prisoner Under Trotsky," p. 42, states: "Their (Red Cross) last piece of 'relief work' was not done to please the sound Russians. It was the donation of hundreds of thousands of cans of condensed milk, sent to the starving babies of Russia, to the Red Army of Trotsky. I found this out when I was in the fortress from one of my jailkeepers who bought me some in the public market and brought it to me saying triumphantly: 'Look at this, the Americans have given it to the lazy Soviet soldiers for nothing and we fathers have got to pay forty rubles a can to the Bolsheviki for it.'" (1918).

ROBINSON, BOARDMAN: cartoonist and painter; advis. coun. A.S.C.R.R.; co-author with Communist John Reed of "The War in Eastern Europe"; accompanied Reed on trip to Balkans and Russia 1915; mem. staff "The Masses" and "Liberator"; Emer. Com. So. Pol. Pris.; John Reed Club, N.Y.C.

ROCHESTER, ANNA: Communist; nat. bd. dir. A.C.L.U.; "New Masses" staff, 1933; staff Labor Research Assn.; nat. coun. Fell. Recon.; ed. "World Tomorrow," 1925; exec. com. L.I.D.; mem. Teachers Un. Aux.; co-author with communist Grace Hutchins; writer of communist Intl. Pamphlets; N.C. to A.S.M.F.S.; Pris. Rel. Fund (I.L.D.); Recep. Com. Soviet Flyers; John Reed Club.

RODRIGUEZ, WM. E.: lawyer; active in Socialist Party; Ald. (Socialist) Chgo. 1915-8; exec. bd. A.C.L.U. Chgo. Com.; former vice pres. Pub. O. Lg. of Am.; sponsor Berger Nat. Found. dinner, 1931.

ROEWER, GEO. E.: nat. coun. L.I.D. for Mass.

ROLLAND, ROMAIN: French Communist; writer; Intl. Com. for Struggle Ag. War; intl. com. W.C.A.W.; writer for "Izvestia" and "Pravda"; headed Anti-Imperialist Lg. of France (see A.A.A.I. Lg.); intl. com. Nat. Com. to Aid Vic. G. Fascism, 1933; corres. for A. Lincoln Center "Unity"; endorser "Letters of Sacco and Vanzetti"; intl. advis. bd. Intl. Literature 1933.

RONN, ESKEL: Communist; born Finland; gen. mgr. Cent. Coop. Exchange since 1922; North. States Coop. Lg.; home Superior, Wis.; died 1932.

*ROOSEVELT, MRS. FRANKLIN D.: Socialist sympathizer and associate; pacifist; Non-Intervention Citiz. Com. 1927 (Opposed to Monroe Doctrine, which the Roosevelt admin. has abrogated; 26 of its 75 members leading Socialists or Communists); active member of socialistic Nat. Cons. Lg. (see) and Nat. Wom. Tr. Un. Lg. (see), both supported by communistic Garland Fund; donated radio fees to Nat. Wom. Tr. Un. Lg. and radical Am. Friends Serv. Com. (see); co-worker with many radicals, some of whom have been appointed to Government positions by her husband; speaker, Nov. 24-25, 1933, Prog. Edu. Assn. (see) meeting with radicals Norman Thomas, Reinhold Niebuhr, Harry A. Overstreet, etc.; sent telegram expressing hope for success of radical pacifist World Peaceways (N. Y. Times, 10/17/33); vice pres. N.Y. Lg. Women Voters; addressed pacifist Conference on Cause and Cure of War, introduced by Carrie Chapman Catt, who exulted that "for the first time in the history of our country we have a woman in the white house who is one of us" (Chgo. Trib. 1/18/34); on advis. bd. ultra radical New Sch. for Soc. Research (see) 1931; communist Daily Wkr. 4/7/34 stated she and Miss Perkins were donating their services broadcasting over socialist Debs Memorial Radio Station WEVD (see) for benefit Intl. Ladies Garm. Wkrs. Un. (which rec'd $100,000 from Garland Fund for one communist-led strike) and suggested that this official cooperation might explain why the Federal Radio Commn. had lately granted this Socialist radio station an increase in wave length.

RORTY, JAMES: Communist; Nat. Com. Def. Pol. Pris.; M.W.D. Def. Com. 1930; contrib. ed. "New Masses"; contrib. ed. "Student Review"; contrib. to "Common Sense"; with Hunger Marchers in Wash. 1932; Communist Lg. P.G. for F. & F. 1932; A.C.L.U.

ROSEN, MRS. K. N.: A.S.C.R.R.

ROSENBERG, JAMES N.: lawyer, vice chmn. Am. Jewish Jt. Dist. Com.; chmn. Am. Jewish Joint Agrl. Corp. (Agro-Joint), which has settled 100,000 Jews on land as agriculturists in Russia and is spending many millions additional toward continued Jewish land settlement in Russia; dir. A.S.C.R.R.; For. Pol. Assn.; contrib. to "The Nation"; home N.Y.C.

ROSENTHAL, HENRY M.: Rabbi; Am. con. W.C.A.W.

ROSS, EDW. A.: Prof. Sociology, U. of Wis.; People's Legis. Serv.; Nat. Pop. Govt. Lg.; Nat. Save Our Schs. Com.; endors. "Professional Patriots"; nat. coun. Berger Nat. Found.; author of books on Russia; "Communist-Recommended Author"; nat. com. A.C.L.U. 1931; signer of Jt. Com. on Unemp. demand for redistribution of wealth (Fed. Press. Wash. Letter 4/7/33; endorser of F.S.U. Soviet recog. campaign; signer of letter to Pres. Roosevelt urging Russian recog.; signer of A.C.L.U. telegram to N.R.A. protesting United Mine Wkrs. of Am. jurisdiction in cold fields (as against Red unions); advis. bd. Lg. for Org. Prog.; dir. A.S.C.R.R.; contrib. to Rosky Golos Decennial (commemorating Russian Revol.); formerly at Stanford U., dismissed because of radicalism.

ROYCE, EDW.: Communist; Am. com. W.C.A.W.; treas. W.I.R.; delg. to W.I.R. cong. in Berlin, 1931; bd. Pris. Rel. Fund (I.L.D.).

RUBICKI, STEVE: Communist Party functionary.

RUBIN, JAY: sec. communist Food Wkrs. Indust. Un.

RUBINOW, I. M.: vice pres. A.A. for O.A.S.

RUEGG, WALTER (alias Paul Nouellens): Communist agitator; sec. Pan-Pacific Tr. Un. Secretariat; arrested in Shanghai with wife, Gertrude, both charged

*Sponsor Wash. Town Hall lectures featuring Communist and Socialist spkrs., barred from U. S. Chamber of Commerce auditorium because of radicalism.

with sedition against Chinest Govt. 1932.

RUGG, HAROLD: Columbia U. Prof.; broadcast speaker of Dec. 26, 1933, for socialist L.I.P.A.; his growing pro-Soviet eulogies in another speech are quoted at length in communist Daily Worker, Dec. 5, 1933 (Mike Gold's column): "'Today 6,000,000 young Russians in the Communist Youth Organization are making a fine constructive contribution to the construction of a new social order. Here is a war psychology of dramatic action which is so dear to youth set to the great building tasks of peace.'" His reference is to the Russian Comsomols (Young Communist League), which are building for world bloody class hate and revolution, destruction of religion and family life; cooperating educator Recon. Trips, 1931; bd. dir. Prog. Edu. Assn. organ 1934.

RUSSELL, BERTRAND A. W.: English author and lecturer; head Eng. section communist Anti-Imperialist Lg.; fined £100, imprisoned for six months, and lost lectureship at Cambridge U. for treasonable actions during War; author of "What I Believe," which advocates sex immorality, and "Why I Am Not a Christian," in which he says: "I believe that when I die I shall rot and nothing of my ego survive."; Daily Worker (Oct. 26, 1931) quotes him as saying in New York: "There is no hope in anything but the Soviet way."; L.I.D. lecturer on Am. tours; debater at Communist New Workers Sch., N.Y.C., 1931-2; vice pres. Freethinkers (atheist); British section A.S.C.R.R.; endorser "Letters Sacco and Vanzetti"; Freethinkers Ingersoll Com. 1933.

RUSSELL, CHAS. EDW.: journalist and author; Socialist; nat. coun. Berger Nat. Found.; mem. spec. mission to Russia, 1917; author of "Russia Unchained" (1918) and "Bolshevism and the United States" (1919); cand. for dir. L.I.D. 1931; vice pres. Pub. O. Lg. of Am.

RUSSELL, ELBERT: Prof. Biblical Interpretation and Dean, Sch. of Relig., Duke U.; nat. com. A.C.L.U.; special lecturer for Am. Friends Serv. Com. in Germany and Austria 1924-5; home Durham, N.C.

RUSSELL, GALEN E.: Socialist; nat. coun. Fell. Recon. 1928; Com. for Thomas 1929.

RUTHENBERG, CHAS. E.: deceased; U.S. Communist Party founder and exec. from 1922 until he died; lived in Cleveland, Ohio, which is designated "Ruthenberg" on U.S. maps redrawn by Soviets for "after the revolution."

RYAN, JOHN A.: Catholic priest; 1920 Lusk Report, p. 1139, cites him as leader of a certain group in Catholic Church "with leanings toward Socialism"; Prof. Moral Theol. and Indust. Ethics, Catholic U., Wash., D.C., since 1915; dir. soc. act. dept. Nat. Cath. Welfare Coun.; co-author (with Morris Hillquit, alias Hilcovicz, radical left-wing Socialist) of "Socialism—Promise or Menace" 1914; a leader of Cath. Assn. for Intl. Peace; nat. com. A.C.L.U.; vice chmn. Labor Def. Coun. (with Communist Wm. Z. Foster, Eugene Debs, etc.) 1923; Nat. Mooney-Billings Com. 1929; Am. Assn. Lab. Legis.; hon. vice pres. Nat. Cons. Lg.; N.C. for P.W.; vice-chmn. Jt. Com. on Unemp.; Nat. World Ct. Com. 1931; vice pres. A.A. for O.A.S.; vice pres. Pub. Ownership Lg. of Am.; Nat. Pop. Govt. Lg.; Nat. R. & L. Found. 1933-4 and book editor, with Ernest F. Tittle and E. L. Israel, of its very Red organ "Economic Justice," which features Soviet atheist cartoons and distributes Communist books such as "Toward Soviet America" by Wm. Z. Foster, "Little Lenin Library," etc.; nat. coun. For. Pol. Assn.; Nat. Save Our Schs. Com.; People's Legis. Serv. and a founder; endors. "Professional Patriots."

RYKOV, ALEKSEI: U.S.S.R. Army Commissar; 1917 revolutionist.

S

SACCO, NICOLAI: beneficiary, with Bartolomeo Vanzetti, of Communist Sacco-V. agitation; executed with Vanzetti for the murder of a paymaster and theft of $15,000 at South Braintree, Mass.; prosecution of these Anarchist-Communists cost the county $36,000; Communist agitation carried case to U.S. Supreme Court, 1927.

SAKLATVALA, SHAPURJI: British Communist from Bombay, India; intl. com. W.C.A.W.; mem. Parliament, England; Intl. Red Aid; intl. com. Nat. Com. to Aid Vic. G. Fascism, 1934.

SALZMAN, R.: Communist; nat. sec. I.W.O.

SANDINO, GEN. AUGUSTO C.: Nicaraguan mine worker; Communist-supported, violently anti-American revolutionary 1928; intl. com. W.C.A.W. 1932; killed Feb. 1934.

SANDINO, SOCRATES: nat. com. A.A. A.I. Lg.; brother of Gen. Augusto Sandino of Nicaragua (communist-supported revolutionary); killed Feb. 1934.

SANFORD, MARY R.: Socialist; exec. com. L.I.D.; exec. com. Conf. Prog. Pol. Act.; formerly sec. Vt. Socialist Soc. and mem. bd. Nat. Cons. Lg.; nat. coun. Berger Nat. Found.; N.Y.C.

SANFORD, REV. RAYMOND: C.W.C. on Unemp. 1933.

SANGER, MARGARET: formerly wife of Dr. Wm. Sanger, now Mrs. J. Noah H. Slee; leading birth control advocate; pres. Am. Birth Cont. Lg.; lecturer and writer on subject; indicted 1915 (charges dropped after petition to Pres. Wilson by radicals) and arrested and convicted 1916, both for illegal birth cont. activities; author of book formerly barred by P.O. Dept.; former associate of Emma Goldman and Alex. Berkman, anarchists; mem. Lg. for Amnesty Pol. Pris. (of Berkman anarchist gang); listed in Freethought Press Assn. (atheist) catalogue as "a crusading freethinker against religious bigotry"; Fell. Faiths speaker 1933 Chgo.; Freethinkers Ingersoll Com. 1933.

SANGER, DR. WM. W.: author of "The History of Prostitution," pub. by the Freethought Press Assn., whose catalogue says of the book: "Tends to prove that prostitutes of our own times come generally from those classes of society where religion is taught most thoroughly—and that the prostitutes themselves are generally ultra-devout."

SAPOSS, DAVID: Socialist; res. faculty mem. Brookwood Lab. Coll. 1932; bd. dir. L.I.D.; edu. dir. N.Y. jt. bd. Amalg. Cloth. Wkrs. of Am. 1920-1; instr. Rand Sch. 1932; John Reed Club.

SAYLER, OLIVER: A.S.C.R.R. (com. on Arts); lect. on the theatre and on Russia; ed. Plays of the Moscow Art Theatre, etc.; author "Revolt in the Arts"; N.Y.C.

SAYRE, JOHN NEVIN: Socialist; brother of Francis Bowes Sayre (Roosevelt appointee and endors. Lane Pamphlet); wartime "peace" worker; minister; exec. com. W.R. Lg.; nat. com. A.C.L.U.; Emer. Peace Fed. 1917; Labor Def. Coun. 1923; exec. com. Non-Intervention Citiz. Com. 1927; Emer. Com. Strik. Rel. 1928-33; Church L.I.D.; Nat. Mooney-Billings Com.; Il Nuovo Mondo Nat. Com.; nat. advis. com. Sacco-V. Nat. Lg.; endors. com. World Peaceways; nat. com. Nat. World Ct. Com.; exec. sec. Fell. Recon. 1932; nat. vice chmn. C.M.E.; sec. Fellowship Press (pub. "World Tomorrow"); pres. "World Tomorrow" 1932; Peace Patriots; Congressional Exp. Radicals; Conf. Prog. Pol. Act. camp. com. 1934; endors. Lane Pamphlet.

SCARLETT, WM.: dean St. Louis Episcopal Cathedral since 1922; nat. com. A.C.L.U.; nat. coun. C.M.E.; Sherwood Eddy delg. to Russia, 1926; nat. coun. For. Pol. Assn.; endors. "Professional Patriots."

SCATTERGOOD, J. HENRY: A.C.L.U. Phila. branch; nat. coun. C.M.E.; People's Lobby; Sacco-Vanz. appealer; For. Pol. Assn.; Am. Friends Serv. Com.; endors. Lane Pamphlet.

SCATTERGOOD, E. F.: vice pres. Pub. O. Lg. of Am.; elec. engineer.

SCHAAR, SARAH B.: exec. com. L.I.D.; advis. com. C.W.C. on Unemp.

SCHACTMAN, MAX: Communist Lg. nat. com.; nat. com. A.A.A.I. Lg. 1928; "Trotskyite."

SCHEVILL, FERDINAND: Prof. U. of Chgo.; A.C.L.U. Chgo. Com.; People's Lobby; endors. "Professional Patriots"; sponsor Berger Nat. Found. dinner, 1931.

SCHINDLER, KURT: A.S.C.R.R.; composer.

SCHLESINGER, BENJ.: Socialist; mgr. Jewish Daily Forward, Chgo.; was gen. pres. Intl. Ladies Garm. Wkrs. Un.; infamous People's Coun.; Workmen's Circle; nat. coun. Berger Nat. Found.

SCHLINK, F. J.: nat. com. Nat. R. & L. Found.; technical director of Consumer's Research (socialist); finan. contrib. I.L.D. 1928; lect. for L.I.D.

SCHLOSSBERG, JOS.: born Russia; Socialist; nat. com. A.C.L.U.; Workmen's Circle; wartime "peace" worker and an org. of infamous People's Coun.; gen. sec.-treas. Amalg. Cloth. Wkrs. of Am. and ed. of their organ "Advance"; L.I.P.A.; Il Nuovo Mondo Nat. Com.; Non-Intervention Citiz. Com. 1927; org. Pioneer Youth of Am.; bd. Russ.-Am. Indust. Corp.; advis. com. Fed. Unemp. Wkrs. Lgs. N.Y.C. 1932; exec. bd. Fed. Press; Conf. Prog. Pol. Act., 1933; nat. com. Lg. Against Fascism; lecturer Rand Sch. 1931-2; endors. Lane Pamphlet.

SCHMAULHAUSEN, SAMUEL D.: see "Recovery Through Revolution"; Sacco-V. Nat. Lg.; sex and spec. lecturer and psych. consultant Labor Temple Sch.; co-author "Sex in Civilization" with V. F. Calverton; consultant communist Wkrs. Cooperative Colony, N.Y.C.

SCHMIES, JOHN: Communist Party cent. com.; Communist Party Dist. No. 7 org. at Detroit.

SCHNEID, HYMAN: Socialist Party; Workmen's Circle; exec. com. C.W.C. on Unemp.; pres. Amalg. Cloth. Wkrs. of Ill.; Am. Com. on Inf. about Russia, 1928; Socialist Cand. for Ill. Congressman-at-Large, 1932.

SCHNEIDER, ISADOR: novelist and poet; Communist Lg. P. G. for F. & F. 1932; leader anti-Jap. parade Feb. 4, 1933; contrib. "New Masses" and Daily Wkr.; home N.Y.C.

SCHNEIDERMANN, ROSE: born Russian Poland; Roosevelt appointee Labor Bd. 1933; Fed. Unemp. Wkrs. Lgs. of N.Y.C. 1933; Communist sympathizer; see Hands Off Committees; pres. N.Y. and vice pres. Nat. Wom. Tr. Un. Lg. since 1917; wartime "peace" worker; Emer. Peace Fed.; Am. Conf. Democ.; an org. infamous People's Coun.; nat. com. A.C. L.U.; cand. U.S. Sen. N.Y. Farmer-Lab. ticket 1920; Emer. Com. Strik. Rel.; nat. coun. Berger Nat. Found.; exec. and org. of Cloth Hat and Cap Mkrs. Un.; gen. org. Intl. Ladies Garm. Wkrs. Un. 1914-1916; has objected, it is said, to the nickname, "the Red Rose of Anarchy"; assoc. of Mrs. F. D. Roosevelt on Non-Intervention Citiz. Com.; Fell. Recon.; nat. com. Nat. World Ct. Com. 1931; Pioneer Youth of Am.; signer of ad. in "World Tomorrow" for Aug. 1925 soliciting money for Garland Fund for use in helping Chinese Communists.

SCHOENRICH, JUDGE OTTO: Garland Fund Com. on Am. Imperialism.

SCHOFIELD, CHAS.: com. Chr. Soc. Act. M.; Ft. Collins, Colo.

SCHUMAN, FREDERICK L.: U. of Chgo. Prof.; lecturer Communist Chgo. Workers Sch. 1932; leader of tour to Soviet Russia for A.S.C.R.R. and Intourist, 1933; Communist Lg. P. G. for F. & F. 1932; Recep. Banquet Com. for Ford 1932; nat. com. and endorser Student Cong. Ag. War, (U. of Chgo. 1932); contrib. "Soviet Russia Today" 1932; dir. A.S.C.R.R. Chgo. branch; endorser Janowicz, Communist cand. Ald. 5th Ward, Chgo., Feb. 1933; sponsor of communist Chgo. Workers Theatre 1933.

SCHWARTZ, BENJ.: com. Chr. Soc. Act. M.; Muscatine, Ia.

SCHWARTZ, CHAS. P.: A.C.L.U. Chgo. Com.

SCHWARTZ, MAUD: org. Pioneer Youth of Am.; Socialist; mem. Workmen's Compensation Bd. of N.Y. State Dept. of Labor.

SCHWARTZ, SAMUEL DISRAELI: Adult Edu. Coun.; L.I.D.; mgr. very radical Hirsch Center Forum at Sinai Temple, Chgo.

SCHWIMMER, ROSIKA: Hungarian Jewess; Minister to Switzerland and mem. radical Nat. Coun. of 15 governing Hungary 1918-19, under communist-aiding Count M. Karolyi, who delivered Hungary to Bela Kun Communist terror regime; org. with Lochner of Ford Peace Party; org. with Jane Addams and others of W.I. L.P.F.; has described herself as an "uncompromising pacifist and absolute atheist, and without a sense of nationalism"; denied U.S. citizenship because she refused to promise to defend U.S. in case of war; her atty. in citizenship fight, an A.C.L.U. atty.; Fell. Faiths speaker Chgo. 1933.

SCOTT, WALTER DILL. pres. Northwestern U., Evanston, Ill.; World Peaceways; Nat. Advis. Coun. on Radio in Edu. (in conjunction with L.I.D.); opponent of Baker anti-sedition Bills at Springfield Hearing, May 1933; denies that James M. Yard's radicalism was cause of his dismissal from U. staff.

SCUDDER, VIDA D.: Prof. Wellesley Coll.; Socialist; nat. coun. Berger Nat. Found.; formerly social worker; A.C.L.U. Mass. Com.; mem. A.C.L.U. com. on acad. freedom; also nat. com. A.C.L.U. 1932; exec. com. Ch. Socialist Lg.; vice pres. L.I.D.; chmn. Ch. L.I.D.; Peace Patriots; Il Nuovo Mondo Nat. Com.; Sacco-V. Nat. Lg.; financial contrib. Commonwealth Coll.; endors. "Professional Patriots"; Cong. Exp. Radicals; home Wellesley, Mass.

SEARS, AMELIA: social worker; formerly sch. teacher; Cook County Commr., Ill.; A.C.L.U. Chgo. Com.; Fell. Faiths; W.I.L.P.F.; Chgo. Forum Coun.; Woman's City Club, Chgo.; acting pres. Urban League Chgo. 1933 at race relations parley; adv. com. Util. Cons. and Inv. Lg.

SEAVER, EDWIN: Communist Lg. P. G. for F. & F. 1932; contrib. ed. "New Masses"; Nat. Com. Def. Pol. Pris. 1931; John Reed Club, N.Y.C.; writer; former publicity dir. A.C.L.U.; Com. for Philippine Independence; Fell. Recon.; Lg. for Mutual Aid.

SEEDS, NELLIE M.: see Nearing.

SEEDS, WM. H.: com. chmn. C.W.C. on Unemp.

SEITTER, CARL C.: com. Chr. Soc. Act. M.; Los A., Cal.

SELDES, GILBERT: assoc. ed. "New Republic"; radical columnist for Hearst papers; appealed for funds for Rand Sch. 1933.

SELIGMAN, EDWIN R. A.: Prof. Columbia U.; A.S.C.R.R.; Fell. Recon. Pet. Russ. Recog.; vice chmn. Fell. Faiths com. of 300; Nat. Cons. Lg.; Freethinkers Ingersoll Com. 1933.

SELLERS, ALBERT G.: Communist; nat. treas. Bonus Exped. Forces Rank and File; U.S. Cong. Ag. War; 524 Walnut St., Allentown, Pa.

SENIOR, CLARENCE: nat. sec. Socialist Party; A.C.L.U. Chgo. Com.; exec. com. L.I.D. Chgo.; advis. com. C.W.C. on Unemp. (Borders); nat. com. L.I.D.; delg. Labor and Socialist (2nd.) Intl. at Vienna 1931, Paris 1933, etc.; tour conductor Russia 1930; nat. com. W.R. Lg.; campaign dir. Socialist Party 1932; wife Ethel Watson; nat. com. Lg. Against Fascism; sponsor Berger Nat. Found. dinner, 1931.

SHAW, GEORGE BERNARD: English author, born Dublin, Ireland, 1856; leader London Fabian Society (Socialist); a founder British Labour Party; lecturer on Socialism since 1883; intl. com. W.C.A.W.; lauded Russia and Soviet regime after short, carefully-supervised visit there in 1931; a London dispatch dated Dec. 12, 1932, pub. in Los A. Examiner, quotes him: "Keep Einstein out of America? They can't do that! I am a Communist and they haven't tried to keep me out. I have a passport."; created furore in China, Feb. 1933, by advising Chinese students to "get into Communism up to their necks" and join in a Communist revolution; latest book bitter attack on religion; British section A.S.C.R.R.; Freethinkers Ingersoll Com. 1933; Intl. Com. for S.A.W. 1933.

SHEDD, CLARENCE: nat. com. Nat. R. & L. Found. 1933.

SHELDON, JAMES HUMPHREY: Am. com. W.C.A.W.

SHIELDS, ART: Recep. Com. Soviet Flyers; Fed. Press corres.

SHIELDS, BEATRICE (ALIAS SISKIND): dir. Chgo. Wkrs. Sch. 1933; Communist Party Agit.-Prop. dir.

SHIPLACOFF, A. I.: convicted during war for issuing and circulating seditious propaganda; Amalg. Cloth. Wkrs.; former Socialist alderman N.Y.C.; Conf. Democ. and Terms of Peace; Non-Intervention Citiz. Com. 1927; Il Nuovo Mondo Nat. Com.

SHIPLER, GUY EMERY: edtl. chief of the Episc. "Churchman" since 1924; rector St. Paul's Ch., Chatham, N.J.; nat. com. Nat. R. & L. Found. 1933.

SHIPSTEAD, HENRIK: U.S. Senator from Minn. (Farmer-Labor Party) since 1922; formerly dentist; mem. of radical bloc in Congress; Garland Fund Com. on Am. Imperialism; endors. Lane Pamphlet.

SHOEMAKER, F. H.: Congressman from Minn. of Farmer-Labor Party; endorsed by L.I.P.A.; Conf. for Prog. Pol. Act. com. 1933; nat. com. Lg. Against Fascism, 1933; urged Pres. Roosevelt to free War-Time prisoners (Times, Chgo. 5-24-33); served jail term before election to Congress.

SHOTWELL, JAMES T.: Prof. Columbia U.; Carnegie Endow. for Intl. Peace; Non-Intervention Citiz. Com.; Griffin Bill sponsor; Lg. for Org. Prog.; advis. coun. Foreign Lang. Inf. Serv., 1933; spkr. at Conf. on Cause and Cure of War ("World Tomorrow," 2-22-33).

SHULTZ, E. B.: nat. com. Nat. R. & L. Found. 1933.

SIEGEL, WM.: Communist writer for Intl. Pamphlets; "New Pioneer"; John Reed Club; contrib. ed. "New Masses" 1931; illustrator and cartoonist.

SIGMAN, MORRIS: Socialist; born Russia; pres. Intl. Ladies Garm. Wkrs. Un.; org. Pioneer Youth of Am.; N.Y.C.

SILVER, ABBA HILLEL: Rabbi; born Lithuania; nat. com. A.C.L.U.; nat. coun. C.M.E.; Nat. World Ct. Com.; vice pres. Cons. Lg. of Ohio; Nat. Child Lab. Com.; endors. Lane Pamphlet; Fell. Faiths spkr. Chgo. 1933; nat. coun. Berger Nat. Found.; home Cleveland, O.

SILVERMAN, HARRIET: Communist Party functionary: Recep. Com. Soviet Flyers, 1929.

SIMONS, WILLIAM: metal worker; nat. sec. A.A.A.I. Lg. of U.S.; Am. com., intl. com., and delg. to W.C.A.W.; Am. Com. for S.A.W.; Communist.

SIMONSON, LEE: scenic designer; exec. com. and dir. A.S.C.R.R.; in Russia 1933 on 2nd. trip; glorifies Soviet Moscow Theatre; home N.Y.C.

SIMPSON, HERMAN: Communist Lg. P. G. for F. & F. 1932; book reviewer for "New Republic"; formerly ed. N.Y. Call (Socialist daily, now discontinued).

SINCLAIR, DAVE: son of Upton Sinclair; instr. in physics, Columbia U.; Socialist; exec. com. of N.Y. L.I.D.; in publicity matter supposedly reproved father as "backslider" for running for Gov. of Cal. as Democrat (N.Y. Trib., 9/22/33).

SINCLAIR, JOHN F.: born Canada; writer, lecturer, formerly Mpls. banker; nat. com. A.C.L.U.; formerly active in Y.M.C.A. work; People's Legis. Serv.; Am. Acad. Pol. and Soc. Sci.; Garland Fund Com. on Am. Imperialism; signer of telegram to Pres. in behalf of Sacco and V., Aug. 1927; endors. "Professional Patriots"; endors. Lane Pamphlet; home Mpls., Minn., office N.Y.C.; appointee NRA review bd. 1934.

SINCLAIR, UPTON: author; Lusk Report calls him "a violent literary Socialist"; Garland Fund paid him $1100 for work in selecting 200 titles for series of cheap radical works in 1925; intl. advis. bd. of Moscows' communist Intl. Literature, organ of Intl. Union of Revol. Writers (Am. section Revol. Writers Fed.) 1933-4; nat. com. communist I.L.D. 1928; Socialist cand. for major offices (N.J. and Cal.); founder Inter-Collegiate Socialist Soc. (now L.I.D.); nat. coun. L.I.D. for Cal.; founder A.C.L.U., Cal. branch, 1923; Sacco-V. Nat. Lg.; Peace Patriots; nat. com. communist Intl. Wkrs. Aid (now W.I.R.) 1927; nat. com. W.I.R. 1928 Berger Nat. Found. 1931; N.C. to A.S.M. F.S.; Emer. Com. So. Pol. Pris.; Nat. Com. Def. Pol. Pris. 1932; permanent contrib. "New Masses" (communist); intl. com. and Am. com. W.C.A.W. 1932; officer communistic Commonwealth Coll.; appealed for funds Rand Sch. 1933; Intl. Com. Pol. Pris. 1933; called Conf. Prog. Pol. Act. 1933; U.S. Cong. Ag. War; Am. Com. for S.A.W.; Freethinkers Ingersoll Com. 1933; Cal. cand. on Democratic ticket, 1933; John Reed Club; see Wkrs. Cultural Fed.

SINGH, RAJAH, OF BANGALORE, SO. INDIA: wealthy Prince of Nepal; backer and speaker Fell. Faiths, Chgo. 1933; founder of "Humanistic Club."

SISKIND, G.: Communist Party functionary; Wkrs. Sch. N.Y.C.; Party org. Sect. 2, Dist. 2, and Agit.-Prop. dir.

SIVERTS, VICTOR: Unitarian minister; arrested, Aug. 1932, in So. Ill. with Midwest College Com. for Investigation and Relief of So. Ill. Miners, of communist N.S.Lg.; Rev. Bragg is reported to have phoned Franklin Co. Sheriff in his behalf.

SKARIATINA, COUNTESS IRINA: her book "First to Go Back" Communist-recommended; spkr. for communist F.S.U. dinner, N.Y., Mar. 2, 1934.

SKINNER, CLARENCE R.; edtl. contrib. A. Lincoln Center "Unity"; nat. com. A.C.L.U. and dir.; Universalist minister; Prof. Applied Christianity, Tufts Coll. since 1914 and vice dean; trustee St. Lawrence U., Canton, N.Y.; home Cambridge, Mass.

SKVIRSKY, BORIS: before recognition was Communist Soviet Govt. unofficial ambassador in Wash. D.C.; head of Soviet Union Inf. Bureau.

SKOGLUND, CARL: nat. com. Communist Lg. of Am. ("Trotskyite"); delg. to Mooney Congress, 1933, Chgo.

SLESINGER, DONALD: Prof. of Law and Assoc. Dean Soc. Sciences, U. of Chgo.; Chgo. Com. for S.A.W.; A.S.C.R.R. Com.'34.

SMEDLEY, AGNES: Communist; Intl. Un. Revol. Writers; perm. contrib. Intl. Lit.; "New Masses"; Revol. Writers Fed.; author "Chinese Destinies."

SMIRKIN, GEO.: Young People's Socialist Lg.; representing Socialist Y.P.S.L. delegation at Communist Mooney meeting, May 1, 1933, he said they were with the Communists not only in the Mooney and Scottsboro cases, but to help put over the revolution; Nat. Mooney Coun. of Action, 1933; arrested; expelled from Y.P.S.L.; now organizer in Illinois for Y.C.Lg.

SMITH, CYNTHIA: assoc. sec. N. C. for P. W.

SMITH, ETHEL M.: left wing Socialist; legis. sec. Nat. Wom. Tr. Un. Lg.; N. C. for P. W.; LaFollette-Wheeler Camp. Com.; Lg. Wom. Voters; Nat. Cons. Lg.; nat. com. Conf. Prog. Pol. Act.; Wash., D.C.

SMITH, MARY ROZET: A.C.L.U. Chgo. Com.; active Hull House supporter; died Mar. 1934, leaving $25,000 to Hull House and $5,000 to Jane Addams.

SMITH, TUCKER P.: sec. C.M.E.; Socialist; asst. treas. Fell. Recon.; former gen. sec. Y.M.C.A.; exec. com. L.I.D.; com. World Peaceways; Nat. R. & L. Found. 1933; pres. Brookwood Lab. Coll. 1933; U.S. Cong. Ag. War Com.; exec. com. W.R. Lg.; Rev. Pol. Com. See p. 337.

SMITH, THOMAS V.: Prof. U. of Chgo.; sponsor Berger Nat. Found. dinner, 1931; A.C.L.U. Chgo. Com.; Chgo. Com. for S.A.W.; signer Fell. Recon. Pet. Russ. Recog. 1932; contrib. to radical "New Republic" and "Christian Century"; pres. Chgo. A.S.C.R.R. 1933.

SMITH, VERNE: Communist Party cent. com.; writer for Intl. Pamphlets; in Moscow now as corres. for the Daily Worker.

SNYDER, PAUL J.: com. Chr. Soc. Act. M.; Minneapolis, Minn.

SOPER, EDMUND D.: Methodist; pres. Ohio Wesleyan U. since 1928; nat. com. Nat. R. & L. Found. 1933.

SOULE, GEORGE HENRY, JR.: ed. "New Republic" since 1924; nat. com. Nat. R. & L. Found. 1933; a dir. Labor Bureau, Inc., N.Y.C.; nat. com. L.I.D.; Com. on Coal & Giant P.; Am. Assn. Lab.

Legis.; Advis. Coun. on Radio in Edu. 1934; co-author, with J. M. Budish, of "The New Unionism in the Clothing Industry" 1920; speaker for Chgo. Forum Coun. Mar. 7, 1933, on "The Chances for Revolution"; as "expert" investigator, assisted in prep. "Report on the Steel Strike" of the Interchurch World Movement, 1919; in this connection, the Lusk Report says (page 1138): "It is not generally known that the direction of this inquiry was not in the hands of unbiased investigators. The principal 'experts' are David J. Saposs and George Soule, whose radical viewpoints may be gathered from their association with Mr. Evans Clark, acting under the direction of Ludwig C.A.K. Martens, head of the Soviet Bureau in the United States; their connection also with the Rand School of Social Science, and certain revolutionary Labor organizations further emphasizes their unfitness to carry on an unbiased investigation"; Communist sympathizer; lect. Rand Sch. 1931-2; nat. coun. L.I.D. for N.Y.; nat. coun. Berger Nat. Found.; home Lyme, Conn.

SPARKS, N.: Communist writer for Intl. Pamphlets; instr. Wkrs. Sch.; Dist. Org. Dist. No. 1; Boston.

SPAULDING, WILLIS J.: pres. Pub. O. Lg. of Am. 1933.

SPECTOR, FRANK: Communist Party functionary; asst. nat. sec. I.L.D.; ex-convict.

SPECTOR, MAURICE: nat. com. Communist Lg. of Am. ("Trotskyite").

SPEERS, J. GUTHRIE: Presb. minister; Non-Intervention Citiz. Com. 1927; nat. coun. C.M.E.; nat. com. Nat. R. & L. Found. 1933.

SPENCER, FANNY BIXBY: leader of extreme radical group, "The Internationale"; active W.I.L.P.F. and A.C.L.U. in Cal.; deceased; author of Women's Peace Union (see) pamphlet "Militarism."

SPOFFORD, REV. WM. B.: nat. bd. dir. A.C.L.U. 1933; Prot. Episc. minister; Socialist; nat. coun. Fell. Recon.; Church Socialist Lg. and signer of its manifesto calling for a "complete revolution of our present economic and social disorder" (June 29, 1919); pro-Soviet; sent appeal to Pres. Wilson for cessation of intervention, characterizing the Soviet govt. "as the one budding system of democracy in Europe" (Lusk Report); exec. sec. Ch. L.I.D. since 1922; Fed. Coun. Chs.; mem. coun. Jt. Com. on Unemp.; treas. Ch. Emer. Com. Rel. Textile Strik.; N.Y.C.

SPRENGLING, MARTIN: U. of Chgo. Prof.; 5th Ward Communist campaign com. mem. with Profs. Lovett, Haydon and Schuman, backing Communist Janowicz for Alderman in company with Communist Party organizations, Feb. 1933.

STACHEL, JACK: Communist Party cent. com.; asst. nat. sec. T.U.U.L.

STALIN, JOSEPH: real name Djugashvili; Tiflis bank robber, bomber, and murderer; present dictator of Communist Intl. and of U.S.S.R.; the guiding spirit behind plans and activity for World Revolution.

STARR, CLARENCE: Prof. U. of Chgo.; A.C.L.U. Chgo. Com.

STARR, ELLEN GATES: Prof. U. of Chgo.; A.C.L.U. Chgo. Com.; appealed for Sacco and V. (in "Survey" appeal) 1927; then lived at Hull House.

STEFFENS, LINCOLN; author; Communist Lg. P. G. for F. & F. 1932; as part of anarchist group, Lusk Report cites his and Louise Bryant's cablegram to Lenin and Trotsky, 1918; went with W. C. Bullitt to Russia, 1919; Lg. for Amnesty Pol. Pris. (anarchist Berkman's); Nat. Mooney-Billings Com.; N.C. to A.S.M.F.S.; contrib. ed. "Labor Defender"; Nat. Com. Def. Pol. Pris. 1932; sent greetings to U.S.S.R. commemorating Russian revolution in "New Masses," Nov. 1932; wife Ella Winter; nat. com. Henry George Foundation; Am. Com. for S.A.W.; sponsor San Francisco communist Workers School, 1933; Cong. Exp. Radicals.

STEIN, CLARENCE S.: advis. coun. and book com. A.S.C.R.R.

STERN, BERNHARD J.: Am. com., and delg. from communist John Reed Clubs U.S.A. to W.C.A.W. 1932; endors. W.I.R. letter for "Hunger Marchers" 1932; Pris. Rel. Fund; N.C. to A.S.M.F.S.; Nat. Com. Def. Pol. Pris.

STERNBERGER, ESTELLE M.: exec. sec. Nat. Coun. Jewish Women; L.I.P.A.; World Peaceways; contrib. "Survey"; Conf. Prog. Pol. Act. camp. com. 1933; 1st. vice pres. Nat. Women's Council (N.Y. Times, 11/25/33).

STEVENS, BENNETT: author of "Church and the Workers," a Communist anti-religious Intl. Pamphlet; "New Masses"; instr. N.Y. Wkrs. Sch.

STEVENS, EDMUND: Am. com. W.C.A.W.; chmn. Student Cong. Ag. War at U. of Chgo.; delg. to Montevideo (Red) Cong. Against War, 1933; N.S. Lg.; contrib. "Student Review" (of N.S. Lg.); arrested in South River, N.J., riot Sept. 1932.

STEWART, GEORGE: minister; nat. com. Nat. R. & L. Found. 1933; Russ. Reconst. Farms, 1925.

STEWART, MAXWELL S.: For. Policy Assn.; nat. com. communist F.S.U. 1933; contrib. ed. "World Tomorrow"; his "Good News from Russia" is "Communist-Recommended"; one of leaders of Intourist Tour, 1933; signer of letter to Pres. Roosevelt urging Russ. recog.; former assoc. ed. communist Moscow Daily News and tchr. with wife at Moscow Institute (Russia); contrib. "Nation."

STEWART, RAY: communist writer for Intl. Pamphlets.

STEWART, WALTER: A.S.C.R.R.

STILLMAN, CHAS. B.: advis. ed. bd. "The Am. Teacher" (radical) of Am. Fed. Tchrs.; former associate Scott Nearing.

STOCKWELL, S. A.: bd. dir. People's Lobby; nat. com. A.A.A.I. Lg.; Emer. Peace Fed. 1917; vice pres. Pub. O. Lg. of Am.

STOKES, HELEN PHELPS: Socialist; active in social settlement work; vice chmn. nat. A.C.L.U.; vice pres. L.I.D. (also while it was Inter-Coll. Socialist Soc.); vice pres. and chmn. finance com. Nat. Cons. Lg.; Wom. Tr. Un. Lg.; Fell. Recon.; Cong. Exp. Radicals; nat. coun. Berger Nat. Found.

STOKES, ROSE PASTOR: Communist; born Russian Poland; active in Wom. Tr. Un. Lg.; sentenced to ten years Mo. State Pen., 1918, for anti-war activities; indicted Chgo. 1919 and Bridgman, Mich., 1922, on charges growing out of illegal Communist Party conventions; Communist Party exec. com. and org.; formerly lecturer for Inter-Coll. Socialist Soc. (now L.I.D.); died 1933.

STOKOWSKI, LEOPOLD: vice pres. A.S.C.R.R.; Am. com. W.C.A.W.; wife on exec. bd. W.I.L.P.F.; nat. com. W.I.R.; Am. Com. for S.A.W.; conductor Phila. orchestra since 1912; spkr. at Lenin Memorial mtg. at Broadwood Hotel, Phila., 1/19/34, on his symphony "Ode to Lenin," played at this mtg.; Ella R. Bloor, Max Bedacht, and other Communists, fellow spkrs.; announced he would play the communist Internationale at Phila. symph. concerts in spite of Am. Legion protests (Chgo. Trib. 1/26/34).

STOLAR, M. A.: Communist, formerly of Ill.; in charge of typesetting for Moscow News in Moscow (1933); bd. dir. 4A; daughter was in charge of Young Pioneer Camp (Communist) at Paddock Lake, Wis. 1930; she was teaching in Russia, 1933.

STONE, NAHUM ISAAC: born Russia; nat. coun. L.I.D. for N.Y.; Am. Assn. Lab. Legis.; Nat. Child Lab. Com.

STOUT, RUTH: Nat. Com. Def. Pol. Pris.

STRACHEY, JOHN: former mem. British Parliament; Communist; author of "The Coming Struggle for Power," a "forthright advocacy of Communist revolution" (Communist "Left Front" for June, 1933); staff corres. communist "New Masses," 1933; "Foresees World Communism" (N.Y. Times, 10/11/33).

STROBELL, CARO LLOYD: nat. coun. L.I.D. for N.Y.

STROMBERG, YETTA: Communist Party functionary; Pioneer Camp conductor; arrested (see A.C.L.U.); nat. com. I.L.D. 1930.

STRONG, ANNA LOUISE: Communist; home in Moscow; founder and asst. ed. Moscow News, an English-language Soviet propaganda paper circulated in U.S.; married a Russian 1932; daughter of Rev. Sidney D. Strong; writer for Intl. Pamphlets; dismissed as Seattle sch. teacher; corres. for Am. Friends Relief Mission in Russia 1921-2; corres. Fed. Press; contrib. ed. "Soviet Russia Today," 1932; hdqts. at Hull House when lecturing in U.S. (Whitney's "Reds in America"); nat. com. W.I.R. 1928.

STRONG, JOS.: Chgo. sec. communist F.S.U.

STRONG, SIDNEY D.: father of Anna Louise; Congl. minister, formerly Seattle, where he was nicknamed "the Red reverend of Puget Sound"; now of N.Y.C.; infamous People's Coun.; Emer. Peace Fed.; Conf. Democ. and Terms of Peace; Fell. Recon.; Peace Patriots; pres. All Nations Fellowship; contrib. to Commonwealth Coll.; edtl. contrib. A. Lincoln Center "Unity"; com. of A.A.A.I. Lg. 1927.

SUGAR, MAURICE: Communist I.L.D. atty.; Am. com. W.C.A.W. and delg. 1932 from Detroit John Reed Club; atty. for A.C.L.U. Detroit branch and exec. com. Nat. Coun. Prot. For. Born Wkrs.; Pris. Rel. Fund (I.L.D.); sent greetings to Soviet wkrs. in "Soviet Russia Today," Jan. 1933.

SUNDERLAND, JABEZ T.: Union Theol. Sem.; various Indian Freedom organizations; edtl. contrib. A. Lincoln Center "Unity"; nat. com. War Resisters Lg. 1930-31.

SUN YAT SEN, MADAME: Intl. Com. for S.A.W.; Chinese Communist; now about 40 yrs. old; was young mistress, or "wife No. 2," of Sun Yat Sen (first Pres.

of Chinese Republic, who introduced Communism into China); the older wife was never divorced; was named Ching Ling; daughter of Soong, a Christianized evangelist with whom Upton Close, sister and husband, lived in China; attended college four years in Macon, Georgia; sister married Chiang Kai-shek, at present anti-Communist military leader, but formerly dominated by Reds. He discarded two Chinese wives and joined Christian church, of which "Mother Soong" was sponsor.

SWABECK, ARNE: nat. com. Communist Lg. of Am. ("Trotskyite").

SWAN, ALFRED W.: A.C.L.U.; Fell. Recon.; minister First Congl. Ch., Madison, Wis. since 1930; nat. com. Nat. R. & L. Found. 1933; mem. com. to welcome Norman Thomas to Madison, 1932; named as "Communistic" at U. of Wis. investigation (Wis. Capitol Times, 7/12/33).

SWEET, WM. E.: Conf. for Prog. Pol. Act. claimed credit for his election as Gov. of Colo.; supporter A.C.L.U. 1922 and either supporter or associate of L.I.D. and Fell. Recon.; endors. of radical pacifist Lane Pamphlet; Public Relations Division NRA, Roosevelt appointee (see article); Colorado Com. Lg. of Nations Assn.

SWIFT, DUANE: treas. A.C.L.U. Chgo. Com.; officer Amalg. Tr. & Sav. Bk., Chgo.; sponsor Berger Nat. Found. dinner, 1931.

SWIFT, HAROLD H.: millionaire packer; mem. Am. Red Cross Mission to Russia, 1917; pres. bd. trustees U. of Chgo., which retains communistic profs., recognizes Communist student activities, and allows its property to be used for Communist meetings in violation of Ill. sedition laws; advis. com. Chgo. Forum Coun.; sister is Helen Swift Neilson of A. Lincoln Center "Unity"; Survey Assoc. 1934.

T

TAFT, REV. CLINTON J.: dir. A.C.L.U., S. Cal. branch office; Socialist; protested attack on Reds (Daily Worker Oct. 13, 1931).

TAFT, JESSIE: Young Pioneer, very active in 1930; "parents born in Russia and her name a recent acquisition; concludes her speeches by such remarks as 'Remember, comrades, the only country we have is Soviet Russia . . . we children of today will be the leaders of the revolutionary movement a few years hence when we will make this country another Russia.'" (U.S. Fish Report).

TAFT, LORADO: sculptor; father-in-law of Paul H. Douglas; Non-Partz. com. Lillian Herstein; Fell. Faiths, Chgo. Com.; wife member of same and also signer resolution for Recog. of Russia of Women's Com. for Recog. of Russia; Chgo. Com. for Strugg. Ag. War; A.S.C.R.R. Com. '34.

TAGORE, RABINDRANATH: see "English Reds"; repr. of A. Lincoln Center "Unity" in India.

TALLENTIRE, NORMAN: Communist Party cent. com.; nat. organizer F.S.U. 1933; formerly Communist Party dist. No. 9 org. at Mpls.

TAMBLYN, RONALD J.: pastor Congl. Ch., Holyoke, Mass.; nat. com. Nat. R. & L. Found.; Ch. Emer. Com. Rel. Tex. Strike; book reviewer for "Christian Century."

TANNER, ARVID B.: A.S.C.R.R. Chgo. exec. com.

TASHINSKY, JOE (ALIAS TASH): Communist Party functionary; Nat. Miners Un. org. in Ill. and Pa.; police record.

TAUB, ALLEN: atty. for Communist I.L.D.; atty. for Scottsboro boys before U.S. Supreme Ct.

TAUB, BELLE G.: wife of Allen; assoc. sec. Am. com. and delg. to W.C.A.W.; petitioned Pres. for Communist "Hunger Marchers," Wash. D.C. 1932; Pris. Rel. Fund (I.L.D.); Am. Com. for S.A.W.; mem. Office Wkrs. Un.; arrested in Portland, Ore. Dec. 1933, in Communist riot.

TAUSSIG, DR. ALBERT E.: chmn. St. Louis A.C.L.U. Com.; Ec. Dept., Wash. U., St. Louis; A.C.L.U. investigating com. in So. Ill. May 1933.

TAUSSIG, PROF. FRANK W.: Harvard U. Prof. Ec.; Nat. Citiz. Com. Rel. Lat. Am. 1927; Com. on Russian American Relations of Am. Found. (pro-Soviet).

TAUSSIG, FLORENCE G.: wife St. Louis doctor; asst. treas. W.I.L.P.F.; sister-in-law of Albert E.

TAYLOR, ALVA W.: Prof. Social Ethics, Vanderbilt U.; sec. soc. welfare, Disciples of Christ Ch.; studied with Graham Taylor; Fed. Coun. Chs. (mem. soc. serv. commn.); mem. com. Interchurch World Movement prep. report on Steel Strike, 1919 (see Soule); Nat. Mooney-Billings Com.; Ch. Emer. Com. Rel. Tex. Strik.; endors. com. World Peaceways; signer Fell. Recon. Pet. Russ. Recog. 1932; exec. com. Nat. R. & L. Found. 1933; contrib. ed. ultra-rad. "Christian Century"; Emer. Com. Strik. Rel. 1933; Nat. Save Our Schs. Com.; Conf. Prog. Pol. Act. camp. com. 1934; home Nashville, Tenn.

TAYLOR, GRAHAM: founder and res. warden Chgo. Commons (social settlement and hdqts. of Karl Borders and C.W.C. on Unemp.); former minister (Dutch Ref. Ch.); Prof. Soc. Ec., Chgo. Theol. Sem.; assoc. ed. "The Survey"; Chgo. Emer. Com. Strik. Rel.; Fell. Faiths Chgo. com.; advis. com. Chgo. Forum Coun.; Nat. Citiz. Com. for Sacco and V.; also signed appeal for Sacco and V., Aug. 1927; Chgo. Com. for S.A.W. 1933; A.S.C.R.R. Com. '34.

TAYLOR, GRAHAM R.: son of Graham; Russ. Reconst. Farms, 1925; res. Chgo. Commons 1896-1900 and 1904-12; ed. staff "The Survey," 1904-16; spec. asst. to Am. Ambassador to Russia 1916-19; exec. sec. Chgo. Commn. on Race Rel. 1920-21; mem. Nat. Inf. Bureau commn. on famine relief in Russia 1922; chmn. exec. com. A.S.C.R.R.; bd. trustees For. Lang. Inf. Serv.; home N.Y.C.

TAYLOR, LEA D.: Chicago Commons executive; C.W.C. on Unemp. 1932-3; daughter of Graham Taylor; opponent of Baker Bills (against sedition) at hearing, May, 1933; aided strikers at 711 W. Lake St., July, 1933, with Karl Borders, Anetta Dieckmann, Maynard Krueger, and a delegation from red Nat. R. & L. Found.

TELLER, SIDNEY A.: Social Worker; sec. Pitts. A.C.L.U. Com.

TENHUNEN, MATTI: Communist; born Finland; pres. Coop. Cent. Exchange, Superior, Wis.; mem. bd. Fed. Press; mem. bd. Daily Worker Pub. Co.

TEXTOR, LUCY: advis. coun. A.S.C.R.R.; Prof. Russian History, Vassar College; leader Open Road tour to Russia, 1933.

THAELMANN, ERNST: German Communist Party leader, now imprisoned by Hitler.

THOMAS, EDWARD: exec. com. Nat. R. & L. Found. 1933.

THOMAS, MARGARET LORING: nat. recording sec. W.I.L.P.F.; Peace Patriots; N.Y.

THOMAS, NORMAN: nat. exec. sec. of Socialist Party in U.S.; grad. Union Theol. Sem.; former Presb. minister; an active wartime anti-American "peace" worker with Lochner and other radicals; Labor Defense Council, 1923, for Bridgman Communists; exposed in Lusk Report and Cong. Exp. Radicals; a founder of Garland Fund and a dir. since beginning; A.C.L.U. founder and mem. of its nat. com.; leading founder Fell. Recon. (Am. branch); exec. dir. L.I.D.; exec. bd. C.M.E.; L.I.P.A.; Emer. Com. Strik. Rel.; N. C. for P. W.; nat. advis. com. Sacco-V. Nat. Lg.; helped form Emer. Com. Strik. Rel. to aid Passaic Communist strike, 1926, led by Weisbord, called "lesson in revolution," and was still chmn. 1933; Nat. Citiz. Com. Rel. Lat. Am. 1927; exec. com. Non-Intervention Citiz. Com. 1927; nat. com. Nat. World Ct. Com.; Berger Nat. Found. 1931; advis. Pioneer Youth of Am.; Il Nuovo Mondo Nat. Com.; endors. com. World Peaceways; vice chmn. Jt. Com. on Unemp.; Com. on Coal & Giant P.; Conf. Prog. Pol. Act.; Russ. Reconst. Farms 1925; lecturer Rand Sch.; arrested Paterson strike 1932; signer of protest to Chinese Govt. in behalf of Mr. and Mrs. Ruegg, alias Noullens, Communist agitators convicted of sedition in Shanghai 1932; exec. com. Nat. R. & L. Found. 1933; contrib. ed. "World Tomorrow," "The Nation," and "The New Leader"; perennial Socialist cand. for major office; voted for united front with Communist Party (cited in "The Communist," May, 1933, page 431), see under Socialist Party; U.S. Cong. Ag. War; nat. com. Lg. Against Fascism, 1933; People's Freedom Union, 1920; Nat. Advis. Coun. on Radio in Edu. 1933-4.

THOMAS, WILBUR K.: exec. dir. Carl Schurz Memorial Found., whose Oberlander Trust is financing Einstein's American activities; advis. com. A.S.C.R.R., also mem. of its Phila. chapter; advis. Pioneer Youth of Am.; vice chmn. C.M.E.; nat. bd. Am. Com. Fair Play to China; Russ. Reconst. Farms; dir. Am. Russian Inst., Phila.; Intl. Com. Pol. Pris.; nat. com. Paxton Hibben (Communist) Memorial Hosp. Fund; speaker for Am. Friends Serv. Com. and its exec. dir. 1918-29; endors. Lane Pamphlet; home Lansdowne, Pa., office Phila.

THOMPSON, CARL D.: Socialist; former Congl. minister; directing head Pub. O. Lg. of Am.; ed. "Public Ownership" (monthly mag.); wartime anti-American "peace" worker; mem. Ford Peace Ship Party; Emer. Peace Fed. 1917; one time nat. campaign mgr. Socialist party; nominated as Socialist Presidential candidate, Victor Berger making the nominating speech; former trustee of the "Yours for the revolution" People's College, Fort Scott, Kans. (the chancellor, Eugene V. Debs), which was closed during the War; Fell. Faiths spkr. Chgo. 1933; sponsor Berger Nat. Found. dinner, 1931; L.I.D. forum lecturer, 1934.

TIALA, ALFRED: nat. sec. communist United Farmers Lg., 1629 Linden Ave., Minneapolis, Minn.; sec. Minn. Farmers Nat. Com. Action; nat. com. Lg. Strugg. Negro Rts.; arrested Feb. 1934 and sentenced to 6 months in jail for inciting to riot (Warsaw, Ind.).

TIERNEY, AGNES L.: nat. coun. L.I.D. for Pa.; vice chmn. Pa. Com. Total Disarm. 1932.

TINKER, WELLINGTON H.: nat. com. Nat. R. & L. Found. 1933; nat. coun. C.M.E.; Com. for Thomas, 1929.

TIPPETT, THOS.: left wing revolutionary Socialist; corres. and bus. mgr. Fed. Press; now edtl. dir. Prog. Miners Un. of Am. at Gillespie, Ill.; spoke all over U.S. in behalf of new trial for Mooney; edu. dir. Brookwood Labor Coll. until 1933; org. Amalg. Cloth. Wkrs. of Am.; connected with Wm. Z. Foster's Trade Union Edu. Lg. (now T.U.U.L.) 1922; bd. admn. Militant Left Wing Miners of Am. Oct. 1933; org. com. American Wkrs. Party.

TIPPY, WORTH M.: Ch. Emer. Com. Strik. Relief; see Fed. Coun. Chs. Sex Pamphlet; Fell. Faiths spkr. Chgo. 1933; Meth. Fed. for Soc. Serv. nat. com.

TITTLE, ERNEST FREMONT: minister First M.E. Church, Evanston, Ill.; prof. Garrett Biblical Inst.; Northwestern U. trustee; A.C.L.U. Chgo. Com.; nat. coun. C.M.E.; exec. com. L.I.D. Chgo.; advis. com. Chgo. Forum Coun.; North Shore chmn. Fell. Faiths; contrib. "Christian Century"; chmn. nat. com. Meth. Fed. for Soc. Serv. 1928; Fed. Coun. Chs.; mem. World Peace Com. of M.E. Ch., which recommends that the Gen. Conf. of the M.E. Ch. uphold those refusing all military service in defense of our Country (see M.E. Year Book 1932); responsible for adoption of Negro social equality resolution at M.E. Gen. Conf. 1932; signer Fell. Recon. Pet. Russ. Recog. 1932; one of signers of telegram to Einstein asking him to address them in Chgo. Mar. 14, 1933 (sent in Feb.); opponent of patriotic activities; notices of Communist and other radical acitivities appear regularly on Bulletin Board of his church (Anna Louise Strong's and Scott Nearing's lectures; The Proletarian Ball to be held April 15, 1933, at Knickerbocker Hotel, Chgo., for the benefit of the Communist I.L.D.; Henri Barbusse meeting, Oct. 23, 1933; John Strachey, Nov. 26, 1933; F. L. Schuman; etc.); nat. com. Nat. R. & L. Found. and book ed. of its ultra-radical Bulletin "Economic Justice," which sacrilegiously prints Communist-atheist cartoons and carries outright revolutionary propaganda and distributes Communist literature; on Jan. 15, 1933, in his sermon (later printed) entitled "Where Is God?", he said that during the War God was in Karl Liebknecht, Ramsay MacDonald, Romain Rolland and Eugene Debs, who were protesting war (see reference to these persons in this "Who's Who"); endorsed and praised by A. Lincoln Center "Unity," Sept. 4, 1933; see article "News"; sponsor Berger Nat. Found. dinner, 1931; F. L. Schuman spkr. in church Sun. aft. Jan. 28, 1934.

TITTMAN, EDW. D.: nat. com. A.C.L.U.

TODD, A. M.: nat. coun. L.I.D. for Mich.; A.C.L.U.; died 1932.

TODD, ARTHUR J.: Northwestern U. Prof.; A.C.L.U. Chgo. Com.; Chgo. Forum Coun.

TODD, LAWRENCE: communistic dir. Wash., D.C., Bureau Fed. Press. and of Tass (Soviet Union News Agency); was Wash. rep. A.C.L.U. reporting on legislation, etc.; now in U.S.S.R. for Tass.

TODES, CHARLOTTE: Communist; Am. com. and delg. W.C.A.W.; writer for Intl. Pamphlets; Pris. Rel. Fund (I.L.D.).

TOOHEY, PAT: Communist Party functionary; former student in Lenin Sch., Moscow; Communist Party org. Dist. No. 19, Denver, until Dec. 1933.

TOPCHEVSKY, M.: Chgo. John Reed Club; artist; teacher Chgo. Workers Sch.; A. Lincoln Center functionary; Communist.

TRACHTENBERG, ALEX: Communist Party cent. com.; born Russia; Wkrs. Sch. N.Y. City; formerly very active Socialist, beginning with radical student activities while attending Trinity Coll. and Yale U.; org. and treas. Collegiate Anti-Militarist Lg. 1914-5; Inter-Coll. Socialist Soc. (now L.I.D.); Rand Sch. 1915-21; sec. Am. Lab. Alliance for Russian Recog. 1921-2; bd. mgrs. N.Y. Call 1916-20; assoc. with Intl. Ladies Garm. Wkrs. Un. 1920-2; delg. 4th Cong. Communist Intl. 1922, delg. exec. com. Communist Intl. 1923, etc.; Teachers Un. N.Y.; now mgr. Intl. Publishers, N.Y., the official Soviet pub. house in U.S.; writer for Intl. Pamphlets; Recep. Com. Soviet Flyers; Cong. Exp. Radicals.

TRENT, LUCIA: husband Ralph Cheyney; both poetry eds. A. Lincoln Center "Unity"; advis. com. Sacco-V. Nat. Lg.; chmn. artists' and writers' com. for Tom Mooney, 1933; Nat. Com. to Aid Vic. G. Fascism; contrib. to communist pub. "Rebel Poet," also "World Tomorrow."

TRESCA, CARLO: anarchist; born Italy; Anti-Fascist Alliance; arrested many times; see Eliz. G. Flynn, his wife; former spkr. for I.W.W.; Recep. Com. Soviet Flyers; John Reed Club; now starting paper again N.Y.C.

TROTSKY, LEON: known as Bronstein while exiled in N.Y. prior to Mar. 1917, when he left for Europe to join Lenin, Stalin, etc.; ed. "Novy Mir" while in N.Y.; People's Commissar for War under Lenin; as such, reorg. the Red Army and ruthlessly carried out the bloody reign of terror which followed the overthrow of the Kerensky regime; exiled from Russia by Stalin and now confined to Prinkipo, a Turkish island; still the leader of a group of Communists opposed to Stalin policies.

TRUAX, WM. R.: Conf. Prog. Lab. Act, 1933; U.S. Cong. Ag. War; pres. Ohio Unemp. Lg.; exec. com. Fed. of Unemp. Wkrs. Lgs. of Am.; bd. admn. Militant Left Wing Miners of America, new Red miners union.

TRUMBULL, MILLIE R.: nat. com. A.C.L.U.; vice pres. Nat. Cons. Lg. 1931.

TRUMBULL, WALTER: Communist; org. Hawaiian Communist Lg. and attempted to form a Communist unit in the U.S. Army in Hawaii (with Paul Crouch); convicted and served prison terms; he and Crouch feted as heroes by Reds upon their return to U.S.; one welcome arranged in Chgo. on anniversary of Paris Commune (Aug. 10, 1928), with Ralph Chaplin (I.W.W.) and Prof. Robt. Morss Lovett as fellow speakers; dist. org. Young Wkrs. Lg. (Communist); active on Anti-Militarist Com. of Communist Party (for boring from within all branches of military service and breaking down all nat. defense); formerly lived in Detroit; writer for Workers Library Pub. communist pamphlets; nat. sec. Wkrs. Ex-Service Men's Lg. 1933.

TUCKER, IRWIN ST. JOHN: Episc. minister; now pastor of St. Stephen's Episc. Ch., Chgo.; leader of Am. Socialist Party during War; convicted under Espionage Act and given 20-yr. sentence in 1919; Ch. Socialist Lg.; an org. of infamous People's Coun.; Emer. Peace Fed.; First Conf. Democ. and Terms of Peace 1917; reported as listed in I.W.W. organizers' bulletin as on payroll of I.W.W. lecturing on "Technocracy as seen by the I.W.W." Jan. 1933 (Advisor); chmn. for Northwest side Fell. Faiths 1933; sponsor Berger Nat. Found. dinner, 1931.

TUCKER, MARGUERITE: N.C. to A.S.M.F.S.; sec. Il Nuovo Mondo Nat. Com.; Pris. Rel. Fund (I.L.D.); Com. for Thomas, 1929.

TUGWELL, REX. GUY: contrib. ed. "New Republic" ("advocate of revolutionary Socialism," Lusk Report); mem. technical staff of communist-organized First Am. Tr. Un. Delg. to Russia and fellow-author of its Soviet propaganda book "Soviet Russia in the Second Decade"; mem. of Pres. Roosevelt's "brain trust" 1933 as asst. "commissar" of agriculture; see "Nat. R. & L. Found." for his writings; as Prof. of Economics Dept., Columbia U., he offered Donald Henderson, ousted as Communist, a research fellowship for one year in U.S.S.R.; Henderson refused because it entailed $700 cut in his salary; Com. for Thomas, 1929; bd. dir. socialist People's Lobby; Nat. Advis. Coun. on Radio in Edu.

TULIN, JUSTINE WISE: daughter of Rabbi S. Wise (see); nat. com. communist F.S.U. 1933; author pro-Soviet articles; com. of A.A.A.I. Lg. (Daily Wkr. 12/14/26).

U

UNTERMANN, ERNEST: Socialist; an ed. Milwaukee Leader; nat. com. A.A.A.I. Lg. 1928; translator of Marx; delg. to formation I.W.W. in Chgo. 1905.

UNTERMEYER, LOUIS: contrib. ed. "The Liberator"; contrib. "New Republic"; author; A.S.C.R.R. book com.; John Reed Club; Emer. Com. So. Pol. Pris.; N.Y.

UNTERMYER, SAMUEL: Emer. Com. Strik. Rel.; endors. "Professional Patriots"; founder Com. for Human Rights Ag. Naziism; advocate of public ownership of utilities; pres. Palestine Found. Fund; N.Y.C.

U'REN, WM. S.: lawyer; sec. Oregon Single Tax Lg. 1909-17; nat. com. A.C.L.U.; Nat. Pop. Govt. Lg.; coun. People's Lobby; home Portland, Ore.

V

VAN DOREN, CARL: author and ed.; formerly coll. prof.; lit. ed. "The Nation" 1919-22; A.S.C.R.R. book com.; Emer. Com. So. Pol. Pris.; N.Y.

VAN DOREN, MARK: A.S.C.R.R.; supporter of communist N.S. Lg.; lit. ed. "The Nation," 1924-28; wife assoc. ed. "The Nation" since 1926; asst. prof. English, Columbia U.

VAN DUSEN, HENRY P.: nat. com. Nat. R. & L. Found.; nat. coun. C.M.E.; treas. "World Tomorrow"; Com. for Thomas, 1929; Fellowship Socialist Christians continuation committee; endors. Lane Pamphlet.

VAN LOON, HENDRIK WILLEM: A.S.C.R.R. book com.; supporter and lecturer Rand Sch. 1932-3.

VAN VEEN, SADIE: wife of Israel Amter; Communist writer for Workers Library Publishers, "New Pioneer," etc.; instr. pub. speaking, communist Wkrs. Sch., N.Y.C.; sec. I.L.D., Dist. No. 2, 1933.

VANZETTI, BARTOLOMEO: see Sacco; a beneficiary of Sacco-V. Communist agitation.

VARESE, EDGAR: dir. A.S.C.R.R.

VEBLEN, THORSTEIN: I.W.W. 1933 pamphlet "General Strike" devotes its inner cover to quotation on revolution from his "Engineers and the Price System"; Lusk Report (p. 1094) cites his aid in preparation I.W.W. pamphlet published by A.C.L.U. in 1918; People's Legis. Serv.; his book "Engineers and the Price System" is considered basis for "Technocracy."

VILLARD, OSWALD GARRISON: ed. and pub. "The Nation," ultra-rad. mag.; nat. com. A.C.L.U.; nat. coun. Berger Nat. Found.; treas. L.I.P.A.; nat. coun. C.M.E.; Fell. Recon.; Peace Patriots; People's Lobby; bd. dir. "World Tomorrow"; was chmn. exec. com. N.A.A.C.P.; People's Legis. Serv.; Am. Medical Aid to Russia; nat. advis. com. Sacco-V. Nat. Lg.; Emer. Com. Strik. Rel.; as mem. of Intl. Com. Pol. Pris., he protested execution of Chinese Communist general, Chen Du Hsui, Jan. 1933; urged wide open trade with Russia, May 1932; signer of A.C.L.U. telegram to Gov. Emmerson, Oct. 1932, demanding removal of troops from S. Ill., where they were quelling Red activities in the mine fields; signer of letter to Georgia prison commrs., Nov. 1932, protesting prison methods "exposed" by Communist John L. Spivak in his "Georgia Nigger," which ran serially in the communist Daily Worker; was active "peace" worker during War; org. Am. Lg. to Limit Arm.; Nat. Peace Fed.; Neut. Conf. Com.; Garland Fund Com. on Am. Imperialism; Non-Intervention Citiz. Com. 1927; treas. com. on action Conf. Prog. Pol. Act. 1933; nat. com. Lg. Against Fascism, 1933; Nat. Save Our Schs. Com.; appealed funds for Rand Sch. 1933; People's Legis. Serv.; Cong. Exp. Radicals; endors. Lane Pamphlet.

VLADECK, BARUCH CHARNEY: Socialist; born Russia; mgr. Jewish Daily Forward, N.Y.C.; nat. com. A.C.L.U.; bd. dir. L.I.D.; L.I.P.A.; Nat. Mooney-Billings Com.; Socialist Ald. N.Y.C., 1918-21; nat. coun. Pioneer Youth of Am. since 1924; Rand Sch.; Conf. Prog. Pol. Act.; Non-Intervention Citiz. Com. 1927; Berger Nat. Found. 1931; hon. mem. Amalg. Cloth. Wkrs. of Am.; nat. com. Lg. Against Fascism, 1933; Workmen's Circle.

VOORHIS, H. J.: nat. com. Nat. R. & L. Found. 1933.

VORSE, MARY HEATON: author; Communist; Communist Robert Minor her third husband; Nat. Com. Def. Pol. Pris. 1932; N.C. to A.S.M.F.S.; employed by Garland Fund; Labor Defense Council, 1923; permanent contrib. Intl. Lit. of Intl. Union Revol. Writers, 1933; Recep. Com. Soviet Flyers; Revol. Writers Fed.; home Provincetown, Mass.

VROOMAN, CARL S.: Nat. Citiz. Com. Rel. Lat. Am. 1927; Pub. O. Lg. of Am.; Nat. Pop. Govt. Lg.; ex-Sec. of Agriculture; Util. Cons. and Inv. Lg.; moderator Cong'l. Ch. of Ill.; Bloomington, Ill.

W

WAGENKNECHT, ALFRED: born Germany; exec. com. Communist Party U.S.A.; admits being employed in revolutionary movement for last 31 years; nat. sec. Friends Soviet Russia; Recep. Com. Soviet Flyers; relief chmn. Gen. Relief Com. for Textile Strik. (of W.I.R.) 1926; sec. Pa., Ohio, W. Va., Ky., Strik. Miners Rel. Com. 1931; N.C. to A.S.M.F.S.; nat. sec. W.I.R.; exec. sec. Nat. Com. to Aid Vic. G. Fascism 1933; U.S. Cong. Ag. War.

WAKEFIELD, JESSIE LONDON: Communist; Pris. Rel. Fund (I.L.D.); I.L.D. organizer at Harlan, Ky. 1932; arrested on sedition charges, released; wife of Lowell Wakefield, dist. organizer for I.L.D.; Seattle, Wash. 1932.

WALD, LILLIAN D.: a founder and head worker Henry St. Settlement, N.Y.C.; lecturer N.Y. Sch. of Soc. Work; vice pres. A.S.C.R.R.; Am. com. W.C.A.W.; nat. bd. W.I.L.P.F.; exec. bd. For. Pol. Assn.; Am. Peace Found.; Russian Am. Indust. Corp.; dir. Survey Associates; stockholder in "Liberator"; was on Dept. of Justice list of leading radicals 1921; exposed in Senate investigation of radicals, 1919; Emer. Peace Fed.; on Emer. Com. Strik. Rel. for communist Passaic Strike, 1926, led by Weisbord; Non-Intervention Citiz. Com. 1927; trustee Nat. Child Lab. Com.; exec. com. N.Y. Child Lab. Com.; N.Y. Lg. Wom. Voters; Wom. Tr. Un. Lg.; Friends of Russian Freedom; vice pres. Am. Russian Inst.; N.Y. Urban Lg.; Am. Assn. Lab. Legis.; exec. com. Emer. Com. Strik. Rel. 1933; Griffin Bill sponsor; Recep. Com. Soviet Flyers; was in Jane Addams' Wom. Peace Party; Cong. Exp. Radicals.

WALDMAN, LOUIS: Socialist; born Russia; Non-Intervention Citiz. Com. 1927; ousted as Socialist Assemblyman of

N.Y. 1920; N.Y. State chmn. Socialist Party and its cand. for Gov. of N.Y. 1930; L.I.D.; contrib. ed. New Leader; nat. com. Lg. Against Fascism 1933; Lusk Report, p. 554, states that as delg. to Chgo. Socialist convention Sept. 1919 he said: "If I knew we could sway the boys when they got guns, to use them against the capitalist class, I would be for universal training"; attorney; announced Mar 2, 1934 reversal by Pres. Roosevelt of conviction of Robert Osman, found guilty in the Canal Zone (1931) of communicating military secrets to Communists (Chgo. Examiner, 3/3/34).

WALDMAN, SEYMOUR: Communist; author of "Death and Profits"; formerly N.Y. World staff; communist Daily Worker (Washington Bureau head, with Marguerite Young, 1933-4); during 1931-2, editor of N. C. for P. W. International Disarm. Notes; exec. bd. N. C. for P. W., 1932; staff of "New Masses," 1933; grad. U. of Pa.; instr. Eng. Dept., Coll. City N.Y. 1927-8.

WALDRON, WEBB: Nat. Com. Def. Pol. Pris.

WALKER, ADELAIDE G.: wife of Chas. R.; asst. sec. Nat. Com. Def. Pol. Pris. 1931.

WALKER, CHAS. RUMFORD: Communist Lg. P. G. for F. & F. 1932; communist "Labor Defender"; N.C. to A.S.M. F.S.; Nat. Com. Def. Pol. Pris. 1932; bd. Pris. Rel. Fund; with "Hunger Marchers," Wash., D.C., 1932; chmn. Theatre Union; home Concord, N.H.

WALKER, CHRISTINE: nat. sec. of the Junior Atheist League of the 4A. until 1929.

WALLACE, HENRY A.: radical Roosevelt appointee as Sec. of Agric.; Nat. Citiz. Com. Rel. Lat. Am. 1927; Nat. Save Our Schs. Com.; exec. com. Des Moines, Ia. "Peace Council"; Ia. Com. Lg. Nations; ed. Wallace's Farmer.

WALLIS, KEENE: John Reed Club; ed. Revol. Writers Fed. "Literary Service"; Communist.

WALSH, FRANK P.: lawyer, formerly of Kansas City, Mo., now of N.Y.C.; chief counsel of the Lab. Def. Coun. 1923 (to defend Wm. Z. Foster, Wm. F. Dunne, and other Communists seized at Bridgman, Mich. on charges of criminal syndicalism); returned with John Haynes Holmes and others from relief work in Moscow, 1922, bitterly condemning U.S. for not recog. Russia; mem. Am. Neut. Conf. Com. 1916-7; worked closely with Roger Baldwin and Nat. Civ. Lib. Bur. crowd in 1917-8, while he was co-chmn. of the War Labor Board, in behalf of indicted I.W.W.'s; cooperated in the writing of I.W.W. pamphlet (see Lusk Report); chmn. Am. Commn. on Irish Independence, which presented claims of Ireland to Peace Conf., Paris, 1919; Am. counsel for Irish Republic; Nat. Citiz. Com. for Sacco and V. 1927; signed telegram to Pres. in behalf of Sacco and V. (Boston Post, Aug. 21, 1927); leader and counsel, First Am. Tr. Un. Delg. to Russia, 1927, and active in raising necessary funds for exp. of delg. (see under Organizations); signed Nat. Pop. Govt. Lg. charges against U.S. Dept. of Justice because of its anti-Red activities, with Felix Frankfurter, Ernst Freund, etc.; mem. N.Y. Commn. on Revision of Pub. Util. Laws, 1929, appointed by F. D. Roosevelt, then Gov.; went to Cal. to plead for release of Mooney, 1932; Nat. Citiz. Com. on Rel. Lat. Am. 1927; Nat. Pop. Govt. Lg.; People's Legis. Serv.; Nat. Save Our Schs. Com.; "When some questions came up about the Friends of Soviet Russia" (Communist) "they were referred to Moscow for settlement, and he went over as the agent and representative of the F.S.R. and was paid $7500 for the service." (Welsh).

WALTMIRE, W. B.: M.E. minister, formerly Des Plaines, Ill. (now a center of communistic activity), now minister of Humboldt Park Community Ch., Chgo.; grad. Garrett Biblical Inst.; vice chmn. C.W.C. on Unemp. (Borders) and mem. ed. bd. of "New Frontier," its official organ; exec. com. Chr. Soc. Act. M. and designated corres. for its "Socialist Ministers' Protective Assn." (org. to give financial aid to ministers who lose their positions for teaching Socialism-Communism in their churches); presented demands of joint Socialist-Communist "Hunger Marchers" to Mayor Cermak, Chgo., Oct. 31, 1932; was on A.C.L.U. Chgo. Com. when it was org. (1930); teacher Workers Training School, 1932.

WANGERIN, OTTO: Communist Party functionary; formerly of St. Paul, Minn., 1933 Chgo.; sec.-treas. Nat. R.R. Wkrs. Indust. Union (now called R.R. Wkrs. Unity Move.); A.A.A.I. Lg. Chgo. branch.

WARBASSE, JAMES PETER: retired from surgery 1919 to devote all time to coop. movement; cent. com. Intl. Coop. Alliance; delg. to four Intl. Coop. Congresses; pres. Coop. Lg. of U.S.A. (145 affiiliated societies); Socialist; exec. com. Civil Lib. Bureau 1919; Com. for Thomas,

1929; Emer. Com. Strik. Rel.; Teachers' Union, N.Y.; mem. Coop. Club, Moscow, Russia; lecturer Brookwood Lab. Coll.; Cong. Exp. Radicals; wife active in Jane Addams' Women's Peace Party; Roosevelt Appointee on NRA Consumers' Bd.

WARD, HARRY F.: born England; M.E. minister, formerly of Chgo.; head res. Northwestern U. Settlement, Chgo. 1898-1900; Garland Fund founder and dir.; vice pres. Garland Fund, July 19, 1922-May 7, 1924; a founder, gen. sec. Meth. Fed. for Soc. Serv. and co-ed. of its Bulletin (with Winifred L. Chappel, mem. of Communist Lg. P. G. for F. & F. 1932); statement in Meth. Fed. for Soc. Serv. Bulletin No. 8, 1932, signed by himself and Bishop McConnell, admits cooperation with Socialists and Communists; nat. chmn. and a founder A.C.L.U.; advis. coun. A.S.C. R.R.; pro-Soviet enthusiast; returned, 1933, from year's stay in Russia; speaker for communist F.S.U., Oct. 1933, also Nov. 1, 1933, Webster Hall, N.Y.C. with Communists Henry Barbusse, Anna Louise Strong, Robert Minor, and Herbert Goldfrank; lecturing under communist F.S.U. auspices, 1934; was wartime anti-American "peace" worker; active in infamous People's Coun.; Emer. Peace Conf.; his admiration for I.W.W. cited in Lusk Report; presided over I.W.W. meeting (Feb. 9, 1920), held at Rand Sch. to raise money for def. of I.W.W. murderers of four Am. Legion men at Centralia; active in aid of Wm. Z. Foster, C. E. Ruthenberg, and other Communists arrested at Bridgman, Mich.; bd. dir. "World Tomorrow," and contrib. to "The Nation" and "Christian Century"; Peace Patriots; Fell. Recon.; com. on Recon. Trips, N.Y.; sec. Social Serv. Commn., Fed. Coun. Chs.; ed. Yr. Book of the Church and Soc. Serv.; Prof. of Chr. Ethics, Union Theol. Sem., N.Y.C.; contrib. "Soviet Russia Today" (Communist); connected with Y.M.C.A. and Y.W.C.A.; Teachers' Union, N.Y.; Cong. Exp. Radicals; see Hands Off Committees; signer of demand that the ban against Communist Party in the Philippines be lifted, signed also by Sherwood Eddy and Harry Elmer Barnes, sent to Sec. War, 1931; given hon. degree by Glenn Frank, pres. U. of Wis., for his A.C.L.U. activities, 1931; home Palisade, N.J.

WARDWELL, ALLEN: nat. treas. A.S. C.R.R.; Russ. Reconst. Farms, 1925.

WARE, HAROLD: Communist writer for Intl. Pamphlets; special student of U.S. farmers assisting Henry Puro in agrarian course at Wkrs. School, 1933; assoc. of Lem Harris and Otto Anstrum in Russia, 1930 and before.

WARFORD, JOHN: nat. com. Nat. R. & L. Found. 1933.

WARNE, COLSTON E.: Prof. Ec. U. of Pitts. 1929, released for radicalism; Prof. Ec. Amherst Coll. since 1930; was mem. Pitts. A.C.L.U. Com.; cand. for dir. L.I.D. 1931; signer Jt. Com. on Unemp. demand for redistribution of wealth (Fed. Press Wash. letter 4/7/33); L.I.D. Russian tour conductor for Open Road, 1933; mem. bd. Cooperative Lg. of U.S.A. until 1928.

WASHBURNE, CARLETON: supt. Winnetka Public Schools (Ill.) since 1919; pro-soviet co-author and technical staff member of communistic First American Trade Union Delegation to Russia (see); contrib. ed. of Journal and mem. Progressive Education Assn. (see revolutionary manifesto); mem. and contrib. ed. radical Nat. Education Assn. journal; endorser of Open Road; admirer of "pacifist" Gandhi; joined party of persons "blacklisted as subversives" by Am. Legion report in welcoming Einstein (Chgo. Daily News); lectured in Moscow, 1931; writer of articles for radical "Christian Century"; held "open house" for Karl Borders (Jan. 20, 1930), who lectured to Winnetka public sch. tchrs.

WATSON, ETHEL: record. sec. L.I.D., Chgo. chapter; cand. Socialist ticket 1932; wife of Clarence Senior; sponsor Berger Nat. Found. dinner 1931.

WATSON, GOODWIN: Prof. Columbia U. Tchrs. Coll.; M.W.D. Def. Com.; Friendship Tours; Peace Patriots; Prog. Edu. Assn. and an author of its revolutionary manifesto; contrib. radical pacifist book edited by Devere Allen, "Pacifism in the Modern World"; organizing a socialistic organization "Forward America," Dec. 1933; Com. for Thomas, 1929; predicts a new social order; contrib. "World Tomorrow."

WEBB, SIDNEY JAMES AND BEATRICE POTTER (WIFE): leaders with George Bernard Shaw of the London Fabian Society (Socialist), a potent force in undermining present form of British Govt. through injection of Socialism into intellectual circles; British branch of A.S. C.R.R.

WEBBER, CHAS. C.: minister; assoc. dir. field work, Union Theol. Sem., N.Y.C.; L.I.D.; Hands Off China Com.; nat. coun. Fell. Recon. 1928; com. Fell. Recon. Trips N.Y.C. 1931; exec. sec. for industry of Fell. Recon. 1933; Emer. Com. Strik. Rel. 1928-33; Ch. Emer. Com. Rel. Tex. Strik.; exec. com. Meth. Fed. for Soc. Serv.; Com. for

Thomas 1929; Socialist; exec. com. Nat. R. & L. Found. 1933; John Reed Club; author "Methodists turn Socialistic" ("World Tomorrow," July 1933).

WEBER, JOE: Communist; T.U.U.L.; teacher of Strike Strategy at communist Workers School, 2822 S. Mich. Ave., Chgo. 1932-3; Nat. Mooney Coun. of Action, 1933; police record.

WEIGLE, LUTHER A.: dean of Yale U. Div. Sch. since 1928; nat. com. Nat. R. & L. Found. 1933; nat. coun. C.M.E.; dir. Congl. Edu. Soc. and Congl. Pub. Soc. since 1917; chmn. commn. on Christian edu. Fed. Coun. Chs. since 1924; chmn. administration com. same since 1929; New Haven, Conn.

WEINSTOCK, LOUIS: Communist; nat. com. F.S.U.; head of communist A. F. of L. Com. for Unemp. Insur.; Nat. Mooney Coun. Act.; expelled by A. F. of L. from Painters Union, Dec. 1932.

WEINSTONE, WM. WOLF: Communist Party exec. com.; Russian Jew; arrested Bridgman Raid; Wkrs. Sch. N.Y.C. since 1923; on exec. com. Communist Intl. as repr. American Communist Party in Russia; former ed. Daily Wkr.; cand. on Communist ticket, N.Y. 1932; director of holding company for the 26-28 Union Square Corp. (Communist property).

WEISBORD, ALBERT: org.; teacher; lawyer; grad. Harvard U.; former Socialist, Communist since 1924; conducted "first lesson in revolution" in strike at Passaic, N.J., 1926-7; nat. com. A.A.A.I. Lg. 1928; now leader Communist Lg. of Struggle; former instr. Coll. City of N.Y. and teacher Rand Sch.

WELLER, CHAS.: dir. Fellowship of Faiths (see); Emer. Com. Strik. Rel., Chgo.

WELLS, H. G.: English author; Socialist; says "Pacifism is not enough; you must be politically unpatriotic"; British section A.S.C.R.R.; Fabian Society; 1917 club "combining pacifism with definitely revolutionary aims"; endors. "Letters Sacco and Vanz."; assoc. of Henri Barbusse in Clarté.

WELLS, WM. (BILL): org. communist Shoe and Leather Wkrs. Indust. Un., Chgo.

WELSH, F.E.A.: colored Communist Party functionary.

WERLIK, JOHN: Communist supporter; born Czechoslovakia; Chgo. bus. agt. Metal Trades Union; Am. Com. on Inf. about Russia; Tr. Un. Edu. Lg.; joined Socialist Party 1912; withdrew at time of split into Communists and Socialists, 1919; Nat. Mooney Council of Action, 1933; C.W.C. on Unemp. 1933.

WEST, GEO. P.: nat. com. A.C.L.U.; was mem. I.W.W. Def. Com.; Labor Def. Coun. 1923; Cong. Exp. Radicals.

WEYL, BERTHA POOLE: bd. dir. L.I.D.; exec. com. W.I.L.P.F.; Emer. Com. Strik. Rel. 1928-33.

WHEELER, BURTON K.: lawyer; Dem. U.S. Senator from Montana; mem. radical bloc in Congress; Prog. Party cand. for Vice Pres. 1924 (with the elder LaFollette as cand. for Pres.); was ardently supported in this 1924 campaign by Wm. F. Dunne, who later became ed. of the communist Daily Worker; visited Russia 1930; pro-Soviet; urged Atty. Gen. O'Brien of Mich. to dismiss Bridgman cases, Feb. 1933; Nat. Citiz. Com. Rel. Lat. Am. 1927; endors. "Professional Patriots."

WHIDDEN, J. L.: Communist Party functionary; Dist. No. 10 org. Communist Party, Kans. City, Mo. 1932; arrested Dec. 1933, Okla. City, and held for federal authorities' investigation.

WHITAKER, ROBERT: Communist; was Bapt. missionary, and minister; chmn. communist F.S.U., Cal. 1932-3; born England; field sec. A.C.L.U. and ed. "Open Forum," 1924-6, gen. publicity 1927; nat. com. W.R. Lg. 1931; Communist Lg. P. G. for F. & F. 1932; Socialist cand. in Cal.; contrib. "Industrial Solidarity" (I.W.W.); nat. com. Nat. R. & L. Found. (see) 1933; supported Communist campaign 1932; admits being Communist in A. Lincoln Center "Unity"; home Los A., Cal.

WHITE, REV. ELIOT: formerly minister of Grace Episc. Ch., N.Y.C.; vice pres. Ch. Socialist Lg.; associated with Margaret Sanger, Eugene L. Swan, etc. as speaker for N.Y.C. Recon. Trips, his topics being "Companionate Marriage" and "Love Art Which Depicts the Art of Love," Mar. 21, 1931; Emer. Com. Strik. Rel.; he and wife members Nat. Citiz. Com. for Sacco and V. and signers of telegram to Pres. in their behalf (Boston Post, Aug. 21, 1927); repr. of A.C.L.U. 1931; N.C. to A.S.M. F.S.; nat. com. Nat. R. & L. Found. 1933; nat. coun. Berger Nat. Found.

WHITE, WALTER: colored; nat. com. Nat. R. & L. Found.; sec. N.A.A.C.P.; attended Rosika Schwimmer's Recep. for Albert Einstein, March, 1933.

WHITE, WM. ALLEN: treas. A.S.C. R.R.; delg. to Russian conf. at Prinkipo, 1919; nat. coun. C.M.E.; Peace Patriots; nat. coun. For. Pol. Assn.; vice chmn. Nat. Citiz. Com. on Rel. Lat. Am. 1927; For. Lang. Inf. Serv.; Nat. Save Our Schools Com.; Am. coms. for Justice to China, Fair Play to China, and Chinese Relief (all

Communist-inspired to prevent Am. interference when Communists were trying to capture the Chinese Nationalist Party); Am. Fed. Russian Famine Rel.; vice chmn. N. C. for P. W. 1932; endorser "Professional Patriots"; attacked D.A.R.; Freethinker's Ingersoll Com. 1933; home Emporia, Kan.

WHITNEY, CHARLOTTE ANITA: active Communist; was Cal. Communist cand.; treas. Labor Unity and Cooperators Press, San F. since 1919; treas. People's Coun. of Cal. 1917-9; treas. Cal. Lab. Def. Coun. 1919-21; stockholder in "Liberator"; convicted under Cal. criminal syndicalism law, 1920; conviction affirmed by U.S. Supreme Ct.; A.C.L.U. and other radical org. active in seeking pardon; Jane Addams sent telegram to Gov. urging pardon; pardoned about 1928; N.C. to A.S.M.F.S.; nat. com. W.I.R. 1928; nat. com. A.A.A.I. Lg. 1928; Pris. Rel. Fund; endors. W.I.R. letter for "Hunger Marchers" 1932; nat. com. I.L.D. 1930.

WILDER, THORNTON N.: author; teacher at U. of Chgo. since 1930; Am. Com. for S.A.W.; Am. com. W.C.A.W.

WIECK, AGNES BURNS: former wife of Belleville, Ill. miner; pres. Women's Aux. of Prog. Miners of Am.; friend of Prof. Robt. Morss Lovett; protested against barring Communist delegates at Continental Congress of Wkrs. and Farmers at Springfield, Aug. 1933; was leader march of thousands of women on Springfield, Oct. 1933; because of radicalism has been barred from speaking before some miners' locals and charged with being "Hell raiser."

WILLETT, HERBERT L.: minister Kenilworth, Ill. Union Ch.; formerly U. of Chgo. prof.; Chgo. Fell. Faiths; C.M.E. Ill. com.; Chgo. rep. Fed. Coun. Chs.; assoc. ed. ultra-radical "Christian Century."

WILLIAMS, ALBERT RHYS: bro. of David R.; Communist social worker; has been in Russia, principally, since before the revolution; People's Freedom Union, 1920.

WILLIAMS, DAVID RHYS: bro. of Albert R.; nat. coun. L.I.D. for N.Y.; advis. com. A.C.L.U.; nat. exec. com. I.L.D. 1928; nat. com. A.A.A.I. Lg. (Chgo.) 1928; former pastor Unitarian Ch., Oak Park, Ill.; home now Rochester, N.Y.

WILLIAMS, HAROLD: colored; one of ten principal Communist Party leaders; mem. Negro delg. to Russia, 1932; bus. mgr. "Liberator"; director of defense activities of Lg. Strugg. Negro Rts.

WILLIAMS, HOWARD Y.: bd. dir. L.I.D.; exec. sec. and nat. org. L.I.P.A. since 1929; exec. com. Jt. Com. on Unemp.; nat. advis. com. Sacco-V. Nat. Lg.; Berger Nat. Found.; A.C.L.U.; Com. for Thomas 1929; studied Union Theol. Sem.; former Unitarian minister; Socialist; Farmer-Labor cand. 1928; camp. com. Conf. Prog. Pol. Act. 1933; U.S. Cong. Ag. War.

WILLIAMS, TYRELL: Prof. Law Sch. Wash. U., St. Louis, Mo.; Nat. Citiz. Com. Rel. Lat. Am. 1927; Nat. Pop. Govt. Lg. (charges against Dept. of Justice); Nat. Save Our Schs. Com.

WILLIAMSON, JOHN: nat. exec. com. Communist Party U.S.A.; was org. sec. Dist. No. 8 (Chgo.); nat. sec. Young Wkrs. Lg. (now Young Communist Lg.) from 1924 on; dist. org. Communist Party, Dist. No. 6, Cleveland, 1933.

WILSON, REV. BEN. F.: brother of J. Stitt Wilson; pro-Soviet spkr. for the Communist celebration of Russian Revolution under auspices of F.S.U. in San Francisco (Western Wkr. 10/23/33) on "My Experiences in U.S.S.R." at Scottish Rite Auditorium, Nov. 3, 1933; coun. Pa. Com. Total Disarm.; Erie, Pa. minister.

WILSON, EDMUND: Communist; Emer. Com. So. Pol. Pris.; author of article "How I Came to Communism" ("New Masses," Sept. 1932); nat. com. W.I.R.; treas. Pris. Rel. Fund 1932; Communist Lg. P. G. for F. & F. 1932; assoc. ed. "New Republic" 1926-31; John Reed Club; address New Republic, N.Y.C.

WILSON, J. STITT: Chr. Soc. Act. M. 1932; nat. com. Nat. R. & L. Found. 1933; lecturer; Socialist; pacifist; active with Lochner in org. of Emer. Peace Fed. 1915 (Lusk Report); "Yours for the Revolution" People's College; Soc. Party cand. for Cong. from Cal. 1932; state convener of Cal. Continental Cong. of Wkrs. and Farmers, 1933; home Berkeley, Cal.

WILSON, LILITH M.: nat. exec. com. Socialist Party; nat. com. Lg. Against Fascism; mem. Pa. State Legislature; sponsor of socialized medicine bill and old age pensions.

WILSON, LUCY L. W.: principal So. High Sch. for Girls, Phila., since 1915; advis. coun. A.S.C.R.R.; on recep. com. for Bertrand Russell, Mar. 1927; W. I. L.P.F.; her "New Schools of New Russia" pub. by communistic Vanguard Press; Young Pioneers' (Communist) organ praised her pro-Soviet attitude.

WILSON, WALTER: Fed. Press corres.; N.C. to A.S.M.F.S.; Nat. Com. Def. Pol. Pris.; financial contrib. I.L.D.; contrib. ed. "Labor Defender"; Nat. Miners Union

(Communist); delg. Prog. Mine Wkrs. of Am., Nov. 1932; convention bd. Pris. Rel. Fund 1932; Com. Def. Scottsboro Boys (Communist).

WINCHESTER, BENJ. S.: sec. Fed. Coun. Chs.; contrib. ed. Fed. Coun. Bulletin; prepared Fed. Coun. Sex Pamphlet (see).

WINSOR, MARY: Socialist; A.C.L.U. Phila. Com.; W.I.L.P.F.; cand. on Socialist ticket; advocate of slacker's oath; advis. bd. Wom. Peace Soc.; Cong. com. of Wom. Peace Union; legis. chmn. Pa. Com. Total Disarm.; ed. "Equal Rights"; signed report of communistic Am. Wom. Com. to Investigate Russian Women; financial contrib. communistic Commonwealth Coll.; nat. com. W.R. Lg.

WINSTON, EDW. M.: A.C.L.U. Chgo. Com.; exec. com. L.I.D., Chgo. chapter; Chgo. Emer. Com. Strik. Rel.; advis. com. C.W.C. on Unemp.; Non-Partz. Com. for Lillian Herstein 1932; Chgo. com. Fell. Faiths; treas. Chgo. Com. for S.A.W.

WINTER, ELLA: Mrs. Lincoln Steffens; Am. Com. for S.A.W.; staff "New Masses," 1933; Communist Lg. P. G. for F. & F.; Nat. Com. Def. Pol. Pris.; lecturer F.S.U.; 1933 wrote letter to movie producer threatening Red boycott if he released Carveth Wells' truthful movies of Russia; signs herself as "sec. to Fanny Hurst" ("Sentinel," Dec. 28, 1933).

WIRDS, JOHN W.: Judge, Iowa Falls, Ia.; pres. United Farmers of Am.; Conf. Prog. Pol. Act. 1933.

WIRTH, PROF. LOUIS: sponsor communist Chgo. Wkrs. Theatre, 1933.

WISE, STEPHEN S.: Rabbi; born Budapest, Hungary; was on exec. com. Civil Liberties Bureau (now A.C.L.U.); was wartime "peace" worker; Am. Lg. Limit Arm. 1914; Am. Neut. Conf. Com. 1916; Emer. Peace Fed.; dir. Peace Soc. of N.Y.; rep. of Am. Lg. to Enforce Peace; trustee Nat. Child Lab. Com.; vice pres. radical Open Forum Nat. Coun.; chmn. (in succession to Justice Brandeis) of Provisional Exec. Com. for Gen. Zionist Affairs; Nat. Mooney-Billings Com. 1929; Com. for Thomas 1929 and 1932; M.W.D. Def. Com. 1930; A. A. for O. A. S. 1931; For. Lang. Inf. Serv. 1931; vice chmn. Jt. Com. on Unemp. 1931; Pioneer Youth of Am. 1931; Fell. Recon.; Recon. Trips, 1931; Il Nuovo Mondo Nat. Com.; Nat. Citiz. Com. Rel. Lat. Am. 1927; Am. Assn. Lab. Legis.; C.M.E. 1932; Lg. Neighbors; was active in the Communist "Lesson in Revolution," the Passaic, N.J., Textile Strike, where he spoke in behalf of strikers; Emer. Com. Strik. Rel.; signer of A.C.L.U. letter sent to members of Congress protesting against Fish Com. Report on Communism and requesting that the Fish Com. recommendations be voted down; signer of open letter of protest to Ex-Judge Sullivan attacking his report on Mooney case, Nov. 28, 1932; Fed. Unemp. Wkrs. Lgs. N.Y. 1933; exec. com. Nat. R. & L. Found. 1933; daughter is Justine Wise Tulin, author of pro-Soviet articles on Russia; Non-Intervention Citiz. Com. 1927; vice chmn. Fell. Faiths com. 300, 1933; named Einstein, Freud, Brandeis, and Henri Bergson "four greatest living Jews," Feb. 1934.

WITT, PETER: nat. com. A.C.L.U.; Nat. Citiz. Com. Rel. Lat. Am.; endors. "Professional Patriots"; Cleveland, O.

WITTENBER, JAN.: org. sec. John Reed Club of Chgo.; staff of "Left Front," its publication; "proletarian painter"; Chgo. Com. for Strugg. Ag. War; bd. dir. John Reed Clubs (national) 1932; contrib. ed. "The Left" Communist mag.; artists' grievance committee at Hull House meeting John Reed Club, Aug. 1933; Communist.

WOLFE, BERTRAM D.: Communist Party (Opposition); edtl. staff "Workers Age" (its organ); New Wkrs. Sch. dir.; former central committeman Communist Party; expelled in 1929 with the Lovestone faction; an organizer of the opposition Communist Party.

WOLFE, JAMES H.: nat. coun. L.I.D. for Utah; Judge Dist. Court, 3rd. Utah Dist.

WOLFSON, THERESA: Socialist; grad. Columbia U.; teacher at Intl. Ladies Garm. Wkrs. Un. U., N.Y.C.; lecturer at Brookwood Lab. Coll.; former field sec. Nat. Child Lab. Com.; Am. Assn. of Soc. Wkrs.; exec. sec. Nat. Cons. Lg.; Teachers' Un.; N.Y.C.

WOLMAN, LEO: former coll. prof.; lecturer New Sch. for Soc. Research; Socialist; chief of research dept. Amalg. Cloth. Wkrs. of Am.; dir. Garland Fund; contrib. ed. "New Republic"; Am. Assn. Lab. Legis.; Roosevelt appointee 1933; N.Y.C.

WOOD, CHARLES ERSKINE SCOTT: N.C. to A.S.M.F.S.; bd. Pris. Rel. Fund (I.L.D.); author of "Heavenly Discourse," sacrilegious scurrilous anti-religious book published by Vanguard Press; endors. W.I.R. letter for Hunger Marchers, 1932, and was with marchers in Wash. Dec. 1932.

WOOD, L. HOLLINGSWORTH: nat. com. and a founder A.C.L.U.; was wartime "peace" worker; Am. Lg. Limit Arm.; Conf. for Democ.; Fell. Recon.; treas.

Fellowship Press 1927; Nat. R. & L. Found. 1933; Non-Intervention Citiz. Com. 1927; Cong. Exp. Radicals.

WOOD, ROBERT: Communist Party functionary.

WOODBURY, HELEN SUMNER: Socialist; author; active in woman suffrage movement; nat. coun. L.I.D. for N.Y.; Am. Assn. Lab. Legis.; Com. for Thomas, 1929.

WOODS, J. B. COLLINGS: Recep. Com. Soviet Flyers; auditor Russ. Reconst. Farms.

WOODWARD, W. E.: author of a scurrilous book "George Washington—The Image and the Man," 1926; Socialist; Nat. Mooney-Billings Com.; Com. for Thomas 1929; People's Lobby.

WOOLFE, ROBERT: A.S.C.R.R. book com.; Com. for Thomas, 1929; nat. com. Intl. Wkrs. Aid, 1926 (now W.I.R.).

WOOLLEY, MISS MARY E.: pres. Mt. Holyoke Coll.; Russ. Reconst. Farms, 1925; A.C.L.U. Mass. Com.; nat. advis. com. Sacco-V. Nat. Lg.; Nat. Citiz. Com. Rel. Lat. Am. 1927; vice pres. Nat. Cons. Lg.; Nat. World Ct. Com. 1931; dir. Lg. of Nations Assn. and vice chmn. of its Mass. br.; endors. com. World Peaceways; delg. Disarm. Conf. 1932; Griffin Bill sponsor; nat. bd. Y.W.C.A.; advis. com. Am. Assn. Lab. Legis.; advis. com. Open Road (affiliate of Intourist of Soviet Govt.); Nat. Coun. Congl. Chs. in U.S.; signer Fell. Recon. Pet. Russ. Recog. 1932; Lg. Women Voters; nat. coun. C.M.E.; Peace Patriots; vice pres. Fell. Faiths nat. com. 300, 1933; Nat. Save Our Schs. Com.; endors. Lane Pamphlet.

WORK, JOHN M.: ed. Milwaukee Leader; Socialist Party executive since its formation; contrib. to L.I.D. pub. "Unemployed"; labor journalist; was on bd. "Yours for the revolution" People's Coll. 1916.

WRIGHT, QUINCY: U. of Chgo. Prof.; bd. Lg. for Org. Prog. 1931; wife very active in Lg. Wom. Voters and spkr. for Am. Friends Service Com. "Peace Institutes" at Evanston, Ill. 1932 and 1933; A.S.C.R.R. Com. 1934.

WORTIS, ROSE: Communist; T.U.U.L. org. N.Y.C.

WYGAL, WINIFRED: nat. com. Nat. R. & L. Found. 1933; Com. for Thomas, 1929; Fell. of Socialist Christians continuation com.

Y

YARD, JAMES M.: A.C.L.U. Chgo. Com.; Chgo. Com. for S.A.W.; nat. coun. L.I.D.; exec. com. Chgo. L.I.D.; Dean of Religious Education of Northwestern U., Evanston, Ill., for five years, discharged 1933; close associate of Ernest F. Tittle and leader of the "peace" activities in his church; frequently preaches from Tittle's pulpit; announced in Chgo. Daily News as speaker for communist John Reed Club, Chgo. 1933; sponsor of Chgo. Workers' Theater (Communist) 1933; advis. com. C.W.C. on Unemp. (Borders); nat. and exec. com. Meth. Fed. for Soc. Serv. (McConnell, Ward, Chappell, etc.); for twelve years a "missionary" at West China U. at Changtu; Hands Off China Com. 1927; yet Pres. Scott states Yard was not dismissed from N.U. because of radicalism; spkr. 11/15/33 at Communist Party local hdqts., 357 W. Chgo. Ave. for communist Unemp. Council. (My husband attended and heard his pro-Communist talk. The Chgo. Atheist Forum until recently held in the same hall under same auspices.)

YARROS, RACHELLE S.: wife of Victor; born Russia; birth control exponent; advis. com. Chgo. Forum Coun.; Lg. Wom. Voters; chmn. Social Hygiene Council, 9 E. Huron St., Chgo., termed by Chgo. Tribune "a marital and pre-marital clinic"; in an interview quoted in the Chgo. Tribune (Feb. 1933), Dr. Yarros said: "Young men of today do not exact chastity on the part of a woman as a requirement of marriage. It is not infrequent that young women of good families and the best education have come to me and in consulting with me have told of previous relations with their fiances. There is a growing evidence of liberality on the part of men and those of the well educated class are the most liberal"; sec. Ill. Social Hygiene Lg.; A.S.C.R.R. Com. 1934.

YARROS, VICTOR S.: husband of Dr. Rachelle; A.C.L.U. Chgo. Com.; Chgo. Emer. Com. Strik. Rel.; book reviewer for Chgo. Daily News.

YOUNG, ART: Communist writer and cartoonist for "New Masses," "Liberator," "Nation," etc.; contrib. ed. "New Masses"; his cartoon of Jesus used by Nat. R. & L. Found. for distribution in churches; John Reed Club.

YOUNG, MARGUERITE: until Sept. 1933 staff writer for Scripps-Howard New York World Telegram; now head with Seymour Waldman of Communist Daily Worker's new Washington bureau, with office in the National Press Bldg. and credentials for admission to press galleries of U.S. Senate and House; staff "New Masses," 1933; Communist.

YOUNG, STARK: A.S.C.R.R.; John Reed Club; edtl. staff "New Republic."

Z

ZANGWILL, ISRAEL: A British radical; was mem. Hands Off Russia Com. of which Lenin was Pres. and Trotsky vice pres.; said at its demonstration Feb. 8, 1919, Albert Hall, London: "The British Govt. is only Bolshevism in embryo and Bolshevism is only Socialism in a hurry, Socialism while you won't wait," etc. ("Socialist Network" by Nesta Webster).

ZARITSKY, MAX: nat. com. Lg. Ag. Fascism, 1933; Conf. Prog. Pol. Act. camp. com. 1933-4; dir. Amalg. Bank, N.Y.; Workmen's Circle; Socialist; born Russia; father a rabbi; pres. Cloth Hat, Cap and Millinery Wkrs. Intl. Un.

ZETKIN, CLARA: German Communist; was oldest mem. Reichstag; was mem. of Spartacus group which staged Communist revolution in Germany with Liebknecht, 1919; mem. Communist Intl.; intl. com. W.C.A.W. 1932; died 1933.

ZEUCH, WM. E.: Communist supporter; was edu. dir. Commonwealth Coll., Mena, Ark.; now Fed. Press corres. in Europe.

ZIEGLER, PHIL: nat. coun. L.I.D. for Ohio; ed. "Railway Clerk."

ZIFF, FANNIE: sec. Detroit br. A.C.L.U. (1976 Atkinson St., Detroit).

ZIGROSSER, CARL: N.C. to A.S.M.F. S.; Nat. Com. Def. Pol. Pris.

ZOGLIN, ROSALIND A.: A.S.C.R.R.

ZUCKERMAN, MAX: Non-Intervention Citiz. Com. 1927; exec. Cloth Hat, Cap and Millinery Wkrs. Intl. Un.; born Russia, 1868; came to Am. 1891; Workmen's Circle; org. Pioneer Youth Am.; N.Y.

ADDENDUM

PART II

ORGANIZATIONS, ETC.

AMERICAN CIVIL LIBERTIES UNION

Roger Baldwin, national director of the infamous communist-aiding American Civil Liberties Union, expresses the very heart of its purpose in communist "Soviet Russia Today," Sept. 1934 issue, saying: "I too take a class position. It is anti-capitalist and pro-revolutionary. I believe in non-violent methods of struggle as most effective in the long run for building up successful working class power. Where they cannot be followed—obviously only violent tactics remain. I champion civil liberty as the best of the non-violent means of building the power on which workers' rule must be based. If I aid reactionaries to get free speech now and then, if I go outside the class struggle to fight against censorship, it is only because those liberties help to create a more hospitable atmosphere for working class liberties. *The class struggle is the central conflict of the world; all others are incidental. When that power of the working class is once achieved, as it has been only in the Soviet Union, I am for maintaining it by any means whatever.*" (Emphasis in original.) Later in the article, he actually refers to Harry Ward, national chairman of the communist American League Against War and Fascism and of the A.C.L.U., as "so unbiased a student of the Soviet Union as Dr. Harry Ward." The Chicago Tribune of Dec. 16, 1934, says editorially: "There is no more inconsistent and hypocritical body in this or any other country than the American Civil Liberties Union. Its name and pretense of liberalism are the most blatant fraud in America." The power of its members in the Roosevelt administration should give Americans cause for thought.

FELLOWSHIP OF SOCIALIST CHRISTIANS

1934 chmn. Reinhold Niebuhr; exec. com.: Francis Henson, Roswell P. Barnes, John Bennett, Buell G. Gallagher, Henry P. Van Dusen, Frank T. Wilson, Winnifred Wygal, Evelyn Orne Young. 157 Montague St., Brooklyn, N. Y. (See p. 155.)

FOREIGN POLICY ASSN.

Its Nov. '34 Bulletin recommends "China's Red Army Marches," communist book by communist Agnes Smedley, a Soviet Gov't. book introduction by bloody Bela Kun of the Communist International, one put out by the Red Garland Fund's Vanguard Press, and two other radical books. Its accompanying leaflet quotes Newton D. Baker's eulogy: "The work done by the Foreign Policy Assn. in the last two or three years seems to me almost beyond praise"; also quotes endorsement of its nat. councilman Wm. A. Neilson, pres. communist A.S.C.R.R. and of Smith College, etc. Among nat. dir. and nat. coun. members who are also listed in this Who's Who, 1934, are: nat. dir. Walter H. Pollak, communist I.L.D. atty.; James G. McDonald, hon. chmn.; Jos. P. Chamberlain; Mrs. Henry G. Leach; Bruce Bliven; Ernest Gruening; Carlton J. H. Hayes; Paul U. Kellogg; capitalist Thos. Lamont (of firm of J. P. Morgan) and Mrs.

Lamont. parents of Corliss, vehement Red; Lillian D. Wald; Jane Addams; Stephen P. Duggan; Manly O. Hudson; Bishop Francis J. McConnell, Wm. A. Neilson, Roscoe Pound; Chester Rowell (see p. 338); Rev. John A. Ryan; Dean Wm. Scarlett; Wm. Allen White; Maxwell S. Stewart; Vera Micheles Dean, editor research dept.; also Francis Biddle, Phila. Roosevelt appointee, signer of appeals for Sacco and Vanzetti, whose verse was published in "The Liberator," of which his wife was a stockholder when Max Eastman was its editor. National hdqts.: 18 E. 41st St., N. Y. City. See also p. 158.

FREETHINKERS OF AMERICA

Atheistic; see also p. 160; following Honorary Vice-Presidents added 1934: Chapman Cohen, Wm. J. Fielding, M. Edouard Herriot, Sir Arthur Keith, Prof. Harold J. Laski, Prof. Chauncey D. Leake, Joseph McCabe, Bertrand Russell, Prof. G. Elliot Smith, Prof. Leslie A. White, Dr. Henry Smith Williams; May Bell Morgan became treas. and Charles Strohmeyer, sec.

REBEL ARTS

Socialist counterpart of communist John Reed Clubs; publishes "Arise" magazine; 22 E. 22nd St., N. Y. City.

RED FALCONS

Socialist counterpart of communist Young Pioneers; started 1933; in June, 1934, had over 1,000 members; organized by "Flights" in two sections: "Young Falcons" for children 8 to 11 yrs. and "Red Falcons" for those 11 to 15 yrs.; each "Flight" is given the name of some socialist hero, as "Eugene V. Debs Flight"; issues a monthly paper "Falcon Call"; hdqts. 7 E. 15th St., N. Y. City.

REVOLUTIONARY POLICY COMMITTEE OF THE SOCIALIST PARTY

Revol. Pol. Com. of Socialist P.

Who state they wish to "make every effort in promoting the world revolution," and to secure "governmental power for the victorious revolution by arming the workers," "by preparing the working class to turn imperialist war into class war" (Lenin's Communist slogan), "seeking a united front" with other Red revolutionaries, and that they "make no fetish of legality" (from their Bulletin of April, '34; Ruth Shallcross, 554 W. 114th St., N. Y. City).

The following Socialist Party members signed this "appeal" for revolutionary action: Allen, Edw., Mich.; Bardacke, Gregory, N. Y.; Berkowitz, Edith Brookwood Lab. Coll.; Bishop, Merlin D., Detroit and Brookwood Lab. Coll.; Blayzor, Irene, N. Y.; Burdick, Roland, Syracuse, N. Y.; Brown, Irving, N. Y. City; Chamberlain, Wm., representative L.I.D., Mich.; Codina, Cicero, N. Y. City; Cohen, Jos. N., Brooklyn, N. Y.; Cohen, Myer, New Haven, Conn.; Connors, John, New Bedford, Mass., Fed. of Tchrs.; Cook, Wesley, Am. Fed. Tchrs., Phila.; Daniel, Franz, organizer Amalg. Cloth. Wkrs. Un., Phila.; Dillingham, John, Nashville, Tenn.; Dombrowski, James, Highlander Folk Sch., Mount Eagle, Tenn.; Dow, Ralph P., New Bedford, Mass.; Duval, Ronald, pres. Rand School fellowship, N. Y. City; Farrell, Wm., N. Y. City; Felix, David, Phila.; Findley, Warren, Tchrs. Union, Local 5, N. Y. City; Fingerhut, Mildred, Cleveland and Brookwood Lab. Coll.; Flynn, Edw. J., State Exec. Com., Mo.; Friedman, Milton, Essex Co., N. J.; Gendral, Fred, former Pa. State organizer; Gianasi, Dominic, Prog. Miners of Am. and Brookwood Lab. Coll., Kincaid, Ill.; Goldberg, Louis, N. Y. City; Graham, Theo. T., State organizer Mo.; Green, John, vice pres. Marine & Shipyard Wkrs., treas. N. Phila. Branch; Hamm, Elmer V., state organizer Rhode Is.; Hanson, Alice, sec. Am. Fed. Tchrs. Union, Local 192, Philadelphia; Hawes, Eliz., Highland Folk School, Mount Eagle, Tenn., and organizer Amalg. Cloth. Wkrs. Un.; Henson, Francis, Conn. State Exec. Com.; Hill, Georganna, N. Y. City; Hillyer, Mary, organizer for Amalg. Cloth. Wkrs. Un. Local 196, Troy, N. Y.; Huss, Julius, Paint, Lead, Varnish Color Makers Union, N. Phila.; Irish, Margaret H., N. Y. City; Jeffrey, Newman, N. Phila.; Johannes, Jos., organizer, Syracuse, N. Y.; Kaempf, E. H., organizer Essex Co., N. J.; Kester, Howard, Tenn. State Exec. Com., Nashville; Kimball, Carl, Mass. State Exec. Com.; Kimberly, Evelyn, Chicago; Kimberly, Paul, Chicago; Kovitz, Sam'l, Mo. State Exec. Com.; Lee, John, treas. Am. Newspaper Guild, Phila.; Lichtman, Harry, State Com. of N. J.; Lipscomb, Brice, Mo. State Exec. Com.; Loftus, Constance, New Bedford, Mass.; Long, M. D., Austin Branch, Chicago; Lorand, Ivan, N. Y. City; McFarlan, H. J., Mich. State Exec. Com., Ann Arbor; McNutt, Waldo, Topeka, Kans.; McNutt, Ernest, Independence, Kans.; Martindale, John, inst. Brookwood Labor Coll.; Matthews, J. B., N. Y. City.; Mendelsohn, Daniel, Exec. Com. Newark Y.P.S.L.; Miller, Ruth, Cleveland, O. and Brookwood Lab. Coll.; Perlstein, Abraham, Conn. State Exec. Com, Hartford; Pickenback, Helen, N. Y. City; Reiff, Donald, N. Y. City; Rheiner, Conard, Maine State Exec. Com., Brookwood Lab. Coll.; Riemensnyder, Elwin, Am. Fed. Hosiery Wkrs., N. Phila.; Reuther, Roy, Detroit and Brookwood Lab. Coll.; Ross, Eric, State sec. and organizer N. J.; Sailer, Agnes, dir. Pioneer Youth Summer Schools in South, N. Y. City; Scheyer, David, Cook Co. Central Com. Chicago; Shaer, Samuel, New Bedford, Mass.; Shallcross, Ruth, N. Y. City; Shapiro, Rose, N. Y. City; Sitko, Leo, pres. Atlas, Pa. Local of United Mine Wkrs., Mt. Carmel, Pa.; Sluder, Cora, N. Y.; Smith, Tucker P., director Brookwood Labor Coll., N. Y. City; Streator, Geo. W., N. C. State Exec. Com., mg. ed. "The Crisis," Greensboro, N. C.; Sweetland, Monroe, L.I.D. organizer, Ithaca, N. Y.; Tisso, John, Brookwood Lab. Coll., organizer Canners Indust. Un., Camden, N. J.; Trimble, Glen, Mass. Exec. Com.; Van Gelder, Philip, Party and Amalg. Cloth. Wkrs. Un. organizer, N. Phila.; Walter, Noah C. A., Jr., nat. exec. com. Y.P.S.L., N. Y. City; Way, Stewart, Wilkinsburg, Pa.; Whitten, Richard Babb, Exec. Com. New Orleans; Zameres, Jos., nat. industrial organizer Y.P.S.L.

Y. W. C. A.

Communist propaganda of its National Board is even bolder in '34: advocating mixture of colored and whites in social affairs and swimming pools; suggesting for Y.W.C.A. libraries the Communist Manifesto by Marx and Engels, "Das Kapital" by Marx, books by communists Michael Gold, Langston Hughes and Alex. Trachtenberg, by the I.W.W. ex-convict Ralph Chaplin, by socialists Norman Thomas, George Soule, Tom Tippett, Theresa Wolfson, Ruth S. Pollak and Mary Beard and other radicals listed in this book (Program Exchange, Sept., '34). See also p. 250.

PART III

"WHO'S WHO"

BEALL, HAYES: chmn. Nat. Coun. of Methodist Youth; nat. com. communist Am. Lg. Ag. War & Fascism (see).

DUBINSKY, DAVID: vice pres. then pres. Intl. Ladies Garm. Wkrs. Un. since 1922; active in Socialist Party; mem. Jewish Socialist Verband; born Poland; served 18 mo. in prison in Russia and exiled to Siberia for revolutionary activities; elected vice pres. A. F. of L. and given banquet of welcome Nov. 4, '34.

McNUTT, WALDO: mem. Revol. Pol. Com. of Socialist P. (see p. 337); nat. com. communist Am. Lg. Ag. War & Fascism; mem. Socialist P. Local., Independence, Kans.

ROWELL, CHESTER: begged to be included in "The Red Network"; claims over 200 radical friends; Sacco Vanzetti Calif. Com. Aug. 1927 (communist agitation); A.C.L.U. Com. of N. Calif. 1926-; nat. coun. For. Policy Assn.; presided at dinner honoring Roger N. Baldwin, Palace Hotel, San F.; contrib. to A.C.L.U. printed attack on Calif. criminal syndicalism law (U. S. Fish Report); ed. San Francisco Chronicle noted for its pro-radical editorials; regent U. of Calif.; pres. Calif. Lg. Nations Assn. (Lg. Nations endorsed by Socialist Party.)

SWEETLAND, MONROE: Revol. Pol. Com. of Socialist P. (see p. 337); org. for L.I.D.; former State org. Socialist P., N. Y.; anxious for "the revolution" and unity with Communist Party; asked to be listed in this "Who's Who" and promised to spare me when the bourgeois victims are brought before him to be executed in the Red Terror.

TALBOT, MARIAN, dean U. of Chgo.; collaborator with Soph. P. Breckenridge; wrote asking inclusion in "The Red Network"; W.I.L.P.F.

VAN KLEECK, MARY: dir. industrial studies Russell Sage Foundation; nat. com. F.S.U.; spkr. at many Red meetings; assumed an "uncompromising Communist position in her declaration for collectivism" at Kansas City Conf. for Social Work ("The Nation" June 20, '34); endors. Communist unemployment insurance bill H.R. 7598 ("New Masses" March 6, '34).

ZIMMERMAN, CHAS.: Communist Party (opposition); vice pres. Intl. Ladies Garm. Wkrs. Un. '34 (Daily Wkr., Nov. 7, '34); nat. com. Am. Lg. Ag. War & Fascism.

INDEX

(See page 255 for Third Printing Supplement on Anglo-Am. Institute of Moscow U.) PAGE

PART I

Miscellaneous Articles

PART II

Organizations, Etc.

Index

B

D

E

F

I

J

K

L

M

N

O

P

R

T

U

V

W

APPENDIX

PART III

"Who's Who"

Anti-Movements in America

An Arno Press Collection

Proceedings of the Asiatic Exclusion League, 1907-1913. 1907-1913

Beecher, Edward. **The Papal Conspiracy Exposed.** 1855

Beecher, Lyman. **A Plea For the West.** 1835

Budenz, Louis F. **The Techniques of Communism.** 1954

Burr, Clinton Stoddard. **America's Race Heritage.** 1922

Calhoun, William P[atrick]. **The Caucasian and the Negro in the United States.** 1902

Ministers of the Established Church in Glasgow. **A Course of Lectures On the Jews.** 1840

Dies, Martin. **The Trojan Horse in America.** 1940

Dilling, Elizabeth. **The Red Network.** 1935

East, Edward M. **Mankind At the Crossroads.** 1926

Evans, H[iram] W. **The Rising Storm:** An Analysis of the Growing Conflict Over the Political Dilemma of Roman Catholics in America. 1930

Fairchild, Henry Pratt. **The Melting-Pot Mistake.** 1926

Fulton, Justin D. **The Fight With Rome.** 1889

The Fund for the Republic, Inc. **Digest of the Public Record of Communism in the United States.** 1955

Ghent, W[illiam] J. **The Reds Bring Reaction.** 1923

Grant, Madison. **The Conquest of a Continent.** 1933

Hendrick, Burton J. **The Jews in America.** 1923

Huntington, Ellsworth. **The Character of Races.** 1925

James, Henry Ammon. **Communism in America.** 1879

King, James M. **Facing the Twentieth Century.** 1899

Kirwan (pseudonym of Nicholas Murray). **Letters to the Right Rev. John Hughes, Roman Catholic Bishop of New York.** 1855

Ku Klux Klan. **Papers Read at the Meeting of Grand Dragons Knights at Their First Annual Meeting.** [1923]

McCarthy, Joseph. **McCarthyism**: The Fight for America. 1952

McDougall, William. **Is America Safe for Democracy?** 1921

Monk, Maria. **Awful Disclosures.** 1836

[Morse, Samuel Finley Breese]. **Foreign Conspiracy Against the Liberties of the United States.** 1835

National Americanism Commission of the American Legion, Compiler. **ISMS**: A Review of Alien Isms, Revolutionary Communism and Their Active Sympathizers in the United States. 1937

Nevins, William. **Thoughts on Popery.** 1836

Pope, Or President? Startling Disclosures of Romanism as Revealed by Its Own Writers. 1859

[Priest, Josiah]. **Slavery.** 1843

Reed, Rebecca Theresa. **Six Months in a Convent** and **Supplement.** 1835

Roberts, Kenneth L. **Why Europe Leaves Home.** 1922

Ross, Edward Alsworth. **Standing Room Only?** 1927

Schaack, Michael J. **Anarchy and Anarchists.** 1889

Schultz, Alfred P. **Race or Mongrel.** 1908

Stripling, Robert E. **The Red Plot Against America.** 1949

Tenney, Jack B. **Red Fascism.** 1947

[Timayenis, Telemachus T.] **The Original Mr. Jacobs**: A Startling Exposé. 1888

Wiggam, Albert Edward. **The Fruit of the Family Tree.** 1924

Anti-Catholicism in America, 1841-1851: Three Sermons. 1977

Anti-Semitism in America, 1878-1939. 1977